The Grid and the Park

Public Space and Urban Culture in Buenos Aires, 1887–1936

Adrián Gorelik

Translated by Natalia Majluf

LASA | LATIN AMERICA RESEARCH COMMONS

Published by
Latin America Research Commons
www.larcommons.net
larc@lasaweb.org

© Adrián Gorelik 2022
© of the translation Natalia Majluf 2022

First edition in English 2022
Original publication: Editorial de la Universidad Nacional de Quilmes, 1998

Cover design: Milagros Bouroncle
Cover image: © Horacio Coppola, *Avenida del Trabajo y Lacarra*, 1936.
Horacio Coppola Archives
Print version typeset: Lara Melamet
Digital versions typeset: Siliconchips Services Ltd.
Copy editor: Melina Kervandjian
Reference assistant: Mauro Lazarovich
Bibliography and index: Valentín Parra

ISBN (Paperback b&w version): 978-1-951634-20-9
ISBN (Paperback color version): 978-1-951634-24-7
ISBN (PDF): 978-1-951634-21-6
ISBN (EPUB): 978-1-951634-22-3
ISBN (Mobi): 978-1-951634-23-0
DOI: https://10.25154/book8

Suggested citation:
Gorelik, Adrián. *The Grid and the Park: Public Space and Urban Culture in
Buenos Aires, 1887–1936*. Pittsburgh: Latin America Research Commons,
2022. DOI: https://10.25154/book8 License: CC BY-NC 4.0.

Work published within the framework of "Sur" Translation Support Program
of the Ministry of Foreign Affairs and Worship of the Argentine Republic.

To read the free, open-access version of this book
online, visit https://10.25154/book8 or scan this
QR code with your mobile device:

Contents

Illustrations

The illustrations are integrated within the text; each time a reference is made to one of them, the illustration number is indicated with a callout placed in the outer margin.

Regarding the maps of Buenos Aires, it is necessary to offer a few explanations: The difficulty of reading them is aggravated by the fact that during the period under study the practice for their orientation changed: in the nineteenth century, they were mostly arranged with the north to the right, and in the twentieth century, with the north toward the top. For this publication, the decision was thus made to always orient the north according to nineteenth-century representations, which means that the port of Buenos Aires is at the bottom of the maps (and the north is to the right). This homogenization (which applies to both complete plans and to details) is intended to make them easier to read, although from the graphic point of view it forces the legends of some historical plans to appear at a 90-degree angle.

The graphic diagrams were made by Silvana Ferraro for the original edition.

Preface to this Edition

It is rare for studies on Latin American cities conducted outside the North American academy to be published in English. The sociology of publishing has proven with overwhelming figures that translations from Spanish to English—and the same could be said of translations into French—are concentrated almost exclusively in the field of fiction, while in the social sciences and humanities the transit between languages moves almost exclusively in the opposite direction. This is not the place to analyze the asymmetries of the international circulation of knowledge, but recognizing them makes the privilege that this edition represents even more evident, an honor for which I must extend my thanks to the audacious translation program carried out by the Latin American Studies Association (LASA) in the launching of this collection and, especially, to the personal commitment of Natalia Majluf, who not only promoted the initiative in her role as editor in chief of the Latin America Research Commons (LARC), but also took charge of the translation itself.

The word audacious also applies to LARC's decision to open the collection with a book that is not too amenable for translation, not because of the typical difficulties of a Spanish full of subordinate clauses and impersonal sentences so refractory to English precision, but because of the number of assumptions about Argentine culture on which it is based. In fact, good friends who like the book very much have often criticized this feature: an excessive immersion in details of local culture that results in a certain hermeticism, making the narrative difficult to comprehend for an international audience.

My response to these concerns is that the approach is not at all a pursuit of a partially nationalist program: on the contrary, the book encourages comparative reflection, examining the case of Buenos Aires in the light of what happened in other cities of the region or the world, as a strategy to denaturalize beliefs settled in historiography and, more generally, in Argentine culture. A comparative reflection is essential in order to accurately ponder the transformation of Buenos Aires in the transition from the nineteenth to the twentieth century as one of the most intense and interesting international urban experiences, not only because of the explosive growth generated by an immigration process with few equivalents in the world—which itself generated singular sociocultural dynamics—but also because of the originality of the urban instruments that were put into play. One of the first consequences of placing Buenos

Aires on the international chess board of cities has been the questioning of the notion of *Haussmannization*, which has hindered in the last half century a proper appreciation of the processes of urban modernization in Latin America.

Any hermeticism would have to be attributed to the rules of the game of what is perhaps the book's biggest challenge: the production of an urban perspective for cultural history. Placing the material city in intimate correspondence with the dimensions of social, political, and cultural life demands very elaborate interpretations of each of these facets. If this book makes it necessary to re-read the work of a writer like Jorge Luis Borges, it is because the focus on the city demands modifications of what we knew about both Buenos Aires and Borges's work. This is, I believe, a test for an urban perspective: when it works, when it is really productive, is when it manages to produce new interpretations of all elements in play, breaking the habit of the writing of urban history, which often takes culture as a given context for its explanations of the form of the city, and that of cultural history, which often reductively positions the city as a neutral setting for its analyses of culture.

The cultural/urban density of a history thus plotted is almost a starting point, a research and writing program. The focus on the city leads us to put very different types of figures on the same plane of analysis, a move that places completely contrasting cultural worlds into collision: for example, a fundamental intellectual such as Domingo Faustino Sarmiento, and an opaque bureaucrat like engineer Carlos María Morales, whose technical work on the plan of Buenos Aires allows us to read a whole state imaginary of late-nineteenth-century conservative reformism that brings new light on Sarmiento's ideas. It also imposes hermeneutic perspectives on urban operations themselves: I think of the analysis of the work of two Buenos Aires mayors, Torcuato de Alvear and Mariano de Vedia y Mitre, who radically transformed, not merely the city but the very weave of urban life and its representations, yet who did not leave behind a single text on their projects or any form of document to support an analysis of their ideas outside of what emerges from their own actions. In order to "read" the city or urbanistic actions, to interpret them ideologically, it is necessary to reconstruct complete sections of social, political, and cultural history, linking the advances in each historiographic field with urban form and with disciplinary traditions of urbanism in a way that can only make the narrative more complex.

It is worth remembering here that this re-centering of the city in history was fueled by the extraordinary vitality that the city gained in the debates on modernity in the 1980s: although it may seem strange to those of us who lived through it, that moment is now part of a history almost as foreign to the present moment as the one revisited in this book. *The Grid and the Park* could not have been written without the powerful updating of some classic interpreters of the metropolis such as Georg Simmel, Walter Benjamin, or Siegfried Kracauer, which those debates updated and revised, nor without the works of Carl Schorske, Thomas Bender, Marshall Berman, or Richard Sennett, or those even closer to us of Richard Morse, Beatriz Sarlo, Carlos Monsiváis, or Nicolau Sevcenko. It was an international conjuncture, with a strong presence in Latin America, in which the discussion on modernity focused on the study of cities and assumed a high political and cultural intensity.

If these works put the city on everyone's lips and showed very well what cultural history gained from *being situated* in a city, they also allowed this book to pose a slightly different challenge: how to extract from the city itself the keys to interpret culture. Perhaps it was an attempt to respond to a demand implicit in much of Morse's work: If modern cultural life has its center in the city, and if a distinct type of culture is produced in each city, how do we identify the specific links that are drawn between the two, that produce them mutually? How can we find, inscribed in the urban form itself, the keys that give a culture its profile? This book does not offer definitive answers, to be sure, but it positions these questions as the basis for a necessary exploration. And I would like to believe that it is this experimental spirit that motivated LARC's gamble on this translation.

The preface to the first edition sufficiently describes the network of intellectual and academic groups from which this book emerged in Buenos Aires in the eighties and nineties: the only thing that can be said here is that after such a long time I am happy to re-sign each of those acknowledgments. Regarding this edition, I would like to make a special mention of the Editorial de la Universidad Nacional de Quilmes, which has been editing this book since its publication in 1998, keeping it alive with continuous reeditions, for the transfer of rights that has facilitated this translation, and to the translation program "Sur," of the Ministry of Foreign Affairs and Worship of the Argentine Republic which supported it.

Finally, I would like to thank the friends who helped me obtain the excellent photographs that illustrate this edition. To Luis Priamo, great expert in the history of photography, who always offers with enormous generosity his time and knowledge; to the heirs of Horacio Coppola, and especially to Jorge Mara, the person responsible for managing his estate, all of whom, with great generosity, have been accompanying and making possible the research on the photographer and the publications that result from it; and to Lucio Piccoli, Eduardo Gentile, and Daniel Becker, whose invaluable collaboration provided me with archival materials that were so difficult to access during the pandemic. And, of course, I would also like to thank Julieta Mortati, who is in charge of the editorial management of LARC, to whom we owe a great deal of the success of this project.

ADRIÁN GORELIK
Buenos Aires, October 2021

Preface to the First Edition

This book is a revised version of a doctoral dissertation on the emergence and failure of metropolitan public space in Buenos Aires that was presented to the Facultad de Filosofía y Letras, Universidad de Buenos Aires. The research was supported by a CONICET Doctoral Fellowship between 1989 and 1994, based at the Instituto de Arte Americano e Investigaciones Estéticas Mario J. Buschiazzo, Facultad de Arquitectura, Universidad de Buenos Aires. Once the scholarship ended, I was able to continue my work thanks to the Programa de Historia Intelectual, Centro de Estudios e Investigaciones, Universidad Nacional de Quilmes, where I am still doing research today. Additionally, between December 1994 and March 1995 I benefited from a stay at the Akademie Schloss Solitude in Stuttgart. I finished the final version in September 1996. With regard to the process of writing the thesis, I would like to thank especially my adviser Jorge Francisco Liernur, who always led the way. Regarding its conversion into a book, I have tried to follow—although I have not always succeeded—the attentive suggestions of those who helped me in reading it again once I had defended the dissertation: Anahí Ballent, Beatriz Sarlo, and Graciela Silvestri, as well as Oscar Terán, director of the series in which this book is published, and María Inés Silberberg, to whom we owe the intelligent editing.

But these are only the most specific acknowledgments. In fact, I believe that if every history book is the result of a series of exchanges—hypotheses discussed, influences received, cultural climates—this condition is amplified in the case of a doctoral dissertation, because its incubation is necessarily more public and, in general, because it is part of a guided, more collective formation. That is why dissertations are usually accompanied by a long list of debts and acknowledgments. I do not pretend to be original: also here the main ideas that structure the work were presented and submitted for discussion in articles, in papers to congresses, and in seminars, participating and feeding on the stimulating academic climate that was forming in Buenos Aires in the eighties, with its intense permeability toward other areas of cultural life; so that a list of all those from whom I learned in those exchanges would be endless. I would simply like to point out the way in which those exchanges were imprinted as the original mark of this book: the (then surprising) initiative that the studies on the city and architecture that I had been carrying out should lead to a doctoral thesis in history was due to a generous suggestion by Leandro Gutiérrez and Luis Alberto Romero, made in the corridors of one of those congresses.

Above all, I would like to point out that, in addition to the academic exchange of knowledge, no doubt fundamental, the climate in which this book was formed has given meaning to my work ever since, from the point of view of its insertion into a cultural fabric and an intellectual project: I know that I would not have written this, or anything else, without the incentive of imagining that this writing could be part of a collective enterprise, even if loosely defined, but with precise cultural and ideological implications. Thus, rather than merely mentioning this or that reading that the preliminary versions received, the acknowledgments take the form of a description—succinct, to be sure—of the intellectual map that made possible not only the writing of the book, but also the very formulation of a perspective from which to begin to think about these problems. It is a perspective that is made up of three types of views on the city, history, and culture, embodied in three distinct, yet always interrelated intellectual groups within which we have shared many years of work and friendship.

First, there is the group on history and criticism of architecture and the city formed by the initiative and under the influence of Jorge Francisco Liernur over fifteen years ago, in which dialogue and training continue. The approach to the problems of the city and architecture that appear in my research are undoubtedly the product of a collective elaboration in that group. Especially to Liernur, Fernando Aliata, Anahi Ballent, Graciela Silvestri, Mercedes Daguerre, and Alejandro Crispiani, I owe so many debts that at times I see my book as just a chapter of a work that we should sign together: in fact, collective writing has always been a common practice among us, and in particular with Silvestri I have signed a number of articles that over time anticipated much of the hypotheses that I develop here.

Second, I must mention the Programa de Historia de las Ideas, los Intelectuales y la Cultura, which was formed by Oscar Terán at the Instituto Ravignani, Universidad de Buenos Aires. With over ten years of uninterrupted operation of the seminar, which, month after month, has allowed a heterogeneous group of researchers to discuss their work. In a very unorthodox way, in the imperceptible ways in which an artisanal knowledge is transmitted, a common horizon to think about cultural history was built in that seminar that has decisively marked my perspective and my writing. Out of that group, Terán formed the program at the Universidad Nacional de Quilmes in which a team of researchers has been working with a now more continuous degree of exchange since 1994. Among those colleagues, I would like to highlight Carlos Altamirano and Jorge Myers, due to the intensity of their influence throughout this time.

Finally, the magazine *Punto de Vista*, which I joined in 1992. In regular meetings and discussions with Beatriz Sarlo, María Teresa Gramuglio, Hilda Sabato, Carlos Altamirano, and Hugo Vezzetti, I have been able to approach a mode of critical intervention on the world of ideas that has completely redefined my perspective on intellectual work; a mode of political and aesthetic

production on the present that necessarily sheds light on the ways of questioning and imagining the past, which gives it meaning. Thus, because it opened
up those paths for me, the reference to *Punto de Vista* is linked more broadly
to other kinds of experiences that have allowed me to think about the history
of Buenos Aires in a more enriching way. On the one hand, a very particular
aesthetic-intellectual enterprise, the cycle of three video essays on Buenos Aires
made by Rafael Filippelli with a script we produced with Silvestri and Sarlo: the
perspective of film, literature, and art showed me a different city and a different
history, which, although I don't know exactly how, I would like to see operating
in my work. On the other hand, a series of political ventures of rather uncertain fortune, linked to the formation of a new left field in the city at the very
moment when a very long cycle to gain its institutional autonomy was closing:
I do not know if my historicist and culturalist approach to the problems of the
contemporary city has been of any use to my comrades at every turn, but I do
know that the more intimate knowledge of those problems, of the mechanics
of political, social, and institutional functioning—knowledge to which I owe so
much to Miguel Cincunegui, director of the Centro de Gestión Urbana, Oficina
del Ombudsman de Buenos Aires, where I collaborated all these years—gave
me innumerable clues that I have applied in my research in an immoderate way.

Debts, acknowledgments, dedications: perhaps because of the kind of experience involved in writing a dissertation, because of the surely ritualistic sen-
sation that in it a whole period is put into action, not only of research but of
life, I have felt the need to pay tribute to all these people so close to me during
these years, so generous, from whom I learned so much, with whom I enjoyed
so much; may they accept this dedication, may they see themselves at least partially in the result that is this book.

With all of the profound feelings one experiences as one chapter in a
long intellectual course comes to a close, I offer a more specific dedication to
Graciela Silvestri, whose influence has indelibly marked my journey.

And to my parents, for so many things that I wouldn't give to oblivion.

ADRIÁN GORELIK
Buenos Aires, June 1998

A Metropolis in the Pampas

In 1887, as a result of the federalization of Buenos Aires carried out at the beginning of the decade, the government of the Province of Buenos Aires transferred to the national government additional land to enlarge the capital, from which, a year later, its definitive limits were to be drawn (the current General Paz Avenue).[1] The municipality had until then a little over 4,000 hectares, although 3 its 400,000 inhabitants occupied a much smaller built-up area; after its extension, it had more than 18,000 hectares, becoming one of the largest municipal jurisdictions among the most important metropolises.[2] At the time of this 4

---

[1] The federalization of the city of Buenos Aires as the nation's capital was achieved after several decades of internal confrontations. It had been considered in the constitution of the Argentine Confederation of 1852, but the Province of Buenos Aires was reluctant to lose its capital city and port revenues, so it became autonomous as the State of Buenos Aires (1852–1861). It rejoined when, after triumphing in the battle of Pavón (1861), it seemed that it could impose its conditions. Thus, national governments since 1862 had provisional headquarters in the city of Buenos Aires while the site of the future capital was still being discussed. Finally, President Nicolás Avellaneda decided for federalization in September 1880; the Province of Buenos Aires rose up in arms to prevent it, but this time it was defeated by the national state, ending a cycle of civil wars, and allowing the consolidation of a modern order in Argentina. The city of Buenos Aires was federalized, and the Province of Buenos Aires was granted the erection of a new city as provincial capital (La Plata). The federal capital began to enjoy substantial investments from the national government, which was to pay for all public infrastructure and, at a time of great economic growth, further set out to turn its capital city into a showcase of the nation's progress. In 1880 federalization affected only the existing municipality of Buenos Aires, but in 1887 the Province of Buenos Aires ceded the neighboring municipalities of Flores and Belgrano for the city's extension.

[2] According to the second municipal census of Buenos Aires of 1904 (Buenos Aires: Compañía Sudamericana de Billetes de Banco, 1906), in 1888 the fully built-up area of the traditional municipality comprised approximately two-thirds of its original 4,000 hectares. To ponder the significance of the extension to 18,000 hectares it should be borne in mind that, with the exception of the more than 30,000 hectares of the County of London, none of the great European cities had such extensive jurisdictions: Paris had 7,900 hectares, Berlin until 1914 had 6,300, and Vienna had 5,540 (though in 1890 it would extend its jurisdiction to 18,000); of course, in all cases these were cities with a

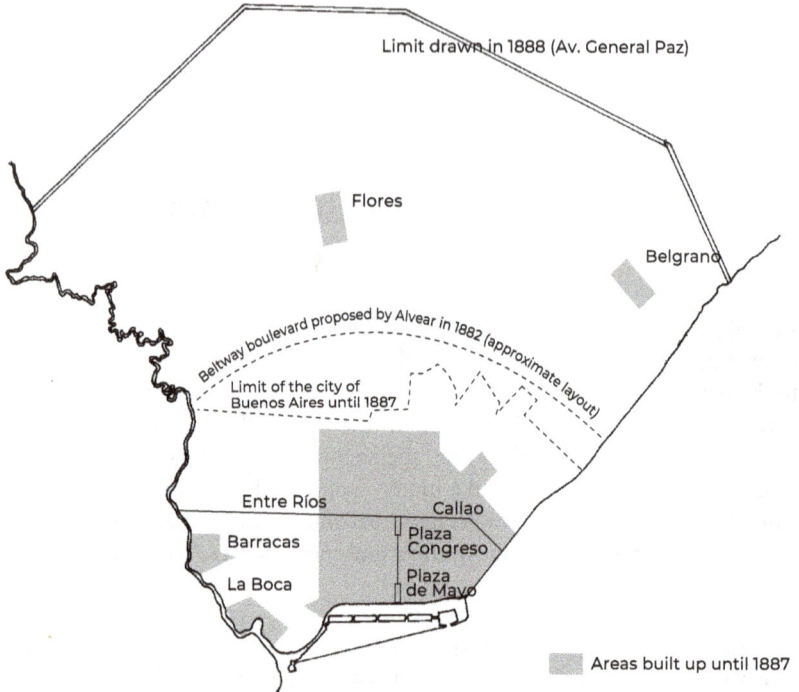

Figure 1. Diagram of the city of Buenos Aires in 1887, showing built areas and the three successive 19th-century "Beltway boulevards": Entre Ríos-Callao (1822), Alvear's proposal (1882), and General Paz Avenue (1888).

Figure 2. Carlos María della Paolera, *Plan of the Regional Expansion of the Metropolis.* Office of the Urbanization Plan, Buenos Aires, 1933.

territorial expansion, there were no more than 25,000 inhabitants in the new 14,000 hectares, and only a few blocks in the villages of Flores and Belgrano had been laid out and built. Five decades later, around 1936, this new territory was already completely urbanized, so that it was impossible to distinguish the original municipality from its annexation. There were also three branches of urbanization outside the Federal District growing northward, westward, and southward to form an emergent metropolitan region. The population of the capital had by then risen to 2,500,000 inhabitants, of which approximately one million lived in sectors corresponding to the old municipality and one and a half million in the land annexed forty years earlier.[3]

This book addresses the temporal and spatial arc covering the half century and the more than 18,000 hectares of what we can call the first metropolitan cycle in Buenos Aires: from the administrative expansion of the municipality, when the annexed territory was nothing more than the boundless expanse of the pampa, to its almost complete urbanization. How is a metropolis formed in the pampa? To answer this question, the book interweaves two histories: that of the progressive occupation of the plains (with the question of the suburban neighborhood as its center); and that of the production of global networks of meaning that in a short period of time completely modified the representations of what the *city* in fact was. It is not intended as a history of the modern expansion of Buenos Aires, of its growth, but an analysis of what happened in that time, with that territory, with its inhabitants and its institutions, that allows us to speak of the emergence of a metropolitan public space in Buenos Aires. Our focus will thus be placed on a handful of relationships, in the framework of which the city is produced as a material, cultural, and political artifact: the relationships between city and society, that is, between form and politics, between material culture and cultural history, between the different temporalities that define the city, that of its material objects, that of politics, that of culture.

For the historical investigation of these relationships, we have chosen to focus on the forms, objects, and material processes of the city, and on the discussions and projects that devised them, through their representations and

---

much larger population than Buenos Aires. This data is taken from *Der* Städtebau, by Werner Hegemann (Berlin, 1910; Düsseldorf 1911–1912), republished as *Catalogo delle esposizioni internazionali di urbanistica*, ed. Donatella Calabi and Marino Folin (Milan: Il Saggiatore, 1975); and Eugène Hénard, *Études sur les transformations de Paris*, a work in installments published in Paris in 1903 and republished in *Alle origini dell'urbanistica: la costruzione della metropoli*, ed. Donatella Calabi and Marino Folin (Padova: Marsilio, 1972).

[3] This information is drawn from the fourth general population census of the city of Buenos Aires, published in 1938. From then on, the population would soon stabilize to the range of three million inhabitants, which remains as the broad general count for the Federal District, while the subsequent population increase would occur outside these limits, in subsequent waves of suburbanization.

the remains of them that have been left to us. The choice responds to reasons of specialty and taste, but it also accompanies the certainty that it is, at the very least, a neglected angle of local historiography. The guiding question that would summarize the approach could be simplified as follows: Why is the city the way it is; or, better yet, why are its forms the way they are; how are they related to culture, society, or politics; what do they allow us to reveal about them? Paradoxical though it may seem, the historiography of Buenos Aires has not often asked these questions: urban images, the forms of buildings, the form of layouts, the form of trees and monuments, of clothing and artifacts, forms in which a culture is matrixed and which in turn contribute to its shaping, are not often exploited for their informative capacity. On the contrary, form is quickly pushed aside, as a mere facade whose surface must be transposed, or as a specular, ideological reflection of another instance on whose surface the key to the real must be read, inverted.

It is not, of course, a matter of maintaining by contrast that the answers to historical inquiry can be found entirely in these forms: it is not a matter of making them the only sources, since in so many ways they are simply mute, and only through numerous detours through other sources is it possible to interpret them, to construct them rather as hypotheses. But situating forms as protagonists, directing the main questions to them, implies more than a choice of sources: even if we take all the detours that their interpretation demands, by placing them in the privileged place of historical narrative we produce new demands; they require new documentary quarries to appear, or new questions to be asked of known sources, or they install an oblique gaze on the usual problems. And this is fundamental for a cultural history of the city: a history that does not separate the history of the city—in material terms—and of society—in social or political terms—but that is a history of the way in which the city, as an object of culture, produces meanings; that is, a cultural history of representations of the city, but with the caveat that the way in which urban artifacts produce meanings affects culture as much as it reverts to its own materiality.

This explains part of this book's title: the *grid* and the *park* are material and cultural figures, they are artifacts that can exist as problems insofar as they have been historically constructed as figures of culture, on whose form a series of interpretations of the process of constituting a metropolitan public space will be based. Through different approaches to these figures—sometimes taken as instruments of public intervention or urban theory, sometimes as a condensation of ideas, sometimes as metaphors of social and cultural processes, and many times as mere materialities, as spaces for the realization of social practices—we will try to prove a hypothesis: that in the years between the end of the nineteenth and the third decade of the twentieth century, peculiar modalities of territorial organization, cultural transformation, popular sociability, and urban public policies were produced which resulted in the emergence of a metropolitan public space in Buenos Aires. From this point of view, the chosen periodization identifies a cycle, in which that conjunction of elements came together

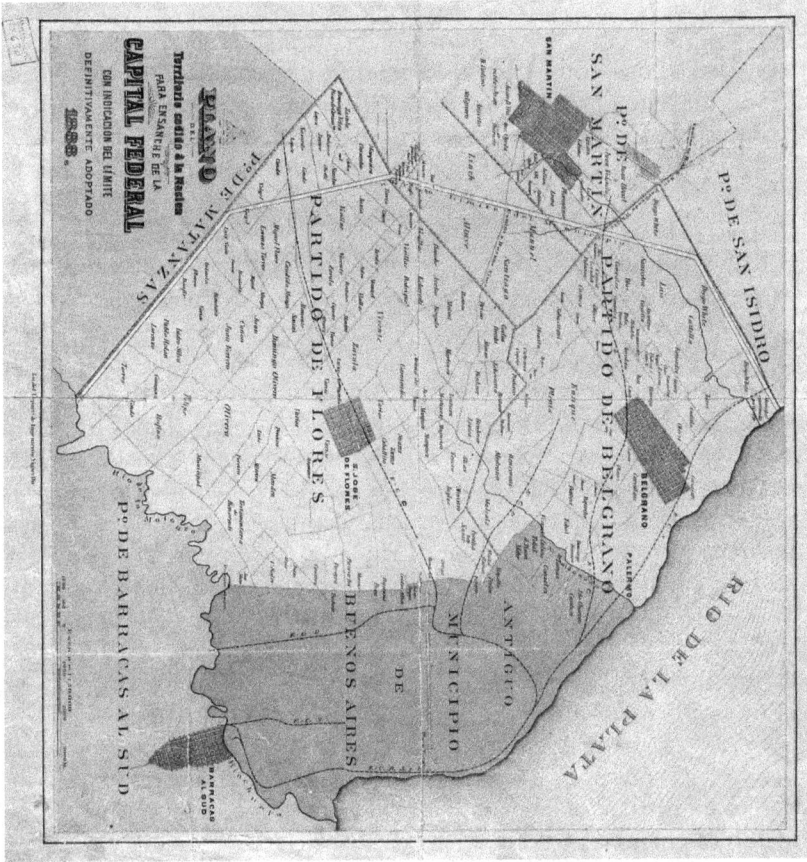

Figure 3. Engineering Department, *Plan of the Lands Transferred by the Province of Buenos Aires for the Federal Capital's Expansion*, 1888. Lithograph. Museo de la Ciudad, Buenos Aires. The plan shows the city limits (now General Paz Avenue), drawn by engineers Blot and Silveyra. It should be noted that the boundary seeks to establish regularity and does not adapt itself to the preexisting form of the transferred districts (Flores and Belgrano). It also includes a sector of San Martín district.

Figure 4. Plan comparing the overall surface of Buenos Aires and London, published in *La Nación*, June 6, 1904.

in what could be characterized as a *reformist cycle*, which toward the beginning of the thirties would be interrupted by an opposite ideological-cultural-urban configuration: that of the triumph of a *modernization without reform*. These are, very briefly, the premises proposed: a specific notion of public space, which the metropolitan qualifier seeks to particularize further; the ambition to construct its cultural history from a pair of figures that allude to material artifacts, the grid and the park; the delimitation of a historical period through a characterization of political terminology—the *reformist cycle*—and its contraposition with a notion such as *modernization*, approached in the terms of recent cultural analyses; more comprehensively, the proposition of a mode of approaching history through the city, of approaching culture through its material forms as they have been historically constituted.

This introduction explores these premises in greater detail through a synchronic survey of the whole historical cycle; but the body of the book seeks to trace an orderly history: each part deals with consecutive periods. The first goes from Domingo Faustino Sarmiento's earliest formulations in the 1840s to the end of the century. It analyzes the opposing figurations of city and public space proposed by Sarmiento and Mayor Torcuato de Alvear, those of the latter as the culmination of a long ideological tradition; and it confronts those figurations with the battery of public actions (especially, the grid and the park) that produce urban expansion at the end of the century. The second part focuses on the moment of the national centenary, as the identity-defining vortex of a period that largely covers the first two decades of the twentieth century: it is a strange moment, in which the acceleration of changes contrasts strongly with their scant visibility; the "traditional city" ignores—because it does not understand it, because it sees it as a threat or as degradation—the emergence of a novel suburb in the annexed territories. Starting from these "omissions," this part analyzes what happens in each sector of the city (and culture) separately: the public space of the "bourgeois city" during the centennial celebrations (the crisis at the moment of apotheosis) and the "silent" transformation in the suburbs of bunches of amorphous and semi-rural local communities into the *barrio* (neighborhood), understood as a cultural device, a new type of public space on a local scale that serves as a bridge between both sectors, and the way in which some isolated figures glimpsed what was happening in those suburbs broken up in the pampas (some travelers, some intellectuals, some technicians). The third part takes on the twenties and thirties; it analyzes the explosive irruption of the suburban neighborhood, the massive presence of its new public and cultural quality in urban management, politics, press, literature, and tango, and shows the different Buenos Aires that this explosion is configuring as confronted imaginaries, but, above all, the metropolitan dimension that the new public space of the neighborhood achieves. Finally, it tries to show the rupture of that expansive experience and to explore its reasons in society and culture, through analysis of the politics of Mariano de Vedia y Mitre's administration.

This very brief guide to the book reveals the many themes involved in the reconstruction of this historical cycle. In some cases, this multiplicity has translated into necessary shifts in focus: some chapters center on urban aspects, others on politics, others on literary, institutional, or social issues. But in all cases the common thread is that of cultural history: the certainty that all these issues take shape in culture is what should unify these approaches; the conviction that a literary quotation can shed light on urban discussions, and an urban plan on the debates of the literary avant-garde. Ultimately, this explains perhaps the book's greatest ambition: to offer an account of a period's "urban culture." That is, to produce a double cultural restitution of the city: to show how city and culture produce each other.

The Grid and the Park: An Approach to Public Space

What are the grid and the park? Literally, the grid of blocks that squares the territory of Buenos Aires and the urban greenery realized in the public parks. Here they are also intended as basic structures of metropolitan public space in Buenos Aires; supports (symbolic and material) for more comprehensive interventions on public space or representations of it, such as monuments or institutions, historical artifacts that contain conflicting ideas about what the public sphere should be, precise cultural and political projects; keys to technical and ideological traditions as long-standing as assertively imposed. They are, at the same time, instruments of urban intervention; that is to say, pragmatic constituents of urban planning in a city without a theoretical tradition in that discipline. Therefore, according to how the urban theory in which they are molded is defined, they are instruments of social reform, formative figures of citizenship and their own metaphors: they are the materialization of models of state and society; traces of conflicts and projects, even those yet unrealized and even those that would never be fully realized; modalities, figures of public space, though not themselves public space.

In our understanding, public space is not the mere open space of the city in the way that urban theory has traditionally conceived it. It is known that public space is a category that carries a radical ambiguity: the same concept names material places and refers to spheres of human action; it speaks of form and of politics, in a way analogous to the way it was inscribed in the word polis. It is a category that has been revalued in recent years as the properly political dimension of social life, capable of illuminating aspects hitherto neglected in both political and social history: public space is a dimension that mediates between society and the state, in which multiple political expressions of citizenship are made public in multiple forms of association and conflict vis-à-vis the state. The aspiration for a politically active citizenship, within the framework of the reconsideration of the democratic problem, is precisely what has made the theoretical and historical discussion on public space so current. But it has also been revalued in its material quality: the public space of the city, in which that citizenship is active, is today a source of concern for theoreticians and urban planners and mobilizes broad sectors of society in a struggle that does not take as a threat what belongs to the state, but that which is private.

Those who have conceptualized public space have taken for granted this connection between urban public space and political public sphere, but, perhaps because of its constitutive ambiguity, there is no theory to guide the analysis of their mutual production, the peculiar unity of form and politics implicit in such reciprocity. This situation has generated a specialized approach, a bifurcated use, so to speak: for those who study the public sphere as the ideal sphere of mediation between society and the state (the press, associations, political parties, "public opinion"), the city and the spaces of public action are usually scenarios, more or less important yet only as the background on which actions develop; on the contrary, for those who study the public spaces of the city (thus, in plural: squares, streets, public buildings), these are models, invariants, typologies, artifacts defined by physical qualities and explained by the evolution of a disciplinary discourse—architectural or urban theory—of very long duration.

Here, on the other hand, we will consider public space as the product of a fleeting and unstable collision of form and politics. If social, cultural, or political processes appear to be involved in certain forms, it is more the product of a clash—as flashing and scintillating as it is ephemeral—than of a pursued and stable relationship. Thus, the emergence of public space could be thought of as a conjuncture, in the double meaning of a specific occasion in history and of an encounter of different spheres.[4] Therefore, it is not defined once and for all in the open and freely accessible space of the city: there is nothing preformed in the city that responds to "public space"; it is not a preexisting scenario or an epiphenomenon of social organization or political culture; it is public space insofar as it is traversed by a social experience at the same time that it organizes that experience and gives it certain forms. It is, therefore, a political quality of the city that may or may not emerge in defined conjunctures, in which different histories of very different durations intersect in unique ways: political, technical, urban, cultural, of ideas, and of society; it is a crossroads. Thus, the hypothesis regarding the existence or not of public space is the product of an

---

[4] I believe I am, in this way, close to the *register* in which Hannah Arendt develops her positions on public space, close to her way of representing it (rather than to a *theory* proper, a formulation which she rejects). See *The Human Condition* (Chicago: University of Chicago Press, 1958), especially chaps. II and VI. On this possibility of reading in Arendt's *register* —that is, in a lateral way to her formulations—a conceptual approach to the issues of public space in the city, see the analysis of her work by Pierre Ansay and René Schoonbrodt, *Penser la ville. Choix de textes philosophiques* (Brussels: AAM Editions, 1989), 62.

interpretation of the relationship between urban form and political culture of a given moment in history.

In our case, this moment is indicated in the category itself by the qualifier metropolitan, which again seeks to name material and social processes. Unlike the usual meaning of metropolis, which refers to the size of cities, here we seek to point out the qualitative change implied by the urban, economic, political, and social phenomenon that is metropolitanization, as opposed to the previous processes of the formation of a public sphere in the traditional city. This is the meaning of the notion of metropolis given by Georg Simmel at the beginning of the twentieth century, which has inspired a great part of the cultural and sociological readings of modernity: the metropolis is the general form of modern "existence," produced by the process of mercantilist rationalization of social relations that modify the quality of the traditional city into a quantified and abstract universe. In the case of Buenos Aires, Mayor Alvear's avenues at the beginning of the 1880s, with their high-rise buildings that promote a new form of urban income, are already setting a new scenario that breaks with the traditional city; but in our hypothesis, the fundamental change that allows us to begin to speak of a metropolis is the territorial expansion of 1887 generated by the transformation and complexification that the market produces—urban, political, and cultural—introducing masses of new popular groups to the city and to citizenship.[5]

Now, this periodization adopted to focus on metropolitan public space is what would in fact prevent the literal application of the most well-known theory of public space—the one formulated by Jürgen Habermas, inspired by the Enlightenment model—since it supposes a previous historical moment and a different historical conflict, the one that takes place between the aspirations of a nascent bourgeoisie and a particular type of absolutist state. In relation to Argentina after the 1880s, we must also incorporate to the notion of public space the founding role of the state in the process of modernization, which eliminates a good part of the classical meaning that is based, precisely, on the belonging of public space to civil society, as opposed to the state. That is, here

---

[5] See Georg Simmel, "The metropolis and the life of the spirit" (1903), in *The Art of the City. Rome, Florence, Venice* (London: Pushkin Press, 2018). On how to conceptualize the problem from the point of view of transformations in the urban market, I follow Italo Insolera, "Europa XIX secolo: ipotesi per una nuova definizione della città," in Alberto Caracciolo, *Dalla città preindustriale alla città del capitalismo* (Bologna: Il Mulino, 1975). Insolera shows the productive role of the Haussmannian boulevards, proposing the Parisian reform as the inauguration, through foundry activity, of the industry-city model: Haussmann not only organized the city as an efficient means for the production and circulation of goods, but he also invented the bourgeois house as a real estate commodity; this the reason for the birth of the boulevards. And this is when the industry-city demonstrates that it can competitively absorb the private capital that until then was invested in industrial production.

we must understand the formation and functioning of a metropolitan public space admitting that, to a great extent, it sought to be built "from above," with the declared objective of giving shape to a society that state reformism perceived in risk of atomization. This originary statism of the notion of the public in metropolitan Buenos Aires will also illuminate the movements coming from civil society, both in its productivity and its aporias. Thus, the notion of public space cannot be subjected here to any theoretical or historical orthodoxy; it will be taken more as a stimulus to focus on a series of problems than as a system of theoretical certainties; more as an access to new zones of historicity, than an explanatory matrix of them.[6]

Public space will be understood as a horizon, in a double sense. A conceptual horizon, which allows us to focus on the contacts between the two very different dimensions that it implies—the political and the urban— and lets us drive a wedge into the intersection of politics and form, to try to understand how one is produced in the other, to see what there is of one in the other. And a political horizon, of democratic politics and the right to the city, which implies the permanent tension toward the construction of a public arena that is inclusive of both social and cultural groups and issues that broaden the spectrum of what is established as the "common good."[7]

---

[6] This has already been assumed by the best works of history that in the local sphere are inspired, however, by the Habermasian notion of public space; I am referring especially to the works of Hilda Sabato on the period after Caseros. She has given a definitive comprehensive version of them in the suggestive book, *La política en las calles. Entre el voto y la movilización. Buenos Aires, 1862–1880* (Buenos Aires, Sudamericana, 1998). For Habermasian theory, see Jürgen Habermas, *The Structural Transformation of the Public Sphere: An Inquiry Into a Category of Bourgeois Society* (1962) (Cambridge, MA, MIT Press, 1991); and "The Public Sphere: An Encyclopedia Article (1964)," *New German Critique 3* (1974), the English version of the article Habermas wrote for the Fisher Lexicon, *Staat und Politik* (Frankfurt, 1964). With respect to the limitations I raise, Habermas himself took care to stress, responding in advance to so many anachronistic uses of his theory, that it cannot be used as a "model": the "bourgeois public sphere" can only be understood historically as a "typical epochal category"; *History and Criticism,* 38. Indeed, every important theoretical formulation of public space has presupposed a specific *moment of realization* (classical antiquity for Arendt, for example), postulating in the concept itself a debate on the problem of periodization in Western culture.

[7] In this last paragraph I am paraphrasing aspects of Nancy Fraser's intervention in the debates generated by the re-reading of Jürgen Habermas's classic text; see "Rethinking the Public Sphere: A Contribution of Actually Existing Democracy," in Craig Calhoun, ed., *Habermas and the Public Sphere* (Cambridge, MA: MIT Press, 1991).

Historiographical Paradigms

The grid and the park are, then, the material and cultural protagonists of the history of the production of that political horizon in metropolitan Buenos Aires. This book builds the historical framework that constitutes both figures into an urban and cultural reality of long duration and multiple effects in the city. In this introduction we will proceed in reverse: trying to understand and discuss their conflictive place in the historiography so as to cut out a new figure from the negative. The grid has always been considered as the spontaneous product of real estate speculation; the parks, as the hygienic, ornamental, or recreational green space, always insufficient and always marching in the rearguard of other processes (land rent, transport, infrastructure). For inverse reasons (one for its excess and the other for its lack thereof), both were taken as a clear demonstration of the absence of public authority to influence the city's destiny. Here, however, they are considered as public space, not because they are in themselves open spaces of free circulation, but because in Buenos Aires they historically functioned as triggers of the emergence of a metropolitan public space, especially through their role as instruments of the public regulation of urban form.

In this sense, the mere presence of the grid and the park as public realities calls into question the main paradigm on which the modern historiography of metropolitan Buenos Aires was built: the conviction that the expansion of the city was the direct product of a combination of technical modernization (the port, the railways, and the electrification of the tramway) and the needs of local and foreign capital (real estate speculation with its famous sale of lots in installments and the private exploitation of public transport). As we know, it was James Scobie who in the 1970s masterfully formalized this paradigm, in the first book on the history of Buenos Aires structured through a set of coherent hypotheses.[8] His work was indebted to the usual precepts of urban history of the period, in which the mark of economicism (with distant Marxist resonances, but carried forward through structural-functionalist developmentalism) led to foregrounding technical processes (also as a way of adapting the functionalist hypothesis that causally links industrialization and metropolitanization).[9]

---

[8] James Scobie, *Buenos Aires: Plaza to Suburb, 1870–1910* (New York: Oxford University Press, 1974). There are two other very important works contemporary to Scobie's that share his vision of the expansion but advance other aspects of the research and are essential for consultation: Charles Sargent, *The Spatial Evolution of Greater Buenos Aires, Argentina, 1870–1930* (Tempe: Arizona State University, 1974); and Horacio Torres, "Evolución de los procesos de estructuración espacial urbana. El caso de Buenos Aires," Desarrollo Económico (Buenos Aires) 58 (July–September 1975).

[9] We have developed this theme with Graciela Silvestri in "Imágenes al sur. Sobre algunas hipótesis de James Scobie para el desarrollo de Buenos Aires," *Anales del Instituto de Arte Americano e Investigaciones Estéticas "Mario J. Buschiazzo,"* 27–28 (1991).

The conceptual keys deployed by the notion of public space, the world of problems and objects that its approach uncovers, allow us to identify processes that seriously question that paradigm. Continuing with the example of the relationship between public and private in metropolitan expansion, the grid and the park show that the urban expansion carried out by the tramway and the creation of plots moved within the very narrow limits imposed by public authorities, following the priority given to a punctiliously and publicly delineated blueprint that covered the entire new territory of the city. At the end of the century there is a battery of public actions that have not been analyzed so far in their specificity; actions not concerted as a joint and organic plan but coinciding in their intention to control urban expansion; the construction of a rational market and the definition, through the form of the city, of the modalities of sociability for the new inhabitants of an enlarged public space. I am referring to the demarcation of the new limits of the federal capital (1888) and the subsequent parallel development, between 1898 and 1904, of two decisive actions: the design of a public expansion plan for that vast territory and the layout of a system of parks around the perimeter of the traditional city, in the border space between the consolidated city and the new areas. It is necessary to recall that the first cycle of private suburban expansion took place precisely from 1904 onwards: it was not until then that the electrification of the tramway became generalized (with the consequent reduction of tickets) and the massive process of the sale of land in installments began.

Let's pause, then, to reflect on this battery of public actions. First, the new limit of the city, the "Boulevard de circunvalación" (beltway boulevard) rules out adapting the new shape of the municipality to the irregular borders of the sum of the two annexed municipalities: a regular and artificial line is drawn (the future General Paz Avenue) fixing an ordered figure for the new city, seeking to preserve, despite the change of scale, the centrality and the symmetry of the traditional city. As if attempting to project geometrically toward the city's new extension—what for Bernardino Rivadavia had been the Entre Ríos-Callao Boulevard and for Alvear would be his own beltway Boulevard project—here a will to form seeks to cut out what is and is not the city, though in this case the line is drawn in the middle of the vastness of the pampa. Second, the public map squares this new territory. Published in 1904, this road map, practically identical to the gridiron metropolis that would materialize a few decades later, covers with a homogenizing grid the vast wastelands that surrounded the city up to its brand-new limit. It manifests the will of the state for the incorporation of those lands to the urban market to be made according to an ideally equitable public delineation in all directions of the potential growth of the city. And, finally, in those same years, there emerged the project and (partial) realization of a series of parks that sought to form a green belt for the already consolidated concentrated city; the idea of an incipient system of parks conceived by the municipality simultaneously with the expansion of the grid; a green belt that coincides with the will to form the new city limits but that openly proposes to limit urban expansion.

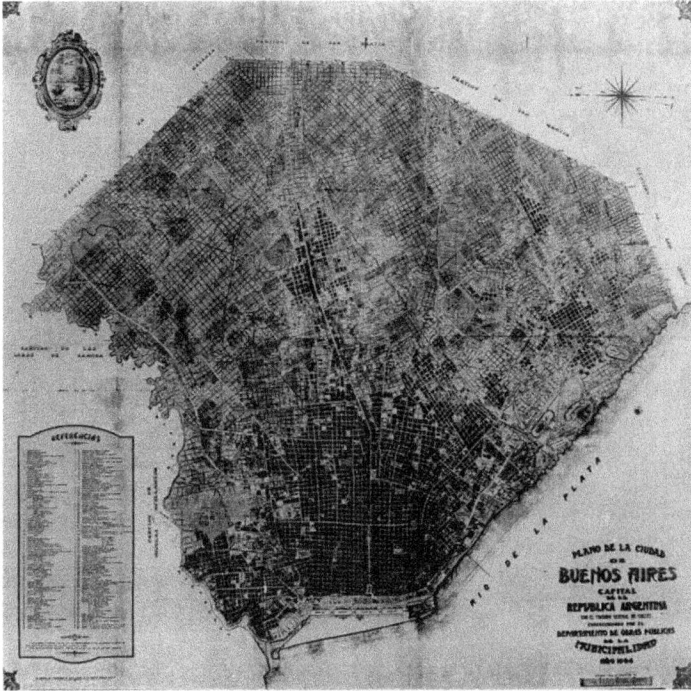

Figure 5. Department of Public Works, Buenos Aires, *Plan of Buenos Aires with Annexed Lands*, 1904. Instituto Histórico de la Ciudad de Buenos Aires.
The plan, drawn between 1898 and 1904 by a municipal commission overseen by Carlos María Morales, an engineer and then acting as Director of Public Works, publishes for the first time the image of the grid over the entirety of the annexed lands. Note the difference between the grid over built areas (darker) and the broad areas of the more uniform grid drawn over the empty territory. The squares drawn on this plan are those that would be open and built, with barely any modification, over the next four decades.

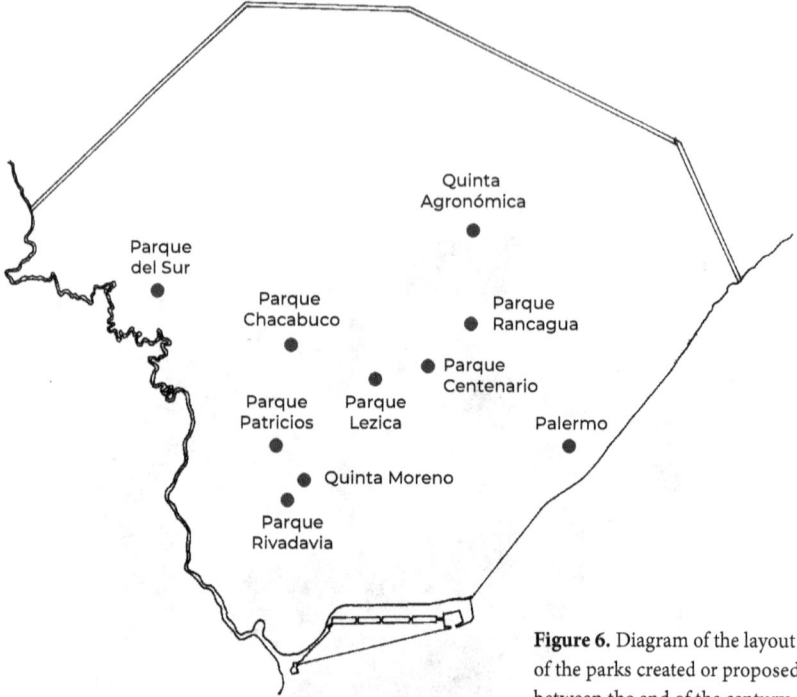

Figure 6. Diagram of the layout of the parks created or proposed between the end of the century and 1904.

Figure 7. Department of Public Works, Buenos Aires, *Plan of Buenos Aires* (detail of the Parque Chacabuco sector), 1904. Museo Mitre, Buenos Aires.

We will analyze the contradictory impulses contained in this battery of public actions, but, in principle, the grid and the park appear there as the incarnation of a public will to project the city, a will whose capacity and consequences are at least surprising for the time, and produces, in itself, enormous modifications to our images of metropolitanization. Possibly, those who are not acquainted with urban plans do not immediately notice the importance that this set of actions—the early public definition of a vast urbanizable territory around the traditional city—had for Buenos Aires. It shows that the undeveloped territory that was annexed in 1887 was not occupied at the mere design of real estate speculation or technical modernization. Perhaps the contrast with what was more common at the time in Latin American cities serves as an illustration: in these cities, faced with a state that did not care or that directly partnered with real estate investors, the new lots lacked any regulation, any contact with each other and any belonging to a global image of the future city they were building, which gave rise to the typical Latin American distinction between a legal and an illegal city. One of the hypotheses of this book is, instead, that the existence in Buenos Aires of a public plan extending not only to the entire built city but foreseeing a growth that would only occur over decades, was one of the urban material bases that generated the possibility of public space and that established in the structure of the city one of the key factors of future social and cultural integration; a gesture, as we will see, comparable to very few international experiences. This public will does not arise from a vacuum: it speaks of the slow and coordinated production of instruments of urban intervention, of the construction of a public administration capable of putting them into practice, of political and urban projects that were outlined during a good part of the nineteenth century through city management but, above all, of intense intellectual and political discussions that put the city and its public space at the center of cultural debates on the definition of the nation. Following a program that had become common sense since the Enlightenment; changing society and changing the city were two faces of the same project that, in the Buenos Aires of the new century, would find definitive and defining form in the grid and the park.

Now, just as this set of public actions appears under the lens of a historiographical perspective that emphasizes the notion of public space, so its absence in the existing historiography could explain the limits of its conceptual perspective: as in Edgar Allan Poe's "The Purloined Letter," one cannot see what is most obvious when it is too obvious—and what could be more obvious than the *porteño* grid?—or, to put it more like Detective Dupin, when its evidence is outside the presuppositions that guide the investigation. The traditional histories of fin-de-siècle Buenos Aires aim to show (to praise or criticize) a "European" city, modernized with British loans and infrastructure, with French urban criteria and Italian builders. This is all undeniable and at the same time, at least today, useless. Because it does not allow us to understand the peculiarity of what was produced as a city and as a society, which is far from being a degraded, incomplete, or parodic version of "original models": it is the very notion of influence that must be called into question. On the one hand, we must contemplate the peculiarities that the mixture itself entails, a subject exemplarily developed in the cultural studies of Adolfo Prieto or Beatriz Sarlo; on the other, we should acknowledge that this mixture took place in a Buenos Aires that, as Jorge Francisco Liernur has shown, was throughout this period a sort of provisional frontier camp.[10] But here I am interested in going further back, to show that such ignorance has deep roots, which appear on the back of a very long tradition of rejection of one of our two protagonists: the grid, and what it represented—the unlimited suburban sprawl. Avoiding the symmetrical Manichaeism of now inverting this rejection, I propose to inscribe it in a new vision of the city's history. By deciphering from the negative the constant presence of the grid in thinking about the city, we are offered in this case a glimpse into the specific characteristics of the culture and society of Buenos Aires; because such denial had a cultural and a socioeconomic side: the first speaks of the images and imaginaries of the relations between the city and the pampa; the second of the vicissitudes of a constellation of reformist views and actions on the city.

City and Pampa

One of the paradoxical effects of the rejection of the grid and of suburban expansion has been its most complete naturalization: as if the foundational grid fixed by the colonial laws of the Indies had genetically determined all future development. This is one of the reasons why neither the outline of the new federalized city nor the grid of the 1898–1904 plan have been visible. Were they not already inscribed in a destiny as inescapable as it was natural? In the line of culturalist interpretation of the city (that is, one that deterministically links urban form and culture, the longest lasting in Argentina), it is an opprobrious destiny imposed by the double barbarism of Spanish tradition and pampean nature. The curious thing is that this culturalist repudiation, initially enormously productive, condensed a series of diagnoses and was crystallized into a sort of common sense that survived long after the conditions and paradigms from which they were formulated had changed.

Sarmiento is one of the first to propose a diagnosis: the identification of the old city with the persistence of tradition, as a synonym of Spanish "lack of foresight" and "ignorance" and of the anomic threat of the pampa; the pampa

---

[10] Adolfo Prieto, *El discurso criollista en la formación de la Argentina moderna* (Buenos Aires: Sudamericana, 1991); and Beatriz Sarlo, *Una modernidad periférica: Buenos Aires 1920 y 1930* (Buenos Aires: Nueva Visión, 1988). Jorge Francisco Liernur, "La ciudad efímera," in Liernur and Silvestri, *El umbral de la metrópolis. Transformaciones técnicas y cultura en la modernización de Buenos Aires (1870–1930)* (Buenos Aires: Sudamericana, 1993).

is the metaphor of the asphyxia of a city that the grid turns into "a vast prison," into "a plethoric body that drowns."[11] It is the portrait of a traditional city that could only reproduce, in Sarmiento's vision, a traditional society. To them he opposes a vision of the city as public space, made possible exclusively by the modernist charge of the idea of the park: Palermo, as the ex-novo beginning of a new city for a new society that could only emerge far away and outside the traditional city. The park is a meeting place for the picturesque and the sublime, for culture and democratic civility, opposed both to formless nature and to the past present in the grid.

15, 16

But Palermo did not constitute a new city, nor its center of gravity; rather, toward the end of the century, it was subsumed in the indifference of the new grid. Thus, when the grid is designed for the whole of the enormous, annexed territory, the two threats of the civilizing model seem to feed into each other: the city, through the grid, realizes the threat of the pampa; its expansion cannot be seen as a culturization of the plains, but as a metamorphosis. Thirty years later, Ezequiel Martínez Estrada sees that "Buenos Aires has been engendered, conceived, and superimpregnated by the plain. Surface: that is the emblematic word. Surface is the essence of the city that lacks a third dimension."[12] During those decades, countless testimonies tend to identify the city as an indeterminate prolongation of the pampa: "One of the peculiarities of Buenos Ayres is that you can see no end of it. Since on the pampas there is no obstacle," Georges Clemenceau would write in 1910; and two decades later Massimo Bontempelli would in turn claim that:

> Buenos Aires is a piece of pampa translated into city. This explains its construction by blocks [...]. By repeating the blocks to infinity, a city is made, without necessary limits. [...] The principle of repetition to infinity, taught by nature with the pampa, has been scrupulously repeated by men when they had to build the human world facing the natural world.[13]

But what for some visitors could be auspicious (understanding it as a peculiarity of the "American city"), was a demonstration of failure for local observers: the city "has no end in sight," the city "has no necessary limits," because

---

[11] Domingo Faustino Sarmiento, "Arquitectura doméstica" (October 15, 1879), in *Obras completas*, ed. A. Belin Sarmiento (Buenos Aires: Imprenta y Litografía Mariano Moreno, 1900), XLVI:104. This edition of Sarmiento's complete works will be cited as *Obras completas (BS)*.

[12] Ezequiel Martínez Estrada, *X-ray of the Pampa* (1933) (Austin: University of Texas Press, 1971), 230.

[13] Georges Clemenceau, *South America To-day; A Study of Conditions, Social, Political and Commercial in Argentina, Uruguay and Brazil* (New York, London: G. P. Putnam's Sons, 1911), 30; Massimo Bontempelli, *Noi, gli Aria. Interpretazioni sudamericane* (1933) (Palermo: Sellerio Editore, 1994), 68–69.

the pampa is no longer an obstacle, but a means for metropolitan expansion: the modern city, as it advances on the pampa, becomes more and more its own metaphor. The culturalist key to the repudiation of the grid is its assimilation to the barbarism that the city was called upon to banish. And we will see how all discussions of expansion and all the projects for public parks will be touched by this culturalist ambition to define the frontier of the pampas.

In this very long refutation of the grid by the pampa (that is, in the identi-fication of the grid with the barbaric, pre-modern tradition), there are several paradoxes that richly inform us about aspects of local urban culture and of the city itself. The first of these is that, at least since William Penn created the modern version of the squared grid for the North American city, in most of the world, and unlike what happened in Buenos Aires, the grid has been the urban planning instrument identified with the crudest capitalist rationality and with the most radical territorial modernization, devoid of any cultural mediation.[14] Here there is a paradox that fed more than a few misunderstandings in the triangular relationship of Europe–North America–Buenos Aires, a relationship always mediated by the generic prestige of a vague image of the European city placed in opposition to the absence of history and the beauty of the American city; it was precisely the vagueness of that opposition that, in the nineteenth century, often made criticisms put forth from absolutely different criteria appear the same. Let us compare two travelers in America: Charles Dickens and Émile Daireaux. In his American Notes, Dickens recalls his mid-century stay in Philadelphia, the city created, precisely, by Penn, as "a handsome city, but distractingly regular." "After walking about it for an hour or two," he wrote, "I felt that I would have given the world for a crooked street."[15] Daireaux, in turn, describes the Buenos Aires of the late 1880s:

> Entirely straight, the streets always continue, with no other object than to prolong in the same line those that were traced or outlined three centuries ago. They lead further than they did then, but to the same place, to the con-fines of the city, which recedes in front of them without changing in any way [...]. You are overcome by a kind of melancholy as you walk along houses that give you only the feeling of having been seen.[16]

---

8 [14] William Penn planned Philadelphia as the capital of the Quaker province of Pennsylvania (1681) with a regular and uniform layout that markedly determined the course of subsequent urban design in the United States. See John Reps, *The Making of Urban America: A History of City Planning in the United States* (Princeton: Princeton University Press, 1965).
[15] Charles Dickens, *American Notes* (1842) (New York: Modern Library, 1996), 129.
[16] Émile Daireaux, *Vida y costumbres en el Plata*, vol. 1 (Buenos Aires: Félix Lajouane, 1888), 119.

Evidently, both travelers have different European models to back up their criticism: Dickens's motley London, Daireaux's radial and baroque Paris. This shows that defining the prestige of the European city univocally—at a time when the dialogue between cities was intense and complexly cut across models and viewpoints—is very misleading, because depending on who it was, or depending on the moment, absolutely contradictory elements could weigh in its celebration: from the rational clarity of Baroque interventions, with their circular and diagonal avenues, to the cultural density of historical centers; that is, the nineteenth-century "modern" city or, in tune with the historicist claims that rejected those interventions, the variety and complexity of the intricate medieval streets, their "organicity," their ability to form communities by contrast to the anonymity of the new metropolis. In this way, Dickens impugns the modernity of Philadelphia and Daireaux the absence of modernity in Buenos Aires, the uncut prolongation of its traditional layout. Yet both do so in practically identical terms, making their different criticisms of cities that they see differently—though not precisely through what they see—coincide in the exasperating regularity of the grid.

The example should prepare us to understand the criticisms that we will find in local culture, because this mixture of motives is what founds the experience of distance that travel offers elites, when from Europe they perceive the contrasts with the endless perspectives of the always similar streets of Buenos Aires, whose low houses with flat roofs matched the tedious regularity of the   27 plain: "the ugliest city I have known among those of the first, second, and fourth order," in the words of Miguel Cané.[17] "Whoever arrives from another continent to Buenos Aires feels the uneasiness of its delineation, because the suppression of perspective is really disturbing," wrote Enrique Prins in 1910. And it is not that Prins did not consider that this maddeningly monotonous outline had been renewed since Cané's times with a deliberate and modern public gesture; he simply linked his impression to an already established culturalist tradition that identified the "congenital vice" from the Spanish colonizers to the municipalities of the end of the century as an inevitable response imposed by the pampas:

> Flat land, edge of the great pampean savanna, the nature of the place did not offer the picturesque model of irregular land. Nothing was more logical in the face of that imperturbable plane than to complete the existing work with the simplest and most elementary geometric expression: the straight line.[18]

---

[17] Miguel Cané, "Carta al Intendente Torcuato de Alvear desde Viena (January 14, 1885)," reproduced in Adrián Beccar Varela, *Torcuato de Alvear. Primer Intendente municipal de la ciudad de Buenos Aires* (Buenos Aires: Kraft, 1926), 481.

[18] Enrique Prins, "Arquitectura de la ciudad de Buenos Aires," *Censo General de Población, Edificación, Comercio e Industrias de la Ciudad de Buenos Aires*, vol. 3 (Buenos Aires: Compañía Sudamericana de Billetes de Banco, 1910), 374. It is curious and indicative

This was a diagnosis that would pass from urban criticism to literature and cultural criticism with great fluidity, gathering a handful of deeply receptive arguments. A few years later Baldomero Fernández Moreno (in one of the first urban poetry books) would thank "Rauch alley" for offering "the simple mystery of (its) curve" to his "spirit tired of so many straight streets;" and still later Eduardo Schiaffino would find the explanation for so much monotony in that the city's founder, Juan de Garay, had been a military engineer: "between him and his imitators they have squared the ground of the Republic."[19] Whether due to the hegemony of picturesque city models or to the later modernist rejection of the rue corridor, the main figures who reflected on the city in the first half of the twentieth century coincided in these judgments, and continued to extract negative interpretations of its culture from the city's chessboard form. Clemenceau's expectant "absence of obstacles" translated into the "vast meanders of the flat city, in the monotonous narrow streets of the capital" of Eduardo Mallea's "visible city." For these authors, as for John Ruskin almost a century earlier, these "square stones are not prisons for the body, but graves of the soul."[20]

49, 51

The absence of obstacles is the primary flaw: the impossibility of setting a stable boundary between the city and the pampa is the cause of a limitless expansion that always imagines the new city as the most exact possible extension of the existing one. Contrario sensu, today it is very suggestive to think that this absence of a natural border that made the grid's lack of charms more notorious, collaborated with the public will to favor an integrated suburbanization without a solution of material continuity; again, it is convenient to recall other Latin American cities (such as Rio de Janeiro, São Paulo, or Caracas), where elements of nature were a factor in the constitution of barriers between social sectors. In Buenos Aires, nature and public will converged in a leveling spirit: the much-repudiated impossibility of establishing a stable border between the city and the pampa constituted one of the main incentives to imagine unlimited expansion as a way of resolving the conditions of overcrowding in the center and allowing an expansion that is at once that of the city and of the citizenry. The operation was possible, again, thanks to the cultural vacuum

---

of the way in which historiography approached the question that a historian like Guy Bourdé takes up these arguments literally and explains the persistence of grid layouts in terms of the "horror of emptiness" that "seems to replace the architectural imagination" of nineteenth-century men; see *Buenos Aires: urbanización e inmigración* (Buenos Aires: Huemul, 1977), 96.

[19] "Callejuela Rauch" (1917), in B. Fernández Moreno, *Ciudad, 1915–1949* (Buenos Aires: Ediciones de la Municipalidad, 1949); Eduardo Schiaffino, *Urbanización de Buenos Aires* (Buenos Aires: Manuel Gleizer, 1927), 232.

[20] Eduardo Mallea, *History of an Argentine Passion* (1937) (Pittsburgh: Latin American Literary Review Press, 1983), 49. John Ruskin, *The Seven Lamps of Architecture* (New York: John Wiley & Sons, 1889), 66.

of the territories that had been annexed, burdened only with values to be over-come: barbarism, tradition.

But to suppose that the pampean plain favored an expansion without fron-tiers does not imply a peaceful expansion with its surroundings. The culturalist repudiation of the pampa's imposition strangely combined the desire for the "picturesque model of irregular land" with a tenacious struggle against every-thing that was perceived as a threat from nature against the city. If one thinks of the continuous filling of the Río de la Plata—the other plain that threatened to spill over into the city—the monumental work of raising La Boca, the piping of the streams or the almost total flattening of the ravine that defined the pla-teau on which the central part of the city extends, one sees a desire to even out the land, aimed at achieving the homogeneous plan of the city that sought to deliberately and conscientiously tame all irregular remains. A will that in each of its manifestations did not cease to lament the scarce goods (in the sense of those that broke the horizontal monotony) that were lost, but whose ideal of regularity was constant and sustained. And this is the crux of the paradox: the grid tries to fill the emptiness of the pampa, tries to build a city on nothingness. Because it sees nature as a material and cultural threat, it founds an abstract, homogeneous, regular form: pure culture (in the only way modernity knows how to achieve it); yet in that regularity, culturalism denounces the triumph of nature (and there is nothing more traditional than nature), because what appears as the main abstraction is the very immensity of the plain, its absence of organicity. As discussed above, this is the restitution promised by the public park since its local creation by Sarmiento. The park as human creation: that is what the Palermo gates are for, to take distance from nature, to create a place among nothingness. And this mark is still present and gives meaning to the parks that are created simultaneously with the grid at the end of the century, in an explicit attempt to form a greenbelt that, starting from Palermo, would border the entire perimeter of the traditional city.

16

6

The other great paradox in the same culturalist framework is that, as is well-known, from the end of the century the vision of the pampa acquired pos-itive value. Faced with the crisis of the civilizing ideal after the financial and political crash of 1890 and the babel of languages and faces that transformed the metropolis, the pampa began to appear as an uncontaminated place, a reservoir of pure values—along with the gaucho, who was transformed into a mythical figure as he became extinct as a real figure—the pampa became an emblem of nationality, the cultural response to the need to build an identity in the face of the migratory flood. And yet, most observers of the process of urban modernization continued to describe the city produced by the grid in negative terms, because of its assimilation with the pampas.

There are few exceptions, such as Borges's most notorious gesture, one that characterizes many of his cultural operations: turning lack into value. He thus imagines the mythical foundation of Buenos Aires in a square block, "a whole square block, but set down in open country," provocatively giving foundational status to the two symbols culturalism condemned.[21] It is precisely on the absence of character of the peripheral city, of the anomic suburb in its undifferentiated foothills with the pampa, where Borges seeks to construct the "epic" that the city dweller lacks, and where he proposes that the modernist construction of cultural identity can fully emerge. But here it is important to show that both the culturalist tradition and its Borgesian inversion only densify the relationship, mediated by the grid, between the traditional city and its modern expansion: it is not a matter of taking sides with one version or the other, but of making room for the number of problems that their contrasts and mismatched junctions reveal. In particular, the imaginary quality with which the abstraction of the grid replicates that of the pampa, a theme that can be identified in the literature and which opens a perspective into the complexity of the dialogues and influences with external urban models.

The Park Against the Grid? The Problem of Reformism

We have identified a specific public will at the moment of the emergence of the grid and the park, and this public will, in the first instance, allows us to postulate a reformist vocation. But when the grid and the park are placed in parallel as a demonstration of a public will to reform, it should be clear not only that two different figures are being brought together, but that two true condensers of meaning that represent irreconcilably opposed conceptual universes in relation to the issue of reform in urban thought are being made to work in the same direction: the park has always been understood as the privileged instrument of reform—social, cultural, and urban—as opposed to the grid, representative of speculative economic interests. This version emerges paradigmatically in the mid-nineteenth century out of the process of formation of Manhattan's Central Park, which became the public park par excellence in the urban imaginary. For although in Europe the park was already associated with hygienic and political reform (environmental sanitation in the increasingly congested city and the opening of the palatial gardens to the bourgeois and plebeian public), the construction of Central Park was a true collective epic of reform that imposed—over more than two decades of fierce debates—the public interest over the interests of landowners, speculators and political bosses, opening in its own heart the rigid grid that ideally covered the entire island.[22] From that

---

[21] Jorge Luis Borges, "The Mythical Founding of Buenos Aires," *Cuaderno San Martín* (1929), translated in *Selected Poems* (New York: Viking, 1999), 53.

[22] It should be noted that this is the "heroic version"; here we are not interested in questioning it critically but in following the history of this idea of the park as a reformist device. For a critical version, see Francesco Dal Co, "From Parks to the Region: Progressive Ideology and the Reform of the American City," in Giorgio Ciucci,

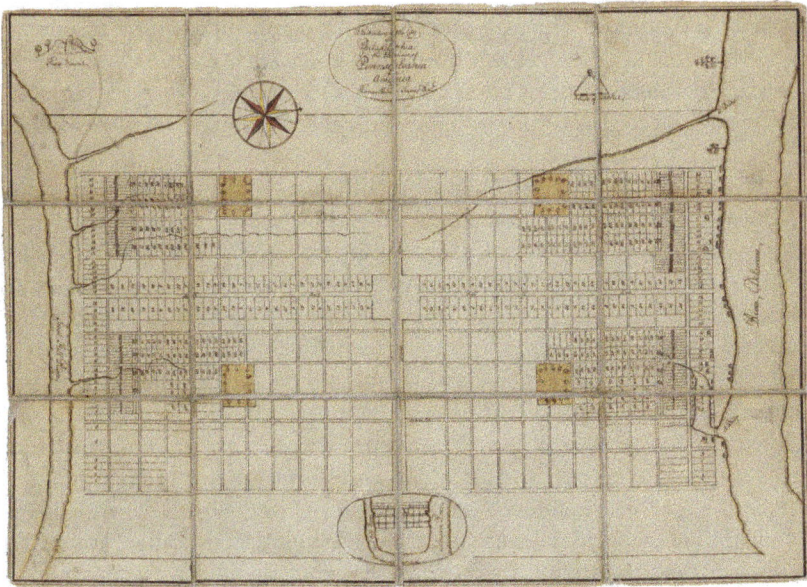

Figure 8. Thomas Holme, *A Portrait of the City of Philadelphia in the Province of Pennsylvania*, 1683. Historical Society of Pennsylvania. The map, commissioned by William Penn, served as a model for innumerable city layouts in the United States.

Figure 9. Drawing by Le Corbusier comparing urban layouts: traditional Paris, New York, and Buenos Aires. From *La ville radieuse*. Paris: Éditions de l'Architecture d'Aujourd'hui, 1935.

foundational moment, the park remains in the urban and political imaginary as the instrument of reform and the grid as its object. As if it had not been a fundamental instrument of modernization, the nineteenth-century park has always been rescued as key in the search to restore a more socially and environmentally harmonious city.

In tune with international experience, in the cycle in which the main parks of Buenos Aires were planned and built—from Palermo to the thirties—the idea of the park will superimpose and densify meanings that give it the quality of exemplary public space: hygienic referent returning the metropolitan experience to nature (the park as nature reintroduced into the city); civic institution of social equality and political freedom (the park as civic center, spatial organizer of republican institutions, and patriotic monuments); pole of community grouping and identity (the park as "new cathedral" in the modern city). We will see the complexity that the superposition of organicist and rationalist valences gives to this public space and to the reformisms that promote it; but it is convenient to pause and reconsider here the opposition with the grid, opposition in which the grid is defined as precise negative to each of those meanings: artificial structure, symbol of the will of the brutal dominion of modern man over nature; diagram of the omnipotent power of the market and of the political submission to its empire; basic scheme of anonymity, demonstration of the impossibility of communitarian grouping.

It is the other, socioeconomic rejection of the block, which, unlike the culturalist one, identifies the grid with what is most modern and criticizes it for the capitalist exploitation of territory and metropolitan anomie. It is a constitutive repudiation of urban planning as such, since in its classic, central European version, urbanistics are formed as a reaction to the plans of squared extension typical of the second half of the nineteenth century, raising as an alternative the English model of the decentralized garden suburb. But even in the imaginary projections of this classical urbanism, those expansive plans that were rejected in European cities did nothing more than refer, once again, to the basic matrix found in American capitalism and in its urban product par excellence: the universal, abstract grid, as the economic control of nature. So it is in the literature on North American cities that the standard account of this rejection is also developed, beginning with Frederick Law Olmsted himself—creator of Central Park and, therefore, a pioneer in the denunciation of the grid—crossing the entire field of North American historiography: from Lewis Mumford, for whom capitalism "treated the individual lot and the block, the street and the avenue, as abstract units for buying and selling, without respect for historic uses, for topographic conditions, or for social needs;" to the historian John Reps, who criticized the New York grid in lapidary terms:

36, 37
49

Francesco Dal Co, Mario Manieri-Elia, and Manfredo Tafuri, *The American City: From the Civil War to the New Deal* (1973) (Cambridge, MA: MIT Press, 1979).

As an aid to speculation the commissioners' plan [of 1811] was perhaps   40
unequaled, but only on this ground can it be justifiably called a great achievement. The fact that it was this gridiron New York served as a model for
later cities was a disaster whose consequences have barely been mitigated by
more modern city planners.[23]

It is a technical, moral, and political repudiation that went through different
moments of revision throughout the century, and still endures in essence until
today.[24] In such a way that we find this disavowal again in the Marxist resonances
of recent historical analysis such as that of Peter Marcuse, for whom the early
capitalist grid (laissez-faire grid) appropriated the territory in such a way that
"the market, not the state, should determine its use;" and also in a more phe-
nomenological analysis of existentialist echoes, such as that of Richard Sennett,
for whom the network is the paradigm of the "neutral city," typical of the "Prot-
estant ethic" of American capitalism:

> [the grid] was a space for economic competition, to be played upon like a
> chessboard. It was a space of neutrality, a neutrality achieved by denying to
> the environment any value of its own. And, like the pyrrhic victory" [...], the
> grid disoriented those who played upon it; they could not establish what was
> of value in places without centers or boundaries, spaces of endless, mindless
> geometric division. This was the Protestant ethic of space.[25]

------

[23] Lewis Mumford, *The City in History: Its Origins, Its Transformations, and Its Prospects*
(New York: Harcourt Brace Jovanovich, 1961), 421; and Reps, *The Making of Urban
America*, 299. Reps distinguishes between William Penn's proposal for Philadelphia,   8
which he judges positively, and the New York grid, with considerations about the   41
appropriateness of the site (a plain in the case of Philadelphia, while in Manhattan the
geography of the island was unknown); but, in this way, he does not take into account
the symbolic charge that he himself recognizes that the grid had for Penn, beyond and
before the site, as the materialization of an ideal of political and religious freedom, and
of social and economic equality.
[24] It went through the vindication of the traditional street initiated by Jane Jacobs in the
sixties, although it was ultimately a communitarian vindication of the neighborhood;
and it survived the formalist rediscovery of the seventies, as developed by Rem Koolhaas
in his "retroactive manifesto" of Manhattan. See Jane Jacobs, *The Death and Life of Great
American Cities* (1968) (New York: Modern Library, 1993), and Rem Koolhaas, *Delirious
New York. A Retroactive Manifesto for Manhattan* (1978) (Rotterdam: 010 Publishers,
1994).
[25] The first quote in Peter Marcuse, "The Grid as City Plan: New York City and Laissez-
faire Planning in the Nineteenth Century," *Planning Perspectives 2* (1987): 295; the
second, in Richard Sennett, *The Conscience of the Eye: The Design and Social Life of
Cities* (New York: Alfred Knopf, 1990), 55. Marcuse's work is one of the first to attempt
a classification of different types of grids, which already represents an enormous

But Sennett builds his metaphor on what is at the very least a one-sided reading of Max Weber, materializing in the grid the image of the "iron cage" of instrumental rationality. Also following Weber, however, the gridiron could be thought of as the fullest manifestation of the state will to build a city in which the market finds a necessary reversal in public space. This relation of necessity is constitutive of the Weberian notion of the modern city: if the origin of the city is to be sought in the market, it is a market that bears a double meaning, economic and political, by which the relation between the economic population and political citizenship is underlined, and the city is defined as the place of homo oeconomicus as well as a political-administrative sphere.[26] Thus, in this definition, the market exists insofar as it allows exchange between free individuals, the emergence of an economic subject such that implies, at least, the "fiction of equivalence." It is by destroying the closed, integrated character of traditional society that this can come about; modern "civil society," of "incomplete integration," generates the two main attributes for the emergence of public space: equity and distance, from which formalized representation emerges: social forms, urban forms, building forms, forms of public presentation (manners, dress), political forms. Forms that allow for a public sphere capable of "bracketing," social differences, to use Jürgen Habermas' figure.[27]

Indeed, the homogeneity of the grid could be thought of as the most extreme materialization of this suspension of difference. It is obvious that it is an abstract and homogeneous matrix, the extreme manifestation of the modern capitalist will of rationalization and control, but is it not necessary to also analyze, along with its implications for social domination, its leveling effects? Along with its stimulus to speculation, its imposition of a framework—formal, juridical, and political—isn't it often too rigid for speculators? As anticipated, it is only possible to answer in a strictly historical framework: the reformist components of the grid depend on a specific moment not only because they are defined according to the available technical knowledge—the objectives and the effects of their layout—but also because reformism itself cannot but be defined conjuncturally, insofar as its essence is the opposition to that which it is called upon to reform, which is necessarily unstable and changing over time. Thus, we formulate these general considerations within the horizon of the gridiron-plan cities produced in the nineteenth and early twentieth centuries.

---

advancement compared to the disregard it has had in urbanistic thought; in any case, it reaffirms the vision of the grid as a scheme exclusively at the service of wild speculation.
[26] Max Weber, *The City* (1921) (Glencoe, IL.: Free Press, 1958), 20. More comprehensive readings than the one proposed by Sennett on Weber's hypotheses on these issues in Hans Paul Bahrdt, *La moderna metrópoli. Reflexiones sociológicas sobre la construcción de las ciudades* (1961) (Buenos Aires: EUDEBA, 1970), and Paolo Perulli, *Atlante metropolitano. Il mutamento sociale nelle grandi città* (Bologna: Il Mulino, 1992).
[27] Jürgen Habermas, *The Structural Transformation of the Public Sphere.* On the definitions of *equity* and *distance* in the modern city, see Bahrdt, *La moderna metrópoli.*

Having clarified this, it is possible to establish a more complex and comprehensive approach to the grid, relying even on the arguments of its fiercest critics. Starting again with Olmsted, who points out what for him was a negative correlation, between the homogeneity that "the rigid uniformity of the system" produces "spontaneously," and the impossibility of social differentiation:

> The clerk or mechanic and his young family, wishing to live modestly in a house by themselves, without servants, is provided for in this respect no otherwise than the wealthy merchant, who, with a large family and numerous servants, wishes to display works of art, to form a large library, and to enjoy the company of many guests.[28]

Undoubtedly, for this description of the urban effects of the checkerboard to continue to seem critical, one would have to share Olmsted's elitist rejection of social leveling. But don't the reasons for this elitist rejection find their local echo, a century later, in Juan José Sebreli's populist refutation of the monotony of the middle-class barrios of Buenos Aires as a metaphor for their social and political misery, barrios whose uniformity makes them resemble "frightening labyrinths of order and common sense where it is as difficult to get lost as it is to find oneself"? To the economic refutation is added a social and ideological rejection of uniformity as a symptom and a cause of alienation.[29]

Also Marcuse offers arguments on the opposite side of this questioning of uniformity, since he must concede that "for representative purposes, the grid is a weak vessel," because it does not favor the formation of centers, nor hierarchical uses, and because in it "all plots are created equivalent and similar."[30] By emphasizing precisely this line of analysis, it has been possible to modify the interpretation of the role attributed to uniformity by the 1811 New York Commission, seeing it now as part of a defense of the preeminence of the public over the private in the expansion of the city: "Thanks to its efforts [the Commission's], the old form of [municipal] government founded on the management of private property gave way to a public bureaucracy whose mission was identified with collective welfare," one innovative paper notes, linking the grid to the emergence of another aspect of the Weberian notion of modernity: the constitution of a state bureaucracy.[31]

40

---

[28] Cited in Albert Fein, *Landscape into Cityscape: Frederick Law Olmsted's Plans for a Greater New York City* (Ithaca, New York: Cornell University Press, 1968), 354.

[29] Juan José Sebreli, *Buenos Aires, vida cotidiana y alienación* (1964) (Buenos Aires, Siglo Veinte, 1965), 69. Beyond his approach to the phenomenon, it is clear that Sebreli is right in identifying the grid with the consolidation of the Buenos Aires middle class, a truly original link for the time and which we will take up again differently.

[30] Peter Marcuse, "The Grid as City Plan: New York City and Laissez-faire Planning," 294.

[31] Jeanne Chase, "New York City reinventata: utili riflessioni su un ordine in continuo evolversi," in Carlo Olmo and Bernard Lepetit, eds., *La città e le sue storie* (Turin: Einaudi, 1995), 243.

For the discussion on the grid implies a deeper interpretative conflict, which opens up a number of central problems for our subject, mainly centered on the political character of public space. For the universalist pretension of this concept has been sharply dismantled by the Marxist tradition, along the lines of Marx's criticisms of the notion of "civil society," pointing out the double meaning of the German term that designates it: bürgerliche Gesellschaft means both civil society and bourgeois society. The same type of responses that the Habermasian notion of public sphere has received over the past few years, whose pretended universality has been questioned not only from the perspective of class, but also for its gender and cultural exclusions.[32] These are responses that, in the face of the recent generalization of a polyvalent use of notions such as citizenship or public sphere, relocate some unavoidable problems regarding their political and social limits. A the same time, faced with a literal continuity of this critical tradition, in recent years some theorists have begun to adopt more heterodox positions, starting precisely from a revaluation of that universalist conviction to question the reduction of citizenship in contemporary Western cities: rather than an instrument of domination or, its opposite, an ideal utopia of political functioning—that is, the terms between which much of the debate between the liberal and the left-wing tradition has passed—for these authors the public sphere—again, as a political horizon—can be an effective instrument of analysis and critique of the limits of existing democracy.[33]

9   If these questions are already problematic in relation to the New York grid, they are much more so if we analyze the emergence of the Buenos Aires grid, more contaminated by different and contradictory traditions. To begin with, because the inheritance of the Spanish checkerboard, of undoubted influence in the formal determination of the grid's expansion, has nevertheless prevented its specific treatment as a modern phenomenon.[34] In the case of the protago-

---

[32] Calhoun, ed., *Habermas and the Public Sphere.*

[33] See, for example, Perulli, *Atlante metropolitano*, and N. Fraser, "Rethinking the Public Sphere."

[34] As noted, this is so much the case that even the historiography has ignored its own
5   public formulation of 1898–1904. One of the few history texts that wonders about the meaning of the grid, although it does not consider its deliberate production as a public plan (in fact, it does not record the existence of the 1898–1904 plan), is Hardoy and Gutman, *Buenos Aires. Historia urbana del Area Metropolitana* (Madrid: Mapfre, 1992). In this text, the grid is explained on two grounds: the ease with which the grid represented for unprepared technical agencies, and, in a more conventional version, that "the checkerboard conformed to the speculative interests that guided and densified the city in those years," 91ff. In a more specifically architectural field, in the last two decades the sensibility with respect to the grid has changed, in the sense of the vindication of basic compositional structures for the city that the neorationalist tendency in Italy and Spain made in the seventies and eighties; for the most serious example of this new sensibility in favor of an acceptance of the grid as the basic structure of the conformation

nists of urban modernization, it could be thought that their inability to address the issue reveals the mixture of culturalist repudiation with a certain feeling of impotence, linked to the incapacity—ideological, political, economic—of the instruments of public governance in the face of private property and the mechanisms of real estate speculation that were activated once the grid was defined. There was almost no municipal administration that did not try to modify, albeit unsuccessfully, the systems of expropriation in favor of greater flexibility for urban reform. The grid thus became the summary of all the city's ills and the explanation of the impossibility of change; always a negative value, the result of a destiny as opprobrious as it was unchangeable: the explanation for Buenos Aires being the "hopeless" city diagnosed by Le Corbusier in 1929.

But in Buenos Aires the phenomenon itself is more complex because, toward the end of the century, the superimposition of traditions and values had become more accentuated and diversified: the fin-de-siècle *porteño* urban culture had to reckon with the grid of the Laws of Indies at the same time as with the North American experience, very attentively followed, in its mixture of capitalist expansion and the search for democratic leveling. Above all, it must reckon with the long tradition of topographic projection "à la française," the tradition of the "regular city," whose enlightenment and strong state imprint had been directly introduced—as Aliata has exemplarily described—through the engineers hired by Rivadavia, shaping by fire a technical bureaucracy throughout the nineteenth century which manifested itself in the Topographic Department's foundation of cities in the Buenos Aires countryside.[35] Finally, the determining influence of contemporary international practices cannot be overlooked: the aforementioned plans of expansion, widening, or road plans (from Ildefonso Cerdá's plan for Barcelona of 1859 to Hobrecht's "Police Plan" for Berlin of 1858–62), which affirmed a public will to control urban expansion (although in a very rustic way, because by meticulously defining a universal grid they produced an incentive for speculation for a very long period of time). 36

There is, however, an even more specific element in the *porteño* gridiron to support the reformist character of its fin-de-siècle layout: its economic irrationality. It can be demonstrated that it was not the most rational modality from the point of view of an exclusive interest in the greater exploitation of land rent for owners and speculators. The evidence is drawn not only from the historical fact that the owners themselves opposed the new layout and the regularization of the existing layout (there are numerous anecdotes at the turn of the century of most of the owners' opposition to having their properties measured for the

---

of Buenos Aires, see Tony Díaz and Damián Quero, *Buenos Aires Ideal* (Buenos Aires and Madrid, 1995), presentation to the Milan Triennial.

[35] Fernando Aliata, *La ciudad regular. Arquitectura, programas e instituciones en el Buenos Aires posrevolucionario, 1821–1835* (Buenos Aires: Editorial de la Universidad Nacional de Quilmes, 2006).

elaboration of the plan and the cadastre), because, as we know, economic actors do not always act according to a rational logic either. This evidence emerges more clearly from the comparison between the Buenos Aires city block and other squared plans. If we compare it with the enormous blocks of Hobrecht's Berlin plan, which favors the concentration of large operators in vast areas; or with New York's own rectangular block, which cancels out any residual element in land rent; the small square block of the Buenos Aires plan (with its residual core, its extreme internal partition, and the front/back ratio of the lots, which is completely unfavorable from an economic point of view) demonstrates its irrationality. This was noticed by a special kind of criticism of the checkerboard that went beyond picturesque or aesthetic objections and emphasized its economic disadvantages; criticism that was later paradoxically homologated in the moral repudiation of speculation.

Already Sarmiento, taking New York as a model, debated the convenience of enlarging the city with a grid layout, criticizing both the irrational extension of public services that it produced, and the scarce utility it offered not only for speculation but also for taxation, because "for direct contribution they waste a useless central land."[36] These positions will continue to be present in the twentieth century, developed especially by urban specialists of the twenties and thirties: whether from the perspective of favoring speculation by again proposing the creation of passages at half blocks, or from a reformist perspective, proposing the prohibition of building at the heart of each block, relying on the scarce economic damage that the expropriation of this sector of the lots would bring their owners.[37]

Understanding that the experts who designed the 1898–1904 plan were also aware of these economic criticisms of the checkerboard, allows us to deduce that the squared layout of Buenos Aires sought a rationality that was not identical to that of the market. It is the public instrument that creates a market but, in the same scheme, imposes on its differentiating mechanisms a reinsurance

---

[36] "El plano de la ciudad de Buenos Aires," *El Nacional 23* (June 1856), in *Obras completas (BS)*, XLII:30. The usefulness of the North American grid in terms of economic rationality is already pointed out by Sarmiento in his *Viajes*, for example, the passages where he comments at length on the benefits of the elongated, rectangular apple versus the Hispanic-American square block, in *Viajes por Europa, Africa y América, 1845–47*, and *Diario de Gastos*, ed. Javier Fernández (Buenos Aires: Colección Archivos, FCE, 1993), 392–93.

[37] In the first case, this search for increased income explains the layout, in the 1920s, of the three neighborhoods now so characteristic of the Compañía de Construcciones Modernas, with their small *tallarín* (spaghetti) blocks (Parque Chacabuco, Liniers, and Floresta). In the second case, the typology of high-rise buildings developed by architect Antonio Vilar between 1934 and 1936 is a characteristic example of the formulation that mixes modernist figuration, hygienist aspirations, and a search for greater economic rationalization in the city.

of homogeneity and urban integration. It was a public will that condensed different traditions and that, toward the end of the century, connected to—and was fed by—the ambition of a rational and equitable universalization of public rights typical of "conservative reformism": homogeneity is equivalent, at least initially, to democratization "from above," which links the grid with the park, showing the internal tensions of that public reformism with its own organicist model.[38] Against the background of this conflict between the search for organicity of the park and the explosion of all form that the uniformity of the grid entails, it may make sense to skip a series of mediations to affirm that these public territorial instruments formalize the public ambition for reform that we find in contemporary institutions such as education and public health, and which is at the base of a series of social processes, but also of the expansion of citizenship, such as the electoral reforms that succeeded one another since the beginning of the century. If the grid is the way to literally box in landowners and proletarians, projecting them as citizens, the park is the model of the community that such citizens should form.

A Cycle of Reform: The Impulse and Its Brakes

Up to this point we have identified the moment of formation of the grid and the park in Buenos Aires as a public, state vocation, and it does not escape me that public will is not equivalent to public space. As we have noted, here appears one of the mismatches with "classical" theories of public space: if, in the Enlightenment conception, public space is conceived as a dialogic arena constructed by autonomous citizens, it is unquestionable that the centrality of the state in the processes of political constitution of society in the case of Buenos Aires demands careful examination. I believe that the grid and the park allow an approach to this key issue. From the very beginning, they offer metropolitan deployment a public, formal, institutional playing board, which potentially favors the appearance of citizen impulses and state incentives for the creation

---

[38] I use the notion of "conservative reformism" in the sense given by Natalio Botana in *El orden conservador. La política argentina entre 1880 y 1916* (1977) (Buenos Aires: Hyspamérica, 1986). There he links "Argentine conservative reformism" with Spanish regenerationism, "also of conservative lineage," and characterizes it as a "conservative ethic—audacious in its political project, strategic in its concrete instrumentation, prudent in the social program of support that accompanies it"—that "seeks to reconcile an inevitable fact of democratization with a handful of values whose predominance must be preserved and even increased," (280, 281). In the course of this book, we will see why "conservative" seems to us to be a much more appropriate label for this state reformism than that of "liberal," recently proposed by Eduardo Zimmermann in *Los liberales reformistas. La cuestión social en la Argentina, 1890–1916* (Buenos Aires: Sudamericana and Universidad de San Andrés, 1995).

of different instances of public space. They are the most general support, it could be said, of the series of specific operations that will define the qualitative transformation of the public space of the traditional city into a metropolitan public space, inclusive of the new suburban reality: monuments, public institutions, citizen associations, modes of sociability and political participation, etc. Therefore, the grid and the park cannot—as material artifacts—exhaust our analysis of the composition of public space; they are, in fact, the double framework that will allow us, from their respective, more encompassing symbolic dimensions, to interpret and give meaning to the set of cultural, social, political, and material phenomena that form it. And those symbolic dimensions exceed the initial moment of public will: the grid and the park carry in themselves long-term effects, which will develop and act from the moment they appear as instruments of public intervention until their material consolidation. In that action, that marks a cycle of expansion and apogee that is realized in the first three decades of the century, we shall seek the emergence of a metropolitan public space.

As anticipated, it is an action shaped by conflicting impulses. The grid and the park imply different conceptions of public space and produce contrasting effects in their realization. While they are public projects, both the park and the grid show the impotence of public power to control the different variables that produce the city. Public authority intervenes on a restricted portion—ideologically, legally, and politically restricted—of these variables (precisely the public sphere), but from there it seeks to control them: in this way, public interventions are charged with the purpose of serving as a global model of a city and, at the same time, counteracting the effects contrary to that model that the real development of the city produces. In this dialectic between will and impotence, public authority tries out different paths and proposes instruments that often contradict each other; instruments that end up fulfilling roles that are completely different and often opposite to those imagined. The grid, by making all the land available simultaneously, not only produces an enormous incentive for speculation, but also leads very partially to the equitable and rational consolidation of a market, and produces that form of spasmodic metropolitanization, characteristic of Buenos Aires, through the formation and aggregation of isolated and unqualified urban fragments. In turn, the park not only does not slow down the growth of the city, but becomes the organic heart of suburban consolidation, the model of a new type of punctual intervention, radiating quality in the grid in which the state decides not to intervene once it has been left to the market.

That is why, in the process of formation of these figures and in the process by which both contribute to the emergence of a metropolitan public space, is where I believe that the vicissitudes and aporias of a complete cycle of reformism in Buenos Aires can be followed: "the impulse and its brakes," according to the suggestive title with which Carlos Real de Azúa analyzed that model reformism that in so many ways was exemplified by the tradition initiated by

José Batlle y Ordoñez in Uruguay in the beginning of the twentieth century. The impulse and its brakes serves to characterize a complete cycle of public reformism in Buenos Aires not only as the two poles of a linear movement that will find its end in the 1930s—when political power reactively redefines the meaning of modernization in Buenos Aires—but also as Real de Azúa uses it, seeking to identify the internal tensions at work in the reformist moments themselves—in turn so different from each other—and at the very heart of the modernization without reform of the 1930s. But the protagonist of Real de Azúa's account is a political movement whose conflicting impulses define a type of reformism. In our case, the main protagonist will be the city itself. This is where the impulses and the brakes appear, the public figures—the grid and the park—in which one can locate the realization and the struggle for certain values contained by the different reformisms and, in turn, with a logic analogous to that of the political movement, to note how

> at the same time that these values are realized in social life, their very affirmation reveals inadequacies and gaps. And these are the ones that, without altering the "table of values," unleash a new process, another sequence that the creator of the consolidated modality [...] is no longer in a position to lead.[39]

The major difference with Real de Azúa's analysis of Batllismo, then, is perhaps that the grid and the park, each carrying and symbolizing impulses and brakes, and each being in some way a brake for the other, define, as urban artifacts constructed and transformed over time with the incidence of multiple social and political actors, a collective dynamic, more anonymous, plural, and thus politically less apprehensible of reformism or, rather, of the public reformisms of Buenos Aires.

Reformisms (in the plural, as we will see enormous differences arising between the technical, political, and cultural sectors): because if we initially focus on the "conservative reformism" produced from the state over the forty years of the cycle we will see acting within its framework a variety of manifestations: starting from those of society, expressed in a number of institutions that flourish in the new suburbs; followed by those of municipal politics, which opens up to the representation of new popular parties in 1918; advancing in the even more contradictory ones of culture. In such a way that we can compose a map that gives an account of the complexity of the ideas and spaces, of the objects and actors that form and pass through these different reformisms, political, cultural, professional, artistic, and social. In reality, this map of reformisms should resemble, above all, a geological map, since in this cycle we will see reformisms superimposed like layers, not always in contact, not always of

---

[39] Carlos Real de Azúa, *El impulso y su freno* (Montevideo: Ediciones de la Banda Oriental, 1964), 102.

similar durations or even densities, in which we will often find identical actors, but whose different institutional or ideological contexts resignify their ideas and actions; in which we will often locate currents of common ideas, but whose different forms of insertion and application generate entirely dissimilar effects.

PART ONE

Figurations

[From Sarmiento to the End of the Century]

Inventing inhabitants with new dwellings.[40]
–Domingo Faustino Sarmiento

To change the city, to change society: the program enunciated by Sarmiento will remain anchored for decades by the local reformist tradition in any of its multiple variants. His two ambitions are really one and the same: Sarmiento is one of the figures most consistently aligned with the Enlightenment premise that emphasizes the educational virtues of urban space. That conviction provides him with a formidable analytical tool to extract observations and to draw social, cultural, and political conclusions from the very shape of the city and to pattern into forms—whether real or ideal—social and cultural programs. That is the double analytical and programmatic sense in which the city enters, almost as a topic, in the horizon of his interests: for Sarmiento, a city materializes the complete system in which a society and a state are organized, and a city shapes—and can therefore change—the society that inhabits it. And for that very reason, a city must change itself if society has already done so. The full conviction of the need for this synchronization is what will guide his search and what, simultaneously, will turn him into an inevitable referent, a builder of the main motives through which the city will be considered in relation to politics, culture, and nature. This conviction is confirmed in his first travels, through the discovery of the North American city, but was already present in the *Facundo*, in the archetypal comparison between the cloistered Córdoba that cannot but look backward and a cosmopolitan Buenos Aires as the model for a new Argentina. To recall that when Sarmiento writes the *Facundo* he knows neither Córdoba nor Buenos Aires only reinforces the deliberately programmatic

---

[40] "La Plata," *El Nacional* (1886) in *Obras completas* (Buenos Aires: Editorial Luz del Día, 1953), XLII:225. This edition of Sarmiento's complete works will be cited as *Obras completas (LD)*.

character of this synchronization, the fictional functionality of the city as artifact in Sarmiento's political narrative.

In Buenos Aires, such a program found an unusual moment of condensation in the Palermo Park project. "Palermo is still very far away, but we will get there someday," Sarmiento says in 1882, a decade after the creation of the park, in a phrase which is more than a lament for the little that was done to achieve its objectives; it highlights the confidence in a collective pursuit that goes beyond the real distance that separates the park from the city.[41] And that distance represented far more than the practical problem of the impossibility of Buenos Aires society to attend the park; it was fundamentally a program. For Sarmiento, there was a double distance to cover: spatial, not because of the considerable number of kilometers between the park and the city, but because the design of the park announced a model of society that could only be developed in a new city drawn outside—and against—the traditional city; temporal, not because of the hours of travel needed to get there, along a road dusty in summer and muddy in winter, but because it was a program for the future, a project.

In this way Sarmiento's ambition outlines a single framework for two issues that will mark the main urban debates during the entire process of the formation of the modern city: the problem of the city's expansion and the theme of the park as a planimetric, social, and cultural model. In this first part of this book, we will go through the different technical and cultural traditions that, by the end of the century, allowed the materialization of a model of expansion and of a type of relationship between the park and the city. The answers adopted will be noticeably different from the formulations anticipated by Sarmiento and, at the same time, they will have lost, in management and discourse, a good part of the projective tension that made them one. But the section on Sarmiento should remind us throughout the extent to which both topics are part of the same problem, that of the construction of the city as a public space producing citizens. If at the end of the century they do not form an organic discourse—at least as organized as Sarmiento's—but rather they need to be traced partially and fragmentarily in forms of management, technical styles, ideological residues, this does not mean that in their materialization they do not impose joint effects nor that they are completely alien to the intentionality of their—often opaque—promoters.

This first part deals, then, with how and why, between the last years of the nineteenth century and the first years of the following, two answers to the problem formulated by Sarmiento in Palermo materialize and find, if not definitive, at least decisive form for a large part of the successive processes of construction of the city: the concretion of a finished model of territorial expansion and the layout of a belt of public greenery around the traditional city: the grid and the park.

---

[41] "Lago Alvear," *El Nacional (1883)* in *Obras completas (LD)*, XLII:157.

The reading of fin-de-siècle urban transformations as responses to problems posed very early on in the nineteenth century (for Sarmiento must be approached within the framework of traditions and polemics that precede him) tends to dissolve the break that historiography has traditionally placed in the eighties, between the "gran aldea" (the great provincial village, as Lucio V. López titled in 1884 his famous novel on the Buenos Aires of his childhood) and the modern metropolis.[42] It also seeks to emphasize the importance of the fin de siècle itself in the history of the city: it is curious that a systematization as decisive for the future of the city as the one we will discuss here, with such a capacity to reorganize the ideological traditions of the urban problem, takes place in one of the least spectacular moments in the history of Buenos Aires. In fact, for the historiography of the city, the years that open with the crisis of the nineties are a kind of parenthesis between the energetic and personalized action of Mayor Torcuato de Alvear in the previous decade and new discussions on diagonal avenues and urban restructuring that emerged with the visit of French urban planner Joseph Bouvard in 1907 and, particularly, with the imminence of the centennial celebrations. This marks a kind of transition, in turn, in the material conditions of urban life, between the dominant presence of tenements in the center and the new modality of the purchase of land in installments in the suburbs that developed after 1904, a parenthesis that would be confirmed in the city's own production: the peak of new construction that occurred in 1888 would not occur again until 1907.[43]

What is generally not noticed when we consider only the aforementioned processes—the material transformation or the intensity of the discussions of the disciplines concerned with urban design—are the dynamics of public management, the procedures of institutional construction, and the administration of the urban phenomenon. In those same final years at the end of the nineteenth century, the transfer of the municipalities of Flores and Belgrano (with the respective increase of more than four times the city's own territory) confronts the municipal management with a major issue, product of a political decision, which forces a series of definitions that, otherwise, would have perhaps awaited the end of the crisis.

Normally this territorial expansion has been attributed to the foresight of Torcuato de Alvear formulated at the moment that the city's federalization was defined, toward the beginning of his administration, which would again place

---

[42] Thanks to Fernando Aliata's recent work on the Rivadavia period, it has been possible to identify technical logics, institutional transformations, and cultural perspectives of great continuity in a process of modernization that runs from the beginning of the independent period. See, for example, *La ciudad regular*, where Aliata has gathered all his previous work on Rivadavia and the urban historiography of the nineteenth century.
[43] See, for example, the tables published in the 1910 census that show the progress in building, in which the increase in population is related to the number of meters built.

the years of the turn of the century in anonymous continuity with previous administrations, though later we will see that such an expansion was not in fact contemplated. It was not even evident then, nor was it later for everyone, that urban expansion was desirable or necessary. In this context, the cession of 1888 could not but generate a situation of enormous uncertainty for the actors in municipal management, which, it should be emphasized, had not yet been fully reorganized and consolidated since 1880, when the city and the Province of Buenos Aires were separated. If the annexation of the suburban municipalities took place in a still brilliant moment of the city, when renovation and reform undertakings were in full force, in just one year the 1890 crisis would further increase uncertainty and strip of funding even the basic needs planned by the old municipality.

Thus, in the last years of the decade, the expectations opened up to speculators and landowners by the expansion of the capital added to the climate of the crisis, provoked in some state officials the militant recovery of an ideal of a small city, not much extended, that should precisely define its limits around the traditional city. To a certain point, this places the "pessimistic" urban thinking of the end of the century at the antipodes of Sarmiento's ideas, although the trope of the park is invoked in order to define these limits—Palermo would in fact be converted into the sketch of a perimetric system of public parks that would function as a limit for expansion rather than as the center of a new displaced city—and although as a result of this reformist search for control, an orthogonal grid of streets was designed for the whole of the enlarged territory.

David Viñas has characterized the passage from utilitarianism to aesthetic consumption in the sphere of the ideas of Buenos Aires elites as a passage from the Romantic generation to that of the eighties.[44] In the city, on the contrary, we see that the two main urban artifacts that could symbolize each of these instances, the "utilitarian" grid and the park as "representation," are produced together at the turn of the century. Tensely contained in each is figuration as a project for the future and figuration as an attribute of an elite seeking spaces in which to recognize itself—that is, the production of figured societies and the reproduction of social figuration as the spectacle of the bourgeois city. But it is precisely in this double movement that nineteenth-century reformism can perhaps appear more complete than in the abrupt break proposed by Viñas's image. And this translates into the relations between reformism and society.

Nineteenth-century reformism is possible as an ideological and cultural operation through the assumption of a strict and distant control of the processes it sets out to reform, but, at the same time, control and distance appear time and again limited, denied, frustrated; and it is this aporia, this tension, that is one of the aspects that define the "conservative reformism" of the end of

[44] David Viñas, *Literatura argentina y realidad política* (1964) (Buenos Aires: Centro Editor de América Latina, 1982), ch. 1.

Figure 10. Juan Manuel Blanes, *An Episode of the Yellow Fever in Buenos Aires*, 1871. Museo Nacional de Artes Visuales, Montevideo.

the century either because, in the reverse of philanthropic discourse, it fails to reform the very social class it represents, or because the new "popular" society against which it seeks to cut itself off reveals, as in a mirror, its own ghosts and the very weakness of its own certainties. This ambiguity is magnificently anticipated in Juan Manuel Blanes's famous 1871 painting of the yellow fever epidemic: in contrast to the figures of the philanthropic hygienists, who appear to dominate the scene, introducing from the door frame the purifying luminosity of the sun and of science, the point of view of the painting subtly changes their roles and transforms the darkness they are called upon to reform into the protagonist, perhaps because what is about to be born in this society is in that same dark space, the space of disease and of the new.

CHAPTER 1

A New City: The Utopia of "Argentine Thought"

From the point of view of the definition of the main characteristics of "modern Buenos Aires" at the end of the century, it could be said that the decisions regarding the whole of the federal territory closed a period of questions and discussions that had been opened in the years of the State of Buenos Aires (1852-1861), although we will also see how logics and traditions that date back even to the first decades of the independent period persist. How should the city be, how should it grow, what should be the relationship between state and society be in that definition? These are some of the basic questions that run through this period and that will find different answers as the century progresses and as the growth of the city—its institutional change and the organization of the state that chooses it as headquarters—generate unforeseen problems.

One of the earliest and most precise formulations—the "new city"—will be elaborated by Sarmiento. It is, in truth, a program that, as anticipated, finds a moment of high condensation in the Palermo Park project. Palermo is formed far away from the city, in symbolically overdetermined lands: the lands from which Juan Manuel de Rosas had organized and administered his despotic order.[45] Facing the tenacious opposition of those who saw in those lands the material emblem of a bloody past, Sarmiento highlights the cathartic value of the park: precisely to close down those meanings, superimposing his model of civilization on barbarism. Political and geographical barbarism: it is the pampa

15

---

[45] During his second governorship of Buenos Aires (1835-1852), Juan Manuel de Rosas bought a large amount of land in the suburb of Palermo, where he built a mansion (the Caserón) surrounded by gardens, ponds, and nurseries. The house functioned at first as a suburban villa, also for productive purposes, but by 1848 Rosas established both his residence and the government of the province there, which for the first time operated from outside the capital city. Thus, after the fall of his government in 1852, his lands in Palermo acquired a special symbolic value among the rest of his properties that were subject to expropriation due to his exile. Sarmiento, who built his entire career as an intellectual and politician fighting Rosas, always defended the need to redefine the lands and the Caserón by changing their functions but keeping them standing, as an example and memory of what he saw as the triumph of civilization against barbarism.

itself that hangs as a threat over the modernizing project that should be "subjected to culture." But, above all, Palermo allows a programmatic distance with the existing city, which must be left behind; Palermo would thus be eccentric only conjuncturally, because it was called to be the Central Park of a new city.

Thus, Palermo becomes capable of receiving contents deriving from the cultural tradition of the nineteenth-century park, but at the same time, of expressing very precise relations with the existing city and with ideas about it. Palermo is created at a crossroads of "influences": Sarmiento was not only directly familiar with the layout of European, continental, and English parks (and we must not forget that the specialists he hired to begin work on the park came from Europe); he was also involved in the debates generated by the North American Park Movement, witnessing during his stay in New York as minister plenipotentiary in 1865–68—precisely the years of the formation and consolidation of Central Park—the confrontations between the real estate interests of developers and the public interests of reformers. Thus, in the creation of Palermo are present both the aspirations of social leveling and civic institutionalization that the park accommodates in the decomposition of the absolutist city, and the hygienic reasons that define it as the "lung" of the increasingly congested industrial city; and both the typical bourgeois practices of figuration and representation of the park and the Haussmannian boulevard and the utilitarian reasons that support the interventions of the North American movement that accompany the evolution of agrarian transcendentalism into urban reformism. But if in this sense Palermo is the inevitable starting point of a history of public parks in Buenos Aires, from the point of view of Sarmiento's thought—moreover, of the relations between Sarmiento's ideas and the reality they sought to affect—it is a point of arrival. A double point of arrival: it is the artifact through which he believes he can capture the complex universe of articulations between education, productive modernization, and social equalization which he has been conceiving since his years in exile; and it is the incarnation of a definitive conclusion regarding the possibilities of the modernizing transformation of the city and of actually existing society, a conclusion that becomes clearer as his relationship with Buenos Aires progresses, from the epic moment of the entry into the city, won over by tyranny, until the years of his presidency.

13, 14

1. From the Quinta Normal to Central Park

> Only in a vast, artistic, accessible park will the people be a people; only here
> will there be no foreigners, no nationals, no plebeians.[46]
>
> –Domingo Faustino Sarmiento

Integration and leveling: the echoes of motifs that make up a good part of the
modern Western tradition of bringing greenery into the city resound notably in
Palermo's inaugural speech. The park as a chemical device capable of amalgam-
ating new social and cultural ties, as an educational machine for modern civic
life, as the main dynamizing factor, in short, the great melting pot in which the
multiple national identities, the persistent rural traditions, and atavistic productive and political practices could be abandoned like old clothes, to give rise
to a new, national, social, and cultural synthesis.

That is why the choice of site for the park is emblematic. For José María
del Carril, it offers the possibility that, "by covering it with flowers, we can
erase, as with a sponge, the memory of that infamous tyrant."[47] There are even
more things to overcome: to erase as with a sponge is the best metaphor for
what the park proposes as a radically new organization of metropolitan life.
"There is no public spectacle," says Nicolás Avellaneda in the discussion of the
project in the Senate, "there is no spectacle that levels conditions as much as
a public promenade. In it and before it all conditions disappear."[48] The notion
of spectacle appears as a new perception of urban sociability and, above all, as
a suspension of all previous categorization, as a tabula rasa. Although what is
really interesting about the park, what shows its constitutive ambiguity, is that it
can be enunciated as most radically new insofar as it is proposed as a means for
a restoration: restoration of the degraded city, of a segmented society; regeneration of deviant behaviors, of nature and memory. It is an *ex-novo* creation of
habits under the naturalizing mantle of greenery in the city; it is, above all, the
recovery of a new communal heart in the disintegrated metropolis, a secular
and hygienic sanctuary around which some unity can be restored.

In this sense, the main tradition that Sarmiento establishes with Palermo is
that of defining the park as a planimetric model of city and society, a typically
North American ambition. Beyond the specific expedients of landscape design,
he places Palermo in the course of an ambition that is born with the North

---

[46] "Discurso inaugural del Parque," *Obras completas (LD)*, XXII:11.
[47] See Congreso Nacional, Cámara de Senadores, *Diario de Sesiones de 1874* (Buenos
Aires: El Nacional, 1875), 165 (regular session of June 20, 1874).
[48] Ibid., 178. I must point out a debt to an acute and innovative work by Pablo Pschepiurca
that has opened a fertile line of research on Palermo; see "El parque metropolitano,"
Materiales 2 (November 1982); and "Palermo, la construcción del parque," *Summa*
"Colección temática" 3 (1983).

American park as opposed to the European park. While the latter *becomes* public, through a series of political and social transformations that only partially affect its internal organization, from royal and aristocratic parks and forests to metropolitan parks, the former is born explicitly as a device for the deliberate production of these public ends.

The American park seeks to establish itself not as the site where a transformation of social practices can take place, but as that of the emergence of a new society. In response to a traveler returning from Europe amazed by its urban parks, Andrew Jackson Downing, one of the leading publicists and reformers who gave birth to the Park Movement, noted in 1848 in *The Horticulturist*: "But these great [European] public parks are mostly the appendages of royalty, and have been created for purposes of show and magnificence, quite incompatible with our ideas of republican simplicity"; Downing's alternative would be the search for an American park program *of his own*, a program for "republican simplicity."[49]

These pioneers of American landscape design were aware of their debts to Europe: in the same article, Downing was obliged to accept the counterexample of some German parks, such as those of Munich and Frankfurt, cities whose medieval walls, demolished at the turn of the century, had been converted into parks designed for the public. Contacts with England were, of course, explicit; its influence through the horticulturalist movements was recognized even in the very name of Downing's newspaper. That influence is embodied in some examples of public parkland, such as Birkenhead. For if Hyde Park, Regent's Park, or St. James's Park were royal parks, only later opened to the public, and even then directly linked to the private speculation of landlords, Birkenhead, on the other hand, designed by Joseph Paxton and opened in 1847, was born specifically as a public park: its design goes beyond picturesque layouts, initiating a program tied to the problem of metropolitan traffic and entirely new services, such as sports facilities and of the active use of leisure, serving as a model for the future development of the American Park Movement.

In the case of England, it is an influence that will pay close attention to institutional and legal precedents: as early as 1833 in London, in the *Report from the Select Committee on Public Walks*, a diagnosis was made which should be

---

[49] Downing's dialogue was published in *The Horticulturist* in October 1848 and is quoted in Frederick Law Olmsted Jr. and Theodora Kimball, eds., *Olmsted: Forty Years of Landscape Architecture* (1928) (Cambridge, MA, and London: MIT Press, 1973), 12. *The Horticulturist* was the magazine edited by Downing to promote the public movement for urban parks. In addition to being a publicist, Downing was a landscape designer (he designed, for example, the Washington Mall in 1851), and his close links with Bostonian transcendentalist reformism make him a key figure in the birth of the American landscape. See Francesco Dal Co, "From Parks to the Region: Progressive Ideology and the Reform of the American City," in Manieri-Elia and Tafuri, *The American City: from the Civil War to the New Deal* (1973).

quoted at length because it will serve as a basis for the most modern representations of the function of the public park:

> It cannot be necessary to point out how requisite some Public Walks or Open
> Space in the neighborhood of large Towns; to those who consider the occu-
> pations of the Working Classes who dwell there confined as they are during
> the week-days as Mechanics and Manufacturers, and often shut up in heated
> Factories: it must be evident that it is of the first importance to their health on
> their day of rest to enjoy the fresh, and to be able (exempt from the dust and
> dirt of public throughfares) to walk out in decent comfort with their families:
> if deprived of any such resource, it is probable that their only escape from the
> narrow courts and alleys [...] will be those drinking-shops where, in short-li-
> ved excitement they may forget their toil, but where they waste the means of
> their families, and too often destroy their health [...] A man walking out with
> his family among his neighbors of different ranks, will naturally be desirous
> to be properly clothed, and that his Wife and Children should be also ; but
> this desire duly directed and controlled, is found by experience to be of the
> most powerful effect in promoting Civilization, and exciting Industry.[50]

The report is part of an incipient and directly Benthamian movement of
opinion in favor of public parks for the poorest sectors of the population: "when
we say public, we mean public, not gentility," said a newspaper article of 1839
that demanded parks for London's East End, for "the poor artisan or laboring
man" of the underworld.[51] If in its origins the baroque park had appeared as a
terrain for experimenting with new urban layouts, now the park is thought of
as a natural antidote to the overcrowding of the poor city and the unhealthi-
ness of factory work. But also as an educational and moral instrument for the
consolidation of the modern family and its values: from savings—with its benefits for increased consumption—to the model of the bourgeois interieur as a
parameter for new building typologies—with the explicit attempt to keep the
worker off the streets, the committee, or the tavern—through the preservation
of the workforce by improving their sanitary conditions; a typical mixture, one

---

[50] In *Report from the Select Committee on Public Walks; with the Minutes of Evidence
Taken Before Them*, [London], The House of Commons, June 27, 1833, 8–9, Reference
originally drawn from Paolo Sica, *Historia del urbanismo. El siglo XIX* (1977) (Madrid:
Instituto de Estudios de Administración Local, 1981), 1:81, 82.
[51] "The Lungs of London," in *Blackwood's Edinburgh Magazine* 46 (August 1839):
212–27, reproduced by Olmsted and Kimball, *Forty Years of Landscape Architecture:
Central Park*, 9. On the Benthamite matrix of the *Report*, see, among others, Monique
Mosser and Georges Teyssot, "L'architettura del giardino e l'architettura nel giardino," in
Monique Mosser and Georges Teyssot, eds., *L'architettura dei giardini d'Occidente. From
the Renaissance to the Twentieth Century* (Milan: Electa, 1990).

could say, of the reformist ambitions of the social legislation of the eighteenth and nineteenth centuries.

The other focus of attention for reform of the urban landscape is, of course, Paris. But it is not only contemporary to the North American proposals but is in itself already a product of the intense mixture that took place in urban practices throughout the nineteenth century: it is a well-known fact that a good part of the proposals for Parisian parks were inspired by English landscape design. It was from his exile in London that Napoleon III imagined the Paris he wanted; as soon as he came to power, he gave precise instructions for the design of the Bois de Boulogne: it was a mixture of the principles with which Repton and Nash designed Regent's Park and Hyde Park, including the Serpentine.[52] In any case, it is not in the planimetric design of the parks where Prefect Haussmann's action is original; in fact, it has been pointed out that the design applied to modern public parks was so systematized in the mid-nineteenth century that from the end of the previous century the routinary aspect of their layouts was jeered at with the formula "belting, clumping, dotting."[53] On the other hand, Haussmann's originality is unquestionable in the use of this new typology as a collective instrument of urban service, as an organizer of metropolitan flows, as an attempt to formally control the growth of the city.

In any case, it is not a question of taking sides in the unproductive polemic about the origins of the public park; a polemic of which its mid-century creators on both sides of the ocean (and on both sides of the English Channel) were well aware. They generally adopted a double discourse that we will encounter again in other topics of urban culture: they celebrated the virtues of foreign examples as opposed to local shortcomings, appealing to the competitive spirit of provincial pride when it came to campaigning in their own cities for political and economic support for their projects; and they stressed the differences and anticipations of their own design, size, characteristics of use, or the ever increasing number of visitors when it came to writing memoirs or participating in international congresses. Beyond these polemics, then, it is worth recognizing that in the first decades of the nineteenth century, and especially from the 1830s and 1840s onwards, public campaigns in favor of urban parks proliferated in European and North American cities, as did mutual stylistic contaminations, influences, and eclectic appropriations of very diverse traditions. Despite the very long tradition of landscape design, the urban park appears as virgin territory for the most daring design experiments, thanks to its radical independence—from its very birth as public program—from the discipline that

---

[52] Françoise Choay, "Haussmann et le système des espaces verts parisiens," *La Revue de l'Art* 29 (1975): 83–99.

[53] Alessandra Ponte, "Il parco pubblico in Gran Bretagna e negli Stati Uniti. Dal *genius loci* al 'genio della civilizzazione,'" in Mosser and Teyssot, eds., *L'architettura dei giardini d'Occidente*, 374.

until then contained it as mere background: architecture, whose crisis would certainly not have favored such a rapid and effective development.[54]

But in such a framework of crossed influences and multiple stimuli, it is still interesting to recognize a certain North American specificity, reinforced precisely by the foundational vocation of these nineteenth-century reformers, by their need to differentiate themselves from England and Europe, to build an original culture based on the values of industrial and plebeian democracy. A vocation not lacking in objective precedents; because that specificity has its origin precisely in the absence of "noble" residues in the North American landscape, which is why the park was born as a public program directly oriented to the problems of urban congestion. Despite the "anti-urban" strands of agrarian and transcendentalist philosophy that are at the base of the Park Movement, the park enters the American city not as nostalgia for a lost nature, but as the recovery of a "natural" key to intervene in the "evils" of the big city, to reform it from a radical redesign in which the public green becomes both an ideological banner and an operational instrument.

Already classic studies on the North American park have pointed out how this tense and creative relationship between metropolitan problems and nostalgia for a lost community (community among men, community with God, and community with nature) appears in suburban cemeteries, as a direct antecedent of the Park Movement. There the relation is clear because the cemeteries that begin to be designed outside the cities as part of the religious and cultural polemic against the traditional disposition around churches appear precisely as a proposal for the recovery of nature from outside the city but pointing directly to its problems. And this allows us to return to Sarmiento, who demonstrates an early understanding of these effects in his first visit to New York. It was already common for the city's inhabitants to visit Greenwood Cemetery in Brooklyn, which had become a real center of attraction for the new uses of leisure and tourism (for which there was a printed guidebook).[55] Sarmiento was taken to visit it and managed to clearly identify many of the peculiarities that make the cemetery a direct antecedent of the park. In principle, its romantic and picturesque character is achieved through the artificial construction of a "state of nature" and the studied design of a series of gradations between artificial park and rustic forest:

11

---

[54] Graciela Silvestri and Fernando Aliata, *El paisaje en el arte y las ciencias humanas* (Buenos Aires: CEAL, 1994), especially part three: "La reorganización del territorio y las ciencias del espacio."
[55] In 1849, Downing estimated that about six thousand people had visited in the summer, "many of these for the pleasures of its foliage and lawns." In Olmsted and Kimball, eds., *Olmsted: Forty Years of Landscape Architecture*, 21–22. Francesco Dal Co locates the suburban cemetery as a very important milestone in the passage from the American landscape tradition initiated with Jefferson to urban parks in "From Parks to the Region."

The landscape is slightly undulating and offers a variety of aspects that change as you penetrate its solitary enclosure. Secular woods shade the low grounds, and even the waters of the rains are deposited in lagoons and ditches. A spacious road for carriages meanders unrestrained at the mercy of the accidents of the ground [...] and on the top of the small hills stand out, either isolated or in groups, graceful young trees of those that make up the varied North American fauna.[56]

But, in addition, Sarmiento identifies the role of architecture in that landscape, a mixture of ruin and world museum (in the provocatively eclectic style that, by definition, the architecture of international exhibitions or zoological gardens would assume, though in the case of cemeteries, that exoticism would rather seek pathetic solemnity): "In the shade of a secular oak a Gothic-style tomb is sheltered, a lantern of Diogenes crowns a mound, and at the bottom of a little valley, among showy saplings, a Greek shrine is displayed [...]." And, finally, he also emphasizes its deliberate contrast with the city: "Is it not true that this system of rustic cemeteries, a true field of the dead, instills feelings of placid melancholy, lightened by the contemplation of nature [...]? At least this impression was made on me by the view, from some elevated part of the cemetery, leaning on a tomb, of New York crowned with smoke [...]." The very conversion of the sacred sphere of death into a space of culture in the face of nature and the city, explains to a large extent the innovation produced by these cemeteries, which already in their origin propose a plurality of contents that in Europe would take time to develop in such fullness: that of the park as cultivated nature, civic institution, spiritual religiousness, and hygienic service to counteract urban smoke and its consequences.

However, and in spite of Sarmiento's accurate intuitions on this first trip, the path he follows to arrive at the proposal of a Central Park for Buenos Aires is not the same as the one indicated for the Park Movement: it is not until much later that Sarmiento will see the park as a specifically urban typology. It could be said that Palermo becomes a park, that it is not the result of the direct importation of a typology already resolved according to the diagnoses of cities that it was convenient to imitate, but that it is the point of arrival of another type of search, always tangentially and complicatedly related to those models. The experimental and propagandist role that cemeteries had in the north, their function of fine-tuning a series of technical and ideological instruments in the search for a renewal of the relationship between city and territory, will be fulfilled here instead by a very particular institution, which links Sarmiento's main obsessions to a single territorial device: the Quinta Normal.

---

[56] Sarmiento, *Viajes*, 372. The quotes in the following paragraph are drawn from the same source.

Figure 11. John Bachmann, *Bird's-eye View of Greenwood Cemetery, Near New York*, 1852. Library of Congress, Washington, D.C.

Figure 12. John Bachmann, editor; Frederick Heppenheimer, printer. *New York's Central Park*, 1863. Lionel Pincus and Princess Firyal Map Division, New York Public Library Digital Collections.

Figures 13 and 14. Illustrations to *Frederick Law Olmsted, Landscape Architect, 1822–1903: Forty Years of Landscape Architecture; Being the Professional Papers of Frederick Law Olmsted, Senior.* New York and London: Putman's Sons, 1923. Pictured are different aspects of the park as explored in Central Park. In the first image, nature is reintroduced in the city in hygienic terms, as a lung and a space for bucolic contemplation. In the second, the park serves as a laboratory of new urban planning techniques, such as the separation of circulation using different levels, where the park was used to separate the upper, "natural" route from the crossing of the "artificial" streets below; this was the basis of much of the criteria for road engineering in modernist urban planning.

The Quinta Normal is, for Sarmiento, a kind of seedbed in which all the virtues necessary to produce the monumental transfer from a traditional society to a modern one could grow and strengthen. It has nothing to do, in this sense, with the usual Jardin d'Acclimatation of the French tradition; it is the deliberate introduction of the seed of a type of organization and modernization that has the United States in its sights, although there its existence as an institution is not necessary precisely because "in that immense laboratory of wealth, there is doubtless no Quinta Normal supported by the government. The whole country is a Quinta Normal."[57] Like so many of Sarmiento's public proposals, the Quinta Normal is then nothing more than a model on a scale created by the state for the establishment of certain conditions that would enable its expansion in society; it is an instrument of transition. The real and effective transformations must be those led by society, not by the state; but the state has the possibility and the responsibility of creating the appropriate conditions for the birth of that will in society. If, for example, the only way to produce the necessary revolution in the agricultural industry is, for Sarmiento, through "the association of all intelligent farmers to smooth out the obstacles and introduce improvements for their own benefit" and this is the basis of his impulse for the creation of the Argentine Rural Society, a Quinta Normal carried out by the state "will be the testing ground."[58]

He perfected the idea of this educational, social, and productive artifact in the years of his last stay in Chile (1852–55), as part of the institutional formulation for the reorganization of the country that he had to again leave after the fall of Rosas. There, he witnessed the formation of the Quinta Normal in Santiago, whose existence in 1854 was, for Carlos Pellegrini, proof that Chile "is ahead of us" and is the country that "most particularly distinguishes itself in this race of progress." From Chile he would write to the Minister of Government of Mendoza, encouraging him to create a Quinta Normal in the city, sending him a French agronomist for its care, in spite of "the systematic resistance" of the society that condemned the initiative as "a luxury establishment," and he would publish his Plan combinado de educación común, silvicultura e industria pastoril, aplicable al Estado de Buenos Aires (Combined Plan of Common Education, Forestry and Pastoral Industry, Applicable to the State of Buenos Aires), in which the Quinta Normal is precisely defined as a basic instrument in his project for the integral modernization for the State of Buenos Aires.[59]

---

[57] Sarmiento, "Quinta Normal de Aclimatación de plantas en Mendoza," La Crónica, November 19, 1853, in Obras completas (LD), X, 214.

[58] Sarmiento, "Quinta Normal," inaugural speech of the Quinta Normal in San Juan, July 7, 1862, in Obras completas (LD), XXI, 168.

[59] Carlos Pellegrini's phrase in La Revista del Plata 11 (July 1854): 160; the quotation on Mendoza's Quinta Normal in Sarmiento, "Quinta Normal de Aclimatación de plantas en Mendoza," 211–13; the Plan combinado .... was a pamphlet published in the printing

In this pamphlet, Sarmiento proposes the creation of numerous Quintas Normales on public lands that should be preserved from the intense subdivision of the countryside that he projected for the reception of immigrant farmers. Those public lands should hold "buildings for schools, forest tree plantations, model stables for dairies, chapels, local libraries, an agronomist schoolmaster's house, a post, and vaccine administration." Sarmiento locates the originality of his proposal only in the organizational aspects, because everything that will make up the Quinta Normal, he points out, already exists in all countries (schools, hospices, farms, and gardens of acclimatization, institutions for foundlings, popular libraries), but "they have not formed until today a harmonious whole."[60]

The function of the Quinta Normal in the countryside was to be, then, that of an educational and productive center of experimentation for the latest technologies and a showcase of economic and social advances; an outpost of civilization in the pampa, that is, a sample of the best of the city in the countryside: an "oasis of culture."[61] But the heart of this whole system was to be found in the outskirts of the city itself, where its function and that of the public park began to be muddled. So it had been with the Quinta Normal in Chile, which soon after its creation became an urban park. And so it would be, when in 1862, during his governorship, Sarmiento built the Quinta Normal in San Juan, for which he had chosen a very central piece of land in a depressed neighborhood, for which the Quinta should also play a role of promotion and progress.[62] This is what was suggested in a Report of the Commissioner of the United States Department of Agriculture for the creation of an experimental hacienda in Washington, which Sarmiento took care to publish in Ambas Américas in 1868: the hacienda was to be next to the Propagation Garden on one of the main roads "not too distant from the city [because] making it both attractive and useful [...] it could fill the lack of a park or public promenade that is noticeable in Washington."[63]

But in Buenos Aires this relationship among the Quinta Normal, the park, and the city becomes more precise and involved from the beginning the lands of Palermo. In 1855, in the Combined Plan pamphlet, Sarmiento postulates in the "Basis of the Law of Common Education" section that

---

house of Julio Belin, in Santiago, in 1855, and reproduced in *Obras completas (LD)*, XXIII, 202–280.

[60] Ibid., 230, 258.

[61] Ibid., 231.

[62] This is what José María del Carril tells the Minister of Government in a letter dated April 26, 1862, in which he mentions that he found an ideal piece of land for the Quinta. Quoted by Natalio J. Pisano, *La política agraria de Sarmiento. La lucha contra el latifundio* (Buenos Aires: Depalma, 1980), 166.

[63] Horace Capron, "Report of the Commissioner of the United States Department of Agriculture," *Both Americas* 1, no. 4 (July 1868).

In the vicinity of Buenos Aires, on both banks of the Arroyo Maldonado, a square league of land will be expropriated for public utility, for the foundation of a Central Farm for the acclimatization of plants and agricultural trials, which will include a Normal School for Teachers of common education, a Hospice for orphans, and a reform house for abandoned children, delinquents, vagrants.[64]

When he writes this pamphlet in Chile, the location is still vague (on both banks of the Maldonado stream); and let us recall that his first visit to Buenos Aires had been fleeting. As soon as he is integrated into the political life of the city, on his definitive return from Chile, the controversy over Rosas's property allowed him to define the ideal location with total precision, inscribing the replacement operation in a prestigious political lineage and giving it symbolic value:

When one dynasty succeeded another in France, policy advised the Emperor to confiscate the property of the fallen king and to devote it to the foundation of rural banks. When liberty has overthrown tyranny among us, the Legislature restored to its sovereignty consecrates the property accumulated by the sum of public power, to the education of the people, for there poverty is the evil, as here it is ignorance.

When I consider Palermo a Normal School for Teachers, Quinta Normal for Agriculture, Redemption Home for badly kept children or Orphanage Hospital, I feel a deep religious recollection, because I can see the hand of Providence teaching with the hand of despotism, and the genius of the Republic making use of the same tyrants to make the happiness of their children.[65]

Rosas's groves and installations in Palermo already functioned, in fact, as a promenade, "where elegant carriages go," but the transformation aimed to correct its character more radically. Because although Sarmiento used the metaphor of the opening of the palace gardens in Europe to the bourgeois public, the truth is that Rosas's gardens were already, during his government, an attractive place for the same carriages that continued to go after his fall. Hence it is not the program of the park that appears in the first instance with the capacity to produce this reversal of contents, but the installation of the center of productive and educational operations, that true central command from where Sarmiento imagines that the whole state that Rosas would have sought to keep in traditional barbarism could be modernized.

---

[64] Sarmiento, *Obras completas (LD)*, XXIII:230.
[65] Sarmiento, "El proceso de Rosas," *El Nacional*, August 11, 1855, in *Obras completas (LD)*, XXIV:61.

The first agricultural exhibition organized in 1858 and located by the state government in Palermo, only confirms this vocation, because "at last a useful destination was (found) for that monstrous construction inspired by the ignorant whim of a despot." In this case, Sarmiento again resorts to the metaphor of revolutionary conversions, but if in Versailles "the useless prodigalities of Louis XIV" were saved to gather "all the artistic glories of France," here, "the semi-barbarous Versailles of our rude tyrant is going to be consecrated to all the Argentine industries, thus filling a need of our situation and a primordial interest of our time." Once again, the contents of the transposition of the park are displaced, and the productivist Sarmiento continues to locate in Palermo a focus of industrial and educational progress for the whole State of Buenos Aires (indeed, for the whole country, which he does not resign himself to seeing sectioned). It is industrial and agricultural education that must produce the exorcism:

> Palermo will thus be transformed into an object of public interest, absolving it from the sort of curse which weighs upon it, and which condemned it to inevitable destruction; and the monuments of savage tyranny like the Model School and the Exhibition of Industry converted into instruments of civilization and progress, a worthy vengeance for the people whom it was intended to enslave.[66]

In this sense, the space of the exhibition also brings together several of the aspirations present in the Quinta Normal, with a not inconsiderable addition: the exhibitions are, in the second half of the nineteenth century, the place par excellence of civilizing contact, the imaginary space where the main metropolises enter into competition, the sphere in which mercantile circulation is embodied in forms and models and, above all, what most connects them with the role that parks will have and that Sarmiento imagines for his Quinta Normal: experiences in scale of urban ideals for the industrial city and focal points of attraction for the direction of the city's growth. Palermo offers a place already naturally predisposed to connect two of the tropes dominating the idea of the exhibitions, technical and landscaping progress: let us not forget that the Crystal Palace was designed by Joseph Paxton, the creator of Birkenhead Park, for the London Exhibition of 1851.[67] Sarmiento will always retain this

---

[66] Sarmiento, "Exposición agrícola," *El Nacional*, January 8, 1858, in *Obras completas* (LD), XXVI, 228.

[67] For this reason, it is interesting to note the reform that Sarmiento imagines for the Caserón de Rosas on occasion of the first agricultural exhibition: its conversion into a "Crystal Palace": "Each of the capitals of the world has been endowed in recent years with a Palace of Industry, and glass architecture has assumed permanent forms. Palermo is admirably adapted to the grandest plan of industrial exhibition. Its square of buildings enclosing an extensive courtyard with immense cisterns, may one day receive a glass roof

technical and landscape advancement as a combined cultural motif. For example, when in 1871 he organizes the Córdoba Exhibition, the Palace of Industry and the multitude of machines and instruments set in the framework of "the beautiful gardens that art has improvised around it," is all that in the inaugural speech allows him to distance himself once again from the double barbarism that obsesses him: that of wild nature, "the pampas I have just crossed," and that of tradition, emblematized in "the monuments that decorate this American Córdoba."[68]

But at this time, what he imagines for Palermo is already a "Central Park;" although its formation would be discussed and approved in the Senate only in 1874, Sarmiento had been working on it since much earlier, starting with a plan by Captain of Engineers, Jordan Wysocki, and including the work of the students of the Military School (installed by Sarmiento in the Caserón de Rosas), "as a practical study of the courses of topography, bridges, and roads that follow."[69]

42

The program of the park is sufficiently explicit regarding the peculiar artifact it projects, a true "technical laboratory," as Pablo Pschepiurca rightly called it: stables, nurseries, greenhouses, facilities for agricultural and industrial exhibitions, observatories, zoological garden, pastures for grazing, dairy farms, experimental facilities for technological innovation in rural establishments, such as artificial irrigation; along with the same proposal that the layout and realization should be part of the training of topographers and military engineers. But in the presentation to Congress, what in the Quinta Normal Central project was exclusive, now appears for the first time displaced by the more usual tropes of the Central Park:[70]

> In the midst of the astonishing development of the city of Buenos Aires, whose suburbs are confused to the south with Barracas and to the west reach San José de Flores, a Park is missing that can give such a large population the ornament and comfort that the Bois de Boulogne, Hyde Park, or

---

to shelter, without depriving them of light and warmth, the numerous plants, flowers, and shrubs which already form our collections, and the four sheds which the ingenuity of the estanciero architect placed at the ends of his singular abode, to shade applicants, welders, and palatial men, may be adapted for collections of birds and animals [...]. [And] the beautiful road that leads to Palermo will present an attraction to visitors that it does not have in any point of the city without counting on the woods and neighboring avenues to keep away the monotony of these meetings." Ibid.

[68] Sarmiento, "Discurso inaugural de la Exposición de Córdoba," October 15, 1871, in *Obras completas (LD)*, XXI, 309.

[69] "Proyecto del Poder Ejecutivo," in Congreso Nacional, Cámara de Senadores, *Sesión de 1874* (Buenos Aires: El Nacional, 1875), regular session of June 20, 1874, 152.

[70] Pablo Pschepiurca, "Palermo, la construcción del parque." See also the sketch of the draft law made by Sarmiento, in Museo Sarmiento, Archive, Box Q.

New York's Central Park offer, not only to the wealthy classes and to foreigners, but to the thousands of artisans and families who find in the exercise and in the spectacle of the natural beauties aided by art, solace to their daily tasks, and innocent and profitable recreation for health.[71]

This is what was new in Sarmiento's discourse in the seventies: to now locate civilizing values in the park itself, as a modern typology for recreation and spectacle; to displace its instrumental character, as center of the vast operation of transformation of the countryside, and to turn it into an end in itself, linked for the first time to the "real" needs of Buenos Aires society. Real, in inverted commas: because what was more figurative, his image of a countryside populated by industrious and happy farmers and modern institutions with the Quinta Normal as their powerhouse, or his image of Buenos Aires going beyond its territorial and social limits?

In order to overcome the resistance to the installation of the park in Palermo—of figures like Guillermo Rawson, who contributed his anti-rosismo with a profuse mixture of hygienic, political, and moral arguments—Sarmiento would emphasize the new needs of local representation, practical fact (the lands are already forested and now belong to the national government) and, above, all symbolic motives: to bury in the cultivated green "the last shoots of the old barbarism," "the summary of all past times [....], the man of the pampean epoch."[72] It is an act of transfiguration and cultural domination: when the remaining parts of Palermo, Sarmiento goes on to say at the inauguration of the first section of the park, "have been subjected to culture, the park will be a model presented to the public of what the whole country can be." That is why, for Eduardo Wilde, before the Park, "around the great city there was nothing but dust and desert, scorching sunshine, or burning wind."[73]

Around the big city: the original mismatch resounds again: if it is now a park, the distance with respect to one of the main models it seemed to be emulating is enormous. Because Central Park is defined, precisely, by occupying the center of the city. Although by mid-century Manhattan was only partially urbanized, the existence of the 1811 plan that laid out the grid of blocks for the entire island showed that Central Park had consciously operated in the heart of the future metropolis. And Sarmiento knew it well, as he described Central Park in 1867 as that "which today is outside the city of New York, but which

41
40

---

[71] "Proyecto del Poder Ejecutivo," in Congreso Nacional, Cámara de Senadores, *Diario de sesiones de 1874*, 152.

[72] Sarmiento, "Discurso inaugural del Parque 3 de Febrero," November 11, 1875, *Obras completas (LD)*, XXII, 13. On the polemic with Rawson, see Osvaldo Loudet, *Ensayos de crítica e historia* (Buenos Aires: Academia Argentina de Letras, 1975).

[73] Eduardo Wilde, "A Palermo," article published on the occasion of the inauguration of the park, in *Páginas escogidas*, ed. José María Monner Sans (Buenos Aires: Editorial Estrada, 1939), IX, 206.

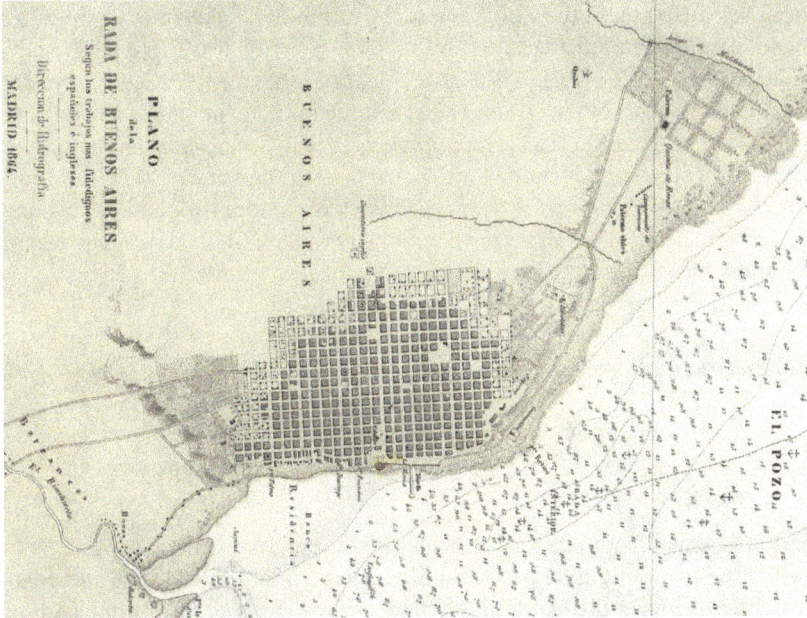

Figure 15. Dirección de Hidrografía del Reino de España, *Plan of the Buenos Aires Harbor* (detail), 1864, Asociación Civil Rumbo Sur. The plan, contemporary with the Palermo Park project, clearly shows the layout of the crops that belonged to Rosas, where the park would be located (above the city, to the right, following the riverbank). Note the distance that separates it from the last confines of the city.

Figure 16. Samuel Boote, *The Gates of Palermo, Built in 1875 at the Beginning of Sarmiento Avenue to Give Entrance to the Park*, c. 1880. César Gotta collection.

occupies the center of the vast layout of the future city."[74] Palermo, on the other hand, is not part of any layout that links it to the city; it is irremediably outside and far away. Central Park is an ideological instrument for the recovery of nature in the heart of the city and an economic instrument for the valorization of urban rent; Palermo is a park eccentric to the city, an inverse device: one for civilizing a hinterland identified with nature and the barbaric past. Lewis Mumford has said of Frederick Law Olmsted's work in Central Park that "by making nature urbane, he naturalized the city;" one may paraphrase him to say that, in Palermo, by urbanizing nature, Sarmiento hoped to culturize the pampa.[75]

2. Palermo and Buenos Aires

> Buenos Aires is a vast prison, a plethoric body that drowns, and cannot walk...[76]
> –Domingo Faustino Sarmiento

But we claimed that in Palermo distance is also programmatic. It does not only reflect the economic and ideological impotence (the absence of legal and political instruments in the hands of the state) of expropriating the central lands of the actually existing city—the main issue for hygienists and urban technicians only a decade later. Palermo, on the other hand, needs that distance and affirms it: the promise and the supposition of a "new city," born out of nothing, far from the city: a displaced city. Because if the park results from the productivist utopia of the Quinta Normal, at the same time, the change of program completely reconsiders its relation to the city. And here we must recognize another itinerary in Sarmiento's thought, in which Palermo also represents a point of arrival: a journey that starts from the consideration of Buenos Aires as a "modern city" as opposed to the "American Córdoba;" it goes through the optimism regarding the possibilities of Buenos Aires to continue its progress and to function as beacon of a broader modernization—in the years of the euphoric discovery of the city, during the times of the State of Buenos Aires—; and after a gradual disappointment, it culminates in the final identification of Buenos Aires as a "traditional city," with all the vices and defects of colonial culture. The role played by Córdoba in the urban application of the classical antinomy "civilization and barbarism," will be taken over by the actually existing Buenos Aires, which will be opposed to an idyllic "new city" that should find its center in Palermo.

The park, then, is destined to oppose its civilizing plan not only to the memory of political barbarism emblematized in the very land it is called to

---

[74] Sarmiento, *Obras completas (BS)*, XXX:277–78.

[75] Lewis Mumford, *The Brown Decades: A Study of Arts in America, 1865–1895* (1931) (New York: Dover Publications, 1955), 88.

[76] "Arquitectura doméstica," October 15, 1879, in *Obras completas (BS)*, XLVI, 104.

counteract; not only to the anomic immensity of the pampa that its groves and arts seek to neutralize. It also offers itself as an alternative, fully modernist in its radicalism, to the traditional city, whose errors and obstacles—material and institutional—hail from the colonial period:

> The street of the Law of the Indies, in checkerboards, the town hall and the jail in the main square, the convents of Santo Domingo and San Francisco, La Merced, Las Catalinas, etc. at a block's distance in all directions. Buenos Aires will continue to be what it is today with its tubular streets, a torture for passersby, and I will not be surprised to see the mazorca [armed group that supported Rosas] reappear. [77]

This radicality with respect to the actually existing city opens up two questions: on the one hand, the series of motives that lead Sarmiento to make this transition in his view of Buenos Aires, from euphoria to disappointment; on the other hand, the series of obstacles that make him believe that it is impossible to modify this city, when in fact he is perfectly familiar with much more traumatic urban transformations than those that would have been required in this case.

Tulio Halperin Donghi has underlined Sarmiento's perplexity, upon his return to Buenos Aires, at the discovery that, against reasonable expectations, after Rosas and in the midst of the colossal political chaos of the fifties, Buenos Aires appeared as a thriving city, with an "insolent present prosperity and [an] unshakable confidence in its future prosperity."[78] These are the years of his definitive return from Chilean exile, when he is enthusiastic and surprised by the social homogeneity of Buenos Aires in terms practically analogous to those he had used in the United States; when he believes he sees a civilizing continuum that has Buenos Aires as the gateway to modernizing transference: "the gaucho abandons the poncho and the countryside is invaded by the city as the city is by Europe."[79] These are the years, moreover, of his councilmanship in "the cultured Buenos Aires," in which he emphasizes again and again the strength of the "municipal spirit," the development of the press, the

[77] "La Plata," *Obras completas (LD)*, XLII:223.
[78] Tulio Halperin Donghi, *Una nación para el desierto argentino* (Buenos Aires: CEAL, 1982), 51.
[79] "Letter to Mr. Mariano de Sarratea," May 29, 1855, in *Obras completas (LD)*, XXIV, 32. There, says a dazzled Sarmiento: "mingling with the crowds that come to the games these days and completely fill the Plaza de la Victoria, I have not found people, rabble, plebs, rotos. The place of the *"rotos"* of Chile is taken by thousands of Basques, Italians, Spaniards, French, etc. The costume is the same for all classes, or more properly speaking, there are no classes." On the homogeneity and social integration, the "education" and "unalterable order" of society, and the "moral and material advancement" of the city, see also "Sobre el Carnaval de 1857," *El Nacional*, February 25, 1857, in ibid., 207–9.

transformation of the institutions, the evolution of industry, the beautification of the city, and its harmony with the main metropolis of the world; and in
which he makes a number of proposals for transformation (demolition of the
Recova, union of the squares of Mayo and Victoria, tree-planting programs,
etc.), demonstrating a practically unlimited optimism regarding the possibility
of the consolidation of a metropolis adequate to the times and to its role in the
country that should be unified under its example.[80]

The initial perplexity, in truth, had to do with a presupposition: the necessary relationship between political progress and economic progress. But to the
extent that the progress that Buenos Aires had experienced, first in political
regression and later in chaos, proved, against all the lessons taught by conservative Chile, that a strong and stable order was not essential to guarantee
development, at the same time, after the initial idyll it would become the irrefutable proof of the obstacles that all change would face. How could a city be
transformed, under the promise of the emergence of a new society, if Buenos
Aires proved time and again, with its "maladjustments," to be adjusted, in fact,
to existing society? Sarmiento would progressively forge—from his time in the
City Council until the last years of his life—a strong disillusionment about the
existing city and society, about the stubbornness of the dominant classes in
opposing the changes that had seemed so natural and attainable in the process of development after the fall of Rosas. Thus, Palermo, in its passage from
Quinta Normal Central to Parque Central, is the manifestation of a double failure, made evident in the change of meaning of the term "central": the failure of
the new territorial organization that would have Quinta Normal as the center
of national operations; and the failure of the transformation of the traditional
city, which was now to be replaced by another city, with a new center occupied
by the park.

The city is incorrigible, because Sarmiento upholds a double correlation:
the first, as we saw, between city and society, and this other one between politics
and economics; his figurations will clash with the reality of both. The conflict
foregrounds two fundamental debates that explain Sarmiento's configuration
of the "new city" as a response to his postulates of the necessary relationship
between social and urban transformation, but which also point to topics of very
long duration in local urban culture: the debate on the political quality of "city"
space, and the debate on the role of the state in its production.

The conception of the city as a political space goes beyond the importance given by most of the constitutionalists of the nineteenth century to the
municipal regime as the basic order of the political system. Because in the most
widespread and hegemonic conception, the city ceased in fact to be a model of

---

[80] On Sarmiento's management as councilor, see F. García Molina and C. Devia de
Ovadía, *Domingo Faustino Sarmiento. Concejal porteño* (Buenos Aires: Honorable
Concejo Deliberante, 1988).

political organization in scale for the whole of national society to become a particular administrative institution, whose role was to decentralize management, even though the communal institution could also be thought of as the basic cell of a democratic society and placed at the center of any projection of development models—according to Tocqueville's widely spread hypotheses—and the ideal Republic—following Echeverría's inspiration—could be considered as "an association of municipalities."[81] Ternavasio has shown how, in the most widespread of these conceptions, a distinction was made between a political sphere, that of the national and provincial states, and an administrative sphere, that of the municipal state: while in the first citizens could act in an egalitarian way, in the second "neighbors" were to act according to property and income qualifications.[82] The municipality is thus defined as the universe of economic interests, whose management can only be entrusted, in terms of good administration, to the interested parties themselves—the owners—without political interference. From this point of view, in the formulations of many thinkers of the nineteenth century, a proposal of traditional organization for the city coincides with the proposal of modern organization for the national state, in which the bourgeois-democratic conception of citizenship prevails, with its correlate in universal suffrage. It is a traditional conception of the municipality as an economic-administrative sphere, which will have a long life and strong ideological presence both in the nineteenth century and during a great part of the twentieth, which not only explains that the political system of the city was modified and democratized later and much more partially than the national political system, but also supports, as we will see, most of the positions and actions of nearly all the social and political actors of this period, generating

---

[81] Alexis de Tocqueville, *Democracy in America* (Garden City, NY: Doubleday, 1969). On his influence on the ideas of Argentine constitutionalists, see Natalio Botana, *La tradición republicana* (Buenos Aires: Sudamericana, 1984). On the constitutionalists and the discussions on the municipal regime, see Carlos Mouchet, "Las ideas sobre el municipio en la Argentina hasta 1853," in Honorable Concejo Deliberante, *Evolución institucional del municipio de la ciudad de Buenos Aires* (Buenos Aires: Ediciones del H. Concejo Deliberante, 1963), 31.

[82] Inequality among taxpaying "neighbors" would thus belong to the "natural right," which lies in the economic-administrative sphere, while equality is circumscribed to the political sphere that does not find manifestation in the city: for Vicente Fidel López, for example, "the essential condition of municipal life is that it be understood that, just as it is different from political life, it is also very different from democratic life, and that municipal power belongs only and exclusively to those who pay the rent and therefore have the right to manage it." Quoted in Marcela Ternavasio, "Municipio y representación local en el sistema político argentino de la segunda mitad del siglo XIX," *Anales del Instituto de Arte Americano e Investigaciones Estéticas "Mario J. Buschiazzo"* 27–28 (1992): 59.

a series of conflicts in the definition of the relations state/society and public space/political citizenship.

Sarmiento inverts the formula that privileged the administrative sphere as a technical space, that is to say, "neutral," and defines the municipality as a space in which every measure "implies option, decision, choice among various alternatives."[83] This explains the importance Sarmiento gives to a series of issues: his vision of the role of the press in the formation of a municipal public sphere, or his proposal for the integration of immigrants into the local political system not merely through their role as taxpayers, but through their nationalization and their acceptance of full citizenship. These are issues on which his position will not undergo profound changes over time. Though in so many other aspects it is possible to find great changes, it could be said that what happens with his ideal conception of the city is similar to that regarding education: these are not only very strong convictions, but they are also not subject to the swings that practical politics introduces in most of the original postulates. This is true for various reasons, but perhaps mainly because of futuristic wager in which the projective character of education and the city coincide. The view of the real city or society may change, and therefore Sarmiento's opinions about the existing "state of civilization" may change, but as concepts, city and education are thought of as instruments for arriving at another society, and therefore their exemplary character is never questioned by the limitations of actual society.

In their necessary future completion, education and the city displace their effects by separating themselves from the present in order to promise a different tomorrow through their own ideal values. The relationship is not new: it already marks one of the most long-standing paradigms in the conception of the city, the one initiated by Moore's *Utopia,* in which urban form represents the pedagogic access to a new social form. However, the "new city" is not, in the Buenos Aires of the second half of the nineteenth century, a utopia in the sense usually assigned to the term; on the contrary, it is strongly rooted in representations prevalent at that time. In a catastrophic common sense that every big city generates in its expansive moments, the idea that the traditional city is exhausted, that in the center "business makes everything cramped," is one that arises and resurfaces periodically in these years: "It is necessary to hurry to build another city; here there is no longer anywhere to live," says repeatedly the chronicler of the *Correo del Domingo* in 1864.[84] But, in Sarmiento, the proposal of the "new city" will go beyond mere negativity by relying on recognizable urban processes; it is a precise model of the city/society relationship, whose

---

[83] M. Ternavasio, "Debates y alternativas acerca de un modelo de institución local en la Argentina decimonónica," *Anuario* 14 (1991).

[84] See Bruno, "La semana," *Correo del Domingo I* (1864), 706–7, 162, quoted in Rodolfo Giunta, "Buenos Aires en el Correo del Domingo," *Seminarios de Crítica 1994* 54 (Buenos Aires: Instituto de Arte Americano, FADU-UBA, November 1994).

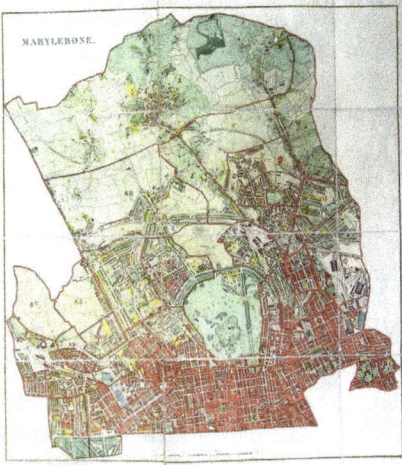

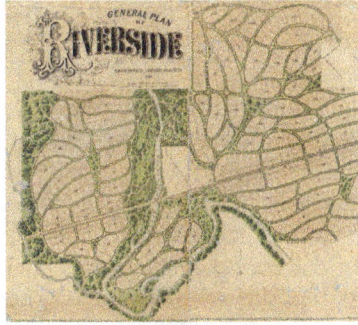

Examples of "new cities," modeled for modern residential developments far from traditional city centers:

Figure 17. *London's Northwest: Map of Marylebone, Regent's Park, Hampstead and Highgate,* 1875. British Library Digital Collections.

Figure 18. Olmsted, Vaux and Co., *General Plan of Riverside,* Chicago, Illinois, 1869. Chicago Lithographing Company. New York Public Library Digital Collections.

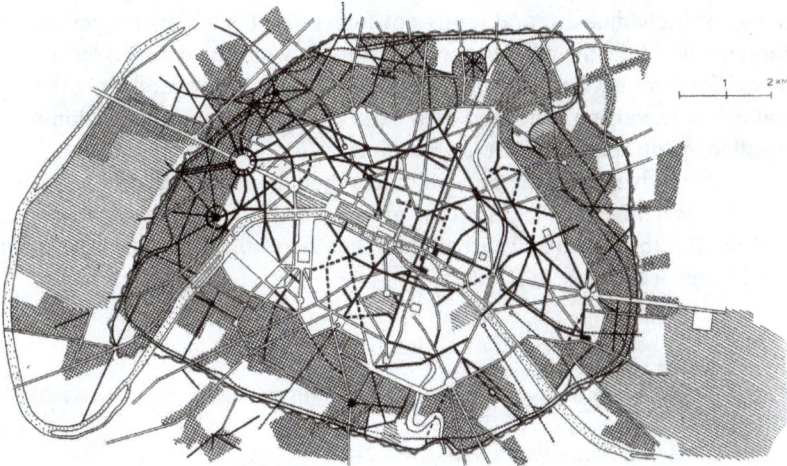

Figure 19. Paris, paradigmatic model of the "concentrated" city which renews upon itself. The plan shows a synthesis of Haussmann's works, most of which are in the restricted area of the old 18th-century municipal boundary, and only a few of which reach as far as the new walled border. Diagram from Leonardo Benevolo, *Diseño de la ciudad – 5. El arte y la ciudad contemporánea,* Barcelona: Gustavo Gili, 1977.

palpable existence in some cities of the world sustains the persistence of Sarmiento's conviction: "cities renew themselves like snakes, leaving the old skin where they did the operation and moving on elsewhere," he would say later on.[85] It is a model that shapes the utopia of a radically new city/society, still without social actors to embody it, but that works in the imaginary because, strictly speaking, it is a real model, which Sarmiento was able to capture in his travels.

In this model, the traditional city should become the "center," the bureaucratic and commercial city, but the residential areas—which is where the wager for the construction of a new society would really be played out—should be displaced: "Englishmen and Americans boast that their wives ignore where their merchant husband's desk is located," Sarmiento repeatedly affirms.[86] This is what happened in London, in fact, from an early process of suburbanization carried out with the peculiar system of residential *estates*, which had allowed a private policy of land occupation favoring a process of expansion of suburban residences. This was also the case in Chicago, where the suburbs (Riverside, designed by Olmsted himself; Oak Park), where the upper- and upper-middle classes moved from 1870 onwards, were formed as the Loop was outsourced; and in New York, though in those years a different expansion process occurred, contained by the public grid, in which Central Park produced the valorization of new areas at the heart of the island. In this Palermo does not deviate too much from its model: "In the conception of Olmsted and the most prominent representatives of the Park Movement, the park enters the city as an organic and organizational element, which must precede and guide the speculative initiative of individuals."[87] And let us not forget Sarmiento's own experience in Santiago de Chile: the neighborhood of Yungay where he lived his last exile, a model for him of a "modern neighborhood," had been the product of the typical urban expansion generated by a park, the speculative urbanization made possible by the opening of the Quinta Normal.[88]

Palermo, then, fixes the possibility of a model and its orientation; it wants to be the incentive for the "new city" and, in its own layout, the indication for its plan. It is the punctual incarnation of that "Argentine spirit" that Sarmiento would later see emerge in La Plata:

[85] See "Un gran boulevard para Buenos Aires," *El Censor* (Buenos Aires), December 20, 1885, *Obras completas (LD)*, XLII: 238.
[86] For example, in *Obras completas (BS)*, XLI:247.
[87] Sica, *Historia del urbanismo. El siglo XIX*, 2: 659.
[88] Armando de Ramón, *Santiago de Chile (1541–1991). Historia de una sociedad urbana* (Madrid: MAPFRE, 1992), 169, reproduces Sarmiento's opinion in 1842 about the neighborhood: a beautiful residential complex where "speculation has had the happiest results and a large population has gathered to make a beautiful little village with lined and spacious streets emerging from the bosom of the earth, as if it had been sown."

The visitor to Buenos Aires feels as if in the world he has dreamed of, because
La Plata is Argentine thought as it has been forming and illustrating itself
for a long time, without anyone noticing it. Where does the Lord Mayor [in
English in the original, referring to Torcuato de Alvear] with his boulevards
and his wide squares come from? From Montevideo, which initiated the
movement [...], from Mendoza, from Palermo.[89]

Montevideo, Mendoza: the choice of models is not arbitrary and, as we saw
in the case of Santiago, is not limited to central cases; the "new city" is a peculiar
modality of urban modernization that Sarmiento is able to distinguish also in
other nearby cities.

Montevideo, due to its peculiar history and location, was one of the few
American originally walled capitals, which places it in a position quite like that
of its European counterparts. But, unlike them, in the nineteenth century it
did not modernize itself by renovating and demolishing sectors of the old lay-   38
out but carried out a truly novel and early "expansion" (1829–36), which is
precisely called Ciudad Nueva (New City), drawing a regular scheme outside
the limit of the walls whose demolition was decreed. When Sarmiento passed
through the city on his way to Europe, he envisioned this layout more than
anything as a promise between the chaos of the siege and the war. Finally, it was
the basis for the early modernization of Montevideo.[90]

Mendoza, on the other hand, also involved an exceptional situation. In
1861 an earthquake had completely destroyed the existing city and, instead of
rebuilding, the decision was made to create a new, displaced city, which, though
it did not completely replace the old, became a modern pole with a completely
different layout from that inherited from the colonial era, one where special
importance was given to regularity, the system of irrigation ditches and profuse
forestation. The popular classes remained in the old city; the upper class kept
their properties there and rebuilt them for rent or commerce but moved their
residences to the new city. New city, new society: "the Mendocinos can boast
of having risen almost transformed from our former way of being," declared
the Legislature in 1864. Sarmiento himself would state in 1886 that "Mendoza
reveals to the traveler that a new type of society and ideas other than colonial

---

[89] "La Plata," *El Nacional*, 1886, *Obras completas (LD)*, XLII:223.
[90] Sarmiento passed through Montevideo in 1846, in the heat of the "Guerra Grande"   38
(Great War, 1839-1851). The demolition of the walls of Montevideo had been resolved
by decree in 1829; the design of the regular widening (the New City) was made
between 1832 and 1836 by José María Reyes; its articulation with the old city in the
Plaza de Independencia was made between 1836 and 1842 by the Italian architect
Carlo Zucchi, a figure of importance in the Río de la Plata in those decades. See Hugo
Baracchini, "Evolución urbanística de Montevideo," in *250 años de Montevideo (Ciclo
conmemorativo)* (Montevideo: GERGU, 1980).

ones begin to prevail. Mr. Gould, on seeing the streets and squares of Mendoza, was reminded of the shaded cities of New England." [91]

The "new city," in this sense, is a pedagogic machine for the political life of the new society that must necessarily emerge, and that will never be able to flourish in the framework of the traditional city. The relationship between city and society is so close for Sarmiento that it is always presented in circular terms: the plan of the "new city" would transform a vicious circle into a virtuous one.

But here appears the other aspect of this conviction: the traditional city is incorrigible not because in Buenos Aires the municipal or provincial government lacks the strength, resources, and instruments to carry out a reform comparable to Haussmann's in Paris, but because this would be undesirable in the educational paradigm. The city is incorrigible, then, because while Sarmiento verifies that society does not do for itself "what it must," he does not believe that a strong state should take over doing it. It is a teaching based on a comparison of the United States and Europe: compared to the responsible freedom of the "yanquee," says Sarmiento, "the European [and he is thinking above all of the French] is a minor who is under the protective tutelage of the state." [92]

The idea of the city as a political space implicitly carries with it this weak conception of the state. Although it may seem to contradict the most frequent characterization of the opposition between Sarmiento and Juan Bautista Alberdi, it is precisely the political space of the Sarmientan city that is presented as the most appropriate to form, by *itself*, the necessary bourgeoisie in the liberal imaginary. Meanwhile, the "neutral space" closer to the Alberdian model—in the sense that Alberdi proposed to keep the logic of the political system (the state) and civil society separate—is the one that historically allowed, and allows by definition, the consolidation of a body of ideas and autonomous "technical" instruments with a strong capacity for public intervention in the territory. We will see the lasting imprint that the latter model will have on the formation of a technical ideology in urban planning. [93] Faced with this tradition, Sarmiento would envision a city that sought to oppose, simultaneously, the qualitative reduction of its character as a political space and the increase of those public instruments that would have made it possible to build this space "from above." But, since he holds on to the idea that city and society

---

[91] Jorge Ricardo Ponte, *Mendoza, aquella ciudad de barro. Historia de una ciudad andina desde el siglo XVI hasta nuestros días* (Mendoza: Municipalidad de la Ciudad de Mendoza, 1987); and Sarmiento, "La Plata," *Obras completas (LD)*, XLII:220.

[92] Sarmiento, *Viajes*, 316ff.

[93] This theme has been developed by Leonardo Benevolo in his classic *Orígenes de la urbanística moderna* (Buenos Aires: Ediciones Tekné, 1967). By the most frequent stylization I refer to the image of the opposition between Sarmiento and Alberdi on the role of the state and its capacity to intervene in society, imposed from the debates on public education. On the "Alberdian model," see Natalio Botana, *El orden conservador* (1977) (Buenos Aires: Hyspamérica, 1986).

must march together, his problem, consequently, is what to do with the existing city, inherited from times when society had other customs and life had other rhythms and directions, and how to define a city more adequate to the times and needs of modern progress, if at the same time it is not possible to actively intervene in the new design.

Palermo will be his most complete answer to this quandary and also the demonstration of all its limitations: it is the public starting point for a new city, the impulse to a development that would only be adequate if society itself were to undertake it from there; a public initiative with enough strength to guide and encourage a private one, to whose responsibility it is addressed as an imperative. It is a shortcut or a detour: "let happen to us in Buenos Aires what happened to England, which, advancing in its political construction and securing institutions, has had to describe detours around the older ones that already occupied the soil."[94] Palermo is a lighthouse placed for the moment of the emergence of a society that agrees with what is already more advanced, ahead of the city and of actually existing society: the "Argentine spirit," the "Argentine thought," that will only be able to manifest itself in a virgin territory free of all hindrance, as will happen a decade after the creation of the Park with the foun-   26
dation of La Plata. Although there, in his last years, Sarmiento also ended up discovering another mirage, self-confirming of his lapidary judgments on local society and politics: that this "Argentine thought" counted him among its very few and isolated representatives.

---

[94] Sarmiento, "La Plata," 223.

CHAPTER 2

A Concentrated City:
The Shape of Order

To understand what Sarmiento expected from Palermo, to interpret his project for a "new city" is what makes intelligible the reasons for his frontal and determined opposition, a decade after the creation of the park, to the centerpiece of Mayor Torcuato de Alvear's project: the Avenida de Mayo, the Boulevard. Sarmiento was one of the few public figures who opposed this sign of the times, and surely the only one who did so in terms of a precise model of the modern city that the boulevard refuted. Because the Avenida de Mayo, by ratifying the central axis of the traditional city, promoted a renewal of the existing city on itself: for Sarmiento, it was the acceptance of that city and that society and its celebration; it was to reaffirm the center of the old chaotic and hopeless Buenos Aires.

Palermo and Avenida de Mayo, the two great emblems of fin-de-siècle Buenos Aires, quickly pacified as complementary postcards, were in fact at the time fragments of mutually exclusionary city projects. And that conflict serves to call into question some recurrent assertions in the historiography of Buenos Aires: such as the "hygienist" explanation of the move of the upper classes to the north of the city; or the "classist" explanation that the intendancies— Alvear's par excellence—which of course represented those classes, favored the development of the north of the city to the detriment of the south.

Sarmiento blames Alvear for projecting Avenida de Mayo, reinforcing the traditional center, while he chooses Callao to the north as a place for his own residence.[95] Was that, in fact, a flagrant contradiction of the "Lord Mayor"? Strictly speaking, two things must be recognized: that the significance of the different sites of the city is in full mutation at the end of the century; and that

---

[95] "Everything has to be explained to *My Lord* who builds a palace in the *Northern* part of the city and sends us to enter Callao Boulevard by the *Southern* part," says Sarmiento, criticizing Alvear's layout of Avenida de Mayo, in "Un gran boulevard para Buenos Aires," where he proposes that the boulevard be built in the north (Córdoba Street, for example), *El Censor* (Buenos Aires), December 20, 1885, in *Obras completas (LD)*, XLII:238.

two traditions of urban thought are in confronting each other. In this case, Sarmiento will again be in the minority in front of the tradition more rooted in local urban culture, for which Alvear will represent, in some way, a point of arrival but also of complete resignification.

1. Centrality and Regularity: The Will to Form

> We are forced, then [...], to open wide streets consulting the physiognomy of the city and the traditional current of concentration habits. We have and will have for centuries, gathered in a short space, the Plaza de Mayo, all the causes that congregate the people, religion, the courts, the municipality, the chambers, the ministries, the main theater, the carriage stations, the civic festivities, finally. That is so and to modify it would be more difficult than all the projected works.[96]
>
> –Miguel Cané, 1885

Alvear's boulevard, Avenida de Mayo, is part of a vast "plan" of works that comes to represent an urban tradition different from the one sustained by Sarmiento, beyond the fact that the technical and formal resources, the type of urban images to which they appeal and the type of artifacts through which the reform is conceived within the nineteenth-century city (regular layouts, boulevards, diagonals, parks) may coincide. This is a tradition rooted in the French urban experience; but it is precisely this case that serves to refute the unilateral link that is generally made when speaking of French influence in Latin American cities through the action of Prefect Haussmann in Paris: operations that—already reductively—had traditionally been attributed to Haussmann there are usually seen here, degraded: demolishing working-class neighborhoods to allow for the maneuvers of military repression or beautifying the bourgeois city. On the contrary, it is a matter of linking Alvear's reform to an earlier line of French experience, in which Haussmann undoubtedly also inserts himself (and, in this sense, the recent characterization of Haussmann's reforms not as a beginning but as the result of a "long incubation" is relevant), rooted in Buenos Aires in the times of Rivadavia and embodied in institutions of great influence in the design of the city and territory during practically the entire nineteenth century.[97]

20, 21

19

---

[96] Letter from Miguel Cané to Mayor Torcuato de Alvear, Vienna, January 14, 1885, reproduced in Beccar Varela, *Torcuato de Alvear*, 484.

[97] In reality, the historiography has produced a double reduction: all urban transformations here are thought of as *Haussmannization*, and *Haussmannization* is conceived through a generalization—which has rendered it ineffective—of Friedrich Engels's original and extremely acute characterization of the "Haussmann method": to cross the workers' quarters with boulevards in order to prevent barricade fighting.

This "regularizing" tradition, born from the needs of the reorganization of the post-revolutionary French state, implied a series of transformations bearing upon the rationalization and systematization of the design of urban equipment. It is a tradition eminently based on engineering, as opposed to the Beaux-Arts tradition of "urban beautification," which tends to define the city as a "perfect machine," "capable of dominating its own economic and sanitary flows," as Fernando Aliata points out in his exhaustive work on the Rivadavian city.[98] "Buenos Aires must fold in on itself," said Rivadavia in 1822, and the Callao Boulevard was then—beyond the fact that since the second half of the nineteenth century it has been seen as the demonstration that Rivadavia had "foreseen" the future expansion of the city—the "Boulevard de circunvalación," the necessary border to delimit the space that could be rationalized and controlled. It is this engineering tradition, of revolutionary state resonance, which marked the formation of the Topographic Department of the Province of Buenos Aires, and which explains the survival of a series of practices of territorial planning, though, in tune with the definition of the city as an administrative space, the increasing assumption of technical "neutrality" implied a transcendental change: from the initial precepts of the Enlightenment that saw these practices as instruments of radical modification of society "from above," to the technical autonomy in which the procedures of regularization and organization of territory become matrices of long-term changes outside of social or political action.[99]

See "The Housing Question," reprint of Engels's polemic with Proudhonism of 1872, especially section III of the second part (multiple editions). The indispensable analysis has nevertheless acted as an obstacle to focus on other aspects of urban reform. But, in recent years, the Parisian experience has not ceased to be reanalyzed: see for example Marcel Roncayolo, "L'esperienza e il modello," in Carlo Olmo and Bernard Lepetit, eds., La città e le sue storie (Turin: Einaudi, 1995), 62, which offers a characterization of Haussmann's aforementioned urban reform as the product of a "long incubation;" also Insolera's, "Europa XIX secolo: ipotesi per una nuova definizione della città," where he explains his hypothesis on Haussmann's invention of the "city industry."

[98] Aliata, La ciudad regular, 162.

[99] I have taken Rivadavia's phrase from Aliata's La ciudad regular, that shows the link between the "regularizing" ambition of Rivadavia's urban administration with precise political and technical traditions: the reorganization of the French state after the Revolution, the models of the "cities of state" created by the Napoleonic administration as part of its territorial consolidation, and the system of Bâtiments Civils, with its design transformations that would be crowned with the formation of the Polytechnic Schools and Ponts et Chaussés. From this training (in France and other European countries) came the technicians, like Pellegrini and Bevans, brought by Rivadavia to work during his administration and who remained in the country influencing urban policies and the consolidation of management institutions throughout the nineteenth century. On these figures see also Alberto de Paula and Ramón Gutiérrez, La encrucijada de la arquitectura argentina, 1822-1875. Santiago Bevans — Carlos Pellegrini (Resistencia, 1974). On the

Indeed, if in Rivadavia's time the experience of technical transformation was accompanied by institutional and political modifications that converged in the will to build the revolutionary city as a political space, after Rosas—a period during which the technical bodies devised by Rivadavia survived without major conceptual changes—the return to Rivadavia's postulates (which Buenos Aires elites happily invoked in the period of its autonomous affirmation), would completely dissociate technical tradition and political tradition. And the former will be the greatest emblem of neutral state interference in the consolidation of modern space and territory.[100]

Characteristic of the growing autonomy of the engineering tradition is the publicity undertaken in the fifties by Carlos Pellegrini (one of the technicians who had been summoned for Rivadavia's reforms) through *La Revista del Plata*, seeking to disseminate technical solutions and organizational methods for the body of problems related to the city's modernization and to territorial knowledge, transformation, and exploitation. From this point of view, Pellegrini's case is interesting because, belonging to an earlier generation, he still shows the traces of a more political enlightenment, in the sense of his ability to tackle great general problems and not to limit himself to partial technical solutions, as we will see would be the habit among engineers toward the end of the century. His whole enterprise is destined to place at the service of rulers, producers, and investors a number of initiatives that become obvious to him in this moment of constructive mysticism that follows the fall of Rosas. But let us see how the question of technical autonomy is being raised.

His vision of the relationship between technique and politics is, in principle, completely instrumental. Beyond the usual diatribes against the Rosas government and the ideological recovery of Rivadavia's programmatic approach, as if in the present situation it were only a matter of saving an unfortunate parenthesis in the path of progress, the skeleton of all his projects has to do with the demand for a growing autonomy between the different technical disciplines within the state apparatus and of all of them in the face of the orientations and political conflicts of the moment. In short, Pellegrini interprets now, Rivadavia

---

French topographic tradition see Georges Teyssot, "Il sistema dei Batiments civils in Francia e la pianificazione di Le Mans (1795–1848)," in Paolo Morachiello and Georges Teyssot, eds., *Le macchine imperfette. Architettura, programma, istituzioni nel XIX secolo* (Roma: Officina, 1980), 82ff; and on administrative issues, Eduardo García de Enterría, *Revolución francesa y administración contemporánea* (Madrid: Taurus, 1981).

[100] From 1853, the work of urban and territorial planning recovers the policy of the Law of Ejidos of 1823, and when the Topographic Department is reorganized in 1857, its competence and powers are described by the same framework; see Amílcar Razori, *Historia de la ciudad argentina* (Buenos Aires: Imprenta López, 1945), vol. 3; and Francisco Esteban, *El Departamento Topográfico de la Provincia de Buenos Aires (actual Dirección de Geodesia). Su creación y desarrollo* (Buenos Aires: Dirección de Geodesia de la Pcia. de Buenos Aires, 1962).

had not succeeded in imposing a "small trial" of a "layout plan" in a suburb of the capital because he had not been able to separate the technical logic from the political one, because he had not been able to reconcile the economic interests of the landowners with the objectively necessary transformation.[101] What is needed, then, is to form autonomous public bodies: "to divide up the work and the professions" by creating various specific departments according to each need in the work of building the state; and, above all, to resolve at once what will happen to all of them "the day the wheel of the state runs up against one of those unforeseen obstacles that frequently divert public revenues toward destruction in revolutionary countries."[102]

The issues are always presented in technical terms, but the fundamental solutions are posed on the administrative level, and it is here where the notion of regularity is most at stake. Regularity to organize the revenues of the countryside, without intervening in the discussion on the structure of the property, but as an abstract device of control and measurement available in any circumstance; regularity to organize the layouts of the city, at a time of strong expansion of Buenos Aires and intense construction of public and private buildings on an administrative and legal board full of litigation, typical of the historical overlapping of domains in the total absence of any kind of public cadastre. Defending his proposed plan for the capital, Pellegrini ironizes on the criticisms of the regularity of the layout, proposing the formation of a commission

> to solemnly trace the direction that each street must follow: whether this direction is carried in a half or full course, whether it is completely straight or somewhat curved; whether its sides are perfectly parallel or not. *This regularity, we agree, is not absolutely essential. What is indispensable is the regularity, the unequivocal legality of the proceedings.*[103]

Therefore, it is a question of an even more all-embracing regularity that also involves, although in the last instance—after the administration, the legality of the domain and the rents—the layout itself, but not as a principle or aesthetic whim, but as a necessary consequence: "Once this sort of trellis (the grid of blocks) has been calculated, we will be able to set it down graphically on paper with exquisite precision; and it is to it as to the foundation of the system, that the subsequent result of the detail operations, that is, the plans of the block fronts, will be coordinated."[104] Precisely, the properties in dispute are the "ulterior details."

---

[101] "Traza y abertura de calles y plano de la ciudad," *La Revista del Plata* 6 (February 1854): 82ff.

[102] "Departamento de Ingenieros," *La Revista del Plata* 7 (March 1854): 94.

[103] "Traza y abertura de calles y plano de la ciudad," 82 (emphasis added).

[104] "Plano de la ciudad," *La Revista del Plata* 4 (December 1853): 82.

It is against this perspective that Sarmiento intervenes in the debate on the drawing up of the city map, a subject around which issues such as the relationship between public space/private space, state/society are defined. Sarmiento postulates that the plan should be executed by the municipality and not by the Topographic Department, but not because of a jurisdictional claim—of which he was so fond at that moment of construction of the municipal institution— but because the municipality is the institution in the best conditions to carry out the plan exactly the opposite of the one Pellegrini wants, the most realistic and less abstract, the one that would respond, inch by inch, to the needs and possibilities of the concrete neighbors as owners of urban lands, outside the impositions of the "hypothetical, ideal plan of the city, to which the Topographic Department is shaping the location of the new buildings. Except for widening the streets, this pretension of *regularity* is an error that brings eternal quarrels and changes."[105]

As we saw, Sarmiento's problem was his simultaneous opposition to the qualitative downgrading of the political character of city space and to the growth of the public instrument that would have made possible its construction "from above," hence his growing displeasure with an institution such as the Topographic Department. From exile he had affirmed that "there still exists in Buenos Aires one of the most beautiful institutions of other times": he imagined the Department nationalized, fulfilling the essential task of measuring and alienating land for the layout of new partitions capable of accommodating immigration in the inner country; but, above all, he imagined it carrying out the tasks of exploration and survey of the entire territory, essential for the construction of a modern national market.[106] Some years later, faced with the concrete practices of the Department, he would refer to it with an acid play on words: "but the Topographic Department put its tail in the sand which, as doctor Ferrera used to say, on the issue of the mapping out of cities had a lot of

---

[105] Sarmiento, "El plano de la ciudad de Buenos Aires," *El Nacional*, June 23, 1856, in *Obras completas (LD)*, XLII:29 (emphasis added). The layout of the new towns was carried out within the principles of the grid, imposing an initial order for the whole. In existing towns, a policy of "squaring" was carried out on the basis of the "pretension of regularity" against which Sarmiento reacted. See his note of June 1, 1860, to the president of the Topographic Department (in Razori, *Historia de la ciudad argentina*, 3:441–42), where he indicates that the attributions of the Topographic Department were inadequate because they imposed precise territorial forms on private individuals, when they were owners of the lands in which the state intervened, or on future neighbors, when it was a question of public lands. Thus, in line with what we saw for the plan of Buenos Aires, he proposes that the layout of new towns should be made by private individuals on their own land, or, in any case, by the justices of the peace on public lands, but at the request and by indication of the neighborhood, limiting the Topographic Department "to indicate the square and one or two streets, twenty *varas* (17 meters) wide."
[106] *Argirópolis*, published in 1850 in Chile, in *Obras completas (BS)*, XIII:100.

topo [mole] and very little of graphic." Beyond the ingenious disqualification, it is evident that what Sarmiento does not accept now is the French, Napoleonic matrix of the Topographic Department, its conception, and the state resulting from it. But it is also evident that, as the century progresses, that engineering tradition will completely unfold its modalities of action, its logics, its vision of the city, and the territory as an abstract board.[107]

So when Alvear became the first mayor of a federalized Buenos Aires, that tradition would already be deeply rooted in urban knowledge. Alvear's request for a greater extension for the city, for example, tends to repeat Rivadavia's operation—although taking into account that the city has grown in the sixty years that had passed, the new border was proposed a little to the west of Callao.[108] Alvear imagines a ring boulevard that surrounds and contains the traditional city while maintaining its centrality around the Plaza de Mayo; that allows to regularize the city's surface, to organize the administration and the perception of rent, and to order the urban figure; and that structures a hygienic belt for a city that is conceived as small and concentrated, surrounded by large reserves

---

[107] The quotation comes from one of the articles he wrote as a correspondent in the United States for the San Juan newspaper *El Zonda* in 1865 while he was Minister Plenipotentiary. In this case, the reference to the Topographic Department is generated in the conflicts over the layout of Chivilcoy; quoted in Eduardo Crespo, *Sarmiento y la ciudad de Buenos Aires*, "Monografías y disertaciones históricas" 9 (Buenos Aires: Museo Histórico Sarmiento, 1942).

[108] It is worth pointing out a traditional error in historiography when listing Alvear's transformations. The request of greater extension for the city that Alvear made has always been seen as a foresight that anticipated and sought the expansion of the city; and the boulevard that Alvear proposed (of which I have not been able to find plans) has always been confused with the one that was drawn in 1888 as the definitive limit of the capital (the current General Paz), giving him authorship. The mere fact that both proposals are called "Boulevard de circunvalación" and seek to draw a definitive and regular limit has prevented the realization that the one proposed by Alvear is displaced just to the west of the limit that the municipality had when it was federalized. According to the *Memoria* of 1881, the widening of the city proposed by Alvear is not linked to the need to enlarge the territory, but to regularize the boundary of the municipality which, in its traditional situation, was completely jagged and irregular, which made it difficult "to receive the income of the municipality and of the surrounding municipalities." The historiographic error starts from the fact that to carry out this regularization Alvear had to request a cession of lands from the municipalities of Flores and Belgrano, but it is a small cession only aimed at the layout of a new regular border, and not what will happen in 1887, when the Legislature of Buenos Aires transfers the entirety of the two municipalities. Alvear speaks all the time of "regularization of the limit" and not of expansion, and besides, in the *Memoria* he describes the boulevard projected by engineer Pastor del Valle (in charge of the office of Public Works), saying that it crosses the "terreno de la Pólvora," that is to say, the current Parque Chacabuco, halfway to the current limit of the federal capital.

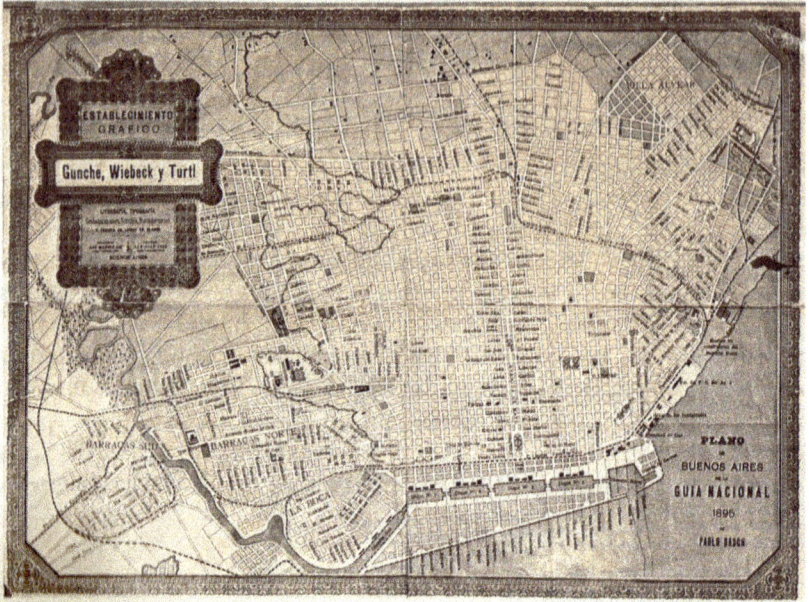

Figure 20. Pablo Basch; Gunche, Wiebeck and Turte, lithographers, *Plan of Buenos Aires from the Guía Nacional*, 1895. Archivo General de la Nación.

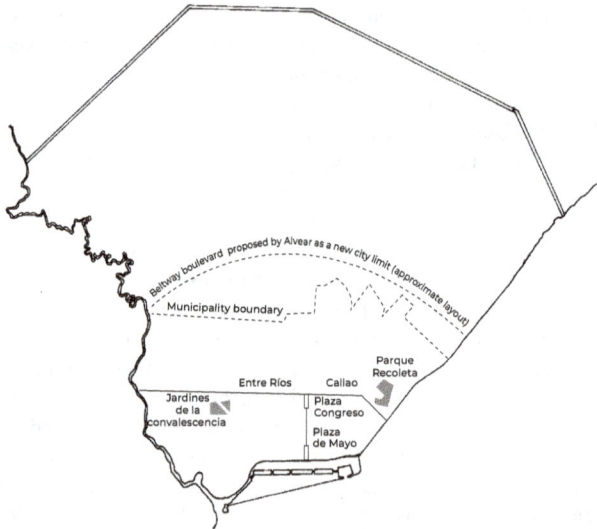

Figure 21. Diagram of Mayor Alvear's main public works mentioned in the text. Note that the works in Recoleta suggest connections with Palermo, though Alvear's entire operation is clearly developed in a still small and concentrated city.

of cultivated green; in short, that serves to limit and control the urban "organism" in the terms of physiocratic thought. It is within this "organism" that the work of modernization is imagined, which implies maintaining and requalifying the traditional center, renewing it on itself. It is upon this ambition that is realized the redesign of the Plaza de Mayo (the square that had concentrated all   20, 21 governmental and commercial functions since colonial times) and the layout of the central boulevard, the Avenida de Mayo, which ratifies the planimetric balance between the south and the north of the city, and which, toward the end of the century, with the decision to finish off its layout with the National Congress, will become the main civic axis of Buenos Aires up to the present.

Along the ring boulevard, as border and sanitary containment, Alvear proposes the disposition among the green of all the "unhealthy" artifacts that characterize the services and functions of a modern city: slaughterhouses, industries, garbage burning, hospitals, cemeteries.[109] A regular beltway boulevard; another boulevard on the very axis of the traditional city, requalifying the center and rebalancing the old south with the new north; and, completing this vision of the city—and now in direct relation to part of Haussmann's plan   19 for Paris—a perimetrical public park at each cardinal point: to the north, the Parque de la Recoleta (Palermo was so far away that it was not even considered as a perimeter to the city), to the west, the Gran Parque Agronómico, and to the south, the Parque de la Convalescencia.

It is simply a matter of accepting, as Cané does in the quotation with which we open this section, the irreplaceable historical condensation of the city center for the cultural constitution of a society, as its command and its guide. But in that text Cané goes further: in 1885 he knows, on the one hand, that after federalization "the street, the appearance, the city, as a whole, belongs to the Republic;" but he also knows that a "republican space" is a pure space of representation and reproduction of values: "since we are republicans, let us think a little about the humble people who do not possess, and let us slowly educate their spirit, providing them with the contemplation of elegant and correct objects." Again, the educational paradigm accompanies the figuration, which is no longer the figuration of a new society but of an order.[110]

It is a project of containment and control, of regularization and order, of renewal of the city on itself, which had found a more finished formalization— for its degree of schematism—in the Lagos Plan of 1869; which is found in a   22 number of private proposals of "building improvement" of the seventies, as the

---

[109] See *Memoria del Presidente de la Comisión Municipal al Concejo de 1881* (Buenos Aires: Peuser, 1882), 71. I elaborated on the interpretation of Alvear's aims in collaboration with Silvestri in "Imágenes al sur. Sobre algunas hipótesis de James Scobie para el desarrollo de Buenos Aires," 27–29.

[110] Letter from Miguel Cané to Mayor Torcuato de Alvear, Vienna, January 14, 1885, reproduced in Beccar Varela, *Torcuato de Alvear*, 487.

"polygonal avenue" of Felipe Senillosa for a "peripheral walk of the old urban area and concentric with its traditional mercantile and civic core;" and that from Alvear on will remain as an urban ideal.[111] It is present in the project of diagonal avenues of Mayor Antonio Crespo of 1887 and, in a more radical project of the same year for a navigable beltway canal that would surround Buenos Aires, joining the Riachuelo and Maldonado streams, to replace—materialize as a geographical cut—the perimetrical boulevard that Alvear had imagined. A reference is necessary to the authors of this project of Saint-Simonian inspiration. One of them, Alfred Ebelot, was a French engineer and journalist who had come to Buenos Aires to participate in an expedition to the pampa in charge of tracing the "trench" (*zanja*) projected by Adolfo Alsina as a kind of local Great Wall of China projected to consolidate the border in the battle against the Indian. The other, Pablo Blot, also an engineer, and also French, was part of the municipal team from the moment of federalization, and we will find him tracing, a year after the canal project, the definitive limit of the city, starting from the annexation of the provincial municipalities of Flores and Belgrano that same year of 1887.[112]

This framework of strong state definition of the urban apparatus as a regular apparatus—in which both social control and urban, hygienic, moral, and social reform could be conceived—is not contradictory either with the "beautification" operations typical of fin-de-siècle urbanism, or with the displacement of social sectors within the city, the origin of new stratifications. This is the framework in which "good society" began to choose the north as a place of residence; and although this tendency was consolidated by Alvear's works in Callao and Recoleta, plus the attraction that the distant presence of Palermo also exerted, it must be understood that they did so in a city that was still small (the "north" was limited to Plaza San Martín and a sector of Callao) and characterized by the homogeneous distribution of a heterogeneous population in all sectors of the city: in 1898, the *costumbrista* chronicler Fray Mocho could make a fully

---

[111] The Lagos Plan was republished by Adolfo Carranza in *La Ilustración Sudamericana* IX, no. 204 (June 30, 1901); it consists of a circular perimeter boulevard with a system of diagonal radii that intersect in the current Avenida de Mayo and 9 de Julio (he already proposed both avenues). On Senillosa's proposal, see Alberto de Paula, "Una modificación del diseño urbano porteño proyectada en 1875," *Anales del Instituto de Arte Americano e Investigaciones Estéticas* 19 (1966): 71 ff.

[112] The navigable canal project proposed the use of the canal as a linear port, reorganizing the city's beltway for strictly productive purposes (and no longer only for sanitation). See Blot and Ebelot, *Proyecto de un canal de circunvalación de Buenos Aires y Puerto de Cabotage* (Buenos Aires: Imprenta de La Nación, 1884). On the canals which, under Saint-Simonian inspiration were being built in those years, see Graciela Silvestri, "La ciudad y el río," in Liernur and Silvestri, *El umbral de la metrópolis*.

Turn-of-the-century projects that maintain the idea of "enclosing" a small city:

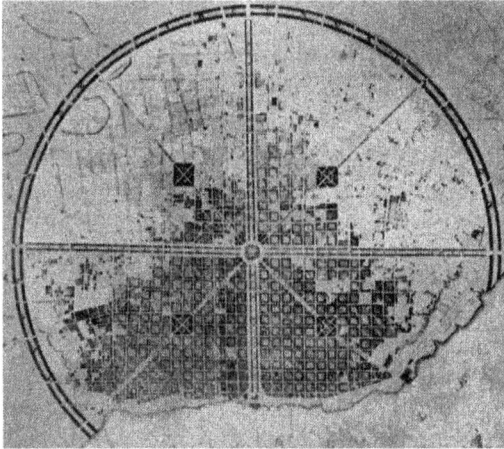

Figure 22. José Marcelino Lagos, *Project for Buenos Aires*, 1867. From Ricardo Llanes, *La Avenida de Mayo*. Buenos Aires: Kraft, 1955. The project circumscribes the built city with a circular boulevard and outlines a series of diagonals and regular squares in its interior, taking the historical east–west axis of the city as the axis of symmetry.

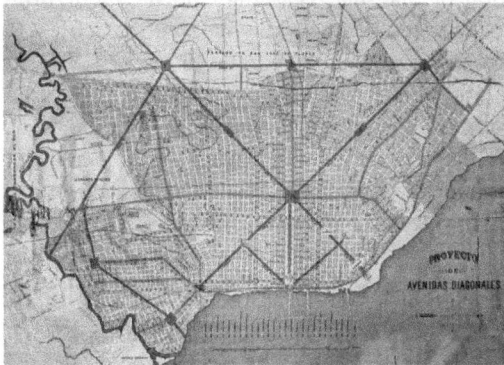

Figure 23. *Plan of the Project for Diagonal Avenues Developed by Mayor Crespo*, 1887. Instituto Histórico, Buenos Aires.

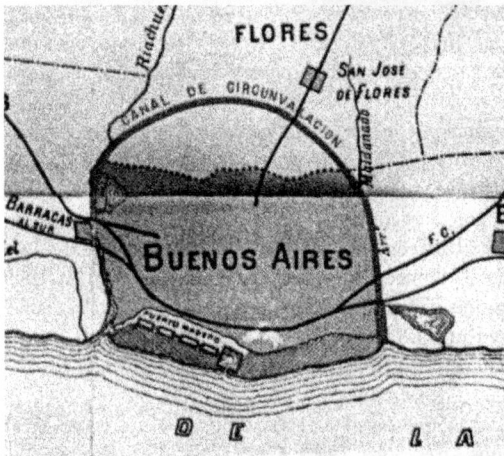

Figure 24. Pablo Blot and Alfredo Ebelot, *Navigable Canal Beltway Project Joining the Maldonado Stream with the Riachuelo, Carried out by Blot and Ebelot*, 1887. Detail from a project in Museo Mitre, Buenos Aires.

popular character say "I'm moving to the north."[113] A homogeneity of the different areas of the city—a strong social heterogeneity in the old quarter as a whole—would continue to be a characteristic of the city, just as the traditional center of Buenos Aires would continue to be increasingly valued, despite the displacements and unlike most of the cities that were already undergoing the

34   renewal processes Sarmiento imagined. It is only in aristocratic rejection of the generalization of "I'm moving to the north" as a bourgeois fashion that Lucio Mansilla would say around the same time:

> [General Alvear] lived on Florida Street, almost in front of Bernardo de Irigoyen's house. This neighborhood is, and continues to be, historic. In a few blocks around, live now, celebrities of note, representatives of glory, of talent, of fortune: Mitre, Roca, Irigoyen, Pellegrini, Tejedor, Anchorena. I don't know what López is doing in Callao![114]

Every displacement, every topological choice in the city, has social connotations, every definition of a position implies taking sides: as Vicente Quesada wrote in the opposite intention of Mansilla regarding culinary modernization in fin-de-siècle Buenos Aires: "the dividing line between the refractory old bourgeoisie and elegant society can be marked on the city plan."[115] To ask again: Was Sarmiento right? Was Alvear contradictory in building the boulevard downtown and going to live, like López, to Callao—emblematic then of the "north"? It is clear that the reasons for the challenge are different for Mansilla and Sarmiento: for the former it was necessary to find anchor in the center, around the aristocratic and elegant but, above all, historical Florida, as

[113] Fray Mocho (José S. Álvarez), "Me mudo al norte," *Caras y Caretas*, December 10, 1898, in Fray Mocho, Carlos M. Pacheco, and others, *Los costumbristas del 900*, ed. with prologue by Eduardo Romano (Buenos Aires: CEAL, 1980), 12; the data on the existence of *conventillos* (tenements) in the city show an even ratio north and south that would remain for at least the first two decades of the century. See Sargent, *The Spatial Evolution of Greater Buenos Aires*.

[114] Quoted in David Viñas, *Literatura argentina y realidad política* (1964) (Buenos Aires: CEAL, 1982), 185. Likewise, Arturo Jauretche could point out as an aristocratic trait that the Anchorenas persisted in living in their house at Suipacha 50; in *El medio pelo* (Buenos Aires: Peña Lillo, 1966), 265. Sargent's book allows us to evaluate the system of changes in the interior of the city between 1887 and 1895: in 1887 60 percent of the population lived within a radius of 2 kilometers from the Plaza de Mayo, while in 1895 only 34 percent lived there; the radius of 2 to 3 kilometers remained practically stable; and the greatest changes occurred in the radius of 3 to 5 kilometers, from 12 to 27 percent, and outside the 5 kilometers, from 16 to 24 percent; see *The Spatial Evolution of Greater Buenos Aires*, 35.

[115] Víctor Gálvez (Vicente Quesada), *Memorias de un viejo. Escenas de costumbres de la República Argentina* (1889) (Buenos Aires: Solar, 1942), 436.

a patrician identification of a social group which condenses power and culture; for the latter, on the other hand, it was necessary to "leave the center to the shopkeepers," something that if Alvear had prevented with the Avenida de Mayo was simply because he was "*porteño* to the bone."[116] What is certain, in any case, is that in the city of the late eighties and nineties, these subtle meanings of domiciliary lineage, this reterritorialization of prestige, is a dance in which few connoisseurs participate in the face of the massification of new processes of urban occupation, and in the face of the alienation, it could be said, that the protagonism of these classes suffers in the new scenario, since, even though they maintain their power, they will see an increasingly strange city multiply around them, like the continuous and solid background against which all their gestures will be cut. This transformation is explicit in Cambaceres's exemplary journey, from *Potpourri*, an 1881 novel in which Buenos Aires is deciphered in the Club del Progreso, to *En la sangre*, of 1887, where the key to explaining the city shifts to the miserable tenements.

From this point of view, operations on the historical center acquire new connotations, of reappropriation and ratification of values, although for this it is necessary to change— "modernize"—its forms. In any case, the contradiction of modernizing the center and going to live in Callao, in the case of Alvear, is of another type: it is the one that arises between the logic of an urban market that will increasingly value the north, and a state that will attribute to itself, on the one hand, the role of preserving the values and, on the other hand—and more importantly for our purpose of unraveling this type of reformism—the role of guaranteeing "urban compensation," in search of recovering the always unstable balance of the city around its foundational axis. Therefore, Alvear is contradictory in a very special way, embodying in his double action (of public management and private residential choice) an ambivalence that from now on we will find again in many other issues as a characteristic of the "modernizing" municipal governments: from the consolidation of the state apparatus—and of the municipality as a federal state apparatus—figures like Alvear seem to gain considerable autonomy, as governors, from their more immediate interests.[117] What will not occur with the members of the Concejo Deliberante (the

20, 21

---

[116] Sarmiento's quotations from "Un gran boulevard para Buenos Aires," *El Censor* (Buenos Aires), December 20, 1885, in *Obras completas (LD)*, XLII:234ff.

[117] Francisco Seeber, who was later to become mayor, did not see such a contradiction as anything but laudatory: "I have told everyone," he writes to Alvear in 1886, "that he has shown his excellent conditions not only as a political man, but also as a private man he has taught our rich men how one should live in palaces outside the center of commerce and not like those who build their houses with storehouses below, in order to get rents, receiving instead the smell of garlic and the rancid oil of frying, or placing their stables under their dining rooms or bedrooms, to economize on land." See "Carta al Intendente Torcuato de Alvear" (London), July 29, 1886, quoted in Beccar Varela, *Torcuato de Alvear*, 511.

elected city board, the City Council from now on)—until the electoral reform some decades later, does not modify its composition—precisely because of the absence of mediation in the type of representation of interests of the "notable" councilors: at the local level the political components weigh much less and direct economic interests much more; and this is consistent with the experience of nineteenth-century urbanization in almost all countries, in which central public power is more innovative than local management groups, tied to immobilizing networks of interests.[118] Of course, this does not mean that the immediate interests of mayors and members of the federal bureaucratic apparatuses do not explain anything about the local social system; it means that they do not explain everything, that a greater subtlety is required to see the specific level in which the more general interests of a class are played out in the city, precisely because a modern and complex state and federal apparatus establishes mediations with the more immediate interests of its individual members.[119]

Thus, it is possible to interpret the Avenida de Mayo and all the projects and layouts that maintain the center in the Plaza de Mayo (at the beginning of the century they will be symmetrical diagonals), also as the manifestation of the will of public power for a homogeneous and equitable city model, against the repeated attempts of different private social actors to define a "specialized" city, with an industrial south and a residential and commercial north. Reformist aporia: for such objectives the state will have few ideological arguments and no legal instruments, but they will be present every time interventions are made, always punctual, always bordering the assumed laissez-faire universe. In a trend that will last for a good part of the twentieth century, the state will intervene actively in the south, seeking to compensate for unequal development toward the north, with the ideal, always in flight, of a balanced city. But I insist, it is not a question of placing in the fin-de-siècle state a generic humanitarian vocation of urban equity, but to see to what extent the choice of a model for the city indicates the taking of sides on more general issues and, at the same time, forces them into being.

---

[118] See Sica, *Historia del urbanismo. El siglo XIX*, 1:60–62.
[119] Guy Bourdé discards the issue by showing, as conclusive evidence, the common social origin of the mayors of the period; therefore, their conflicts with society are not such, but "rather manifestations of the inconsistencies of the institutions than of class oppositions," in *Buenos Aires: urbanización e inmigración* (Buenos Aires: Huemul, 1977), 80.

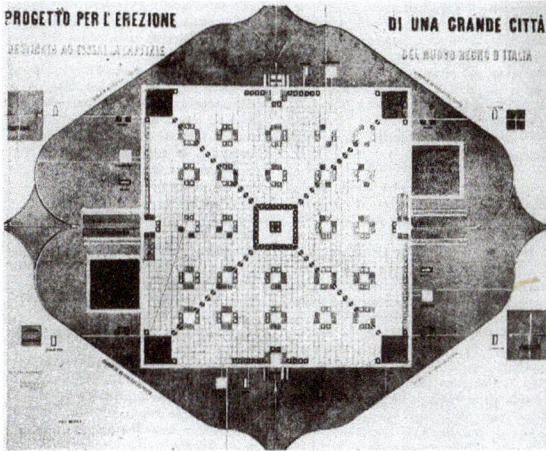

Figure 25. Napoleone Tettamanzi, *Plan for a New Capital for Italy*, 1863. Plan reproduced in Paolo Sica, *Storia dell'Urbanistica. L'Ottocento 1*. Rome: Laterza, 1977. The plan applies the notion of the "regular city." Note the greenery surrounding the beltway boulevard, designed to hold unsanitary services.

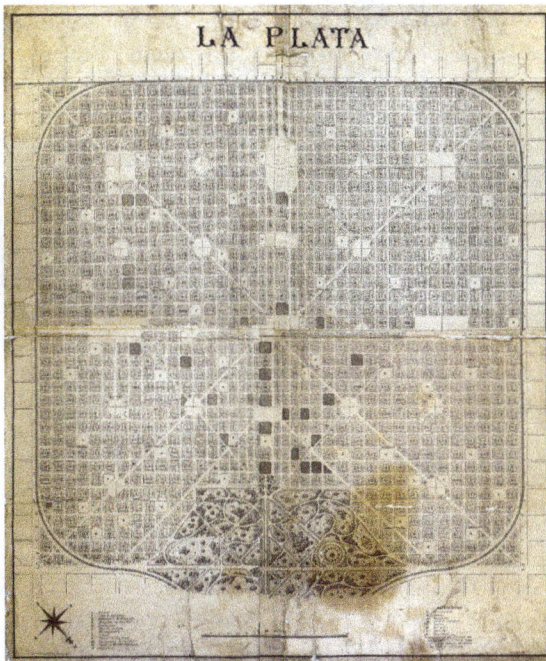

Figure 26. Department of Engineers of the Province of Buenos Aires, Julio Vigier, engraver, *Plan of La Plata*, c. 1882. Biblioteca Nacional Mariano Moreno.

2. A New Public Space and Its Figures

> I can perfectly explain to myself the sympathy with which the people of Bue-
> nos Aires accompanied the Municipal Mayor [Alvear] in the conflict with
> the Council; and I explain them, because without being from there, nor
> residing there, I had them, remembering the zeal and activity with which
> more than once, and more than ten times I have seen him devoted to the
> performance of his duties, taking them on no longer as a faithful and strict
> administrator in the fulfillment of his duty, but as owner, watching over what
> belongs to all as if it were his own, like a neat and avaricious owner, who exa-
> mines one by one the bricks that are to be placed in his building, activating
> here, ordering there, communicating to all the liveliness of his innovative
> and progressive spirit.[120]
>
> –Sansón Carrasco, "La gran Capital del Sud," 1884

To place Alvear's administration in an ideological tradition of urban intervention is not to ignore his radical innovations. To identify them, we must start
from what the main historiography has already highlighted: Alvear has been
identified as the archetype of the mayor, and "his city" as the ideal model of a
Buenos Aires that should be "completed," but always according to that initial
inspiration. It is evident that the originality of Alvear's proposals and the validity of the appellative "the Argentine Haussmann"—which has served to identify
his administration both for those who celebrate him and for those who for that
very reason denigrate him—must be qualified.[121] The validity of this label must
be relativized on the basis of a philological analysis of his effective urbanistic
inspiration and an evaluation of his reforms' lack of radicalism. And, at the
same time, it must be recognized that, in nineteenth-century urban culture, it
was not only impossible for a reformist mayor not to appear as an emulator of
Haussmann, but that each country, each city, had to compose its own provincial
Haussmann, mainly through the press, so busy since then with urban issues in
which it found a privileged pattern of comparison in the symbolic market of
progress. But there is, nevertheless, much that is true in that foundational character of Alvear on which it is convenient to dwell. If the city of the eighties is an
extremely complex artifact, in which interests and jurisdictions overlap in the
process of restructuring public power, there is no doubt that Alvear knew how
to cut a powerful presence within that framework.

---

[120] Sansón Carrasco is the pseudonym of the Uruguayan journalist and politician Daniel
Muñoz. The quotation is taken from an article republished in *El Nacional* (Buenos
Aires), June 12, 1884, reproduced in Beccar Varela, *Torcuato de Alvear*, 500.
[121] Already in Alvear's obituary, the *Revue Illustrée du Rio de la Plata* calls him
"l'Haussmann argentin," according to the quotation in Ricardo Llanes, who continues
without argument that tradition; see *La Avenida de Mayo* (Buenos Aires: Kraft, 1955).

There is a double reality in the foundational character attributed to Alvear. On the one hand, there is the weight that those contemporary representations had in the very conformation of the reality whose description they were try- ing to describe. On the other hand, there is Alvear's unquestionable capacity to compose new figures for a public space that wanted to be new: urban fig- ures that take charge of the symbolic need latent in federalization, proposing to reconstruct memory to configure a public space no longer of the city but of the nation; and figures of public management capable of simultaneously and suc- cessfully attending to the growing complexity and bureaucratization of munic- ipal administration, and to the wager of embodying the identity of the "soul of the city" in the intense personification of its government. That is to say, a rad- ical recomposition of traditional public space, both in its urban forms and in its appeals to historical memory; both in the anonymous administration of the state—in which it is possible to see a municipal manifestation of the vast trans- formation that began in 1880 with the government of Julio Argentino Roca— and in the creation of the figure of a leader that is only possible in the city and that, though not necessarily opposed to the model which that transformation presupposed, poses a difference of degree that lends it originality.

Struggles for Memory

The first level of transformations, that of the urban public space, is linked to the reinforcement of the traditional centrality that we analyzed in the previous sec- tion. But this reinforcement implied, in this new framework, a deep alteration of the significance of centrality in the city before the 1880s. Alvear's historiog- raphy has highlighted two projects as the most emblematic of his administra- tion: the formation of the Plaza de Mayo—from the demolition of the Recova   31, 32
Vieja and the consequent union of Victoria and 25 de Mayo squares—and the
opening of the Avenida de Mayo. It is evident why these works stood out for   28
contemporaries and memorialists: their high degree of visibility, their effective- ness in the very heart of the city. The same reason that allowed later detractors to think of Alvear's work in terms of cosmetic gestures "à la Potemkin," allud- ing to the famous metaphor of the Russian minister who built majestic papi- er-mâché scenographies to hide the miserable streets of the villages through which Catherine the Great would pass.

The two works affected the traditional civic center and, as we saw, encour- aged the development of the main axis of growth of the city to the west, rein- forcing the foundational symmetry that concentrates all public and private   20, 21
activity around the Plaza de Mayo. One of these works, the Avenida de Mayo, preceded Alvear's administration, since its necessity had been proposed in var- ious urban renewal projects since at least the Lagos Plan of 1869; at the same   22
time, it would only begin to be built in 1888, a year after the end of Alvear's administration. On the other hand, unlike Haussmann's boulevards, or even

Figure 27. Sociedad Fotográfica Argentina de Aficionados, *Buenos Aires Rooftops*, 1891. Archivo General de la Nación. Rooftops were rejected as emblematic of the flat and extended character of the city.

Figure 28. Harry Grant Olds, *Avenida de Mayo*, c. 1915. Mateo Enrique Giordano collection, Buenos Aires. The building of the National Congress is barely visible in the distance.

the later avenues of Pereira Passos (the mayor of Rio de Janeiro at the beginning of the century who was known as the "Brazilian Haussmann"), which opened communication routes between the motley massiveness of the traditional city and neuralgic points necessary for the modern functioning of the capitalist city as productive apparatus (railway stations, port, etc.); unlike those modalities of urban renewal, the Avenida de Mayo not only reinforces existing orthogonality but also limits itself to opening an exit to the Plaza de Mayo toward what then functioned as the limit of the consolidated city, the Callao-Entre Ríos boulevard, without seeking productive connections. Not even the civic-monumental axis that was later established was formulated in the original plans: it should not be forgotten that the decision to install the National Congress at the other end of the avenue was made afterward.

This double evidence undoubtedly relativizes the importance of Alvear, who after all was only partially responsible for the layout of an avenue that, on the other hand, did not structurally modify the city along the lines of Haussmannian action: the definitive consolidation of the avenue as a civic axis has more to do with the ceremonial function of the Washington Mall than with the circulatory-productive function of the Parisian boulevards. However, in both senses, in a perspective such as the one we propose, Alvear's importance is capital: from the point of view of his role in the realization of the avenue, because he produced the administrative transformation and the juridical reform that made it possible and set the precedent—with all the limitations we will see—of the main reforms of the city; from the point of view of the very importance of the avenue and the square in the city, because it marked a fundamental transformation of the public space of the traditional city.

Here it may be convenient to introduce the other project that has characterized his administration in most accounts: the Plaza de Mayo, which Alvear could not see finished either, but whose foundational gesture, the union of the two squares, he personally carried out. Again, putting into practice long-standing projects, Alvear demolished the old Recova that separated the two squares 29 and proposed a remodeling of the unified square based on a project by the engineer Pablo Blot and the architect Juan Buschiazzo, marked by a rigid geo- 31 metric and symmetric composition, and the disposition in the center of the commemorative monument to Independence that would replace the old pyramid. It was a rather poor project, by the way, if we look at the international precedents on which Blot and Buschiazzo were supposed to base their work, but which, in any case, at the time of the diffusion of the project appeared as the emblem of the modernization and Frenchification of the city desired by the governing elite.

The new design appeared on the smoking rubble of a living piece of the traditional—colonial, but above all, Creole—city, the Recova, and proposed a monumental new scale for the heart of the city. The mere visual enlargement, with the duplication of the scale, and the creation of a central symmetrical axis that would open the projected avenue of 30 *varas* (24 meters) in width, punctuated by the monument in the center, and finished by the Triumphal Arch proposed as the entrance to the Casa de Gobierno (Government House), already changed the framework, bringing a new Baroque monumentality to Buenos Aires. Spatial context and uses: although the square had always been the preferred site for civic festivities, ceremonial parades, or public protests, the Recova not only circumscribed the visuals, but its function as a market produced a daily life and a mixture of uses that gave the square a completely different character. After its demolition, and above all according to a widely disseminated image in newspapers and posters in the months following the first May commemoration without the Recova, the Plaza de Mayo appears as the first monumental public space in Buenos Aires.

It is important to emphasize the issues of scale and perspective to accurately evaluate the proposed change and its impact, because there had already been other reforms that had strongly modified the colonial character of the two squares into what we could generically designate as a "Frenchified" image. It was in the years of the State of Buenos Aires, when the first installations that sought to convert the traditional square into a *promenade* began to take place. In the very few squares existing at that time in Buenos Aires, differentiated pathways began to be designed, regular borders between the square and the street established; trees were planted; and a battery of artifacts were introduced that radically modified the sense of use and perception of the traditional environment: benches, streetlamps, bandstands, fountains, monuments. In Victoria Square, the first Chinaberry trees were planted in 1856—following Prilidiano Pueyrredón's dispositions—benches and lanterns were installed, and in 1857 the pyramid—also designed by Pueyrredón—was remodeled. It was crowned with the Statue of Liberty-Republic set on a base with four statues representing the Sciences, Arts, Commerce, and Agriculture, all made by the sculptor Joseph Dubourdieu, to great public acclaim. And over the following decade, the surface of each square was partitioned with geometric gardens, set with fountains, railings, and a perimetrical lighting system that turned the squares into ceremonial and festive enclosures. Toward the middle of the seventies, the statue of General Belgrano was finally installed in the Plaza 25 de Mayo. That is to say, the image that appears in the lithographs of the first half of the century, in which the square is a great empty space for trade, through which men, carts, and animals pass in all directions, had already been completely modified, with a certain regulation of forms, uses, and manners that the upper classes had been rehearsing for a long time in their private gardens. Here, as in Europe, this transformation took over public space—and gave it shape—after a slow experimentation in the private realm. The country houses and residences on the edges of the city, such as the Caserón de Rosas in Palermo, or the country houses of Lezama and Moreno, or, even further away, Dr. Castro's farm in Los Olivos, where Santiago Calzadilla recalls concerts performed and attended by high society, were, from very early on, the spaces where French gardening was

Figure 29. Félix Achille Saint-Aulaire after Alcide d'Orbigny, *Plaza de la Victoria with the Pyramid and the Recova Vieja*, c. 1830. Lithograph published in *Voyage dans l'Amerique méridionale*. Paris: Pitois-Levrault, 1835–47.

Figure 30. Benito Panunzi, *The Pyramid and the Recova Vieja*, 1867. Carlos Sánchez Idiart collection, Buenos Aires. The view is taken from the opposite side of the square. Note the transformation of the walk executed by Pueyrredón, with its trees and iron fences, as well as the new profile of the pyramid, now crowned with the statue of the Republic-Liberty and four statues at its base, following Joseph Dubourdieu's design.

introduced and where new social rites associated with "English" fashions (inso-far as they involved a new enjoyment of nature and the open air) were becom-ing common among local elites.[122]

Thus, Alvear's transformations have a long tradition of reform, also in terms of the civic and ceremonial character of public space. Pilar González has recently pointed out how in the years of the State of Buenos Aires—paradox-ically, the period of the "anti-national" city par excellence—there appeared "a historical civility of strong local connotations" but on which the memory of the nation was built, so that national history was identified with the feats of Bue-nos Aires, with its history but also with its urban space. That is, Buenos Aires became the location of national memory.[123] Therefore, Alvear acts on a strongly resignified space that had already lost much of its colonial traces. However, the change of scale he proposes goes beyond consummating an established trend. If the squares had already begun their conversion into promenades, and if the "memory device"—in the terms used by González—had already been put into action, first to fix the national memory of Buenos Aires with urban landmarks and then to reconcile the city with its national destiny, Alvear's reform, in turn, materializes the conversion of the heart of the city into the heart of the nation. What Alvear has to carry out in the square is a symbolic operation opposed to that of twenty years earlier: during the State of Buenos Aires the city had appropriated the memory of the nation; now it is the nation that is in a position to reorganize the memory of the city, but no longer in the terms of the inner country/Buenos Aires polemic, but in the sense of the new reality of the nation-state, insofar as this reorganization of memory comes to sanction at the urban level the possession already established and guaranteed by federalization. It is upon this possession that Alvear executes his plan for the total removal of the remains of local identity and the construction of a completely new scenario, capable of building, in the very heart of Buenos Aires, a new memory for the nation-state but, above all, of integrating the masses of newcomers into its rit-uals. A scenario that would not only interpellate, through the symbolic charge of its locus, those already initiated in the forms of national memory, but that,

---

[122] Santiago Calzadilla, *Las beldades de mi tiempo* (1891) (Buenos Aires: Editorial Sudestada, 1969), 185. O. Troncoso suggests that it was the English who imported to Buenos Aires the habit of summering in the quintas, which only confirms the already consolidated mixture of influences in the development of gardens and parks; see "Las formas del ocio," in J. L. Romero and L. A. Romero, *Buenos Aires, historia de cuatro siglos*, (Buenos Aires: Abril, 1983), 2:95.

[123] Pilar González Bernaldo, "L'Urbanisation de la mémoire. Politique urbaine de l'État de Buenos Aires pendant les dix annés de sécession (1852–1862)," a paper presented at the *Colloque International de l'AFSSAL*, "Les enjeux de la mémoire. L'Amérique Latine à la croisée du cinquième centenaire. Commémorer ou remémorer?" Paris, December 1992, 2.

Figure 31. Pablo Blot and Juan Buschiazzo, *Project for Remodeling the Plaza de Mayo*, 1883. Diran Sirinian collection, Buenos Aires. From the photographic album by Emilio Halitzky, *Mejoras en la capital de la República Argentina. Intendente Torcuato de Alvear, 1885.* The proposed monument is placed at the center of the square formed by the two merged plazas. Toward the left, the opening for Avenida de Mayo, to be flanked by the municipality and the courts, and by the presidential palace.

Figure 32. Unknown photographer, *Plaza de Mayo*, c. 1910. Archivo General de la Nación. The pyramid was not demolished (though it would be relocated to the center of the two squares in 1914). The new buildings and the opening of Avenida de Mayo have changed the scale of the plaza. Note the Cabildo, now without its tower, mutilated by the opening of the avenue (it would be reconstructed in a smaller scale in the 1940s).

through the monumentality of urban space itself, would be capable of proposing the new history for the entire new society.

It was a question of scale (spatial and symbolic) that was acutely noticed by contemporaries who witnessed the change. In order to achieve spatial monumentality, the project affected several landmarks symbolic of the Creole city. Not only the already demolished Recova: also compromised were the Cabildo (city hall), already mutilated and whose almost total destruction was presupposed in the opening of the avenue as a result of an "excessive attachment to symmetry"—in José María Estrada's condemnatory terms—the Government House, which the Triumphal Arch project sought to convert definitively into a unified building that erased all remains of the old fort, and, above all, the pyramid, whose replacement by a new monument at the center of the complex meant that its total removal was to be discounted.[124]

Andrés Lamas, in the middle of the discussion about the reform of the square, lamented:

> The historical Cabildo is already deformed; and the square, which was the forum of the people of 1810, is going to be stripped of its historical and severe nudity, under the inspiration of some stranger who will transform it into a vulgar imitation of a small garden or park of his land. All that is ours is gone! Gone, never to return, are the fort and the arch [of the Recova] that were the material pages of the history of the reconquest of 1806 [...]. All that is ours is gone! Will the pyramid be gone?[125]

---

[124] José María Estrada, letter to the City Council of November 11, 1883, reproduced in *Revista Nacional* XIII (1891), 19. On the modifications of the Cabildo and the Fort see, among others, A. Taullard, *Nuestro antiguo Buenos Aires* (Buenos Aires: Peuser, 1927). The Cabildo was mutilated because, at the beginning of the decade, two floors had been added to the tower, completely modifying its colonial stylistic profile; the Avenida de Mayo project, in turn, implied its complete demolition (as we know, the existing Cabildo is a reconstruction in scale of the old one, of which only the Sala Capitular [Chapter House] remains). The fort was demolished in 1853 by the government of Pastor Obligado; in its back part, the Customs House was built; from the front part there remained a central portico and one of the inner sections that continued to be used as the Government House in the corner of Rivadavia and Balcarce. In 1873 Sarmiento built in Victoria (Hipólito Yrigoyen) and Balcarce the house of the post and telegraphs (already in 1860 Sarmiento himself had had everything painted pink). In 1882 Roca demolished the right wing, which was the last material remains of the old fort and built in its place a structure quite like the post office house; the two wings began to function as the Government House. Finally, around 1885, the central portico that joins the two wings was installed and the block would be completed with new additions toward the back.

[125] In *La Nueva Revista de Buenos Aires* VI, vol. X, new series (1884): 413.

The question of the pyramid puts the focus on the most questioned and discussed issue in the press: when, in October 1883, Alvear presents his reform project, he must ask the City Council for authorization to demolish the "mean masonry construction whose origin is not well-known" and to which, he says, due to the difficulties and the scarcity of funds of the first national governments, have been introduced "reforms and ornaments of bad taste, which place that construction outside all architectural rules and very far from the forms with which we must preserve in the imagination of our children the glorious memory of the work of our fathers."[126] The City Council, then, was tempted to oppose Alvear—as it opposed practically all his initiatives—but forced by a first approval of the Senate, decided to conduct an opinion poll on the fate of the pyramid among prominent local and national figures, many of them, moreover, protagonists of the entire historical cycle that was in question as well as its interpreters or historians: Bartolomé Mitre, Sarmiento, Vicente Fidel López, Estrada, Andrés Lamas, Nicolás Avellaneda, Carranza, among others. In fact, it is a remarkable occasion, for which the same people who were founding the historiographic perspectives on the facts that this space was destined to commemorate were asked for their opinion on the refoundation of the historical space of the city. The survey thus brings face to face the judgments on historical construction and on present transformations, on the capacity of the monument to contribute to the foundation of that memory that was sustained in the literary field, and on the character of the urban public space that could bring it to life. And the divergent answers, which go far beyond celebrating or denigrating progress or appealing to change or preservation, constitute an excellent record of the complexity of the operation set in motion by Alvear.[127]

In principle, it is worth noting that the rejection of the "reforms and orna-   30 ments of bad taste" of the pyramid to which Alvear refers is, in the eighties, universally shared. It is the rejection of Prilidiano Pueyrredón's reforms in the square and the remodeling of the statuary of the pyramid executed by Dubourdieu, although not everyone rejected them for the same reasons. Not for everyone were its "architectural extravagances" due to the repudiatory "invasion of

---

[126] Alvear's message to the City Council, October 18, 1883, reproduced in Beccar Varela, *Torcuato de Alvear*, 70. Alvear had already obtained from Congress a law, approved on October 5, which authorized and gave him the budget for the "erection, in the center of the junction of the '25 de Mayo' and 'Victoria' squares, of a bronze column to commemorate the events that raised the Argentine Republic to the rank of Sovereign Nation"; quoted in Rómulo Zabala, *Historia de la Pirámide de Mayo* (Buenos Aires: Academia Nacional de la Historia, 1962), 79. As Alvear's request had been made through the presentation of Buschiazzo's plan, in which the old pyramid directly disappears, Alvear considered himself authorized to demolish it, and on this subject a strong controversy was unleashed.

[127] The answers to the survey were published in the press daily with great success. In 1891 the survey was reproduced in full in *El Nacional* XIII, no. 57 (1891): 4–67.

Genoese masons," as it was for a journalist of *El Nacional*; nor did all, unlike Estrada, condemn the statue that recalled "the revolutionary art [...] which is rather the symbol of Jacobinism."[128] But it is evident that, once national unity was resolved and Buenos Aires was consecrated as capital, all coincided in considering illegitimate the transformations that took place during the first years of the State of Buenos Aires, during the autonomist governorships of Pastor Obligado and Alsina, and saw in Dubourdieu's statue the best example of their "ephemeral and unauthorized whims," to use López's terms.[129]

In any case, the most important questions do not lie as much in the different views on the past as in their relationship to the present. There is only one voice in the survey, that of Manuel Tréllez, who celebratorily identifies the reform proposed by Alvear with the idea of progress, and who maintains that only that idea allows the values that the original monument represents to be updated. He places, precisely, the issue in terms of the complexity of the relation permanence/change that affects new nations as products of modernity. We must not forget that if everyone discusses a monument that they recognize as "foundational" of the history on which they feel called upon to build a national memory, that monument is barely seventy years old and was erected in the name of a revolution that questioned all precedence. If a revolutionary version of May is upheld, how, Tréllez asks, can homage be paid with punctual respect to the form of a monument erected to those who precisely demonstrated that no form should be respected in order to build the future? Why "subject posterity to invariable and narrow limits," if what is at stake is to "pay homage to the great evolutions of nations"?[130]

For the most ardent opponents of the demolition, on the other hand, it is patriotic virtue and not the transforming impulse that should be preserved as a memory of the revolution. In this case, it is precisely the modesty of the monument, its artistic "imperfections" that, according to Estrada, "enhances the merit of the authors in the event it symbolizes" and allows the ability to keep alive a document that, according to Miguel Estévez Saguí, is "memory and historical testimony of the poverty and virtues of our fathers [....] so that those who later were born rich may understand well." The interpretation of the revolution in light of the pyramid thus allows the process of modernization to be judged in terms of public morality: it is the poor materiality of the monument that challenges the ethical conscience in the face of the crass materialism that reigns in the present. Thus, for Lamas, the richer and more artistic the new monument, the less it would represent the revolutionaries of May: the real issue, for him, with the whole reform project—and his challenge encompasses

---

[128] See *El Nacional*, November 15, 1883, and the letter of J. M. Estrada in *Torcuato de Alvear*, 86.

[129] Letter to the City Council, November 8, 1883, in *Revista Nacional*, 15.

[130] Letter to the City Council, November 7, 1883, in *Revista Nacional*, 17.

the whole "project" of the 1880s—is that "at certain moments in the life of peo-ples, the development of material riches usually produces obfuscations that veil the truth, that pervert criteria, that break the compass."[131]

However, not all those who advocate the restoration and preservation of the monument would be willing to subscribe to such judgments about the ongoing modernization process, and certainly not all those advocates of its demolition are enthusiastic about it. Most of those surveyed are members of a generation that looks askance at the direction taken by Julio Argentino Roca's government, the new state that is emerging with full powers and an unknown degree of autonomy, and the "anomic" society that is emerging when everything is placed under the cloak of "material progress," a coincidence that allows us to outline with greater precision specific alignments. Because if all seek to celebrate the May revolution as a foundational moment, if all resort to the same figures already consecrated in the fifties and sixties, and all agree on the national qual-ity of the space in which this celebration should take place, the dissidence arises in terms of the value of the monument and the character of the public space that it would contribute to forge.

Avellaneda and Lamas present the problem of value in exceptionally clear terms, exposing a conflict in the definition of the monument that is born with modernity, when the historical, commemorative, traditional monument, which brings into play living memory and brings together in a single mark (in a sin-gle locus) the event and the sign that has fixed it, must share space for the representation of memory and the construction of identity with a new type of artistic monument, whose value no longer resides in referring without medi-ation to a shared memory, but in its capacity to provide knowledge and aes-thetic pleasure.[132] Avellaneda defends the pyramid by differentiating precisely between these two kinds of monuments, maintaining that if the value of the artistic monument lies in its beauty, the value of the historical monument lies in its *authenticity*; and Lamas points out that while the former can be required to accompany "the development of wealth and the progress of the arts," historical monuments "are not subject to the laws of progress and perfectibility, because they are of the past, the consummated, irrevocable, untouchable fact."

Lamas is undoubtedly the one who most emphatically defends the need for preservation, because his romantic conception that the main function of his-tory is not to teach about life—as proposed by Cicero's famous sentence, which Lamas refutes—but to link a community backward, is based on the need for

---

[131] See letters to the City Council of Estrada (already cited), by Miguel Estévez Seguí and Andrés Lamas, both dated November 11, 1883, in the aforementioned *Revista Nacional*.
[132] This distinction was made by Aloïs Riegl in his classic work *Der Moderne Denkmalkultus: Sein Wesen und seine Entstehung* (Vienna: Braumüller, 1903). Translated as "The Modern Cult of Monuments: Its Character and Its Origin," trans. Kurt W. Forster and Diane Ghirardo, *Oppositions* 25 (1982): 21–51.

monuments whose authenticity is capable of mimetically invoking the cultural identity of a social group, of making present with their own materiality a series of moral codes in which the legacy they commemorate is synthesized. As for Lamas "poverty has been the greatness of the revolution," only the poverty of the authentic monument offers "a regenerative course of patriotism, of virtue." But this demand can be formulated exclusively by a social group for which the monument has not lost a primitive referential function. The public space, for this group, is a sphere of familiar signs, as is national history itself, which is not only confused with that of Buenos Aires but also with that of a social class or even that of a group of families.

There are those who accept the reform proposed by Alvear reluctantly, like Mitre or Avellaneda, assuming the possibility of coexistence between the old signs of the traditional community and the new landmarks demanded by the new referential functions of the metropolis. And there are those who, like López—in an attitude analogous to that of the antiquarians who emerged in the heat of the French Revolution—do not link the preservation of traditions with real objects, but with the preservation of knowledge, for which is sufficient the museographic and archival preservation of images in a catalogue of memory that does not hinder action, but shows "the historical value of the events that have prepared and produced the development and progress of the present."[133] But there are those who, like Sarmiento and Alvear, not dwelling on the value of authenticity of the original monument, notice two things: on the one hand, and in full harmony with the spirit of Roca's modernization process, that the "imperfections" of the pyramid vindicated by its "authenticity" do nothing more than keep alive the provisional nature of the revolution at a time when what is sought is to close the cycle of temporariness and exceptionality; on the other hand, that the familiarity of the place is a real obstacle for the incorporation into national rituals of broader and more diverse groups and the consolidation of the metropolitan character of the new city as a means to achieve the universalization of representations and the staging of memory. While Lamas wants to maintain the pyramid as a remnant of the "anthropological place" that he sees in the square—that is, an identifying, relational and historical place—the renovation project wants to turn the square into a "place of memory": that is, a place where the image of what a society is no longer, its difference is captured precisely to produce a new process of identification and community building.[134]

---

[133] Vicente Fidel López, letter to the City Council, November 8, 1883, in *Revista Nacional*.

[134] I am following the differentiation established by Marc Augé between "anthropological place" and "place of memory," in *Non-Places: Introduction to an Anthropology of Supermodernity* (1992), trans. John Howe (London and New York: Verso, 2008), especially the chapter "Anthropological Place," 35–60. Augé takes, in turn, the category

In this sense, if until then the plaza had been built on an always recognizable base of signs, whose material restoration could even be considered, what is now sought is a complete substitution of contents and forms. For the first time in Buenos Aires the conflict between historical time and urban space is staged in such a way that it becomes clear that a new public space must emerge from the most complete destruction of the previous one. It is a change of scale that attempts to take charge of the fact that the capital's status, but above all immigration, imply a reconsideration of the terms of identity. The discussion surrounding the pyramid can thus be placed as the prolegomena to what Bertoni described as a real wave of monumental and historical construction between 1887 and 1891, as a reaction of the elite to the increase of the celebrations of immigrant collectivities, which finds its keys in the creation of the museum as an institution, in the urban monument—but also in the museification of the city, in the public recovery of its historical places—and in the ritualization of patriotic school celebrations.[135]

In the end, the pyramid was not demolished (around 1911 it was placed   32
in the center of the two squares in place of the other monument proposed by Alvear, and it is the one that still stands, with some variations), but the urban space at the heart of the city—the heart of the nation—was completely modified. A modification that indicates the moment in which public space is constructed as an artificial scenography where the values of a community are redisposed in function of a general effectiveness and not for their *authentic* reference value; the moment in which the need to redispose all the marks of identity appears, because there is no gesture more integrative, but also more enlightened regarding the adequate means to found a new hegemony, than being willing to found history and its signs anew.

The "Argentinian Haussmann": What Is City Government?

Finally, we should reflect on Alvear's transformations, the problem of management, the problem of the construction of a local bureaucracy, but also the problem of the construction of that very special figure of Alvear as mayor, as "Lord Mayor." Among the transformations that must be attributed to his

---

"place of memory" from the work directed by Pierre Nora, *Les lieux de mémoire*, 7 vols. (Paris: Gallimard, 1981).

[135] Lilia Ana Bertoni, "La educación 'moral': visión y acción de la elite a través del sistema nacional de educación primaria, 1881–1916," (Buenos Aires: Ravignani Institute, April 1991), 37–38, Bertoni mentions the initiative taken by the municipality in 1889 to carry out a survey of buildings significant for the nation's history, commissioning Vicente Fidel López to locate the houses and places where historical figures had been born or lived or where important events had taken place, and to write the texts to be placed on plaques marking these sites.

administration, it is convenient to insist on the meanings and implications of the *ex-novo* construction of a local bureaucracy. As soon as the city was federalized, the new mayor lacked technical bodies under his command with any tradition of intervention in the city: the Department of Engineers of the Province of Buenos Aires (formerly the Topographic Department), which until then had been in charge of the city, ceased to have jurisdiction over it and, together with the technicians, took with them all the documentation, plans, and projects on which it had been working for Buenos Aires (for example, the new municipal Public Works Office would unsuccessfully request again and again from its provincial counterpart the cadastral plan that the latter had been drawing up for years).[136] At the same time, the Department of Engineers of the Nation acquired automatic jurisdiction over the entire capital, but without having to give explanations to the mayor on its works and projects, so that local power was left in a clamp of overlapping and conflicting jurisdictions (and this conflict has marked urban management in Buenos Aires to this day). In this framework, Alvear must organize the whole municipal state apparatus, starting in almost all cases from an absolute vacuum, although counting on the extra offer of prestige that the government of the capital city came to have at its disposal. The most significant cases, in this sense, are those of the presence in the government team of José María Ramos Mejía, creator in 1883 of Public Assistance in the municipal area, and Guillermo Rawson, Alvear's adviser for the creation of the Civil Registry a year later. But, also, a whole staff of offices—the Statistical Office, the Public Works Office, the Chemical Office, etc.—was formed, and their regulations established.

In any case, there is an "administrative" issue in which Alvear established his identity as the second bastion in the lineage of the great mayors initiated by Rivadavia: conflicts with private property and its expression in urban law: expropriations. It is curious to note how liberal culture has always celebrated as great mayors—and a great mayor is always a modernizer—those who fought against the most paradigmatic manifestation of individual rights. This is not by chance, as what is at stake in that battle is the capacity of the ruling class to impose an order that, in the modern city, is necessarily associated with the growing capacity to intervene in private property in the name of the "public good." When it comes to hygienic regulations for the interior of workers' housing, the problem is placed in the classic terms of class rule: the "housing question," as it has been called since Engels so titled his pamphlet, has always been a prerequisite of social order. But when urban reforms affect the properties of the powerful, a much less studied conflict arises, one that affects the symbolic order within dominant groups themselves. This conflict is inevitable, because there is no urban reform without a battle against property, even if that reform is destined to reproduce and increase more generally, in the short, medium, or

---

[136] For this example, see *Memoria de la Municipalidad* (Buenos Aires: 1881), 109–110.

long term, the value of property. That is why urban planning itself, as a disciplinary body, has remained so closely associated with the positions of political reformism. The battle will be more or less limited by the membership or greater or lesser respect of public management groups for the status quo, and by the ideological, legal, and political limits of the society in question; this is obvious. But what I want to point out is the fact that it is precisely in the sometimes embarrassed discovery of these limits that the reformist image of management is constructed. And it seems to me that this makes the characterization of "conservative reformism" a little more complex: it could be said that, in this case, the idea of reformism is defined more by the conflictive relationship that the state group maintains with the interests of its own class—economic but also political, as in the case of electoral reform, and above all cultural, as in the laws on common education and civil registration—than by the task of assistance and institutional modernization aimed at the classic recipients of reform: the subaltern sectors. A reformist, modernizing mayor is the one who realizes that the interests of his class in the city are not equivalent to the sum of the individual interests of the members of that class, and to think through the structural relationship of the series reformism-modernization-urbanization-expropriations, allows us to analyze this not inconsiderable—let's say, inverse—side of reformism.

Already Sarmiento—not to return to Rivadavia, whose government went into crisis every time he wanted to impose general criteria on the plot of properties, precisely the crises that a memorialist historiography has taken to invest him as the "first mayor of Buenos Aires"—already Sarmiento, then, in the years of his tenure on the Council, had asked for a system of expropriation like the one that in Paris had allowed the construction of one of the emblems of pre-Haussmannian urbanism: the rue de Rivoli.[137] International jurisprudence had also advanced very slowly: from the first expropriations almost obligatorily required by the logic of new forms of communication—the typical example is that of the railways—to expropriations for reasons of hygiene or ornament, a legal corpus was generated that allowed the main urban reforms of the nineteenth century, which in turn grew and consolidated with each major reform, often enabled by authoritarian operations on the city and society. It is not strange, therefore, that many of the main legislative advances were made by governments during the conservative reaction in Europe, such as those of Napoleon III, Bismarck, or Disraeli, who, thanks to the recovery of absolute powers, carried out great

---

[137] Sarmiento, "Plaza de Mayo," *El Nacional*, May 28, 1857, *Obras completas (LD)*, XXIV, 217–19. The rue de Rivoli is one of the main achievements of the Empire; Louis Bergeron, ed., *Parigi* (Bari: Laterza, 1989), 197–98. Alvear's connection with Rivadavia is present from the earliest historiography, generally linked to the conflicts over property. See, for example, Ismael Bucich Escobar, *Buenos Aires Ciudad*, 1880–1930 (Buenos Aires: El Ateneo, 1930).

urban reforms, which allows us to situate the other side of urban planning, the point at which it has remained faithful to the slogan—not so paradoxical in the case of the city—of enlightened despotism: absolute power for reform.

Toward the end of the century, legislative advances on expropriations were noticeable, and Buenos Aires was as conscious of them as of their relationship with the urban reforms to which they had given rise. Alvear was inspired by them when he proposed the expropriation law that was to allow him to open new streets on private land (that is, to plan the extension of urbanization in directions fixed by public authorities and not by the market); to impose retroactively on properties alignment regulations dating back to the times of Rivadavia which had not been enforced in the absence of any kind of public control; and to make possible specific public works such as the Avenida de Mayo. To make possible in the double sense, juridical and economic. Because the great advance put into practice in the rue de Rivoli had been that the state no longer expropriated only the fractions of the private properties affected by the project of "public necessity," but complete properties. In this way, by expropriating a larger strip of land than was strictly necessary, the greater value that public works could produce would benefit the state when it resold the surplus land—or the buildings it decided to construct there—at the new values, and in this way it could more than finance the projects carried out. This, on the one hand, is fundamental. But no less important is the fact that, in this way, the state assumed full control of the times, costs, and results of the urban operation, also in aesthetic terms, constructing the buildings itself or imposing on the new constructions on the expropriated land building regulations that would guarantee the desired image. The homogeneity of the Haussmannian boulevards—the model for all these interventions—had that modality of expropriation as an inseparable instrument, showing the homogeneity of the massive presence of the state in the regulation of society.

In the demolition of the Recova (owned by the Anchorena family) expropriation had not been the main issue, because it was part of the litigation over the properties of Rosas, on whose confiscation everyone agreed. The expropriations for the opening of streets in the suburbs, on the other hand, was in fact a kind of mortgage that started to be paid later. But the Avenida de Mayo, by contrast, because of the visibility of the operation and the value of its properties, became a true leading case. Congress passed the broad expropriation law proposed by Alvear, but the owners filed lawsuits which, having failed in the first instances, reached the Supreme Court through appeals. The arguments of Eduardo Costa, representing the interests of the commune, resorted to international precedents: from the Napoleonic Code—and the change it had established from "public necessity" to "public utility," greatly expanding the casuistry to justify expropriations—to the most recent cases of North American jurisprudence. For Costa, to prevent the municipality from obtaining, through a broad law of expropriation, its own resources to pay for major works, meant "condemning all progress;" but, above all, what was under discussion was whether it should be public authority or private owners who were in charge of "deciding whether an improvement should be carried out or not."[138]

The Supreme Court ruled against the expropriations, laying down one of the principles that made it practically impossible in the future to undertake any reform in the city center. In 1907, defending the need for extensive expropriations for the implementation of the Bouvard Plan, Joaquín V. González blamed this principle for the fact that Buenos Aires had developed "without any order," forming "a city stripped of any general aesthetic idea." Moreover, in the case of the opening of new streets, the ruling guaranteed, also for a long time, the perverse system by which the "affected" owners were compensated by the state for the land they ceded for a public street that greatly enhanced the value of their properties (it introduced them into the urban market), and often the state had to pay for that piece of land at the price it would acquire after it opened the street itself.[139] In the case of Avenida de Mayo, the unfavorable sentence postponed and delayed construction in difficult case-by-case negotiations and forced borrowing large amounts of money to acquire the affected sectors of land at prices that grew day by day—the peremptoriness of public works with this system of limited expropriation turned against the state, which, instead of forcing individuals to accept its conditions, was forced to accept theirs. This was to be repeated in every attempt to build a diagonal avenue or a widening of streets, in a true "expropriation business" benefiting owners, lawyers, and diligent civil servants who proposed measures in the knowledge of the subsequent course lawsuits would take. Strictly speaking, this system of expropriation meant that public action could only be taken on the edges, first on the "outskirts" of the consolidated city, and later along the river.

But, at the same time, the demand for a broader law of expropriations, as well as the protests against "selfishness, greed, or individual caprice before the common good," as the *Memoria de la Intendencia* (Memoir of the Intendancy) of 1884 put it, would be characteristic of the reformist mayors, who always find in Alvear their anchor and model. And perhaps even more interesting: this conflict modulates different registers until it connects with one very dear to the "cultural coalition of the new state"—as Josefina Ludmer calls the group of officials-intellectuals of the reformist elite of the eighties: the rejection of the

---

[138] See Eduardo Costa, "Avenida de Mayo," in *Memoria de la Intendencia Municipal de 1887* (Buenos Aires: Imprenta La Universidad, 1888), 150. The whole of Costa's intervention and the court's replies are reproduced there.

[139] One of the cases that established jurisprudence based on the conflict over Avenida de Mayo was that of Isabel A. de Elortondo against the commune. There is an exhaustive description of the conflict, with lists of all the affected owners, in Ricardo Llanes, *La Avenida de Mayo*, especially chaps. II and III. See Joaquín V. González's phrase in *La expropiación en el derecho público argentino* (Buenos Aires: Librería La Facultad, 1915), 14.

meanness and materialism of the urban bourgeoisie, characteristics that can be qualified from their incurable *rastacuerismo* and bad taste, to their practically principled refusal to pay taxes.[140] Especially from that point of view, Alvear would be for the elite a standard bearer "who had to fight a pitched battle, at least, with each of the landowners to get them to accept his reform plan—Calzadilla notes—How much eagerness and patience!"[141]

At the height of his tenure as mayor, Cané writes to him from Europe:

> You must understand that it is not my hope to turn our honored neighbors of Buenos Aires into Greeks of the time of Pericles [...]. No; but between that finished perfection of taste, never repeated on earth, and our present state of artistic education, there is an abyss, the whole abyss of history, the whole distance between primitive instinct and the harmonious conception of the peoples who have reached the intellectual summit. No; I do not ask for Pericles in Buenos Aires, and even if I did ask, it would be difficult to deliver. But it is legitimate that when Mr. Salas or Mr. Chas wish to build a house, they will find architects somewhat more inspired than those who built the present mansions of those honorable citizens. [Although] the architect needs to be sustained by public taste, to respond unconsciously, if you will, to the intellectual atmosphere he breathes. And so much so, that most of our fellow citizens are ecstatic before that building without style, heavy, flat, overloaded with three-meter figurines [...] Poor architects! By dint of applauding those who shout, paradise ends up losing the good artists.[142]

Francisco Seeber writes to him, also from Europe:

> Our excellent friend and minister in Paris, Doctor Paz, told me, ashamed of the few attractions for life that Buenos Aires presents in its streets and parks, and of the timorous spirit of our municipalities, when it is a question of obtaining money to beautify, clean up, and enlarge our streets, that it would be convenient to establish that those who have not spent at least two years in Europe should not be municipal electors. We agreed to this, but on condition that it was immediately before the election, because soon they are influenced by the atmosphere that reigns there where no one wants to pay taxes, and everyone thinks they are burdened with them, especially the richest who pay nothing.[143]

---

[140] Ludmer's expression in "Latin American Cultural Coalitions and Liberal States," *Travesia. Journal of Latin American Cultural Studies* 2, no. 2 (1993).

[141] *Las beldades de mi tiempo*, 160–61.

[142] Letter from Cané to Alvear, Vienna, January 14, 1885, in Beccar Varela, *Torcuato de Alvear*, 482.

[143] Letter from Francisco Seeber to Alvear, London, July 29, 1886, ibid., 510.

The European travels of elites is a journey in search for models and the discovery of the reasons that allowed them to understand why, as Cané lamented, "poor and beloved Buenos Aires" is one of the ugliest cities in the world. The traveler is in Europe and cannot remember Buenos Aires but with European eyes; as Viñas says, in travels after the 1880s "the traveling gentleman frees himself from his country, Argentina or Buenos Aires are the contemptible matter, the sinful body or evil."[144] But that is one side of the problem: at the same time there is a misaligned mirror effect. "The whole of Europe talks about us, because our progress imposes itself," says Cané; in spite of which Buenos Aires is light years away from the image such progress would have for anyone like Cané, whose eyes are full of the European cities whose inhabitants, paradoxically, celebrate the progress of Buenos Aires. It is a matter, therefore, of making an adjustment: to bring Buenos Aires up to the image that the Europe "that talks about us" should be able to see. In the correspondence of all these travelers, there is a permanent rhetorical appeal to what a European tourist "attracted by our fame" would say if he came to Buenos Aires and found the truth of the village provincialism whose memory shames them so much.

What characterizes Alvear and makes him a figure of importance in urban history is that he faithfully represents elite desires for reform, in this case, in terms of social and cultural modernization; of being, precisely, the one capable of not being influenced by "those who shout from paradise" or by "the atmosphere." They all write to him from Europe as the peer that he is, encouraging him, pointing out novelties, and promising clarifications ("I close my eyes," writes Nicolás Avellaneda from Paris, "and I think of the amount of water that is poured daily into the streets and promenades [to water the trees], trying to transfer the fact to our country in imagination. I will look for the data and send it to you"); giving him indications which confound technique, aesthetics, and fashion ("the last word is the paving of wood" or "No palm trees, sir and friend, or alamo trees of spread foliage, or firs, or eucalyptus," Cané prescribes from Vienna at the same time that Eduardo Madero sends him palm trees from Petrópolis); inciting him to energetic measures ("An ukase, if necessary, Mr. Mayor, a dictatorial measure, tasty, since you are accused of taking so many," continues Cané); but also showing understanding ("Many great projects," writes Seeber from London, "were indicated to me by Dr. Paz as indispensable for the civilized life of Buenos Aires, but I observed that with but part of them, which you wanted to carry out, they had already pretended to declare you mad [...] I have too much appreciation for you to propose projects of this nature that endanger your existence"); and, above all, ratifying the elite's support ("the friends [in Congress] will help you with this," Pellegrini wrote to him from

---

[144] Viñas, *Literatura argentina y realidad política*, 50.

Paris, "if you manage to interest the President, the problem will be solved").[145] Such support was ratified in every conflict, not only with the City Council— which was closed or suspended whenever the political situation demanded it—[146] but also with parliament itself, as in the case of the demolition of the Recova: the vote in Congress was won by only two votes after very intense negotiations carried out by the Minister of the Interior himself, Bernardo de Irigoyen, who, referring to the episode, said that it had involved "more work than a great question of state."[147]

Alvear capitalizes on all those conflicts, because he knows how to take to his side the new spectacular character of the city, turning his own action into spectacle: the conflictive demolition of the Recova was carried out uninter-ruptedly, during the night, with full illumination of the square *a giorno*, replete with curious people, with the press participating in the conflict and reporting on the reform day after day, and with Alvear, like a general in battle, poised on the rubble and personally directing the whole operation. This chaotically growing city has finally found someone to oversee its growth in such a way

---

[145] Letter from Avellaneda to Alvear, Paris, August 8, 1885, in Beccar Varela, *Torcuato de Alvear*, 493; letter from Cané to Alvear, Vienna, January 14, 1885, in Beccar Varela, *Torcuato de Alvear*, 488, 492, and 489, respectively. See also, letter from Francisco Seeber to Alvear, London, July 28, 1886, 510; Carlos Pellegrini, letter to Torcuato de Alvear, Paris, August 3, 1883, in Beccar Varela, *Torcuato de Alvear*, 304.

[146] The laudatory historiography of Alvear has shown, in general, the illegitimacy of the Council and its defense of spurious interests; in contrast, the critical historiography of Alvear has wanted to see in the successive closings the demonstration of the authoritarianism of the management leaning, symmetrically, for a defense of the councilmen that in nothing relates to their proposals or political practices. The relationship between the executive and the deliberative council was in fact very complex and has remained so throughout the institutional history of the municipality due to the delegated nature of the government established by the Municipal Organic Law as a result of federalization: the municipal executive is delegated by the president of the nation, and the Council dictates ordinances by delegation of the National Congress (with little capacity to impose these ordinances on the mayor). But we must also distinguish how the Council was composed in each moment: before the electoral reform of 1918, the representation was exercised by the "notables" of each parish, generally political leaders, and economic lobbyists, with logics of confrontations with the executive that rarely had to do with the problems of the city; in turn, the mayors used the city as a stomping ground for the ruling party. For example, when in 1901, faced with the closure of the Council by Roca for reasons of strict political expediency, Joaquín V. González could justify it with arguments of public morality and democratic adjustment to a flawed institution, in Congreso Nacional, *Diario de Sesiones de la Cámara de Diputados*, October 25, 1901. A detailed chronicle on the closures of the Council and its relations with the intendancy, is offered in Eduardo Antonio and Fernando García Molina, "Las tres clausuras del Concejo Deliberante," *Todo es Historia* 329 (December 1994).

[147] Cited in Beccar Varela, *Torcuato de Alvear*, 20.

that it is not ruled by the ignorance of the local bourgeoisie. Personally: like a general or, better, as the Montevidean Sansón Carrasco pointed out in the chronicle quoted at the beginning of this section, like a good boss: "watching over everyone's business, as if it were his own." In a city, it is convenient to insist that, increasingly alienated, the elite need more than an administrator, an "owner" to give it back to them, even if that personalized owner is the head of a bureaucratic apparatus in the process of complexification and autonomy. It is thus not secondary that Alvear should be visualized—and celebrated—by public opinion as a whole as someone "outside politics," which takes us back to the tradition that had established the non-political character of the city: the city is not governed, like the country or the provinces, with politics, but rather like the ranch or the factory, with the wisdom of the owners, *with presence.* In this widespread version, politics in the city is equivalent to "politicking"; those who practice it are the councilors, who obstruct all action for petty parish or committee interests, or directly for personal business—and let's not forget that the "other" politics, that of the nascent class conflict, will always be managed at a different level from that of city management, although the city increasingly serves as its stage and motor.

In this way of giving his all, Alvear is constituted as a paradigmatic mayor, not merely because he responds to the need of his social group, but because he is able to transform it into a collective need, into a matter of public opinion. And this is possible also—and perhaps above all—because each gesture is already inserted in a specific lineage of international urban culture: the caricaturists of the time portray him with a pickax in hand, on a mountain of rubble, giving energetic orders, with techniques and iconographies that are practically the same as those other caricaturists had used to portray, first, Haussmann in Paris, later, Vicuña Mackenna in Santiago and, afterward, Alvear, Pereira 33 Passos in Rio, and so many others. Again, a game of mirrors: Do the mayors pose according to that prestigious lineage whose images they know, and do the caricaturists resort to them because they already have the generic capacity to automatically invoke that lineage? We can now weigh Haussmann's "influence" with greater precision: much more than a "fashion," much more than the "partial" or "mistaken" application of a system of urban reform, Haussmannism in Latin America was the construction of similar figures of mayors as administrators and owners, the "Lord Mayors" whose main tics Haussmann founded and which have remained, one could almost say to this day, as the ideal administrators of the city. They are similar figures because they proposed processes of transformation that condensed similar motives, but also because they were comfortably installed in a literary-iconographic genre that was already widespread at a time when the relationship between city, journalism, and *costumbrista* or travel literature was beginning to be decisive regionally in the construction of social imaginaries.

DEPRESSA ! DEPRESSA !

Figure 33. The figure of the "Lord Mayor": *George-Eugène Haussmann*, 1854. Image drawn from Leonardo Benevolo, *Diseño de la ciudad, 5. El arte y la ciudad contemporánea.* Barcelona: Gustavo Gili, 1977. Caricature of Mayor Alvear, drawn from *El Mosquito*, April 24, 1887, and of Prefect Pereira Passos, Rio de Janeiro, drawn from *O Malho*, March 18, 1905.

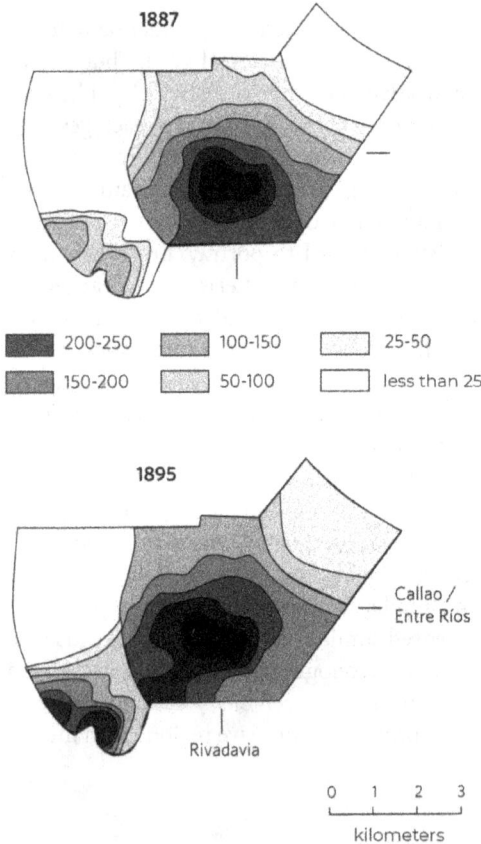

Figure 34. Diagram showing the population of Buenos Aires in 1887 and 1895, from Charles Sargent, *The Spatial Evolution of Greater Buenos Aires. 1870–1930.* Tempe: Arizona State University, 1974. The city's traditional centrality is preserved, with a slight shift toward the north.

CHAPTER 3

An Extended City:
The Metropolitan Dimension

Homogeneity and equity, control, and containment: if the two models of the "new city" and the "concentrated city" under analysis coincide in something, it is in this double ambition, although they radically disagree on what kind of state/society relationship should produce it and on how to generate a market and a public space that guarantee it. That is why the creation of La Plata will 26 coincide so well, at first, with all the expectations about how a "modern" city should be, because it seems to realize both models of the ideal city: in one case, as the manifestation of the purest cultural creation over nothingness, with all the benefits of modernity over territorial and social pre-existences; in the other, as a regular and finished figure, defined by public will, whose pure geometry also offers an also ideal size. It is remarkable that the surface of La Plata strictly coincides with the "concentrated" Buenos Aires that the boulevards or canals tried to circumscribe.[148]   22, 23, 24

In this sense, it could be said that neither of the two models fully incorporates a metropolitan perspective, insofar as they are "closed" models, without a clear position on the great nineteenth-century urban issue: metropolitan expansion. By the end of Alvear's administration, we are still in a small city, 35 "the flat city par excellence," in Cané's terms, fully shared by the modernizing 27 elite as a whole: "An opulent queen full of health and vigor, dressed in rags."[149] A city in the midst of a transforming whirlwind, but whose most characteristic image must have been that of a provisional camp, with shacks and sheds made of sheet metal and wood. The erroneous impression that has remained of a consolidated bourgeois city, in any case, shows how memory officialized the "opulent queen," preventing us from seeing the "rags" that contemporaries recounted with horror.[150]

---

[148] I am indebted to Jorge Francisco Liernur for this observation.

[149] Miguel Cané, "Carta al Intendente Torcuato de Alvear desde Viena" (January 14, 1885), reproduced in Beccar Varela, *Torcuato de Alvear*, 486.

[150] On the idea of fin-de-siècle Buenos Aires as a "provisional camp," see Liernur, "La ciudad efímera," in Liernur and Silvestri, *El umbral de la metrópolis*.

It was not until the beginning of 1888, during the short administration of Antonio Crespo, when the annexation of the provincial municipalities of Flores and Belgrano took place, quadrupling the surface of the capital, that the problem of expansion appeared in all its magnitude: What were these lands that were added, how should they be managed, how did they relate to the city and to existing ideas about how it should be and grow? In this climate of public uncertainty and private euphoria—it was the urban market that had quadrupled—the public actions of the end of the century must be interpreted to understand the extent to which the expansion that took place in Buenos Aires was contentiously linked with the two models we are analyzing, showing, in fact, its own limits and contradictions.

1. The Grid as Public Project

> I do not wish to create one Buenos Aires of workers and another of well-to-do people. I want to place in the city of more or less large groups, in continuous contact with other people, because of their work, because of the means of communication, for a hundred other reasons.[151]
>
> –Domingo Selva, 1904

The first action that must be considered is the layout of the new borders of the city. We explained already that Alvear's request for the cession of lands of the municipalities of Flores and Belgrano to the Province of Buenos Aires in 1881 for his boulevard beltway project had not been, strictly speaking, a project of "extension," but of regularization, in so far as the new territories were only destined to rationalize the broken and capricious traditional limit of the municipality of Buenos Aires and to form a hygienic belt that should, of course, be distant from the consolidated area (because a project of that nature was also economically and legally unfeasible if it affected already urbanized and valuable lands), but precisely to serve as a limit and containment. That is why a distance of approximately seven kilometers from Plaza de Mayo was proposed (let's imagine a straight line along Rivadavia Avenue, at the height of the current Acoyte Street, in Caballito). Approved by the National Congress but stopped in the legislature of the Province of Buenos Aires from 1884 on by various political conflicts, when the cession was resolved in June 1887 it already considered the incorporation of the entirety of the municipalities of Flores and Belgrano. This under the reasonable argument that both were in fact appendices of the capital, unpopulated municipalities not productively developed,

---

[151] Domingo Selva, "La habitación higiénica para el obrero" (paper presented at the 2nd Latin American Medical Congress), *Revista Municipal* 46, 47, 49 (December 5, 12, and 19, 1904).

extensions that served the urban, wealthy classes for recreation and seasonal rest—let us not forget that the same legislators of the province who discussed the cession lived in Buenos Aires, and several of them had country houses in the outskirts of the city. The cession expanded the radius of the capital to over fifteen kilometers, if we take the same straight line from Plaza de Mayo. It was more than the double what Alvear had imagined.[152]

The same response from the province would not have been forthcoming if the annexation of Barracas to the south (Avellaneda) had been requested. This was more logical—and in terms of surface, a smaller—annexation of an area inextricably linked to the production and commerce of the capital, and which formed, with Barracas to the north a single, homogeneous urban sector. It is remarkable how, until very late in the twentieth century, with the new limits having been established, the usual plans of commerce or industry insisted on continuing the historical tradition of depicting a Buenos Aires horizontally placed on the Río de la Plata, including Barracas to the south and not the new lands to the west.[153] But, as soon as the wounds produced by federalization were healed, the province was not going to also renounce its main industrial settlement and the exit to the Riachuelo that still functioned as the main port at the end of the century. Thus, despite what a certain productive logic could suggest—if we think of the city as a productive artifact and accordingly define its administrative forms—and despite repeated attempts starting with federalization to expand the capital to the south, the Riachuelo remained as a jurisdictional limit, hindering the local structuring of the port and a consolidation more closely linked to urban developments of the metropolitan industrial axis.[154]

So, the jurisdictional extension was made only toward the west, in fact the "natural" direction of expansion of the residential market in Buenos Aires, mainly for topographical reasons (the "highlands"). That direction would now be favored even more by the way in which the extension was conceived, opening up the city onto the pampa. But the cession of the province was of two municipalities and, nevertheless, the limit drawn for the capital dismissed the adaptation of the new form of the enlarged municipality to the mere addition

3

---

[152] On the definition of the limits, their parliamentary debates and their respective laws, see the two classic texts of Arturo B. Carranza: *La cuestión Capital de la República, 1826–1887* (Buenos Aires: Talleres Gráficos Rosso, 1927); and *La Capital de la República. El ensanche de su municipio, 1881 a 1888* (Buenos Aires: Talleres Gráficos Rosso, 1938).

[153] On this subject, I follow the hypotheses that we developed together with Graciela Silvestri in "Imágenes al sur. Sobre algunas hipótesis de James Scobie para el desarrollo de Buenos Aires."

[154] Carranza mentions that, years later, in his speech to the Legislative Assembly in 1912, President Roque Sáenz Peña requested the annexation of Avellaneda to the capital as something "impostergable por razones de orden político, económico, de higiene y seguridad" (unavoidable for political, economic, health, and safety reasons). Cited in *La Capital de la República. El ensanche de su municipio*, xxxiv.

of the surface of those two with its irregular borders. Concretely, the new limit cut part of Flores and Belgrano and incorporated a sector of the municipality of San Martín. This is a formal decision which merits reflection. In February 1888, the engineers Pablo Blot (for the national government) and Luis Silveyra (for the provincial government) finished the layout and the survey of the 100-meter wide beltway that would divide the capital and the province until today: repeating much more toward the west the regularizing gesture initiated by Rivadavia's Callao Boulevard, followed by Alvear's beltway boulevard project, the engineers traced a regular and arbitrary line (the current General Paz Avenue) that fixes an orderly figure for the new city, seeking to preserve, in spite of the change of scale, the centrality and symmetry of the traditional city, maintaining that *will to form* that, as Graciela Silvestri showed, also makes *pendant* with the aspiration of the new urban front that was materializing contemporarily in Puerto Madero (Madero Port).[155]

But, while this gesture is inscribed without conflict within the regularizing tradition, the second great public decision requires more detailed analysis. I refer to the design made by a municipal commission in 1898 and that would be officially published as a plan in 1904 of a mostly uniform squared grid for all that immense territory, defining the future city with precision, block by block, covering with a homogenizing mesh the vast wastelands that surrounded the traditional city up to the new limit. Simply by comparing the topographic plan of 1895, which more or less faithfully reproduces the existing city limits, with that of the municipal Public Works Department of 1904, which presents the layout of the new grid, one can see the excesses of the latter, at a time when only the traditional city was very relatively densified, the first suburban area (San Cristóbal Sur, Almagro, Palermo) was just beginning to be developed, and the periphery (with the exception of the small preexisting nuclei of Flores and Belgrano) was a great extension of pampa.[156] At first glance, it would seem that this plan is complying, as we saw with La Plata, with both traditions: with the tradition of "squaring," the "ambition of regularity" of the master line of local urban engineering and, at the same time, with Sarmiento's call for "decentralization," to build the new city outside the limits of the old one.

However, this plan was produced by the municipality in the very years in which that public will to control the expansion, pointed out again and again

[155] Graciela Silvestri, "La ciudad y el río," in Liernur and Silvestri, *El umbral de la metrópolis*. In their report of January 17, 1888, Blot and Silveyra say that they drew up the layout for the future boulevard "which together with the Ríos de la Plata and Matanza would enclose a fairly regular area of land." Quoted in Carranza, *La Capital de la República. El ensanche de su municipio*, 197 (emphasis added).

[156] Carlos María Morales, "Algunos datos relativos al trazado general del Municipio," *Anales de la Sociedad Científica Argentina* 46, (second half of 1898). See also, by the same author, *Las mejoras edilicias de Buenos Aires. Memoria presentada al Segundo Congreso Científico Latino-Americano reunido en Montevideo* (Buenos Aires, 1901).

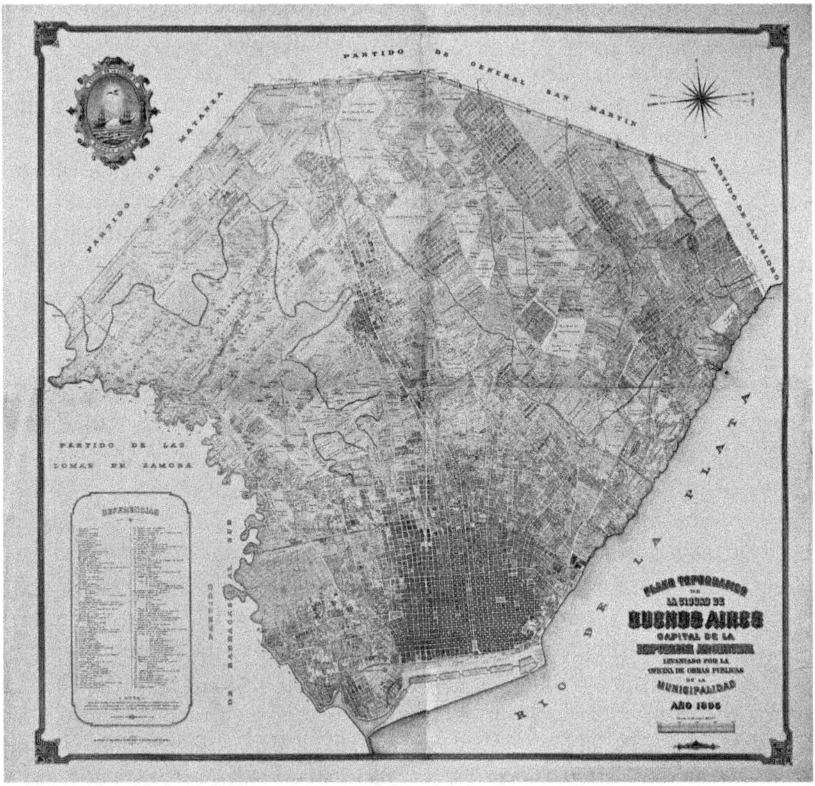

Figure 35. Office of Public Works, Buenos Aires, *Plan of Buenos Aires*, 1895. Instituto Histórico de la Ciudad de Buenos Aires. Compare the existing public lands in 1895 with the plan drafted in 1898–1904.

by the definition of beltway boulevards, had become more notorious. Because to the thunderous public crisis of the nineties, not only of resources but, above all, of a large part of the premises of the expansive civilizing project, must be added the effect caused in public authority by the expectations that the annexation itself raised in speculators and landowners. Between 1887 and the beginning of the century, private requests for approval of layouts for the sale of lots and private proposals for "extension plans" for the capital multiplied, which boosted in the municipal management the militant recovery of the ideal of the small and concentrated city, now, in tune with the ideological climate of the nineties, spiced with a strong "moral" condemnation of real estate speculation. But just as it must be noted how public governance begins to deposit in that speculation all the evils of the city, taking the first step that will turn it into a "metaphysical evil," as if the real estate business did not have protagonists and concrete reasons and, above all, as if its performance was independent of the actions of public power itself. At the same time, the value of that condemnation should not be neglected, in evaluating its implications for the urban policies undertaken and to identify, as we began to see with the issue of expropriations, the progressive consolidation of bodies of public officials who, in their state role, will tend to autonomize themselves, through an ideology of the public, from the sectors and interests of the elite to which they belong, placing them more than once in situations of conflict.[157] Here we can see how, toward the end of the century, the actions that in Alvear were assembled together, become detached in different types of "conservative reformisms": in the case of civil servants who carried out the plan, we must speak of "technical reformism" to indicate motivations and instruments that are very different from political and, in turn, cultural reformisms.

It is in the direction of the contradictions of this "technical reformism" that one must interpret a good part of the objectives of the design of a series 6, 7   of public parks surrounding the consolidated building area of the traditional city at the turn of the century: as the expression of the (impotent) search for a boundary capable of limiting expansion and stabilizing an urban figure; and in the same way, one must see the long campaign, taken up again and again

---

[157] Giorgio Piccinato lucidly points out the conflictive and circular relationship established between two logics: the logic of the complement "expropriation / greater value of private property" and the inverse logic of the complement "expropriation / autonomous rationality of the urban plan": "The demand for expropriation arises from the need to subtract from private property the control of land necessary to guarantee the orderly expansion of the city. And being, as we have seen, one of the objectives of an orderly expansion a gradual increase in land values, expropriation appears ultimately as an instrument to support private property. But if this is the *philosophy* that is at the basis of one of the most debated questions, there is no doubt that the need for a rational design of the urban plan leads more than one technician to always extend the boundaries of the areas subject to expropriation," in *La costruzione dell'urbanistica. Germania 1871–1914* (Rome: Officina, 1974), 87.

by the intendancies of these years, to stop the process of opening streets in the suburbs, a process that functioned as a real public subsidy to the real estate speculators and, therefore, as an incentive to expansion. But these issues will come up in the next section. Here I want to analyze the reasons why the public plan of 1898–1904 is carried out precisely in this climate of anti-expansion and condemnation of speculation when it is the most resounding refutation of that same condemnation by making all land simultaneously available on the market; and, above all, the reasons why the grid is universalized for that expansion, as the only possible layout. That is to say, the reasons why, in the face of the pronounced and ratified *will to form*, a plan is made with an abstract grid that annuls, by definition, all possibility of form. Because if the first dissonance of the 1904 plan is the way it favors building expansion to an extreme degree, the second, and perhaps greater contradiction is the choice of the much repudiated "Spanish" grid.

First of all, the issue of expansion must be analyzed. Indeed, the public endorsement of a completely urbanized federal territory was an explosive revitalizer of real estate activity. But effects should not be confused with objectives: the contradiction between the generalized distrust of expansion and the drawing up of this plan is, strictly speaking, one more manifestation of the impotence of preventing suburban subdivisions, since the plan could be interpreted as an instrument, inadequate by the way, to control expansion.[158] An instrument in search of urban order, primitive and crude though it maybe, but whose negative results were only just beginning to be diagnosed and combated by central European town planning: the "widening," "police" or "alignment" plan, which attempts to guide and control the real estate market by meticulously defining a universal road network, although what it achieves in this way is an incentive for speculation over a very long period, since by simultaneously making all developable land available, without distinguishing between main expansion and network roads, it produces an artificial increase in value.[159]

5

36, 37

---

[158] In fact, for Carlos María Morales, the new continuous border around the federal territory—the riverside road, the beltway, and the rectified Riachuelo—would allow a circuit that would "enclose" the city "in this beautiful frame"; see "Algunos datos relativos al trazado general del municipio," 316.

[159] This is, strictly speaking, the criticism that the nascent European urban planning will make of such plans; in fact, it could be said that it is in the practice of this diagnosis and this dispute that classical urban planning is constituted as such. It was not until the series of international urban planning exhibitions of 1910 (Berlin and London) that the responses to road plans were systematized. Accepting that the expansion of the city is irreversible, and that "authoritarian" attempts to control it (such as the *police plan)* are counterproductive, the nascent "classical" urban planning opposes speculation insofar as it implies a deformation of "natural growth" by exploiting the "waiting rent" (based on the acquisition of land around the city and its subtraction from the market while awaiting its valorization). From then on, in European and North American cities, the

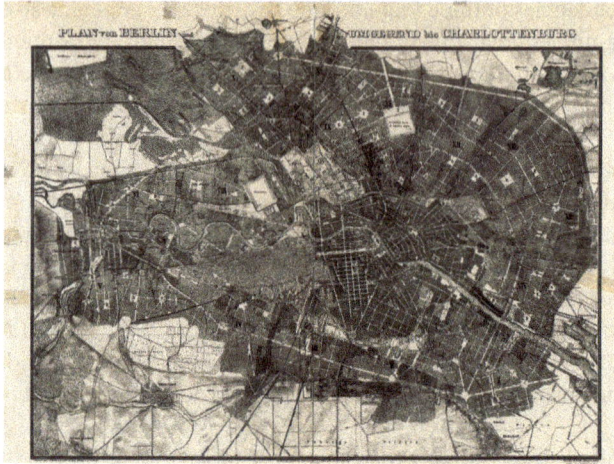

Figure 36. Ferdinand Boehm, cartographer; W. Bembé, engraver. *Hobrecht's Plan of Berlin* ("the police plan"), 1858–62. Zentral und Landesbibliothek Berlin. Note the size of the squares of the expansion toward the north of the consolidated city.

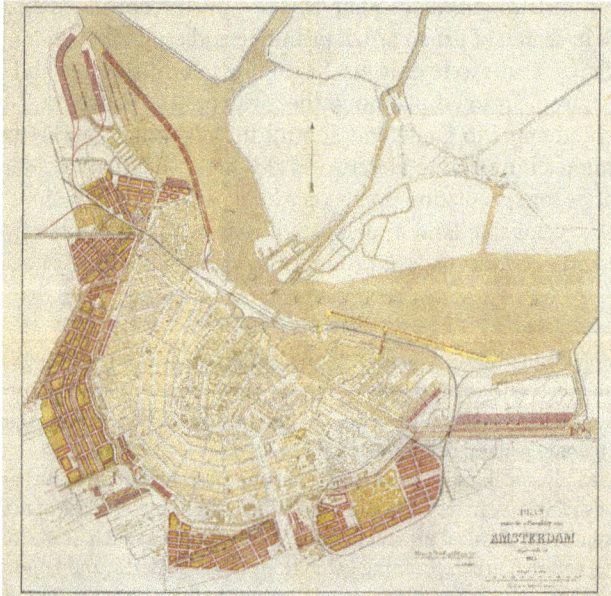

Figure 37. J. C. Loman Jr.; Smulders & Co., *Plan for the Expansion of Amsterdam*, 1875. Amsterdam City Archives (KOKA00396000001). Toward the end of the 19th century, the reaction against such expansions would shape both "classical urbanistics" and the vindication of the qualities of the traditional city present in picturesque urbanism and civic art.

Therefore, due to its character as an instrument to control expansion, beyond the precedents that could be sought throughout the nineteenth century—from the widening of all the avenues from Callao to the west decreed by Rivadavia, to Pellegrini's discussion with Sourdeaux and the Topographic Department in the sixties to draw up an expansion plan for the city—this plan must be seen in direct dialogue with and response to the different private advances on the definition of the new urban area from the very moment in which the certainty of federalization modified the rules of the game in the city. Already during the seventies there were frequent widening proposals submitted by individuals, such as the aforementioned one by Senillosa, but from 1880 onwards there was a flood of proposals. Now, just as the "widening plan" is the basic instrument for the design of urban expansion in the second half of the nineteenth century, its realization required an essential first step: the topographic survey of the existing city, its road and cadastral knowledge. As we saw, for reasons of administrative competence, after federalization the city lacked the surveys that the Topographic Department of the province had been developing; that is to say, it lacked the basic knowledge that public power must have in a city to define such daily operations as approving the alignment of a land whose owner wants to sell or divide it. In March 1881, for example, Carlos Hernández y Cía. presented a "Triangulated plan of the municipality of Buenos Aires with its widening and improvement."[160]

It is worthwhile to dwell on the argument made by this businessman in defense of his project, since it implies a strong criticism of the way in which the growth of the city was being left to chance—to the market, strictly speaking: everything that continues to be built without real knowledge of the situation of the city and without a plan, he says, constitutes enormous "obstacles to improve and expand Buenos Aires." He proposed to draw up a plan of what exists, to rectify "the endless imperfections of our streets" (such as Venezuela, which joins Rivadavia "and yet they are called parallels") and, above all, to know the reality so as to proceed

---

mechanism of the purchase of extra-urban agricultural land by public authorities will become frequent, to then use it as part of a policy of "guaranteeing the naturalness" of expansion, gradually releasing it to the market and in specific sectors, while reserving large green areas. See Werner Hegemann, *La Berlino di pietra. Storia della più grande città di caserme d'afitto* (1930) (Milan: G. Mazzotta, 1975), 246ff. The most suggestive analyses of this moment in urban planning in Giorgio Piccinato, *La costruzione dell'urbanistica*; Donatella Calabi, "Nota introdutiva" in Werner Hegemann, *Catalogo delle esposizioni internazionali di urbanistica. Berlino 1910-Düsseldorf 1911-12* (Milan: Il Saggiatore, 1975); Françoise Choay, *The Modern City: Planning in the 19th Century* (New York: Braziller, 1969).

[160] "Propuesta de Plano Triangulado del Municipio de Buenos Aires con su Ensanche y Mejoramiento" (Proposal of a triangulated plan of the Municipality of Buenos Aires with its Widening and Improvement), by Carlos Hernández y Cía, March 1881, in Archivo Histórico Municipal, Caja 12, 1881, Serie Obras Públicas.

with an adequate expansion: What is the most logical layout, he asks, what is the most beneficial expropriation? Can the municipality decide that? The only plans that are made, he answers, have no accuracy, no matter how beautiful they may seem: "it is very useful, to draw them, to take the draftsman's square and draw parallel lines at 150 varas (120 meters) that say *This is Buenos Aires.*" Governments have concentrated public buildings, and commerce follows them, he states, which produces a fabulous increase of the value of urban property that makes impossible any future reform. That's why it is the very governments, he continues,

> the ones called upon to mark out the new direction of expansion, inspired by public justice and expediency. It is well-known that if the government points out the outlines of new streets for the expansion of the capital in direction A or B, and establishes public buildings, the value of property rises instantly. Now, when Buenos Aires has doubled and quadrupled in population, it remains to be known which will be the most convenient direction of expansion, which will be the great arteries, squares, streets, public buildings.

I believe that these arguments point to the extent to which there were different types of actors with an awareness of the situation that cannot be explained only through the interests of the proposed business. In this case, the company asks in exchange for its work in triangulation and drawing up of the plan, approval to pave 150,000 square meters of street at a fixed price per meter. The proposed deal demonstrates the type of interest that the new situation of the city awakens—the budget for public works increases notably since the national government takes jurisdiction over it—and it is evident that this company's approach to the problem is explained in good measure in that its business is the public works contract, therefore it depends precisely on the state to set the guidelines for expansion. This is a very different situation from that of private actors with an interest in land development who are interested in the city developing around their properties in order to increase their value. But, in any case, the argument with which they defend the proposal shows that the knowledge of urban issues is not limited to elite travelers and their informative epistolaries: here other actors who build the city begin to appear.

And no less significant is the response given by the municipality barely a year after its creation: the report of the recently created Commission of Public Works headed by the engineer Pastor del Valle considers that the proposal is correct in its diagnosis, and agrees with the need for the expansion plan, but rejects it precisely because the importance of that plan confirms that it should not be undertaken by "a private individual motivated by profit" but by the municipality.[161] The Commission of Public Works establishes in this way a

---

[161] Report of the Public Works Commission of April 13, 1881, in Archivo Histórico Municipal, box 12, 1881, Public Works Series.

principle that will guide public action from here until the definitive realization of the 1898–1904 plan: it does not have the instruments to carry out such an enterprise, again and again it unsuccessfully asks the Department of Engineers of the province—which does have them—the cession of the documents and collaboration in the realization of a new layout, tries to form its own resources to realize it, but meanwhile does not yield the will of absolute control on each street that is opened or each alignment that is approved, on each corner of its territory.[162]

A situation that we could define as a complicated impasse: a state that has as its model a strict control of expansion and its subjection to a predetermined layout but lacks the instruments to exercise control and design the layout. We are still at the beginning of the eighties; when in 1888 the new limits are defined and the proposals for subdivision of land, now urban, multiply, because what has multiplied is its potential value, the situation will no longer be one of impasse, but simply of chaos: on the basis of what criteria should a proposal for subdivision in the middle of the wastelands of Flores be approved or disapproved? How should it be aligned? As long as the definitive plan has not been drawn up—in a situation that report after report by Public Works officials keep describing as provisional—the criteria that prevail as common sense, as public ideology, let us say, are those of guaranteeing the greatest continuity with the preexisting layout or with the main roads and guaranteeing the regularity of the layouts, which were generally made as private commissions by engineers and surveyors trained in the tradition of the Topographic Department or directly by the municipal Public Works Office at the request of the owners. For example, on April 24, 1889, a company that owned the land surrounding the Nuevos Mataderos (New Slaughterhouses) presented a project for the layout of the "Town of New Chicago" drawn up by Carlos de Chapeaurouge, a prominent surveyor who in those years was commissioned to draw up public plans in several cities. The justification for the layout developed in the request for municipal approval is to demonstrate that the layout considers the directions of the outlines of the ring road Boulevard (General Paz Avenue), the roads to Cañuelas and Campana and the Mataderos (Slaughterhouses) project, trying the propose the largest number of streets to access them "and the greatest regularity in the blocks." Continuity and regularity: those are the keys to defend a layout project before the public authority. The approval of the municipality,

3

---

[162] Beccar Varela cites an ordinance of 1881: "Since that date, any sale of fraction of land belonging to another major, or the division into lots of land in the municipality, must be made with the intervention of the Municipality, for which they must submit the respective plan, raised by Surveyor or Engineer patent. The Municipality shall indicate on the said plans the streets to be opened according to the approved layouts and it shall be the obligation of the owner to transfer the land destined for the street free of charge," in *Torcuato de Alvear*, 239.

however, notes that such continuity is not the desired one for the future city since the layout is not the imaginary extension "in any direction" of the existing streets in the municipality. Nonetheless, as it is a large extension in which "a (very) important urban center" will soon be built, it should be approved with similar criteria, says the report, which has already been applied in cases such as Villa Catalinas, Villa Devoto, Chacra de White, Villa Ortúzar, etc.[163]

These were all important undertakings, capable of exerting strong economic and political pressure; the Public Works Commission saw them as inevitable evils in the face of the "provisional" absence of a general plan. Carlos María Morales, a key figure throughout these years as director of the Public Works Office, in a paper given to the Sociedad Científica Argentina (Argentine Scientific Society) toward the end of the century, describes the work of the commission that designed the 1898–1904 plan, and explains why the layout of
5   the city departs, outside the central part "delineated by Don Juan de Garay," from the regularity of the checkerboard:

> The cause of this irregularity is evidently due to the lack of a general layout project; as the owners of land requested the delineation of the streets that were to cross them, these layouts were made partially, without relating, in general, one to the other and obeying only the individual criterion of the employee in charge of the operation. It is enough to observe in the map of the city the layout followed in different neighborhoods, to be convinced that things have happened as mentioned above.

The definitive layout should have been made, precisely, "in order to overcome this inconvenience and adopt a uniform criterion."[164]

The commission of experts for the project of a definitive layout "of the streets, squares and avenues, according to which to proceed in the future," was formed by the municipality after the topographic survey of 1894 as "official plan of the municipality" (published in 1895), and its project was approved by
35   the City Council in November 1898, after being published as a plan, as we saw, in 1904.[165] That is to say, from 1898 to 1904 the municipal officials already had

---

[163] Archivo Histórico Municipal, file 10, 1889, Obras Públicas.

[164] The first quote is in Carlos María Morales, "Algunos datos relativos al trazado general del municipio," 305. The second, in Morales, *Las mejoras edilicias de Buenos Aires*, 5. Morales was born in Uruguay in 1860; he was a surveyor, civil engineer, and held a doctorate in physical and mathematical sciences; he was an honorary member of the Sociedad Central de Arquitectos and several times president of the Sociedad Científica Argentina. Toward the end of his career in Buenos Aires, he returned to Uruguay, where he became an outstanding member of the National Party and president of the Senate; he died in 1929.

[165] Carlos María Morales, "Estudio topográfico y edilicio de la ciudad de Buenos Aires," in *Censo General de Población, Comercio e Industrias de la Ciudad de Buenos Aires*, vol.

the instrument they needed for at least a decade, and could align lots according to a master plan, but the design of the future city that was born in that great extension of the pampa was not public; likewise, when it was published in 1904 it would be as an administrative document, devoid of the relevance and publicity of a "city project." And this opacity, which in any other bureaucratic act would not attract too much attention, in this case seems to me full of meaning. It is enough to compare the public diffusion through the press, even with advertising posters in the streets, that Alvear gave to the proposal for the reform of the Plaza de Mayo, or the later proposals of Joseph Bouvard in 1907 or the Noel Plan in 1925, with public polemics in all the newspapers, to notice the magnitude of the fact that the layout of the future of the city was handled from an absolutely "technical" perspective, in bureaucratic offices, outside of public debate and knowledge.

This opacity explains, in my opinion, the scarce transcendence that one of the most important measures taken in the history of the city, and one with the greatest future consequence, has had. Just as it was not a subject of debate for its contemporaries, the 1898–1904 plan never existed for later historiography as the product of a deliberate act of public design, but merely as a drawing of the city that resulted from private actions: what was not noticed was that it had designed with millimetric precision the outline of a complete city on the desert. But if this "technical" opacity could explain such an omission, it is the opacity itself, on the other hand, that must be interpreted.

---

1 (2° Censo municipal levantado en septiembre de 1904) (Buenos Aires: Compañía Sudamericana de Billetes de Banco, 1906). Members of the commission included Carlos Olivera (former member of the Department of Engineers and of the Council of Public Works), architect Juan Buschiazzo (former Director of Public Works of the Municipality), surveyors Juan Girondo and Eduardo Castex (former vice president of the Road Commission of the Province of Buenos Aires and former president of the Argentine Rural Society), Carlos Thays (Director of the Office of Parks and Walks of the Municipality), and Morales himself as director of the Office of Public Works. Most of them were members of the Sociedad Científica Argentina, at that time the seat of the main debates and initiatives regarding the city. The plan, in addition to the completion of the grid, gathered a set of specific projects for the city center that had been proposed in the last two administrations (Mayors Crespo and Seeber): the North–South Avenue 5 (the current 9 de Julio, proposed with a shorter route); four diagonals that would each depart from a corner of the future Palace of Congress; the Avenida de la Ribera from the Dársena Norte to Avenue Sarmiento (the current Costanera Norte, projected by Morales); the arrangement of the Paseo de Julio; the conversion into parks of the Chacarita lands, the Parque del Oeste (Rancagua), the Gran Parque del Sur (in the lands of La Tablada), and the park in the lands of Piñero (the future Parque Centenario). Additionally, it was proposed to clean up the Flores marshes, the Medrano stream and, as mentioned, the rectification of the Riachuelo.

In principle, it is worth insisting on the comparison with the publicity of
Alvear's actions. We said that he founded a model of mayor, as a modernizing
and reformist public man, and he set up a local technical bureaucracy with growing autonomy. Both things will continue to work, the model and the bureaucracy, but while the first will be part of an always unrealizable imaginary, the
second will guarantee the anonymous continuity of public management. The
permanence of Alvear's model as an unrealizable ideal cannot be explained—at
least not only—by the fact that his figure was irreplaceable, but also by political
reasons and the logic of urban management itself: Alvear governed the city for
about seven years (first as president of the Municipal Commission, between
1880 and 1882; from then until 1887, as mayor), most of the time during the
stable presidency of Roca, in whom he found great support for conflicting measures. During the following twelve years, nine mayors succeeded each other,
of which only two finished a two-year mandate, in a framework of political
instability, financial crisis, and budgetary shortage, in which the place of the
intendancy became one more box, and not one of the most important, in a
board commanded by the logics of the national political situation.[166]

---

[166] It is worth quickly enumerating the mayors to see the material impossibility, due
to the short time of each mandate, for them to carry out a memorable task: there was
barely enough time for them to present a project—impossible to put into practice—
and to get acquainted with the administrative twists and turns, when they succeeded in
doing so. Upon the departure of Alvear—who did not want to renew his mandate under
another president: in October 1886 Juárez Celman took office—Antonio Crespo was
appointed, remaining in office for a year and three months (May 1887–August 1888)
until he resigned. During the Juárez Celman presidency, two more mayors succeeded
each other: Guillermo Cranwell (August 1888–May 1889), who replaced Crespo as
president of the City Council and had to resign seven months later in the midst of a
public scandal due to suspicions about his handling of public finances; and Francisco
Seeber (May 1889–June 1890), who a year after his appointment traveled to Europe
to make financial arrangements for the municipality and while there resigned upon
learning of the 1890 Revolution. In August 1890, when President Carlos Pellegrini
assumed office, he appointed Alvear again in an attempt to return a degree of prestige to
the city government—the Minister of the Interior was again Roca; Alvear accepted from
Europe with great public success but set a record for the brevity of his administration:
he died before taking over the mayor's office. In December 1890, Francisco Bollini was
appointed in his place. He had to take office in the middle of a crisis and managed a
neat administration until he resigned due to the change of president in October 1892.
President Luis Sáenz Peña appointed a well-known man of the "cultural coalition of
the eighties," Miguel Cané, who lasted eight months. He was succeeded by Federico
Pinedo for a year and two months until he resigned (August 1894). And it was only then
that the first two mayors succeeded each other in their two-year terms: Emilio Bunge
(September 1894/1896), the first mayor to go through a presidential crisis without being
removed (in January 1895 Sáenz Peña resigned and José Evaristo Uriburu took over), and
Francisco Alcobendas (September 1896/1898), but both in a context of severe budgetary

In the same period, the technical bureaucracy—at least as far as the material management of the city is concerned—remains practically stable, consolidating teams of officials and a series of practices whose horizon necessarily seeks to gain a maximum of autonomy from the ephemeral political climate and the instability of the city's leadership. And this means, precisely, to look for the continuity of structural works that require long periods for their realization, to maintain the operation of initiated projects, to manage the slow administrative reforms, but with a low profile, in the sense that it is practically impossible, from that space of management, to carry out an ambitious—and therefore conflictive—plan of urban reform, that is to say, what is normally considered a Plan.[167] This is why the 1898–1904 plan is a *plano* (map) and not a *Plan* (project): it is proposed as a solution to an administrative and managerial problem, and not as a city project.

The authors of the plan were evidently aware of this difference and accounted for it within the limitations with which they had to carry it out: "the commission had to respect the existing layouts, improving only what could be corrected in order to make work practical and feasible," was Morales's assessment.[168] From the point of view of a plan, the "existing layouts" remained irrelevant in comparison with the virgin surface on which the commission laid   35, 5

---

restrictions. Finally, Roca, who became president again in 1898, appointed the mayor who would serve two terms, Adolfo Bullrich, who achieved four uninterrupted years in office. It would be necessary to wait eight more years until another mayor, Joaquín de Anchorena, managed to stay so long in office. It is true that it could be argued the other way around: as no mayor was able to reach the level of a figure like Alvear; they all succumbed to the obstacles of management or politics. However, I think the example of Cané, a figure of undoubted prestige, is demonstrative of the place that the mayor's office had come to occupy: eight months after the beginning of his administration he was summoned as a minister to the national cabinet. It seems to me that, beyond Alvear, Bullrich, and Anchorena, this issue of time is not unrelated to the mayors with the most notable works during the period of the conservative mayorships: the times of the city, the drawn-out periods in which public works can be carried out, are incompatible with ephemeral governments.

[167] Among other administrative measures, in 1892 the Reglamento General de Reparticiones was given, which reorganized the municipal organization chart, and the same year the cadastre was started; in 1895 the first municipal population census was carried out. The continuity in long-term structural works is remarkable in the framework of the incessant change of mayors: the filling of La Boca or the Avenida de Mayo itself, for example. While these ephemeral mayors have left few marks on the city and the urban culture, figures such as Blot, Morales, Thays, etc. formed a management team that developed some central topics for the development of the technical and professional ideology—mainly in engineering—in the twentieth century.

[168] In "Estudio topográfico y edilicio de la ciudad de Buenos Aires." With "the existing layouts" he refers to the preexisting settlements of Flores and Belgrano and to the partial subdivisions already approved by the municipality before the existence of the plan.

out the grid for the whole capital, but how to make them compatible with the idea of the Plan, which precisely requires a great capacity for maneuver on all pre-existences? The plan of 1898–1904 carries out a work of embroidery that seeks to avoid all conflict: its focus is not on the reform of the existing city but on the completion of the future city. For example, the plan incorporates a few residues of a Plan: the North–South Avenue, a long-standing project, a riverside avenue, and four diagonals that should start from the Congress (not yet built) crossing the whole city, as part of a more ambitious project of diagonals carried out during the administration of Intendente Crespo. However, Morales's diagnosis of their feasibility was more than cautious—and let's point out that he was presenting his diagnosis at one of those international congresses that officials attend to show the "progress" of their cities: the two projected diagonals that start from the plaza toward the southeast and northwest, that is, toward the consolidated part of the city, "perhaps [...] will not be carried out"; the other two, which start where the city opens out onto the pampa, "I believe that they will become a beautiful reality [...] because they affect less valuable lands and buildings"; and the North–South Avenue would be easy to carry out because it follows the criteria of the Avenida de Mayo of crossing the heart of the blocks, but "provided that the Honorable Congress passes the law requested by the municipality and without which it will be very difficult for this great work [...] to be carried out," Morales warns, when the legal, legislative and economic conflict caused by the Avenida de Mayo has not yet ended.[169] It is evident that a part of the opacity to which we were referring must be linked to the fact that the Commission visualizes the plan as a compromise solution, and that it cannot proudly show the achievements of a Plan, in spite of the fact that, in retrospect, the magnitude of what was "realistically" carried out by the plan reduces those attempts of a Plan to a simple empty gesture.

Now, this is the plan that marked the entire future of the capital city throughout the annexed territory. Does its administrative character, its bureaucratic opacity, its *patchwork* realism really indicate that it is not a city project? This question is crucial to advance new perspectives in our concern to characterize this "conservative reformism." My hypothesis is that precisely insofar as it cannot be a Plan, what appears most strongly in the plan, being the remainder of its "concessions," what resists, is the series of assumptions that are not discussed: continuity, regularity, homogeneity, integration. That is why we must speak, in those years, of a reformist role of the expansion plan. In the absence of more advanced technical alternatives at a time of political instability and economic crisis, the layout of the plan was the mechanism with which the state covered its control reflex, as a guarantee of income but also as public support of a potential urbanism. The plan functions as a promise of equity and integration, by the simple procedure of supposing, in the face of the plurality of actors that

---

[169] In *Las mejoras edilicias de Buenos Aires*, 6.

intervene in the realization of the city, a common, public board that seeks to ensure the future communication of multiple and uncontrollable private operations. The plan, thus, puts into action the tradition of public reform because it is the only thing it cannot fail to do amid the compromises with existing reality; but it is a tradition that has become a method of state: the plan is the product of a "reformist machine."

But perhaps the strict meaning of this "promise of equity" to which I refer, as something implicit in the urban structure itself, can best be seen in comparison with other expansion processes. Mexico City and Santiago de Chile, for example, are two opposing paradigms of growth, each showing alternative modalities to that of Buenos Aires and its effects. In Mexico, metropolitan expansion took place through extra-urban *colonies*, carried out mainly in the first decades of the century by private developers with direct access to the levers of power (the "portafolieros," often local front men for foreign investors), without any broader public plan in which these colonies were forced to be inserted and without any public control over their layouts. In Santiago, on the other hand, Benjamín Vicuña Mackenna's 1873 plan had laid out a "camino de cintura" (beltway) within which public authorities established their rules; but, unlike the successive Buenos Aires "boulevards de circunvalación" (beltway boulevards) projected by Rivadavia and Alvear as well as the definitive one of 1888, such a beltway, far from incorporating everything that really existed around the traditional city, was proposed as a differentiating cut—according to the author's statement—between "the proper city subject to the charges and benefits of the municipality, and the suburbs, for which a separate, less onerous and less active regime should exist." The "proper, enlightened, opulent, Christian" city should thus be opposed to the suburbs, "an immense sewer of infection and vice, crime, and pestilence." "The proper city," Vicuña Mackenna wraps up, "needs to separate itself from the city of the grasslands."[170] In one case due to the absence of public policies and in the other due to their segregating nature, structural barriers were imposed from the beginning in both cities between social sectors, separating the city of *one's own* from that of *others*, the *legal* from the *illegal*.

The obligatory reference, on the contrary, to a public gesture of the magnitude of the 1898–1904 plan, is the already mentioned 1811 plan of the New   40
York Commissioners: the grid that traced the expansion of all Manhattan when

---

[170] See Benjamín Vicuña Mackenna, *La transformación de Santiago. Notas e indicaciones respetuosamente sometidas a la Ilustre Municipalidad al Supremo Gobierno y al Congreso Nacional por el Intendente de Santiago* (Santiago: Imprenta de la Librería del Mercurio, July 1872). On Santiago, see also Armando de Ramón, *Santiago de Chile. Historia de una sociedad urbana* (Madrid: MAPFRE, 1992); on Mexico, Jorge H. Jiménez Muñoz, *La traza del poder. Historia de la política y los negocios urbanos en el Distrito Federal, de sus orígenes a la desaparición del Ayuntamiento (1824–1928)* (Mexico City: Dédalo-Códex, 1993).

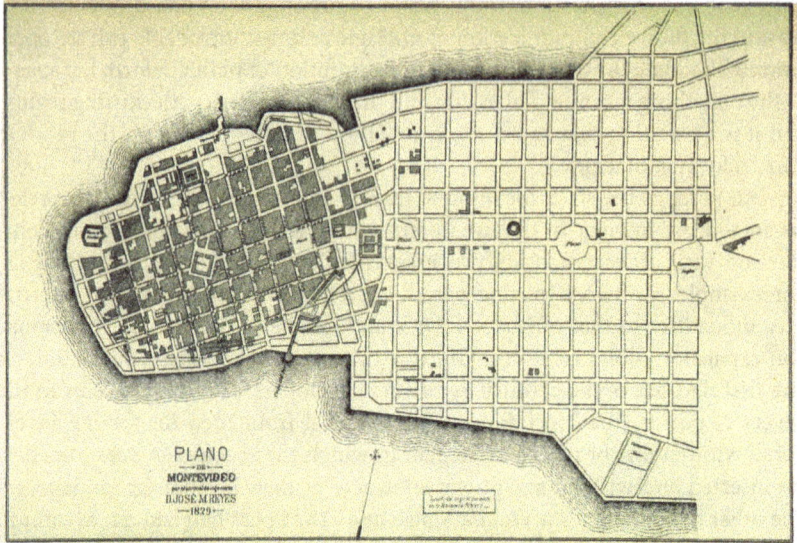

Figure 38. José María Reyes, *Plan of Montevideo*, 1829. Mechanical Curator Collection, British Library Commons. The New City is placed outside the city walls (the dark area of the peninsula is the old city grid; the New City is defined by lighter areas).

Figure 39. *Plan of the City of Montevideo*, 1889. Plan of the "Ciudad Novísima" (Newest City) structured through "Boulevard de propios" (Boulevard Artigas), which surrounds the city, seeking to include in the regularity of its layout a great part of what preexisted in what was then the suburb.

the old Dutch city on the lower tip of the island, lower Manhattan, was built.[171] In nineteenth-century Latin America, in turn, it is only possible to homologate the plan of Buenos Aires with but a few cases, such as the layout of Artigas Boulevard in Montevideo in 1878, although it defines a smaller area than the extension of Buenos Aires (leaving out some suburbs already developed), and although the grid designed for the "Ciudad Novísima" must compete with the pre-existence of many more layouts, which explains the peculiar cut of some Montevideo neighborhoods.   39

But these two cases lead us to the other theme present in the 1898–1904 plan of Buenos Aires: the choice of the checkered layout as the ideal universal grid for all the new layouts. Although it is true that such a choice can be linked to the "regularizing" engineering tradition, by the end of the century urban design had incorporated much more sophisticated models than the mere continuation of the grid, as the example of La Plata locally proved. In fact, a negative opinion of the grid was already completely hegemonic toward the end of the century, also among the technicians of the municipal teams. Synthetically, they gave continuity to Sarmiento's criteria, although the disdain for Spanish heritage that had been typical then was no longer common. For example, Alberto Martínez—another official with a long career in the municipality—criticizing in 1887 Garay's checkerboard, no longer explains it as a sign of Spanish "lack of foresight" and "unculture," to which Sarmiento used to refer, but justifies it insofar as that layout would have sought to answer "the tortuous, narrow, and capricious" character of the medieval layout of the European cities from which the colonizers departed.[172] That is to say, the grid is criticized from the perspective of the Baroque urban paradigm that endured from the middle of the century (wide avenues, diagonals, roundabouts), but is considered a lesser   26

49, 50, 51

---

[171] One of the arguments of the members of the commission that drew up this plan is suggestive for our case: "To some it may be a matter of surprise, that the whole Island has not been laid out as a City; to others, it may be a subject of merriment, that the Commissioners [the report is written in the third person] have provided space for a greater population than is collected at any sport on this side of China. They have in this respect been governed by the shape of the ground. It is not improbable that considerable numbers may be collected at Haerlem (*sic*), before the high hills to the southward of it shall be built upon as a City; and it is improbable, that (for centuries to come) the grounds north of Haerlem Flat will be covered with houses. To have come short of the extent laid out, might therefore have defeated just expectation, and to have gone further, might have furnished materials to the pernicious spirit of speculation." See "Commissioner's Remarks," in William Bridges, *Map of the City of New York and Island of Manhattan* (New York: self-published, 1811), 30. Quote originally drawn from Reps, *The Making of Urban America*.   40

[172] Alberto Martínez, "Estudio topográfico de Buenos Aires," *Censo General de Población, Edificación, Comercio e Industrias de la Ciudad de Buenos Aires* (surveyed in 1887) (Buenos Aires: Compañía Sudamericana de Billetes de Banco, 1889), 1: 67.

evil compared to completely irregular layouts. These, however, would soon be vindicated by the picturesque paradigm, setting the tone of the hegemonic climate of urban ideas from the first decade of the twentieth century, in which the criticism of the grid will be relentless in terms of the search for a model of a less "monotonous" and more "varied" city. Variations and superimpositions that demonstrate another of the central themes in the problem of "influences": what did travelers actually see in European cities that they so wanted to imitate? In the nineteenth century we can only see the layouts that sought to regularize, modernize, and expand the medieval city, whose "charms" could only be discovered when they became (especially through the work of Camillo Sitte) urban theory.[173]

What persisted of Sarmiento at the end of the century was not so much the cultural matrix of the repudiation by which the grid was the materialization of the anomic threat of the pampa, the deterministic metaphor of the plains, but functional and economic arguments. The functional criticism of the grid, because it lengthens distances, which implies as an unfailing counterpart to the proposal of diagonals that "more rationally" unite different points of the city. The economic criticism, in turn, unfolded in two lines of argumentation: on the one hand, the "irrational" extension of infrastructure enforced by the checkerboard; on the other hand, the "irrationality," once more, of the square module, in terms of the loss of rental value of the center of the block. The interesting thing about this argument is that it relativizes what will be the most recurrent argument against the grid throughout the twentieth century: the accusation against its direct and exclusive functionality to speculation, as the most favorable modality for the exploitation of land rent. As we saw, in order to criticize the checkerboard, Sarmiento took the example of the New York grid, whose rectangular rather than square blocks avoid the economic "inconvenience" of the absence of value at the end of the lots, and consequently proposed "to divide the blocks from north to south or from east to west by streets of twenty

9

---

[173] In 1904, when the plan is published, Morales himself will review his own grid layout from the perspective of picturesque criticism (since the beginning of the century, Sitte's text was known in Buenos Aires in its French translation, and already in 1897, the *Revista Técnica* had published lectures by Cornelius Gurlit, one of its main disseminators). Making a very interesting re-reading of the role played in the layout by "pre-existences" (roads and previous layouts) to which it was necessary to submit and that very shortly before had seemed to him the main limitation of the resulting plan, Morales now considers that those pre-existences allowed the plan to have some of the irregularities that are celebrated in European cities as their urban beauty. Within a few years, under the influence of changes in theory, the "obstacles" had been transformed into vehicles of greater "beauty." See Carlos María Morales, "Estudio topográfico edilicio de la ciudad de Buenos Aires."

Figure 40. William Bridges after John Randel, *This map of the city of New York and island of Manhattan as laid out by the Commissioners appointed by the Legislature.... 1811*. The Miriam and Ira D. Wallach Division of Art, Prints and Photographs: Print Collection, The New York Public Library Digital Collections.

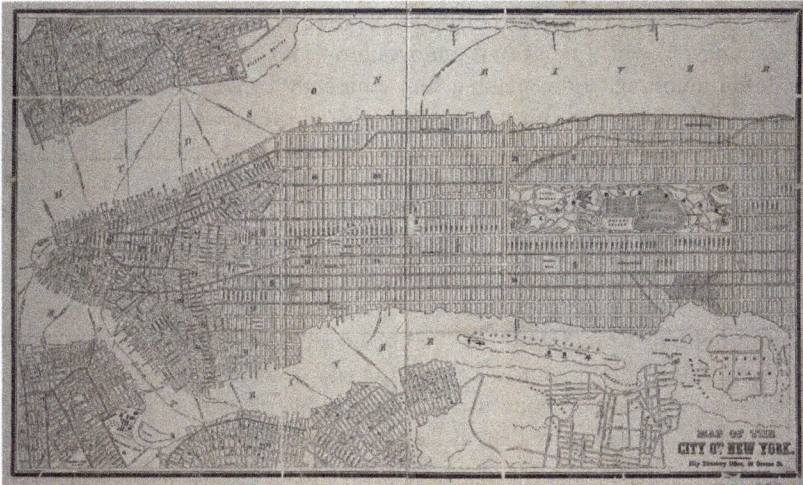

Figure 41. *Map of New York City South of 118th Street*, 1858–62. The consolidation of the grid showing the layout of Central Park. Lionel Pincus and Princess Firyal Map Division, The New York Public Library Digital Collections.

varas (16 meters)."[174] The undifferentiated grid does not favor, for example, the definition of industrial areas, which by the end of the century required the availability of much larger and more flexible surfaces: the grid ratifies and prescribes the bureaucratic and above all residential character of the capital city.

Because the technicians who drew up the 1898–1904 plan were aware of these economic criticisms of the grid, it is necessary to approach the design of the Buenos Aires grid from the perspective that it sought a rationality different from the economic one and a homogeneity that could not be homologated exclusively with the market. The grid had a double connotation: to generate a uniform framework, in which not every speculative operation was possible, and to lay out the guidelines for a type of integrative social distribution. That is why I think it should be read, rather than as an instrument of speculation, as a means of expansion of public space throughout the city, as a means of social integration of the new popular sectors to the heart of the city. It was intended, of course, as a way of guiding an agitated society toward the ideal of a community of small landowners; but not only that. In his project to solve the problem of workers' housing, Domingo Selva linked, precisely in 1904, both aspects. On the one hand, small property, because "it contributes to the desire to spend it with a certain ease, it links him [the worker] to the generous soil that houses him, it makes him a quasi-citizen, no longer indifferent to the pains and joys of the country in which he lives; it removes him from any misunderstood party or trade union agitation, making him eminently conservative." But, on the other hand, along with this conservative idea of the role of property—which ratifies the belonging of this "technical reformism" to the political horizon of "conservative reformism"—Selva takes as obvious the conditions for the location of these "quasi-citizen" workers in the city: a search for integration that discards the "garden suburb" models already in vogue—whose isolation favors social stratification—and that presupposes the maximum continuity between the different urban and social sectors—"for their work, for the means of communication, for a hundred other causes," he says in the sentence with which we open this section—coinciding with the way in which the state contemporarily sought a homogeneous distribution of public services in the territory.[175] A search for homogeneity that, at least at an initial moment, is also a search for social leveling, one more strategy of *induced citizenship* put into practice in public institutions of reform such as the school or the public hospital, and that is at the base of a series of processes of socialization, but also of consolidation of the institutions themselves, such as the electoral reforms that take place between the beginning of the century and 1912. In this way, the grid, as a reformist machine, metaphorizes and materializes a variety of expressions of

---

[174] "El plano de la ciudad de Buenos Aires," *El Nacional*, June 23, 1856, in *Obras completas (LD)*, XLII:30.

[175] Selva, "La habitación higiénica para el obrero."

that ambition of rational and equitable universalization of public rights typical of the reformist cycle.

But let's look at some of its peculiarities at the end of the century. The 1890s have been stigmatized by the *stock market syndrome*: speculation and public corruption, social ascent without cohesion, anomie and lack of control. It is at least unsettling to imagine in those same *babelic* years this group of technicians and bureaucrats "silently" designing the outline of a plan that embodies, on the one hand, the attempt to domesticate a convulsed and heterogeneous society, but that, on the other hand, in that same movement produces the main material gesture to favor the most complete realization of citizenship; the necessary conjunction of public space and market realized "from above." Returning then to our question about the projectual quality of the 1898–1904 plan: possibly it is not a project, in the sense that the notion of project involves a certain idea of will located in specific subjects and in an individualized and punctual moment. But then perhaps it is convenient to think of the plan as a structure or, better still, as a device, taking up the inspiration (although, as is evident, not all of its implications) with which Foucault has posed the notion of *dispositif*: the plan can be thought of as the incarnation of a *reform device* insofar as it brings into play, condenses, a sum of practices and conventions formed over time by a collective of diverse actors, and at the same time has the capacity—impossible to notice for its authors and contemporaries—to define toward the future a dense mesh—and in this case it is much more than a metaphor—of conditions and consequences that will tend to continue working according to their own logic, beyond specific actors. It is, we could say, in abuse, a reformism without a subject.

2. For a System of Parks: Center and Border

> The Patricios Park in the Corrales had at one o'clock in the afternoon a huge crowd of young and old. In the distance, a curtain of smoldering smoke indicates the burning of garbage. Nowhere as there, is it necessary to purify the air with good vegetation.[176]
>
> –Chronicle of *El Diario*, on the inauguration of Parque de los Patricios, 1902

From the small lawn that in 1902 anticipates and promises the future gardens of Parque de los Patricios, the group of people attending the inauguration perceives, "there in the distance," the smoldering smoke of fire. The counterpoint between the Brooklyn Cemetery and smoke-crowned New York that had struck Sarmiento more than fifty years earlier is almost exactly reproduced. The smoke here is not the product of that "infernal machine" that is the modern metropolis, but of one of its peripheral excrescences, the burning of

46

---

[176] *El Diario* (Buenos Aires) September 11, 1902, evening edition.

garbage; the motif of rejection has shifted from the modern city as such to its unhealthy suburbs, but the cycle has closed and the park as a hygienic motif, converted into a universal formula of urban reformism, has made its irruption into the city.

The new reference to Sarmiento is not accidental: in Buenos Aires the cycle keeps the memory of each of its steps, as counterpoint or reflection that seeks to reproduce the symbolic function of the park with the thoroughness of a rite. Adolfo Bullrich, the mayor who inaugurated the Parque de los Patricios at the opposite end of the city, is the same man who four years earlier, at the beginning of his administration, had dynamited the Caserón de Rosas—an isolated and already disfigured remnant of the Tyranny in Palermo—to erect in its place Rodin's statue of Sarmiento.[177] The new park, in turn, rises over other barbaric remains: those of the Old Corrales del Sur, the slaughterhouses, like the Caserón also linked to that past and to the nature of the pampa that the city must leave behind and outside it. Appealing to an identical act of exorcism, barbarism is buried under the greenery. And, to leave no room for interpretation, the inauguration of the new park in the south of the city takes place on September 11, the anniversary of Sarmiento's death, the day of the "feast of the tree," later "of the teacher," again raising the analogy between the city, greenery, and education.

67, 68
69, 70

In this tree festival of 1902, five thousand pupils of the San Cristóbal School Council planted sixteen hundred trees as the starting point of the park that was to sanitize the most unhealthy area of the city, but also to offer a normalizing mantle to the neighbors of a neglected and marginalized area, whom the smoke from the burning, "on the rare occasions they come to the center makes them immediately recognizable as inhabitants of San Cristóbal by the acrid smell they carry with them."[178] The park against polluted air; like public education, against traditional culture and social segregation, but also against deviant behavior: other children attend the festival as involuntary protagonists: inmates of the Male Correctional Prison will be in charge of turning, with their work, the old slaughterhouses into a park, to be "regenerated" by the green. According to the inaugural words of the reformist mayor, "these children, more wretched than guilty, also receive the fruits of this park. Their instincts, their perversity [...] will be replaced by work habits, by the

---

[177] Sarmiento did not agree with the decadence of the building, "remarkable and worthy of preservation, as for its historical importance the den of Louis XI," and complained, in 1885, that "they have made [of the Caserón] a dovecote, for rooms, closing the arches of the gallery, showing the foreigner who visits Palermo [...] no longer the dwelling of Rosas [...] but the barbarism of the generation that has succeeded him, exempt even like the Indians from all notion and architectural modesty," in "Arquitectura y paisajes isleños," in *Obras completas (LD)*, XLII:181.

[178] *El Diario* (Buenos Aires) September 15, 1902.

instruction of arboriculture and they will become useful citizens for country and family."[179]

From the smoke of industry to the smoke of rubbish; from the soldiers who did their topographical apprenticeship in the park to the children-inmates who must be regenerated by the green; from the north to the south of the city; from the search for a new green heart for a new city to the sanitization of its squalid borders. Against the continuous background of a series of long-lasting motifs, contrasts, and displacements stand out: a system of identities and ideological symmetries is established between Palermo and the parks of the turn of the century, at the same time as a large part of their more specific purposes and meanings as instruments of urban intervention are inverted. That is to say, a cultural line and an ideological use of the park in the city is reinforced, while its urban function is inverted.

The park is one of the new urban artifacts in which the most reformist ambitions are deposited. Thus, unlike the grid, we must speak here of a reformism *with* actors, of a discursively elaborated reformism that is supported and projected in the park, giving it an unparalleled semantic density. Although these discourses should not hide from us the fact that, at the same time, the park is the urban artifact that—at least in Buenos Aires—is most active in the *silent* reorganization of modalities of land occupation. In a city without great traditions of urbanistic thought and without refined public instruments of intervention, the park will also be one of the mechanisms of qualitative transformation of the city through which public authorities will carry out a progressive experience of metropolitan management. The park will thus become, from Palermo to the parks of the new century, a privileged instrument of punctual, "corrective" interventions in the course of a laissez-faire strategy in which the limits to reform make themselves felt with juridical and ideological force. But, for all the same reasons, the park becomes, in turn, an always incomplete ideal: an instrument that in its explicit objectives always lags behind the "reality" of the city, but whose "silent" effects are not always acknowledged.

The first thing to analyze is how the park functions, the kind of public space it forms in fin-de-siècle Buenos Aires. Unlike the grid, which is of obscure filiation and whose elaboration is modestly hidden, the park is one of those urban artifacts with a lineage, incorporated within a closed device of discourses already completely elaborated and available, from which it is impossible to escape at the time. In this modernizing tempest that then seems unstoppable because each of its pieces infallibly refers to the others as in a clockwork mechanism that is assembled dizzyingly under the eyes of its protagonists, with their complete certainty that the well-oiled operation will cause a definitive transformation of society, in this whirlwind of progress, few

47

[179] "Discurso del Intendente Bullrich," *El Diario* (Buenos Aires) September 11, 1902.

artifacts are so saturated with meaning, interpretations, and diagnoses as the park. Sarmiento presages with modernist fervor that movement, that coincidence less fantastic for being inevitable, of the events and transformations that lead to the spread of progress:

> There is never a useful idea in the world that, abandoned to possibility and counseled by the feeling of goodness, does not move like rain or dew to fertilize the whole extension of the country where that idea reaches [...]. The square of San Luis is, I was saying, planted with trees. When I visited the hidden city of Santa Fe, I found it planted with trees; Mendoza's was planted with trees; Tucumán's was planted with trees; and those of Santiago de Chile and Buenos Aires were already planted with trees or are covered with trees from one year to the next. What Government, what Congress has ordered the planting of trees in public squares in all parts of America? I will offer a hint. When I left Europe in 1848, I left all the nations that compose it, planting with trees public roads, boulevards, and squares that were not yet shaded, and it is astonishing how remote San Luis, San Juan, and Tucumán follow a movement impressed upon mankind by the progress of public hygiene.[180]

But the fact that in the case of the park the device is inseparable from its discourses means that, along with the trees, the San Luis Plaza is populated by interpretations and diagnoses of "public hygiene" that were made for metropolises with radically different problems. If we do not want to produce either a history of the "progress" or a symmetrical one of the "blunders" of a peripheral urban modernization, what remains to be seen in the theme of the park is that mismatch, the functioning of a device that solidly links typology and discourses in cities and societies in which the processes they responded to were not yet activated.

That is why this new artifact, this new component of the mechanism, must be installed with instructions for its use in the modern metropolis. It is not only a problem of transculturation. The parks of central cities also have tour guides, like the one Sarmiento was offered in the Brooklyn Cemetery: they serve to ratify the cultural character of the natural promenade, to convert its entire enclosure into a museum in which natural beauties and monuments can be enjoyed equally as works of art. The difference is, as always, only of degree: in our city parks, the guides will additionally be conceived, as *instruction manuals* of a future metropolis. Such is the one drawn up by Mayor Vicuña Mackenna in 1874 for the Santa Lucía hill promenade in Santiago, and such is the one proposed by Juan de Cominges in 1882 for Palermo.[181] The park gates (Portones

---

[180] "Quinta Normal," San Juan, September 7, 1862, in *Obras completas (LD)*, XXI:159.
[181] See *El Santa Lucía. Guía popular y breve descripción de este Paseo para el uso de las personas que lo visiten* (Santiago: Imprenta de la Librería del Mercurio, 1874), and

de Palermo, as they were known) have similar implications: the construction of the enclosure within which that anticipatory ritual could be carried out. In Parisian parks, the gates and the continuous system of decoration with the city (street lamps, drains, benches, drinking fountains) are the symbols of urbanity and denaturalization that transform the park into a metropolitan unit, into a structural component of the city; in Palermo, on the other hand, the gates not only separate the park from the pampa as culture from nature, but also separate it from the real city to link it to an ideal city of which this closed system of decoration—imported with difficulty and effort by Sarmiento and the subsequent park commissions—is intended to be an anticipation and guide.

It is the combination of Palermo's frontier character and the anticipatory virtues that are attributed to it with respect to the future of the city that explains the other mismatch: the full adoption of French gardening even though at that time the prevailing ideological discourse on greenery was Anglo-Saxon. The needs are different. Olmsted could affirm in relation to New York of 1870 that

> the park should, as far as possible, complement the town. Openness is the only thing that you cannot get in the buildings. Picturesqueness you can get. Let your buildings be as picturesque as your artists can make them. This is the beauty of a town. Consequently, the beauty of the park should be the other. It should be the beauty of the fields, of the meadow, the prairie, of the green pastures, and the still waters.[182]

13

Here, on the other hand, it is not a question of complement but of replacement, and the French park is the most irresistibly urban at the same time as its form of urbanism, that of Paris, is the most irresistible. Having lost the original battle to install a productive center in Palermo, and having subordinated all initial proposals to the dominant function as "park," the plan will follow the manual by Jean-Charles Adolphe Alphand—Haussmann's gardener—which, as we have seen, already processes the three models that are recognized in the origin of the public park: the landscaped park of the eighteenth century, with its idea of the aesthetic fruition of nature; the botanical garden, with its pedagogic impulses later to be continued by zoos and museums; and the Vauxhall-type pleasure garden, with its ludic prolongation in amusement parks and sports facilities.[183] It is not in the layout, then, where we can expect original

Juan de Cominges, "Informe sobre Palermo," (1882), republished in *Revista del Jardín Zoológico de Buenos Aires,* (May 1916), 40ff.
[182] F. Law Olmsted, "Public Parks and the Enlargement of Towns," *American Social Science Association* (Cambridge: Riverside Press, 1870). Republished in Nathan Glazer and Mark Lilla, *The Public Face of Architecture: Civic Culture and Public Space* (New York and London: The Free Press, 1987), 246.
[183] See the classic book by G. F. Chadwick, *The Park and the Town: Public Landscape in the 19th and 20th Centuries* (London: The Architectural Press, 1966).

contributions from Palermo, both in the initial works of Jules Dormal and in the later extensions of Charles Thays, the designer of most Buenos Aires parks during his long tenure as head of the General Directorate of Parks and Walks (1891–1914).

43

From the beginning, the park's execution met with enormous difficulties in carrying out engineering works, ornamentation, and gardening, but also in society incorporating the new uses it proposed. In 1882, within the framework of the general impulse for the construction of parks that Alvear's administration produced, Juan de Cominges would make, through an imaginary walk, the ideal enumeration of what there should be in Palermo, gathering ecumenically all the models and all the aspirations with which the role of the park in society was charged: from mixed public toilets to a cable car, from funfair (with roller coaster and balloon ride) to theaters and popular choirs, from aquariums and ponds for fish farming to gymnasiums and sports parks (with national games, such as the *sortija*), from dance halls for "seamstresses and students" to productive orchards and dairies, from zoos and botanical gardens with a great display of picturesque architecture to quiet meadows for walking, from the "great aristocratic hall" that is Sarmiento Avenue to the national immigrant clubs and societies.[184] An ecumenical ambition from which financial issues are not absent, not only for the park—unfeasible until then—but, through it, for the city: "It is necessary that Buenos Aires be an amusing city that attracts the passenger," wrote Pellegrini in 1883, for they "are generally rich and spenders, and it is necessary to give them something for their money. Museums, promenades, theaters, gardens, etc., etc., become money for commerce and prosperity for the city."[185] The very formation of executive park commissions was the international solution of the moment to solve the problem of management and financing, but in Buenos Aires, the one formed by Sarmiento and Pellegrini (the names themselves indicate the initial importance given to it) was not very successful in obtaining disinterested contributions from society.

35
20, 21

The creation of Recoleta Park, carried out by Alvear in the eighties, was the first important change to affect Palermo, since it incorporated it into a more complex and varied circuit that is part of the city. It must be recalled that Recoleta was one of Alvear's three perimetrical parks, one at each cardinal point, and that the fate of each is emblematic of the complex relationship between the theoretical homogenizing aspirations of public authority and the reality of the city's development to which it contributed: while the Parque del Sur—the Gardens of the Convalescence—remain restricted in function to serve as the inner

---

[184] Juan de Cominges, "Informe sobre Palermo." Cominges was an official of the National Directorate of Agriculture to whom the report was entrusted. I am grateful to the kindness of Pablo Pschepiurca for allowing me to consult this report.

[185] Carlos Pellegrini, letter to Torcuato de Alvear, London, July 18, 1883, in Beccar Varela, *Torcuato de Alvear*, 300–302.

lung of an area of services and seclusion, completely marginal to urban life, the Paseo de la Recoleta, with its foothills toward Palermo, becomes the meeting place and the space of representation par excellence for the Buenos Aires bourgeoisie, giving a precise direction to the modernization of the city.

Although, as we anticipated, whether that modernization to the north should or should not be aristocratic was not yet evident in those years. When Sarmiento imagines the expansion to the north, he follows what seems to be an undeniable economic logic: in all cities real estate development has to do with pre-existences in which economic value and the prestige of power are combined; if we follow the logic of good businessmen, Sarmiento reasons, we will understand what is the "natural" sense of the expansion of Buenos Aires.[186] But that must apply for society as a whole: even if the most luxurious residences are located next to the park, because that luxury only encourages the aesthetic education of those less favored by fortune. And we can say the same of Alvear, as a counterpart of the evident imbalance with which he promotes some works in the north: besides his already analyzed search for equilibrium in the general plan (the boulevard of Avenida de Mayo, to begin with), even his impulse to the north is so contradictory that in its own wake he was led to place there the first working-class barrio of the city. [187]

The fact is that these artifacts—the park, in the first place, and the urban expansion it would produce—had not been conceived as a mere reproduction of existing social practices. As we have seen, in its own layout the new park was called upon to impose new uses, to which the upper classes of society would not easily yield: rather than exercise, Sarmiento complained bitterly, people seem to prefer "to exercise the gaze of others, making them admire their horses and carriages."[188] Exercise or looks: it is always, as Avellaneda had lucidly stated in the parliamentary discussions, a spectacle, the "public spectacle" in which "all conditions disappear." But this contradiction between the spectacle of sight (the exchange of hats in the park) and the spectacular transformation of the old into the new on the leveling stage of air and light is a conflict that has always been present since the formation of the modern park. During his stay in London,

44
45

[186] Sarmiento says, in his preaching against the old city: "The art of buying land in big cities is a profound art that takes into account the history of the country, the course of events, and individual action. We saw in Chile a wide stone sidewalk that went out of the city, and we said to ourselves: a minister has lived here. Yes, we were told, it goes to the Quinta de Portales. Cities are like water; the current follows the inclination of the plane. Buenos Aires slopes to the north, a little north-northwest, and the talent is in knowing the *agachadas* (schemes) to get in the way." In "Un gran boulevard para Buenos Aires," *El Censor*, December 20, 1885, in *Obras completas (LD)*, XLII:237.
[187] The first working-class neighborhood was built according to Juan Buschiazzo's plans in 1887–89, on Larrea, Melo, Azcuénaga, and Las Heras streets; see, among others, Samuel Gache, *Les logements ouvriers à Buenos Aires* (Paris, 1899).
[188] "El parque," *El Nacional*, October 12, 1882, in *Obras completas (LD)*, XLII:78.

Hippolyte Taine had taken it upon himself to highlight the peculiar, modern use of English parks as a critical counterpoint to the ways in which the Parisian upper classes enjoyed greenery: the Amazons "come here (to London parks) not to be seen, but to take the air."[189] It is here that the English example weighs heavily: against the French tradition of reinforcing the representative character of the park, as a "theater of regulated behavior," all the promoters of the renewal of the park's uses in the city will turn almost exclusively to the English model in their explicit search to produce a direct, physical relationship with a "natural" environment, and to affect the life of all social sectors.[190] That is why in 1882 Vicente Quesada considered it appropriate to hide behind the authority of a "North American traveler" to criticize the scarce use of the park:

> The Parque 3 de Febrero is a very good walk [but] it is lonely every day, and only on Sundays and holidays is there a notable turnout in excellent carria- ges with expensive trunks. But why aren't there people every day? These rides are not mere luxury, it is hygiene that demands going out to breathe the fresh air. These walks cannot be taken as a mere exhibition of good taste; it is necessary to think that ladies, young people, children, and men of all ages and conditions, need rest and distraction [...]. The obesity of ladies has its origin in the lack of exercise: young girls do not acquire the develop- ment that nature demands for the same reason, and if children are pale, it is because they live shut up in their houses.[191]

Once again, we face a question about the type of reformism that comes into play in the park: Can the reformism of philanthropic hygienism be easily separated from the reformism with which elites target the bourgeoisie itself? On the one hand, we find the typical discourse deriving from Bentham that we saw in the London *Report* of 1833 and that is introduced in Buenos Aires as the ultimate meaning of the park, from the very beginning, giving rise to a family of discourses that will not cease to feed itself until the reality of the city and society adjust to it. Although then it will not be easy to understand what in

---

[189] Hippolyte Taine, *Notes on England* (London: W. Isbister and Co., 1874), 24, quoted in Monica Charlot, "El spleen de los exiliados franceses," in Monica Charlot and Roland Marx, eds., *Londres 1851-1901. La era victoriana o el triunfo de las desigualdades* (Madrid: Alianza, 1993), 60.

[190] The definition of the park as a "theater of regulated behavior" is drawn from Choay, "Haussmann et le système des espaces verts parisiens," 83–89. It is inspired by César Daly, for whom the urban spectacle of the park is equivalent to that of an opera in which everyone plays his part: "both spectator and actor must conform to the rules of staging." Quoted from Daly, *Revue générale de l'architecture*, XXI (1863): 249.

[191] Lucy Dowling (Vicente Quesada), "La ciudad de Buenos Aires. Apuntes de una viajera," originally published in the *Nueva Revista de Buenos Aires* in 1882 and republished in Gálvez (Vicente G. Quesada), *Memorias de un viejo*, 65.

those discourses is generic reiteration and what is diagnosis or response. To the point that when the socialists adopt the issue of the expansion of public parks, for example, it will be difficult to know how much their demand corresponds to a true analysis of the life of the Buenos Aires urban masses—who, for long will live in a small city surrounded by countryside or, later on, in semi-rural suburban lots—and how much corresponds to the mechanical ideological reproduction of the hygienic, social, and moral virtues of urban greenery, in fact elaborated for the peaceful socialization of those masses in capitalist society.

It was not only Sarmiento who started promoting the park for its integrating virtues (so that there would be no more "foreigners, nationals, or plebeians") and to appease the latent class conflict in mass democracies. In the same discussion of the law promulgating the creation of the park in Palermo, in 1874 Avellaneda says:

> That is why these public walks serve at last even to soften, to improve, to purify, to ennoble the feelings of the multitudes, giving softer forms to these hard and severe struggles which democracy engenders, so that the chairman of the New York Central Park Commission has been able to say, in one of his speeches: "when our public walks are more crowded, our elections will be less agitated."[192]

This is the other side of the issue of distance: the difficulty of walking to Palermo not only affects the possibility of transforming the sedentary habits of high society ("it is said that it is far, which is not true; the truth is that we do not know how to walk and that it is necessary for us to know how," writes Pellegrini, precisely from London), but also makes access difficult for the sectors to which it is presumably dedicated.[193] In fact, the distance of parks in large cities becomes the great motive for criticism of reformism, because it reveals the insurmountable obstacle implicit in the very economic functioning of the modern city: the impossibility of "opening lungs" in the most congested sectors due to their high values, and, consequently, the impossibility for parks to act socially and hygienically where they are most needed. Mayors and reformers will complain bitterly about this limitation imposed by a real estate speculation, which they nevertheless do not cease to favor, even with those distant parks that they impose with such difficulty. That explains the symbolic importance of the name Central Park, representing a battle won against speculation and in favor of social and hygienic reform. Olmsted shields himself when he explains, in 1870, that if the poor still do not reach the New York park it is because it is

---

[192] Congreso Nacional, "Cámara de Senadores, Sesión ordinaria del 20 June 1874," Buenos Aires, 1875, 178.
[193] Carlos Pellegrini, letter to Torcuato de Alvear from London, in Beccar Varela, *Torcuato de Alvear*, 300.

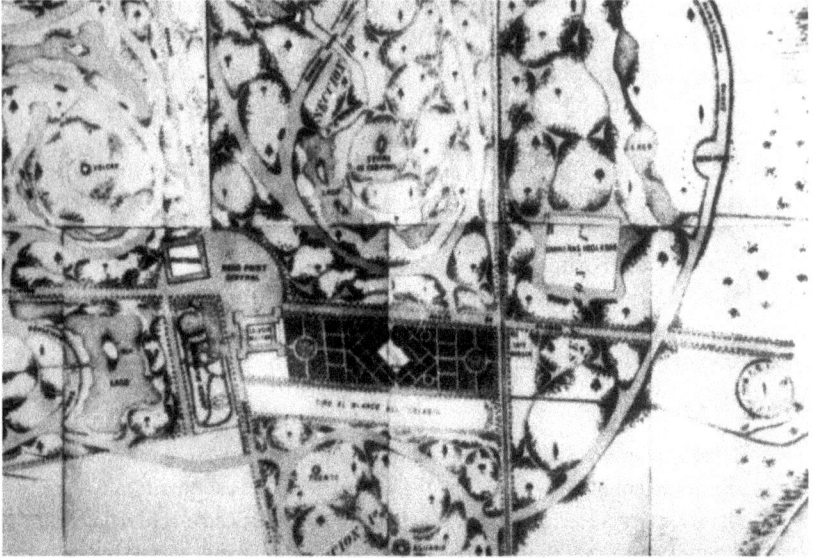

Figure 42. Captain Wysocki, *First Plan for Palermo Park*, c. 1870. Commissioned by Sarmiento, before the law ordering its construction. It preserves the layout of the Rosas plantation and transforms the Caserón (house) into a military school. Holmberg Library Archive, courtesy of Pablo Pschepiurca.

Figure 43. *Detail from a Plan of Buenos Aires*, c. 1890. From Sonia Berjman, ed., *El tiempo de los parques*. Buenos Aires: IAA, 1992. View of Carlos (Charles) Thays's design for Palermo, including the zoological and the botanical gardens, as well as the Exposición Rural in their final locations. Note how Caserón de Rosas (Rosas House) remains as the Military School to the northeast of the first section of the park.

thought for the future, for when the city reaches it and surrounds it. The great promoter of the "representative park," Haussmann, who in his *Memoires* uses terms significantly like those of English or American reformism, laments the absence of this centrality of green in Paris:

> In spite of all my efforts to make these two splendid promenades easily accessible to all classes of the population of Paris [...] I could not succeed in making them widely used except on Sundays and holidays [...] because of the distance, the time, and the cost of transport [...]. Conceived and built in terms of the satisfaction they were meant to bring to all the inhabitants of our capital, these two creations became during the week—the Bois de Boulogne, above all—the almost exclusive usufruct of the most fortunate, especially of those who, considering themselves too noble to do nothing, devote most of their beloved idleness to the daily exhibition of their luxury.[194]

The same issue makes the comparison not with the central cities, but with Santiago de Chile, so unfavorable for local reformers. Considering how little had been achieved in Buenos Aires, and confronting the isolated and never completed Palermo, by the end of the seventies Santiago by contrast already had the Alameda, Cousiño Park, the Quinta Normal, and the Santa Lucía Hill. Above all, because Santa Lucía Hill is located in the heart of Santiago, thus becoming "the favorite walk of the middle classes, that is, of families who cannot always have a carriage at their doorstep"—and that this should have been achieved by the people of Santiago, traditionally accused by *porteños* of being aristocratic, turned the comparison into a scandal for local reformers.[195] Thus, the first important public work, the paving of Sarmiento Avenue, was justified on the grounds that it put the park in immediate contact with Santa Fe street, which, being illuminated along its entire length and served by trams, "would give easy access to people of modest conditions of existence."[196] Along the same

43

---

[194] Georges-Eugène Haussmann, *Memoires* (Paris, 1890–93), 224–25, quoted by Choay, *L'orizzonte del posturbano*, 84.

[195] The quote is from Benjamín Vicuña Mackenna, *El Paseo de Santa Lucía. Lo que es y lo que deberá ser. Segunda Memoria de los trabajos ejecutados desde el 10 de septiembre de 1872 al 15 de mayo del presente año, presentada a la Comisión Directiva del Paseo por el Intendente de Santiago* (Santiago: Imprenta de Santiago, Librería del Mercurio, 1873), 83. In the project that Sarmiento presents to Congress in 1874, he already makes the unfavorable comparison with the parks of Santiago, as he will in countless articles; see "Proyecto de Ley del Poder Ejecutivo," in *Cámara de Senadores, Sesión de 1874* (Buenos Aires, 1875), 151.

[196] "Primer informe de la Comisión del Parque '3 de Febrero,'" Buenos Aires, November 11, 1875. Domingo Faustino Sarmiento, president and Carlos Pellegrini, secretary. Sarmiento Museum, Archive, box Q. Also, Rawson, in his radical opposition to the installation of the park on Rosas's lands, had used in the legislative debate the arguments

Traditional social practices and new uses in Palermo:

Figure 44. Samuel Boote, *Palermo Park*, c. 1885. Archivo General de la Nación. Round of carriages in the "aristocratic salon" of Palms Avenue (as Sarmiento Avenue was then called), with the usual salute.

Figure 45. Unknown photographer, *Woman Cycling in the Lagoon Pavilion* (Pabellón de los Lagos), c. 1908. Archivo General de la Nación.

lines, Sarmiento would defend Alvear's initiative to impose the Sunday holiday in the city, establishing early on the typical reformist association between the park and the reduction of working hours for popular sectors.[197]

As can be imagined, the appraisal of advances made on these uses of the park at the beginning of the eighties is, however, devastating for its own creator:

> Frequented exclusively by luxury equipment [...] children do not arrive in   44
> Palermo.... The artisans, the mothers with children and without equipment,
> are content to know that it exists [...]. Whose fault is it? [...] There are in the
> city a hundred thousand Europeans of all classes and in all situations. In the
> Park you do not find a hundred, nor more than Americans, which proves
> that they come in this respect as badly educated as they find us here. The
> government has done its part as much as was indispensable. The public has
> done nothing, nor have public manners changed at all, or very little.[198]

The blame returns to society. Although he admits that not much has been done to attract the popular classes, Cominges, the great defender of the park in the face of criticism from the right and the left, concludes that everything is due to the irremediable absence of culture among those classes, ratifying a not very "modern" function for the park: "if the proletarian classes do not attend [...,] let us not blame the distance that separates it from Buenos Aires; let us blame, in the first place, their state of culture, which still does not allow them to enjoy the purest pleasures provided by the spectacle of beauty."[199] In this generalized meaning, already far removed from the initial inspiration, the park is a point of arrival, of enjoyment and refined appreciation, it is a ratification of the culture of those who already have it rather than a chemical transformer of habits and traditions. It is the element that the elegant society of Buenos Aires was lacking, and in any case, what might be surprising is that its necessity was not noticed earlier:

> How could the cultured capital of the Argentine Republic—continues
> Cominges—have been satisfied until June 1874 with its clubs, its Colón and
> its Florida Street? Was such a narrow orbit enough for those dazzling stars
> of luxury, beauty, elegance, grace, and courtesy that today embellish and
> enliven Palermo Park to revolve with the majesty of which they are worthy?

---

of distance, pointing out that it would prevent access to the mass of poor people, crowded in the tenements of the center. See *Escritos y discursos* (Buenos Aires, 1891).
[197] See Sarmiento's letter to Alvear, October 10, 1881, in Beccar Varela, *Torcuato de Alvear*, 373ff.
[198] Sarmiento, "El Parque," *El Nacional*, October 12, 1882, in *Obras completas (LD)*, XLII:77.
[199] Cominges, "Report on Palermo," 47.

144 THE GRID AND THE PARK

That is the vision dominating the main descriptions of the park in the eighties: its function as a "green and flowering salon," as Alphand had characterized Parisian parks. "Sarmiento Avenue is, in short, an aristocratic salon, of sufficient proportions to contain the high society of Buenos Aires," Cominges concluded.[200] In Adolfo Bioy's exemplary description, on the other hand, it is not possible to find differences, in the ritualized exercise of social representation, between the Palermo walk and that of Florida Street:

> On ordinary weekdays, few people went to the Palermo promenade [...]; but on Sundays and Thursdays, the Palermo walk was crowded: the ladies, with their daughters, wearing suits and hats of the latest fashion, went in their coupes, *victorias* and *landós*, pulled by select yokes and driven by luxuriously uniformed coachmen, among whom a few blacks surviving from former times, when most of the charioteers were black. Four rows of coaches filled the avenue. The men or young men, who drove their carriages, took some friend, of the ugly sex, as a companion, and those without carriages, mostly young men, rode, in threes, parading in *victorias* in the square. The affair was reduced to going round and round the avenue for a long hour, at the pace of the horses, alternating each time the central rows with the side ones, so that no one would fail to meet. The first time in the afternoon that acquaintances passed by, they greeted each other ceremoniously, with a bow and a smile, and the men would tip their hats; the next time they met, they were not supposed to greet each other; at most, they could give each other a sidelong glance. A farewell salute was allowed on the last lap. When the hour of the walk was over, all the cars left at a long trot along Alvear Avenue, which was suddenly covered by vehicles that rivaled each other in lightness, in an unacknowledged racing joust, to reach Florida Street, where the walk was reproduced, in two rows, one toward the south, the other toward the north.[201]

We find the same equation in Ricardo Hogg: the classic walks of Palermo and Florida were, until the end of the century, "the most romantic social attraction of the time."[202] Hence, Palermo could also have been an adequate metaphor for the moral condemnation of that society in two authors so different—and with such different works—as Lucio V. López and Julián Martel: it is the scene that in *La gran aldea* serves to represent the duplicity of modern society, when the protagonist goes with Don Benito on a profane romantic excursion as soon as the burial of Aunt Medea is over; and it is also the place in *La Bolsa* (The

---

[200] Alphand's phrase in Choay, *L'orizzonte del posturbano*, 74; that of Cominges in his "Report on Palermo," 42, 61.

[201] Adolfo Bioy, *Antes del Novecientos (Recuerdos)* (Buenos Aires, 1958), 265–66.

[202] Ricardo Hogg, *Recuerdos del siglo pasado*, quoted by Ricardo M. Llanes, *Historia de la calle Florida* (Buenos Aires: Municipalidad de la Ciudad de Buenos Aires, 1976), 2:178.

Stock Exchange) where all the characters gather in an admonitory row, to stage the chaotic mixture that Martel repudiates and, above all, to foretell in the walk "the immense apocalyptic vision" of an unbridled race toward the abyss into which they will plunge, "in horrible and heartbreaking confusion, horsemen, horses, magnates, prostitutes."[203]

The incorporation of Palermo into a circuit with Florida and Recoleta brings there the typical *flânerie* that had been taking place on the Parisian boulevard and the New York promenade since mid-century. But the same memorialists alert us to how inadequate it would be to extract for Buenos Aires the already famous observations that have been made for those cities, in the sense inaugurated by Baudelaire and used as a category of analysis by Walter Benjamin to understand the cultural and social transformations in the modern metropolis. The still provincial character of the social circuit—if not of the city itself—in turn-of-the-century Buenos Aires, eliminates the condition of anonymity that was indispensable in those new rituals of metropolitan public space. According to Bioy, "everyone (those who strolled in the Palermo walk) knew who the others were. A stranger who showed up one day attracted so much attention that after a while they had all found out who he was."[204] These are not distortions of memory: contemporaries themselves pointed out with disgust that provincial character by contrast to what they saw in their travels. For example, Vicente Quesada makes his "North American traveler" say contemptuously:

> At sunset, that is, at 4 p.m., the hour when business ceases, I gave myself up to the pleasant pleasure of *flânerie*, an inveterate custom of those who have frequented Broadway in New York, the Strand in London, the Boulevard des Capucines or des Italiens in Paris, Ringstrasse in Vienna, Unter den Linden in Berlin, the Newsky Prospect in St. Petersburg, the Via del Corso in Rome, or the Puerta del Sol in Madrid. In Buenos Aires, this is faintly represented by Florida Street, which is narrow, with narrow sidewalks; adorned with buildings, some sumptuous and others modest; the circulation of cars interrupted by the tramway that occupies half of the cobblestones and by the traffic carriages. [...] It bears little resemblance to the great arteries which I have mentioned [...]. Rich families live there, who like to show off on their balconies on fine days, a Spanish custom, since neither in London, Paris, Vienna, Berlin, nor Rome is such a thing done. We Americans go for walks, but we do not show off in our homes.[205]

---

[203] Lucio V. López, *La gran aldea* (Buenos Aires: CEAL, 1980), 112; Julián Martel, "Corriendo al abismo," chap. 9 of *La Bolsa* (1891) (Buenos Aires: Editorial Huemul, 1979), 146ff.

[204] Bioy, *Antes del Novecientos (Recuerdos)*, 264.

[205] Lucy Dowling (Vicente Quesada), "La ciudad de Buenos Aires. Apuntes de una viajera," 69. In that paragraph, Quesada's opinion articulated through his traveler is very

And in the same sense, Cané observed: "We lack the indispensable agglomeration of people so that the individual and his acts disappear in the whole."[206] The absence of crowds is equivalent here to the absence of metropolitan social habits, to the absence, then, of a modern society. The image of the multitude appears in reformist discourse of the park no longer as a threat or as the subject of reform, but as a trigger for changing the traditional habits of high society. Enthused by the idyllic spectacle of metropolitan masses pacified by greenery, local reformers of the end of the century bet on a transformation that will frighten them when it is realized, but that in the meantime functions as a trigger for urban figurations and, above all, as an instrument for the criticism of actually existing society. If the complaints of reformers are directed equally at the type of "representative" use that the upper classes make of the park and at the fact that popular sectors do not reach it, it is unquestionable, at the same time, that in Palermo's first period, emphasis is placed on the first of these terms. As we saw in the case of expropriations, for the reformist elite it is the upper sectors of society that must be reformed first, because their habits are perceived as the most difficult obstacle to remove to produce the desired transformation, whose expansion alone, if possible, would come to affect the rest of society, *naturally*, without hindrance.

The important thing, in any case, is to perceive this game of mirrors, to see that in the eighties it is still possible for them to think that both reformist intentions are really one and the same. The warning that things are changing will come from one of the main municipal officials of the period, Juan Buschiazzo, who in 1893, as president of the Commission of Parks and Municipal Walks, maintains that the humble sectors of the city need another park like Palermo, where they do not have to suffer the affront of the wealth to which they cannot have access.[207] At the same time that he is accepting, in fact, the aristocratic character of Palermo—which implies altering this foundational ideological tradition that places in the park an alchemical converter of society as a whole—Buschiazzo is posing a question that is tantamount to accepting the growing complexification of the city: Can a remote, eccentric park, to which one must go especially "for change," to be transformed, fulfill its mission of philanthropic

---

similar to Sarmiento's on the need for a "new city" capable of separating residence from work. In fact, in his preaching against the Avenida de Mayo, Sarmiento will quote this note, mistakenly attributing it to an "American traveler."

[206] Miguel Cané, "Sobremesa," Archivo General de la Nación, sala VII, 2.214, Leg. 13, quoted by Elisa Radovanovic, "El modelo ideal y la realidad de la traza. Buenos Aires en el pensamiento de Miguel Cané," in Instituto Histórico de la Ciudad de Buenos Aires, *Pensar Buenos Aires (X Jornadas de Historia de la ciudad de Buenos Aires)* (Buenos Aires, 1994), 175.

[207] Juan Buschiazzo, "El parque Tres de Febrero," *La Prensa* (Buenos Aires) March 21, 1893, quoted by Sonia Berjman, "Los espacios verdes de Buenos Aires, 1887–1925," (PhD diss., University of Buenos Aires, 1987), 153.

Figure 46. Unknown photographer, *Inauguration of Parque Patricios*, 1902. Archivo General de la Nación. Mayor Bullrich surrounded by schoolchildren during the opening.

Figure 47. *Gymnastic Exercises at Parque Patricios*, illustration in *Caras y Caretas*, October 3, 1908. The image illustrates a note on the Patronato de la Infancia (Children's Foundation) that operated in the park.

reform? Ultimately, it is a matter of inverting the problem of distance, albeit from an elitist idea of social specialization in the city. When proletarians and immigrants do not have to go as far as Recoleta-Palermo to be "integrated," but rather

6   when it is the parks that go out to integrate all the sectors of the city as a fan open equally—albeit with gradations—from the Plaza de Mayo in all directions of the new city, there will be an attempt to apply, to generalize, the same instruction manual for the use of the metropolis; seeking, once again, to extend through the unifying green the same model of life. In principle, starting from the incontrovertible reality of the consolidated social uses and defining, consequently, the new parks as degraded mirrors, as a "Palermo of the poor"; but, in the same movement, accepting that public authority is responsible for bringing the "joys of beauty" to produce the radical transformation of the "state of culture" of the new urban multitudes. Such is the price that municipal reformism is willing to pay for the park to begin to function in the "modern" way that, with more idealism, the founding reformism pursued: as a hygienic and civic regenerator, as a moral and economic unifier. If the important thing is to emphasize the educational role of the park, then it must be everywhere, like the school, distributed homogeneously on the municipal level; and if this supposes that not everyone goes to the same school, but that in each one there is a representation of the society of each sector of the city, at the same time it supposes the universal presence of the institution: everyone goes to the same institution, guaranteed equitably by the state. In a way, then, we could say that with the turn-of-the-century parks, with their search for the articulation of a still very fragmented "park system," we would be moving from the park as an artifact of modernization to the park as an institution of the modern city, definitively completing in Buenos Aires the cycle of the replacement of the traditional content of the park (the search for the beautiful, the sublime, and the picturesque) by the new content defined by the much more encompassing and much more ambiguous concept of *civilization*.[208]

46, 47
71   As we saw in the opening of this section, that is the main sense given to the inauguration of Parque de los Patricios, one of the most emblematic of the new parks, precisely because over time it will materialize the ambition of a "Palermo of the poor," with a zoo, botanical garden, and entertainment on a scale for the southern neighborhoods. In the words of Mayor Bullrich, its objectives were "to combat depopulation [...], alleviate misery [...], overcome ignorance [...]

6   and prevent disease."[209] And he is not the only one: the whole series of parks that were planned on the edges of the traditional city, at the same time as the drawing up and publication of the plan with the layout of the streets through-

68   out the new federal territory, had identical aims: besides the Parque de los

---

[208] On the notion of civilization in discussions of nineteenth-century parks, see Alessandra Ponte, "Il parco pubblico in Gran Bretagna e negli Stati Uniti. Dal *genius loci* al 'genio della civilizzazione'," 369–82.

[209] "Discurso del Intendente Bullrich," *El Diario* (Buenos Aires) Thursday, September 11, 1902.

Patricios itself, the Parque Rivadavia (today Florentino Ameghino, over the old
Cementerio del Sur), the Perito Moreno country estate (although the efforts to
buy it were fruitless), the Parque Chacabuco (the first specifically programmed
for "physical exercises"), the Gran Parque del Sur (on the lands of "La Tablada"
in the Bajo Flores), the Parque Lezica (the very long process of purchase began
in these years and ends only several decades later), the park in the center of
the federal territory (which later will be called Centenario), the Parque Rancagua, the Parque del Oeste (Quinta Agronómica). Parks that seek to constitute
a "system" behind the explicit ambition to form a greenbelt that, starting from
Palermo, would border the city around its entire perimeter.

Once again, we are dealing with peripheral parks, but, like Sarmiento in his
own way at the founding moment of Palermo, the aim is to turn this lack into
a value. In the first place, because having accepted with resignation the impossibility of opening the necessary "lungs" in the congested center, the voices of
hygienist reformism had already focused their campaigns for some time on the
public purchase of cheap land on the outskirts of the city for park reserves, in
anticipation of the city's growth. At the end of the century, it is already known
that in urban expansion, what today is the edge, tomorrow will be part of the
city, and the role that is demanded of public governance is that it knows how
to anticipate growth. Of course, we are far from central European urbanism,
which in these same years is already proposing the need for municipalities to
transform all lands surrounding urban centers into public lands, to define the
"greenbelt," but above all to control the direction of urban expansion, reserving
for public authorities not only the possibility of designing the layout—as happened in Buenos Aires with the 1898–1904 grid—but the total decision regarding which lands are released to the market and when. In Buenos Aires, these
perimeter parks are seen as an incipient greenbelt, but not so much to direct
growth as to prevent it, by defining a stable and definitive border for the city.

This border has as one of its central tasks the sanitation of unhealthy settlements, within the framework of the "regularizing" tradition (remember the
functions proposed for Alvear's "perimeter boulevard"), although with its productivist connotations already completely weakened. It is a question of replacing with the greenbelt of the park the blackbelt of urban waste:

> The Arroyo Maldonado, the swampy lands [south] of Flores, the municipal
> slaughterhouse, the Riachuelo, La Boca, the lagoons of the port surround
> the city like a chain; the links are the marshes, mudhouses, pools of stag-
> nant water, and garbage dumps, reinforced by a rosary of factories, plants
> and other industrial establishments which have no way of throwing off their
> waste without endangering the hygiene and health of the city.[210]

---

[210] *Revista Municipal* III, no. 263 (January 8, 1896), 2, quoted and translated by Scobie,
Buenos Aires: Plaza to Suburb, 180.

But, above all, it is a question of stopping growth: once again the great problem of Buenos Aires, the impossibility of a clear definition of its limits with the
pampa. The idea of a "system of parks" is elaborated in the municipal sphere
simultaneously with the expansion of the urban fabric, but as part of an explicit
attempt to oppose the growth of the city. Unlike the original function of Palermo,
the park belt is not proposed as an urban revitalizer, but as a spatial brake, as a
border, as a limit to the "irrational flat building of Buenos Aires," as the municipal
report of 1902 characterizes it. As anticipated, in contrast with the design of the
grid, the model of the small and concentrated city is more alive than ever in the
municipal imaginary of the end of the century: "the most serious defect of our
city [...] is its great extension," writes the architect Víctor Jaeschké in an "open
letter" to Mayor Bullrich in 1898; and the parks are going to be one of the main
instruments to try—unsuccessfully—to arrive at that model.[211]

Precisely in 1904, the year the street plan is published, the *Revista Municipal* places those ideological arguments in the mouth of a fictitious "New York
traveler": "[Buenos Aires] is a great city with a great defect. It lies down instead
of standing upright. We who do nothing without consulting its practical aspect,
[densify] building in search of height. You spread out and despise aerial space."
A diagnosis on which the magazine—with direct links to municipal management—launches its proposal: "How much reason and practicality this judgment
reveals! [Here] services are becoming more expensive, distances impose on the
inhabitants wasted time translated into wasted money, taxes are increasing [...].
The time has come to change our tendencies."[212] Two years earlier, Mayor Bullrich
had published in his annual report a proposal for the densification of the capital
that circumscribed the built-up area to a quadrilateral inscribed in the traditional
center—a quadrilateral that significantly responds to the "ideal" measures of the
urban plan of La Plata; in this scheme, the parks that were being created were to
function as perimeter "forests," much like the role they had in European cities,
where the traces of the old walls were transformed into green beltways.[213]

---

[211] Víctor Jaeschké, *A propósito de mejoras y embellecimientos urbanos en Buenos Aires.
Carta abierta dirigida al nuevo Intendente Municipal de la Capital de la República
Argentina, Señor D. Adolfo Bullrich* (Buenos Aires: Imprenta y Encuadernación de Juan
Schurer Stolle, 1898), 5.

[212] *Revista Municipal* I, no. 2, second series (November 1, 1904). Already in the General
Census of 1887, the first municipal and national census, when the municipalities of
Flores and Belgrano had just been incorporated but the definitive limit had not yet
been defined, Alberto Martínez, in charge of the aforementioned "Topographic Study
of Buenos Aires," was confident that in the fifty-nine blocks gained from the river by the
works of Puerto Madero "a considerable mass of population could be accommodated"
and this would stop "the unconscious growth that until now [the city] has operated
toward the west," in *Censo General de Población*, 1:59, 60.

[213] Municipalidad de la Ciudad de Buenos Aires, *Memoria de la Intendencia Municipal
1898–1901* (Buenos Aires: Martín Viedma e hijo, 1901).

Again, the paradoxes of public administration: in moments of intense land subdivision, at the beginning of the expansion of the city, it was Bullrich, a well-known auctioneer turned mayor, who proposed stopping the *irrational* "agglomeration of family houses" in the suburbs. To this end, he interrupted compensations for the opening of streets (as we have seen, the problem that had been dragging on since the judicial defeat of the municipality in the Avenida de Mayo case, and that was not yet solved), stating that "the city extends too much and the services it provides are harmed," and emphasizing the need to "monopolize" all available space for public parks on the edges of the city: "What is being allowed is absurd [...]. Everything is being built on; every vacant lot is given over to speculation, and when density demands these lungs or public gardens, it will be necessary to pay exorbitant prices for them and, in all justice, the administrators of today will receive the sharp criticism of the men of tomorrow."[214] We have already raised the issue in the case of Alvear, when we pointed out the growing differentiation—within the framework of the consolidation of the state—between individual interests and public figures. And it is no mere coincidence that Bullrich is President Roca's mayor: in this too Bullrich fulfills a kind of ritual, but one that does not have Sarmiento as its model but rather Alvear. President Roca once again chose for the post of mayor someone from "outside politics," not only because it reaffirmed the administrative idea of city government, but also because this avoided party mediations in the link between the president and the mayor and, above all, between the latter and society.[215] Thus, relatively distanced from the turbulences of petty politics, Bullrich becomes the first mayor since Alvear to serve two full terms, adding a four-year term at the head of the municipality after countless ephemeral administrations: his capacity to propose, the energy of his claims, are also proportional to his distance from the pressures and interests of political *caudillismo*, the presidential support for his administration, and the continuity of his projects.[216]

---

[214] Ibid., 34.

[215] See Natalio Botana when he defines the "presidential control" of Roca's management of the city, in "Conservadores, radicales y socialistas," in Romero and Romero, *Buenos Aires, historia de cuatro siglos*, 113.

[216] The comparison of Bullrich with Alvear is already made by Ismael Bucich Escobar, *Buenos Aires Ciudad, 1880–1930,* (Buenos Aires: El Ateneo, 1930). See in the previous chapter the note referring to the continuity of the mayors. On the contrary, in his quest to prove through the social origin of the mayors the meaning of their public actions, Bourdé says of Bullrich only that he was "mixed up in real estate speculation." See Bourdé, *Buenos Aires: urbanización e inmigración,* 80. He does not contemplate that the commercial function of the Casa Bullrich was still much more linked to the auctioning of fields and animals than to urban land (which is clear from the auction advertisements appearing in newspapers of the period), but also that the function of the auctioneer was still conceived as incompatible with speculation in personal real estate investments. In this last sense, see

The same continuity is what allows Bullrich the businessman, relying on a much more oiled and strengthened bureaucratic apparatus, to begin to understand some of the rationales for the city's operation. And, at the same time, it is the very functioning of the city that makes his proposals generate unthinkable effects that go beyond the discourses that sustain them. That is, as an individual figure, Bullrich can hardly repeat as commonplace the hygienist and reformist discourses that sustained the park as a public artifact: his discourse in front of the children-inmates is nothing more than a vulgarization of the discourses of a Wilde or a Ramos Mejía.[217] Without those discourses the park could not be realized, and it is not precisely a Bullrich who gives them new airs. But, vice versa, the materiality of the park, made possible by the place that Bullrich manages to occupy in the state and through the strengthening of public bureaucracy, is pregnant with unforeseen consequences for the future of the city, generating other discourses and other practices, when, at the pace of a new urban expansion in the disqualified universe of the grid, the park begins to play a completely different role from the one assigned to it as limit and frontier.

10   If, as Blanes's painting that we already discussed at the beginning reveals, hygienist reformism proposes to bring the light of the sun and science to the immigrant home, the task will only be fulfilled when it is the immigrant's home that is arranged in a new city around the park, betraying its urban objectives as city limit. At this point, and beyond the discourses that give it such a different character from the grid, the park will also act as a reformist machine. And the different expressions that we have covered to arrive at this result are representative of urban reformism toward the end of the century: we have gone from the figurations of Sarmiento to the figure of Alvear and, finally, to the more or less mechanical rituals of Bullrich, accompanied by the de facto actions of a group of anonymous municipal bureaucrats. I believe that it is precisely this passage that allows us to see the process of metropolitanization of Buenos Aires "working" in its double aspect: as the urban formalization of the massive incorporation of new social sectors resulting from immigration, and as the radical transformation of the old habits of the traditional city, when politics ceases to be a "virile sport" and becomes the "orderly administration of the state."[218]

José Bianco, *Transmisión inmobiliaria* (Buenos Aires: G. Mendesky e Hijo, 1912), where the role of auctioneers in real estate speculation processes is portrayed.

[217] Bullrich's hope in the regeneration of these children-inmates coincides with Ramos Mejía's sympathetic view of "street children," a sympathy which, as Oscar Terán, commenting on *Las multitudes argentinas*, rightly pointed out, attenuates the biological component of his discourse, and even makes him find in them "the future feeling of nationality in its modern conception." See Terán, *Positivismo y nación en la Argentina* (Buenos Aires: Puntosur, 1987), 24.

[218] Tulio Halperin Donghi, "Un nuevo clima de ideas," in G. Ferrari and E. Gallo, *La Argentina del ochenta al Centenario* (Buenos Aires: Sudamericana, 1980), 20.

This is punctuated until the end of the century with the various modifi-cations of the place of the park as urban artifact, and the importance that the public grid acquires in the process. Even if only potentially—because the dis-tance with the "real city" would remain great for a long time—the layout of the street plan had placed Palermo within a comprehensive urban structure, and no longer as an elegant appendix of the city. *Post facto*, the 1904 grid offers Palermo the framework that the 1811 grid had provided Central Park *ab initio*, as the very meaning of its "central" function. Palermo is thus finally integrated, if not to the present, at least to a foreseeable future of the city, although, as we have seen, no longer in Sarmiento's sense as the heart of a "new city," but only as a call for attention, as a rupture and punctual distraction: either from the actually existing monotonous and limitless extension of the pampa or from the homogeneous universe of the grid ideally extended in all directions of the plan. That is to say, as a distraction from the blinding routine of what was older and the mercantile anomie of all that was newer.

But the creation, toward the turn of the century, of a "system of parks" sur-rounding the city reveals changes of meaning, not only the vocation to define a green frontier against speculative growth which, as we repeat, denies the layout of the grid, but the conversion of Palermo into the beginning of a sanitary, moral, and civic chain that was to border the whole city from north to south. The park denies the grid in its expansive potential but accepts it insofar as it makes avail-able a whole new border with the pampa, and it is this space that it seeks to ratify, to culturize, with a green border. So, practically at the same time that Palermo is integrated into a grid that designs the city of the future, it is integrated into a crown of public green that begins to form a system—which again seeks to restore the system's imbalance—with Avenida de Mayo: the border of a traditional city that renews itself, renewing above all its public space. The layout of the perimeter parks is what gives the park in Buenos Aires a "modern" public function, anal-ogous to that proposed by the reform of the symbolic function of the Plaza de Mayo: an urban layout that stages the will to integrate. But also, in this first stage, it ratifies the stratification of public space in a central area, the Plaza de Mayo and the boulevard, to which discussions on the renovation of public space, the rela-tions between national civic space, monument, and memory remain restricted; and a peripheral area, edge or border, in which the park, or parks, will begin their task of radical renovation of the urban figure and metropolitan habits, calling into question any notion of traditional centrality. An area that, in step with the occupation of the grid that it originally sought to contain, will be alternatively center, border, and new center of a new dimension of public space, no longer of the modern city, but of the modern metropolis.

PART TWO

Omissions

[Around the Centenary]

One of the peculiarities of Buenos Ayres [*sic*] is that you can see no end to it. [...] on the side of the Pampas there is no obstacle.[219]

Georges Clemenceau, 1911

[Buenos Aires...] that immense enigma that for twenty years has been growing in silence.[220]

–Jules Huret, 1911

How is the radically new produced in the city? From what region of the old do the forces that compose it emerge? What degree of evidence touches its novelty? During the first two decades of the century, the grid will guide a continuous occupation of the territory recently incorporated to the federal jurisdiction, and around the parks—which sought in vain to limit it—the most resounding novelty of modern urban society in Buenos Aires will take shape: the appearance of a new type of public space, local and limited, as a sphere of production of barrio culture and germ of the most complete transformation of public space in the traditional city. What is striking is the silent way in which this happens, completely ignoring the problems and uses of the city, its debates and proposals for transformation. If, for an observer like Clemenceau in 1910, the city's expansion in the pampa did not encounter any obstacles, what were the other obstacles, those that prevented this process from having visibility in the traditional city?

In a few brief pages full of suggestions, José Luis Romero characterized the city of these first decades as "the Buenos Aires of the two cultures." There

---

[219] *South America To-day*, 30. The book is the English version of the *Notes de voyage* that Clemenceau wrote for *L'Illustration*.

[220] Jules Huret, *De Buenos Aires al Gran Chaco* (1911) (Buenos Aires: Hyspamérica, 1988), 1:27.

was a constituted culture, the "culture of the center," of the upper classes, the traditional middle classes and the new middle classes; and an unprecedented, "marginal" culture, the culture of the barrios, in which very different groups intermingled: immigrant groups and children of immigrants, uncomfortable in their marginality, and a range of Creole and immigrant sectors that thrived in it, "a formidable experiment, forced by the presence and contact of different groups placed in the same situation, and for whom segregation acted as a catalytic agent."[221]

A hasty reading of Romero's brief text could evoke the category of the "segregated city," so much in vogue in urban sociology then and which inspired the main histories of Buenos Aires written in the 1970s. Without explicitly forcing a polemic, the richness of Romero's text nevertheless lies in an intuitive opposition to that category and to the literature that produced it. By shifting the focus from economic conflict to cultural conflict, Romero is able to see that the peculiarity of Buenos Aires in the first decades of the century, its most pressing enigma, does not consist in the progressive crystallization of exclusion, but in a conflictive but growing integration, which he locates in the interweaving of "a thousand subtle threads between the two cultures that ended up creating a common fabric for both in the Buenos Aires of 1930." It should be clarified that this idea of integration is not conceived as a linear extension of dominant values which, in reaction to accounts of "segregation," neoliberal historiography began to raise also in the seventies: Romero's sympathy for the strength of the new, popular, and marginal cultures, makes him identify in that common plot the traces of their triumph. It is simply a matter of a complete change of perspective in the face of polarized interpretations.[222]

This was a change of perspective for which Romero's diverse selection of sources was by no means secondary. Being a very good reader of Ezequiel Martínez Estrada, he would rarely be as faithful to his interpretations as in this case, taking from the essayist his original way of defining the conflicts of

---

[221] José Luis Romero, "Buenos Aires: una historia," in *Historia Integral Argentina*, vol. 7: *El sistema en crisis* (Buenos Aires: Centro Editor de América Latina, 1972), 105.

[222] The best example of polar interpretations is given by the only open controversy recorded on these issues, the one manifested in the eighties, in the pages of *Desarrollo Económico*, between Francis Korn and Lidia de la Torre against the work of Oscar Yujnovsky of a decade earlier. The authors defend the hypothesis of a seamless success of the model of "outward growth" of the conservative order, against Yujnovsky's Marxist-inspired analysis that focused exclusively on the processes of social and urban segregation. It was, in truth, a settling of scores within the framework of the new hegemony of neoliberal ideas. See Oscar Yujnovsky, "Políticas de vivienda en la ciudad de Buenos Aires, 1880–1914," *Desarrollo Económico* 54 (July–September 1975); Francis Korn and Lidia de la Torre, "La vivienda en Buenos Aires, 1887–1914," *Desarrollo Económico* 98 (July–September 1985).

Buenos Aires, modifying its traditional geographical orientation.[223] Indeed, if all the specialized literature—in a simplified vision of structural conflict—had traditionally revolved around the denunciation of the inequalities between the north and the south of the city (that effective phrase by Mario Bravo about the city being divided into two parts, the rich neighborhoods in the north and the poor neighborhoods in the south), then, *X-ray of the Pampa*, already suggested that in order to understand the deepest conflict of modern Buenos Aires, one must change course, focusing on the conflict of east versus west. This confronts Europe versus the inner country, manifested in the city as the conflict of the river versus the pampas, the center versus the "frontier barrios." The north and the south would be relatively non-homogeneous parts of a homogeneous city: the traditional city ("one is rich and the other poor, as happens in the bosom of any family" Martínez Estrada would later specify in *La cabeza de Goliath*). The west, on the other hand, is opposed to the whole. And it is precisely in the tension that arises in this new territory between the expansion of the city and the resistance—and persistence—of the pampa that the Buenos Aires of metropolitanization is best understood.[224] Today it is possible to make Martínez Estrada's clarifications even more precise, suggesting that while the first conflict, rather than referring to economic and class tensions, refers to the tensions established and contained in traditional urban and social frameworks, the second, highlighting the production of the new in the city, allows us to return from a cultural to an economic interpretation, because it sheds light on the most complex and characteristic structural phenomenon of Buenos Aires society: the emergence in those years, thanks to the expansion of the city on the pampas, of new popular sectors on course to becoming a middle class.

The north/south conflict thus omits the new. Behind its back, I insist, silently, a pressure cooker of continuous mixing begins to form out of which the city will emerge transfigured, incubating in a frontier that is much more geographic and cultural than social. Because it is easy to see that in these first decades of the century the borders, for example, between the "new middle classes" of established culture and the immigrant groups eager for social ascent are very tenuous and in constant redefinition. But what is fluid socially is much more rigid geographically and culturally: these peripheral regions and cultural practices will not, in these first two decades, be visible to the center. The "two

---

[223] Adolfo Prieto has developed Romero's relations with Martínez Estrada in a beautiful article, in "Martínez Estrada, el interlocutor posible," *Boletín del Instituto de Historia Argentina y Americana Dr. E. Ravignani* 1 (1989).

[224] *X-ray of the Pampa* (1933). Only one of its six parts is specifically dedicated to Buenos Aires, one of whose chapters begins with the subtitle "Oeste contra este" (West against East), under which he develops these hypotheses that he will later expand as the general basis of the text already entirely dedicated to Buenos Aires, *La cabeza de Goliath* (The Head of Goliath), of 1941.

cultures" are irreducibly anchored in the center and in the new frontier barrio, although their members often share spaces and strips of society: more than two cultures, then, strictly speaking, it is a matter of different ways of being in the city. This means that social subjects will not function in the same way in one and another sphere. The Creole bureaucrat who in the office approaches the themes and problems of central culture and of the traditional city; the immigrant craftsman who is integrated in the workshop, or the son of immigrants who is integrated first in the school and then in the university; all of them in the barrio—along with those others who do not move from there—are part of the product of a social and cultural compound that, while it will operate as a system of cultural translation, will remain in these early years ignorant of these other points of contact and, above all, will be ignored by them. The construction of the new is silent, and only when, in the twenties, its potential is very frankly unfolded and its features defined, will we see the "thousand subtle threads" that recompose the urban scenario geographically, culturally, and socially: only then will the effects of the formation of the barrio appear as a translation device and as a mechanism for the reassembly of the city as a whole.

In this second part I will try to show how these processes take place in mutual ignorance: how in "the city"—the one that incorporates the metaphorized conflict in the north versus the south—the circuit of a traditional public space comes to be defined, with clear hierarchies and stratifications inherited from the urban modernization of the eighties, while in "the periphery" the new public space, the barrio, is simultaneously formed. Between the two processes, we will intersperse the way in which a few observers—foreign visitors, in the first place, perhaps because their off-centered gaze allows them to notice the "absence of obstacles" or to appreciate processes that remain silent to locals— glimpsed, in the formless jumble of the boundless expansion over the pampa, some features of the emerging metropolis. Contrary to what much of the literature on the first decades of the twentieth century tells us, that mutual ignorance does not imply a stereotyped contrast of a "central" culture traversed to the point of paralysis by decisive conflicts, in the face of which what is "peripheral" will reveal itself as a quarry of innovative responses. Therein lies the main *omissions* of "central" culture: not understanding the logic with which the device of the grid and the park had been launched into the future, not understanding the city they contained. That device had been part of a reformist, integrating, and conservative state policy, which also quickly showed its effects in the framework of social conflict: in those years it is notorious that the city, opening its borders to peripheral residence, offers a buffer space that displaces and diverts social conflict, shelling it on the territory, producing a fabulous experience in which geography imposes laws on society and reveals the other "function" of expansion, helping to unlock the conflicts of traditional society.

CHAPTER 4

The City and History: First Birthday

Every anniversary imposes a reckoning. In February 1909, in the midst of the public euphoria over the preparations for the celebration of the centenary of May 1810, the illustrated weekly *P.B.T.* published a humorous page contrast- ing two images: in the first, a group of gigantic figures, the patriots of 1810, emerges proudly from a very small and primitive village; in the second, in the middle of a modern and powerful city, a group of pygmies, the rulers of 1910, deliberate in disorientation. A legend, categorical in its obviousness, reads: *"Quantum mutatur ab illo!* (Alas, how much is it altered from what it once was!). The centenary, it is known, was a consecrating moment for the city and for established culture. A young country and, above all, its young capital, sought to show the world the degree of progress made in merely thirty years, to present a proud and optimistic balance. It is also known that this "trial of the century"—as Joaquín V. González titled his work—was complex and took place amid contradictions and conflicts. The remarkable economic growth was far from preventing inequality and social and political tensions, and this was made public in strikes, demonstrations, and street attacks, which led to the ultimate paradox celebrating the "anniversary of freedom": that it took place within the framework of a state of siege. The splendor of the oligarchic regime was not enough to hide the fraud, corruption, and pettiness of its leaders (sati- rized, as in *P.B.T.*, by public opinion), but this did not prevent the development of a political reform that would lead in 1912 to the Sáenz Peña Law (which imposed male universal, secret, and obligatory vote) and, a few years later, due to the electoral success of the Partido Radical, to the extinction of its cycle. The anathema of the immigrant as responsible for the "importation" of social con- flict and the dissolution of nationality (put into action by the state, moreover, with the Residence Law), took place in the course of a successful process of social integration actively undertaken by the state through public education. The materialistic cult promoted by the establishment was harshly contested by the spiritualistic regenerationism of a broad sector of the cultural and political elite, many of whose members participated in that same establishment to a high degree of commitment.

Official optimism and economic progress, inequality and social mobility, moral criticism, national renaissance, spiritualism, social conflict: this "climate" of the centenary, in its ideas, in its social, political, and economic complexity,

¡Quantum mutatur ab illo!

El 1810 dejó un pueblo muy pequeño con hombres muy grandes.

Y el 1910 va á encontrar un pueblo muy grande con hombres muy pequeños.

Figure 48. "¡Quantum mutatur ab illo!": *P.B.T.*, Buenos Aires, February 13, 1909. The inscription above reads: "1810 left a very small town with very large men." The inscription below reads: "And 1910 will find a very large town with very small men."

has been dealt with in some of the best texts of Argentine critical and historic literature, and it would be difficult, at least for now, to add much.[225] However, it could be said that we have barely begun to see—apart from the primary ver- ification of the contrast between the splendors of the palace and the sordidness of the tenement house—the roles played by the city in the composition of that climate, the way in which the public space of the traditional city completed its definitive articulation in its folds. The "bourgeois city," whose beginning can be located in the administration of Torcuato de Alvear, becomes visible toward the years of the centenary; a date that condenses the urban conflicts of the "center" of the first two decades. The image of the city that consolidates in those years is supported by some "palaces" of the Creole aristocracy in the northern part of the city and a series of public buildings of magnitude that, as observers of the period point out, try to give "respectable" shelter to a national and a local state that did not cease to grow in a handful of inadequate buildings, most of the time in dark, rented dependencies.[226] These buildings design a policy of public space for the traditional city, but we will see above all how this public

---

[225] The texts that have most influenced me in the understanding of the different aspects of the period are Carlos Altamirano and Beatriz Sarlo, "La Argentina del Centenario: campo intelectual, vida literaria y temas ideológicos," in *Ensayos argentinos. De Sarmiento a la vanguardia* (Buenos Aires: CEAL, 1983); Jorge Liernur, "Buenos Aires del centenario: en torno a los orígenes del movimiento moderno en la Argentina," *Materiales* 4 (December 1983); José Luis Romero, *Las ideas políticas en Argentina* (Mexico City: FCE, 1956); Botana, *El orden conservador*; Tulio Halperin Donghi, *El espejo de la historia. Problemas argentinos y perspectivas latinoamericanas* (Buenos Aires: Sudamericana, 1987); Adolfo Prieto, *El discurso criollista en la formación de la Argentina moderna*; Hugo Vezzetti, *La locura en la Argentina* (Buenos Aires: Folios, 1983); Oscar Terán, *En busca de la ideología argentina* (Buenos Aires: Catálogos, 1986).

[226] The problem of the lack of public buildings appears in a multitude of sources; Víctor Julio Jaeschké makes a merciless enumeration of the few existing examples toward the centenary in "Ver para creer. ¿A dónde están nuestros edificios públicos?" *El Tiempo*, April 21, 1909, 5. Some of those built in those years are: Teatro Colón, project by F. Tamburini, 1890, begun by V. Meano until his death, 1904, concluded in 1908 by Julio Dormal; Congreso Nacional, project by V. Meano, concluded around 1906; Palacio de Tribunales, Correo Central and Colegio Nacional Buenos Aires, arq. N. Maillart, 1906–1910; Aduana, Lanús and Hary, 1909–1911. Regarding private residences, we can highlight the Fernández de Anchorena residence (present Nunciatura, Av. Alvear and Montevideo), arch. Le Monnier, 1909; Quintana Palace (Rodríguez Peña 1874), architect Prins, 1907; Salas Palace (Callao 1451) and Devoto Palace (Plaza Lavalle), architect Buschiazzo, 1904 and 1913 respectively; Anchorena Palace (the current Chancellery), architect Christophersen, 1909; Ortiz Basualdo Palace (Arenales and Maipú), arch. Dormal, 1905; Le Breton (Arenales 982) and Vivot (Uruguay 1288) residences, by Lanús and Hary, 1904 and 1908; Mihanovich Residence (Maipú 720), architect Morra, 1905; De Bary Residence (Alvear Avenue), architect Nordmann, 1907; Plaza Hotel (Plaza San Martín), architect Zucker, 1910. For an overview of architecture of the period, see

space reveals its main modulations in three themes that occupied all attention at the time: the debates on urban reform, the massive occupation of the streets for celebration or protest, and the erection of memorials to figures or events of the past. In all three, a public system is defined, and its conflicts presented, embodying the roles of the city in the constitution of the centennial climate.

48   The illustration that appeared in *P.B.T.* introduces us to some of these roles. For all observers, the city was the most emblematic materialization of that progress that was characterized as "material," whether to celebrate it or to stigmatize it. For those who were enthusiastic about it, as in the case of the magazine, the city was the place par excellence to exercise in the "gloating of figures," as Real de Azúa rightly defined the way in which the period's optimism was expressed.[227] What amazed them, then, was the contrast between that development and the smallness of the ruling sectors, as if that fantastic result had been produced outside their will and capacity (and here we can only recall Sarmiento in the early years of the State of Buenos Aires, impressed by the strength and development of the city *in spite of* tyranny and political chaos: that vision, which entails a definition of the relationship between city, society and politics, has proved to be long-lasting). For those who found in this "material" progress the best proof of the resounding failure of the entire modernizing project, on the other hand, the city appeared as the symbol par excellence of "philistinism," the objective mark of foreignization, with its babel of "exotic" languages and faces and its carnival of architectural and urban styles that replaced the nation's historical heritage with nouveau-riche insolence; further, as the place whose growing and ostentatious wealth had to take into account the proportional impoverishment of an inner country in which values began to be discerned that would soon reverse the antinomy of civilization and barbarism. What amazed them, on the contrary, was that all this could happen in the face of the passivity and complacency of the ruling sectors, as if this result had been part of a premeditated public plan.

Both positions, however, have more in common than it seems. In the first place, because there are number of intermediate positions that touch on aspects of one and the other: for example, that of those who defend material progress—and therefore can be proud of the city they produced—but as part of a process to be completed with a stage of "spiritual progress;"[228] or that of those who in

Federico Ortiz, J. Mantero, Ramón Gutiérrez and Abelardo Levaggi, *La arquitectura del liberalismo en la Argentina* (Buenos Aires: Sudamericana, 1968).

[227] Real de Azúa, *El impulso y su freno*, 102ff.

[228] This position could be seen as emblematic of the cultural elite of the eighties partially disappointed with the course of "progress"; for example, Miguel Cané in 1902 writes to Quesada: "I assure V. that 30 years ago, the village called Buenos Aires, with its rough stone pavement, its tile-roofed schools, its sidewalks with posts and its river carts, was an incomparable center of culture, moral and intellectual, next to the sumptuous capital of the same name, with its central pavement superior to any other city in the world, its

the name of a more effective material progress point out and denounce that the facade of urban wealth in very localized points of the center only unsuccessfully hides the abscesses that emerge behind (here appears one of the most recurrent themes in the aesthetic-ideological-urban discussion of the period which, turning aesthetics into moral parable, confronts facade and truth, appearance and content, as opposite qualities of society). Second, because the great element common to both extreme positions must be identified: the contempt for the regime's political leaders, accused of being inept and immoral in the course of a process that would remain for years stigmatized in collective political memory as "the scandals of the centenary." But, above all, they have many points in common because at the heart of each of these extreme positions it is easy to find a similar ambiguity toward the city.

It is evident that in *P.B.T.*'s illustration the relations in the two scenes between men and the city are mutually defining: the greatness of the patriots of 1810 is not independent of material humility, just as the smallness of the men of 1910 cannot be understood without the disproportionate size of a city whose development seems to them out of control. Symmetrically, the regenerationist critique uses the city as a metaphor for all the ills it diagnoses in society, but again and again it will choose it as the most appropriate territory in which to battle for memory and identity, not only because it was so ordered by the fatality of the concentration of the entire political and cultural movement in Buenos Aires, but because, far from accepting it with resignation, Buenos Aires is also for them the material and potentially spiritual sum of the Argentineness they are looking for. More than a mere example, though in 1924, is Ricardo Rojas's attitude in *Eurindia*, which in a way is completely in tune with the climate of the centenary. In a chapter entitled "The Cosmopolitan Life," he reproduces all the commonplaces of moral criticism against "the progress of Buenos Aires," but a few pages later, in the chapter "The Harmonious City," he develops his thesis that Buenos Aires is "the predestined city of Eurindia," clarifying that it will be so despite "its current individualistic mercantilism [and the] nickname of Cosmopolis or Carthage with which we artists, in our thirst for the ideal, sometimes censure it."[229] He does not, however, bother to explain how this miracle will occur or why it should necessarily happen in the city that provokes its excesses. The ambiguity in both cases recognizes different causes, but it generates a wide zone of contacts in which nationalism and history are going to be linked to the city in complicated ways. The centennial celebration, far from hiding those conflicts behind their "masks," is going to put them in the most visible of places: public space.

---

school palaces, its wide avenues and its marvelous port." Quoted in Alfredo Rubione, *En torno al criollismo. Textos y polémica* (Buenos Aires: CEAL, 1983), 239.

[229] Ricardo Rojas, *Eurindia* (1924) (Buenos Aires: Librería La Facultad, 1924), 165 and 199–200, respectively.

1. Celebration and City Performances

> It is necessary to call a competition of ideas [...] for the general layout of the
> avenues, parks, squares, etc.; in a word: the plan for the rectification and
> beautification of the capital. This will be, in my opinion, the best legacy of
> the capital in honor of the festivities that will be celebrated in four years.[230]
> —Alejandro Christophersen, 1906

> Some, perhaps intoxicated by the dance of millions that planners have develo-
> ped before their eyes, perhaps indulging in unbridled jokes, dare to propose:
> Since it is about something big, why not found a model city, to be called Inde-
> pendencia or 25 de Mayo, or with some other commemorative name, and that
> gathers all the perfectionism that can be desired, from the great working-class
> barrios to the most beautiful public buildings? The names of the streets, the
> names of the palaces, promenades, squares, everything would refer to that
> glorious date. It would be, at the same time, a city, and a history book.[231]
> —Roberto Payró, 1906

Throughout the second half of the nineteenth century, universal expositions
sealed a relationship between patriotic celebrations and demonstrations of
national progress based on the symbolic needs of imperial expansion (the
consolidation of national industries competing in world markets). This relationship was not only always embodied in cities but tended to turn each host
city into the ultimate manifestation of that relationship, into a true exposition.
Paris is, of course, as "capital of the nineteenth century," the emblematic case:
in 1889, the first centenary of the revolution was the occasion for the exhibition
that achieved its most resounding success in the tower built by Gustave Eiffel,
which for the first time turned pure technology into a monument, one whose
only technological function was to offer the unprecedented spectacle of the
view of the city from great height. But this is not the only case: in 1876 it was the
Philadelphia exhibition for the centenary of American Independence; in 1893
it was Chicago for the fourth centenary of the discovery of America; in 1904
Saint Louis for the centenary of the Louisiana Purchase; in 1911, a year after
Argentina, Rome and Milan, for the fiftieth anniversary of the unification of
the kingdom of Italy, and the examples would not cease to multiply throughout
the twentieth century. In all cases, expositions were the occasion of important urban renovations, annexing new areas and systematizing the expansion
of the city, experimenting with urban technological advances that would later

---

[230] "Conmemoración del gran centenario. Proyecto sometido a la Comisión Nacional,"
Arquitectura: Suplemento de la Revista Técnica 39 (July–August 1906).
[231] Roberto Payró, "Las píldoras del centenario" (August 4, 1906), in *Crónicas* (Buenos
Aires: M. Rodríguez Giles, 1909), 19.

be massively applied, or setting a deadline for the completion of long-standing projects that were difficult to carry out.[232]

From the point of view of urban culture, then, it was reasonable to suppose, as does Christophersen—one of the most renowned local architects of the period—in the opening quote, that the best celebration of the festivities should be the city's own reshaping, as a monument and as a legacy, in that irrefutable official equation of the period: capital city/image of the nation. From the perspective of someone like Payró, alien to this chain of thought, which is only partly exclusive of urban disciplines, the question is the opposite: "The celebration of the centenary should be more moral than material," he argues; for which it would be enough that "the people take part with all their soul" and that, then, "any tangible thing [...] monument or simple inscription," would perpetuate its memory. If, like Payró, it is assumed that "what is praiseworthy is the 25th of May 1810 [and] not the 25th of May 1910," then the "dance of millions" of urban projects becomes senseless. For "the least outlandish" of those projects are "those which, under the pretext of the centenary, would compromise the country's finances for another century"; hence the ironic description of the "model city" in the opening quote. We will see in what follows that the relationship "model city/history book" which Payró ironizes, contains one of the main dilemmas of the centenary. Here I am interested in pointing out the range of positions opened up regarding the nature of the city/celebration connection, once the imminence of the centenary places the city at the center of the balance. And this will happen as soon as the century begins: all urban debates of the first decade are organized with the centenary as a fixed deadline, and almost all of the second decade maintains the same goal by inertia.

Among whom is the discussion taking place? The climate of the centenary produces the paradox that an urban progressive like Payró has already ceased to see the progress of the city as the primary task of government: the "unbridled *chirigota* [troupe]" of projects for the city center reproposes in one way or another the discussion on expropriations so dear to urban reformism—and that is why it would compromise the finances for another century. His call for sanity at this juncture does nothing more than distance itself from nineteenth-century conservative reformism to coincide with the anti-modernizing demands that would equate urban transformation and political corruption or, at least,

---

[232] For a general approach to the problem of universal exhibitions, see Sica, *Historia del urbanismo. El siglo XIX*, 2:1064ff; more specific studies: E. Schild, *Dal palazzo di cristallo al Palais des Illusions* (Florence, 1971); and John Alwood, *The Great Exhibitions* (London: Studio, 1977). Francisco Foot Hardman, *Trem fantasma. A modernidade na selva* (São Paulo: Companhia Das Letras, 1988), especially chap. 2 "Exposiçoes universais. Breve itinerário do exibicionismo burguês," 49ff., which explores the relationship between exhibitions and national celebrations, focusing on the contradiction between the explicit objectives of "brotherhood of peoples" that the exhibitions set themselves, imperial competition, and war.

with the spurious needs of representation of the regime, which confines discussion on city reform to official voices and technical debates. This is another consequence of the omissions: until socialism in the 1920s did not find in the issues of suburban expansion a field for the development of positions on the city in line with its political positions, the focus of political progressivism would close in "the housing question," leaving aside more global problems of urban public space, so that the debate on urban reform would remain restricted.

Doubly restricted, because a peculiar symmetry is established with another element absent from the debate: private capital. It is notorious that in the modernization of traditional Buenos Aires there are no major private initiatives outside specific building renovation (private capital is restricted to operate in speculation in peripheral lots and transport infrastructure). The last initiatives by private companies to carry out large-scale urban transformation projects involving entire sectors of the traditional city (opening of boulevards and avenues, renovation of public buildings, etc.) date from the end of the nineteenth century. By the twentieth century, a growing and drastic distance emerges between a state that carries out all major operations and builds a board of fixed rules, and a private capital that limits itself to moving within that framework with "retail" operations, without showing any interest in homologating its own logic to the variety of aspects that make up urban space and economics beyond the maximum exploitation of the increase in real estate income.[233]

Urban reform in the opening decades continues to propose modernizing the traditional city, in terms almost identical to those of Alvear's time. There is a continuous series of proposals from the end of the century that coincide in a limited stock of resources: boulevards and diagonal avenues, whose layout will be tirelessly discussed. At the same time, it must be recognized that a series of imbalances and displacements appear with respect to nineteenth-century urban debates. On the one hand, because two themes are added that demonstrate a progressive change in the climate of urban ideas: public buildings and, in connection with these, the monumentalization of public space in an extended circuit, themes put on the table by the new lines of picturesque urban

---

[233] As the Cadaqués writer Rahola y Tremols acutely observed in his 1905 visit, the great freedom for private urban business (which would know an unbridled expansion throughout the first decade) was manifested in the scale of the lot, which generated a notorious image of temporariness, while "everything that implies action by the state or the municipality, that is, when it reaches the community or the health of the people [paving, sewers, lighting, cleaning services, running water], is solid or definitive [...]: houses are provisional, but streets are definitive." See Federico Rahola y Tremols, *Sangre nueva* (1905) (Buenos Aires: Institución Cultural Española, 1943), 21. In any case, in this attitude of the state we should not only see philanthropy, since most often street layouts favor—by the system of expropriations, as we saw—big owners; as Mayor Bollini complained in the *Memoria Municipal* of 1892: "it is due to it that in many parts where there are no buildings nor any traffic we observe big, paved surfaces."

Garden Suburb and picturesque models as alternatives to the usual expansion plans:

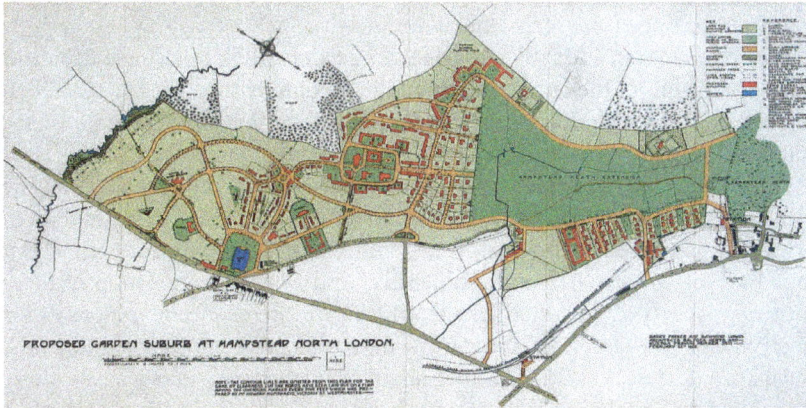

Figure 49. Raymond Unwin and Barry Parker, *Garden Suburb Design for Hampstead, London*, 1905. Hampstead Garden Suburb Archives, Hampstead.

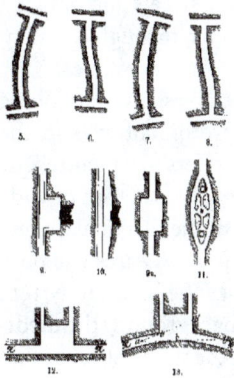

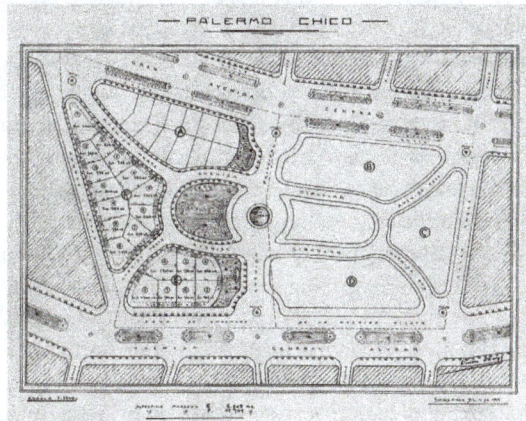

Figure 50. K. Henrici, *Deutsche Bauzeitung*, 1894. Models for curved streets: the generalization of Camilo Sitte's ideas in fin-de-siècle manuals.

Figure 51. Carlos (Charles) Thays, *Plan of Palermo Chico*, Buenos Aires, 1912. Dirección General de Fiscalización de Obras y Catastro, Buenos Aires.

planning, of rapid diffusion in the period. On the other hand, because the other omission, the great novelty with respect to Alvear's city—the extended territory and its public grid—never ceases to seep through. Although we will study these filtrations in the following chapter, it is convenient to point them out here in reference to one of the main difficulties of urban debates, aggravated in periods of marked transition, like this one: the accumulation in a single debate of different visions of the city, each responding to different theoretical and urban moments, and which, therefore, referring to objects that seem to be the same, move in truth in completely incompatible conceptual dimensions.

The diagnosis regarding downtown reform is generally common to all the protagonists of the urban debate. It can be summarized in a generic ambition: to set limits to a laissez-faire attitude that translates into controversies about building regulations, heights, and density. And in the identification of three negative aspects of the inherited city, which give rise to specific proposals for intervention: the streets are too narrow for a traffic that grows day by day; the regularity of the checkerboard does not allow picturesque perspectives; there are no monumental complexes of value in the city. We had already seen the first item diagnosed since the second half of the nineteenth century; in these years it refers unilaterally to Haussmannian proposals: to open avenues that favor circulation as a rational mesh that overlaps the continuous background of the traditional city. In a city like Buenos Aires, where that continuous background is already "rational," in that it is orthogonal and regular, proposals of this type do not cease to pose paradoxes, generally sticking to widening streets and drawing diagonals that connect important points of the city directly, through a system of monumental public focal points (the equivalent of the Parisian étoiles).[234]

The second item, the claim for the absence of perspectives, also has a long history; but if before it meant exclusively absence of prominent axes in the homogeneous grid, in the Parisian baroque sense, it now refers to a picturesque sensibility that is no longer satisfied with the subtle change of rhythm of wide avenues on the checkerboard or with the direct rupture of the diagonal. In any case, the paradoxes that the checkerboard of downtown Buenos Aires will pose to these picturesque pretensions will not be minor. Just as the baroque system sought to superimpose its new rationality on a formless background (the medieval city), the Central European picturesque is based on the vindication of that background, which becomes the giver of historical and cultural form. Therefore,

19

---

[234] This is what the 1869 Lagos Plan, the 1887 project of Mayor Crespo, the specific projects incorporated in the 1898–1904 plan, the diagonals of Desplats, Chanourdie, Jaeschké and the North–South avenue variants of Eugenio Badaro and Emilio Mitre were trying to do, all of them proposed around 1906–1908, and those that would be finally realized over a period of thirty years, the conversion of the main east–west streets into avenues, the diagonals that converge in Plaza de Mayo, and the North–South Avenue (today's 9 de Julio).

in the historical center of Buenos Aires, the picturesque seeks respect for mon-   50
uments and a modernization that establishes points of contact with its historical logic—understood literally through a compendium of formal resources that
can be mimetically adapted to new designs: curved avenues, always limited perspectives, public and monumental spaces secluded and closed to open visuals,
etc.—while in the suburbs it proposes to replace orthogonal extensions with a
typology of picturesque neighborhoods that will be developed along the lines
of the British-American Garden City. In the old center of Buenos Aires, the   49
picturesque logic would imply superimposing an "irrational" mesh of jagged or
curved avenues on the existing checkerboard. This introduced an aestheticist
load even less tolerable than that of the already repudiated French urbanism, in
which hygienic and functional codes still allow, despite their growing discredit
in urbanism at the beginning of the century, a greater capacity of response in
cities like Buenos Aires. In this way, in the consolidated center, the picturesque
has no choice but to renounce global proposals, indicating extremely punctual
projects, very difficult to integrate into the grid, and arguing endlessly over
details. It could develop the typical proposals of picturesque urbanism of garden-neighborhoods for the suburbs, discussing the grid expansion; but the fact
that it hardly does so—and only rhetorically—shows better than anything else
the impossibility of urbanistic debates to observe attentively what was happening outside the traditional center. For picturesque urbanism the omissions generate the central paradox of not being able to engage the issue of expansion, the
only thing about which it could offer global instruments of analysis.[235]

Lastly, the third item, the need for monumental ensembles, responds well
both to rationalist logic and to picturesque sensibility, although they differ
notably in the concrete design solutions they propose and their general distribution in the city. In turn, public expectations will be focused mainly on
this point, since these monumental groupings maintain their emblematic force,
condensing meanings of a political and cultural order, of urban advancement
and state representation, encompassing the specific discussions on commemorative monuments, that produce one of the most characteristic meeting grounds
between national celebration, international exhibition, and urban reform. In

---

[235] The emblematic case is Víctor Jaeschké, the main disseminator of picturesque ideas.
Faced with a parliamentary proposal in 1911 to build three neighborhood parks "on the   51
outskirts of the capital" (so he says, although it is Palermo, Parque Centenario, and San
Cristóbal, in the first suburban cordon *within* the capital), Jaeschké will point out that
"it is plausible as a work of foresight for the future, but there is another similar work
that is no less useful and that is surely of *greater urgency* than that one: the widening
and creation of new squares [...] not in the outskirts or in the periphery, but *in the most
densely populated part of the city*" (underlined by the author), *Las Avenidas* (Buenos
Aires) January 25, 1912, 18. According to these priorities, urban planning professionals
would obsessively discuss the angle and meeting points of the diagonal avenues in the
traditional center.

Figure 52. Unknown photographer, *Congress Plaza*, 1911. Colección Lorenza Trionfi Honorati, Buenos Aires. The view shows the plaza a year after its inauguration (the construction site that is visible is for the first subway line). It was built following plans designed by the Centenary's Municipal Commission.

Figure 53. Joseph-Antoine Bouvard. *Proposal for Congress Plaza*, 1907. *Revista de Arquitectura* (February 15, 1909). Bouvard follows criteria shared by local urbanists on the need to close perspectives.

fact, the resolution of the Plaza Congreso (Congress Plaza) is undoubtedly the   52
main urban development of the centenary. In the first place, because it brings
the discussion on expropriations up to date, showing the profound obstacles to
any urban transformation, to the point that, in the face of the Supreme Court's
traditional obstruction to expropriations, a call for a constituent assembly is
even proposed.[236] Second, because of its very rapid implementation, which
not only contrasted with the ineffectiveness of all provisions for the centenary,
but also recalled the good times of Alvear, after decades in which every public transformation had found only obstacles and delays, recovering the image
that municipal progressivism had so sought to cultivate.[237] In third place, for
its compositional success, that was in fact imposed as evidence to a very hard
initial opposition (the "longaniza square" (long sausage), as engineer Barabino
mockingly called it); the truth is that this project of great longitudinal dimension solved in a masterly way the ending of the Avenida de Mayo in the Congress, raising a type of perspective much more American than European and
granting the avenue a coherence which it originally lacked, establishing from
the Plaza de Mayo the most representative unitary civic-monumental axis of
the whole century.[238]

But surely Plaza Congreso is the most important initiative because it manages
to bring together the two ambitions that almost never converged in the Buenos
Aires that was preparing for the centenary celebrations: the representative needs
of the ruling elite and the reforming ambitions dominating urban debate. It could
be said that in almost everything else these ambitions marched separately, not
because urban debates did not contemplate the representational qualities of its

---

[236] The call came in the editorial "La ciudad de Buenos Aires," *La Prensa*, June 24, 1907, 3.
It is for this discussion that Joaquín V. González makes the intervention in the Congress
mentioned in chapter 3.

[237] Jules Huret writes in his chronicle of the trip: "Two phrases constantly come to the lips
of the *porteños* that reveal their pride in the road traveled and their self-confidence: 'If
only you had seen' and 'You will see! [...] On leaving Buenos Aires for an excursion into
the inner country, the Plaza del Congreso was small, consisting of a simple avenue and
four streets that bordered it. In front of it there was a theater, a barracks, a market, and
some streets on which stood multi-story houses. When I returned after three months,
the municipal mayor, the nice Mr. Güiraldes, took me to it. Instead of the streets, the
houses, the theater, the barracks and the market, there were gardens!" Huret, *De Buenos
Aires al Gran Chaco*, 1:40–41.

[238] Its elongated layout in front of the Congress building had already been proposed by   52
Carlos María Morales in the 1898 plan as a more economical solution (according to
the expropriations to be made) than annexing the Lorea square. Specialized opinion
generally preferred, however, a solution that would limit perspectives, leaving the free-   53
standing building surrounded by gardens around its perimeter. Barabino's phrase in "La
Plaza del Congreso," *Arquitectura. Suplemento de la Revista Técnica* 9–10 (September
30, 1904).

proposals, but because it already subjected them to the resolution of the problems of the city included in a general plan that primarily addressed the issue of circulation. Political elites, on the contrary, more urgently required a scenographic resolution of monumental public space that would accompany what was considered the vertiginous progress of the city. But here lies one of the main paradoxes of a possible reckoning of what the centennial left the city: while urban planners, behind their technical and functional debates, maintained the ideally symmetrical scheme of a city plan increasingly contradicted by actual urban development, the government, concerned with the ephemeral arrangements of the celebration, exhibition pavilions and commemorative monuments, left an indelible stamp on the city, ratifying the definitive impulse of expansion to the north. It is only toward the centenary that the "bourgeois city" begins to define itself in some important buildings, and this is already definitely done in "the north," with the completion of it paradigmatic space, San Martín square, and the beginning of its expansion in a progressive deployment along the streets connecting with Recoleta.

54

This relationship between urban debate and representational needs of the government will reveal its double face in the visit of the French town planner Joseph-Antoine Bouvard, hired in 1907 by the administration of Carlos Alvear (Torcuato's son) for the realization of an improvement plan. The results of this plan will be analyzed in the following chapter, but it should be noted here that, as far as the traditional city center is concerned, they confirm in general terms the main trends of local debates, continuing or reinterpreting existing projects and maintaining in essence all the characteristics of the development of traditional public space, with its strong axiality and symmetry and its centrality on the Plaza de Mayo. On the other hand, the few specific projects that he was commissioned to carry out (or at least that considered his indications) are located in the northern axis of the city: the urbanization of the Quinta de Hale, the design of Alvear Hospital, and the Centennial Industrial Exposition.[239]

In this sense, the main urban role of the centennial celebrations was to legitimize and dynamize that line of expansion, saturating with symbolic content what was already the most prestigious area of the city. It was evidently a conservative attitude, compared to the examples of cities that took advantage of these occasions to generate new zones of expansion or to activate depressed areas; to impose with a great urban event a logic different from that of the market, which in Buenos Aires was spontaneously privileging the northern zone. But what such an attitude reveals in a more drastic way is the national government's lack of willingness to implement a general urban plan: if this variable is discarded, it was logical to rely on the most modern area of the city to enhance the celebration. The area was, it is worth reiterating, far from being homogeneously

---

[239] On these specific projects by Bouvard, see Sonia Berjman, "Proyectos de Bouvard para la Buenos Aires del centenario: barrio, plazas, hospital y exposición," *DANA* 37/38 (1995).

modern: all observers of the period highlight the unqualified mixture of "palaces," precarious shops, shanties, garbage dumps, and tenements that border Alvear (del Libertador) Avenue on the way to Recoleta and Palermo, so the celebration is a way of revitalizing and completing that modernization. There were even more conservative positions, which feared that the layout of the exhibitions in "distant" Palermo would limit attendance, proposing that they be held in more central and consolidated areas.[240]

All the exhibitions are finally set up between Plaza San Martín and Palermo: 54
the International Art Exhibition in San Martín square, where the (reassembled) Argentine pavilion of the Paris Universal Exhibition of 1889 already functioned as the Museum of Fine Arts; the International Exhibition of Hygiene on Alvear and Tagle Avenues; the Exhibition of Spanish Products on Alvear and Castex Avenues; the International Exhibition of Agriculture and Livestock in the grounds of the Rural Society, in Palermo; the Industrial Exhibition (national) on Alvear Avenue in a new section of Palermo; the International Exhibition of Railways and Land Transport, on the banks of the Maldonado stream on the current Bullrich Avenue. All of them implied some sort of consolidation of the adjacent urban area: the enlargement and redesign of San Martín square, the annexation of new landscaped areas to Palermo, the infrastructure works in the Maldonado stream to link the agriculture and railway exhibitions through a bridge that gave continuity to Santa Fe and Cabildo Avenues (favoring the cleaning and urbanization of one of the most degraded areas of the city in the nineteenth century), the use of the landscaping of the Industrial Exhibition for the project in 1912 of the first *barrio-parque* (a small neighborhood with a picturesque layout).

The main attractions were, of course, located in that same area, such as the scenographic reconstruction of the old Plaza de Mayo carried out by the Sociedad de Beneficiencia in the Roses pavilion in Palermo, with student representations of historical scenes, within the framework of a format already imposed in the universal expositions: the nostalgic recreations of urban scenes of the past.[241] The main monuments inaugurated by the government were also located there. These included the complete renovation of the base of the monument to General San Martín and all the donations of foreign nations: the monument of the Spanish and the Germans, located in different points of Alvear Avenue, the

---

[240] For example, see Enrique Chanourdie's criticism of the Centennial Commission for the "eccentric" location of the exhibitions in Barrio Norte and Palermo, in *Arquitectura. Suplemento de la Revista Técnica* 45 (August 1907).

[241] On the papier-mâché reconstruction of the Plaza de Mayo, see *Caras y Caretas* (Buenos Aires), December 4 1909 and January 15, 1910, 583–89. At the 1884 Turin exhibition, a medieval village had been reconstructed, which was widely celebrated by Camilo Boito, in the line of Art and Crafts recreations, and a section of old Paris was reconstructed at the 1900 Paris exhibition. These reconstructions were well received by a public that had learned to value the past as a relic among all the novelties of the progress of the exhibition.

monument of the French in Recoleta, and the English Tower in British Square in Retiro. The main foreign visitor, Spain's Infanta Isabel, was lodged in a new residence near Recoleta, that of De Bary, which generated a permanent public mobilization in the area. Of course, the Avenida de Mayo, with the recently inaugurated the Congress building and its square, was a main attraction for public events and civic and military marches, but no longer as the axis of symmetry of a city that was represented concentrically, but as the southern edge of a public space that now clearly extended north. The entire public circuit was structured there, from Plaza de Mayo through Florida to Plaza San Martín, and from there to Recoleta and Palermo through Santa Fe and Alvear: military parades in honor of foreign visitors; concentrations of school battalions, floral offerings of the "centennial youth," patriotic marches, and civic demonstrations of foreign collectivities. While seeming to ratify an already consolidated public space, the centennial provokes a subtle shift by bringing together two relatively different circuits in one: the ceremonial and civic (Avenida de Mayo and Florida) and the playful and festive (from Plaza San Martín to Recoleta and Palermo); both had already been definitively crystallized as the monumental and at once elegant circuit of the city.

There are, of course, other ways of occupying public space, other ways of tracing routes, creating legitimacy and disputing hierarchies in the city of the centenary, those of workers' and social protest; but from the point of view of the urban representations they generate, they are not so different. The workers' socialist and anarchist demonstrations burst into the city of the nineteenth century with their threatening charge, but also with their irrecusable modernity, as an emblem of a society that completes its metropolitan character through urban industry. This is clear in the way in which some newspapers and illustrated magazines deal with the subject. Caras y Caretas, for example, an enthusiastic admirer of all expressions of "modern life," not only reserved an important space for it—in a practically fixed section called "Movimiento obrero" (Worker's Movement)—but also showed a marked sympathy for protests throughout the decade, as a spectacle that aroused similar enthusiasm to that of military and patriotic parades. Thus, the legitimacy of their claims will be emphasized, but, above all, the seduction of the overwhelming spectacle of the crowds in the street, the "civilized" participation of women and children, flags in the wind, and their rhythmic and informally martial step. The magazine would comment ironically on all this regarding "the fright suffered by some timid bourgeois and some priests" who stand on the sides of the demonstration looking "at the socialists with suspicion, trying to discover the place where they kept the dynamite bombs"—and if this phrase is from 1901, when there had not yet been expressions of violence, the tone would not change substantially, not even in the most critical moments of attack and repression.[242]

---

[242] The quotation in "El 1° de Mayo en Buenos Aires. Manifestación de socialistas," Caras y Caretas (Buenos Aires), May 11, 1901; see also Donato Chaquesien, Los partidos

In any case, it is a question of sustaining different legitimacies in the occupation of public space: How was the multitude of raised fists connected to the multitude of Argentine flags? There is a whole host of answers that social and political history has given a subject that is the most perfect emblem of the contradictions of the country in the centenary: official repression and the organization of informal repressive groups, state of siege, Residence Law, the bombing of the Colón theater during the celebration's gala performance, the death of the police chief Falcón, and so on. But from the point of view of the demarcations of public space I think two questions can be raised. The first is that there is a strictly urban component to the repression, which is linked to a tradition of "young patriots" who come out in defense of public space when they feel it has been endangered: it is a struggle to impose a certain visibility and representative emphasis on the streets, which must be linked to the new patriotic identity of public space aggressively constructed through the marches of school battalions. It does not seem unwise to link the frenzied groups that set fire to anarchist and socialist premises in the centenary or who broke up public demonstrations, with the students who nourish their patriotic spirit by "correcting" what they consider are injudicious decisions in the design of the festive facilities: it was common for students, "representing an aggrieved metropolitan culture"—as one publication celebrates them in a tone similar to a certain coverage of the fires against anarchists and socialists—to "participate" in official decisions on urban ornamentation for patriotic festivities, by beating down or setting fire to elements they considered in "bad taste."[243]

The other urban component of the protest is linked to the demarcation   54
of territories based on the routes of the different demonstrations. And here it could be said that the usual circuit complements that of official celebrations: while virtually maintaining the centrality of the civic axis of Avenida de Mayo, the weight of the protest representations shifts south. Thus, the image of the city split in two is constructed: to the south, the working-class city of protest; to the north, the elegant city of celebration. The traditional symmetry seems to be replaced by an image of unequal but complementary parts that, for various reasons, share the central axis. This reveals the objective of protesting sectors to occupy the center; time and again regulations or repression will try to prevent it, but during the whole period it will grow in importance as an explicit

---

porteños en la vía pública (Buenos Aires: Talleres Gráficos Araujo, 1919).
[243] I cite two examples throughout the decade: May 25, 1903, when Colegio Nacional students demolished by blows the kiosks with which the municipality had "disfigured" the Plaza de Mayo; and May 25, 1910, when another group set fire to Frank Brown's circus which had been installed on Florida Street as part of the attractions arranged by the centennial commission; for the first, see "La manifestación contra los quioscos," *Caras y Caretas* (Buenos Aires), May 23, 1903; the second in *Revista Municipal* 328 (May 9, 1909).

objective of demonstrations. This was undoubtedly favored by the crystallization of the civic axis Congreso-Plaza de Mayo, since previously demonstrations
could go indistinctly to other points (the socialists from Plaza Constitución to
Plaza Rodríguez Peña, crossing the civic axis, and the anarchists from Plaza
Lorea to Plaza Once, to the west of the civic axis).[244] And it shows, at the same
time, the growing identification of protests with the working-class south: traditionally, socialist rallies were already held in Constitución square and from
there they marched toward the center, but some events of the first decade ratify
this identification, although traditional social homogeneity in the city had not
been substantially modified: the first electoral triumph of socialism in La Boca
in 1904, the concentration in San Telmo and La Boca of the main organizational
activity in the 1907 tenants' strike, turn the south into not just another point of
concentration, but the region from which the workers "come" to the city.

The South as Ideology

But if we were to remain simply with this ratification of the terms of the north/
south conflict, we would not understand much of what was to happen later in
the city, and not only in its old traditional center. Because it is also for the centenary, and as a reaction to this crystallization of the traditional city into two
opposing universes, that a sort of *municipalist perspective* will be formalized,
demanding active public intervention in the south as a counterweight to the
development of the north. If all private action and all public representational
efforts are concentrated in the north, to preserve the old symmetrical scheme of
the city it is no longer sufficient to ratify it again and again abstractly in urban
plans as technical debates pretend to do. Who takes charge of the fact that the
city is developing in a different way from the ideal indicated in plans and urban
projects? In these years, this verification produces two positions. One seeks
to legitimize this difference by proposing the advantages of the complemen-
tarity between an industrial south and a bureaucratic and commercial north;
based on long-standing proposals that sought to consolidate the Riachuelo as
an industrial channel complementary to the commercial functions of Puerto
Madero. This position will now be presented with the prestige of a new technical concept of urban planning—*zoning*—key to modern urbanism that in
Buenos Aires will paradoxically justify the processes of spatial segregation

---

[244] I have analyzed the demonstrations with data from *La Vanguardia* and *Caras y
Caretas,* both during the first decade of the century. On the May Day demonstrations,
see Aníbal Viguera, "El primero de mayo en Buenos Aires, 1890–1950: revolución y
voz de una tradición," *Boletín del Instituto de Historia Argentina y Americana Dr. E.
Ravignani* 3 (first half of 1991).

that this very concept rejects.[245] The other position is that of the aforementioned *municipalist perspective*, which is the mode that technical reformism
will assume in this decade, denouncing every public action that tends to favor
the north and demanding an increasing governmental dedication to the south.

It is a position that embodies in many sectors, especially in those directly
affected (organized neighbors of the south zone), in the political parties of
opposition and, it could be said, in public opinion, shaping from then on one
of the main urban commonplaces of the entire twentieth century. But here it is
interesting to see how, in the centenary, that position becomes far more than a
claim for urban justice and, for a certain sector, in fact becomes the driving core
of an ideology, as the crystallization of representations that organize collective
experience. I refer to a sector of the municipality, the technical and bureaucratic
bodies, in which that ideology will be a structural component of something that
it is convenient to call, using Martínez Estrada's expressive characterization,
"municipal nationalism."[246] In this group, technical reformism and municipal
nationalism will be interchangeable figures difficult to distinguish from one
another. We will see it paradigmatically expressed in an episode of monumental commemoration that involves one of the most important and urgent aspects
of the centennial: faced with the evident preference for the north as the location
where official celebrations organized by the National Centennial Commission
are organized, the municipality decides to distribute honors as a way to restore
territorial balance. The City Council, at the suggestion of Adolfo Carranza,
director of the Museo Histórico (Historical Museum, then a municipal institution), approved in 1907 an ordinance for the erection of statues to the members of the First Junta (with the later addition of the statues of Rodríguez Peña,
Garay, and Vieytes); the argument moves in the typical logic of the centenary,
as we will see in the following section, of constituting historical remembrance
through the confrontation between nationalism and cosmopolitanism. But the
most interesting thing is that the location of the statues is manifestly situated
in the south of the city: the few official acts produced in that sector will be for
the inauguration of these statues. With the exception of Rodríguez Peña, in the
square of the same name, and Alberti, in the Barrancas de Belgrano (although
the original location chosen by the municipality had been Alberti square) the
rest are located from Rivadavia to the south: Castelli in Constitución square,
Paso in Independencia square, Larrea in Herrera square (Barracas), Vieytes in

54

---

[245] On the Riachuelo proposal, see Graciela Silvestri, "La ciudad y el río," in Liernur and
Silvestri, *El umbral de la metrópolis*.

[246] Martínez Estrada uses the expression in "X-ray of the Pampa," listing among the
city's oppositions that of "municipal nationalism against snobbery" (244). Although he
does not do so in the same sense as here (since he refers to the west–east opposition),
nevertheless I think he captures the mood of these technical bodies at this moment in
their definition of the *south* as a metaphor for other conflicts.

Moreno square, Saavedra and Matheu in the squares carrying their respective names (La Boca), and Moreno, Azcuénaga, and Garay in the same downtown axis of the city, the first two in the Congreso and Primera Junta squares, and the third in the intersection of Rivadavia with the Bajo (the eastern border of the city facing the river).[247]

The decision is not attributable to mere chance: each location and each commission involved discussions between the National and Municipal Commissions for the organization of the centenary. For *Atlántida* magazine, unofficial spokesman of the National Commission, the City Council exceeded its functions by trying to be "interpreter of national thought": it should not be responsible for the placement of monuments or the decision on urban toponymy, municipal "usurpations" that create "the risk [...] of subjecting the whole country to a localist docility."[248] For the main spokesperson of *municipal nationalism*, the *Revista Municipal* (Municipal Magazine), on the other hand, the tributes consecrated by the municipality are the only thing that can "save the metropolis from the ridicule that is prepared for it with the insignificance of the festivities organized" by the National Commission, which accumulated lavish initiatives to end up with a poor handful of official events.[249] The tone of the confrontation is unusually violent, especially if we consider the official character of the *Revista Municipal*: "we are fatally destined to show off with the centenary," it states sarcastically again and again in view of the imminence of the celebration. The only thing that will save the celebration is what the municipality does: "the Plaza del Congreso, the public gardens, the statues,

---

[247] See *Memorándum sobre las estatuas inauguradas en 1910* (Buenos Aires: Talleres Gráficos Rinaldi, 1912). Though his name does not appear on the cover, Adolfo Carranza writes this memorandum on the vicissitudes of the commission and installation of the statues. The commission designated for the project was formed by Carranza himself, Vicente Fidel López, José María Ramos Mejía, C. Saavedra Lamas, José Luis Cantilo and Ernesto de la Cárcova.

[248] "Crónica del centenario," *Atlántida* 2, n° 6 (1911): 407. The magazine was directed by David Peña, member of the Comisión Nacional del Centenario (and, it could be said, intellectual bridge between the official establishment and the new nationalist generation that was to recognize him as a fundamental mentor). The National Centennial Commission was composed of Interior Minister Marco Avellaneda as president, Mayor Manuel Güiraldes as first vice president, former president Quirno Costa as second vice president, A. Z. Paz as treasurer, and D. Peña as secretary. Among the members were: B. Terán, V. Casares, J. de Apellaniz, Garmendia, F. P. Moreno, C. Estrada, E. Pellegrini, J. de Guerrico, P. Olaechea y Alcorta, and C. Pereyra Iraola. See *1810-1910. La República Argentina en el primer Centenario de su Independencia* (Buenos Aires: Talleres Gráficos Rosso, 1911), which describes the monumental inaugurations; and the documentation in the Archivo General de la Nación organized under the title "Comisión Nacional del Centenario," room 7, files 18-1 to 18-6.

[249] *Revista Municipal* 315 (February 7, 1910).

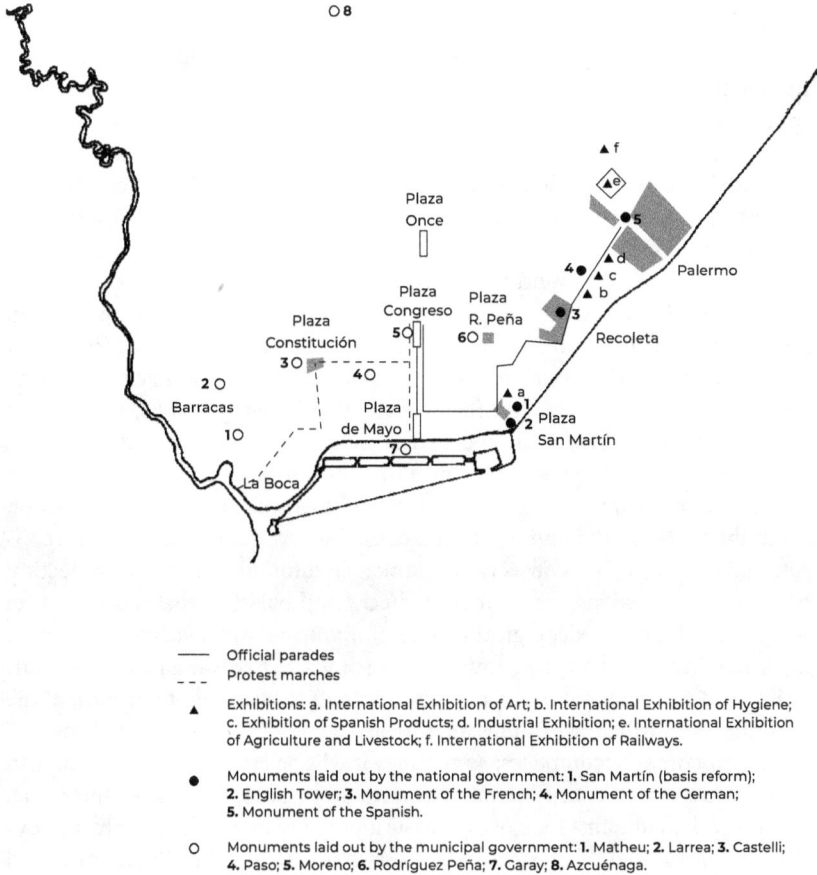

○ 8

Plaza
Once

▲ f

◆▲ e

● 5   Palermo

Plaza
Congreso   Plaza
R. Peña

4 ●   ▲ d
▲ c
▲ b

Plaza
Constitución   5○
6○ ■   ● 3

Recoleta

3○   4○
Plaza
de Mayo

2 ○
Barracas

1 ○

▲ a
● 1
2   Plaza
San Martín

7○

La Boca

——— Official parades
– – – Protest marches

▲   Exhibitions: a. International Exhibition of Art; b. International Exhibition of Hygiene;
c. Exhibition of Spanish Products; d. Industrial Exhibition; e. International Exhibition
of Agriculture and Livestock; f. International Exhibition of Railways.

●   Monuments laid out by the national government: 1. San Martín (basis reform);
2. English Tower; 3. Monument of the French; 4. Monument of the German;
5. Monument of the Spanish.

○   Monuments laid out by the municipal government: 1. Matheu; 2. Larrea; 3. Castelli;
4. Paso; 5. Moreno; 6. Rodríguez Peña; 7. Garay; 8. Azcuénaga.

Figure 54. Diagram showing the route of official parades and protest marches in the years of
the Centenary, with the location of exhibitions and monuments as laid out by the national and
municipal governments.

the lighting, the banners," that is to say, the representations of the city itself
as spectacle; everything the National Commission does is considered horrible:
"Buenos Aires thus ornamented," it says of a project of floral ornamentations,
"would present the aspect of the principal parts of a tenement on a feast day;
the snobbery of the inhabitant carouses over the most frightful ridicule, in its
eagerness to approach the characterization of an aristocratic salon."[250]

For the *Revista Municipal*, the activities of the "great pompous commission" of the centenary are an intrusion of national government in the city. Here
appears, for the first time in such a direct way, a conflict that would mark urban
management throughout the twentieth century, that of the definition of com-
petences between municipal and national government, in the framework of a
legislation that, as we saw, since the establishment of the capital, sponsors a diffuse and superimposed territory of attributions with an explicit subordination
of the municipality. Around the centenary is when all municipal expressions
begin to point out with growing discomfort every situation in which national
institutions impede or hinder municipal urban management (the Ministry of
Education, which does not whitewash schools or demands a very high contribution from the municipality; the Directorate of Health Works, which does
not make drains where indicated by the city; the Ministry of Public Works,
which projects buildings without consulting the municipality, etc.), to the point
that, in the municipalities of the city, the *Revista Municipal* raises the question
about the need—in the middle of debates on the new electoral laws—for a con-
stitutional reform that consecrates municipal autonomy with direct election
of the mayor, breaking the system of checks and balances that federalization
sought. But here the ideological charge of *municipal nationalism* will also be
made manifest, in its attempt, impossible in practice, to distinguish the respon-
sibilities of national and municipal government: for the *Revista Municipal* the
"building authorities" will sometimes be impotent victims of national government, sometimes accomplices; sometimes it will be convenient to distinguish
between mayor and councilmen; sometimes they will represent the same thing;
in this it will maintain a tone of deliberate ambiguity in which the only immov-
able certainty is that the municipal interests are represented by its technical and
bureaucratic bodies.

In spite of the obligatory ambiguity of the denunciation, the interesting thing
is that this conflict crystallizes a chain of associations whereby the national
government is blamed for the unequal development of the north as opposed to
the ideal of equitable development. Celebrating the burning of Frank Brown's
circus next to San Martín square as a "popular reaction" to another blunder
by the National Commission, the magazine ironically states that the arsonists
had no right "to save national decorum at the expense of the tranquility of the
aristocratic barrio: precisely the barrio from where the expression of supreme

---

[250] *Revista Municipal* 328 (May 9, 1910); 322 (March 28, 1910).

Argentine culture stereotyped in the commission of notables [of the centennial] emerges"; the south, on the contrary, will be in this equation the "poor Cinderella [....] condemned to dress with the spoils of her aristocratic sister."[251] The installation of the municipal statues in the south takes place then in the midst of the elaboration of this ideological corpus that, with an unusual charge of violence in its discourse, is going to claim for itself all the virtues that it denies its adversary: morality, social sensitivity, patriotism. It is the resurrection of a confused mixture of *porteño* slogans of the eighties, rebellious slogans of the nineties, urban populism, and technical nationalism, in which *the south* will begin to embody a precise constellation of multiple meanings. Mainly, *the south* will be everything that the intrusion of an aristocratic and corrupt national government neglects: the south itself and the new working-class suburbs that surround the traditional city in all its extension with their misery, from the Maldonado to the Riachuelo—that is, both the old city, the traditional south, and the suburbs where the old and the new are mixed. Within the framework of this frank imbalance between the aristocratic and modern city and the rest, the interesting thing about this *municipalist perspective* is that it will construct a very special south: south and north appear clearly as much more comprehensive metaphors for the city's conflicts, and it is with this content that they will transcend urban common sense, as an ideological representation of these conflicts, the creation of a municipalist imaginary of good guys and bad guys.

Finally, the south will also become a metaphor for an equitable, honest, popular, and technically correct way of carrying out urban practices; a mode of practice which—as Silvestri has shown—Luis Huergo's defeated project for the port in the 1880s will be the most complete emblem: the north is backstage politics, government corruption, imperial business, finance, the hollow formalism of the aristocrats; the south, on the other hand, the technical perspective appropriate to poverty, industry, the project of a modern and autonomous development.[252] Perhaps the best example of the ideological character of this *south* is the fact that Huergo was always a supporter of the model of the complementary city that separated industrial and bureaucratic-commercial sectors, the model against which *municipal nationalism* reacts; but the important thing here is not to point out its contradictions but its efficacy as a representation. For this *municipal nationalism* of Buenos Aires, technicians and bureaucrats will also be a manifestation of the interests of the emerging disciplinary fields of engineering and architecture, which will be defined precisely in the framework set out by the great urban public works and the consolidation of state technical bodies. In this they follow to a large extent the advocacy initiated by the Sociedad Científica Argentina (Argentine Scientific Society) in the last decades

---

[251] *Revista Municipal* 328 (May 9, 1910), 340 (August 1, 1910).
[252] Silvestri, "La ciudad y el río."

of the century, fundamentally empowered by the condensation of ideological topics and the complexity of disciplinary fields of the centenary.

The city will be for them the epicenter of a reformist and, therefore, *nationalist*, exemplifying action. In principle, those who build the city should be Argentines; this is, as we know, the first function of the institutions formed at the turn of the century: Centro Argentino de Ingenieros (Argentine Center of Engineers), Sociedad Central de Arquitectos (Central Society of Architects), Escuela de Arquitectura (School of Architecture)—shared functions and shared ideologies, although conflicts of all kinds quickly appear in their own bosom: between architects and engineers, between public office technicians and liberal professionals, and so on.[253] Second, the very city they build should be *Argentine*. Amid the crisis of eclecticism and of the nationalist unease of the centenary, this will mean two things. On the one hand, the emphatic advocacy for the use of national materials and for the technical experimentation that would allow the development of local industries: Carlos María Morales proposing the use of local wood for paving; Domingo Selva taking advantage of minimal infrastructure works to experiment with reinforced concrete; Carlos Thays selecting examples of national flora for trees. On the other hand, there is the search for an architectural and urban style that expresses a "new art," its own, national, from the colorful searches of Alejandro Christophersen to the surveys of colonial architecture by Juan Kronfuss.[254] Municipal nationalism, technical nationalism, professional nationalism: how telling the appearance of different nationalist aspects is in the very core of those who build and shape the city, the quintessence—for the nationalists—of the foreign disorientation of the *porteño* society. What are those nationalisms so naturally established as a premise of technical reformism; how are they linked among themselves and with other expressions of the nationalism of the centenary? The richness of the possible answers appears in the more specific issue of monuments, no longer focused as a territorial dispute but as a field of definition and demarcation of different visions of nationalism: here the dispute will be about the role of history in the nationalization of city and society.

---

[253] The Argentine Center of Engineers is formed in 1897; in 1895 the Society of Architects and Builders of Works; the Central Society of Architects is formed definitively (after a failed attempt in 1866) in 1901, and in 1904 it begins to publish *Architecture*, at the beginning as a supplement of the *Revista Técnica*; finally, also in 1901, the School of Architecture is created within the Faculty of Exact Sciences. Liernur has developed these questions in an essential article, "Buenos Aires del centenario."

[254] On Christophersen's proposals for a "new art," see the suggestive work by Alejandro Crispiani in which he delves into the conceptual aporias of that search, "Alejandro Christophersen y el desarrollo del eclecticismo en la Argentina," *Cuadernos de Historia* 6 (April 1995); on Kronfuss's surveys, see Marina E. Tarán, "Juan Kronfuss: un registro de nuestra arquitectura colonial," *summa* 215/216 (August 1985).

2. The Pedagogy of Statues

> History is not taught only in the classroom lesson: *the historical sense*, without which History is sterile, is formed in the spectacle of daily life, in the traditional nomenclature of places, in the sites associated with heroic memories, in the remains of museums and even in memorials, whose influence on the imagination I have called *the pedagogy of statues.*[255]
>
> –Ricardo Rojas, 1909

At least since the idea of an international competition for the May memorial was launched in 1902 as a way of starting in time the organizational tasks for the celebration, it could be said that all aesthetic, cultural, and political polemics regarding the present will become inseparable from a perspective on the past, since the focus of the centenary will favor several initiatives linked to history and, above all, with its monumental appropriation in the city. This is verified in a double expansive movement. On the one hand, everyone is called upon to give their opinion, discuss or propose alternatives within the framework of an extremely widespread consensus on the need to monumentalize the past in the city. On the other hand, the monument, the statues, and especially the foundation stones, become a sort of allegory representative of political or social conflicts: from the humor in illustrated magazines, which as the date approaches will increasingly appeal to the figure of the monument to satirize issues of everyday politics, to the ideological polemics in literary magazines. The monument seems the most socially effective way to take sides, and at the same time it is imperative to take sides on monuments because this time, as we saw, they are finally being built.

It would be necessary to specify, in any case, what is specific to the centenary on a subject that recent specialized literature has tended to trace to earlier moments. We saw in the discussion on the pyramid in chapter 2 how, since the early eighties, discussion of monuments had involved the issues of the preservation of memory and its articulation with progress, within the framework of a redefinition—a radical modernization—of traditional public space in the heart of the city, the Plaza de Mayo. This debate was presented as the prolegomenon of a whole cycle that by the end of the century was already manifesting itself in a ritualization of the practices of memory, aiming at the reproductive role of primary education and finding in the city the space par excellence to materialize it: commemorative plaquettes in historical buildings, a new nomenclature memorializing patriotic figures or events in streets and squares, an articulating center in the history museum to provide a coherent weave to that multitude of dispersed signs, and the civic processions, massive

31, 32

---

[255] Ricardo Rojas, *La restauración nacionalista* (1909) (Buenos Aires: Peña Lillo, 1971), 139. This edition is based on the second, expanded edition of 1922.

and martial, of school battalions as a modality of periodically insufflating it with meaning.[256] From this point of view, the concern that Rojas expresses in *La restauración nacionalista* (Nationalist Restoration) does not imply, in 1909, an innovation in the official climate of ideas. But, throughout the first decade, the mutual nourishment between this tendency and the initiatives for the organization of the centenary were producing a true historicist saturation of which his book is symptomatic.

Some data is well-known: in 1908 a "patriotic teaching"—which Halperin Donghi characterized as a "civic liturgy of almost Japanese intensity"—was formalized by the National Council of Education for schools, which gave a prominent place to visits to museums and monuments and the massive provision of historical iconography, along with the uniform celebration of anniversaries and the daily salute to the flag.[257] To this end, the state commissioned a series of reports that would be referents of the debate on education, history, and nationality, which include the book by Rojas mentioned above and the publications of Ernesto Quesada or Leopoldo Lugones. Directly linked to the preparations for the celebration is a sequence of official commissions that result in the first texts on the country's architectural and historical heritage, especially in Buenos Aires—and it could be said that a complete line of nationalist historiography is born of those official commissions. A similar qualitative leap can be found in toponymy, with a massive renaming of streets and walks based on patriotic history.[258]

---

[256] Lilia Ana Bertoni "La educación 'moral': visión y acción de la elite a través del sistema nacional de educación primaria, 1881–1916," Instituto Ravignani, Buenos Aires, April 1991 (mimeo).

[257] Halperin Donghi's quote from "¿Para qué la inmigración? Ideología y política inmigratoria en la Argentina (1810–1914)," in *El espejo de la historia*, 226. To see the novelty and radical nature of these practices so naturalized in the twentieth century in Argentine schools, it is useful to refer to the astonishment of a foreign visitor: pointing out the patriotic character of teaching in Argentina, evident in the "pictures and (the) inscriptions on the walls" of the schools, Clemenceau shows in an explanatory note how surprised he was by their practices: "It appears that on the day of the National Fête the pupils of the primary schools have to take an oath of fidelity to the Flag, which is called the *jura de la Bandera*, and is accompanied by speeches and patriotic songs that cannot help making an impression on the children," in *South America To-day*, 93.

[258] I mention but a few of the more significant titles in the long list of texts commissioned for the centenary. On education: Ernesto Quesada, *La enseñanza de la historia en las universidades alemanas*, 2 vols. (La Plata: Universidad Nacional de La Plata, 1910); Juan P. Ramos, *Historia de la instrucción primaria en la Argentina, 1809–1909 (atlas escolar)*, 2 vols. (Buenos Aires: Peuser, 1910); Leopoldo Lugones, *Didáctica* (Buenos Aires: Otero y Cía., 1910). On colonial architecture and urbanism: Enrique Peña, *Documentos y planos relativos al período colonial en la ciudad de Buenos Aires*, 5 vols. (Buenos Aires, Peuser, 1910); José Antonio Pillado, *Buenos Aires colonial. Edificios y costumbres* (Buenos Aires: Compañía Sudamericana de Billetes de Banco, 1910); Serafín Livacich, *Buenos*

Something similar was happening with monuments: the change was quantitative, but the spectacular proliferation of initiatives will soon make it qualitative. Although the problem had already been stated, at the beginning of the century there would still very few historical and patriotic monuments erected in public places, which were now even more necessary to satisfy the demands of a growing ritualization. To the Pyramid of May and the equestrian statues of San Martín (1862) and Belgrano (1873), had been added only their own mausoleums (that of San Martín in the cathedral and that of Belgrano in the church of Santo Domingo), the statue of Adolfo Alsina in the Plaza Libertad (1882), the column of Lavalle in the Plaza del Parque (1887), the statue of Falucho in Florida and Charcas (1897), and Sarmiento's statue by Rodin in Palermo which, inaugurated on May 25, 1900, became the first great local sculptural episode to mobilize public opinion, reproducing, in scale, the scandal that the French sculptor had generated in Paris with his Balzac.[259] Each monument was integrated with great pomp to that network in formation, but they were still too few for the desired density. There were some other sculptures, but either they do not belong in this category or, on the contrary, they appeared as threats to the construction of the nationality with which they should collaborate. In the first case, the profuse statuary of Recoleta Cemetery, the destination of many public demonstrations and the first place where the *porteños* were educated in sculptural polemics between general admiration and elitist contempt for the many "mamarrachos de la marmolería criolla" (rubbish of Creole marblery, as an irritated López described in *La gran aldea*), but which does not count for nationalizing purposes because the concentration of such monumental profusion in a single site has the opposite pedagogic meaning than would a broader distribution

---

Aires. Páginas históricas para el primer centenario de la Independencia (Buenos Aires: Compañía Sudamericana de Billetes de Banco, 1907). This is the context in which Paul Groussac sends Gaspar García Viñas to the Archivo de Indias in Seville to form the *Colección de copias de documentos* for the National Library in Buenos Aires; Lugones was in turn sent on a documentary excursion to the Jesuit missions (he publishes *El imperio jesuítico* in 1904), and the Faculty of Philosophy and Letters of the University of Buenos Aires extended its archaeological expeditions to the northeast with the work of Ambrosetti (begun at the end of the previous century) and Debenedetti (who began work precisely in 1909). On toponymy, see Adolfo Carranza, *Origen del nombre de las calles de Buenos Aires* (Buenos Aires: Kraft, 1910), and Beccar Varela and Enrique Udaondo, *Plazas y calles de Buenos Aires (significación histórica de sus nombres)* (Buenos Aires, 1910), both titles edited on the occasion of the centenary.

[259] The statue was commissioned from Rodin by Miguel Cané and was installed on the site of the recently demolished Caserón de Rosas. We will return to the general displeasure caused in Buenos Aires by Sarmiento's statue later. The fact that Cané took advantage of the inaugural ceremony to make harsh criticisms of the educational reforms that Roca's government was carrying out was no small part of the scandal.

over the entire city's public space.[260] In the second case are the sculptures that appear as a threat to national identity, among which the statue of Mazzini, in front of the government house in Roma square, controversial since its inauguration in 1878 because the city's legislature sanctioned its erection with opposition from the government of Buenos Aires, and which would become for Rojas an emblem of the cosmopolitan politics of Buenos Aires (together with the statue of Garibaldi erected in 1907 in Italia square).

But, from the beginning of the century, already in the course of the centennial celebrations, statues multiply; often literally, since the first reproduction of the statue of San Martín was made at the request of the government of the province of Santa Fe in 1902, provincial city squares would soon be populated with duplicates.[261] In Buenos Aires, the discussion about the May monument that would replace the pyramid is reopened, for which an international contest of great repercussion is called; monumental donations of foreign collectivities are arranged; the statues of the members of the First Junta, of Rodríguez Peña, Garay and Vieytes are ordered, and many of the existing ones are reformed, in a kind of race against the clock to populate the centenary with inaugural acts. In the rest of the country, the proliferation is repeated, not always with copies, but with large-scale projects, such as the monument to the Army of the Andes in the Cerro de la Gloria in Mendoza.[262]

Proliferation produces changes. First, the effect of empowerment itself: as soon as the pantheon of heroes eligible for monumental representation expands, the demand for new recognition takes the form of an unstoppable spiral, to the point that here begins something so common since then but unimaginable only a few years earlier, the conversion of toponymy and monuments into polemical evidence. It is significant that, when confronting the ideas of Ricardo Rojas's *La restauración nacionalista*, Roberto Giusti decides to specify his differences by choosing different monuments, proposing "not only Moreno, Rivadavia, San Martín, respectable champions of an already ancient ideal, not only the symbolic Dante that Rojas admits, not only

---

[260] See Lucio V. López, *La gran aldea. Costumbres bonaerenses* (1884) (Buenos Aires: CEAL, 1980), 112.

[261] On the casts, see Eduardo Schiaffino's polemic with Ernesto de la Cárcova in *La Nación*, May 21 and 22, 1926, reproduced in the "Documentary Appendix," Schiaffino, *Urbanización de Buenos Aires* (Buenos Aires: M. Gleizer, 1926), 271ff; there they offer data on the first casts, blaming each other for not having prevented them, because of the obvious harm to the sculptors.

[262] The law for the erection of the Monument in Mendoza dates to 1888, but its project is only entrusted to the sculptor Juan Ferrari for the centenary, when actual work begins, though the monument would be completed much later; see Comisión Nacional del Centenario, "Expedientes relativos a monumentos del Centenario con intervención del Ministerio de Obras Públicas, 1911–1920," Archivo General de la Nación, room 7, file 18-4-9.

Garibaldi and Mazzini, which he proposes to throw into an attic, but also—and why not?—Karl Marx, Émile Zola, Leo Tolstoy, champions of the new ideals."[263] In the same way, the fact that Olegario V. Andrade has no statue or street named after him, "while our prodigality of glory raises monuments to all the subaltern generals of our wars and names the streets of the 'Athens of the South' with the names of every mediocre politician our fertile democracy has produced," serves Manuel Gálvez in 1910 as a rhetorical strategy to show that Buenos Aires despises its poets and, of course, everything spiritual. In addition, for Gálvez, the rejection of the port city and its "fertile" democracy must also be manifested in a list of monuments that is different from the official one.[264] As in the case of Giusti, what goes unquestioned is that this is how values should be represented.

Second, the proliferation of monuments produced an extraordinary "patriotic" diffusion in society. In addition to the centenary commission itself, which dealt with official assignments, these years saw the spread of commemorative commissions in search of public and private subscriptions (which, in this ideological climate, must have been difficult to resist) for the most varied monumental initiatives. According to the importance of the hero or the event, the commissions were formed by more or less distinguished members, from the political and cultural establishment to parish celebrities; they would commission their monument to foreign or national artists, famous or unknown; and they would see their proposal realized or postponed for years. The proliferation favored all kinds of practices: the *Revista Técnica* denounced mediocre sculptors who formed ad hoc commissions of scarce prestige to pay due homage to a forgotten hero as blackmail for funds for their own monumental projects. Patriotic arguments, it is known, have everywhere been the origin and material support of local arts, but what is not always considered is the role of these civic commissions in the broadening of traditional public space: that ambiguous intermediate space of maneuvering between the state and society which deals with irrecusable initiatives that neither one nor the other can confront but which dignify both, and which in its less prestigious borders sheds light on its expansive reach of new social sectors. The local artist, on the one hand, and the

---

[263] Roberto Giusti, "*La restauración nacionalista* por Ricardo Rojas," *Nosotros* V, no. 26 (February 1910): 151.

[264] Manuel Gálvez, *El diario de Gabriel Quiroga* (Buenos Aires: Arnoldo Moen y Hno., 1910), 191–92. There is a certain peculiarity in this ecumenical call for monuments: in a country with a much longer and more prolific monumental tradition, such as France, it is possible to recognize, following Agulhon's studies, an ideological watershed between those in favor of monumental representation, who throughout the nineteenth century can be placed on the left—with the ratification in the secular monument of its modernizing pedagogical vocation—and those who systematically oppose it, placed on the political right—with their conservative will reluctant to extend the cult to "the new gods" of politics, science, or the military; see *Histoire vagabonde* (Paris: Gallimard, 1988).

committee politician, on the other, the barrio dignitary, up-and-coming merchant, or new professional, find in these mixed initiatives of civic commissions
a practical, social function of the cult of the homeland that does nothing but
guarantee its reproduction.[265]

The Monument Against the City

We have already covered the controversy over the placement of the statues,
in which a kind of municipal nationalism seeks to counteract the "northern" effects of the occupation of urban space by the national government. But
there is another use of monuments for a "cultural nationalism," whose postulates could be said to develop in the shadow of official optimistic nationalism—shadowed in a double parasitic sense: nourished by it and in confrontation with it. For this new nationalism it is no longer a matter of preference for
one or another sector of the city: the whole city is enemy territory, and this is
the main difference with preceding monumental discussions, not only with
respect to municipal nationalism. From Rosas's overthrow onwards, all the
monumental polemics—the attempts to identify the deeds of Buenos Aires
with national history, as in the State of Buenos Aires; or, conversely, to re-ap-
propriate the city for a national public space, as in the 1880s—began from
an identitarian recognition of the city. This is the first time that a desire for
change in the city operates from the most radical estrangement. For Manuel
Gálvez, for example, in El diario de Gabriel Quiroga, the city is, in its materiality, the incarnation of everything that traditional society has lost through
modernization. Again and again, he denounces its commodification, its commercial and foreign materiality, structuring the armored series Buenos-Aires/
port-city/Phoenician-city: "We don't mind that our houses, passing from hand
to hand and being sold daily, have something of the prostitute." But the metaphor can be even more encompassing, because all of Buenos-Aires (with a
hyphen, as Gálvez writes with an archaizing gesture, as if to make present the
contrast with the traditional city) is, in truth, "a beautiful prostitute who is
learning to beautify herself and who, under the splendor of her cosmopolitan

---

[265] On the role of the commissions, we find in costumbrista notes acid criticisms on the
reverse of which it is possible to understand their leveling social sense. For example, the
chapter "Las comisiones" in Santiago Rusiñol, Un viaje al Plata, translated from Catalan
by G. Martínez Sierra (Madrid: V. Prieto y Compañía, 1911), chap. XXX, 161ff; Roberto
Gache, "La estatua de un general desconocido," in Glosario de la farsa urbana (Buenos
Aires: Cooperativa Editorial Ltda, 1919), 29 ff. The continuity of these social practices
appears clearly—again in a strongly critical tone—in a suggestive text by Roberto Arlt,
"La gran manga," El Mundo (Buenos Aires), March 24, 1929, compiled in Sylvia Saítta,
Tratado de la delincuencia. Aguafuertes inéditas de Roberto Arlt (Buenos Aires: Biblioteca
Página/12, 1996).

flesh and the mimicry of her loud and complicated luxury, lets her crude condition be perceived at every moment."[266] Materialism versus artistic spirit, fetishistic veneration of money versus worship of national values, cosmopolitanism versus nationalism, falsehood versus honesty, the complication of luxury versus the simplicity of true beauty, aristocracy versus the *nouveau riche*: a sequence of oppositions that would ceaselessly reproduce and expand over the following decades, setting the tone for a climate of anti-urban ideas so widespread as to bring up many points of contact with technical nationalism, so different in so many ways (which means that when this sequence appears, whole or in parts, it will not necessarily be accompanied by the full argumentation of someone like Gálvez, with its warlike chauvinism, its anti-Semitism, and its aristocratic discrimination of "mulattoes" and "gringos," as European immigrants were then called).[267]

Much has been written about this intellectual generation from which the main figures of the "national renaissance" emerged: idealism, spiritualism, their condition as poor and bohemian provincials in an indifferent metropolis—which, by the way, some of them could hold responsible for the decline of their provincial family glories.[268] A figure in many ways different from that group, as Alberto Gerchunoff will recall a few years later, how they had nurtured an anti-metropolitan ideology: "we were incredibly unfair to Buenos Aires," he will say precisely in a banquet honoring Gálvez.[269] What are, then, monuments for them? A redemption: the network of monuments is now seen as a purifying mantle over the alien and forgetful metropolis. For the first time, the web of historical and national signs is thought of as something alien to the city, to be imposed on it: the forcible implantation of a spiritual skeleton that could twist the course of its "cosmopolitan flesh"; a sensitive plane of elements that, superimposed on the homogeneous city, organizes and qualifies its mercantile anomie.

This is the tone of *La restauración nacionalista*. As was made clear in the opening of this section, Rojas knows that monuments and public art in general

---

[266] *El diario de Gabriel Quiroga*, 204 and 64–65, respectively.

[267] His proposal to go to war with Brazil as an indispensable step for the formation of a national sentiment is only less scandalous to our present eyes than the reason why he ends up considering it unnecessary: the "transcendent revelation" of the "patriotic" fires against anarchists and socialists, carried out by students "while they were blowing the notes of the national anthem" (232). This has been highlighted by Oscar Terán in "El decadentismo argentino" (Buenos Aires), mimeo, 1990.

[268] See Carlos Payá and Eduardo Cárdenas, *El primer nacionalismo argentino en Manuel Gálvez y Ricardo Rojas* (Buenos Aires: Peña Lillo, 1978); Adolfo Prieto, "Gálvez. Una peripecia del realismo," *Estudios de literatura argentina* (Buenos Aires, Galerna, 1969); and Carlos Altamirano and Beatriz Sarlo, "La Argentina del centenario: campo intelectual, vida literaria y temas ideológicos," in *Ensayos argentinos*.

[269] "Comida en honor de Manuel Gálvez," *Nosotros* 22, no. 85 (May 1916): 220.

are the main instruments through which the city guarantees the nationalizing task. He learned this in Europe, where public art is abundant and its quality, sedimented for centuries, and for centuries indissolubly associated with the city, had already given Romanticism the arguments to bridge history and folklore, cultured and popular art, political and cultural nationalism. The problem for Rojas is that in Buenos Aires he finds himself in a very precarious situation: a city that must first be transformed itself so that it can be counted on to perform the task. To bridge the impasse he will produce the most detailed manual of the necessary relationship between new monuments and the heritage conservation, between the museum and the school, art and architecture, toponymy and municipal archives, as a symbolic reappropriation of a city affected to the point of dissolution by "the prolongation of foreign nationalities, which, sending their armies of men with their *penates* (household gods), carried out, as in an ancient rite, the symbolic occupation of our territory."[270] But this phrase can be misleading: concerned with the elaboration of a cultural policy rather than with spiritualist denunciation in the manner of Gálvez, Rojas does not focus his reaction on the immigrants themselves. His diagnosis and his recommendations place him much closer to a Ramos Mejía, in a way that allows us to understand the transformations of local liberalism itself in its view of the city; even, or above all, by the change pointed out by Halperin, from the ironic instrumentality of Ramos Mejía (typical of an intellectual of the eighties), which leads him to formalize an educational program that he believes is as necessary as it is ridiculous, to the romantic candor with which Rojas assumes the task.[271]

Rojas does not invert, like Gálvez, the values of Sarmiento's antinomy of civilization and barbarism; what has changed for him is the scenario and the form, but he continues to define the values of that struggle in the same terms: the theater of barbarism "is the city, not the countryside, and the *montoneros* no longer use the horse but electricity: Facundo rides the tram," he explains.[272] The problem, in any case, is that this change of scenery is not neutral with respect to the antinomy, because what will be produced in the city is an undifferentiated mixture of its terms: this is the metropolitan babel, the impossibility of deciding what is civilization and what is barbarism, the permanent concealment of one in the other. And here it is appropriate to dwell on another monumental issue, a central one in the centenary and in itself very complicated in Buenos Aires: the preservation of historical building heritage, an issue that allows us to identify the wide gray area of contacts

---

[270] Rojas, *La restauración nacionalista*, 222. As seen in Giusti's reply, Rojas proposes the removal of the statue of Mazzini, because "the statue of a foreigner [...] cannot remain at the very gates of Buenos Aires."

[271] Halperin Donghi, "¿Para qué la inmigración?," 229ff.

[272] *Nosotros*, III, nos. 13–14 (August-September 1908): 126.

between nationalist regenerationism and other forms of nationalism until it reaches its official expression, showing the typical ambivalences that the theoreticians of nationalism have pointed out between essentialist and the epochalist currents.[273]

A first zone of coincidences opens up from what seems to be an irreducible opposition. There is an emblematic enemy of the nationalist reaction, the press, because it is the medium par excellence that reflects and reproduces—in a fatally effective way, judging by its growth—"exotic" metropolitan life. Nationalist intellectuals establish a structural relationship between the press and what they repudiate in the city. "What was once priesthood and tribune, is today a business and a market hawker," says Rojas: service advertisements that reflect "the starving immigration that congests the city;" commercial notices that reflect "our abnormal economic life of speculations and auctions;" portraits and details of the European nobility; frivolous social chronicles; cablegrams with trivial events of Italian and Russian villages; a racing page to satisfy the curiosity of urban crowds that "give to a horse or its jockey the admiration that other people dispense to their great poet or their first dramatist."[274] This is undoubtedly the reaction of the cultural elite against the massiveness of the periodical press; but what also arouses the anti-modern reaction is the new structuring of modes of experience analogous to that of the city that appears in the press, and which therefore reproduces ad infinitum the new dissolution of values: as Julio Ramos points out, the newspaper and the city are traversed by the same logic, "unhierarchized, by an accumulation of fragmented codes." And if this is assumed by the newspaper, which more and more explicitly embodies its urban character until it develops formats "to read on the tram," the "miscellaneous system of the magazine"—as Sarlo called it—will take it to a level of paroxysm, because, in the urban chronicle, illustrated magazines find the vehicle for the construction of their new publics, exasperating the fragmentation and the multiplicity of meanings.[275]

The illustrated magazine makes a bastion out of its materialistic cosmopolitanism; it takes on, as its militant enterprise, the promotion of the values of progress and urban modernity as a key to the spirit of the times. In its series

---

[273] The formula is drawn from Clifford Geertz, *The Interpretation of Cultures* (London: Fontana Press, 1993), esp. chap. "After the Revolution: The Fate of Nationalism in the New States." See also Tom Nairn, *The Break-up of Britain: Crisis and Neo-nationalism* (London: NLB, 1977), esp. the chapter "The Modern Janus."

[274] *La restauración nacionalista*, 134.

[275] Julio Ramos, *Divergent Modernities: Culture and Politics in Nineteenth Century Latin America* (Durham [NC]: Duke University Press, 2001), 124. On the reaction of the elite against the massiveness of the press, see Adolfo Prieto, *El discurso criollista*. The reference to Sarlo is from *El imperio de los sentimientos. Narraciones de circulación periódica en la Argentina (1917–1927)* (Buenos Aires: Catálogos, 1985).

"Modern Buenos Aires," in 1900 *Caras y Caretas* promoted the construction of a hotel on Avenida de Mayo in the following terms:

> Buenos Aires has been transformed in five years. And if it is true that "such progress is almost exclusively material," we must not forget that this phrase is as hollow as most: there is no body without a soul; there is no form that does not envelop its corresponding idea. If our capital city progresses in its external aesthetics, it responds to a feeling that is perhaps not very well defined but which is a real and effective progress. The constructions of the Avenida de Mayo have done more for our culture and our education, than twelve hefty volumes of artistic doctrine or pedagogical pedantry. [276]

The clear polemical imprint shows how early the accusations against "material progress" that the magazine considers its duty to raise appear. Rojas seems to take up the discussion at the same point: protesting against the official disregard for architectural heritage, he points out how Enrico Ferri, "foreigner and champion of internationalism," was nevertheless indignant with that disinterest and stated that Sarmiento's house, "as architecture and as historical relic," had caused him "a greater aesthetic and civic impression than the Avenida de Mayo."[277]

Not only for Rojas, but for the entire elite, the Avenida de Mayo was ceasing to be an emblem of modernity and becoming instead an emblem of the aesthetic masked ball of a new civic barbarism: that of the gaudy bourgeoisie and nouveau-riche immigrants; in its eclectic chaos, the Avenida de Mayo is a synecdoche of metropolitan Buenos Aires, while Sarmiento's house in San Juan is a synecdoche of history and the nation. In this way, Rojas creates a program of patrimonial preservation in which monuments are thought of as an intrusion of civilizing memory in a barbaric territory. The "authenticity" of that memory does not matter, nor does its original location: his objective is to transform the public space of the city, "to disturb the party of its cosmopolitan mercantilism."[278] Two decades later, Rojas commissioned Ángel Guido to design his house (today a museum) on Charcas Street, whose external facade reproduces that of the historic Tucumán House, then demolished, as a way of brutally confronting the dememorialized city with an icon of the patriotic past. The past as a *patriotic icon*: this is how Rojas sees history in the city.

But it is here that the distance with the illustrated magazine begins to shrink in a double sense. On the one hand, because the magazines and the press were the great builders and disseminators, in these years, of the patriotic

28

55, 56

---

[276] "En la Avenida de Mayo. Metropole Hotel," *Caras y Caretas* (Buenos Aires), January 20, 1900.
[277] *La restauración nacionalista*, 56–57.
[278] Ibid., 22.

iconography that has lasted almost to the present day. The proximity of the centenary and the figurative demands of nationalization programs through schools, lead to maximizing the need, raised since the end of the century, to fix a repertoire of official patriotic imagery: portraits, symbols, historic recreations, reproductions of objects for a new nationalist consumption, marking the beginning of a cultural industry that poses a fetishistic relationship with history and produces the main motifs with which the patriotic liturgy will be populated with images.[279] This very modern need for "clear," recognizable images for massive and effective patriotic consumption, poses narrow limits to a search for modernity on the other side, so to speak, of the historical function of monumental representation: art. The polemics about the resemblance of the heroes and the verisimilitude of the scenes are reiterated in each commission and each inauguration. But not only in terms of a demand for traditional realism in the face of the "distortions" of artistic expression; it is a demand for archetypal figures for the foundational needs of an imagery that is thought of in its capacity not for representation but for iconic reproducibility: like the spiraling columns inspired by those of the historic Tucumán House in Rojas's house.[280]

---

[279] Regarding the fetishistic relationship with history generated by this new cultural industry, a good example is that of Aceite Bou (Bou Oil), which gives "Argentine children" in commemoration of the centenary a copy of General San Martín's plate exhibited in the Historical Museum, appropriating the slogan with which the English reproduced, in turn, Admiral Nelson's crockery: "to eat on the plate of a hero is to be inflamed in the flame of the most cherished patriotism." See, among others, *Caras y Caretas* (Buenos Aires), January 21, 1911. As an example of the treatment—and the relevance—that this magazine gave to history, see the special issue, *Caras y Caretas* (Buenos Aires), May 21, 1910. Here it is already possible to find the type of representation that would later be developed and popularized by the magazine *Billiken*.

[280] The episode of Rodin's Sarmiento is a good example: unlike the scandal that the sculptor had caused with his Balzac in Paris, here almost no one discusses his artistic stature or the beauty and expressiveness of the monument as a whole; the problem is only one—and "doblemente capital" (doubly capital), as Lugones would say: the head bears no resemblance to its subject. Rodin's symbolist sensibility can be accepted in the whole monument, but it is not enough for the head to be a symbol of Sarmiento—as its defenders would say; what is demanded for the iconic pantheon that is being built are synthetic images, easily apprehensible, reproducible. It is curious that many years later the same monument is being discussed for similar reasons: Eduardo Schiaffino, defender of the Sarmiento since its inauguration, proposes around 1926 that in the face of the profusion of coats of arms "badly translated into tin" on the fronts of public buildings, the Argentine coat of arms "so happily stylized" by Rodin on the plinth should be universalized; Ernesto de la Cárcova—then president of the National Commission of Fine Arts—while recognizing the beauty of Rodin's coat of arms, replies that the image of the national coat of arms "cannot be left to the more or less brilliant imagination of foreign or even Argentine artists; this will lead, as time goes by, to not knowing which

Figure 55. *Ricardo Rojas's House on Charcas Street,* designed by Ángel Guido, Buenos Aires, 1927. Photograph by Adrián Gorelik.

Figure 56. *Tucumán House,* reconstructed by Mario Buschiazzo in 1943. *Summa,* Buenos Aires, nos. 215–16 (August 1985).

And there is yet another question: the distances between nationalism and the illustrated magazine diminish, above all, because the magazine embodies in an emblematic way that wide gray zone extending from official optimism to nationalist regenerationism, which manifests itself in the radical ambiguity with which everyone faces the aporias of an impossible articulation: between the celebration of civilizing progress and the cult of the past that the centennial has placed on the agenda. What should the city do in the face of the double demand for preservation and change? *Caras y Caretas* deals with the ambiguity through a growing schizophrenia: while the "modern Buenos Aires" type of notes continues to define the general tone of the magazine, critical articles on the loss of urban heritage, in which all the arguments of regenerationism are reproduced, will gain ground in the years leading up to the centenary (in fact, in 1913 the magazine will publish the first operative revaluation of the colonial architecture of the Río de la Plata in an article by Christophersen). "We have nothing left but the parody of what we were," laments a chronicler in front of an old mansion converted into a tenement house in the southern barrio, at the same time that in other pages one reads daily the criticism—very extended in the period—that the south does not "progress" because owners, keeping their old one-story houses, ensure themselves a very good rent, hardly improvable in the perilous process of the sort of building renovation that the magazine proposes.[281]

Let's take a case in which the tension between both values is at its maximum: a large house in Belgrano Street between Bolívar and Defensa is demolished to build a "modern palace." "The frequent modernizations that our streets, squares, and promenades undergo," the chronicler notes, "are gradually destroying all archaic corners." The ambiguity of this sentence, in the context of the magazine that most strives for urban modernization and that simultaneously most searches for picturesque corners in its "walks through the municipality," makes the valuation assigned to the terms modernization and archaic undecidable.[282] This is, moreover, a special demolition: General Belgrano was born in the mansion, and the owner is Julio Peña, politician and historian, a "notable" of Buenos Aires directly committed to the historicist restoration of the city (he will carry out official missions to Europe to acquire statues and will publish compilations of old documents for urban history).[283] Moreover,

---

[image] to follow. In the modern industry of patriotic images that has been set up since the years prior to the centenary, the main thing is to know what to stick to; see Eduardo Schiaffino, *Urbanización de Buenos Aires*, his proposal on p. 160; de la Cárcova's response on p. 272.

[281] The quote in *Caras y Caretas* (Buenos Aires), May 21, 1910.

[282] See *Caras y Caretas* (Buenos Aires), March 6, 1909.

[283] Vicente Cutolo, *Nuevo diccionario biográfico argentino, 1750–1930* (Buenos Aires: Elche, 1978), vol. V.

five years have passed since the much reviled demolition of the Rodríguez Peña house, and it could be said that the alert on the subject is generalized. How is the conflict resolved? From the ambiguity of the magazine, we return to that of the "official" view of the city and history: the demolition is "inaugurated" with a public act practically the same as the inauguration of a monument, with the full municipal cabinet, headed by the mayor himself, receiving in solemn donation from the hands of the owner, the ironwork of the house to be exhibited in the Historical Museum, like stumps of the past forever protected from building progress. The tension between the two equally powerful certainties in the centenary is precariously resolved, in a way already notoriously torn, accepting that the place of memory in the city is the icon or the museum, and giving this renunciation the character of a patriotic donation.

From Classicism to Abstraction

The split, at any rate, is smaller than in the case of urban specialists. In 1905 the journal of the nascent architects' corporation reacts unanimously against a legislative proposal, in line with the many iconographic reconstructions for educational purposes, to rebuild the Cabildo and turn it into a historical museum.[284] This occurred in the midst of the historicist outpouring, in the midst of the search for a militant technical nationalism, in the midst of the expansion, moreover, of the picturesque theories that already brought as added value the articulation between the new urban historicism and the nationalism of the intellectual and artistic circles of central Europe, highly functional to the climate of the centenary, and which since the end of the century had given the historical monument a methodological centrality in urban design. The magazine opposed the project in the most forceful way: with a survey of renowned architects which was to be considered a true "technical plebiscite."

Among those surveyed there are very divergent positions, but they converge in opposition. Those least affected by the new urban planning theories cannot see the relationship between material remains, history, and the city: the Cabildo seems to them to be an eyesore, and it makes no sense to preserve the

---

[284] The Cabildo was then completely disfigured not only, as we saw in the first part, by the opening of Avenida de Mayo; before that, its tower had already been replaced by a larger one, in academicist style, which later collapsed. But in addition, numerous projects foresaw the construction of a monumental entrance to the square, with a building on the site of the Cabildo that would produce an effect of symmetry with the building of La Prensa (one of the most celebrated of the new constructions of the avenue). The reconstruction project was presented to the Chamber of Deputies by General M. Campos and published in *Arquitectura. Suplemento de la Revista Técnica* nos. 26–28 (June–July 1905), 47.

memory of eyesores. Therefore, it should be demolished, and, if history is to be commemorated, a new building should be built, appropriate to its modern function: "Great towns should commemorate their civic ideals, but they should also avoid ridicule," says one architect surveyed.[285]

Those who, on the other hand, already see the intimate unity between material remains, urban memory, and modern urban planning, will place the absence of authenticity at the center of their refusal to reconstruct: from this point of view it makes no sense to preserve fragments and even less to carry out reconstructions; the answer, in short, will be the same: better to demolish, build a monumental building, and make a plaster model of the whole of the old Plaza de Mayo, to recreate the complete environment. Víctor Jaeschké, the main introducer of the Sittean picturesque in Buenos Aires, takes this position: after so many alterations, that shapeless remains is anything but the Cabildo. But there is no doubt that for Jaeschké the absence of authenticity is a dep-roblematized verification, a quick expediency to get rid of a problem that is secondary to him, which is reaffirmed when in 1908 he discusses the diagonals of the Bouvard plan which meet at Plaza de Mayo: what he is going to criticize is not the French urban planner's formalist disinterest of local tradition, but his "petty and timorous spirit" that prevented him from "frankly attacking our old cathedral to reach [with the layout of the Diagonal Norte] the center of the square."[286] But, then, is the picturesque without history admissible? Did they read Sitte so badly? Is it logical that in the paroxysm of the nationalist histor-icism of the centenary this vein of the urban picturesque, so principal and so functional, should be squandered?

A first attempt at a response should, above all, acknowledge the versatility of Sitte's theory, the plural history of its various receptions. While in continental Europe the historicist and aestheticist reading predominated, vindicating the value of singular monuments—as demanded by the growing displeasure with the destruction and renovation of historic centers—in England, with a lon-ger historicist tradition, the picturesque was translated into a formula for the ex-novo resolution of garden districts, taking from Sitte the revaluation of the "square" as an articulating space of the suburban community and as a specific instrument for the technical resolution of a new road network.[287]

[285] The architect Ernesto Moreau's answer to the survey carried out by *Arquitectura*. The survey is completed in the following issue of *Arquitectura* 29 (August 31, 1905).

[286] The quotation from *Arquitectura. Suplemento de la Revista Técnica* 47 (May 1908): 110.

[287] See Donatella Calabi, "L'arte urbana e i suoi teorici europei," in Guido Zucconi, ed., *Camillo Sitte e i suoi interpreti* (Milan: FrancoAngeli, 1992), 37ff. In American urban culture, on the other hand, Sitte's theory, stripped of all historicist picturesqueness, was read as a formal resolution of monumental ensembles, which, if it resorts to historical examples, is only to be translated into classical typologies in availability; this version will serve precisely to oppose the anti-urbanism of the Garden City, as exemplified in the work of Werner Hegemann and Elbert Peets, *The American Vitruvius: An*

Another line of possible answers must depart from urban logic: it starts from the question about the value of colonial architecture in the modern city but takes us much further, to the prototypical debate of the centenary about the relationship, in a new country, between modernity and tradition. What does it mean that the Cabildo is an "eyesore"? The first thing to rule out is that it is a simple Europeanism, whereby valuable monuments would originate there. It is discussed under the impact of the reconstruction of the campanile of the ducal palace in Venice, recently demolished, which, for Santiago Barabino—one of the most emphatic engineers in his technical nationalism—is also a "*mamarracho* (a monstrosity) [...] that fell down as a tribute to good taste"; its reconstruction is as big a mistake as the one that would be committed with that of the Cabildo.[288] There is a simple and tautological explanation for these positions: the Cabildo is an eyesore because the "poor" colonial architecture of the Río de la Plata cannot yet be valued. It is only about 1915 that colonial revaluation will acquire the form of a neocolonial manifesto. But this would be to suppose that the neocolonial stand offers architectural culture a real solution to the problem posed, and we will see that this is not the case. Moreover, they are but a few years apart, and it is clear that we are facing the same climate of ideas. As we have seen, since 1904, with Lugones's trip to the Guaraní missions, the colonial heritage has begun to be systematically documented, the Hispanist revaluation has already given its first revisionist fruits, the trips to the Archives of the Indies are becoming more frequent. Likewise, the revaluation of other architectures of Spanish colonization has already earned its place: not only the artistic and cultural density of the Peruvian or Mexican Baroque is celebrated, but also North American colonial architecture, as "poor" as the Río Plata, and which under the influence of the Ruskinian Arts and Crafts—so influential also in Buenos Aires—has produced since the end of the century a whole fashion of Hispanic revival in California.[289]

The problem is another, and it is exemplarily raised in the answer that Christophersen gives to the 1905 survey—let us remember, he is master of the academic architects, one of the first, in 1913, to propose an operative rereading of the colonial architectural legacy:

Architects' Handbook of Civic Art (New York: Architectural Book Pub. Co., 1922). See the introductory study by Christiane Crasemann Collins to the Princeton Architectural Press reprint of the book (New York, 1988).

[288] Reply of the engineer Santiago Barabino, *Arquitectura*, 26–28, 49.

[289] On the theme of the different uses of colonial inspirations see Jorge Liernur, "¿Arquitectura del Imperio español o arquitectura criolla? Notas sobre las representaciones 'neocoloniales' de la arquitectura producida durante la dominación española en América," *Anales del Instituto de Arte Americano e Investigaciones Estéticas "Mario J. Buschiazzo"* (1992), 27–28.

The old town hall, apart from the memories and traditions that it contains, has never had real artistic merit, because this building, like most of
those that were erected in the colonial period in the capital, were the work
of modest "*alarifes*" [master builders] and not the inspiration of the many
good artists who lived in the mother country. And it is to be deplored that
all these colonial works did not have real and true architectural merit, since
many or almost all of them were built with good sense and perhaps with
more adaptability to climate and the environment than many of the new
buildings of which Buenos Aires boasts.[290]

The technical nationalism constitutive of the nascent disciplinary fields
involved in the construction of the city already offers positive readings of "sensibility" and the "adaptability to climate and the environment" as distinctive
contributions in the face of the modern city: the spirit of place, nature, original
materials, as quarries for a local artistic and architectural expression. In this
context, the absence of "architectural merit" in colonial architecture reveals the
impossibility of the architectural discipline (marked by academic parameters)
to seek in colonial figuration an adequate response to metropolitan problems,
as Christophersen himself will later argue, when he proposes the neocolonial as
a figuration only possible, due to its picturesque character, for the countryside
and the suburbs. This means, in short, that architecture and urbanism cannot
accept the answer of iconicity to the question—also anxiously formulated since
the beginning of the century—for an authentic and national expression: the city
cannot be seen by them as a stage for patriotic representation.

Thus, we are faced with a strictly disciplinary imposition: history, for
technical nationalism, cannot enter the city, neither as urban distribution—
because here history is the modern grid that, from the picturesque perspective, blocks history—nor as image—because the question to be solved is the
one posed by the profusion of images of eclecticism. In fact, the great problem facing culture in Buenos Aires—and in this diagnosis practically everyone agrees toward the centenary—is eclecticism, understood as stylistic chaos
and plurality of languages. The problem is far from being local: the crisis of
academicism internationally has imposed since the end of the century in the
French Academy of Beaux-Arts itself, under the influence of Taine's theories,
the need to develop "national styles" as a counterpart to eclectic indifferentia-
tion. But in Buenos Aires this problem is aggravated, because elites of foreign
collectivities also share this need, which they will develop by hiring architects
of their own nationality or by demanding allusive images, which may not necessarily translate into eclecticism technically speaking but develops an urban

---

[290] Alejandro Christophersen's response to the survey, in *Arquitectura*, 29, 65.

image of growing heterogeneity.[291] This means that the problem of Argentine architects cannot be solved with the generic characterizing claim of "national styles": here it is necessary to find *a* style of the Argentineans, imposing it on other figurations.

The truth is that at the very moment when the "bourgeois city" finally seems to consolidate itself, it is difficult to find anyone proud of its image: with the exception of a few "official" voices that will immoderately celebrate the centenary—for them the plurality of languages will be synonymous with the generosity of the land that opens its arms to all races and all cultures and, therefore, to all styles—the *image* of the city becomes part of that spiritual duty that the *materiality* of the city disregards with arrogance.

Between the absent spirit and overbearing matter: to resolve this hiatus, the naturalistic functionalism of this technical nationalism is developed: the image of things must respond to what things are, without any embellishments or masks. The demand for transparency as a modern reaction to the also modern mismatch between form and content manifests itself again and again in fields that go far beyond the well-known architectural claim of coincidence between form and function: Enrique Chanourdie's criticism of Rodin's Sarmiento in 1900 is pictured in his ironic proposal to set up a sign saying "This is Sarmiento"; for Augusto Bunge, in 1916, in the petty monstrosity of the *barrio-parque* of Palermo (today Palermo Chico) only a tree "represents" the park as in an allegorical theater set: "That tree is saying to the passersby: 'this is a *barrio-parque*, not to be confused.'"[292] The eclectic masks produce an unreal public space, in which it is impossible to distinguish truth from appearance. The only thing that consoles Julio Molina y Vedia in the conclusive assessment he makes in that same year of 1916 is that this present city "is not ours," because it was built by foreign architects and builders. But what architecture should these brand-new Argentine architects make in the name of whom Molina y Vedia postulates his assessment? Here regenerationism plays a dirty trick on functionalism and its demand for transparency: for as long as the material background of the city is not accepted, as long as it is maintained that this eclecticism reveals the deep evils of both city and society ("this ostentatious architecture is the mirror of the falsity and emptiness in which we all

---

[291] See Jorge Liernur, "Buenos Aires del centenario." This profusion of styles must not be confused with eclecticism, since in reality in many cases they are in fact a counterpoint; eclecticism refers to works where motifs from different historical styles are used indistinctly. See Mercedes Daguerre, "Eclecticismo," in Jorge Liernur and Fernando Aliata, eds., *Diccionario de arquitectura en la Argentina* (Buenos Aires: Agea, 2004), vol. 3.

[292] Chanourdie's quotation in "Sarmiento y su estatua," *Revista Técnica* 104–105 (June 15, 1900), 72; Augusto Bunge in "El anticarrasco," *Nosotros* 21, no. 81 (January 1916): 81.

live" says Molina y Vedia in harmony with Rojas), what else should the task of a new image be but to conceal?

The iconic response to this dilemma is simple and will end with an oxymoron in the neocolonial style: as a "true mask." We can now better understand why this only accounts for a very limited part of the problem: if the public space of the bourgeois city is presented to them as an unbearable polyphony, the *cocoliche* (Italian-Argentine slang) turned to stone, what the neocolonial offers with its historicist allusions are more images: it doubles the bet of eclecticism for a hyper-eclecticism. Rojas's iconic pedagogy can serve for a patriotic education or for a notion of public space as didactic scenario, but it does not even come close to a usable answer in the field of language in the city, because the very tradition of architectural discipline leads to an aporia that the neocolonial does not take on: if in the midst of the crisis of academic languages one can turn to the climate, materials, and place to find the hard core on which to anchor a national style, at the same time those references are mute; they do not yet constitute language; they point to the future. It is evident that we are facing a debate and a search analogous to those of the "national language of the Argentines," recalling the title of Lucien Abeille's polemic book of 1900; but, unlike what the different nationalisms can sustain in the idiomatic debate, technical nationalism cannot find its answers for the city in any past, but must appeal to the future construction of a "new style," as Christophersen will propose with dramatic lucidity.[293]

This moment of "transition"—it is easy to speak of transitions from the future—of irresolution, of uneasiness, of a situation in which the old does not offer answers and the new does not yet appear, is going to be translated in the disciplines that build the city in a call to order, in the formation of a "party of sobriety"—according to Liernur's precise denomination—that will tempt different stylistic searches: return to a severe classicism, colorism, "technical" architecture; in this ambiguous terrain, the neocolonial will be just another quarry.[294]

Having raised this debate we can return, then, to the role of the monument, to finish analyzing the problems of the configuration of the public space in the traditional city. Because only starting from a more thorough understanding of the peculiar crossroads of the aesthetic, cultural and urban debates of the centenary, can the exceptionality of Leopoldo Lugones's proposals for the May commemorative monuments be discerned.[295]

---

[293] On Abeille's book, the polemic in which it is inserted and the one it generated, see *En torno al criollismo. textos y polémica*, critical study and compilation by Alfredo Rubione (Buenos Aires: CEAL, 1983).
[294] See Liernur, "Buenos Aires del centenario."
[295] I am grateful to María Teresa Gramuglio for informing me of Lugones's prolific preoccupation with the monumental question; as will be seen in the following pages,

As we saw, one of the fundamental aspects of the celebration was the call made in 1907 by the National Centennial Commission for an international contest for the realization of the main monument in the Plaza de Mayo. The competition received a considerable response, with a majority of French and Italian submissions; in May 1908 the projects were presented to great acclaim in an exhibition at the Rural Society. To better or worse effect, all the works presented responded to the strict frameworks of the academic tradition.[296] In a first selection, six works were chosen, which—with modifications requested by the jury, including the preservation of the pyramid so often condemned—were to participate in a final competition from which the winner would emerge.[297]

In the course of this process Lugones wrote two articles, "El templo del himno" (The Temple of the Anthem) and "El monumento del centenario," (The Monument of the Centenary), which he published in 1910 in the book *Piedras liminares*, along with his lecture, "La cacolitia (ensayo sobre antiestética moderna)" (La cacolitia [Essay on Modern Anti-aesthethics]), in which he rejects the construction of the Luján basilica in neo-Gothic style.[298] These incursions into monumental debates are linked to very basic concerns of his aesthetic-political project, which lead him to propose a new monument to Sarmiento in 1911 and another to José Hernández in 1913: for Lugones, only monumental architecture has the same capacity as poetry to incarnate the homeland. Here the book's debts to Ruskin become evident. Beyond the familiar air of the title and the citation of authority in the argument regarding the Gothic, his inspiration is summed up in a central conclusion: "there are but two strong conquerors of the forgetfulness of men"—Ruskin had pointed out in *The Seven Lamps*

---

her work has been extremely important for my own work. My analysis of Lugones is also informed by her "La primera épica de Lugones," *Prismas* 1 (1997), 157–63.

[296] At the beginning of the century, the architectural monument is one of the most rigidly defined themes of academicism, with its restricted universe of formal and allegorical possibilities. As an example of a larger scale, but with important analogies, it is worth bearing in mind that in these years the monument to Vittorio Emanuele was being built in Rome, which had been selected through a competition several years earlier, but which would only be inaugurated (incomplete) at the 1911 exhibition for the fiftieth anniversary of the Kingdom of Italy.

[297] See the album organized by the Comisión Nacional del Centenario for the exhibition of the projects, which includes the rules of the competition and all the works presented with their respective descriptive memories, *Concurso para el Monumento de la Independencia Argentina* (Buenos Aires: Kraft, 1908); see also the documents of the Commission in Archivo General de la Nación, room 7, folder 18-4-8. The opinions of the jury in "Resultado del Concurso del Monumento a Mayo," *Arquitectura. Suplemento de la Revista Técnica* 49 (June–July 1908), 134ff.

[298] Leopoldo Lugones, *Piedras liminares. Las limaduras de Hephaestos* (Buenos Aires: A. Moen y Hno., 1910).

of Architecture: "Poetry and Architecture."[299] The problem is that, because of this Ruskinian starting point, Lugones is confronted with the zero degree of the debate on national character in architecture, because it is no longer even enough to search for a national architecture—an architect's problem—but rather—as was the problem of the national poet—an architecture in which *everything* expresses the nation.[300]

From that perspective he will judge the exhibition of projects with a categorical conclusion: it is a set of "projects for sepulchers"; what is worse, "sepulchers for military men" (and Lugones's anti-militarism is in these centenary texts only equal his anti-clericalism and anti-republicanism).[301] To a large extent, the absence of quality proposals is the natural result, for Lugones, of the type of competition, conceived as an institution and with commissions of notables as obligatory bureaucratic decision-making bodies (a perfect example of the failure of democracy, he will add, which makes all value depend on the "chimerical virtues" of the parliamentary system).

The institution of the competition presents two contradictions in the development of a peripheral technical and artistic culture. The first, between quality and the creation of opportunities: quality is associated with the artist of foreign genius who is directly hired, because he would never "lower himself" to compete in a competition, while the transparent opening of opportunities is fundamental for those who are concerned with the construction of a stable system of disciplinary legitimacy; that is why artists like Lugones or Cané, oblivious to the institutional problems of the constitution of professional fields, were in favor of direct commissions, while architects and engineers are going to make the public competition the sine qua non condition of the whole institutional scaffolding of the liberal profession. The second, more critical contradiction is that between the prestige granted by an international competition (prestige with which most of the projects in the universal exhibitions were associated)

---

[299] John Ruskin, *The Seven Lamps of Architecture* (1849), 169.

[300] Jorge Monteleone has analyzed Lugones's quest in the centenary texts to "give sense" to the secular nation; see "Lugones: canto natal del héroe," in Graciela Montaldo, ed. *Yrigoyen, entre Borges y Arlt (1916–1930)* (Buenos Aires: Contrapunto, 1989).

[301] "El monumento del centenario," *Piedras liminares*, 201ff. On his anti-militarism, see his *Didáctica*, which today could also be read as one of the most fully liberal and Sarmientine educational analyses of the period, especially in comparison with the reforms of Ramos Mejía and Rojas's text (Lugones does not accept the notion of "patriotic education" and proposes that of "democratic and rationalist education"). On his anti-clericalism, "La cacolitia" was written among other reasons to prevent the May celebrations from taking place in the basilica of Luján. It is not my intention to propose, from the reading of these relatively marginal texts, a Lugones different from the one that the critics of the last decades have accustomed us to; it is only worth remembering that Lugones can be seen in the centenary as a much more complex figure than the fascist intellectual of the twenties and thirties.

Figure 57. Luigi Brizzolara and Gaetano Moretti, *First Prize for the Competition for the May Monument*, 1907–1910. Centro de Documentación e Investigación de la Arquitectura Pública, Ministerio de Hacienda, Buenos Aires.

Figure 58. Joseph-Antoine Bouvard, *Proposal for the Remodeling of the Plaza de Mayo*. Note that the proposal considers tearing down the Government House to open a view toward the river, replaces the Cabildo (municipality) to build a symmetrical building at the entrance of Avenida de Mayo, opens up two diagonals, and places at the center the monument that won the first prize in the competition. Virtually the entire local professional field agreed on these reforms. *Censo Municipal*, 1910, Municipalidad de la Ciudad de Buenos Aires.

and the nationalism that presides by definition over monumental initiatives, a contradiction that had already generated major scandals in other countries, as in the case of the monument to Vittorio Emmanuelle: "But why should the competition be worldwide when what was asked for was most Italian?," a critic from Italy wrote justifying the cancellation of the first prize awarded to the Frenchman Nénot.[302]

Thus, while the *Revista Técnica*, in its concern with guaranteeing a system of competitions, is going to reject the inclusion of the only Argentine among the six preselected—Rogelio Yrurtia, because his project does not comply with the bases ("the triumph of a national artist cannot be preferred to the triumph of Justice")—Lugones is going to found a good part of his criticism on the incomprehension that foreign projects showed with respect to the monument's purpose: their main mistake was to represent "independence and liberties for all service," not noticing, for example, that if the lion is the symbol of the monarchy whose defeat is celebrated, "it was a trait of elementary good taste to avoid the lion. [....] That, however, tingles with lions."[303]

Independence, liberties, and abstruse lions: Rojas will make a similar criticism of the base for the San Martín monument designed for the centenary by the German sculptor Eberlein, for its "nonsensical" scenes, in which the young Creole girls turn out as "a Margarete with an Alsatian bodice and high heels, and the Creole cattleman, as blond young man of the Prussian guard."[304] But, beyond these similarities, Lugones points out the mismatch only as a first step to completely subvert the logic of academic rhetoric. Indeed, while the local debate on the monument remains within the framework of academic legitimacy—pointing out compositional successes or errors and the greater or lesser appropriateness of allegorical solutions—Lugones ignores, in a completely avant-garde gesture, its conventional referentiality and, with a perspective external to its norm, turns allegory into parody:

In a healthy and sincere individual, the spectacle of people who deliberate seriously, having climbed on a ledge, an abacus or a lintel is absurd of course; [...] "What will those guys do over there?" will be the obligatory and natural question, followed by the consequent laughter. This is, in fact, the fundamental procedure of parody: heroes or gods who represent scenes foreign to their character or are placed in places inappropriate to their character. When we see, then, the personifications of liberty, of the Fatherland, of glory, perched on a pillar or lintel, *without any rational cause*, and only

---

[302] The scandal produced by the triumph of a foreigner led to a new competition, in which the winner was an Italian; quoted in Sica, *Historia del urbanismo. El siglo XIX.*
[303] Quoted in *Revista Técnica* in "Resultado del Concurso del Monumento a Mayo," 135. The quotation from Lugones is in *Piedras liminares*, 207.
[304] *Eurindia* (1924), 2:41.

> because such an inadequate position seemed to the designer [...] we can call
> it parody, and ask ourselves without irreverence: "But what on earth have
> the Fatherland, Liberty, and Glory gone up there to do? Isn't that to go and
> absurdly and solemnly dispute the cats their mewling love?[305]

Without any rational cause: Lugones's criticism of academicism strikes at its
weakest point, in the sense that the monument is the program most subject to
conventions: being pure rhetorical condensation, when its intrinsic rationality
is broken nothing justifies it, everything in it is subject to mockery. But, in
addition, the monument is the weakest point of academicism because, precisely
due to its conventionalism, it cannot be a field of linguistic innovation: unlike
architecture, its only meaning is the communication of meaning. And as long
as there is no desire to communicate the meaning of technical progress—to
which Eiffel's tower has already answered—in 1910 the rejection of academicism confronts the artist with a complete void of references. Consider that,
internationally, these years see the first outlines of a post-academicist monumental art, such as can be seen in Sant'Elia's sketches or in Adolphe Appia's
scenographic spaces.

Already in the field of formal suggestions for the monument, Lugones's
whole proposal is an attempt to escape that crossroads, the same one faced,
without much success and with a still diffuse conscience, by the architects'
search for a "new style."[306] It is obvious that they rely on the same resources. In
the first place, the appeal to "function" as the social anchor of art: "in the aesthetics of the people, it is necessary to match what is useful, because among
the people the poor are many more than the rich, and therefore necessity
is always superior to pleasure," says Lugones in proposing that the monument should serve as both pantheon and museum. Second, the appeal to the
materials, nature, and spirit of the site to establish the Argentine ownership
of the work: "a monument erected with the most valuable materials of the
country would also be more flesh of its flesh." To this end, one could begin
"with that beautiful pink stone of Misiones that the Jesuits tried out in their
old churches," and which Lugones knew, thanks to the official commission of
the 1904 survey:

---

[305] *Piedras liminares*, 210, 211.

[306] The analogies with the anti-eclectic and anti-historicist sensibility of the architects
are extremely precise in each case in which Lugones refers to the real city. For example,
the aesthetic displeasure caused by the Plaza de Mayo: about the inconvenience of
placing the monument in that square, Lugones says that "no aesthetic creation would
resist such a neighborhood [...], the government house alone would be enough to make
the Colossus of Rhodes sick"; the square is "the old well of the viceroys"; he calls the
congress building "a bastard heap," etc. (ibid., 214–15).

A palace of the natural color of that stone, with white sculptures, would carry, by that detail alone, positive originality in itself, being destined by our light and our environment to acquire over the years a golden patina, a kind of permanent solar warmth, like the temper of certain late clouds, which is perhaps the ultimate beauty of the stone ordered by man. [...] The mere idea of a colossal frieze that would show off our most beautiful onyx and jasper involves a stupendous pomp, to which our woods could add their wonders in suitable compositions.[307]

As with technical nationalism, Lugones also sees here an opportunity for local industry: "Dare I add, to the satisfaction of commercial scruples, that this would be at the same time a permanent exhibition of our products," he adds in a footnote. Finally, Lugones's proposal will coincide with architectural explorations in its recourse to the most severely classical forms in its call for order. But this is where their differences begin.

On one level, there is the rigor with which he will appeal to the most elementary geometry, to the point of referring to certain images of eighteenth-century French revolutionary architects. As when, for example, after discarding Greek and Egyptian "styles," he proposes a square inscribed in a giant circle for the Temple of the Anthem. The appeal to primitive geometries has in these years the additional charm of occult signs, but that link between national materials and geometric severity already appears in other previous proposals, such as that of Congressman Aldao, who in 1905 imagined the centennial monument as "an agglomeration of anonymous stones brought from all parts of our territory," piled up like Egyptian obelisks, since "it is in geometric purity and simplicity that symbolic expression can be given to the cult of ancestors."[308] Of course, this is a rigor that is uncompromisingly disengaged *ex profeso* from any constructive realism ("one never has to build it," says Lugones to emphasize the necessary idealism of his Temple), but perhaps it is this lack of commitment which allowed them to take complete distance from the blind spot to which the local architectural debate seemed to have arrived.

In any case, Lugones's most innovative suggestion occurs at another level, when he proposes a relationship of greater complexity: between national materials, geometric rigor, and a geographic-cultural quality that allows him to move from the sobriety already associated with demands for order, to a celebration of geometric abstraction as the most direct representation of the characteristics of the landscape of the pampa. If the monument, like the poem, must *be* the homeland, its essential matter must be capable of embodying the material essence of the homeland, sought in Taine's terms, in the spirit of the place:

---

[307] Ibid., 228–29.
[308] Honorable Cámara de Diputados, *Diario de sesiones,* 1905, sessions of September 20.

[H]ere we have natural elements of extraordinary value for the inspiration of our aesthetic realizations. Three gigantic units emerge, so to speak, from our topography. First, the pampa, whose immense horizontality would be enough to engender a whole reserved and philosophical art. Then the colossal flow of the internal waters, which the Plata mixes in its formidable knot. Then the earth begins to ascend, until it presents on the horizon, as if sketched for future giants, the immense blue city of the Andes. We Argentines have, then, an eye for greatness; and these three units, to which the prodigy of the jungle must be added, are aesthetic elements that cannot be ignored when it comes to projecting commemorative monuments of the nation where they are located. Undoubtedly, in every country there are mountains, waters, and plains; but not every country has the pampas, the Plata, and the Andes.[309]

A generic relationship—large dimensions, pure geometric forms—made even more precise in Buenos Aires, which also "presents peculiarities worthy of note": it is "low and extensive," which highlights "the clarity of its environment;" "its horizons are vaster; its air masses more powerful." These are the peculiarities of the pampa, and it is the first time that the analogy between city and pampa begins to be celebrated and, even more, that in the search for representation of its quality, abstract motifs are introduced to "a reserved and philosophic art."[310]

It should be clarified that this original relationship between the quality of the pampa as positive value in the city and classicizing geometric abstraction would not be taken into account at all in the debates on monuments—nor in the immediate architectural and urban discussions; the prize for the monument was decided by a vote in favor of the project of the Italians Brizzolara and Moretti over that of the Belgians Lagae and Dhurcque, in the well-known academicist resolution.[311] In spite of it, Lugones's positions open the way to the most radical approach with which, more than a decade later, the architectural and literary avant-garde will seek to give new answers to the same problem. And if it is worth anticipating, among other things, Borges's poetry and essays of the 1920s, it is simply to point out that just as the debate on the final crystallization of traditional public space has placed on the table a major issue of the

---

[309] *Piedras liminares*, 217–18.

[310] Ibid., 218.

[311] In the epilogue of the book, Lugones writes about the result: "The pantheon of the mutual aid society, with its fatal niches. That will be the monument of the liberating Revolution. The usual covered-brick bump, erecting its share of marzipan on the tray of the Plaza de Mayo." Ibid. In fact, the first two prizes had tied, which necessitated the tie-breaking vote of the Minister of the Interior and president of the National Commission, Marco Avellaneda; of the first prize, only the foundation stone was placed; the second one was the one that was finally built in the Plaza Congreso.

specificity of modern culture in Argentina, it will also be the new "peripheral" suburb—still omitted in the 1910s—the one in charge of offering to this crucial crossroads of "central culture," one of the most remarkable solutions of twenti-eth-century local culture.

CHAPTER 5

Envisioning the New City

One of the many visitors of the centenary, the Catalan Santiago Rusiñol, on his return to Buenos Aires after the standard tour of the interior of the country, shows his astonishment for one of the characteristics most emphasized by all observers of the period, the vertiginous expansion of the city: "it seems that it had grown," he writes,

> it grows at all hours, it grows at every moment, one could say that one sees it grow, or better, that one hears it grow: that it goes plain forward, filling the immense board with pieces, lining up to infinity, numbering itself to infinity decimally, like a problem of houses; making meridians of the streets and arcs of meridians of the squares; and one feels it so grandiose, that, a moment comes in which what one sees does not seem to be a great city, but the plan of a city in a project made on canvas by a dreaming geometrician.[312]

And, in fact, while the main public attention is devoted to the debate on the monumentalization and reform of traditional public space, the city has grown and, it could be said, has changed its composition in just five years, turning massively to the new suburbs, initiating a trend that would only increase in the following decades. The census taken in October 1909 for the centennial celebration—nothing better than a census to feed "the gloating of the figures"—showed overwhelming data in comparison with that of 1904. On the one hand, population growth: an annual rate only slightly lower than that of Hamburg, slightly higher than that of New York, almost double that of Berlin, and three times that of London.[313] But, above all, what stands out is the novelty in the dis-

60

---

[312] Rusiñol, *Un viaje al Plata*, 295.

[313] The population of Buenos Aires increased from 950,891 inhabitants in 1904 to 1,231,698 inhabitants in 1909, which means a 29 percent growth, in comparison to 30.5 in Hamburg, 28.5 in New York, 16.9 in Berlin, or 9 in London in the same period; the information is calculated by Alberto Martínez in the *Censo General de Población, Edificación Comercio e Industrias de la Ciudad de Buenos Aires* (Buenos Aires: Compañía Sudamericana de Billetes de Banco, 1910), vol. 1 (the census was taken on October 16 and 24, 1909).

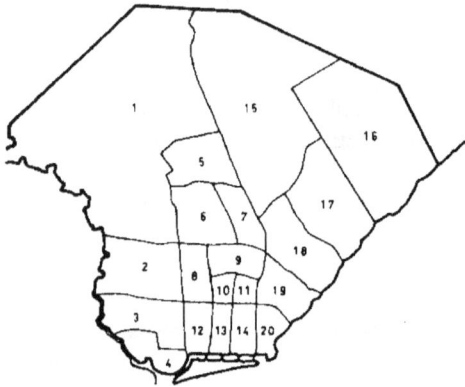

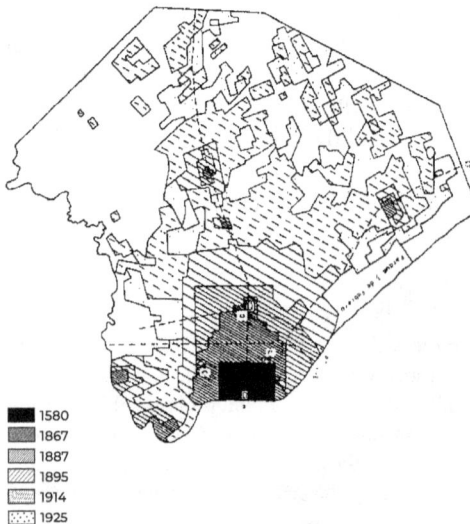

Figure 59. *Census Sections of the Federal Capital*, 1904. References: 1. Vélez Sársfield; 2. San Cristóbal Sur; 3. Santa Lucía; 4. San Juan Evangelista; 5. Flores; 6. San Carlos Sur; 7. San Carlos Norte; 8. San Cristóbal Norte; 9. Balvanera Oeste; 10. Balvanera Sur; 11. Balvanera Norte; 12. Concepción; 13. Montserrat; 14. San Nicolás; 15. San Bernardo; 16. Belgrano; 17. Palermo; 18. Las Heras; 19. Pilar; 20. Socorro. To approximate the more common names (as this is a nomenclature that the city only recently attempted to fix but that is not generally recognized as such): 1. Southwest barrios, Nueva Pompeya, Villa Soldati, Villa Lugano, Mataderos and Flores sur; 2. Parque Patricios, with a sector of Barracas and Nueva Pompeya; 3. Barracas; 4. La Boca; 5. Caballito and Flores; 6. and 7. Boedo, Almagro and part of Villa Crespo; 8–11. Once and Congress; 12–13. San Telmo; 14 and 20. Center and Retiro; 19. Barrio Norte; 15. Northeast barrios, from Villa Crespo and Chacarita to Villa del Parque and Villa Devoto; 16. Belgrano and Núñez; 17 and 18. Palermo.

Figure 60. Diagram of progressive urbanization of Buenos Aires from the city's foundation to the 1920s. From Charles Sargent, *The Spatial Evolution of Greater Buenos Aires, 1870–1930*. Tempe: Arizona State University, 1974. Great stretches of empty land are still visible in the mid-1920s.

1580
1867
1887
1895
1914
1925

tribution of that population: of the almost three hundred thousand people that were incorporated in five years, 90 percent settled in the new suburbs, which implies that while the population of the traditional city remained practically stable, that of the new suburbs doubled.

In any case, this sharp division between old and new city sectors hides a recomposition of the city that is revealed in population indices. Urban density continues to show a traditional symmetry, with its maximum point of concentration around the central axis of the consolidated city, but the variation in growth shows a new plane in which the qualification of the center-north has resulted in a shift of focus toward the Plaza San Martín. In the area bounded by Córdoba Street, Callao Avenue, and the river (downtown-north and Retiro areas), we find the peak of population decrease of the city (about 10 percent fewer inhabitants than in 1904); in the adjacent area, taking Independencia and Boedo-Medrano streets as external limit (downtown, Once and Recoleta areas) the growth was almost nil (barely 5 percent); in the south of the traditional city (San Telmo, San Cristóbal Norte, La Boca, and Barracas) the growth was minimal (about 10 percent); in the first cordon surrounding the traditional city (San Cristóbal Sur, Almagro, and Barrio Norte) the average growth was 50 percent; and in the entire new perimeter (the southwest—Bajo Flores, Mataderos—Flores, the northwest—Colegiales, Chacarita, Villa Urquiza, Devoto—Belgrano and Palermo) the average growth was 140 percent, with peaks of 200 percent in the northwest and 180 percent in the southwest. That is to say, the traditional city tends to decongest from its most valued areas, while the new city tends to be massively populated from its less valued areas, which shows a completely peculiar process of suburbanization, both for its homogeneity in all cardinal directions and because, in its framework, the traditional center—with a slight displacement toward the north—has increased its value.[314]

The census also shows the economic movement that has been recorded in the new suburbs, both in real estate transactions and in transport infrastructure. For, if in 1904 only the horse tram lines had been increased in the Once and Barrio Norte area and electric trams had been laid out to Flores-Mataderos and Belgrano, in 1910 the densification of lines—all electric—had been completed in the first suburban belt, and the service to the farthest west and northwest areas already had its main routes laid out.[315]

These remarkable changes were obviously registered and, in keeping with official optimism, celebrated profusely. It is not ignorance of the process that

[314] The data is drawn from the census itself, in its constituency-by-constituency analysis. I have preferred to name the areas of the city with their conventional names and not with the strict name of the constituencies or their numbering.
[315] On tramway layouts in 1904 and 1914, see Sargent, *The Spatial Evolution of Greater Buenos Aires*, 67–68. Later, in Chapter 9, I dwell specifically on certain problems of transportation development.

216 THE GRID AND THE PARK

generates the effect of omission, but, as we shall see, the impossibility of accepting that it is producing a new city and not mere suburbs of the traditional city.
To see how this new city is being formed, we can turn to a few contemporary
voices: on the one hand, to those who describe what is happening because their
public role imposes it on them—in the case of the municipal government—
because their reformist ideology leads them to take an interest in the fate of
these new urban settlers, or because their character as occasional visitors facil-
itates a view that is precisely *off-center* with respect to that of their hosts. On
the other hand, one can turn to the even fewer who, at the very beginning of
the movement, already foresee the city that is being produced and propose to
act accordingly.

Rusiñol's phrase with which we open the chapter brings together most of
the problems that this expansion generates in the urban culture of the centenary for those who describe or propose it. First, the mathematical metaphor
to allude to the whole process, which allows Rusiñol to establish a series of
homologations between real estate speculation, the grid and mercantile provisionality of the modern city, bringing to the suburb the main topics of regenerationism; second, the symbiotic relationship between that style of unlimited
growth, its degree of abstraction, the infinite dimensions, and the pampa, as a
condition to understand Buenos Aires.

1. Eccentric Excursions

> The city is formed, in that area of its expansion, as the future towns emerge
> in the middle of the Pampa.[316]
>
> –Adolfo Posada, 1912

Although not all of them devote many pages to it, the new suburb is one
of the most significant themes in the relationship of the travelers of the centenary with Buenos Aires. As narratives of contrasts—and all travel accounts,
by definition, record with one attentive eye what they see and with another
the reading conditions of their own public—compared to the European urban
experience, travel accounts find no greater peculiarity in Buenos Aires than
the emergence of a city out of nothing. But first, it is worth pointing out what
kind of travelers' stories appear in the centenary to then ponder the space that
the suburb occupies in them. As we know, travel narrative is a genre that was
already highly formalized in the mid-nineteenth century, starting with the
increasingly famous texts on non-European nature and culture by Humboldt
(1809–1825) and Darwin (1839), among others. Unlike memorialist literature,

---

[316] Adolfo Posada, *La República Argentina. Impresiones y comentarios* (Madrid, 1912)
(Buenos Aires: Hyspamérica, 1986), 54.

these texts were offered—as Adolfo Prieto points out in relation to Humboldt's book—"as a powerful textual montage in which scientific annotation, aesthetic effusion, and humanistic concern could alternatively be coupled with or separated from the narrator's voice and his captivating account of revelations and personal accidents."[317]

Throughout the nineteenth century travelers' accounts of Argentina do not cease to multiply within the framework of this generic tradition, but to read the stories that are produced around the centenary it is necessary to recognize some important changes. First, the nature of the commission: in the centenary we already find the figure of the professional traveler, who makes a living from publishing his or her stories, but, in addition, in many cases the travel account is commissioned to well-known writers, sociologists, or politicians, which reaffirms the importance not so much of informative description as of narrative quality and interpretative approach. For the public, it is now a question of evaluating the perspective of one or another author in an already densely canonized relationship and in a very specialized cultural market. The other important change is nationality: it could be said that in the centenary Latin visitors displace the predominance of British visitors in the previous century. There was a considerable increase in the number of visitors, especially from the Iberian Peninsula, as part of a reconsideration of Latin culture that also included French interests, a constant presence since the previous century, and Italian interests, which had already been evident since the end of the century in orienting, organizing, and capitalizing as far as possible the flow of immigrants.[318]

The additional stimulus for the Latin component toward the centenary is the emergence of Buenos Aires as a world metropolis, which becomes a sort of Latin counterpart to New York: if the United States has already shown that America is the future, Buenos Aires allows Latin visitors to imagine "the future of the race." It is largely in Latin Europe that the specular relationship New York/Buenos Aires is constructed, triangulated with its own unsurpassable culture but which does not hide from itself the traits of decadence in the face of American emergence or German power. This is important to bear in mind when we find in contemporary sources certain local critical voices that, with good reason, denounce as a delusion of Argentine grandeur the representation so recurrent in the centenary of Buenos Aires as "the second Latin city after Paris," showing that the euphemism only manages to hide the fact that between Buenos Aires and Paris are the unattainable Berlin, Vienna, or New York. The truth is that this euphemism was carefully nurtured by foreign visitors, not as

---

[317] Adolfo Prieto, *Los viajeros ingleses y la emergencia de la literatura nacional argentina. 1820–1850* (Buenos Aires: Sudamericana, 1996), 17.

[318] To establish relative numbers of travelers, I have worked with the very complete study by Susana Santos Gómez, *Bibliografía de viajeros a la Argentina*, 2 vols. (Buenos Aires: FECIC/IAHH, 1983).

the polite deference of a guest—in many areas customary, moreover—but as their own need to be part to some extent of this new phenomenon that they, just as much as Argentines, would like Buenos Aires to embody.[319]

Some passages from Georges Clemenceau's travel book are highly illustrative of the questions of the hour. In the chapter "The 'Latins' of South America," he asks:

> Latin idealism keeps these South American nations ever facing toward those great modern peoples that have sprung from the Roman conquest. I cannot say I think we have drawn from this favourable condition of things all the advantage we might have derived from it, both for the youthful Republics and for our Latinity, which is being steadily drained by the huge task of civilization and by the vigorous onslaught that it is called on to sustain from the systematic activity of the Northern races. The great Anglo-Saxon Republic of North America [...] has taken over a continent to make it a modern nation whose influence will count more and more in the affairs of the globe. May it not be that South America, whose evolution is the result of lessons taught to some extent by the Northern races, will give us a new development of Latin civilisation corresponding to that which has so powerfully contributed to the making of Europe as we know it?[320]

And if this is how it is perceived from France, for a Spaniard like Posada the situation presents fewer doubts:

> Remember that in Spain there is no city of that position, nor of that youthful force, nor of such enormous expansive action. Only Paris, among the Latin cities, surpasses Buenos Aires in population; in the Castilian language there is none that equals it. [...] And that is why for us, from European soil, who preserve its past and who could—what an admirable program!—be the guardians of its spirit, as depositaries of the soul of the race, Buenos Aires offers the exceptional and most curious phenomenon of an enormous city, which walks without ceasing [....] forming, on the basis of what we have been, one of the most powerful propelling centers with which humanity is honored today, [which] sings its epic of greatness, of economic expansion [...] in the language spoken in the austere and depopulated and sometimes desolate Castilian plain.

---

[319] Rómulo Carbia writes a harsh note on Argentine jingoism in relation to travelers and the absurd expectation that Buenos Aires be called "the second Latin city after Paris." See "El alma nuestra," *Nosotros* 3 (November–December 1908): 270ff.

[320] Clemenceau, *South America To-day*, 63–64.

It is through Buenos Aires, then, that the spirit of Spain, despite its present decline, "has and will have its future in the world":

> The great English merchants, the commission merchants and travelers from Germany, the French importers, must learn the language of the good noble-man from La Mancha in order to get rich on the shore of the River Plate. The present moment of Buenos Aires is very symbolic of a subjective symbolism to an extreme degree. It is the symbol of a possible empire that is still drawn as an ideal, but which is certain to be realized.[321]

The differences in emphasis between Clemenceau and Posada are not merely a product of Buenos Aires being comparatively more important in relation to Spain than to France; it is also evident that in the first decade of this century new channels have opened up between Buenos Aires and the peninsula, so that the possibilities for enriching contact appear so strong: here much progress has already been made in a positive reconsideration of the Hispanic heritage, and a whole generation of Argentine intellectuals seeks to answer the typical cente-nary questions of cultural identity by drawing on the arsenal of issues raised by Spanish regenerationism of '98.

Thus, the two changes in relation to the tradition of travel narrative—the new intellectual profile of travelers and their Latin origin—also produce a fur-ther novelty: these artists or intellectuals are linked in a relationship of intense parity with their local counterparts, taking sides in their conflicts and dialogue with their works, which implies a new responsibility for the travel writer toward a specific local public that he or she takes as a reference, and the generation of an intertextual network much more direct and, at the same time, diversified than in the previous century.[322] This perspective allow us to organize, then, a productive series within the multitude of travelers of the centenary, trying to understand, in the specific point of view of their visions of the suburb, what positions and debates they embodied.

Santiago Rusiñol reactively reveals the strong preponderance of the Latin per-spective, when he defines himself as someone who does not want to "tighten ties, nor unite frontiers, nor join Latin races" with his writings; a statement needed, on the other hand, as a preamble to one of the most lapidary conclusions about Argentina lavished in a traveler's account.[323] A renowned playwright, poet, and painter, Rusiñol is the perfect intellectual *partner* of local nationalist regenera-tionism, with the not inconsiderable difference in favor of his certainties, that

---

[321] Posada, *La República Argentina* 33, 30, and 34 respectively.
[322] I follow Prieto's notion of "intertextual networks" to think through travel narratives. See *Los viajeros ingleses y la emergencia de la literatura nacional argentina*.
[323] Rusiñol, *Un viaje al Plata*, 77.

he does not need to fall into the contradictions and ambiguities of those who propose to regenerate Buenos Aires. He is simply dedicated to taking to the ultimate consequences the kind of criticism we saw in authors like Gálvez or a Rojas, with whom he was in regular contact, but who, when it came to proposals, managed to find ways out of the "Phoenician city." Rusiñol never ceased to show compassionate deference to these attempts, which he saw as desperate and useless; for him, the only way out was the port, the return to the land where the true nourishment of the spirit is found, "that which we call tradition": cathedrals, art, beauty, feelings, "everything that cannot be bought or sold."[324]

Let us return, then, to his excursion out of the city into the suburbs:

> One goes on walking and walking, and finds streets: first of two floors, then of one; one goes on walking and finds nothing but low floors; one goes on walking and the floors are flattened, and after being flattened, they become clearer; and when they have become clearer, one finds palisades, and after the palisades, wires that mark the city, until that of tomorrow, and when they finish, the immense pampa also bounded with intention, like a dream of greatness.[325]

The city is a homogeneous continuum in which the only difference between the center and the suburbs is given by the height of the houses or their more or less compact agglomeration; but what stands out in his observation is that such homogeneity is produced by the virtual plan that guides the city toward its future, which Rusiñol sees in each wire fence as a universal design and which his local interlocutors do not perceive directly. What is common to them, as to other travelers, is the repudiation of the most sensitive manifestation of that plan: the grid. If in the introduction we were able to play with the misunderstanding typical of the late nineteenth century between the romantic and the rationalist critique of the grid (embodied respectively by Dickens on the North American grid and Daireaux on the Buenos Aires grid), in these centenary texts there is no longer any misunderstanding: the complete hegemony of the picturesque sensibility makes everyone reject in the grid its monotony and its irremediable absence of culture. Unlike Sarmiento, they no longer see in it the iron heritage of the colonial city, but the presence of the most radically new, the capitalist city.[326]

---

[324] Ibid., 305ff. These are the final pages of the book in which he emphatically recommends his compatriots not to go to Buenos Aires.

[325] Ibid., 69.

[326] "Of course, with so many straight lines there comes a moment when the spirit would like to find a narrow or blackish street in front of its eyes," says Rusiñol (69), almost paraphrasing Dickens in the quotation we reproduced in the introduction: the "straight line" has become the main characteristic of America, the fundamental change that defines the journey from Europe.

Figure 61. Alfredo Berisso, head of the Drawing Department; Manrique Ruiz, Adolfo Kliman, draftsmen, *Plan of the City of Buenos Aires with the General Layout of the Streets*, 1916. Buenos Aires, Department of Public Works of the City of Buenos Aires. The University of Chicago Map Collection. Note the "spasmodic growth" of neighborhoods in the suburbs.

Figure 62. Unknown photographer. *Mataderos*, c. 1918. Dirección de Paseos, Museo de la Ciudad, Buenos Aires. The suburban image in the same period.

But perhaps more important is the other change that Rusiñol's phrase shows, directly linked to that of the grid: the immense pampa is also delimited with that "gridded intention." One of the main topics of travel literature in the Río de la Plata, the pampa, has ceased to be the archaic realm, mysterious by definition, and has become the territory of capitalist expansion. In Clemenceau's case, to show the "natural" disposition of the plain for an unlimited extension of the city; in Rusiñol's, taking advantage of the contrast with the romantic cliché of the nineteenth century and already sensitized by local Creole literature, to denounce that this untamed extension has finally been domesticated by the city grid, which has been commodified. Just as the grid is now repudiated as the instrument of predatory modernization, its traditional peer in Sarmiento's rejection, the pampa, also inverts its valuation, and becomes the true bastion of Argentine culture: now the grid is the cage that is relentlessly stretched over the most authentic part of the land's culture, the pampa and its inhabitant, the *gaucho*. It is precisely in the suburbs where this conflict of cultural domination appears in all its crudity, where everything becomes "business":

65
62

> Imagine a country of zinc, where a whole people housed on plots of land that will go up in price, have become switchmen with no switches. The streets, of what will be a city in a few years, are marked in the intention, and the intentions are galvanized wire fences, which enclose... precisely that; a town that is waiting to be and that, while waiting, has spent everything in feet and meters and has no money to build, has built some little bars that are not houses; they are sentry boxes that watch over the city that is to become. These houses (and we call them houses as it is customary to call the places in which one sleeps) are built (and we say built because we have to say something) with all the tin sheeting, with all the zinc, with all the *electroplating* that the importation of biscuits, sardines and oil has brought to this country from the colonial era to the colonized era. [...] Surrounding these, which we will call houses, the fantasy of the inhabitant has planted his garden, but as he knows that in time this garden will have to be built on, he does not take much care in planting it [...]. This is the barrio we are passing through, but what gives it the most character, and what is of great importance, are the fences of these plots, the stakes that separate them and that galvanized wire, which we are going to find all over the pampa.[327]

For an anti-modern sensibility like Rusiñol's, the suburb is the worst of this "new" society, where the abstraction of the universal grid of galvanized wire embodies its unredeemable materialism, its exclusive interest in business and wealth, its inability to see in the land "the homeland," but only "the lot": the

---

[327] Ibid., 188–89.

desacralization of what is most dear to traditional culture, the land, the home, swept away in the whirlwind of the perpetual movement of merchandise.

All travelers indeed establish the same link between the new suburb and speculative fever, which they coincide in pointing out as a salient feature of Buenos Aires society of the centenary. But for a reformist like Adolfo Posada, it is a link that reveals problems: "all the luxurious living, the banking and financial movement, and the world credit of the republic rest on the assumption that the land is valued. That is why the atmosphere of Buenos Aires and of the whole republic is an atmosphere of *speculation*," he says in full harmony with the general tone of moral criticism. But from there he must take on an aspect of the speculation/urban expansion *entente* that complicates his judgment: the possibility of decent housing accessible to all social sectors: "But land is not valued without people. [...] The interest, then, of the land speculators of the city is in making the backwater of Buenos Aires pour into the Pampa [...]. They can always repeat, with Alberdi, that 'to govern is to populate.'"[328]

Posada is, in many aspects, a counter-figure to Rusiñol: sociologist, academic from Oviedo—intellectual headquarters of social reformism in Spain—he comes invited by the University of La Plata as part of an exchange program inaugurated with the visit of Rafael Altamira; his local interlocution describes an ideological arc bounded between Joaquín V. González and Juan B. Justo, between the public reformism of the members of the National Department of Labor and the Socialist Party; his problems are institutional and political.[329] His vision, therefore, of the new city growing behind Buenos Aires' back connects with the reformist positions of officials and technicians who are seeking, with the census data, to draw the first local conclusions about the suburban phenomenon. There are two reports that explain and develop, in many ways, Posada's positions: those of F. R. Cibils and Domingo Selva, two representative figures of the technical reformism that has been consolidating in the conservative state. With differing tones, what both authors say is that the market (the speculation and the tramway companies), by itself, had solved the problem of workers' housing that only a few years earlier had seemed on the verge of exploding, "naturally" ending the factors that kept alive the economic and social need of the tenement. "The eviction and demolition of those old and dirty dens of infections and of physical and moral degeneration, *has been imposed, then, without laws or ordinances*," writes Cibils in the publication of the National Department of Labor.[330]

---

[328] Posada, *La República Argentina*, 66.

[329] On Posada's trip and Spanish reformism, see Zimmermann, *Los liberales reformistas*, 73–74.

[330] F. R. Cibils, "La descentralización urbana de la ciudad de Buenos Aires," *Boletín del Departamento Nacional del Trabajo* 16 (March 31, 1911): 88 (emphasis added).

It is not surprising that, after celebrating all that the working-class population has gained by moving to the suburbs (light, sun, space, comfort), Cibils devotes himself to an incisive critique of everything they have lost (mainly sewers and running water, but more generally the urban infrastructure they had in the downtown tenement) and to an indignant description of the new conditions of degradation imposed by these deficiencies. But it is not possible to ignore the new framework in which this critique takes place: such deficiencies are the responsibility of the state, which is required to expand its services as an indispensable complement to a positive transformation that has been brought about by the market. It could be said that, according to Cibils's version, the capitalism so long awaited by public reformism in Buenos Aires has finally appeared: the one that initiates the action that must then be seconded by the state. The much criticized speculator finds in this hypothesis a side of unexpected nobility, while connecting with the concerns of a whole reformist sector that tries to modernize the rules of land speculation, even relying on its less "modernizing" aspects in classical terms: "ant speculation," typical of the process of urban expansion in Buenos Aires, is not only read as a generalization of non-productive practices for society more broadly, or directly as moral and cultural corruption in the manner of regenerationism, but as a form of social process to be encouraged.[331]

A change of emphasis in the critique of suburbanization appears more clearly in Selva, promoter, as we saw earlier, of public solutions for workers' housing since the end of the century. For him, "the housing problem," defined in the dramatic terms in which he had posed it just six years earlier, was "in fact solved" in 1910. It was the land market that by itself had carried out the fundamental task of popular housing: to convert the worker into a property

---

[331] On this subject, the positions of José Bianco—director of the Land Registry since 1908—are interesting, proposing the elaboration of a National Land Registry law to give guarantees to the buyers of small lots in installments. According to Bianco, public auctions until then spread false land values to inflate the market, something that was avoided with the system of deeds and the publication of the *Land Registry Bulletin* with real values. But the main problem to be solved by the proposed law is that, when sold in installments, the lots were not deeded for several months, being kept as the only evidentiary element by the buyer during the installments, serving as the purchase-sale ticket and the "booklet" of the installments, devoid of any legal formality. This allowed fraud. The speculators who plotted and sold in monthly installments were rarely the owners: they bought large extensions in installments, paying a part and guaranteeing the rest with mortgages; then they plotted and sold in turn, and with the monthly installments they received they paid their own debt, a process that often failed, as they were unable to cover it, leaving all the small buyers without any title. The law proposes the deed at the time of purchase and the regulation of the profession of auctioneer. On this subject, see *Transmisión inmobiliaria* (Buenos Aires: G. Mendersky e hijo, 1912); especially chap. VI: "Venta de inmuebles por mensualidades. Proyecto de Ley."

owner. His description of the new homeowners offers a completely opposite assessment to Rusiñol's and shows a very acute vision of a process that from then on would do nothing but unfold, transforming the social composition of the urban population:

> With these constructions, reduced to the minimum expression of economy and representing the *summum* of the diminutive as a dwelling house, all the outskirts of the densely built-up part of the capital have been populated [...]. It is evident that they are not what the hygienist and the sociologist have devised for workers' housing. Hygiene, comfort, and convenience have no place there, and the Municipal Inspectorate should have made itself felt in an effective way [...]. But, with that, the problem of *one's own house* is solved. The occupant knows that the piece of land he has fenced off—perhaps with staves from old barrels—and the room where he lives—which serves as a dining room, a bedroom, an infirmary, a storeroom, and sometimes a kitchen—is *his*, and *his* very *own*. He knows that he has acquired it without waiting the twenty years—or in the best of cases the fifteen years—that the ad hoc companies need to ensure a tenant the ownership of the house he lives in. And although he understands that the latter would be more comfortable, more hygienic, more comfortable, and perhaps better situated for communications with the center of commercial and industrial activity, he also thinks that he has, with what he has managed to acquire in the third part of that time, a base on which his future desires for property will develop.[332]

62

Starting from this observation, Selva will also direct his complaints to the state: in addition to infrastructure, demands must be made for health, education, and recreation, distributed equally in all areas of the new suburb, and a system of state housing for rent as the definitive end of the tenement. These claims, it should be clarified, remain within the framework of the issues already assumed by the state—after all, Selva and Cibils come from its bosom: for example, in 1908 sanitation works had, in fact, been projected onto the whole new radius, where the different services would be inaugurated in stages over the following three decades. But the important thing to point out is Selva's astonished discovery of the commendable consequences of a process so loathsome on so many counts. If already that discovery generates ambivalence in a state reformer like him, it will further profoundly mark the future of socialist reformism in the city over the following decades, undecided between the criticism of speculation and

---

[332] Domingo Selva, "Edificación obrera," *Arquitectura. Suplemento de la Revista Técnica* 63 (May–June 1910): 52. The text is the first part of a paper delivered to the American International Scientific Congress held in Buenos Aires as part of the centenary celebration; the second part was published in the following issue of the same magazine.

the recognition of its direct incidence in the formation of its own public: the Buenos Aires middle class.

The case of Jules Huret is different: a journalist and professional traveler, when he comes to Buenos Aires he has already written travel accounts of great impact for *Le Figaro* on the United States and Germany. His literary format is possibly the most conventional, combining accounts of customs, natural and urban description, meticulous portraits of the economic, productive, and institutional aspects of society, with a double focus on the interest of a public eager for travel literature and on that of potential markets for his country, in search of protagonism in the inter-imperialist struggle. His interest in Latin America is reduced to that: throughout the book, the matter at hand is focused more on bringing a flourishing economy such as Argentina's into the French orbit than on asking a question about "the future of the race," as we saw in Posada.

With the eagerness of someone who wants to see everything, to tell everything (and if it is with abundant figures, all the better), Huret goes to the suburbs to find two landscapes. On the one hand, the picturesque misery of the Barrio de las Ranas (Neighborhood of Frogs), which serves as a rhetorical counterpart of economic success, as a metaphor of the latent conflicts in the vertigo of progress—and it is worth saying that most of the travelers resort to this formula of embodying in specific examples the "dark" face of Argentina; Rusiñol and Clemenceau in fact coincide in closing their accounts with the suicide from the boat of an immigrant who returns in failure to his country. On the other hand, there is the provisional and unfinished camp landscape, which nonetheless follows the invisible iron guidelines of the order of the grid that guarantees its future integration to "the city." In any case, both landscapes form part of a unitary picture, because the very picturesqueness of the Barrio de las Ranas, with its exceptional character, serves in this narrative to highlight the *normality* of the massive process of suburbanization:

> We find ourselves in the eccentric barrios, amid all that is provisional and unfinished of which I spoke earlier as characteristic of certain parts of Buenos Aires. Here, unpaved streets are, however, lined almost entirely with new houses. Some are handsome-looking, but the more modest are clerks' or workmen's quarters, ground-floor, with facades painted pink or white, and nearly all with art nouveau trimmings. There are others built with stamped brass, imitating slate, which give the impression of a "nomadic" camp of settlers. [...] They are separated by undeveloped land and fields of alfalfa and corn. Large white signs with letters placed on tall stakes indicate that an "auction" will take place the following Sunday. The plots of land will be auctioned and purchased by workers who will have to pay for them monthly, and within six months they will be covered with houses under construction. This is how in fifteen years most of the suburbs or eccentric barrios of Buenos Aires were formed, the "villas," Malcolm, Santa Rita, the Catalinas,

Devoto, etc. In these outlying districts the streets are very wide, but not very lively. You can still find there the milkmen in Basque berets milking their cows in the middle of the street and then distributing the milk to their customers. [...] In these extreme barrios there are hundreds of streets, sometimes close to very populous avenues, which only exist on the plans, distinguished by the depth of the roads.[333]

Again, as in Rusiñol, it is the omnipresence of the plan, perceived by these travelers with extreme acuity, that gives meaning to this multitude of frayed *vecindarios* (local isolated communities) on the plain: the hundreds of streets that exist only in plans critically point to the delays of municipal action in the face of real estate development, but at the same time weave the only half-visible network of containment of this explosion of land and houses; they point to the potential passage from the nomadic camp to the *villa* (isolated neighborhood) and from there to the city.

But, to complete the series of travel accounts, perhaps the most interesting case is that of Enrique Gómez Carrillo, a Guatemalan writer and journalist who developed his career in the artistic circles of Madrid and Paris. With *El encanto de Buenos Aires* he does not seek to understand or explain the country as a whole; he proposes an urban chronicle in continuity with his previous book, *El encanto de París*, placing himself in front of his local interlocutors not as an expert or an intellectual, but as an urban artist, an exquisite taster of cities. Who better than a Latin American trained in Paris—that is, someone who knows the two possible extremes of urban culture very well—to judge impartially the great problems of identity of the *porteños*: Does Buenos Aires have a culture, what cities does it resemble, what is its own character? Gómez Carrillo's entire book flirts with these questions, answered in advance by the similarity of the titles: Buenos Aires belongs to the cultural family of Paris, with very little to envy. It has many characteristics of other "new cities" like New York or Berlin, but unlike those "improvised capitals" in which only the economic reigns, it has culture, beauty, and elegance.[334]

Just as Rusiñol is the ideal *partner* of regenerationism, so Gómez Carrillo is the ideal partner of the cultural establishment to which he offers their desired city; also like Rusiñol, his character as a foreigner allows him to double all bets, in this case to refute the *porteño* cultural inferiority complex in the face of Europe precisely in the clichés that the cultured *porteños* qualify as defects: the foreign dilettante is the one who can discover the richness of urban culture in its frivolous folds, because as an artist he does not run the risk of being confused

[333] Huret, *De Buenos Aires al Gran Chaco*, 1:57.
[334] Enrique Gómez Carrillo, *El encanto de Buenos Aires* (Madrid: Perlado, Páez y Comp., 1914).

with the frivolity he celebrates. In contrast to the essentialist preoccupations of Buenos Aires intellectuals, Gómez Carrillo pays attention to the value of appearances as a peculiarity of modern society: the beauty of women extended to all social classes, which he connects, suggestively and deliciously, with that of racehorses to sustain the superiority of racial mixtures, the great problem of Buenos Aires, as well as absolute social integration in the Colón Theatre and Palermo, the once sacred precincts of the aristocracy. Paying no attention to the authenticity of lineages, but merely to the "charm" of what he sees, allows him to celebrate the ethnic and cultural mix of Buenos Aires as the construction of a new synthesis and as the full democratization of public space.[335]

Gómez Carrillo is the last of the series: he comes to Buenos Aires in 1914 and the book is published the same year as a result of his discussions in *La Nación* with Enrique García Velloso. Of additional interest is that he consciously and polemically links himself to his predecessors:

> But then, on reflection, I thought that there was something to be said, or, at least, certain things still had to be said in a way that the Hurets, the Clemenceaus, the Baudins and other serious publicists have not used in their books. And I also thought that this "something," something apparently frivolous, but at bottom transcendental, perhaps I could write it better than my predecessors, not because I had more talent than them, no, but because my soul feels the grace of certain cities with an intensity that great ministers and great journalists disdain.[336]

Thus, the place of authority or documentation that in the other books become internal references to the series, in Gómez Carrillo is inverted to give way to irony or, in the case of Rusiñol, to open polemic: the entire book is a great refutation of the Catalan's criticisms.

The only two times that Gómez Carrillo leaves the city center, its landscapes and its types, to go to the suburbs—and we must insist that, as befits the social sector with which he relates, these are true excursions, presented as such—he does so to prove his thesis on the urban and cultural equivalence of Buenos Aires with European cities, with the added bonus of democratic originality, impossible to find in "old" stratified cultures. The first excursion is guided by Mayor Anchorena, "rich, young, active, with a thirst for progress and reform that does not let him sleep, it could be said that he embodies the insatiable soul of this city." As for the most enthusiastic apologists of Argentine progress, what he finds in his path indicates an urban and social mobility without fissures or conflicts:

---

[335] Ibid., especially the chapters "En los grandes teatros," 71 ff. and "Entre flores y sonrisas," 201 ff.

[336] Ibid., 6–7. Gómez Carrillo had translated Huret's book into Spanish in France.

The automobile rolls along streets paved in such a way that Paris and Berlin would envy. We are no longer, however, in the elegant districts. We have crossed immense spaces in which the buildings are modest. From time to time, an enormous factory chimney lets us see that we are in the working-class suburbs. Nothing, however, of what in Europe indicates the poverty of the lower classes shocks us. The grocery stores, though smaller than in the center, boast the same tempting victuals. The little boys playing on the sidewalks are dressed like the children of the bourgeoisie. Only occasionally, from time to time, a dirty man, with a deformed hat and broken shoes, smokes his pipe on a street corner: he is a recently arrived immigrant who, in a month's time, will be dressed as well as the Creole workers. After twenty minutes we arrive at a suburb in formation. The streets are not yet asphalted and there are already shops.[337]

It is much more than an account of what he sees, as we might find in a Huret; it is the X-ray of a social process that Gómez Carrillo believes he can guess *in nuce* in the clothes of the children or in the tempting victuals of the stores. In the same way as these, the whole *vecindario* is like the center in scale, with its social mobility in scale (the unemployed emigrant can become a worker in a month), its building in scale, and its paved streets that connect it with its future: the city itself.

The second excursion to the suburb—as expected from a member of the journalistic bohemia like Gómez Carrillo—will be to visit in its own cradle the cultural product that in a decade will be recognized as one of the main "threads" that sewed the culture "of the two cities": tango, already famous in Paris and still bearing an aura of proscription in Buenos Aires. A group is formed with other visitors—including Blasco Ibañez—which, as it should be, is led by a *baqueano* (an expert guide). This time it is "a distant, sordid, and almost deserted barrio." Everything here is ordinary: the streets, puddled and full of water; the joint where the dance will take place, "barely lit by a few gaslights" and populated by "a few dirty tables;" the "showy rags" of the women who, for the only time in the whole book, are described as ugly, pathetic, or infamous. The diaphanous and progressive clarity of the working-class barrio finds its exact opposite in the sordidness of the tango district. Clearly, in this case it is La Boca which, as we shall see, occupies precisely that place in the local imagination, as the opposite of the new suburb. But in Gómez Carrillo the intention of the contrast points to another objective: nothing could be further from the author than to initiate here a critical description "à la Huret," because all this descent into the hells of the suburb is nothing but the rhetorical preamble necessary for the marvelous appearance of art to produce the most contrasting revelation: "In the *bouge* where before we saw nothing but misery and vice,

[337] Ibid., 154–55.

crispness and sordidness, [the tango] has created, on the spot, with the magic of its leisurely and stately rhythm, which seems to elongate the silhouettes and refine the waists, an atmosphere of gallant, worldly, and restrained festivity." The transfiguration is complete:

> I do not recognize, in fact, in these couples neither the *compadritos* (troublemakers), bowler tipped to the ear, nor the sad women sinners in crazy rags. Without connecting, almost without touching, looking more at their steps than at their faces, they smile with a grave smile, the same on all their lips, and undulate in complicated steps, as if they were celebrating a rite of ceremonious harmonies.

For a refined spirit like Gómez Carrillo, what is to be admired in tango is not any "American" naturalness, impossible in such an elegantly contrived dance; no appeal to the savagery of the "land covered with amorous sweat": "the people of the countryside and the plebeians of the provinces have no time to learn complicated dances." It is, then, the highest product of European culture: "a brother of those languid *pavanas* (Spanish dances) and those ceremonious minuets of the eighteenth century. It is a court dance." In the background, there is always Paris as a praiseworthy counterpoint; and both the daytime working-class suburb, integrating and neat, and the nighttime one, sordid and marginal, come to prove, each in its own way, that, as the Buenos Aires elite would like to believe, Buenos Aires has nothing to envy.[338]

2. Suburban Grid: The Pampa Map

> The plan shows that the real city, the great city of the not distant future, the city that will fill America and the race with pride, must develop from Callao and Entre Ríos to the west, where the layout meets the requirements of modern cities.[339]
>
> –Benito Carrasco, "La ciudad del porvenir," 1908

There is another suburb in the years of the centenary, the suburb of the few—very few—that distract their attention from downtown reform to imagine, in those shapeless borders of the city with the pampas, "the city of the future." When we see the illustrations with which *Caras y Caretas* published Carrasco's article in 1908, we notice the difficulty of such an operation: deserted cobblestones crossing the plain, wire fences, some trees; the only urban features are the names of the streets below the photographs and, in one of them, the image

65

---

[338] All quotations, in ibid., 220–21.
[339] *Caras y Caretas* (Buenos Aires), February 22, 1908.

of a streetcar in the distance, framed in a perspective of lighting poles. Is that the city of the future?

The treatment of the suburbs in magazines and newspapers in these years is scarce: "the outlying barrios" are the places of picturesque events and great natural disasters, never part of "the city." The complaints of Mayor Manuel Güiraldes in the municipal reports of 1908 and 1909 are fully justified: "for the general concept, the municipality of Buenos Aires is the area of its great streets and promenades," but the city that must be taken care of with practically the same resources is four times bigger, and nobody appreciates the public works carried out in the new suburbs (pavements, lighting, clearing, bridges, drains). Of course, also for the mayor's office, the main problem is that the municipality has acquired an "exaggerated extension [...] that indisputably threatens municipal services and aesthetics due to this ocean of one-story houses that are detrimental to income and value," which shows to what extent the ideal of the concentrated city was kept in force in the municipal imaginary, although now there was no other choice but to accept with resignation "the consummated facts."[340]

The most important project in these years which contemplates the whole of the new city is Bouvard's plan (1907–1909), well-known in the specialized literature only for its proposal of central diagonals, but without an analysis of its ideas for the suburbs. The overshadowing of the 1898–1904 plan subjected Bouvard's plan to a double misunderstanding: that of contemporaries, who discussed it as just another proposal for diagonals; that of historians, who always catalogued it as a plan that sought to impose an inappropriate Haussmannian model (utopian or colonialist), or, at best, as an initiative that simply arbitrated between local proposals in dance for the city center.[341] When, on the other hand, Bouvard's plan is placed in relation to the 1898–1904 plan, and when one finds the name of Carlos María Morales in the local commission formed by the City Council to accompany the Frenchman's work, one sees that the importance of the Bouvard plan lies in its proposals for the suburb. Morales had been largely responsible for the previous plan and, after twenty years directing the municipality's Commission of Public Works, knew the city best. The Bouvard

---

[340] "Memoria del año 1908," in *Memorias de la Intendencia Municipal de Buenos Aires correspondiente a 1908* (Buenos Aires: G. Kraft, 1908), viiff.

[341] The main historiographical versions to which I refer: Jorge Tartarini, "El Plan Bouvard para Buenos Aires (1907–1911). Algunos antecedentes," *Anales del Instituto de Arte Americano e Investigaciones Estéticas Mario J. Buschiazzo"* (Buenos Aires), 27–28 (1992); Jorge Enrique Hardoy, "Teorías y prácticas urbanísticas en Europa entre 1850 y 1930. Su traslado a América Latina," in Hardoy and Morse, eds., *Repensando la ciudad de América Latina* (Buenos Aires: GEL, 1988); Sonia Berjman, "Los espacios verdes." Without departing from the framework that limits its consideration to downtown projects, Alicia Novick provides the most measured analysis of Bouvard's visit by considering him an "arbitrator," in "Técnicos locales y extranjeros en la génesis del urbanismo argentino. Buenos Aires, 1880–1940," *Area* 1 (1992).

plan was, in truth, an adjustment of the 1898–1904 grid to the reality of Buenos Aires' first expansive cycle: the attempt to adjust the plan to the real city.

We have already seen that Bouvard was hired by Carlos Alvear's administration to draw up the plan of improvements for the centenary. The French town planner had been engaged to carry out preparatory work in Buenos Aires from 1907 onwards (he would be here for three months that year, three months in 1909, and another three in 1910). In this early moment in the international formation of the discipline of urban planning, this type of commission—largely given to French, and to a lesser extent, German planners—was not uncommon even in less peripheral countries such as the United States or Spain. The exchange of experiences between specialists from different countries was very intense within the framework of the beginning of the cycle of international congresses that would define city planning as a profession and a science. To understand Bouvard's specific appointment in Buenos Aires, it should be made clear that he was by no means the most internationally renowned professional of the moment, but he had extensive management experience in post-Haussmannian Paris, especially in relation to the urban organization of the Universal Exhibitions, the specific objective for which he was hired in the run-up to the centenary.[342] And this evaluation is very important in the face of the often capricious imputations of the time which, in reality, were motivated by rivalries or professional spite: the paradigmatic case is Jaeschké, but no less significant is Schiaffino, who several years later still oscillates between comparing the Bouvard plan to "the rumbustious projects of Bouvard and Pécuchet," or describing it as "the beautiful Bouvard project," according to whether the themes he is interested in defending in each case coincide or not with his own proposals.[343] Perhaps the best demonstration of the average acceptance in the professional field of this commission in particular and of the mechanism in general is that the magazine *Arquitectura*, the mouthpiece of the Sociedad Central de Arquitectos, extremely jealous of the recognition and hierarchical status of local professionals, it does not contest the hiring but only the conditions, questioning the short time Bouvard was required to stay in Buenos Aires and arguing that in those conditions he should have been called upon simply as an adviser to collaborate in the formation of a local team, while at the same time admitting that foreign experts are still necessary in these matters.

---

[342] Joseph-Antoine Bouvard was director of the Parisian exhibition at the Universal Exhibitions of 1878 and 1889, for which he designed the Champ de Mars; at the 1900 exhibition he was director of parks and gardens. For the most complete and precise information on Bouvard and on the specific circumstances of his hiring in Buenos Aires, see Anne-Marie Châtelet, "Joseph-Antoine Bouvard, 1840–1920," in Programa Internacional de Investigaciones sobre el campo urbano, *Documento de Trabajo N° 1. Seminario Internacional Vaquerías* (Buenos Aires: 1996).

[343] Schiaffino, *La urbanización de Buenos Aires*, 22 and 115.

Figure 63. Joseph-Antoine Bouvard, *Bouvard Plan*, 1909. Biblioteca Esteban Echeverría, Legislatura de la Ciudad de Buenos Aires. This image shows Bouvard's interventions in red over the lighter grid. This visualization of the project emphasizes the specific character of his proposals for the suburbs, intended to connect specific points on the grid. This manner of "stitching" is far from the "utopian" operations for which he is criticized when attention is paid only to the circuit of diagonals at the city center. At the same time, it is clearly evident that in most of the areas that are to undergo reforms the grid is still but a drawing over the pampa.

I believe that a productive reading of the whole episode of Bouvard's hiring lies, then, in noticing that in reality what took place was something quite similar to what the architects' society demanded: in a way Bouvard functioned as a consultant, since the local commission, embodied in the figure of Morales, had a decisive place in the drawing up of the plan.[344] In order to see this, we must shift the focus of the debate from the avenues and diagonals in the city center and pay attention to Bouvard's overall plan for the city as a whole: the precision and extreme realism of each of the reforms proposed for the suburb is striking, to the point of producing, rather than the image of an ambitious urban project, that of a petty patchwork of micro-projects for avenues and parks.

But what does realism mean in the suburban context, when the plan was still mostly an imaginary tracing projected on the pampa, the delusions of grandeur of a dreaming geometrician, in Rusiñol's terms? In this context, realism can mean different things. In a broad sense, it means the acceptance, detail by detail, of the 1898–1904 grid, that is, the acceptance of the conditions of a plan that the municipality imposed on the land market on a juridical basis. To see the exceptionality of this realism in urban debates of the period, it is enough to compare the Bouvard plan with the contemporary reforms proposed by Chanourdie, the only one of the technicians active in the debate who does not reject the idea of the gridiron as a matrix for the expansion of the city. Over that grid he proposes a geometric system of regular diagonals, but which he never defines or designs outside the radius of the traditional city, as if the suburb could still be a motive for free disposition of streets outside the juridical commitments implied in the 1898–1904 grid.[345]

In a more specific sense, realism means to operate consciously on this plan in terms of very specific reforms. One type of proposed intervention goes in the direction of a greater abstraction of the grid: it seeks to increase the universality of communications, partially hindered in the 1898–1904 plan by the pre-existing lots and the already materialized sectors of the layout (both obstacles are referred to by Morales as limitations of the 1898–1904 plan; both objectives are referred to in recalling Bouvard's plan). The other type of proposed intervention goes in the direction of greater concreteness: it seeks to favor mutual

63

---

[344] The Commission that appointed the intendancy was formed by Carlos María Morales, Francisco Beazley, Carlos Thays, Fernando Pérez, and Ramón Bravo. In Jaeschké's accusations against the Bouvard plan it is clear that he holds Morales responsible for its main lines, establishing continuity with the plan of 1898–1904: the "phenomenal and deformed development" of the city is the fault of "one of the most conspicuous members, the only technician of the commission of amateurs who accompanied M. Bouvard in his studies [...]. Let us remember in passing, that in 20 years of direction of Public Works, the mentioned engineer did not know how to do anything, but let auctioneers and speculators do everything," in *Las avenidas*, 3.

[345] Chanourdie's project in "Conferencia sobre transformación edilicia de Buenos Aires," *Arquitectura. Suplemento de la Revista Técnica* 39 (July and August 1906): 57ff.

communication between the few already populated nuclei of the homogeneous grid. In the first case, the aim is to improve the grid fan and, above all, the continuity of transversal communications, in a north–south direction; in the second case, the aim is to make specific contacts demanded by the real occupation of the suburb with avenues and articulation centers. And it is in this type of realism where we find the most interesting confirmation of the conjunctural significance of the Bouvard plan, because it comes from a source that shows us the exact opposite of the recusations of which it was the object, revealing how the plan could be understood from the again decentered perspective of the suburb: it is the vision of the plan from a suburban "subintendence."

Since the Güiraldes administration (1908–1910) there had been an outline of administrative decentralization in three subintendencies that responded to the traditional "towns" of La Boca, Flores, and Belgrano; in the Anchorena administration (1910–1914) the fourth, Vélez Sársfield, was formed to attend to the expansion of the southwest. The municipal official appointed to head this brand-new subintendency, Luis Mohr, presents in his 1912 *Report* one of the very few sources of the period that show the other side of the vision of urban expansion, that of the concrete problems of the real settlements in the universal checkerboard. In the chapter "Neighborhood Roads," he demands that Bouvard's "plan of diagonal roads" be fulfilled, in order to open and pave those that would join Villa Devoto with the center of Vélez Sársfield, and Liniers with Nueva Chicago. In defense of that idea, Mohr points out that the universal roadway that appears in the plans of the Department of Public Works (the 1898–1904 grid) can be found only in the layout, since very few streets actually exist. Also, materializing these streets (and then maintaining them) would be much more expensive than making only the "diagonals" that he sees in the Bouvard plan, which directly connect the populated points (the typical economist criticism of the checkerboard, which sees it as a huge superstructure of great cost only to draw a virtual city, since in reality only some urban nuclei are developed). For Mohr, then, the Bouvard plan would "remove the difficulties that the existing fields between the villas Urquiza, Devoto, Real, del Parque, and Liniers offer for all communication."[346]

Mohr's claim shows us the inverse misunderstanding that generates the relation of the Bouvard plan with the 1898–1904 grid, because, in short, it shows us another aspect of the omissions: the incomprehension of the effects of the grid on the part of the same civil servants who should manage its development. For the "conjunctural" view of the subintendency, the few really populated centers in the suburb are isolated "villas," separated from each other by huge

---

[346] See "Vélez Sársfield," in *Memoria del Departamento ejecutivo presentada al H. Concejo Deliberante por el Intendente Municipal Dr. Joaquín S. de Anchorena, Municipalidad de la Capital Federal, República Argentina, ejercicio de 1912* (Buenos Aires: Talleres gráficos del Ministerio de Agricultura, 1913), 434.

"fields," which it does not imagine as necessarily expanding until they join one another; and in this it is entirely consistent with the perspective in which the subintendencies were created, modeled on the towns that had been annexed to London's municipal administration while maintaining their individuality.[347] The only obstacle in the analogy is that the London model not only assumes the existence in the outskirts of the city of very old settlements, resistant to the absorption of metropolitan expansion—the contrast with the emptiness of the pampa could not be greater: the "village" of Belgrano had been created barely fifty years earlier, not to mention the whole of the suburb that is *a direct product* of metropolitan expansion of the beginning of the century—but also implies a mechanism for expansion exactly opposite to that of Buenos Aires, not through the universal grid, which presupposes the future homogeneous occupation of the whole territory, but through the "garden suburbs," with its system of installation of conclusive urbanizations in a rural territory.

The utility that Mohr finds in the "diagonals" of the Bouvard plan shows that he has not understood how it operates its embroidery on the 1898–1904 grid, but at the same time it reveals much of the careful design with which each one of those "diagonals" had sought to solve precise questions of the actually existing expansion: the fact that Mohr can understand them as "neighborhood roads" destined to solve pressing situations, implicitly demonstrates that those punctual reforms were not drawn at random (and for that reason they can only be attributed to someone like Morales). The other thing that is striking, if we contrast this "realism of the grid" with the incomprehension of the municipal administration's own officials regarding its effects, is the continuity of management and conception that a group of technical officials, here represented by the persistence of Morales, has managed to impose, outside of political changes and foreign hires.

That is why, from the point of view of the autonomy required of an "urban plan," the one designed by Bouvard is incomprehensible: because it thoroughly reforms something that does not exist. It traces one abstraction on top of another. Looking at the drawings, it is disturbing to recognize that the avenues and diagonals that in the original European models were intended to open up dense sectors of compact, historic cities, are here thought of as rural roads to connect population centers, or as a careful embroidery in a regular grid over the desert, to regularize even more, connect even more, and universalize even more the 1898–1904 grid, ratifying the material and conceptual impossibility

---

[347] Mayor Güiraldes says in his 1908 *Report*, justifying the subintendencies: "In a word, Buenos Aires will eventually require, like London, a numerous series of subintendencies, dependent on the central administration for the time being, and that little by little, given their importance, will allow an absolute division of complete municipal life (in each subintendency), which today is lacking": see *Memoria de la intendencia municipal de Buenos Aires correspondiente a 1908, presentada al H. Concejo Deliberante* (Buenos Aires: G. Kraft, 1908), viii.

(in the sense of the urban theory and the cultural meaning that sustains it) of a Haussmann in the pampa.

A second intervention on the future of the suburb that is worth analyzing is that of Benito Carrasco himself, with whose quote we opened this section. Carrasco is an agronomist dedicated to urban planning; during the administrations of Arturo Gramajo (1914–16) and Joaquín Llambías (1916–19), he succeeded Carlos Thays in the direction of Parks and Walks (from 1914 to 1918), where he was responsible for the creation of the Balneario Municipal (Municipal Resort) in the Costanera Sur and the Rosedal (Rose Garden) in Palermo. In the 1920s, from within the Amigos de la Ciudad association, from the columns of *La Nación*, or collaborating with the Democratic Progressive Party in the City Council, he was to play an important role in public debates on the city.[348] His 1908 article is part of the discussion opened by the hiring of Bouvard and the consequent proposal of the plan of improvements for the centenary. The publication in *Caras y Caretas* not only indicates the spread of public interest on the subject, but also a constant in Carrasco's career: his consistent exclusion from the professional spaces of architecture, where he will never find legitimacy as an urbanist. And it would not be wrong to suppose that, in 1908, such distance from the cenacles of professional urban discussion is directly proportional to the originality—eccentricity, it could be emphasized—of his approach:

64, 65, 66

> All the projects and plans presented [for the modification of the urban plan of Buenos Aires] are limited to the opening of costly avenues that are difficult to implement, or to the widening of streets by slow and impractical procedures; all within the radius surrounded by Callao and Entre Ríos [...] as if these boulevards were the impassable limits of the municipality.[349]

But if that eccentricity allows him to see the whole of the city plan without prejudice and thus to understand as myopia to continue considering "the nucleus that we call 'center' as the city of Buenos Aires," at the same time it is important to recognize that such a perspective is made possible by a theoretical disciplinary position that is not marginal; on the contrary, it is the fullest assumption in the local context of the postulates of picturesque urbanism in its version of the Garden City, a position, as we have seen, completely hegemonic in the professional ideology of the period.

---

[348] For a biography of Benito Carrasco (Buenos Aires, 1887–1958) see Sonia Berjman, "Carrasco, Benito," entry in Liernur and Aliata, eds., *Diccionario de arquitectura en la Argentina*, vol. 2.

[349] Benito J. Carrasco, "La ciudad del porvenir," *Caras y Caretas* (Buenos Aires), February 22, 1908. All subsequent citations refer to the same article.

Illustrations to Benito Carrasco, "La ciudad del provenir," *Caras y Caretas*, February 22, 1908:

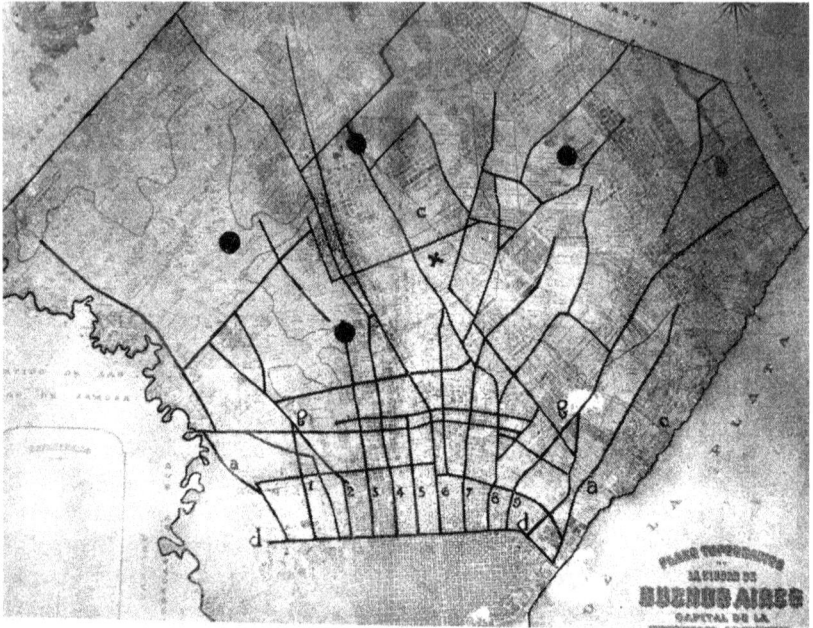

Figure 64. "Plan for the future Buenos Aires," to the West of Callao-Entre Ríos Avenue, with a system of zonal park-centers (encircled) and with a cross over the barycenter of the new city where government should be located.

Figure 65 and 66.
Photographs of the areas in which Carrasco imagines "the city of the future": the streets stretching out over the pampa are also Joseph Bouvard's "boulevards" or the "neighborhood roads" projected by Deputy Mayor Mohr.

Beyond the heterodoxy and precariousness with which Carrasco assumes the theories of the Garden City, the interesting thing is that they lead him inevitably to the positions of the first great decentralizer of Buenos Aires, Sarmiento, who not coincidentally relied on the experience of the British-American city, in which he naturally embodied the type of suburban expansion that later picturesque urbanism would theorize.[350] Like Sarmiento thirty years earlier, Carrasco defends his position in terms of the economic cost of downtown reform. Here we see how the acceptance of the new climate of ideas in technical debates allows him to convert the moral reaction against the "fantasmagorias as costly as unrealizable" of downtown expropriations—which in someone like Payró is necessarily limited to postulating a quietism that is conservative despite itself— into a reformist wager in favor of expansion. Also, like Sarmiento, Carrasco organizes the possible eccentric expansion around large parks combined with public buildings, as generating nuclei of urban quality and civic and community structuring, *equitably distributed throughout the plan.*   64

This is the obvious difference with Sarmiento's times: now decentralization has as inevitable reference the new limit of the municipality enlarged in 1887, which implies considering as a future city a figure already designed in the territory, which proposes by itself a regular expansion, fanning from the nucleus of the traditional city toward all cardinal points. This is the novelty with respect to Sarmiento that generates Carrasco's main contribution to the decentralizing debate, the innovation that will return in the twenties and thirties, again and again, as a reformist demand: if the new territorial figure of the expanded municipality is accepted as an urban unit, then the need for a physical and symbolic "recentralization" becomes evident. That is why Carrasco proposes   65 the location of the municipal palace "in the center of the 'true' municipality and not at an extreme as the present one." Unlike Sarmiento, for whom decentralization implied the creation of a "new city" far away and outside the traditional city, as two independent entities, what Carrasco is saying is that the new city is the whole of the new territory generated by the jurisdictional enlargement. Thus, it can only be understood from an eccentric perspective because it is that enlargement which *decentralized* the traditional city, leaving it at one end of the future city.

It is difficult to overestimate the radical nature of such a proposal in 1908, when the most audacious decentralizing projects in the professional field were

---

[350] Carrasco's heterodoxy in his assumption of the picturesque theories can be seen above all in his citing "in defense" of his position the examples of the "modern" enlargements of Berlin, Barcelona, and Vienna, all expansions planned through regular grids—the "police plans"—repudiated by the new urbanism in its picturesque version of the Garden City or in its classic versions of the theory of expansion, a confusion that is attributable to his lack of training, but, as we saw when we analyzed other positions, also to the precariousness of the field.

limited to the erection of the municipal palace in Plaza Once. It is not just a matter of a few kilometers more or less to the west; it is the comprehension of the future meaning of the new urban figure and its most resounding acceptance: the need for a complete symbolic recomposition of the traditional city. At the same time, Carrasco offers a solution to the municipalist postulates of clear discrimination between city and nation: by proposing that the municipality take charge of the new complete figure of the city, installing its government in the "true" center, he is also proposing the separation of the municipal government from the traditional center of the national government, the Plaza de Mayo, proposing a resolution of the conflict of powers and attributions that, as we saw, begins to arise crudely toward the centenary. One has only to return to the aforementioned photographs with which Carrasco illustrates his article to understand how a proposal like his could be received: the photograph showing the intersection of Chubut and Camargo streets, with its path of trees as if it were the private access to a farm in the middle of the countryside, is the closest image to the central point of the "real municipality": it is about placing the new "center" in the same vortex of the provisional camp that everyone repudiates or tries to ignore.

But Carrasco does not equally take charge of all the consequences of the expansion plan: he attends to the new urban figure created in 1888, but is unable to accept that, since the 1898–1904 plan, it has also been covered by the grid in its full extension. And this is the point at which the omissions become more interesting, because they no longer imply the incomprehension of the whole process of urban expansion but appear in someone extremely alert to some of its novelties. It is not only that Carrasco does not see the grid; what is more important is the aporia nested in this omission: the reasons why he *cannot* accept the grid lie, precisely, in his picturesque conception, which is what allows him to accept suburban expansion in some of its most radical consequences. For a series of reasons that have to do with picturesque aesthetics, the territory to the west of the traditional city can be for him a field of experimentation for a *truly modern* city: because he finds there "unevenness and undulations that make the much-criticized 'flatness' of the capital disappear;" because its entire extension is crossed by a stream like the Maldonado, whose canalization and widening "will contribute greatly to beautify the city;" and, mainly, because there the layout "abandons the famous 'checkerboard' arrangement," which will enable "the formation of model barrios—'cottage' or other types." Carrasco abstracts himself from the grid and in the plan, he only sees what coincides with his image of a "modern city": a more varied landscape— which, it is worth saying, shows a remarkable imagination—and a system of avenues (Chiclana, Santa Fe-Cabildo, Camino Puente Alsina, Alvear) "as perfect diagonals that fan out."

In his own way much as Mohr with the Bouvard plan, Carrasco selects from the 1898–1904 plan only some elements, as if the empty territory could also become an empty plan, without seeing how much they have been mutually affected by the grid or, at least, without proposing any alternative way to overcome it, overcoming not only its juridical implications but also its conception of the city as a universally communicated whole. That grid, ominously present to travelers as an unappealable universal diagram, is simply ignored by Carrasco, because his idea of modernity can no longer accept the modernity of the grid. And if this is the point in which he coincides with the whole urbanistic debate of the centenary beyond the theoretical limits with which the picturesque hypotheses were assumed, the contrast between the modernity of the "varied layouts" and the reality of the grid will only deepen. In 1916, in one of his first public interventions, the very young Carlos María della Paolera, renovator of local urban debates and a continuator in the twenties and thirties of decentralizing positions such as those of Carrasco, wrote in the *Revista de Ingeniería* that "the monotonous checkerboard devised by Don Juan de Garay [...] has been transplanted without modification to the various barrios into which [the city] has been expanding"; a "narrow criterion" that does not intervene "in the aesthetic part" because it has "a horror of the diagonal and the curve." The straight line and the block are only transgressed by "petty conditions": "by the convenience of the owners, by the direction of an old road," that is, traditional privileges or remnants of the old city. This "desolate monotony" in fact combines respect for tradition and the "crushing supremacy of utilitarian tendencies" and is only contradicted by the "small stain of modernization" of the curved layout of the streets of the *barrio-parque* under construction in Palermo Chico.[351] So these judgments about the grid, these omissions with respect to its public role in the suburb, will be repeated again and again and are largely co-responsible for the continuation, again and again, of the grid plan, which in the meantime was limited to fulfilling its regularizing purpose without hindrance, completing itself lot by lot, block by block, in the face of a generic but impotent repudiation, which will turn the absence of alternatives into an innocent victim of a predatory speculation, to which more and more the authorship and the responsibility of the checkerboard will be attributed, as if outside of any public design.

Finally, a third approach to the expansion of Buenos Aires in these early decades; its interest, in terms of its capacity to illuminate and project a new city, lies in exactly the opposite of Carrasco's: the understanding of the grid, its incorporation into a reading capable of celebrating it as an essential mark of modern

---

[351] Carlos María della Paolera, "Servidumbres estéticas en las construcciones edilicias," *La Ingeniería* XX, no. 5, January 9, 1916, 293 and ff. Palermo Chico was laid out, as already mentioned, on one of the sites of the Centennial Exposition designed by Bouvard; in 1916, its realization was largely the responsibility of Carrasco, then director of Parks and Walks; Bunge sarcastically described its landscaping in "El anticarrasco," as we remember from chapter four, which shows that hegemonic picturesqueness allowed quite contrasting meanings.

Buenos Aires. We find it in an article by Alberto Gerchunoff, in which he some-how transfers to the city the foolproof optimism about the Argentine future that he had already expressed in his most famous book, *Los gauchos judíos* (The Jewish Gauchos of the Pampas). Peace, prosperity, and integration: as Viñas points out, the book, from the very meeting of terms proposed by the title, is seamlessly connected to the official optimism of the centenary, and the same can be said, also starting with the title of the article "Buenos Aires, Continental Metropolis," published in Paris in 1914.[352] There is a point in which, indeed, Gerchunoff limits himself to modulating variants of the immoderate songs of Argentine progress found in some commemorative albums or poetry books; but there are, on the other hand, other features that show a very different oper-ation at work. The first, in any case, is to break with the climate of anti-modern and anti-metropolitan pessimism of his literary generation. We have already quoted him repudiating, in 1916, the "injustices" committed against Buenos Aires by his generation, but we should simply recall that the circumstance was the banquet in honor of a Gálvez increasingly crystallized in that anti-metro-politan sensibility to see to what extent this was an issue of principles.[353] But the most important novelty is that his mode of optimism will lead in the article to one of the first literary formalizations of a futuristic modern imaginary for Buenos Aires.

In "Buenos Aires, Continental Metropolis" Gerchunoff will seek to dis-pel one by one the charges, common among the local elite and most for-eign visitors, of the absence of culture in the city, understood as the absence of tradition as perceived by a European gaze. But unlike Gómez Carrillo, who, as we have seen, pursues the same objective, Gerchunoff will not try to show that Buenos Aires shares the refinement and beauty of European culture, but he will postulate its most extreme "Americanness," in the sense given the term since the previous century in central Europe. There, *Amer-ikanismus* referred, positioned between admiration and distrust, to North American utilitarianism, to the universe of technical progress, to its peculiar way of extending without "cultural" obstacles the processes of appropriation of territory and the rationalization of social relations. It referred to the social and cultural model that makes the Weberian capitalist possible, a model from which an important sector of the European artistic and architectural avant-gardes would take very diverse elements—from the assembly line to the skyscraper—to translate them into powerful aesthetic-ideological motifs,

[352] See the chapter "Gerchunoff: gauchos judíos y xenofobia," in Viñas, *Literatura argentina y realidad política*, 295ff. "Buenos Aires, metrópoli continental" was published in two parts in *La revista de América* 23 and 24 (January–April and May 1914), respectively; see M. E. Gover de Nasatsky, *Bibliografía de Alberto Gerchunoff* (Buenos Aires: Fondo Nacional de las Artes and Sociedad Hebraica Argentina, 1976).
[353] "Comida en honor de Manuel Gálvez," *Nosotros* 22, no. 85 (March 1916): 220.

into icons, and, at the same time, into condensing metaphors of an imaginary of modernity. Gerchunoff says:

> Buenos Aires lacks, not historical tradition, but local tradition. There are no medieval castles that evoke the life of princes and legends of dramatic loves and tenebrous crimes; there are no corners of somber sadness, no crooked streets of gloomy neighborhoods that synthesize before the contemporary spectator old episodes. Everything is young in Buenos Aires, everything is of yesterday, everything will be of tomorrow. And to scornfully pout for that is like looking with disdain at a robust and exultant adolescent because, in his virile beauty, he does not show the traces of old age, the melancholy of gray hair, the melancholy of wrinkles.[354]

In reality, Gerchunoff's operation is to double the wager on the parallel already drawn between Buenos Aires and New York. Now it is not a matter of showing the former as the "Latin counterpart," that is, as the spiritual counterpart of the latter's utilitarianism, as peninsular visitors wanted and, above all, as proposed by the dichotomy Rodó's *Ariel* spread in Latin America from 1900 onwards. Now it is a matter of identifying them in their Americanness, so as to capitalize in favor of Buenos Aires the charges of futurist vitalism against Europe: the same reasons that postulate the decadence of the West are those that can be optimistically reversed to point out the virtues of the "young," "healthy," "robust" peoples, for which Gerchunoff is going to use all the artillery of the syncopated rhetoric of "machinist progressivism":

> A city that piles up factories, that accumulates power stations, that agglo-merates comfortable houses for the popular classes, that breaks its streets and turns them into avenues, that weaves floors and floors for offices, that erects universities, schools, hospitals, where mechanics combine aqueducts, bridges, cranes, where chemists study formulas, it is the modern city, the city of man who travels by railroad, who trades in swift ocean liners, who invents aviation.[355]

As the city in this imaginary must be defined by "technical and scientific progress applied to well-being," the superiority of Buenos Aires, *thanks* to its absence of traditions, knows no limits:

---

[354] "Buenos Aires, metrópoli continental," quoted from its reprint in Alberto Gerchunoff, *Buenos Aires, la metrópoli de mañana*, Cuadernos de Buenos Aires, 13 (Buenos Aires: Municipalidad de la Ciudad de Buenos Aires, 1960), 15.
[355] Ibid., 17.

It has no tradition, it is said, and this is to its immediate benefit. How can we demolish an old column, an old wall that impedes the logical development of a street, of a city, if that column, if that wall revives for the sleepy scholar and for the distracted tourist a gloomy poem or a supposed fact? We do not possess, over there, ancient columns, evocative walls […].

The ruins, Gerchunoff explains, make for endless hesitation when it comes to modernizing these old, rather than traditionalist cities, which are cloistered in their prejudice "and are therefore, under the guise of technical progress, incomplete and cramped." Well then, "We do not know these obstacles. We do the marvelous on a daily basis. We are the barbarians, the beautiful and rough barbarians of civilization."[356]

The refutation of regenerationism is what appears in the first place: if for Rojas the great problem of the metropolitan Babel, what should be abolished, was the confusion between civilization and barbarism, the eclectic and cultureless mixture; and if in any case for Gálvez the valuation between the terms of Sarmiento's formula should be inverted in order to discover new virtues in barbarism, understood then as "true" culture; Gerchunoff's formula proposes a reuse of the antinomy that rejects all spiritualism, proposing the positivization of that which was doubly demonized. "We are the barbarians of civilization" is the distortion of the *Facundo* formula as the full recovery of Sarmiento's celebration of the United States: it is the recovery of a Sarmiento that allows us to trace relations with another American barbarian, Walt Whitman; as Gerchunoff himself admits, the recovery of his "language of bellows." To understand the eccentricity of the approach, it must be recalled, as Oscar Terán demonstrated, that starting at the end of the century spiritualist anti-Americanism had been politically renewed through an anti-imperialist profile.[357] In any case, this is Gerchunoff's way of opposing both regenerationism and local positivism, which, although it came to denounce European "decadence," had never celebrated American utilitarianism as a value. It is enough to recall Cané's 1884 observations on New York or to see the "idealist" solution of the late positivism of José Ingenieros and the *Revista de Filosofía* in the years following the centenary, to see that Gerchunoff's materialist vindication took him in a different direction.[358]

---

[356] Ibid., 18–19.

[357] See Oscar Terán, "El primer antiimperialismo latinoamericano," *Punto de Vista* 12 (July–October 1981): 3.

[358] See Miguel Cané, *En viaje* (1884) (Buenos Aires: Claridad, 1995). It is also evoked by Oscar Terán in "El decadentismo argentino," where he mentions paragraphs by Groussac about Chicago that point in the same direction. On the "idealist solution" in the *Revista de Filosofía*, see Luis Rossi, "Los primeros años de la *Revista de Filosofía, Cultura, Ciencias y Educación*: la crisis del positivismo y la filosofía en la Argentina," mimeo (Buenos Aires: CEI-UNQUI, 1996).

The person who best perceives the implications of this New Yorkization of Buenos Aires is Gómez Carrillo. At the beginning of his book, he explains that reading "Buenos Aires, metrópoli continental" in Paris, just before embarking, made him believe with disgust throughout the trip that he was going to arrive in yet another one of those cities "similar to the famous 'electric houses' of the Universal Exhibitions": "To go to see another New York, another Chicago; to go to live among tumults of iron, among the vertigo of elevators, among the vibrations of rails!... Ah, no!" Gerchunoff's article seemed to him to have been written by "a machinist" rather than by an artist; fortunately, Gómez Carrillo would realize with joy on his arrival in the city that Gerchunoff had invented a nonexistent Buenos Aires, which sought to hide, out of provocative eagerness, his express familiarity with Paris, Rome, or Vienna, those "retrograde loves" of the exquisite dilettantish that "have the audacity to be less comfortable than Chicago or Berlin."[359] If Gómez Carrillo describes the Buenos Aires that the cultural establishment wants to see, Gerchunoff makes a paradoxical celebration of a city in which very few would want to recognize themselves. Of course, at one point the Argentinean also reserves for himself the aristocratic place of the artist who can celebrate the youthful and uncultured voracity of the American *pioneer* because he also understands European high culture, proposing himself as a bridge between the two, as a translator. But what is certain is that, in his defense of a modernity without roots for Buenos Aires, he gives shape to a plebeian gesture that practically isolates him from intellectual culture, linking him to the adoration of North American progress that in the period is only found in the illustrated magazines—also with nuances and contradictions— and that would begin to unfold in popular culture through the mass media and cinema. It is, in short, the confrontation of an aristocratic imaginary against a *progressive* one, in a strict sense.

And the highest point of friction between the two imaginaries will occur precisely on the subject of the grid: Gerchunoff relies on the already generalized change of characterization of the grid, but now to vindicate in it the radical modernization that everyone has discovered with horror. This brings together on the opposite side, as we have seen, all the observers, from Rusiñol to Gómez Carrillo: the only difference between them on this point is that, while for Rusiñol the grid, installed "in the streets, in the hearts and in customs," is also the explanation that "Buenos Aires is sad," for Gómez Carrillo it is not sadness but "an undeniable and insurmountable urban ugliness": "In Buenos Aires, so clean and so cheerful, beauty would be entirely Parisian were it not for the damned straight lines, which make perspectives impossible and impose

---

[359] In *El encanto de Buenos Aires*, cited above, Gómez Carrillo devotes almost the entirety of one of his opening chapters, "Las calles de la City," to refuting Gerchunoff's text; 37–53.

monotony [....] Ah, the blocks, the hateful blocks of the Americas!"[360] If in the grid what is now rejected is the decharacterization and anomie of metropolitan society and capitalist territorial exploitation; and if for the disciplines that deal with the city, moreover, it is a modernization that should be corrected by the action of "modern" urban planning—the picturesque—Gerchunoff's originality lies, simply, in completing the inversion, also inverting the relation of value: in the progressive and utilitarian Buenos Aires that he portrays, all the modern implications of the checkerboard are a cause for celebration:

> That is Buenos Aires. It doesn't have the picturesque crossroads of the old cities, it doesn't have the patina, like Rodin's *Thinker*, it doesn't have the cracks of the *Venus de Milo*. The streets are straight, long, and the city is laid out in the perfect squares of a checkerboard. Is it ugly? It is beautiful! The straight line is beautiful when it is infinite, and Buenos Aires is laid out on straight and infinite lines, because its founders, its continuators, and its men of today, conceive beauty in the infinite.[361]

The change of perspective is complete: not only is rejection abandoned, not only is the resigned acceptance of the consummated fact—of fatality—also abandoned, but the grid becomes a value that characterizes that which is most powerful in Buenos Aires. All this now derives, not from the logic of nineteenth-century rationalism, but from the avant-garde passion for abstraction and geometry. But a few years later, one of the main opponents of the hegemony of picturesque urbanism, Le Corbusier, would coin the famous remark that the curved line "is the way of donkeys," the straight line is the "way of men."[362] It is also a passion for the clarity of functions, extracted from the logic of the machine:

> the exact and successive square shows the easy symmetry, the rigorous order, which allows the activities of an industrious people to develop without artificial complication. Imagine an industrious housewife who carries out during the day the multiple household tasks [...] Can she carry out her work in a house with complicated stairs and superimposed floors? She needs the house of adjoining rooms, which is logical because it is easy, which is beautiful because it is clean. [...] Thus, Buenos Aires, a populous, boiling, industrious, industrial city, needs strict order, which does not exclude infinity,

---

[360] See Rusiñol, *Un viaje al Plata*, 185; and Gómez Carrillo, *El encanto de Buenos Aires*, 38–39.

[361] "Buenos Aires, metrópoli continental," 21.

[362] As part of his polemic with Camillo Sitte and picturesque urbanism, Le Corbusier would title the first chapter of his book *Urbanisme* (Paris: Éditions Crès, 1924) "The Way of Donkeys. The Way of Men."

which does not reject, but characterizes grandiosity. It is sumptuous because progress, which is the exploitation of action, is sumptuous, as is shown by the observation of a locomotive or an ocean liner: the bronze ornament is a rivet, it is a reinforcement; it serves the primordial by being ornament. We blindly employ mechanics. We channel the elaboration of all the scientific workshops of the world and for that reason, Buenos Aires is so comfortable, so elegant, so graceful in its absolute simplicity.[363]

With the typical rhetoric of the "modernism of modernization"—as Guilherme Merquior so well characterized Brazilian modernism—Gerchunoff peeks into the revulsive edge of the aesthetic avant-garde.[364] We know that this is a type of aesthetic avant-garde that will not have too many followers in Buenos Aires, where the type of modernism that derives from classicizing abstraction outlined in the variants of the "party of sobriety" will develop massively. It is enough to point out that the skyscraper is even more unanimously repudiated than the grid by local urban and architectural renovators in the first decades of the century. We also know that Gerchunoff paid little attention to it in his later artistic and intellectual practice; but it is highly suggestive that he adopts that posture to refer, in complete solitude, specifically to the grid.[365]

It could be said that, in 1914, Gerchunoff's Americanist utilitarianism, more than a deliberate aesthetic option for the artistic avant-garde, is an ideological provocation against the hegemonic spiritualism in Buenos Aires. He finds in the grid the best instrument of defense of a progressive and plebeian culture, without roots, because he himself, as an immigrant, notices that all the other paths in search of identity tried out by his generation exclude the features of local culture and society that make his own existence possible. Obviously, this is then an abstract vindication of the grid that omits its effective role in the actual suburbs, which at the same time was scattered across the pampa, fulfilling the squared form of the block; but it opens the way to a completely new contemplation of the same phenomenon. If Carrasco marks a turning point with respect to the perception of the overall metropolitan territory, Gerchunoff marks it with respect to the checkerboard that turns that territory into a cultural object; both views are completely marginal, and it is not clear that they have received much attention, even less than the "neighborhood roads" of Bouvard's plan. Seen from the present, they are, with their limitations, more partial

---

[363] Ibid., 21–22.

[364] José Guilherme Merquior, "El otro Occidente," in Felipe Arocena and Eduardo de León, eds., *El complejo de Próspero. Ensayos sobre cultura, modernidad y modernización en América Latina* (Montevideo: Vintén, 1993), 112.

[365] Gerchunoff cultivated these positions on very specific architectural and urban themes, which he emphasized in the 1930s with his close relations with the magazine *Nuestra Arquitectura* and with the Russian architect Wladimiro Acosta, who immigrated to Argentina in 1930.

omissions on the process of suburbanization than those of established culture, they allow us to understand other aspects of that new city that was being built, huddled behind the edges of the traditional city.

CHAPTER 6

From the *Vecindario* to the *Barrio*

Infinite provisionality, extension, and movement: a generalized representation of the suburb in these first two decades; even more acute in those who discern behind the whole process the rigid matrix of the grid, because that is exactly what it produces by definition: an abstract, inflexible matrix, on which any expression of the concrete can be only contingent; a structure. Only by the end of the 1910s will it clearly appear that on that abstract structure, or rather, on the modernizing whirlwind that it allows and stimulates, a new urban unit has been formed: the barrio. Barrio is not, in this sense, a jurisdictional definition, applicable to sectors of the city at any moment in history, but points to the appearance of a phenomenon specific to Buenos Aires: it is the modern suburban neighborhood, as a material, social, and cultural phenomenon; the very new production of a local public space that will restructure the identity of the heterogeneous popular sectors in the suburbs.

The process of constitution of the local public space barrio leads us, then, to a first question: How is a *form* produced on that homogeneous and universal structure, in the middle of that modernizing vertigo? Because this is how the construction of the barrio could be considered: as the aggregation of bunches of dispersed and semi-rural *vecindarios* (local isolated communities), amorphous and uncharacterized, in a new urban compound, a recognizable, social, and cultural *form*. That is why it can be said that the neighborhood as a public artifact is not the product of the quantitative expansion of the city on the pampa: the expansion produces those small border communities that I prefer to call *vecindarios*, nuclei often as close as they are separated by impassable barriers, material and social; minimal corpuscles of the spasmodic process that the grid generates when it abruptly converts an immense territory into an urban market. In these *vecindarios* there are immediate social relations, products of necessity and isolation, *private* relations in a classic sense: the relations of the *oikos*. They are the domestic outposts of that provisional encampment that surprises all observers, its frontier installations. The barrio, on the contrary, is its *public* reconversion, the production, *over* the quantitative expansion of popular sectors to the suburb, a territory of identities, a much more complex cultural device in which an accumulation of actors and public and private institutions participate, articulating economic and social processes with political and cultural representations. It is a modern artifact produced on the same course of modernization, the appearance of a *form* on the anonymous undifferentiation of the grid.

From this point of view, it is necessary to review Scobie's influential position on the expansion of Buenos Aires, his vision of suburbanization as a modernizing continuum—guided by the tramway and the lot sales in installments—that advances from the traditional city to the barrios. In Scobie's version it is not important to distinguish between suburb and barrio—in fact, in the English and Spanish titles there is an overlap: *Buenos Aires, Plaza to Suburb/Buenos Aires, del centro a los barrios*—but, above all, his study ends around 1910, that is, he interrupts the narrative precisely when the main change affecting the suburb is just beginning to take shape, thus failing to establish the differences with the barrio cultural device. Thus, the image he gives of the suburb is that of a homogeneous territory of continuous economic expansion that extends the traditional city like an oil stain—we could add: a vision very much in accordance with the urbanistic position of the functional-developmentalism of his time—and not that of a socially and culturally produced territory.[366] If we respect the synchronic break in the years of the centenary it is impossible to find something similar to a barrio formed in the suburb; simply *vecindarios*, in which nothing indicates that a cultural aggregation such as the one that the neighborhood supposes could be produced.

But at this point we face a second question, fundamental for the precision we seek (and fundamental to counter the bibliographic inverse to Scobie's economicism, the most abundant on the barrio, that memorialist bibliography that is sustained in the anachronistic feeding of the community myth). Is the notion of barrio relevant to the case of Buenos Aires?[367] Evidently not, at least if we adopt the traditional term according to its meaning in old European cities. The difference was described masterfully, moved by the contrast, by that very special traveler Jean-Paul Sartre when he arrived in New York in 1945. One of the first things he discovered, astonished by the modern and regular American city,

---

[366] Scobie, *Buenos Aires: Plaza to Suburb*, especially the chapter "Streetcar and Neighborhood."

[367] The memorialist barrio bibliography in Buenos Aires has manifested itself above all in the *Cuadernos de Buenos Aires* collection that the municipality has been publishing since the 1960s on different neighborhoods of the city. The participatory spirit of the nascent democracy in the 1980s, with a new emphasis on the local, also placed its emphasis on a recovery of the barrio, and from there came undertakings such as the Talleres de historia oral (Oral history workshops) organized by the Instituto Histórico de la Ciudad de Buenos Aires (Historical Institute of the City of Buenos Aires), which in fact produces materials not very different to those *Cuadernos*. Beyond memorialism, from an approach based on a communitarian defense of the barrio as *existential place*, Mario Sabugo, for his part, has been producing a series of works seeking the recovery of the barrio through the circulation of its mythological motifs. See especially "Placeres y fatigas de los barrios," *Anales del Instituto de Arte Americano e Investigaciones Estéticas "Mario Buschiazzo"* 27–28 (1992).

was that he could not distinguish neighborhoods; he also discovered something about his own city: Europeans have "round cities," he acknowledged, "divided into similarly rounded, closed districts" in which the "tangle of jumbled houses weighs heavily on the ground."[368] *They weigh heavily*: few images would illustrate so well that existential peculiarity attributed to the *locus* in the traditional city: as a transcendent vertical that connects human history with an original design; it is the weight not of history but of tradition, in which it is possible to recognize one's own ancestors, the materials of the place, the sum of human work, family and community events. In the European neighborhood, houses are heavy because they form a horizon of urban and social consistency in which everything leads back to the same place:

> Streets run into other streets. They are closed at each end and do not seem to lead out of the city. Inside them, you go round in circles. They are more than mere arteries: each one is a social milieu. These are streets where you stop, meet people, drink, eat and linger.[369]

We could add: repeating an ancestral ritual that gives them back the representation of a common origin; that is why in Europe, Sartre points out, "we cleave to a neighborhood, a block of houses or a street corner, and we are no longer free."[370]

The dimension of the American city, on the other hand, does not allow for the internal differentiation of identity circles: it is an abstract structure. Its streets are limitless, infinite highways that always lead out of the city; they are streets that have emerged from nothing, produced in a very short time through a territory without history, in which the existential dimension of "place" cannot be recognized. The modern grid city emerges as part of the modernizing process that closes that circular experience, and nothing better than the grid, homogeneous in all directions, to visualize the rupture. All the travelers who arrived in Buenos Aires from the "narrow and blackish" European city streets that Rusiñol longed for, carried the weight of the contrast between the rational clarity of the grid and its existential indifference; Sartre in New York portrayed it like no other: "I am never astray, but always lost."[371]

Except for the "towns" of La Boca, Flores, and Belgrano, which were born separate from the city—although it should not be forgotten that they also did so because of a structural link with its modernization—the "suburban barrios"

---

[368] Jean-Paul Sartre, "New York, Colonial City," in *The Aftermath of War (Situations III)* (1949) (London and New York: Seagull Books, 2008), 122 (the following quotes from Sartre refer to this edition).
[369] Ibid., 123.
[370] Ibid., 131.
[371] Ibid., 127.

in Buenos Aires are the most direct product of that fulminating process. How to find a barrio, then, in a place where, as Arturo Cancela said, houses live less than men? This territory changes day by day, "today an utterly featureless place of English-style roofs, three years ago a place of smoky brick kilns, and five years ago a jumble of small pastures," as Borges pointed out not without irony, showing the difficulty of finding a local essence to which to cling.[372] Nonetheless, at the same time, the existence of the "hundred *barrios porteños*" has become so undeniable almost since the very beginning of the process that it has become commonplace to say that they are the most characteristic thing about the city. This indicates that we are facing a problem: Which barrio is it? The distinction I propose lies in the fact that the production of this suburban barrio of Buenos Aires is not the production of an anthropological *place*—impossible by definition—but of a political *place* (in the broadest sense of the term): it is not the production of a *community* space but of a *public space*: as we know, modern public space, with its load of conventional and formalized behaviors and its social functioning of "incomplete integration," is exactly the opposite of that *place* of "complete integration" that the traditional barrio would emblematize.[373] In Buenos Aires, *vecindarios* can be transformed into *barrios* when that territory is radically resignified by the appearance of a public space of local scale, constituted in a complex process of formation of neighborhood institutions and production of a modern popular culture, some of whose characteristics have been developed in the pioneering studies of Leandro Gutiérrez and Luis Alberto Romero.[374]

But to establish the distinction between community space and public space and, based on that, to demystify the Buenos Aires barrio is all too simple (unlike Scobie's book, barrio memorialism is not concerned with subtlety or rigor in its hypotheses). What is interesting, in any case, is to see that the barrio artifact could not have been born in Buenos Aires without a mythologized relationship with original traditions: as a barrio, the Buenos Aires neighborhood is a product of modernization, while at the same time it is condemned to deny it. And just as the process of public construction of the neighborhood is in the hands of that accumulation of social institutions that make it a novel public space, it could be said that the process of its mythical construction will remain in the hands of literature and, above all, of tango, with all its links to a nascent popular

[372] See Arturo Cancela, "Buenos Aires a vuelo de pájaro," in Municipalidad de la Ciudad de Buenos Aires, *Homenaje a Buenos Aires en el Cuarto Centenario de su Fundación* (Buenos Aires, 1936); and Jorge Luis Borges, *Evaristo Carriego: A Book About Old-time Buenos Aires* (1930), trans. Norman Thomas Di Giovanni (New York: Dutton, 1984), 42.

[373] I use the classical sociological categories following the formulation of Hans Paul Bahrdt, *La moderna metrópoli. Reflexiones sociológicas sobre la construcción de las ciudades* (1961) (Buenos Aires: Eudeba, 1970).

[374] See the compilation of his articles on the subject in *Sectores populares, cultura y política. Buenos Aires en la entreguerra* (Buenos Aires: Sudamericana, 1995).

mass culture. In later chapters we will see how the political and mythological aspects relate to each other at the moment of the emergence of the suburban barrio as a cultural topic; it is only important to anticipate here that the speed with which both are produced makes it a particularly interesting phenomenon: few myths so firm and so productive in the cultural order have been born in such a short time and with so few original or distinctive attributes. In this chapter we will see how the role of the park in suburban expansion is linked to both processes, both as an urban typology and as an ideological topic: in the same way as the barrio, the park is also a public space that is a product of the urban, social, and political modernization of the city, while at the same time calling for an organic restitution, and in that sense its impact will be decisive in the future representations of the barrio imaginary.

Knifers and Strollers: The Park in the Formation of a Local Public Space

> The decaying *arrabal* [popular suburb] took refuge in Parque de los Patricios. It is no longer a fact of blood. It got rid of its fame as *guapo* [thug] achieved in quarrels and in discussions where the dagger carved; it kept the laurels of the *compadrito orillero* [tough man of the outskirts of the city] in the *viola* [guitar] box left silenced in the wardrobe; it transformed into *fondines* "uso Nápoli" [cheap restaurants Italian-style] its *bodegones orilleros* [suburban taverns] [...]; it hung its indolence with the six strings of the guitar and prepared to regenerate itself through work.[375]
>
> –Enrique González Tuñón, 1925

According to González Tuñón's description of Parque Patricios, it seems that in the two decades that have passed since we saw it created in 1902 on the remains of the Corrales del Sur slaughterhouses, the park has completely fulfilled the civilizing task with which it had been conceived. *Regenerate*: significantly, the writer uses terms identical to those already used by the reforming mayor at the inauguration and even before him, by Sarmiento; but not so much the terms as their urban meanings have been subtly modified. In 1900 it was a question of incorporating a marginal population into urban habits,

67, 68
71

---

[375] Enrique González Tuñón, "Parque Patricios," *Caras y Caretas* (Buenos Aires), December 12, 1925. This section is based on collective work previously published in the following collaborative writings: Graciela Silvestri and Adrián Gorelik, "San Cristóbal Sur entre el Matadero y el Parque: acción municipal, conformación barrial y crecimiento urbano en Buenos Aires, 1895–1915," published in the *Boletín del Instituto de Historia Argentina y Americana Dr. E. Ravignani* 3 (first half of 1991); Jorge Liernur, ed., "Formación y desarrollo del barrio de San Cristóbal (1870–1940)," Informe Final PID-CONICET, Buenos Aires, 1991.

that of San Cristóbal Sur; to turn into a city that "corner of life characteristic
69   of the old Creole way of life," as described with ambiguous nostalgia by *Caras
y Caretas* when it described the transfer of the slaughterhouses.[376] The park
was not offered, at the beginning of the century in Buenos Aires, neither as a
natural antidote against the evils of the big city, like the American parks, nor
as a new center for the creation of a new displaced city, as Sarmiento had imag-
70   ined in Palermo, but as the last frontier of the consolidated city, a modernizing
shield against the remains of the traditional urban system that should remain
outside, a clear border between the city and the pampa, between the present
and the past.

Two decades later, when González Tuñón writes, the park has almost
inadvertently become the center of something else: a "cordial barrio."[377] The
expansion had quickly surpassed any idea of a border, scattering patches of
urbanization throughout the area previously characterized by the industries
of the slaughterhouse. In this process, the park would play a novel role for
which it had not been designed: to become *post facto* a public heart, re-signi-
fying the entire sector. *Regeneration* has not only been that of a marginal population that through the example of the civilizing green has exchanged the
dagger for modern factory work; the park has also *regenerated* a fragmented
urban fabric, emptied it of meaning with the eviction of its traditional productive center—the slaughterhouse—superimposing on it a new meaning,
one of whose main manifestations will be the nomenclature itself: the new
barrio that emerges at the end of this process in the traditional San Cristóbal
Sur will be called Parque Patricios.[378] The *knifer* and the *stroller* are the social
types that embody each extreme of the modernization process, and this is one
of the elements that gives interest to the study of the formation of the barrio
in this specific area of the suburb: unlike other areas of the expansion, in San
Cristóbal Sur/Parque Patricios there is a "past," fundamental at the time of
constructing the myth, although we will see that it can only be realized as
nostalgia once the complete removal of the old has been accomplished. But
what material transformations and what changes in representation allow this
new place of the barrio in the 1920s? What is the urban framework on which
the extraordinary flourishing of a new popular barrio culture in the 1920s
and 1930s is based?

In truth, the passage from the knifer to the stroller encloses in its parable other reasons that justify the attempt to explain such transformations

---

[376] Martín García, "Inauguración de los nuevos mataderos," *Caras y Caretas* (Buenos
Aires), March 31, 1900.
[377] González Tuñón, "Parque Patricios."
[378] The old name San Cristóbal Sur encompassed the electoral district no. 2, whose main
part is now called Parque Patricios, while the southern sector, bordering the Riachuelo,
is divided between Barracas and Nueva Pompeya.

through the specific example of a barrio that is, further, quite exceptional: Parque Patricios is special because of the centrality that the park assumes in its formation—since it is obvious that not all the barrios of the city were formed around parks—and because of its preeminently "working class" character. As we will see, although one of the main characteristics of the suburban barrio as the seat of formation of the *porteño* middle class, is its ethnic, social, and labor heterogeneity, the representation of "working class neighborhood" was common throughout the suburbs in these early decades. What is certain is that in this sector of the city the construction of the figure of the stroller acquires density in a triple passage of urban representations: from the traditional marginal area of the knifer to the factory neighborhood of the worker, and from there to the "cordial barrio" of the humble and modern working family: the "model working-class barrio" that Tuñón portrays in his chronicle is an integration and normalization device against differentiated strata of threatening otherness.

In this sense, it could be said that its position as a fulcrum of urban modernization is what makes San Cristóbal Sur a privileged observatory for the formation of the *porteño* barrio: a hinge insofar as it is a frontier of the consolidated city, which allows us to see the formation of the neighborhood in the most complex territory of the first suburban cordon; and a hinge as a point of cleavage within the south-southwest axis—the axis of development of an incipient metropolitan industrial system—between the two traditional working-class neighborhoods (La Boca and Barracas) and a "new south," the barrios that would emerge from San Cristóbal Sur along the line of the Riachuelo and the western edge of the city. This border territory is where the complete passage from knifer to stroller takes place, a model transformation that could only be achieved with an unusual condensation of public interventions of which the park is both consequence and foundation. And this is the point at which the "exceptional" can explain the "normal": by its character as a laboratory of a model, the passage from *vecindario* to *barrio* in this area of the city is a publicly assisted passage, which implies interventions and enhanced representations of what a barrio should be: thus, the "model working-class barrio" becomes the quintessence of the middle-class neighborhood and its symbolic horizon, not from the point of view of its material formation but of the imaginary that it generated in its successful outcome.

Modernization without Quality: The "Working-Class Barrio"

Between 1867 and 1872 the slaughtering pens were moved from the Convalescencia (where the slaughterhouse that inspired Esteban Echeverría was located) to the edge of the San Cristóbal Sur ravine. In 1888, when these New Slaughterhouses of the South were barely finished, it was decided to move them further west, to the new slaughterhouses of Liniers, which became effective in

67

1900, so that, despite the tradition they established, the Slaughterhouses of San Cristóbal Sur operated in the area for less than thirty years and in a condition of permanent instability.[379] The successive relocation indicates concretely the type of relationship proposed by the hygienic criteria in force during the nineteenth century between the city and its "unhealthy services": to move the services to the ever-changing edges of the city, while at the same time imposing on them, with each relocation, a modernizing transformation. During their stay in San Cristóbal Sur, slaughtering activity structured the whole area through the development of a variety of establishments: tanneries, grease factories, candle factories, etc. The coherence was not only productive: it was also territorial, due to the forms of land occupation and the morphology of these establishments that modified little of the natural geography of the area overlooking the ravine (open and not very formalized layouts, rudimentary rural structures); and social, due to the demands of the peculiar modalities of a job "where the dagger carved."

69

Two other elements complete this "traditional system," coloring the legendary character of the area: the burning of garbage and its Barrio de las Ranas, and the route of the Western Railway, the "Tren de las basuras" (the Garbage Train), which stitched the area transversally, signaling an early productive connection with the industrial axis of the Riachuelo. This is a productive and service coherence acceptable beyond the edges of the consolidated city, but which ceases to be perceived as such when, toward the end of the century, the expansion of the city tends to modernize sectors of the area, creating the image of an urban advance on a primitive territory; the replacement of the remains of the slaughterhouse by the park in 1902, in addition, will empty it of the neuralgic center of its traditional coherence.

That same year, in a series of notes denouncing the situation of the inhabitants of "La Quema," the garbage burning area, the hygienist reformer Gabriela Coni, describing her tour of the area, shows how a sharp division can already be discerned between modern and traditional sectors: "On one side, electricity in its different forms, smooth paving, water supply, and sewers; and on the other side, swamps, infectious and acrid smoke from the burnings, pestilential odors

---

[379] "In fact, the building of the Nuevos Mataderos del Sud is almost a ghost building: whenever the *Memorias* announce that it is built, we find a new tender or a new project the following year. However, its mark on the neighborhood was so strong that, even today, many inhabitants think they remember the time when Parque Patricios, then San Cristóbal Sur, was characterized by the slaughterhouse," Fernando Aliata and Graciela Silvestri, "Continuidades y rupturas en la ciudad del Ochocientos. El caso de los mataderos porteños (1820–1900)," *Anales del Instituto de Arte Americano e Investigaciones Estéticas "Mario J. Buschiazzo"* 26 (1988). The formation of traditions in Buenos Aires is thus sudden and decisive; in fact, today a whole ritual of rural memory is celebrated in Mataderos, when the establishments installed there in 1900 were the product of a radical modernization of slaughtering practices.

from the grease factories, tanneries, pigsties, and slaughterhouses."[380] For the gaze of the modern and progressive city, the suburb has been dislocated: the meat processing establishments that remain in the area despite the removal of the slaughterhouse (they will remain there for a long time yet), the Barrio de las Ranas and the burning, have become strange pampean remnants, pustules that urgently need to be eradicated. The codes to understand their former coherence, the social and territorial logic of these urban functions—functional to a previous type of modernization of the city—have been lost.

Behind those functions of the modern city, there is only chaos and sordidness, obstacles to a modernity that seeks preeminence. In fact, the logic of these areas affects the whole city, expanding a mixture of uses that will become increasingly unacceptable: the railroad that carried the garbage from Plaza Once to La Quema at the same time served to take the butchered animals from the slaughterhouse to the edge of the Riachuelo, from where they continued on barges to the Central Fruit Market in Barracas to the south to be sold. The burning affected the development of a much larger area, as descriptions of its operation show, in which it appears that "a little less than a thousand carts" converged during the first half of the day, first alongside lengthy Caseros Street and then along Rioja, painted red and advancing in line, "with the slowness of crustaceans, the carts resemble a procession of gigantic and heavy spider crabs."[381]

Thus, the Barrio de las Ranas will be throughout the first decade the incarnation of the "persistent, tenacious vestige of the Buenos Aires of yesteryear," in the words of Jules Huret.[382] As a counterpoint to the park, the demonization of marginality and misery is deposited there, but also the celebration of the picturesque in a city determined to raze all remnants of its "past." This shows that there is another gaze that focuses on these transformations: one cannot otherwise understand the interest that this neighborhood of kerosene-can houses arouses in journalism and foreign visitors, an interest only comparable, albeit at a considerable distance, to that of the "Tierra del Fuego" on the outskirts of Palermo at the other end of the suburb. The Barrio de las Ranas comes to be simultaneously described as a place inhabited by the underworld and prostitutes, the "*mala gente* (bad people) who carry in their blood the instinct of crime"—as García Velloso condemned it in a play performed in 1910—and the legendary site of autonomous and self-marginalized anarchist organizations of

---

[380] Gabriela L. de Coni, "El barrio de las ranas," *La Prensa*, February 7, 1902, with a continuation about the burning the following day.

[381] Quoted by M. Bernárdez, "La quema de las basuras," *Caras y Caretas* (Buenos Aires), January 21, 1899. See also "Primer informe de la Comisión de Estudio de las Basuras" of 1899, with a profusion of data and photographs, in Municipalidad de la Ciudad de Buenos Aires, *Tratamiento y eliminación de las basuras. Informe teórico práctico de la Comisión especial* (Buenos Aires), June 1904.

[382] Huret, *De Buenos Aires al Gran Chaco*, 1:55.

Series of plans of San Cristóbal Sur/ Parque Patricios, 1895–1904 (to the left the Riachuelo, southern limit of that sector):

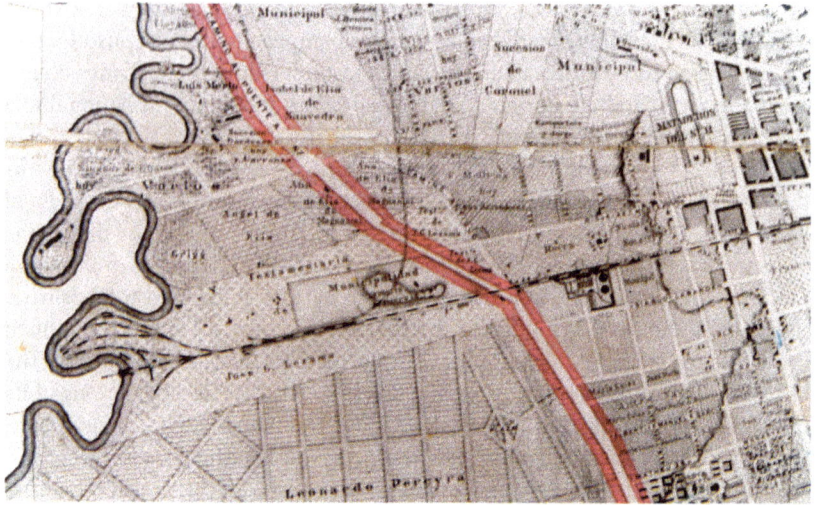

Figure 67. *Plan of Buenos Aires* (detail), 1895. Museo Mitre, Buenos Aires. The establishment of the Southern Slaughterhouses (Corrales del sur) in the upper part of the ravine (upper right corner), the "garbage" railway, and the municipal burning field (over the Lezama lands) are visible.

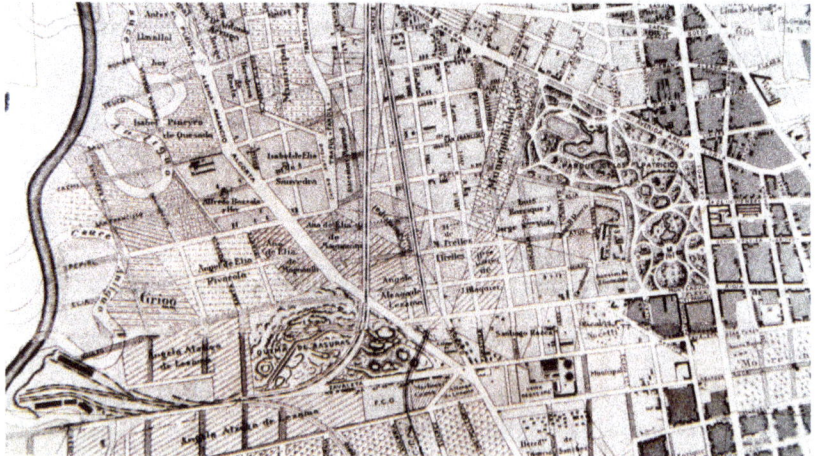

Figure 68. *Plan of Buenos Aires* (detail), 1904. Instituto Histórico de la Ciudad de Buenos Aires. The same area, showing the grid as projected by the 1898 Commission and Carlos (Charles) Thays's layout for Parque Patricios, where the slaughterhouse stood. The relation between the grid and the park is clearly visible, as are the "preexistences" of the previous plan: roads, ravine, railway, burning areas, etc.

Images of the transformation of San Cristóbal Sur/Parque Patricios:

Figure 69. Unknown photographer, *Grocery Store on the Corner of the Slaughterhouses*, 1899. Published in *Caras y Caretas* (March 4, 1899), Archivo General de la Nación.

Figure 70. Unknown photographer, *Construction of the Park*, c. 1905. Archivo General de la Nación. New factories begin to be built in the area.

"libertarians who prefer misery and independence to the official or bourgeois solicitude," as some will take up toward the centenary.[383]

That is the *costumbrista* production that finds the possibility of a recovery of singular features of the Creole tradition on the margins of the modern city at the moment of its transformation. As we saw with building preservation, on this topic the ambiguity between the growing appreciation for the picturesque past that is lost in the name of modernity—and that can be appreciated in the name of that modernity—and modernizing ambitions appears clearly, in such a way that all activity linked to the area will fall into a contradictory zone, between criticisms in the manner of Coni and celebrations of the peculiarity of the place. These contradictions appear emblematically in an article in *Caras y Caretas* in which the new installations of the slaughterhouses of Liniers are celebrated and its transfer lamented, with the aggravating factor that here it is not only about monumental or picturesque traditions that are lost, but the end of a social type that is in the process of ideological and cultural recovery: the *gaucho*. Thus, the writer can affirm that

> The work of the slaughterhouses of Liniers is a work of vast scope, and once the natural difficulties of such a complex mechanism and those of the interests rooted in the old and nauseating theater of the bloody slaughters have been overcome, the slaughterhouses of Buenos Aires may be shown as one of the most ostensible aspects of the culture and progress of our great metropolis.

And, at the same time, without interruption, he can lament that what was lost in San Cristóbal Sur, along with "the old and nauseating" slaughterhouse, is "a corner of life characteristic of the old Creole way of life": "The old country soul, sheltered in the tangle of hedges and fences, among the acrid and healthy emotions of the life of the stockyards [....] now shrinks back, self-conscious and sullen, on being taken to an enemy *medium*, where mechanics reigns and courage is not needed."[384] The fact that this "country soul" was instrumental

---

[383] The phrase "la mala gente" in "Un pueblo misterioso," *Caras y Caretas* (Buenos Aires), November 4, 1905. Enrique García Velloso's play, *En el barrio de las ranas*, was staged by the Podestá-Vittone company in November 1910 at the Apolo theater to great acclaim (it is worthwhile remembering the theatrical boom in Buenos Aires in these decades). The quotation about the anarchist legend of the barrio, in Huret, *De Buenos Aires al Gran Chaco*, 1:55. On the fascination of the *costumbrista* vision of the marginal, R. I. Ortiz writes in *P.B.T.* 109 (December 15, 1906), specifically on the burning, that if "the suburb is the grimace of the city," at the same time it is what gives it "color": "They are the diverse gestures of the great metropolis"; together they "form that immense, bubbling, polyform panorama called the city of Buenos Aires."

[384] See Martín García, "Inauguración de los nuevos mataderos." The article develops the idea that because of the modernization of the slaughterhouse, not only is the artisan

in the actions of the Unión Cívica during the revolution of 1890 (through the backing of the slaughterhouse entourage) and in the mythical foundation of Radicalism—that is, the party of the urban middle classes—only shows the multiple expressions of the same paradoxical relationship between tradition and modernity in the Buenos Aires imaginary, in the midst of which the barrio is produced.

Faced with the forcefulness of this symbolic pole of degradation and local color, during the first decade the park fails to offer a real alternative, as it consolidates with great difficulty, remaining for many years as a dark and dangerous paddock, another obstacle to transformation, which ratifies, by default, that ideological vision of the beginning of the century: the park as a brake on speculation (in fact, in its delay, the park does not allow Caseros Street to be valued, keeping it as an unqualified edge of urban development). Curiously, this "anti-speculative" function that seemed to guide initial postulates is articulated with the strong rejection of the big landowners of the area to the replacement of the slaughterhouse by the park. From very early on, this sector of the suburb shows an oiled organization of landowners behind a productive project for the whole southwest area of the city, through the consolidation of an axis that would unite Barracas-Flores, with its center in the meat establishments of San Cristóbal Sur and in its railway-port junction: the "old country soul" finds a correlate in the resistance to modernization—or, in any case, in the resistance to a model in which modernization is equivalent to urbanization—of the traditional owners of the area. This is not just a localist position: Moreno, Navarro Viola, Gowland are part of a large group of interests that, as already mentioned, defends a complementary vision of the city, with an industrial south and a residential and commercial north. The truth is that they will stand as defenders of the "interests of the south," although that defense does not pursue urban development but large-scale territorial and productive projects, demonstrating great influence on decisions on urban infrastructure, such as the railway layout or the opening of land to the market. As urbanization progresses, these positions will oppose the homogenizing vision of the municipality—and that is why they will oppose the park proposal and the universal grid—but will generate a complicated relationship with the more immediate interests of the new suburban dwellers, who objectively need a city model more similar to the municipal one,

---

quality of work and its association with courage lost, but now any foreign newcomer will be able to work there, so the loss is double: "The gaucho of rough frown and hard claw, who looked with ironic disdain to the *nation* clumsy for the knife and surly for the *guampa*, now is humiliated, matched to any first-time *faenero chambón*." And he makes one of the displaced workers say, pointing to an immigrant now skilled in the task, that "even the animals themselves have changed," because now they obey even an "Italian muzzle," with which the chronicler embarks on a description of the effect of modernization on men and animals, through which he explains the end of the gaucho.

but who will find banners for their struggle for improvements in the area in that "defense of the south."[385]

Because of these delays, resistances, and indecisions in the consolidation of the park, the neuralgic center of the old system will remain as arrested, a blind center in the framework of a territory that suffers an accelerated but discontinuous and fragmentary transformation. In these first years of the century, different sectors of the area develop autonomously, separated from each other by natural obstacles (the ravine, in the first place, but also the multitude of streams that cross the Bajo, as the lowlands below the ravine were known), by traces of service infrastructure (such as the railway network that will densify throughout the decade with a logic different from that of urban development), by land withheld from the market by its owners (for reasons of speculation or, as we have seen, by different projects of territorial occupation), or by differences in the grid (being an area bordering the river, the plan finds severe obstacles to its homogeneous extension, and each change of grid produces differentiated sectors). Thus, modernization produces the fracture of a previously homogeneous area, turning it into a mosaic in which each of its pieces acquires a life and a physiognomy of its own around a multitude of small "dynamizing foci" of suburbanization: a factory, a street through which the tramway passes, a train station.[386] Each of these *vecindarios* is self-sufficient in everything related to daily life, with at least one store in the manner of the general countryside stores, so that they appeared as scattered nuclei, incommunicated and isolated materially. In their contrasting development they form a strange landscape, in which sectors of high urban consistency are interspersed with others in which the small, improvised housing on lots lacking infrastructure generate a still semi-rural image. If we consider that many of its inhabitants had never really lived in a

---

[385] For example, due to Lezama's efforts, the branch of the West Railroad projected in 1867 to join Once de Septiembre with the Central Fruit Market of Barracas to the south modified the initial route, resolving a new route that crosses San Cristóbal Sur to the Riachuelo between Lezama's and Pereyra's lands. The change of route, besides adding to the original function of transporting goods from the west to the market, meat from the slaughterhouse, and garbage to the burning site—which will give name to the branch—indicates the productive vocation of the big landowners who did not dislike the fact that the area was defined as a service area for the city. See "Antiguo ramal al Riachuelo y Mercado Central de Frutos," *MOP. Leyes, contratos y resoluciones referentes a los ferrocarriles y tranvías,* IV, part II, compiled by Eduardo Schlatter (Buenos Aires, 1902).

[386] For the case of San Cristóbal Sur, see Liernur, ed., "Formación y desarrollo del barrio de San Cristóbal (1870-1940)," which studies one of these neighborhoods, that of the lands of Coronel. Regarding the surrounding area of Nueva Pompeya, I must thank Mabel Scaltriti who generously shared her unpublished research carried out at PEHESA; see, for example, the author's "Surgimiento de las sociedades barriales en Buenos Aires. El caso de Nueva Pompeya," *VII Jornadas del Instituto Histórico de la Ciudad de Buenos Aires,* September 1990.

big city, it is understandable that in this isolated community they managed to recreate customs that intermingled in a confusing way with the new routines of factory work and of the emerging metropolis.[387]

The process described so succinctly is far from being specific to San Cristóbal Sur; in fact, it could be generalized in these early years of the century to the entire first cordon of the suburbs surrounding the traditional city: the areas we pointed out with 50 percent population increase between the censuses of 1904 and 1909—in addition to San Cristóbal Sur, Almagro, and Barrio Norte—which since the end of the century had begun its modernization on partially occupied territories.[388] When one processes the few sources that give an account of this *silent* development—municipal acts requesting the opening of streets, plans, officials' reports, news scattered in the newspapers—one can see the extreme similarity of modernization in Villa Crespo, Palermo, or San Cristóbal Sur. In all these areas there is a process that could be called *modernization without quality*, in which each of the fragments in which the traditional systems exploded are produced with relative spontaneity regarding the social actors that intervene in the urban market: no regulatory interventions or qualifying elements of sufficient impact to reestablish a hegemonic character for the entire area are recognized, and local communities proliferate with absolute autonomy. In any case, the important difference to notice within this first suburban cordon would be given by the greater or lesser regularity of the grid, that is, the public board on which all operations take place: in the axis of expansion to the west, from Once to Flores, the regularity of the layout is almost perfect, which makes the different fragments be completed with very similar schemes; in the border cases, such as San Cristóbal Sur and Barrio Norte, the imperfections of the layout and natural obstacles tend to crystallize fragmentation into very contrasting urban landscapes.

And if I highlight the more crudely morphological aspect as opposed to the social one for this sketch of a typology of expansion, it is because I believe that, in a city of explosive growth like Buenos Aires, urban morphology was often decisive: social homogeneity, recognizable in a short time in the entire western axis of the expansion and later—with differences and contrasts—in the southern and northern edges of the city, was a social construction produced on the results of suburban expansion. In effect, it is notorious that at first the entire new suburb (with the few exceptions of the urbanizations produced early around the first railway stations to the northwest) shares the social characteristics that

---

[387] The rural origin of much of the immigration to Buenos Aires is a widespread hypothesis in immigration studies. See, for example, Fernando Devoto, "Los orígenes de un barrio italiano en Buenos Aires a mediados del siglo XIX," *Boletín del Instituto de Historia Argentina y Americana Dr. E. Ravignani* 1 (first half of 1989).

[388] Specifically, in the area around San Cristóbal Sur, the number of inhabitants increased from 36,985 in 1904 to 53,466 in 1910, according to the censuses.

explain its generalized representation in those years as a "working-class barrio": a neighborhood composed of lower middle-class sectors, of immigrant origins, artisans and small merchants, and of state employees generally of local origin. To this we can add the even presence, in the whole suburb, of a mix of modern and traditional production and services: the northwest axis is sensibly symmetrical to the southwest, with its factories and workshops, with its burnings and its power plants, its "Tierra del Fuego" and its "Bajos"; the west, different in its greater regularity, nevertheless maintains zones strongly marked by the presence of large or medium-sized factories and by a multitude of small workshops. In contrast to the representation of the "bourgeois city" of the modern center that was consolidated in the centenary, this distribution of "the working class" throughout the suburbs was ratified by the first Industrial Regulation of 1914. The regulation symmetrically distributes industrial zones throughout the suburbs: those of maximum danger to the southwest of the capital and to the west of Chacarita; as "industrial neighborhoods" it designates Parque Patricios, Nueva Pompeya, Villa Urquiza, and Villa del Parque.[389] Faced with this initial homogeneous suburban heterogeneity, society and the city will gradually work out their differences, building their particular homogeneities, that which will later be defined as a gradation from the upper middle classes in the northwest axis to the lower middle classes in the southwest.

But the issue is to determine how the social and the morphological are linked. Having accepted this characterization of the suburb in its beginnings, there is no doubt that in the first moment of expansion, morphological homogeneity favored social homogeneity. As we saw in the first part when analyzing the meanings of the Buenos Aires grid, the regular small block promotes a model of the residential and commercial city for at least two reasons. First, because it does not favor the installation of large factory complexes: the "working-class neighborhoods" are composed of manufacturing establishments of low industrialization, "workshops" that still in 1930 represent 70 percent of the total of the industry and that, as Silvestri has shown, by its low index of machinization, its low concentration of labor and capital, its specialization in consumption and the absence of a Taylorist organization, conforms a type of strongly integrated citizen-producer. We could say that just as the grid produces a type of "ant speculation" that involves the entire society, this type of industrialization also produces an "ant modernization" of as low intensity as broad extension.[390]

[389] See J. Auza, "Buenos Aires y sus reglamentos industriales desde 1900 hasta la actualidad," *II Jornadas de Historia de Buenos Aires* (Buenos Aires: IHBCA, 1988). See also on the industrial installation in the city, Fernando Rocchi, "La armonía de los opuestos: industria, importaciones y la construcción urbana de Buenos Aires en el período 1880–1920," *Entrepasados* 7 (Buenos Aires), late 1994.
[390] See Graciela Silvestri, "1880–1910: la federalización de Buenos Aires y la construcción de los barrios," in A. Ballent, A. Gorelik and G. Silvestri, "Para un estudio de la ciudad y

The second reason is that the small block favors an easy building replacement, and therefore a quick material adaptation to social changes. In the sectors of faster social ascent, the residence can gain preeminence over workshops and shops without traumatic changes; this generates a type of neighborhood, of which Almagro or Villa Crespo are good examples, in which morphological regularity is translated in regularity of prices in the market and in social regularity: they are the sectors where the *porteño* middle-middle class is "naturally" produced. In the areas on the edge of the suburbs, on the other hand, a strong morphological heterogeneity—produced by the ravine, the difficulty of urbanization of the lowlands, pre-existences, etc.—tends to produce jumps in market values which crystallize in social fragmentation. With a strong investment in the north, a product of the qualitative development of the traditional city in that direction, these jolts tend to produce the "difference" on which the greater wealth of the city will be based, as well as the strong contrasts of the late tenements in Recoleta and the degradation of the Maldonado stream in Palermo and the Bajo Belgrano; in the south, however, these contrasts will be less pronounced because they will be produced between the lower-middle and lower classes. This explains the modernizing value attributed in this first moment of suburbanization to urban regularity in its clearest expression, the block: the block guarantees "normality" in the future, it is a module of a larger city. The "alluvial" society of the beginning of the century sees in homogeneous integration a reassurance of social ascent that completely erases the traces of its miserable past: in these years, the picturesque *barrio-parque* (neighborhood park) so often mentioned by urban planning is an acceptable offer only for the upper sectors of society. Thus, one can understand not only the predilection for the regular block of the popular and middle sectors, but also the stubborn erasure of any natural "irregularity"—the ravine, the lowlands, the streams—seen as obstacles to homogeneous expansion. Far from being the exclusive product of a vision "from above," this flattening of territorial differences also had its "ant" expression in the proliferation of small brick kilns that combined topographic regularization with real estate speculation and private self-production of popular housing.[391]

Thus, in contrast to the greater homogeneity of the city's central plateau, in the mosaic produced by modernization in a border area such as San Cristóbal

---

sus barrios," *Actas de las Primeras Jornadas del Instituto de Historia Mario J. Buschiazzo*" (Buenos Aires: FADU-UBA, 1985). These conclusions are also shared by Fernando Rocchi, who argues that "the city developed a peculiar framework, free of sharp definitions," in "La armonía de los opuestos: industria, importaciones y la construcción urbana de Buenos Aires en el período 1880–1920," 44.

[391] The brick kilns operated by leasing the land to owners who sought to level the area's topography, so that with the same land they produced the materials with which they then built houses in the suburbs.

Sur, one can find different forms and moments of the transformation of the abstract grid into the urban fabric, so that the entire phenomenon of metropolitan expansion could be analyzed in a single sector. From the point of view of its typological articulation, it is possible to find in the area at least four types of expansion. There are sectors which, being closer to the consolidated city and in perfect continuity with its layout, develop in the usual way along the main line of expansion of the city, through a dense fabric of residences and small workshops and shops (to the north of the park, between Caseros Avenue and San Cristóbal Norte); also, sectors where the early installation of modern factories, as large "palaces of industry" that occupy entire blocks changes the scale, turning the urban block into a monumental unit of measurement and representation of the urban (east of the park) and sectors, already in direct connection with the Riachuelo, where huge factory complexes are developed with a typological and territorial layout that will respond directly to the needs of productive circulation from the river, without seeking "urban" representation. In the interstices of these large sectors is where the neighborhoods most closely linked to the speculative mechanics that articulate train stations or tram lines with popular lots will emerge. Likewise, from the point of view of the moments of modernization, as the infrastructure problems of this first suburban cordon move westward (toward the new cordon of suburban neighborhoods: Villa Soldati and Villa Lugano, Mataderos, Villa Urquiza), simultaneously within the area there will remain "pockets of backwardness" that can point us to a second and even a third suburbanization.

The Park and the "Model Working-Cass Barrio"

On that *modernization without quality*, on that mosaic of spatial and temporal fragments, in a second moment we see the park acting, both in its own role as a park as it consolidates and in the complex web of qualifying public interventions that it begins to concentrate, like a powerful magnet whose attractive capacity will be reinforced with each intervention, promoting others to finally transform the "working-class barrio" into a "model working-class barrio." But first, what kind of park is it now? What kind of park in this southern corner of the city?

It is a park that in its consolidation comes exemplarily close to the foundational program: a green to shelter, in its normalizing mantle, institutions of the state and civil society. At the same time, as it was already proposed at its inauguration, it is an idea of a park as a public complement to the qualification that the market produces in other areas of the city: a popular park, a "Palermo of the poor." A double program that was also affected by changes in the representations and uses of the park in these first two decades. On the one hand, the expansion of the public users of the park throughout the city, starting with Palermo itself: if already in the centenary foreign visitors saw in the crowds that

Series of plans of San Cristóbal Sur/Parque Patricios, 1916–41:

Figure 71. Department of Public Works, Buenos Aires, *Plan of Buenos Aires* (detail), 1916. Museo Mitre, Buenos Aires. The park holds a zoological garden, a sporting area, a garden, the Escuelas Patrias (Patriotic Schools), and the municipal housing complex La Colonia, shown to the left. A few blocks toward the river, to the left of the park, the San Vicente de Paul housing complex is visible.

Figure 72. *Land Register Plan* (detail), 1941. Instituto Histórico de la Ciudad de Buenos Aires. The layout for the municipal barrio La Colonia forces the regularity of the grid. The typical partition of squares into small properties holding housing, workshops, and stores is also visible.

frequented it the best example of the social integration of Buenos Aires, since 1916 an author like Roberto Gache will be able to criticize that Palermo has become "the absurd festival" of a new middle class, denouncing it as another symptom of the "urban farce." It is significant that in the year of the rise of Radicalism as the political representation of these new middle classes, Gache inaugurates a series of rapidly generalized clichés of urban *costumbrismo*, presenting "Sunday in the park" no longer as a cultural ideal for the whole of society, but as an expression of the incurable tedium and mediocrity of the *porteño* petty bourgeoisie.[392]

On the other hand, we must note the spread of a different park concept, a park of use and not of representation. We saw that this concept sought to impose itself since the end of the century, but it will increasingly mark both the design of new parks and the very consolidation of existing parks. With the more explicit search for a "reform park," reformist discourse will make room for utilitarian proposals that impose a consensus on the need for an equitable distribution of parks in the city, but above all for a design that focuses on the "true" benefits of greenery as opposed to the superfluous and wasteful nature of conventional park models. This is a discussion analogous to the one that developed over the character of school buildings, between advocates of "educational palaces" and advocates of republican austerity: it is no coincidence that as early as 1890 the official publication of the National Education Commission took the lead in the debate over parks with an article calling for the multiplication of "playgrounds" for children. If the park is to play an educational role complementary to that of the school, the article proposes—in complete harmony with the most advanced American reform movements—that its design should be simple and economical, with landscape resources limited to

> what is strictly necessary: space and trees. Let us not allow ourselves to be moved by those who demand the effects of perspective. We are forewarned against those who would use this beautiful pretext to restrain places of recreation [...]. A square of this kind could be established in a new or transformed neighborhood.[393]

Faced with the reality of a still aristocratic park at the end of the century, the "playgrounds" appear as a "school of equality," in a double sense: because

---

[392] Roberto Gache, *Glosario de la farsa urbana*, especially chapter IV, "La historia de un día domingo," 66ff. This book of *costumbrista* criticism is mostly composed of a series of articles that Gache began to publish in the magazine *Nosotros* around 1916 under the generic title "La vida de Buenos Aires" (Life in Buenos Aires). With a strongly aristocratic decadentism, Gache constructs a series of motifs and topics for the analysis of the "porteño soul," which will endure when in the 1920s and 1930s urban *costumbrismo* essay expands as a genre.

[393] *El Monitor de la Educación Común* XI, no. 184 (July 15, 1890): 244–45.

Figure 73. Unknown photographer, *Tambo Criollo Dairy in the Central Zoological Gardens,* c. 1916. Dirección de Paseos, Museo de la Ciudad, Buenos Aires. This installation is similar to the goat dairy that functioned at the Parque Patricios Zoological Garden and other parks.

Figure 74. Unknown photographer, *Children's Theater at Parque Avellaneda,* c. 1916. Dirección de Paseos, Museo de la Ciudad, Buenos Aires.

of their spatial capillarity, which allows their reproduction in working-class
neighborhoods, and because of their capacity to promote, again like the school,
social and cultural community activities. In 1906, in the midst of the process
of consolidation of the first belt of parks, the *Revista Municipal* published an
article by the French landscape architect J. C. N. Forestier—of long influence
in Buenos Aires—in which he proposed the notion of "neighborhood gardens,"
not only for beautification or hygiene, but to "save children from bad influences
and criminal associations."[394] If still in 1908 Benito Carrasco could structure
the whole "city of the future" around four large parks, increasingly this already
traditional idea of the equitably distributed "metropolitan park" will share a
place with proposals of small playgrounds/neighborhood gardens destined to
organize communally new neighborhood cores.

73, 74

This transformation of uses and representations accompanies and is nourished by the development of a park like Patricios, precisely because of its dual
condition both institutional and as urban complement: unlike, for example,
Parque Chacabuco, which was created exclusively for "physical exercise," in
Parque Patricios the combination of the different practices and the different
qualities of institutional and representative spaces will seek a more complex
balance. Starting from a conventional design—by Carlos Thays in 1902, conceived as a small Palermo with its picturesque layout—as the different fragments of the park and its successive enlargements are carried out over the first
fifteen years, it suffers the impact of new conceptions guided by a strong public
presence. From its very inauguration, it began to be the seat of institutions,
such as the Asociación Popular de Educación (Popular Education Association),
which was installed in 1903 for the practice of sports. In any case, until the end
of the decade the park would not be much more than the quadrangle inaugurated in the eastern sector, standing out as a square in the open lot, between
virgin land, wild forest and the remains of the ravine.

68

Between 1909 and 1916 the main material qualification of the area took
place, associated with a number of public and philanthropic initiatives. In the
first place, walking, education, and charity: the building of the South Zoological Garden, a sort of branch created on the hemicycle of the old slaughterhouse by the director of the central zoo, Clemente Onelli, quickly became
"the instructive, obligatory, and frequent walk of the numerous state schools
and asylums, very numerous in these popular neighborhoods."[395] One of these
institutions, and undoubtedly the most important, has been working since
1908 to consolidate the southern arm of the park: the Escuelas Patrias del
Patronato de la Infancia (Patriotic Schools of the Childhood Board). For its

71

---

[394] J. C. N. [Jean Claude Nicolas] Forestier, "Los parques de juego o jardines de barrio en
las grandes ciudades," *Revista Municipal* 146 (November 5, 1906).

[395] See Clemente Onelli, "El jardín zoológico en 1916," *Revista del Jardín Zoológico de
Buenos Aires* XII, no. 48 (December 1916): 513.

inauguration, *Caras y Caretas* published an article that narrated how the board
"removes from vagrancy and a miserable existence" more than a thousand boys
and girls from La Quema, heading with a more than eloquent phrase the way
in which the combination of park and institution is represented in the *regenerating* action: "God has come down to the park."[396] Even further south, at the
gates of the burning, the municipality cedes a block for the construction of the
monumental pavilion of the Madres Argentinas Society (Argentinian Mothers
Society), the vanguard of the reorganization that will be completed in 1911
with the eviction of the Barrio de las Ranas.[397]

Second, housing for workers: in 1911 the first municipal workers' neighborhood, La Colonia, for which construction had begun in 1909 at the southern
end of the park, was inaugurated, and in 1912 the workers' housing complex,
built with funds from the Jockey Club by the San Vicente de Paul Society a
few blocks away, was unveiled. The presence at this second ceremony of an
official retinue headed by President Roque Sáenz Peña and Mayor Joaquín de
Anchorena, plus select members of the Commission of the Ladies of the San
Vicente de Paul Society, and the Jockey Club, is illustrative of the importance
the establishment gave these initiatives. The fact that the ceremony continued
with a tour of the park, a visit to the zoological garden, and a glass of milk at the
"municipal goat farm," which was also being inaugurated, indicates even more
eloquently that philanthropy was thought of in relation to the modernization of
the park and its expansive capacity to affect the whole area.[398]

The subject of housing initiatives in the area goes beyond these two examples: between 1907 and 1919, a considerable number of popular housing projects were to be concentrated in the vicinity of Parque Patricios. Except for the
isolated Alvear workers' complex in the previous century, they represented
the first official steps toward a housing policy: in addition to La Colonia and
San Vicente de Paul complexes, the Buteler block (1907–1910), the unrealized
project for a municipal neighborhood designed by Thays on the grounds of La
Quema (1911), and the first collective house of the Comisión Nacional de Casas

[396] "Los chicos de la Quema," *Caras y Caretas* (Buenos Aires), October 3, 1908. The
methods of regeneration do not seem to be very different from those of Mayor Bullrich
with the children-prisoners: "We do not wait for their parents to take them or for them
to go on their own—the chronicler explains—we hunt them in the street (because) the
Patronato counts on the disinterested help of people who pick up the beggars and take
them to the house in Parque de los Patricios."
[397] The Argentinian Mothers Society was formed in 1905 to take care of the children of
single mothers (somehow linked to the lurid affairs of "decent families"); in 1908 the
municipality gave it a piece of land on Monteagudo and Ambato, in front of the burning,
and in 1910, with public donations, the engineer Arturo Prins built the huge building of
panoptic typology that partially survives to the present day.
[398] R. Llanes, *El barrio de Parque de los Patricios, Cuadernos de Buenos Aires*, XLII
(Buenos Aires: Municipalidad de la Ciudad de Buenos Aires, 1974).

Baratas (National Commission for Cheap Houses) in front of the park (1919). In a city in which until the 1940s there were practically no public housing projects, this concentration of initiatives—in some cases of high architectural and urban quality, and in all cases of clear effect in the dilution of the wildness of the suburb—could explain almost by itself the identification of Parque Patricios as a "cordial barrio" in the 1920s. The concentration of experiences in this sector of the city turns the issue of popular housing into a laboratory at an urban scale comparable to the process of typological debate and experimentation taking place since the beginning of the century for the construction of the "modern family." Thus, in 1922, in the "moral map" that Manuel Gálvez designed in *Historia de arrabal*, "a small house with two rooms facing the park" could already represent the only space of salvation for its protagonist—the future of a *family* and the integration into a community—in the face of the dangers embodied by La Boca and Barracas or by the center.[399] The combination of modern housing and park functions in the representation of the barrio, activating a diffuse imaginary of a Garden City, with its promise of a friendly domesticity for the suburb, rescued from the consequences of a "working-class" crystallization.

But, unlike the picturesque images of garden-neighborhoods, what stands out in these housing estates is their active commitment to the materialization of the grid in still vacant areas: a commitment that prevents them from carrying out any experimentation in housing prototypes—where the *modern family* was to be formed—because in the last instance they are submitted to the ultimate test of the general disposition in the grid—where the *modern barrio* was to be formed—thus showing an extreme concern for fulfilling their role as vanguards of regularization, assuming in the midst of true wastelands full protagonism in an *urban* consolidation of the suburb. These housing complexes, which if seen at the time of their emergence might appear to be self-sufficient fortresses contrasted with the formless suburb, in truth represent the future integration of an environment that only exists as a promise in the plans of the municipality; unlike the typologies of the American or British *suburb*, the idea of a modern family in Buenos Aires is inseparable, even more than from the *home*, from the integration into the grid that the barrio will allow.[400]

---

[399] In an acute analysis of the urban implications of Gálvez's novel, Anahi Ballent proposed the notion of "moral map" that I use here; see "Manuel Gálvez: barrio y reforma social. Algunas relaciones entre literatura y ciudad," in Ballent, Gorelik and Silvestri, "Para un estudio de la ciudad y sus barrios." The hypothesis about popular housing debates as part of the construction of the "modern family" is from Jorge Liernur, "La estrategia de la casa autoconstruida," in Diego Armus, ed., *Sectores populares y vida urbana* (Buenos Aires: CLACSO, 1984).

[400] In the case of the municipal neighborhoods, the acceptance of the grid as a homogenizing matrix with the future of the city is a conscious choice, which clearly prevents the typological experimentation of the housing cell and that does not arise from legal impositions, since these sets were made on municipal land, which could have

Toward the middle of the 1910s, then, on the general modernization of the first suburban cordon (that is to say, the private densification of the urban fabric and the public layout of sewage and pluvial networks, light and paving, that in this area finds a punctual and symbolic manifestation in the eviction of the Barrio de las Ranas and the replacement of La Quema by an incinerating plant); on that modernization, the concentration of public and philanthropic initiatives around the park has produced an unplanned qualitative improvement. The consolidation of the park, with its modern housing complexes, its nurseries, its zoo and dairy, its municipal library, its schools and sports fields; the correlative conversion of Caseros Street into a boulevard, with the growth and complexity of residences and commerce; and the proliferation of new public and private institutions, creates a new reference that reorganizes the identification of the neighborhood: it forms the basic material and institutional framework, on which the *vecindarios* will be woven into the barrio artifact, as a public space on a local scale.

Let us dwell on the composition of this public space in the passage from *vecindario* to *barrio*. The first transformation takes place in the contact between different nuclei based on the recognition of a common center: the park. While in each vecindario the forced union of the small community around material shortages reproduced the family ties typical of the traditional village, the integration of these vecindarios into a larger unit involves them in a series of mediating institutions, which fracture the extended family space of the "community." If in the vecindario the street can still be thought of as an extension of private space, in the barrio, on the other hand, the street opens its borders making explicit its belonging to a larger public system, where the appearance of the unknown is possible and where, therefore, the institutional production of mechanisms of integration and differentiation, of forms of recognition and distance are necessary. This production mixes political, social, and urban dimensions.

Fundamental to this is the role of three types of institutions that in these years of transition construct a variety of possible relations between civil society and the state, with the peculiarity that they give them territorial and urban form: they are *localized* institutions. One institution, the school, is produced "from above," by the state; the other two are produced by local society, although one of them is recognized for its capacity to establish a dialogue with the state, the sociedad de fomento (here translated as neighborhood advocacy association), while the other, the club, appears as an associative product with greater autonomy from politics, whose success is affirmed in the development of a novel mass culture in these decades, under the protection of the growing availability in popular sectors of free time. Each of them contributes different ingredients

---

been drawn with enough compositional freedom toward more "organic" models, as in fact is going to happen in the case of Palermo Chico.

to the formation of a local public space.[401] The school has a leading role in the constitution of socio-spatial identities, according to its symbolic and material capacity to embody a set of public values, as a chain of transmission and inclusion in them: the most important ones, social and national integration, explicitly offered by the "Argentinization" school program; and social ascent, insofar as for this society in movement, "culture" has become a key capital, as demonstrated by the boom of popular libraries and the institution of courses and conferences studied by Luis Alberto Romero, but also by the privileged place of the *maestra normal* (primary school teacher) in the provincial world of the neighborhood, as Sarlo has proved.[402]

The neighborhood advocacy associations, on the other hand, structure local society according to needs that make the very definition of belonging to an urban area cut against a state that, in the confrontation, also finds a territorial identification in the "traditional city," "the center." Its emergence, its modes of social, cultural, and ideological production, have been very convincingly analyzed in the most recent historiography.[403] As a practice on a scale of institutional functioning, as an aggregation of social actors in pursuit of objectives that put them on an equal footing with the state, and as an efficient apparatus for organizing local society, this type of institution appears clearly in the mid-1910s, when the densification of the suburbs began to delimit the ambiguous field of interests with the "improvement commissions" that we had seen bringing together large landowners since the previous century. Their spectacular flourishing, as we will see, will take place in the twenties and thirties at the pace of the complexification of municipal politics and a growing capacity for negotiation with the state. But in these early years, when political democratization barely promised to reach the new inhabitants of the suburbs,

---

[401] I have not studied another undoubtedly "localized" institution: the parish, of great importance in the production of neighborhood identities in some areas of the city. It would be important to confront its functioning with those that I discuss. I refer to the study by Luis Alberto Romero, "Nueva Pompeya, libros y catecismo," included in Gutiérrez and Romero, *Sectores populares, cultura y política. Buenos Aires en la entreguerra*.

[402] See L. A. Romero, "Buenos Aires en la entreguerra: libros baratos y cultura de los sectores populares," in ibid.; also Carlos Mangone, "La república radical entre *Crítica* y *El Mundo*," in Graciela Montaldo, ed. *Yrigoyen, entre Borges y Arlt*; Beatriz Sarlo, "Cabezas rapadas y cintas argentinas," *Prismas* 1 (1997): 187–91.

[403] In addition to the texts already cited by Gutiérrez and Romero, for the most comprehensive hypotheses, see the work of Ricardo González, "Lo propio y lo ajeno. Actividades culturales y fomentismo en una asociación vecinal. Barrio Nazca (1925–1930)," in Diego Armus, ed., *Mundo urbano y cultura popular. Estudios de Historia social argentina* (Buenos Aires: Sudamericana, 1990); Luciano de Privitellio, "Inventar el barrio: Boedo 1930–1940. Origen y desarrollo de una modalidad urbana" *Cuadernos del Ciesal* 2–3, 1994. Mabel Scaltriti, "Surgimiento de las sociedades barriales en Buenos Aires: el caso de Nueva Pompeya."

the advocacy society produced a concrete practice of expanded exercise of citizenship, in the sense of making effective the ownership of rights in the more traditional meaning of "right to the city"; an announcement of civic integration insofar as its inclusive capacity is guaranteed by the need to collectively self-manage improvements for the material conditions of life in an immediate environment.[404]

The club, finally, presents two aspects: from the point of view of the complexity of a type of sociability, it fulfills a similar purpose to the neighborhood advocacy associations, sharing a series of activities, such as cultural ones (the existence of a library is essential in both institutions), and offering a larger stage for the flourishing of dances, a central aspect of popular culture of these years. But it also presents a fundamental difference when it comes to the definition of the barrio itself as a localized public space: the football team, that neighborhood creation of great capacity to crystallize territorial identities. This is peculiar to Buenos Aires, for though the construction of identity around popular sports is common to all modern cities, what is frequent is the regional competition between cities or, at most, the presence of two big teams per city, and not this proliferation of rival teams in the same city. The main football clubs in Buenos Aires are a territorial creation, arising from a floor of hundreds of initiatives favored by the type of fragmented urbanization of the *vecindarios*: all the foundational histories of the first football teams are epic stories of young neighbors prevented, by material or social isolation, from participating in other sporting or cultural institutions. Once some of these clubs were consolidated in the framework of the professionalization of sports and the fabulous explosion of the mass media in the twenties, their transcendence will again have repercussions in the barrio favoring the composition of identities of enormous referential capacity.[405]

---

[404] This distinction between political citizenship and citizenship as entitlement to rights, in this case as the "right to the city" (which, among other things, is inclusive of all those who did not vote, such as women, foreigners, or children), we will also see it at work in the park and in the set of problems that define the neighborhood; it is a fundamental distinction because it will later allow us to understand the demarcation between the "social" character of citizenship in the local public space of the *neighborhood* and the "political" in the expanded public space of the metropolis. I owe this distinction to Beatriz Sarlo's observations, for which I have found support in Henri Lefebvre's classic "The Right to the City" (1968), in *Writings on Cities* (Oxford and Cambridge, MA: Blackwell Publishers, 1996).

[405] In the area of Parque Patricios and Boedo there will be two emblematic clubs of the first period, Huracán and San Lorenzo, with their origin in youth groups of small neighborhoods that consolidate and superimpose themselves over a dense network of minor clubs—still today the dense network of "social and sports" clubs that subsist in the area is remarkable; these two will define for decades the identities and rivalries in this suburban area. On the role of clubs in the city, see Mario Sabugo, "Las canchas,

For different reasons, then, these institutions are patterned by an important *urban* component, in the sense that they constitute societies defined locally in terms of a concrete territory and a place in/against a larger city. By producing a localized public space, a space furrowed by social and cultural relations mediated and formalized by them, they transform the small everyday universe of streets and buildings of the neighborhood into a historical space. But this historic space will not be defined by a *tradition*, like the neighborhood of the traditional European city, nor by a *destiny*, like the *vecindario* of modernization without quality, but by a *project*: in the first years of the formation of the barrios, the *patria chica* is made of promises, of integration, of ascent, of improvements, of triumphs; it is, in this express sense, *progressive*.

Public vocation, social structuring, territorial identification: in this local public space, the park offers an identity tradition already built: a *heart*, modern and organic at the same time. The *civic* and *natural* components, which oscillate ambiguously in each of these institutions (the school, the advocacy association, and the club), find in the park a sanctioned articulation, because it is also strongly sanctioned, throughout a history much denser than that of this new historical space that is born, the capacity of the park to pattern into a city, in urban forms, an experience of civic rights. All institutions build citizenship as a right to the city; the park *is a* right to the city. That is why it contains them, that is why it magnetizes them, signifies them, and empowers them; that is why they all revolve, in this first moment of suburbanization, around its model, explicitly configuring it into the ideal of the suburban public, an experience that is repeated in the exemplifying force of each of the parks that form this incipient "system": Patricios, Chacabuco, Centenario, or Avellaneda, as well as in the later debates on the "Great Park of the South." The model of intervention that originates with the park is the one that is most quickly identified with the "progressive," civic, and organic aspects of the idea of barrio, forming the first dimension of the public in the suburbs.

6, 7

In this sense, if Palermo was first conceived as a technical laboratory and then as a laboratory of public practices of the traditional city, Parque Patricios should be thought as a laboratory of production of a new metropolitan category: "spare time"; as a field of experimentation for the production of the park as a recreational, sanitary, transcendent, educational and moral focus, of a morality of work that paradoxically can be established in its modern mode when work is evicted from the center (the slaughterhouse) and is replaced by the supreme representation of spare time (the park). In this area that was initially a peripheral *arrabal* (popular suburb) and then experienced that modernization without quality that created the *vecindarios*, the park introduces the

---

monumentos bohemios," *Ambiente* 40 (1984); on football and identity, see Eduardo Archetti, "El imaginario del fútbol: estilo y virtudes masculinas en *El Gráfico*," *Punto de Vista* 50 (November 1994): 32–39.

very notion of free time as time radically opposed to work although functional to its reproduction. The park produces a first homogenization of the barrio as a local society, gathering around the use of free time a multitude of dispersed experiences: precisely the "institutions of free time"—park, club, library, neighborhood advocacy associations, the *modern family*, that can recognize itself as such in a new shared time outside of work—as new organizers of daily experience in the city and as a now global structuring of the time of the popular sectors, are those that can reestablish a "system," fill the gap opened up by the removal of the slaughterhouse, and produce the modern neighborhood. The knifer becomes a stroller, that is, a modern citizen and not a modern "worker," precisely because of the role of free time in the definition of his new place in the city. It is in the production of this institutional framework—*separated from work* not only by the mobility that allows the worker's home to be located far from the factory, but also because the system of small workshops in the neighborhood itself does not form a working-class culture—that the idea of public space can be densified because the modern right to the city will be increasingly equivalent to the availability of free time to exercise it. This process is not merely the general application to the whole city of new forms of sociability that find their patterns of public behavior in *family strolls*, sports and cultural practices, and social organization for the material improvements of the area. What is significant is that all these forms are intertwined in localized institutions that consolidate the representation of a historical and cultural territory.

This is a laboratory, then, of a new type of suburban public space, but only one aspect of the transformation. In Parque Patricios, because of its explicit character as an urban complement, because of its role as a "model working-class neighborhood," this process will have consequences on wider representations of the city and the suburb. The park will become a laboratory for other practices: when, toward the end of the 1910s and the early 1920s, this *silent* transformation became public—in literature, in the press, in municipal representations—the conversion into a "cordial barrio" of what in 1913 was still represented as "an extreme, dirty, smelly neighborhood where families did not dare to go for fear of a bad encounter with some gang of *compadres* and *malevos* (ruffians)," the success of a device for rethinking the entire production of the city became evident.[406] Public authorities discover, at the end of a process, that a series of specific interventions without global intention, product of institutional overlapping, of the "natural" role of the park as a condenser of representations, but also of the impotence of the municipality to intervene more decisively on the whole grid, have demonstrated a capacity to convert an artifact originally thought as a brake to urbanization, into a device capable of radiating a certain urban quality, as an alternative to the "anomie" produced by the market left to its own impulses. Modernization without quality produces

---

[406] Quoted in *Revista Municipal* (January 19, 1914).

neither neighborhood nor city; what public authorities begin to discover, in this aspect, is a new potential capacity to impose models on the market without the need to intervene in it drastically, but concentrating interventions at the margin, let's say, of the laissez-faire model for which it assigns the main portion of the grid. It is a modality of reformist intervention that we will see affirming itself throughout the twenties as an urbanistic instrument; a modality that proposes to advance on the abstract equity of the grid, already turned into a homogeneous market through the production of qualitative focuses for a reorganization of the popular experience in the city. The municipal "not doing" (a starting point if we think that interventions are concentrated in very reduced locations in comparison with the sectors in which there is no intervention) could be conceived, then, as a different form of "doing," a qualification through elements of urbanization that operate over long periods, that put symbolic representations at the command of urban transformation.

Here appears another reformist role of the suburban park, a role that is more urban than social: it is no longer just a "reform park" because it regenerates habits, puts into action the right to the city, or saves children from the threats of the street, but because it proves capable of completely changing the urban physiognomy of a sector like San Cristóbal Sur. In the process of demarcation, between the suburb considered globally "working class" and the growing concentration of factories to the south of the city, San Cristóbal Sur becomes a place of redemption of the south, where it is repeated as a demonstration of all the best that the city can offer and from whose emulation the modern industrial axis must grow. But in addition to the generation of urban policies that this supposes—and that we will analyze in the third part of the book—here appears a fundamental change in public representations of the south, which goes beyond both the simplistic vision of the north/south opposition, and of the *south as ideology* that municipal technical nationalism offered in the centenary to deal with the conflicts of the traditional city. This new representation of the city supposes, in the first place, a partition within that ideological, abstract south, that reunited in the same "marginalized" flank the south of the traditional city with the new "working class" suburb as the forgotten areas in the process of "northward" modernization. Now the progressivism of the "cordial barrio" allows for a more subtle differentiation between the old working-class neighborhoods (La Boca and Barracas) that, as we saw in Gálvez's novel, are perceived as incorrigible, and a "new south" that for public authority begins in Parque Patricios, where the economic-moral device has shown its effects in the ideal of a "decent working-class suburb." The advantage of the park is that it turns the "working-class barrio" into a "model working-class barrio" and designs an ideal of aggregation that is going to be fundamental in the imaginary of the new neighborhoods that arise to the south and west of the suburb, as a contrast with the old working-class neighborhoods. It is now useful to recall the Industrial Regulation of 1914 to notice that if, on the one hand, it considers as "industrial" neighborhoods of the whole suburban range, at the same time it omits any mention to the only actually existing working-class neighborhoods, La Boca and Barracas, natural objects of any industrial regulation. In contrast to mechanistic conceptions that see the municipality as a mere "agent" of capital, it is also possible to find in this industrial legislation traces of the public search for models, projects and figures that are separate from what is sanctioned by the market.

Now, this process of ideological differentiation that cuts out the old and new south with the bevel of the "decent working-class suburb," allows us to understand another fundamental transformation in public representations: the "new south" is no longer simply the place of compensation, but the place of the most advanced experimentation of city models. Because these "progressive neighborhoods" are seen as detached from any past—they are, again, seen as *projects*—during the first half of the century and a great part of the second half, the southwest axis of the city, from Parque Patricios to Gran Parque del Sur first, and—as Anahí Ballent showed—to Ezeiza later, will be represented as a tabula rasa, as a place where the most advanced models of the *modern city* that the saturation of the market in the north makes unimaginable can be experimented. At the same time that it is the space of symbolic and material poverty—and paradoxically for that very reason—the "new south" will be the site of the urban avant-garde.[407]

Finally, the example of San Cristóbal Sur/Parque Patricios helps us understand to what extent the formation of the barrio as a public space is produced in a double process of differentiation and generalization marked by a public tension. The differentiating aspect is carried out territorially and socially: the barrio cuts out territories in order to rename them, gathers *vecindarios* and reorganizes them as new internal units according to certain sociomorphological identity guidelines. Likewise, the barrio stratifies local society with new values in a complex pyramid according to specific criteria, linked to parish-scale prestige, outside the global conflicts of politics and work, placing leisure time, and through it, a precise representation of culture, at the center. The generalizing aspect is what multiplies this experience and turns it into an ideal model in each of the neighborhoods, imposing on public power a strategy of specific interventions that qualify the whole grid, and on society a privileged representation of how community aggregation should be produced. Differentiation and generalization find their urban representation in the grid and the park: in the first place because, to be produced, the barrio as a *form* must be distinguished from the abstract structure of the grid, and there the referential and disruptive capacity of the park enters into operation. But, at the same time, we have seen that in the restricted scope of the neighborhood, the block, as the module of a

---

[407] Anahi Ballent, *Las huellas de la política. Vivienda, ciudad, peronismo en Buenos Aires, 1943–1955* (Buenos Aires, Editorial de la Universidad Nacional de Quilmes, 2005).

greater unit (the grid), produces urban quality for a first level of identity in the local public space: that of urban regularity as guarantee of social integration. It will only be in a second moment of metropolitanization when the contradictory roles appear, when the difficulties of maintaining the delicate balance between differentiation and generalization become apparent: just as the park organizes and qualifies, the grid does not favor any nostalgia for the recovery of a center. It should be emphasized: by prefiguring the new city as an exact prolongation of the traditional city, projecting to an ideal future the disappearance of the limits between new and old city, but also between neighborhood and neighborhood or between neighborhood and center, the grid projects, announces, and lays the foundations for the loss of any city attribute in the quantified regularity of the metropolis.

Here the importance of the myth appears: but not only the communitarian myth, supported by the organic aspects of the park as a regenerating institution, but, above all, the literary myth. This will be, as we shall see, the main paradox of the "progressive barrio" and its internal gash. If up to this point we have seen its *silent* production, insofar as it was not recorded as a narrative but had to be reconstructed in scattered and fragmentary documents, when we analyze its narrative production as barrio in the 1920s—central to the very configuration of the neighborhood as a cultural device—we will see that, starting from that modernization, it will end up contradicting it point by point. Indeed, when modernization erases the last remnants of the traditional area, when the promises of the *progressive* public space are realized, it is only then that nostalgia will show its effectiveness in the construction of a "tradition" that is inseparable from the production of identity. Enrique González Tuñón, still celebrating the achievements of "cordial" progress, was able to foresee it in 1925, at the very moment when it was beginning to happen: "With the rusty zinc sheets that covered its shacks, Parque Patricios will one day raise the pantheon of its *malevo* past, where it will devoutly keep the memory of the *compadrito* who danced tango on the sidewalks to the plaintive chords of the *organito del arrabal* (suburban hand organ)."[408]

---

[408] González Tuñón, "Parque Patricios." The original Spanish reads: "Con las chapas de zinc oxidadas que cubrieron sus ranchos, Parque Patricios ha de levantar un día el panteón de su pasado malevo, donde guardará devotamente el recuerdo del compadrito que bordeaba de cortes la vereda en los acordes quejumbrosos del organito del arrabal."

PART THREE

Modernization or Reform

[The Twenties and Thirties]

> The urbanization of Buenos Aires within the present administrative limits would be a fiction since such limits are fictitious within the integral organism of the agglomeration. It would be of little use to solve problems to organize traffic, to suppress level crossings, to build healthy and economic housing, to create free spaces and to beautify some neighborhoods of the capital, if such solutions [...] suppose the translation and the subsistence of such problems in the dilated zone of influence that surrounds the city.[409]
>
> –Carlos María della Paolera, 1929

> Florida Street will not resist with the years the advancement of the legions that are incubating in the frontier barrios.[410]
>
> –Ezequiel Martínez Estrada, 1933

At the very moment when the suburb is acquiring its full profile as a local public space, the almost abrupt leap from its silent formation and subaltern place to the most emphatic and diversified publicity takes place. In a very short period, between the late 1910s and the early 1920s, the suburbs *advanced* over the center, rapidly occupying the main political, cultural, and urbanistic attention. It would not abandon them until it became clear that urban growth had not been a phenomenon independent of the qualities of the traditional city but had affected them to the point of dissolving even their meaning, rethinking the very bases on which public space had been considered up to that time. Thus, in the twenties and thirties, it was in the thinking about the suburbs that the ideological positions on the definition of Buenos Aires and its future were played out.

---

[409] *Urbanismo y problemas urbanos de Buenos Aires* (pamphlet) (Buenos Aires), (lecture, September 13, 1929, Instituto Popular de Conferencias, 3; also published in *La Ingeniería* 660 (October 1929).
[410] Martínez Estrada, *X-ray of the Pampa*, 245. We have slightly modified this translation, replacing "frontier districts" with "frontier barrios."

The first sphere of cultural production of the suburban neighborhood as a metropolitan problem is the political one. Since the electoral reform that brought Hipólito Yrigoyen to the presidency in 1916, the need for a democratizing reform of the city began to be discussed: "the administration of qualified suffrage builds diagonal avenues and resolves the widening of streets, neglecting attention to the most elementary needs of a large part of the city," wrote Mario Bravo in 1917. It is important to note that the 1912 electoral reform promoted by Sáenz Peña, which universalized the male vote, was applied at the national and provincial levels, but in the city voting continued to be restricted to income-qualified neighbors until 1918. For Bravo—promoter of municipal reform in the Chamber of Deputies—as well as for a good part of public opinion, qualified suffrage represented traditional public space, the modernized center with its traditional citizenship of owners and its corresponding urbanistic ostentation. By logical opposition, democratic expansion should attend to the postponed aspirations of the other city, the suburb, allowing its new popular voices to be heard, making them citizens.[411] When the first communal elections with universal suffrage were held in 1918, the absolute majority achieved by Socialists and Radicals materialized that prediction, turning the City Council into an effective sounding board for neighborhood problems, not so much because those problems were solved immediately, but because they were placed at the top of the public agenda. As part of an imaginary that claims the expansion of "progress" and the "integration" of the new popular sectors in the city, the barrio finds a field to project itself publicly toward the whole city as public space, making that metropolitan transcendence coincide with the material contact of all the neighborhoods with each other and with "the city" by the effectiveness of the universal grid. Local barrio public space explodes and affects decisively the emergence of a metropolitan public space.

The press of the period played an important role in this projection. In the process of political publicity of the neighborhood, the suburbs became a journalistic theme of the first order: in the same way as political parties, the new journalism built its main clientele there, which is why in the twenties it began to give it a privileged space. Between the modality of "excursion to an unknown territory," with which the press took on the suburban theme in the first two decades of the century to narrate natural disasters or exotic border epics, and "Buenos Aires complains," as Roberto Arlt titled his daily column in *El Mundo* in 1934 to denounce the municipal authority's neglect of the neighborhoods, there was a spectacular transformation in the production and orientation of the news, in which the barrios gained a growing presence as an inseparable, if not

---

[411] *La ciudad libre* (Buenos Aires: Ferro y Gnoatto, 1917), 17–18. In this book, the socialist deputy Mario Bravo reproduces his interventions in parliament since 1913 in favor of the democratization of the city in terms of the effect of electoral reform of the Sáenz Peña Law at the national level.

the most characteristic, part of the city. Faced with the now widespread sensitivity to the situation of the suburban barrio, the press will be a sounding board for the denunciation of the neighborhood advocacy movement, the conflicts and the socialist claims in the City Council or the policies of the Radical intendancies. There is no newspaper that does not have its municipal section, that does not commission a series of specialized articles (like *La Nación* did with Eduardo Schiaffino or Benito Carrasco), that does not go out of its way to recognize the new popular city (like *La Prensa* in its weekly rotogravure), or that does not carry out surveys on the transformations in course (like *Crítica*, that will question both notable figures and unknown passersby, inaugurating the first periodical column on urban issues with opinions of "the people of the street").[412]

In all these cases, it is about the *publicity* of the neighborhood as "cordial barrio," the progressive and industrious neighborhood that we saw silently forming in the first years of the century. That is to say, the homogeneous representation of the *modern barrio* that political reformism will raise in tune with the reasons and objectives of *fomentismo* (here translated as neighborhood advocacy movement) that it tried to question and represent. But almost simultaneously another line of representations of the neighborhood arises, that of the folkloric neighborhood of literature and tango, that will be fundamental in its cultural production and in its new "centrality," although we will see that it is opposed, point by point, to neighborhood progressivism. Also, in a very short period, this neighborhood fulfills Tuñón's prediction with which we closed the previous chapter: to become a reservoir of a past whose extinction had been, however, a prerequisite for its own existence. And in the cultural results of that same operation lie some of the main keys to understanding the *advance* over the center: Martínez Estrada identifies, as cultural "means for assault" the "legions" of "frontier barrios," the "lyrics of the tango," the "infamous novel," the "bludgeon-like criticism," to which we could add the growing success of soccer.[413] Because of them, modern popular culture in the twenties and thirties is going to revolve around the cultural device of the barrio, turning it into a space of cultural production and consumption of as much innovation as capacity for social reproduction.

---

[412] For example, the column "Qué haría si fuera Intendente," which appeared in the mid-twenties, or the survey "¿Qué se le ocurre a usted para embellecer Buenos Aires?" with which, from January 16 to February 14, 1926, he questioned a list of notables, from President Alvear to Alfonsina Storni. See Richard J. Walter, *Politics and Urban Growth in Buenos Aires: 1910–1942* (Cambridge: Cambridge University Press, 1993), 100; for the information on the survey of notables I must thank the generosity of Sylvia Saítta, who shared her research, later published as *Regueros de tinta: el diario "Crítica" en la década de 1920* (Buenos Aires: Editorial Sudamericana, 1998).

[413] *X-ray of the Pampa*, 245. We have slightly revised this English translation. In *La cabeza de Goliath* (1940), Martínez Estrada would explore the theme of football.

How does this abrupt and massive *publicity* of the suburb, this proliferation of representations, this advance of the local barrio public space over the
whole city, this universalization of its themes and problems affect the city? In
a double sense, as the apparent contrast between della Paolera's and Martínez
Estrada's quotes point out: the traditional center, "the city," must be recognized as *part of* the new quality of the extended city, at the same time that the
suburb is advancing over the center. Borders tend to dissolve outwardly in the
territory and inwardly in society, producing two complementary impulses in
the classic cycle of the reformist expansion of the city: *metropolitan expansion*
and *social integration*. In turn, temporally, both imply a third forward impulse:
the idea of *project* and the primacy of the new. In the framework of this triple
reformist, modernizing tension, *progressive* in a strict sense, not only do cities
grow, but municipal socialisms and urban planning as profession, as management and public ideology, proliferate in the West. This framework of continuous expansion defines the very foundational premises of urban modernity: an
idea of expansive progress in which something new is continually "added to
what already exists until it is submerged, substituted, transformed, and eventually denied."[414]

The origins of this expansive cycle in Buenos Aires go back, as we saw,
to Sarmiento's proposals of the mid-nineteenth century. The end of the century, with its battery of public actions, represents, in the long duration of this
process, a turning point, because it is then that the material structure of the
expansion in which integration will be possible is defined as a project. That is
why we inscribe the production of the grid and the park in the process of the
constitution of public instruments and urban, political, and cultural debates
throughout the nineteenth century, as an inflection, as a point of arrival and, in
turn, as a condition for a new reformist moment. The public appearance of the
barrio in the 1920s, for its part, turned the question of expansion into a pressing political and cultural problem: this explains its capacity to condense the
entire reformist debate. The existence of the barrio incarnated the expansion,
it gave a name to the new city. From then on, a plurality of reformisms will be
able to find expression, struggling to influence the production of a democratic
and popular city, confronting another plurality of conservative interests that
will seek forms of restitution of the city and traditional public space. The public
appearance of the barrio as a social, cultural, and political artifact, as a novel
local public space that competes with the qualities of traditional public space,
gives a completely different connotation to the polemic between expansion and
concentration that we have seen presiding over the entire urban debate since
the previous century. For, if it could then be considered an internal polemic

---

[414] Bernardo Secchi, "Le condizione sono cambiate" (1984), in *Un progetto per
l'urbanistica* (Turin: Einaudi, 1989), 49. I have developed the hypothesis of the triple
expansive tension from a fertile suggestion in this short essay.

between different reformist traditions, now it has become for the first time a transparent polemic between reformism and conservatism.

From the point of view of urban culture, this transformation of the terms of the polemic has had decisive consequences: the neighborhood brings with it the incarnation of the social problem in an urban form, and this identity allows an unprecedented approximation of political reformism to the city. Thanks to this, for the first time, actors, conscious of their urban reform programs, will tend to appear outside the state apparatus. They will interpret and question the program implicit in the "reformist machine" of the grid and the park from other reformist paradigms, different from that of the state technical tradition that nourished it; in some cases to reaffirm it, in others to deny it, but always as an inseparable part of the same expansive impulse. In this way, due to the changes introduced by the barrio in the political-urban debate, the twenties became the reformist moment par excellence within the classic cycle of reform.

The grid and the park will here play out their contradictory roles. The necessary identification of the many reformisms with the city's expansion will imply the appearance of political and technical actors that will develop a more committed relationship with the 1898–1904 plan. In this way, there is a tendency to formulate a transcendent criticism, which contemplates the territorial impact of the grid and is organized around the new role that a distribution of regional parks, as new organic and civic centers, can promote. What is certain is that the new articulation between state technical reformism, urban theory, and political reformism will place the grid and the park in their moment of fullest agreement, as a key for interpretation and projection of the processes of a progressive transformation of the city.

What is it that changes in the mid-thirties so that we see this cycle come to an end, specifically in the administration of Mariano de Vedia y Mitre (1932–1938), the mayor who will prove to be the most faithful realizer of the "Alvear project," the one who will "complete" modern Buenos Aires by crystallizing its main themes? In reality, there are a number of issues deriving from the debates of the 1920s that are still valid in the 1930s, but what we will see happening is a general reorganization of themes and positions that converge in a new climate which will no longer be *reformist*, but *modernizing*, as if with the same pre-existing ideological and material components a different constellation is being structured, almost unnoticed, again nucleated around the changes in the mood of state policies. What is changing is the relationship of public policies with the triple reformist tension in each of its aspects: expansion, integration, and culture of the project. While many of the debates and proposals continue, a different global logic begins to prevail that overlaps with the previous one and tends to appear as the dominant characteristic of the moment: the logic of dislocation between reformist debate (political, cultural, and technical) and urban policy, which is the dislocation between the reformist debate and the actual management of the city, annulling the tension that had characterized urban public management until then between concentration and expansion, modernization and reform. And we will see how this dislocation is analogous to that which is increasingly taking place between the local dimension of barrio public space and the global dimension of metropolitan public space, in which the evolution of relations between neighborhood advocacy associations and municipal politics will play a decisive role. Thus, while in many of the specific fields and in many particularized proposals reformist themes and intentions are maintained, a governmental, political intervention gives a completely different meaning to urban modernization.

Modernization or reform. Until then, modernization had been synonymous with *what was happening*, with what the city's own evolution had established, a *must be* of the city, its "nature": the market, whose vigor already surprised Sarmiento in the years of the State of Buenos Aires. Reform, on the other hand, was the way in which the state and, from the electoral reform, the political system, should control and regulate the meaning of that modernization. Modernization was happening; in the twenties, lots were multiplying, houses were being built, the urban fabric was densifying and consolidating; in other words, there was *progress* rooted in civil society. Reform, on the other hand, was a public need, the need to build urban and political instruments that would link the sphere of *civil progress* with that of the *political integration of the citizenry*. Despite the contradictions, in the drive for the transformation of the reality of the market that had guided public administration until then was structured by the complex range of compromises between modernization and reform, as were the relations between reformist politics and the triple expansive tension; the effectiveness of de Vedia y Mitre lies in annulling that tension from the state orbit, setting in black and white the aporias of political reformism.

In this book, the opposition between modernization and reform also attempts to open a way of interpreting the complex universe of cultural transformations that took place in the thirties, thinking about them through the evidence of the reconsideration of the "progressive" cycle of expansion in the context of a brutal modernization. The very distinction between modernization and reform is based on many of the contributions produced in recent decades in the debate on modernity, which have contributed to enrich our conception beyond the simplified perspective of early theories—especially in the architectural and urban fields—of postmodernity.[415] From that point of departure, it is

---

[415] The distinction between modernization and reform attempts to unblock the univocal relationship between modernity, modernism, and certain ideological values and principles, simultaneously answering canonical modernism, which understood modernism as synonymous with progressivism, and postmodernism, which symmetrically postulated the inverse relationship. This distinction has been the driving force behind Manfredo Tafuri's reinterpretation of the cycle of modernity; see, for example, *The Sphere and the Labyrinth: Avant-gardes and Architecture from Piranesi to the 1970s* (1980) (Cambridge, MA: MIT Press, 1987). Likewise, although I do not take his argument literally, it is present in the very title of Jeffrey Herf's book, *Reactionary*

possible to propose a paradoxical idea such as *reactive modernization* to characterize the peculiar operation produced in Buenos Aires in the thirties. That is, until now, interpretation of the period has confronted unilateral images, whereby when the caesura of the 1930s is emphasized, a society and a political culture in serious crisis appear, and when the processes of continuous modernization of the city and society are emphasized, an integrated and rising society appears, building a new culture of synthesis. On the contrary, perhaps a more multifaceted and, precisely, paradoxical idea, such as that of *reactive modernization*, allows a path of interpretation capable of incorporating the imbalance between the different processes of the city, society, politics, and culture, and their different temporalities.

Modernism: Technology, Culture, and Politics in Weimar and the Third Reich (Cambridge and New York: Cambridge University Press, 1984).

CHAPTER 7

Toward a Metropolitan Public Space

"A thousand subtle threads": better than any other, the idea with which José Luis Romero traced the rich relationships that began to develop between the "two cultures" in Buenos Aires lends itself to the capillary metaphor of the gridded city: a *thousand subtle streets.*[416] The grid embodies precisely the universal communication of all the initially cloistered construction experiences of barrio culture with each other and with the "center." The consolidation of the public space of the barrio confronts urban culture in the 1920s with the evidence that those wastelands are not only becoming a city, but that it is no longer possible to clearly differentiate between "center" and "periphery," since that abstract layout, the grid, has almost unnoticedly merged them without return, pushing toward the conformation of a new metropolitan public space. This change can be celebrated or reviled, but it can no longer be ignored: the "search for the center" that was unleashed in the 1920s, marking political debates until the mid-1930s, is the product of the realization that there is a loss to be repaired. The debate will be organized around the question of priorities for the investment of resources, with the emphasis on public action, but it will connote different positions with respect to the quality of public space in the new, expanded city: How to attend, in the urban figure itself, to the reality of the territorial expansion of the new city?

In this chapter we will see different expressions of this debate. First of all, public initiatives for an urbanization plan begin in the early twenties, materializing in the Proyecto orgánico para la urbanización del municipio (Organic Project for the Urbanization of the Municipality) of the Carlos Noel intendancy in 1925: it is the first systematic attempt to think and respond to the new city, to understand the urban status of this until then "spontaneous" phenomenon of suburbanization, to gather in a single interpretation the devices of the grid and the park according to the very experience of its results in the qualification of expansion and in the constitution of the barrio public space.

There is no tradition in our historiography to ponder politically and culturally the urbanistic ideas of a plan: the historiography of the city has rather accustomed us to consider plans as eminently technical artifacts or, more often

---

[416] I have expanded on this figure of Romero in the introduction to the second part.

than not, as naive or interested products, abstract and misaligned with respect to local reality, ratifiers of elitist and Europeanist visions of the problems of the city and society. I would like to show, instead, that the plan and the polemics it generated in the 1920s prepared the ground for a new reformist conception of the city: it could be said that if for the first time reformism can interpret the present and envisage a future for the city, it is not only because the political conditions for a new type of representation were produced, but also because for the first time technical and conceptual instruments were available that raised new questions and generated the need for new answers. That is, at the very moment in which the city is constituted as a political terrain for reformism, urban theory functions as a source of problems that until then had no place in the horizon of politics, without which the question of expansion as the emergence of a new public space could not have had an urban existence.

I believe that the itinerary described by municipal Socialism in Buenos Aires, with its advances and its aporias, is a good demonstration that urbanistic ideas are configured in the 1920s as a *condition of possibility* for the interpretation of the process of the modernization of the city and for the generation of instruments to imagine its global reconfiguration in metropolitan public space, as a way of democratizing the city by integrating the new metropolis and its new inhabitants. But, in any case, what the relationship between this itinerary and urban debates indicates is that the process of socialization and politicization of the urban condition is in Buenos Aires mediated by public administration. It is public management that produces the plans on which debate is organized; that combines ideology, politics, and technical knowledge and formalizes it in a conception of public space. We shall see that this primacy of the state will not fail to have consequences in the very definition of that space.

1. The Search for the Center

> The role of authorities is not very graceful. Hundreds of millions are distracted in promenades and external and possibly postponed roads, while the center, the heart of the city, the focus of commercial and administrative life, is suffocated and oppressed.
>
> –Gerónimo de la Serna, engineer, 1927

Electoral reform in the city brought as an immediate consequence the enrichment and the complexification of municipal political life, with the appearance of a multiplicity of new actors. The young Socialist, Radical, and even Democratic Progressive politicians (despite the conservative origin of the party) arrive in 1919 to the City Council not only as genuine representatives of all the sectors of the new urban society, but as part of a chain of transmission of the ideas and the conflicts of their national parties to the municipal sphere. To understand the magnitude of changes implied is enough to compare them with the composition of the previous councils of "notables," elected by qualified suffrage, in which the "backstage" practices of national government policy alternated with the most direct interests of employers' groups and commercial pools.[417] At the same time, together with the new importance of the interests they defended, neighborhood advocacy organizations themselves became prominent political actors on the municipal scene: the process we are analyzing, by which they build new networks of sociability in the neighborhoods, shows its other side by turning them into recognized interlocutors with the state; this is the double process by which "the inhabitants simultaneously become full members of the city and of the political system," as Gutiérrez and Romero pointed out.[418] The relations of political sectors with neighborhood institutions, now "natural" representatives of the suburban interests, will become more complex and varied in the twenties. This will range from the pragmatism of the Radical Party that, expanding its system of neighborhood leaders and using all the instruments that the municipal power grants, sought to incorporate them into its well-oiled electoral machinery, to the oscillation between recognition and distrust with which Socialists viewed not only the neighborhood institutions but also the very urban expansion that gave them meaning and through which the social sectors it sought to represent had found a place in the city.

The municipal political struggle is transformed, to a large extent, into a struggle to respond to the "urbanistic" problems of the suburbs. In the City Council, this is verified in a veritable flood of proposals for paving streets, building bridges, sanitizing lagoons, clearing land, installing drains, according to a competition in which each political sector establishes a heterogeneous list of priorities based on its visualization of urban problems, to their clientelist relationships with neighborhood advocacy associations or leaders, or to the greater or lesser permeability to local pressures. This is when the phenomenon of neighborhood advocacy associations that go to the Council or invite politicians to visit their area to learn about their problems and push to resolve them begins. It could be said that this flood of multiple and different needs worked in an analogous way to the flood of requests for the alignment of lots caused in the eighties by territorial expansion: at that time it had been about the multiple and diversified specific interests of a real estate market opened explosively toward the suburbs; in this case, it was about the explosive opening toward the suburbs of the political space with the multiplication and diversification of clienteles. As then, its necessary counterpart was the demand for an "organic" response from public administration.

---

[417] For a detailed analysis of the municipal political course in these years—indeed a detailed chronicle of the relations between the City Council and the municipal executive branch, see Walter, *Politics and Urban Growth in Buenos Aires: 1910–1942*.

[418] "La construcción de la ciudadanía, 1912-1955," in Gutiérrez and Romero, *Sectores populares, cultura y política. Buenos Aires en la entreguerra*, 154.

Thus, the voices that began to demand a "Regulatory Plan" expanded a chorus formed until then exclusively by the universe of the urban planning discipline: in 1921 the Democratic Progressive bench of the Council presented a draft "plan" for the suburbs prepared by Benito Carrasco, and in 1924 the association Los Amigos de la Ciudad was formed, which based its raison d'être on the dissemination of the need for a "plan" for the city.[419] In order to meet this demand, in 1923 the City Council made two moves that guaranteed them initiative and control: it formulated a plan of works "for the hygiene of suburban neighborhoods," which would be financed by a municipal loan, and it created a Comisión de Estética Edilicia (Commission for Building Aesthetics)—with part of the funds from this loan—for which it hired as adviser the landscape architect Jean-Claude Nicolas Forestier from Paris. The commission was made up of representatives of different institutions linked to the construction of the city: the Central Society of Architects, the National Ministry of Public Works, etc.[420] The City Council was not involved, generating its predictable opposition, since the proposal excluded any kind of political control. Far from being an oversight on the part of the administration, the exclusion indicates a good part of its objectives: an aggressive policy of direct linkage with the problems of the city through social and professional institutions, without the mediation of an almost completely adverse Council—besides the strength of Socialism, the imminent division of Radicalism between *Alvearistas* and *Yrigoyenistas* was already clear—which, in any case, should be assigned an obstructionist role in the face of the progressive energy of the executive. The policy of Radicalism to incorporate as far as possible the neighborhood advocacy movement to its electoral machinery, in the case of Mayor Noel became an essential practice as a legitimation of his action outside the "politics" (of the Council). Thus, from the beginning of his administration he appointed officials to maintain direct contact with neighborhood associations and turned the personal tour of the barrios in a periodic ritual widely celebrated by popular media such as *Crítica*

---

[419] On the outline of Carrasco's "plan," see Sonia Berjman, "Carrasco, Benito," entry in Jorge Liernur and Fernando Aliata, eds., *Diccionario de arquitectura en la Argentina* (Buenos Aires: Agea, 2004), vol. 2. On Los Amigos de la Ciudad, see *Cinco lustros al servicio de la ciudad, 1924-1949* (Buenos Aires: Ediciones de Amigos de la Ciudad, 1951).

[420] The Commission was composed as follows: one member appointed by the mayor (architect René Karman), one appointed by the Department of Architecture of the National Ministry of Public Works (its director, engineer Sebastián Ghigliazza), one appointed by the National Commission of Fine Arts (its president and brother of the mayor, architect Martín Noel) and one appointed by the Central Society of Architects (its president, Carlos Morra); the presidency was reserved for the mayor, Carlos Noel. Victor Spota, general director of the Department of Public Works of the municipality, was appointed secretary. See Intendencia Municipal y Comisión de Estética Edilicia, *Proyecto orgánico de urbanización del municipio* (Buenos Aires: Peuser, 1925).

or *Caras y Caretas*, which focused on the "politicking" of the City Council as their main targets of attack. The situation—frequently repeated in these two decades—of an opposing Council, soon revealed the limits of the institutional scenario implicit in the electoral reform: a popular deliberative and a delegated executive. As Luciano de Privitellio has observed, in that framework the partisan struggle becomes an institutional confrontation (council vs. municipality) from which different criteria of legitimacy and representation come into dispute.[421] We will develop this issue further on; what is certain is that, more directly linked to the issue of urban plans, this scenario leaves almost exclusively in the hands of the executive the possibility of making proposals on the scale of a "plan"; the very possibility of having a global vision of the city and translating it into technical instruments of intervention.

This dispute over the legitimation of popular representation is, then, one of the explanations for the centrality that "suburban barrios" have in the package of measures given in 1923: the "plan of hygienic works" for the suburbs and the very building program with which the City Council summons the Commission of Building Aesthetics, one of whose objectives is dedicated to "working-class neighborhoods, gardens, and sports stadiums, suburban beautification." At the same time, the way of enunciating the problem that appears already in the title of this programmatic item speaks to the urbanistic, commonly held view on the suburb prior even to the idea of metropolitan public space that from 1925 this same "plan" will contribute to establish as part of the new centrality of the suburban question. *Working-class neighborhoods, gardens, and sports stadiums, suburban beautification*: in consonance with a diffuse Garden City imaginary, in 1923 the suburb could still be thought of as a necklace of new neighborhoods, arranged around the city as autonomous "units" (precisely the British-American *neighborhood units*) where the "workers' neighborhoods" (planned and built through public or philanthropic initiative) and parks were to be located, as a resource for their "beautification" and physical health; the addition of the "sports stadiums" speaks to an also extended imaginary on the free time of the popular sectors. It is evident that the experience of silent formation of the barrio public artifact in the first two decades influences the diagnosis: the initial program proposes the articulation of working-class neighborhood and park as qualifying centers of metropolitan anomie, capable of restructuring new identities around them. But it is also evident that the potential homogenization of these "units" in the universe of the grid that has not ceased to consolidate

[421] Luciano de Privitellio adds: "In the heart of this conflict, the neighborhood advocacy associations became privileged actors in Buenos Aires politics." See *Vecinos y ciudadanos. Política y sociedad en la Buenos Aires de entreguerras* (Buenos Aires: Siglo XXI, 2003), 69–70.

cannot yet be visualized, or that, at least, to recognize it would imply a flagrant contradiction with the prevailing common sense on the "garden suburb."[422]

The Organic Project will work through these contradictions, within the framework of a pragmatism that will allow it to articulate the two *spontaneous* characteristics of previous suburban development, the universal grid and the conformation of local public spaces that emulate the model of the park, to open the debate on the need to base on them a new urban design capable of structurally incorporating the suburb to the city—and its inhabitants into citizenship—qualifying this new major unit through the hierarchization of local centers communicated between them. The Organic Project is the highest point of urbanistic enunciation of the expansion of the city through a model of conjunction between the grid and the park, articulating the experience of spontaneous formation of the neighborhoods with new theoretical approaches that allow projecting it to a regional dimension.

In truth, the Organic Project thus proves to be the highest point of development of the outlines of public technical reformism. Until then—starting from the evidence of the jurisdictional enlargement of the city—we had encountered two modalities of technical reformism in public administration. A *defensive-conservative* modality, embodied in a figure like that of Mayor Bullrich, who sought to prevent expansion with a model of a small city concentrated in the master regularizing tradition of local urban culture, and another, *expansive-progressive* modality, embodied in figures like Cibils or Selva, who identified expansion early on as a solution to the popular housing problem through the housing market on the public grid. It is obvious that the use of the terms conservative and progressive to qualify the different gradients of this public technical reformism are relative and can be handled by cautioning that they belong to the same conceptual framework of the public mentality: in the first case, for example, one can speak of a reformist vocation because the major hostility to expansion was centered on the impossibility of controlling the role of speculators and was rooted, by opposition, in the park, the organic nucleus of civic transcendence that could restore community; and one can qualify it as conservative because of its search to resolve its reformist impotence with a reconcentration on the traditional city. In these cases, the conflict epitomized by the abstraction of the grid and the organicism of the park served as a litmus paper—one of many possibilities—to test the reformist positions within a public administration that accepts capitalist development as a time frame: reformisms that looked *forward*, betting on modernization, the abstraction and

---

[422] For example, the program proposes that in "new" neighborhoods, when the layout of the street meets with large estates or wooded land, it should make a curve to save "the beautiful plantations" and "increase the picturesque sense"; likewise, the hills should be used so that the streets and avenues "lose their apathetic horizontality"; IM and CEE, *Proyecto orgánico de urbanización del municipio*, 17 and ff.

rationalization of relations, the expansion of urban and political rights, accepting the failure of laissez-faire and the need to found a modern state of great intervening capacity; reformisms that looked *backward*, toward the recovery of quality and totality lost against metropolitan alienation, the recovery of a last residue of community.

Faced with these public traditions, the Organic Project takes expansion as an auspicious fact, combining those reformist positions that, already in the decades between the wars, will oscillate between the impulse for a civic and metropolitan public space and the defense of communitarian models of suburban expansion: by returning to the park its civic character, the Organic Project imposes a compromise solution to the opposition between *progressivism* and *communitarianism*, articulating the egalitarian individualism of the grid with the civic republicanism of the park in a tense equilibrium, guaranteed "from above" by the selective intervention of a regulatory state. What is certain is that by taking the initiative in accepting the specific conditions of the metropolitanization of Buenos Aires, the Organic Project constructs, within the public tradition, a new scale for thinking the city. But let us contemplate the type of theoretical combination it proposes and the different polemics it involves.

In order to back up its proposals, the Commission of Building Aesthetics analyzed what has happened in the city since 1900, concentrating on two moments: the elaboration of the 1898–1904 plan and the Bouvard Plan, the main antecedent with which it must contend.[423] Despite the fact that in 1925 the grid was far from being completely occupied and despite its Garden City premises, the first thing that is striking in the way the Commission considers the 1898–1904 plan is the naturalness with which it takes its fulfillment for granted: it is not the analysis of an administrative, artificial fact, which has founded form on emptiness, but the acceptance of a *reality* of the city. The Commission replaces in an almost brutal way the voluntarism characterizing urban planning projects until then, which always assumed an unlimited capacity to maneuver on the structure of urban property and settles on the realism of the technical tradition exemplified at the turn of the century by a figure like Morales: the grid, as the original public pact of the new city, is irreversible and unmodifiable. If we consider that the Organic Project designed the Costanera Norte, that is, a 10 kilometer-long operation to fill in the Río de la Plata and move fifteen million cubic meters of earth, it is easy to see to what extent for this state reformism the intangibility of a drawn grid is incomparably greater than that of nature, indicating a priority that will define a large part of subsequent choices.

The Bouvard Plan, on the other hand, is adopted by the Commission in all its artificiality, inaugurating the criticisms that, focusing on Bouvard's proposals for the city center, saw in it a "utopian" attempt to apply Haussmannian

---

[423] See ibid., chap. "El concepto de partido adoptado."

precepts to Buenos Aires. In the interpretation of the polemics that the local technicians held with Bouvard, the Commission chose to slip by its own urban position: if in the centenary the opposition to Bouvard's "French school" ideals had been formulated from a combination of "the precepts of the [...] English landscape school [and those of] the German irregular and picturesque system," the new attitude proposed by the Commission is to merge them all, incorporating the French ones:

> fusion [that] has been so formally studied in the United States, for its application in the plans of Chicago and Philadelphia—cases, by the way, very interesting for us, since those cities have a similarity with ours; it is enough to remember that the latter was established on the geometric checkerboard [...]. This system evidently defends the advantageous disposition of the distribution and division of the lots."[424]

It must be not only the first time in urban debate that theoretical heterodoxy is assumed so fully, but surely the first such direct reference to the North American urbanistic models after Sarmiento. The Commission refers to the proposals of the City Beautiful movement, and in some paragraphs it is demonstrated that such heterodoxy also reveals ignorance of the precise moment of international debate: in the enumeration of the theoretical antecedents that would have allowed a successful fusion with the "French precepts" in the United States, the Commission cites the Town Planning Conference held in London in 1910, without noticing that what took place there was the most intense confrontation between supporters of the City Beautiful, which had already passed its peak, and defenders of the British model of the Garden City, which, as we saw, was then in vertiginous ascent in international urban thought.[425] And this directly informs our problem, because what had been confronted in London is an idea of the city in which the urban figure is ordered through the representative—institutional and monumental—significance of public spaces, and an idea of the city decentralized and extended through the private space of the *cottage*;

75, 76

49

---

[424] Ibid., 58–59.
[425] The City Beautiful movement arose from the action of Daniel Burnham in the design of the Chicago Columbian Fair of 1893, where—against the nationalist tradition of Chicago—he imposed an urban model that combined the precepts of French classicism with the very rich previous tradition of American landscape architecture, in particular around the experience of Frederick Law Olmsted, the designer of Central Park, who was in charge of the *landscape* at the Fair. The movement reaches its maximum expression—after the systematization of Washington's monumental center in 1902—with the 1909 plan for Chicago and finds its final spurs in the plans of New Delhi, New Guayaquil, and Canberra, in the second decade of the century; see Mario Manieri-Elia, "Toward an Imperial City: Daniel H. Burnham and the City Beautiful Movement," in Manieri-Elia and Tafuri, *The American City: From the Civil War to the New Deal* (1973).

76
75

that is, the tradition of classicist Civic Art and political republicanism versus that of romantic landscape architecture and individualism, which symbolize, respectively, the metropolitan celebration and the defense of "the architecture of a city as the clothing of the body politic," versus the bucolic and anti-metropolitan utopia of the small cottage in a rural and productive suburb.[426]

The interest of the Organic Project in the resolution of differentiated qualities of public space, considering its institutional values and representation, directs the gaze to the North American experience, although it does not hinder it from maintaining as a suburban ideal the much more prestigious models of the Garden City which, for its part, contradicted the structural respect of the grid. The mixture actually speaks of two things. On the one hand, as we have pointed out, with respect to previous urban debates, it evokes the very mixture in which the traditions of urban planning in central countries were being shaped. For example Joseph Stübben, one of the main referents of German town planning, explained around 1910 the progress made by this tradition—and Germany was then the country that undoubtedly could count the greatest progress in urban reform—with the formula that they had managed to combine in a mixed concept French baroque influence (symmetry, long perspectives, radial stars) and the vindication of the picturesque character of the medieval city popularized since the publication of Sitte's book.[427] Of even more direct influence for our case, Werner Hegemann and Elbert Peets published in 1922 in the United States the book *The American Vitruvius: An Architects' Handbook of Civic Art*, with the explicit aim of culturally densifying the City Beautiful tradition through the diffusion of Sitte's formulas. There is, in fact, a baroque side little appreciated in Sitte, through which Hegemann and Peets develop a radical criticism of the picturesque, presenting a vast catalogue of classicist and monumental urban situations, since "(m)odern civic art can learn from a study of the achievements of the seventeenth and eighteenth centuries, which in turn were deeply influenced by classical antiquity."[428] *The American Vitruvius* is possibly the most recent book cited in the Organic Project's bibliography (it appeared in the United States barely a year before the Commission was formed), and its pragmatic, textbook-like manner of offering answers to infinite urban situations with the guarantee each time of the civic prestige and institutional enhancement of classicist public architecture must have been closely followed.

---

[426] The phrase in quotes reproduces the title of a lecture by one of the defenders of City Beautiful at the Town Planning Conference, cited by Mario Manieri-Elia, "Toward an Imperial City," 110.

[427] See George R. Collins and Christiane Collins, *Camillo Sitte and the Birth of Modern City Planning* (1965) (New York: Random House, 1965).

[428] Werner Hegemann and Elbert Peets, *The American Vitruvius. An Architects' Handbook of Civic Art* (New York: The Architectural Book Publishing Company, 1922), 29.

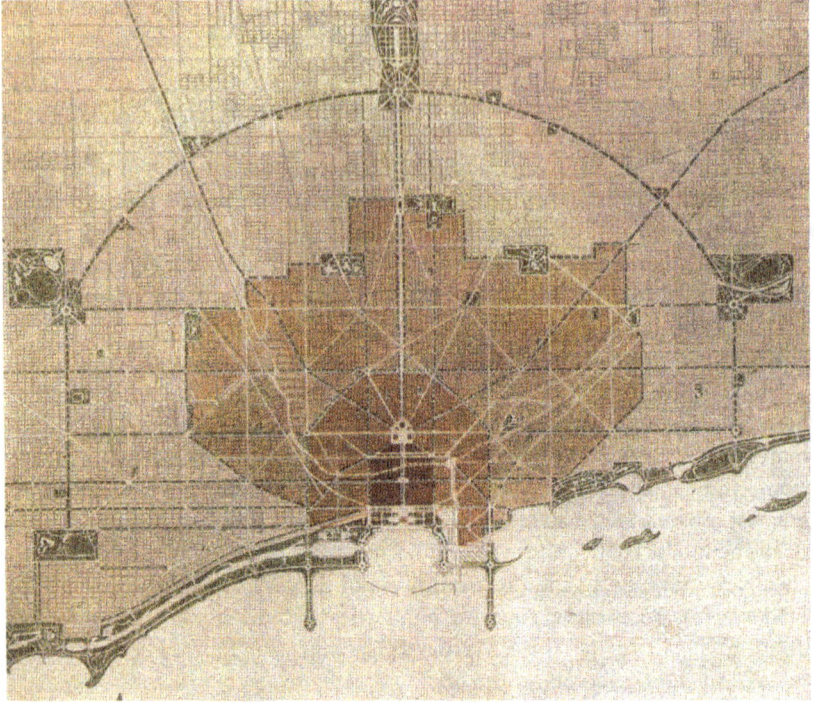

Figure 75. Daniel Burnham and Edward Bennett, *Plan for Chicago*, 1907–1909. The Art Institute of Chicago. Detailed plan of the park and boulevard system. The Chicago plan is the great example of the City Beautiful movement and makes visible the functionality of the proposals for regular grid cities.

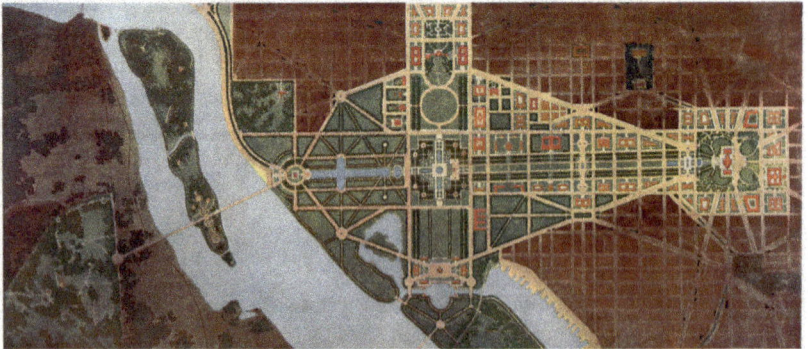

Figure 76. United States Senate Park Commission and U.S. National Geographic Society. *The Mall, Washington, D.C. Plan Showing Building Development to 1915 in Accordance with the Recommendations of the Park Commission of 1901.* Map drawn with the participation of Daniel Burnham and Charles McKim. Library of Congress Geography and Map Division, Washington, D.C.

Thus, the City Beautiful may have appeared as the most pertinent way of thinking about Buenos Aires, surely because it must have appeared as the most appropriate way to continue to look to Paris from local conditions and from the present: as the North American updating of the Parisian classical-baroque tradition. But beyond its transitive prestige, the City Beautiful was already in itself a pragmatic attempt to apply the main urbanistic traditions and, above all—and this is the second reason for the presence of fusion in the Organic Project— it had successfully resolved the combination of the best of each of them with a frank respect for the grid, which brings us back to the intangibility of the 1898–1904 plan: the City Beautiful is the only theoretical referent that founds the necessity of *quadrillage* in its double aspect, as an intensive exploitation of land rent and as a material expression of a principle of order that gives value to the civic-institutional dimension of the city. In this sense we could speak of a "reformist realism" of the Organic Project.[429]

From this consideration of its sources, the Project's main proposal could then be summarized as the combined attempt to define a new urban figure through a continuous system of avenues and a continuous system of parks. 77 Combined, because both should connect public spaces of different scales that would structure the city and, therefore, in this civic tradition, public life: in the central sector, through the configuration of monumental civic centers; in the suburbs, through the reinforcement of local civic centers, whose public and urban life, "already on the way to an evident prosperity," would be increased through the enlargement of green spaces and the decentralization of all the functions of municipal government.[430] And here we can ponder the importance of the hiring of Forestier, whose local reception should also be interpreted in terms of the City Beautiful: indeed, one of the keys of the North American model is the necessary relationship between urban design and *landscape*, a relationship in which realism should be the responsibility of urban design (and it was thus not appropriate to hand it over to foreign urban planners who would repeat Bouvard's mistakes and "utopias"), while *landscape* could have a freer role, so that a certain distance from real conditions would allow the landscape architect to propose solutions that were not as subject to the meager possibilities of reform. In any case, the functionality of Forestier's proposal to the needs of the reconfiguration of metropolitan public space in Buenos Aires

---

[429] In a previous article, I developed this subject, showing that the influences of the 1925 Organic Project are far from being explained only by the North American model, as it incorporates an eclectic combination of varied elements of classical German urban planning, the models of the Garden City, and Sittean picturesquism. See "La búsqueda del Centro. Ideas y dimensiones de espacio público en la gestión urbana y en las polémicas sobre la ciudad, 1925–1936," *Boletín del Instituto de Historia Argentina y Americana Dr. E. Ravignani* 9, third series (first half of 1994).

[430] IM and CEE, *Proyecto orgánico de urbanización del municipio*, 93.

could not have been more complete: he designs a double system of parks that attempts, on the one hand, to open the city to an indispensable connection in a "regional plan," pointing out the arbitrariness that "the lands surrounding the city are found under a different political administration"; on the other hand, to structure it internally, connecting with avenues-pathways the different public spaces-parks-civic centers, "whose new center would be the Plaza Centenario," the geometric center of gravity of the extended city.[431]

The Organic Project, then, can appropriate the most varied theoretical fragments to the extent that they allow it to interpret and capitalize the keys of the "spontaneous" experience of public management in the modernization of Buenos Aires. It is now a question of linking together, enhancing, and giving metropolitan meaning to the specific public interventions that had functioned by qualifying the amorphous mass of private division of lots in which it still will not intervene, taking as a minimum basis of order for speculation the joint diagram of rationality and homogeneity of the universal grid. The park, as civic articulator of local public space, and the grid, as a means of universalization of its experience, come together in an urban project, placing the *neighborhood*—until then "suburban"—for the first time as unit and model for the development of the whole city.

Even before it was published, the Organic Project became the center of urban debate: by putting expansion in the spotlight, aggregating into an organic unity its hitherto dispersed manifestations, the Project builds the agenda for the coming years. As we have seen, it is not that these issues were not part of public debate: what the Project produces is a global and unitary vision that institutes the new city as an indisputable reality to which it is only possible to respond in a global and unitary way. And that is what we find in the intense polemics of the period: the conservative reaction against the positive sanction that the Organic Project gives this new reality or the radicalization of its consequences, as the two extremes of a very wide and varied range, although undoubtedly inclined toward the first position. In fact, many more point out the absurdity of

---

[431] Quotes drawn from IM and CEE, *Proyecto orgánico de urbanización del municipio*, 386 and 423, respectively. The "double set of parks" in Forestier's proposal to the Building Aesthetics Commission is configured as follows. On the one hand, a ring system of continuous parks surrounding the capital, connecting Puerto Madero with the northern bank of the river (the Costanera Norte), the latter with the avenue-boulevard-circumferential forest General Paz, and closing with the landscaped bank of the Riachuelo. The system would be tangential to a linear green waterfront from Tigre to La Plata as a way of opening up the city in a "regional plan." On the other hand, a system of parks within the city, connecting the different public spaces-parks with avenues-promenade that would rest on the new barycenter of the extended city: the geometric center of the city, as Carrasco had proposed two decades earlier. It is noteworthy that it is no longer a matter of mere "beautification," but rather that Forestier has located structural problems of the city in terms of the need to reconfigure its public space.

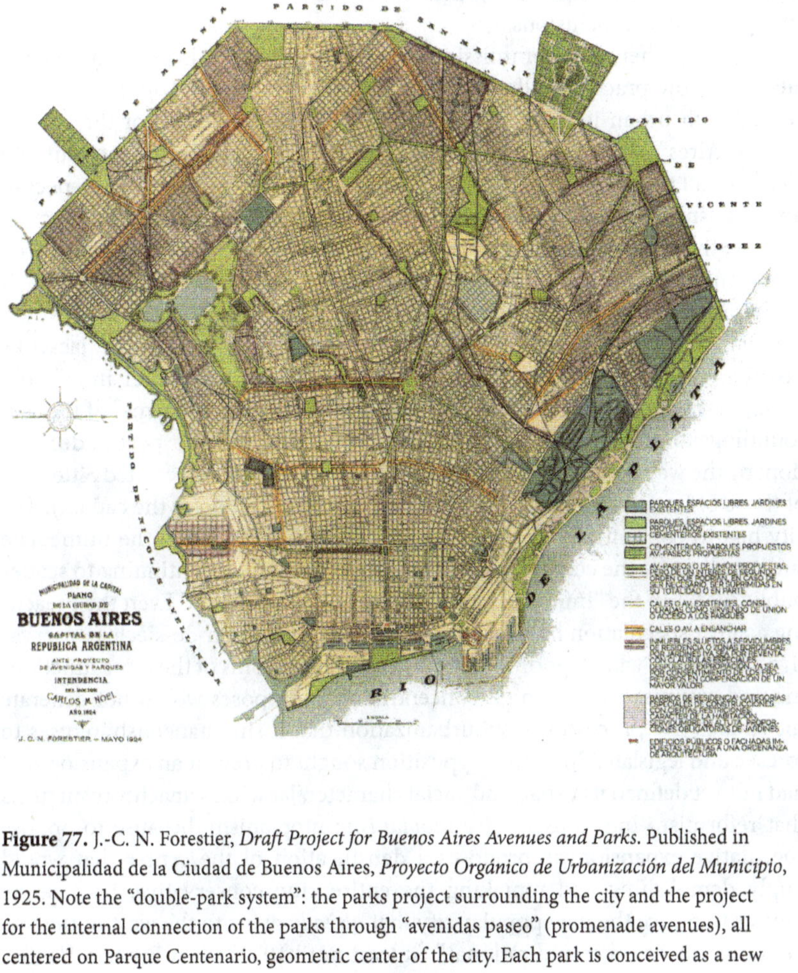

Figure 77. J.-C. N. Forestier, *Draft Project for Buenos Aires Avenues and Parks*. Published in Municipalidad de la Ciudad de Buenos Aires, *Proyecto Orgánico de Urbanización del Municipio*, 1925. Note the "double-park system": the parks project surrounding the city and the project for the internal connection of the parks through "avenidas paseo" (promenade avenues), all centered on Parque Centenario, geometric center of the city. Each park is conceived as a new neighborhood center.

the attention paid by the Commission of Building Aesthetics to the process of consolidation of suburban neighborhoods (which, beyond the technical opinions it deserves today, shows again the strong reformist tinge with which it was received by its contemporaries), than those who rely on the same evidence to strengthen their conclusions.

In 1924, when the Commission's studies had not yet been made public, Jaeschké, now practically the only voice in the *Revista de Arquitectura* concerned with urban issues, titled an article "Useless Expansion of the City of Buenos Aires" in response to Forestier's proposal to "incorporate into our city all the small towns near the capital."[432] Without much variation with respect to his criticisms of the Bouvard Plan, Jaeschké rejects the expansive tendency of the city: the Organic Project had reached the extreme of favoring expansion by proposing the need for the administrative creation of Greater Buenos Aires, a proposal from which, in his opinion, only auctioneers and speculators would benefit. As Mayor Bullrich proposed more than twenty years earlier, Jaeschké insisted that the city should be densified on its traditional center in a "more sober, more open and more rational" way, leaving the "small towns" of the surroundings to preserve their rural character and their poetic aspect (a description, by the way, more typical of the small German towns that excited Sitte than of those of Buenos Aires that were formed by the attraction of the capital). The city had to concentrate, and for that purpose, what existed in the immediate surroundings of the center had to be improved instead of continuing to scatter public works in the "immense municipality of Buenos Aires." Even the preaching against speculation has the same moralistic tone of fin-de-siècle conservative reformism, which ignores the economic mechanisms of the city's functioning and assumes that the high concentration it proposes would not generate the speculative processes of suburbanization that it simultaneously refuses to foresee and legislate. But if that opposition sought to prevent an expansion that had not yet defined its urban and social character, Jaeschké's anachronism turns that reformism into *conservative utopianism*: utopianism, because to oppose speculative expansion he proposes a densification of the center that would imply demolishing and remaking the entire city; conservative, because he refuses to notice the new popular city that *already exists* to the west of the one he wants "more sober and rational." At least until 1932, when Ernesto Vautier took editorial charge of these issues from a different position, the official organ of architects will support this vision.[433]

---

[432] Víctor Julio Jaeschké, in *Revista de Arquitectura* 45 (September 1924), 269.
[433] Even in July 1931, in the editorial of *Revista de Arquitectura*, 127: "It is necessary to reform the Law of Expropriations," the accusation against the Organic Project is to have "broken the financial balance [and] fomented the particular speculation sown in the four directions of the city by so many projects of impossible immediate realization, as they have been launched in the last years."

The other important voice to react energetically is that of engineer Gerón-imo de la Serna: as soon as the Organic Project is published, he refutes it globally, now from the perspective of a realistic and consistent conservatism, with no attenuating reformism. From a standpoint of incontrovertible and harshly effective technical seriousness, the Project is presented by de la Serna as "a series of sketches and an exposition of general ideas, repeated and diluted in streams of *flamboyant* literature, and collected here and there, by chance, among the most vulgarized and well-known; without concrete data, without precise calculations." But the criticisms quickly cease to be technical (or at least technically unobjectionable): "The Commission did not understand that what was essential resided in the old part of the city and ventured into the suburbs and new neighborhoods." From there, de la Serna's criticism is directed, on the one hand, to impugn all the municipal reforms that gave rise to the need for the plan, in the terms we discussed: while "hundreds of millions" are squandered in "external" suburban works, "of possible postponement," "the center, the heart of the city, the focus of commercial and administrative life is suffocated and oppressed." On the other hand, in a more comprehensive way, he contests the very idea of a "regulatory plan," because "cities of great progress like Bue-nos Aires are not directed as one wishes, but as one can." With a doctrinaire orthodoxy from which conservative reformism has always taken distance, de la Serna denounces the ineffectiveness of the plan in the city of capital: the future is unpredictable in the market; what would be desirable would be a minimum regulation that does not restrict or put molds on the energies of the incessant and changing movement of progress: "To each era its own labor. Generations to come will know how to develop on the basis of what we do now that is useful, practical, profitable, and far-sighted. Let us reduce then, for now, great public works to the primitive hull of the city."[434]

The voices of Jaeschké and de la Serna are very important for the Commis-sion of Building Aesthetics, so much so that in its preliminary study they are the only ones it cites as local sources.[435] In the years immediately following the pub-

---

[434] "Disquisiciones edilicias referentes al 'Proyecto de la Municipalidad para la urbanización del municipio,'" lecture delivered at the Centro Argentino de Ingenieros and published in *La Ingeniería* (1927).

[435] Benito Carrasco also opposed it in a series of notes published in the cultural supplement of *La Nación* between 1923 and 1926 (republished in 1927 as a pamphlet by Los Amigos de la Ciudad, in *Algunas consideraciones sobre la urbanización de ciudades*). But he does not contribute any relevant element. On the contrary, in chapter 5 we saw that Carrasco had been among the first to assume the need for expansion to the west of the traditional city, proposing, in 1908, a decentralization to the "true center" of the new city, which would be taken up again in Forestier's proposal (the center of his park system in Centenario Park). Likewise, we mentioned his schemes for the Democratic Progressive Party in 1921 with an organization of zonal civic centers that also takes up the Organic Project literally; in fact, his name had been proposed by the Deliberative

64

lication of the Organic Project, a number of developments and initiatives that seek to reinforce, in line with those criticisms, the traditional center of the city follow one after another. In fact, the Commission of Building Aesthetics itself also proposed the redesign of the Plaza de Mayo as one of the strong points of the Project, with the grouping of all the national ministries into a monumental environment, the demolition of the Casa Rosada for the continuation of the views toward the river, and the erection of a "skyscraper" on each corner as a "monumental gateway" to the central axis of the city. But such was the impact of the attention given to the "suburb," the resources allocated for its reform, the decentralization of the entire municipal administration, and the formation of zonal civic centers that the main reactions fed the polarity between expansion and recentralization. Thus, projects such as that of Jorge B. Hardoy of 1927 appeared, which sought to redesign the city with a huge, elevated platform that would connect Plaza de Mayo with Retiro (a kind of Catalinas Norte *avant la lettre*), giving finished form to the tendencies to displace the tertiary sector of the city to the north and opening the series of projects for the remodeling of Plaza de Mayo. The epicenter of those projects will be the contest organized by Los Amigos de la Ciudad in 1934, based on the literary evocation of the square that Enrique Larreta had made in *Las dos fundaciones de Buenos Aires* (The Two Foundations of Buenos Aires).

A faded echo of the voices of Andrés Lamas in the early eighties and Adolfo Carranza in the centenary, Larreta listed dejectedly:

> The fort no longer exists. Of the Cabildo there is nothing left but a disfi-gured and absurd stump. The Recova has disappeared. Since none of that would last, a little patriotic foresight could have been placed in projecting some noble grouping in its replacement. It was not just any square; it was the principal square, the main square, the historical square of Buenos Aires. Its agora, its forum, its proscenium. Let those who have traveled say if they have seen anywhere anything so monstrous as that disorder, anything that could give a less favorable idea of the inhabitants of a city.[436]

Council as an alternative to the hiring of Forestier at the time when the item requested by the mayor had to be approved. His opposition, in truth, is motivated by rivalries in the definition of a professional field for urban planning: it is as significant that Carrasco does not recognize the undeniable points of contact between his ideas and those of the Organic Project, as it is that in the latter he is neatly excluded from any reference or antecedent. In the twenties, Carrasco is already a recognized professional in many fields, but he will always have difficulties being accepted in the architectural field, with preeminence in the Commission of Building Aesthetics.

[436] Enrique Larreta, *Las dos fundaciones de Buenos Aires* (c. 1929) (Buenos Aires: EMECE, 1943), 67; the episode has been previously analyzed in Mariana Arcondo, Eduardo Gentile and Juan Carlos Pignataro, "Centros cívicos para Buenos Aires: 1923–1943," paper presented at the conference Buenos Aires moderna. Historia y perspectiva urbana,

The historicist recovery that had its apogee in the centenary finds at the end
of the twenties the cultural and political elites united in the need for the requal-
ification of the traditional center in its own heart. Larreta offers that restorative
ambition a complete image: the square transfigured into sober lines, with a
continuous stone floor that restores the unity lost at the hands of the stone-
masons and the *pelouses* of the successive Frenchified reforms, with a rebuilt
Cabildo—in 1933 it will be declared a National Historic Monument—and the
Casa Rosada demolished to facilitate the view of the river, coinciding with the
Organic Project and showing once again the constant ambiguity with which
building heritage is still viewed (it is the reforms introduced from the 1880s
onwards that must be undone in order to rehabilitate it). Los Amigos de la
Ciudad form a commission chaired by Larreta himself, giving rise to a number
of projects behind which the whole architectural discipline is mobilized, and
which will appear as an explicit attempt to requalify the old center of the city,
recovering its traditional lines and reinstituting it as a modern center of government and business, against the trend toward decentralization and dehier-
archization of the square.

And it is in this same direction that the intervention of a very special visitor
to Buenos Aires in 1929—amid the debate on expansion—must be interpreted.
Le Corbusier's visit, so rich in cultural connotations, has been studied; here I
am only interested in pointing out that the main keys of his proposal implied
a conscious taking of a position in the debate on expansion opened in urban
terms by the Organic Project.[437] As we know, the key nucleus of Corbusier's
design for Buenos Aires is the *cité des affaires*: the skyscraper platform over the
river. By superimposing on a detailed reading of technical precedents a grand
design gesture that completely overturns the terms of the polemic between
expansion and concentration, Le Corbusier tunes in to the restorative ambition
of the local elite by quickly uncovering the deepest and most deeply rooted
myths of the relationship between Buenos Aires and its history. The equilibrium of the decentralized city had to be recovered, not by displacing the old
center toward the new suburbs, but by inventing a new city on the river, capable
of returning centrality to the traditional heart of the capital and recreating the
"spirit" of the colonial city. A refoundational gesture that seeks to prove the
validity, in terms of modernist figuration, of the models of the concentrated

IAA, Buenos Aires, 1990 (mimeo) (I owe to this intelligent work the first visualization
of the subject of civic centers in its specificity; and particularly to Gentile for generously
sharing his sources). Jorge B. Hardoy's project, in "Consideraciones sobre urbanización
de la ciudad de Buenos Aires. Contribución al estudio de su plano regulador," *Revista de
Arquitectura* 83 (November 1927).
[437] The best and most complete study on Le Corbusier in Buenos Aires is by Jorge Liernur
and Pablo Pschepiurca, "Precisiones sobre los proyectos de Le Corbusier en la Argentina
1929/1949," *summa* 243 (November 1989); from a cultural perspective, see Beatriz Sarlo,
"Arlt, ciudad real, ciudad imaginaria, ciudad reformada," *Punto de Vista* 42 (April 1992).

city in the manner of the Parisian tradition, with great modifications in the heart—the "forum of commercial and administrative life" according to de la Serna—and an enormous hinterland populated by suburban *quintas*.

If the Organic Project, then, was read in the framework of that polarization, between recovery of the traditional center or decentralization and qualification of the suburbs, between denial of what expansion implied for the city or the search to articulate its growth in a new way, it should be noted that the second position, with the implicit support of public administration, although stressing its more reformist aspects, will be restricted, fundamentally, to the City Council; that is to say, it will develop more in political than technical terms. And in this regard, it is important to recall the initial opposition of the Council to the Organic Project and the objections that produced in that seat the policy of Mayor Noel. However, this is where a line of thought that will organically link improvement of suburban conditions with political and administrative decentralization is generated. For example, in 1926 an Yrigoyenist councilman like Guillermo Faggioli, confronted with the mayor's office (1924 saw the schism of the radical party between Yrigoyenists and Alvearists), joins the type of criticism that points out the "inorganicity" of the Organic Project as a mere sum of disaggregated reforms. Nonetheless, what he proposes is, by contrast, greater regulation and greater decentralization. Taking advantage of the institutional experience of production of local public space and with a view to enhancing it, he proposes a subdivision of the city into proportional zones, each with its civic centers with municipal services and its own institutions (schools, police station, hospital, neighborhood societies). Replicating almost directly the type of objections we analyzed, he says that "while we have the prejudice that everything has to be done from Callao Street to Paseo Colón, no urbanism will be possible."[438]

In any case, councilman Faggioli represents a line of proposals that still seeks to reconcile, as the Organic Project did, a partial governmental decentralization with the simultaneous reinforcement of the traditional city center around the Plaza de Mayo. On the contrary, more radical proposals will be developed within the Council that postulate the global reformulation of the traditional city and see in the transfer of all governmental functions to the "true center" of the new city the main resource to achieve it. Vicente Rotta, another radical councilman, raises it in the same debate for the formation of the Commission of Building Aesthetics: as a response to the intendancy's initiative, Rotta proposes that the City Council organize its own Commission (of Hygiene and Building Aesthetics) for which he proposes a program whose first two points contemplate a general plan of sanitation of the suburban neighborhoods

---

[438] *Actas del Honorable Concejo Deliberante*, Municipalidad de la Ciudad de Buenos Aires, December 15, 1926.

and the total decentralization of public offices.[439] This position will be solved architecturally by Julio Otaola ten years later in The Civic Center of the City of Buenos Aires, a project based explicitly on the City Beautiful principles that postulates the formation of a monumental government center out of the union of Lezica Park and Centennial Park, as a solution to the need to recover the form of the extended city, to restore its organicity, as corresponds to an idea that is structurally City Beautiful: that of supposing that a monumental civic center can rearticulate around itself the whole functional and civic organization of the city.[440]

78, 79

---

[439] Ibid., December 24, 1924.
[440] Julio Otaola, *El Centro Cívico de la ciudad de Buenos Aires* (Buenos Aires: Los Amigos de la Ciudad, 1933).

Julio Otaola, Project to Move the Government Buildings to the City's Geometric Center, 1933. Illustrations for *El centro cívico de Buenos Aires*, 1933:

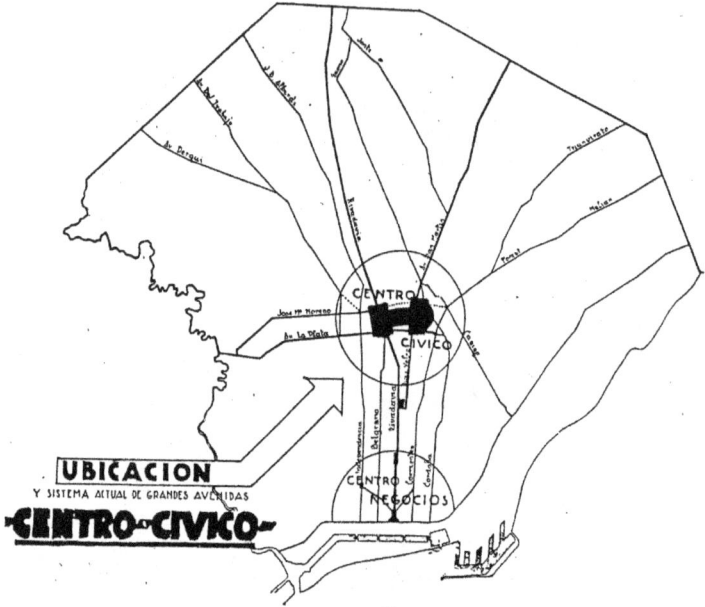

Figure 78. Location of the new civic center.

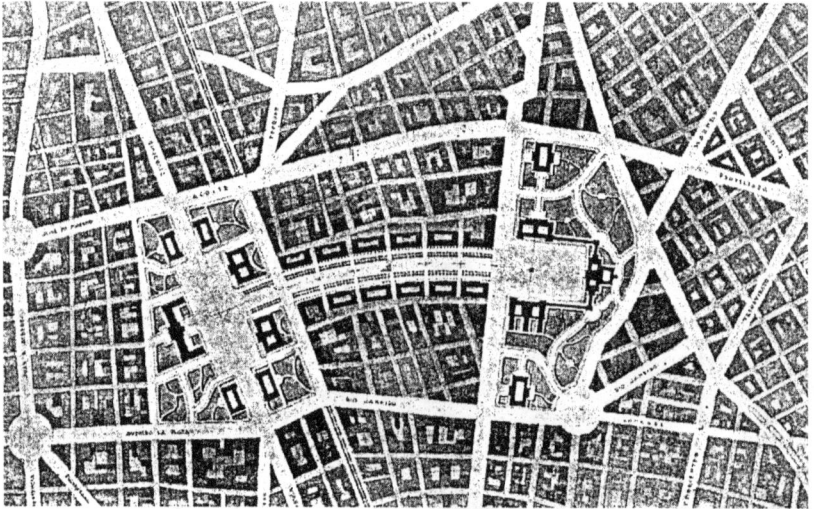

Figure 79. Detailed plan of the new civic center designed to connect Rivadavia and Centenario Parks. The spirit of the City Beautiful movement is clearly evident.

2. "Socialist" Buenos Aires

> The new Buenos Aires must be built by going to its still almost virgin center.
> –Werner Hegemann, 1931

At this point it is convenient to reflect on the socialist position in the City Council, because it is the one that best indicates, in my opinion, the evolution and the limits of municipal political reformism. It has already been mentioned that ever since the first election after the reform in 1918, Socialists became a determining presence in the Council, not only numerically, alternating with Radicals as first and second minority: above all, because Socialists make all of parliamentary life revolve around it. Its practice of hierarchizing the City Council, placing on the lists leaders of the highest political and intellectual presence who did not seek local office only as a launching pad for national careers (there are several cases of important socialist leaders who were councilors after having been national deputies); the disciplined functioning of the bloc, which reproduced the methods of the deputies and proposed the City Council as a field of experimentation of forms of political and parliamentary elaboration; its specific work in the realization of proposals, and its way of introducing social vindications of a national level into the city; all this speaks of a solid party with growing roots in society, which manages to enlist the bulk of reformism behind its initiatives. Thus, in a social and political context highly prone to reform, the other parties end up supporting them or reproducing them with slight variations. This happens with the councilmen of the radicalized Left, including the International Socialist Party, later Communist, that came to have two councilmen between 1920 and 1924, and always maintained at least one councilman over the whole period, the Progressive Democrats, who attained a bloc of three councilmen, large part of the Radicals, and the Independent Socialist Party, recently separated from the Socialist bloc, but that maintained at the municipal level more commonalities than the conflicts that confronted them at the national level of politics.[441] Thus, for over two decades we will be facing a City Council strongly hegemonized by a socialist *mood*.

---

[441] A detailed account of each of the elections in the "reformist" period (1918–1941) can be found in Walter, *Politics and Urban Growth in Buenos Aires: 1910–1942*. The thirty councilors were renewed by halves every two years, so in order to see the composition of the Council it is not only the election results that must be analyzed; in this period the Socialists equal the Radicals in the first minority in the elections of 1918 (ten councilors each); they surpass them from those of 1920 (eleven Socialist councilors against ten Radicals, but, in addition, the Socialists achieve their own majority, voting with the three councilors of the Progressive Democratic Party and the two of the International Socialist Party); they come second in those of 1922 (the Council remains with twelve radicals and ten socialists); and in those of 1924 (seventeen Radical councilors against

It is important to emphasize the common universe of *reformist* ideas in which this coloration of the municipal institution is produced. So far we have focused on different manifestations of state public reformism, implanted through a slow accumulation and consolidation of technical traditions in a series of institutions and in bureaucratic and professional teams; the state as an apparatus that, as far as urban management is concerned, carries implicit logics of reform "from above": a moral, social, political, and hygienic reform that places the city as a privileged recipient of the complex range of issues that make up the "social question." But by the 1920s these public traditions began to share spaces (and to compete for them) with more varied reformisms in society, in the cultural and political fields, as a manifestation, one might say, of the civilizational crisis of the interwar period, in which the terms right and left seemed to lose relevance in the face of the mixture and confusion of ideological motifs. Thus, we can certainly identify a more diffuse reformism, such as the one we are analyzing in neighborhood associations, clubs, cultural production centers in the barrios, due to their integrating character and their shaping of citizenship in the extension of new qualities of public space. And, although mutual relations are increasingly complex, it is clear that the expansion of more specifically ideological or cultural reform movements, which are produced in such different but interconnected orbits—and of such weight in a city like Buenos Aires— as the university, the literary and artistic avant-gardes, the figurative renovation movements in architecture, and more specifically urbanistic proposals, all contribute to the preparation of this *reformist climate;* the intervention of the literary and journalistic fields in the city since the end of the 1910s will finish coloring the reformist cycle with all its complexity and its social and ideological ambiguities. This is a climate in which it is possible to find antagonistic tendencies running through groups and institutions, from fascism to Bolshevism, romantic populism and positivism, nationalism and state socialism, Juvenalianism, mass social democracy, and aristocratic rejection of the immigrant; or, in more specifically aesthetic terms, traditionalism and avant-garde, *criollismo* or indigenism and modernism, within the framework of a curious optimism that is justified in the field of ideas by the paradoxical adoption of European decadentist tropes, read in the light of a territory—the American one—in which the future seemed open.[442]

---

ten Socialists, although the Radicals are already divided into personalists (Yrigoyenists) and antipersonalists (Alvearists) leaving the hegemony) they remain in the second bloc despite the division in 1927 of the Independent Socialist Party; and between 1932 and 1936 they are largely part of the majority bloc thanks to the abstention of radicalism.

[442] This is one more of the variables of an extremely complex period in which the whole ideological and cultural framework is undergoing an explosive historiographic revision. On local Socialism, I build on the lessons of José Aricó, of which unfortunately only his notes on Juan B. Justo have been published. See, for example, "La hipótesis de Justo," *La ciudad futura* 30–31 (special issue dedicated to Aricó) (December 1991–February

The visualization of the complexity of this framework, with all the confusion of which the growth of Radicalism from state power is not at all alien, allows us to understand some of the reasons why the relative doctrinaire and organizational solidity of Socialism must have appeared as a differential advantage of great effectiveness on the institutions of society and politics, which allows it to prevail in the local parliament, in the debate of ideas, and in the visualization of the new popular place of the city, the suburb. It is not only a correlation between political reformism and the place of application of the reform (the municipality): as has been pointed out for the case of the European city, in the first decades of the twentieth century there is an identification between reformism and municipalism, in which the municipality is proposed by reformism as an overcoming of old philanthropic organizations, tending to transform it into the agent of political mediation between state interests, economic interests, and local needs, acquiring a preponderant role in new areas of daily life outside spaces of production. Even Argentine Socialism, with its strong liberal anti-state tradition, from its effective insertion in local politics, will progressively see in the municipality an intermediate scale of public intervention, closer to social needs and to the construction of instruments of political participation, differentiating it from the national state. The formation of production and consumption, housing, and construction cooperatives; the demand for the municipalization of transport and infrastructure services; the *localization* of social rights as urban rights: common characteristics in the experiences of social democratic management of the period, such as "red" Vienna or Weimar Berlin, and that we will see guiding the debates and the problematization of urban issues in the "socialist" City Council of Buenos Aires.

Yet with a differential nuance in this city: Socialism organizes its main causes around a global struggle on the issues of housing and public services, without incorporating specifically urbanistic proposals in its platforms and being incapable of postulating a global image of the city. We will see later how, in its own way, images of the city appear in the political struggles for public services, but if the "socialist Buenos Aires" is above all the Buenos Aires of the suburbs, in the sense that it is the Buenos Aires that incorporates as a central problem the popular sectors that have settled there, how did a reformist party without a clear urban development project envision the suburbs? The first thing to point out is the unequal relationship at this point between Socialism and the state "reformist machine" that it embodies in the Organic Project, bringing

---

1992). On the positions of Socialists in relation to the city, I base my conclusions on the exhaustive analysis of Anahi Ballent, *Socialismo, vivienda y ciudad: la Cooperativa El Hogar Obrero. Buenos Aires, 1905–1940* (1989). Digital document available through the historical section of El Hogar Obrero's web page. See also, Sergio Berensztein, *Un partido para la Argentina moderna. Organización e identidad del partido socialista (1896–1916)* (Buenos Aires: Documento CEDES, 1991).

together and strengthening its various technical traditions. Public reformism is born in the state, from the place where the rules of the game and the reformist logics of public intervention are generated early on: its very meaning lies in its capacity for intervention "from above." That is why it is not a "political" reformism, although its consequences certainly are: state mediation in Buenos Aires stifles the development of urban policies as the realization of immediate class interests and lays the foundations for a conception of urban policy as a reform device toward the construction of social actors who accept the rules of the game of a homogeneous city for their own economic prosperity in the more strategic framework of social peace. Socialist reformism undoubtedly shares these objectives, but it lacks the instruments to identify them in one or another urban policy, to distinguish the implicit precepts from the concrete practices that municipal governments then carry out, contradicting them; it is a reformism, as we saw, which is in principle refractory to state intervention, and it is now its own definition that is at stake, since Socialism is born in the public sphere confronted with a state that it visualizes as the main object of reform. The need for political reform, it could be said, simplistically, prevents it from seeing the political effects of technical reform and its potential in society.

Anahi Ballent has acutely pointed out a double socialist tradition of connection with the city, which in these years survives as an unresolved conflict: on the one hand, a "political" tradition, which visualizes the city as a public space and which demands its free possession by the people as "materialization and symbol of our democratic spirit," in the words of Américo Ghioldi; on the other hand, a "medical-hygienist" tradition, centered on domestic reform and the transformation of social customs in the very heart of the family nucleus.[443] Ballent analyzed the conflictive coexistence of both traditions in the proposals of the cooperative El Hogar Obrero (The Working-Class Home), which oscillate between collective housing on the edges of the traditional city, with the hyper-politicized model of the workers' complexes of red Vienna, and individual suburban housing as a "modern program," with the model of the *home* and the small community of the Garden City, not coincidentally affiliated with utopian socialism. In relation to urban policies, it could be said that this double tradition allows us to understand that Socialists confront the Organic Project by disaggregating two inseparable components in its urbanistic premises: expansion and the recomposition of the urban figure starting from a new center; that is, it separates that combination typical of Civic Art between the celebration of urban public space and the application of the theory of indefinite expansion, by which *the search for the center* is an inseparable part of a regional vision of urban growth. Socialism separates them, and just as in the 1920s it bets more emphatically on collective housing projects, so too in urban plans

---

[443] See Anahi Ballent, *Socialismo, vivienda y ciudad.* For Américo Ghioldi's expression, see "Las reuniones en las plazas y esquinas de la ciudad," *La Vanguardia,* October 27, 1929.

does it opt for the former over the latter, that is, for the reformist aspects of a recomposition of public space in the expanded city over those linked to urban expansion; it is not only that it cannot see the close link between one and the other in the Project, but that from its entry into municipal politics, socialism's own relationship with urban expansion will be marked by distrust.

Is expansion progressive? Such is the doubt that marks the actions of social-ism in urban policy in these years: it is impossible not to notice in its interven-tions and projects a paralyzing ambivalence between the justice of the claims of the new inhabitants of land that for most of the year is underwater, and the flagrant injustice that lies in the very process that puts that land on the market, with the "lagoon landowners" as the only beneficiaries. Expansion is experi-enced by socialist reformism as a relentless circle: the few improvements that the state can bring to the suburbs to make them more habitable once they have been plotted out only result in even more uninhabitable land being more easily looted. For this reason, far from considering it "progress," suburban expan-sion is interpreted by Socialists, in the words of one of its councilmen, Manuel Palacín, as a "flight of tenants to the periphery, to the unhealthy marshes, to the neighborhoods without electricity, without pavements, without sanitary works, fleeing in terror from the tenements, and above all, from the criminally expen-sive tenements.[444] The absence of an image of the city forces all urban problems to pass through the restricted light of "the question of housing"; in such a way, expansion cannot but appear as the undesired consequence of the absence of public policy for popular housing and tax reform. Palacín continues:

> Every time the phenomenon [of expansion] has occurred, our city counci-lors, with the criteria of estate auctioneers, have celebrated it as a demons-tration of the "dynamism" of our city. [...] At the same time, all the resour-ces of the commune fell short; an astonishing inflation of the budget; an enormous lack of cleaning and urbanization services, increasingly deficient; the absence of these services in many "progressive" neighborhoods, built on ponds of putrid water [...]. The municipality will make a great deal by preventing the "swamp" auctioneers from continuing to do theirs.

Against the experience of public reformism which, as we have already seen in Selva and Cibils toward the centenary, had come to produce a com-prehensive vision of the phenomenon of expansion as a private "solution" to the problem of home ownership for popular sectors, Socialists will oppose a negative vision of "ant expansion," postulating as an alternative a "society of tenants." That is why, amid the whirlwind of the formation of the popular sub-urb, Enrique Dickmann spoke out against the division of urban property: it is

---

[444] Manuel Palacín, "Vivienda, expansión y urbanización," *La Vanguardia* (Buenos Aires), September 1, 1929, 6.

not in the multiplication of property owners that Socialists see the possibility of reforming society; nor in compulsory expropriations. This image of a society of tenants indiscriminately housed in an economically homogeneous territory by force of the progressiveness of tax policies responds, as Ballent rightly pointed out, to the influences of Georgist theories; but that is precisely what makes it incompatible with a specifically urban perspective on housing problems.[445]

To a large extent, this restriction explains why Socialism's initial municipal policy is based on two extremes: the global struggles for tax reform, housing, or public services; and the proposals for urban improvements that are strictly particularized in relation to the demands of neighborhood associations. Faced with the global urban vision of the technical reformism of the Organic Project and with its own ambition to conceive of the city as a political space, the conceptual framework of Socialism necessarily translates "city" as the basic infrastructure of consumption and popular habitation. We are already going to see the impact that this restriction will have on its relations with society; but here we must incorporate the other restriction that is associated with this distrust of expansion: the evolutionist restriction of socialist thought, incompatible with the idea of a plan.

This is possibly the most solid tradition in Socialism, in spite of the fact that along this path it only ended up coinciding with a consistent conservative like de la Serna, and in spite of the fact that international experiences of social democratic administrations in the period show excessive confidence in planning, to the point that, through scientism, another aspect also paradoxically present in local Socialism, socialism and plan become almost synonymous in European progressive urbanistic culture. On the contrary, amid the debate opened by the Organic Project, in 1928 Nicolás Repetto says:

> cities develop according to their needs [...]. Man can [...] accelerate or improve the evolution of a city, but on condition that he respects its proper functions [...]. And it is good not to foresee or anticipate too much in time, because the mutation or dislocation of commerce or industry tends to render superfluous not a few forecasts made at great cost. What is practical in

---

[445] Dickmann says in 1915: "in the city we are not only enemies of the division [of property], but we would like the land to be made up of large blocks, so that [collective] houses could be built in the European style, covering a block." Ballent (*Socialismo, vivienda y ciudad*, 35) quotes this sentence showing how, in the line of Henry George, for socialism "property was not the central question, but the appropriation of the rent of which it was the condition"; what he proposes, therefore, is to confiscate the rent of the soil through taxation as a gradual and implicit form of collectivization: property would not thus be abolished but would become a mere nominal title. This moderate proposal is opposed both to socializing expropriation and to the "ant" speculation that multiplies small landowners.

these matters consists more in accompanying the movement of cities than in arbitrarily directing it in the name of aesthetics.[446]

However, this double restriction of Socialism is only the basis from which we can begin to understand the conflicts and transformations that its thinking and proposals will undergo in the heat of the experience of the municipal Council in its years under a *socialist climate*. On the one hand, during the years of Noel's mayoralty and the agitated discussions regarding the Project, Socialists discover that they lose the initiative in front of the global vision of management that the municipal executive puts into action. In fact, in 1923, despite all the objections not only to the idea of the Project, but more specifically to Noel's *caudillo* politics and, even more specifically, to the elimination of all control by the City Council in the proposal for the formation of the Commission of Building Aesthetics, Socialists had to support the loan requested by the Council to finance the "improvement plan" for the suburbs and the Organic Project. It is appropriate to reproduce *in extenso* the intervention with which councilman Ángel Giménez expresses the positive vote of his bloc:

> Here we have the mania of urbanism, the supposed science of improvement and reform of cities by which in our country it would have to be done all over again. The Spaniards knew about war and many other things, but they did not know how to plan cities. [...] Then, years later, we find our great city that has not responded to any kind of plan. There are streets laid out with different orientations. In addition, due to speculation in the sale of land for monthly payments, lots have been built on impossible terrain. [...] I have had the opportunity to visit one of the points that appear [in the Plan presented by the Executive Department to support the request for the loan]: Coronel Roca Avenue [...]. All of that would have to be filled in. We wanted to check by sight if the points where [the Plan states that] the bridges should be established were suitable and in reality, we have seen [that it would be necessary to build] a much larger series of bridges. And the same thing that happens in the south of the city happens in the north. In the lower part of Belgrano, in the western part as well [...] and in that way impossible rooms are built, houses of wood, of tin, narrow streets in some parts, and in others deficient pavements.
>
> We have signed this dispatch [...]. It will not, I repeat, be able to meet all the needs of the population, but there will at least be some of the practical things that can be done within the limited resources. [...] And we have something against us, something that hinders us: we will bring hygiene, improvement

---

[446] N. Repetto, "Lo útil a condición de lo bello. A propósito del plan regulador," *La Vanguardia* (Buenos Aires), December 19, 1928.

to a whole area, and we will find that we will have valued the land, improved the properties by giving them a higher value than they had when their owners acquired them, and on that basis we will not be able to obtain any benefit, because we lack the instrument that will authorize us to establish the tax on the higher value [...]. It is in this sense that I have voted and signed this dispatch [...]. More cannot be projected, and we cannot be here in this room flattering the electorate, deceiving them with continuous minutes, with promises of bridges, passages, and pavements that are never done. If we were to make a statistic of the projects of the gentlemen councilors promoting the paving of streets, there would be enough to make a street from here to Valparaíso and a bridge that crosses the Río de la Plata.[447]

I believe that this intervention exposes all the issues and their complexities: the global vision of the suburb as the place of deprivation against which all action is insufficient and, at the same time, the need to establish a priority of actions. In this framework, the contemptuous disdain for the "urban planning mania" can only contrast with the clear identification of the absurdity to which the electoralist and populist logic of the functioning of a deliberative body without a strategic vision of the city leads, with councilmen who request an infinite number of specific arrangements to bring "progress" to the areas of their constituents without caring about the viability of their requests, and without caring that by adding to an impossible list of specific proposals "demanded" of the Executive Department, the only thing they achieve is that the latter rations them according to the needs of their own zonal constituents and of electoral times. The mere existence of Noel's initiative for the realization of the Organic Project highlights the corrupt burden of that "political" logic of the City Council and leads Socialists to necessarily lean back on the realistic search for *organicity* of the executive, a movement in which the mayor's proposal to modify taxes on urban income was not secondary; and the same will happen when in 1928 socialism votes in favor of the new building regulations proposed by Noel's administration.[448] In such a way, the conflictive relationship of Socialism with expansive urban dynamics, whose perversity it lucidly points out but

---

[447] Intervention of Ángel Giménez in *Actas del Honorable Concejo Deliberante*, Municipalidad de la Ciudad de Buenos Aires, September 20, 1924.

[448] See, for example, the speech of councilman Américo Ghioldi upon the resignation of Mayor Noel, *Actas del Honorable Concejo Deliberante* (Buenos Aires), Municipalidad de la Ciudad de Buenos Aires, May 3, 1927. The building regulations were voted unanimously on June 30, 1928. Contrary to what has usually been maintained, Gentile points out that the new regulations (which replaced the previous one of 1910) had little to do with the recommendations of the Organic Project, and we will see later that from the point of view of its urbanistic and social implications it was highly criticized. See Eduardo Gentile, "Los centros cívicos y el ideal City Beautiful. Propuestas para Buenos Aires 1925-1943," in Fernando Aliata and Fernando Gandolfi, eds., *Materiales para la*

whose social connotations it cannot renounce, will end in a hesitant acceptance of the regulation of the Plan, but without being able to forge a position of its own and without being able to gather together its different dimensions. It may be revealing to contrast the hesitations on this point with the approach toward Socialism of a very important foreign visitor, the German urban planner Werner Hegemann, who will reveal the different possibilities of reformist understanding of the processes opened up in the city by expansion.

Hegemann is an outstanding theorist of urbanism (with training in political science and economics) who came to the country in August 1931 invited by Los Amigos de la Ciudad at the zenith of his career as a scholar and propagandist. We mentioned him a few pages back as the main theoretical inspiration of the Organic Project and through a manual coauthored by him—*The American Vitruvius*—that proposed the complexification of the notions of the City Beautiful movement in the direction of Civic Art, but his greatest importance lies in having been one of the outstanding organizers of international congresses on urban planning at the time when the "scientific" profile of the discipline was being defined: the 1910 and 1911 Berlin and Düsseldorf congresses. After a stay of several years in the United States, in the 1920s Hegemann directed the magazine *Der Städtebau* in Germany and, in 1930, a few months before arriving in Argentina, he published one of the first works on urban history, with his famous call to solve the conditions of overcrowding in the rental buildings of the German capital: *Das Steinerne Berlin* (The Berlin of Stone).[449]

During the four months of his stay in the Río de la Plata, at the end of 1931, Hegemann was intensively active in Buenos Aires, Rosario, Mar del Plata, and Montevideo, organizing exhibitions of urbanism and architecture, offering conferences analyzing the cities he was getting to know, making proposals for legal and administrative transformation, advising on specific projects

---

historia de la arquitectura, el hábitat y la ciudad en la Argentina (La Plata: FAU-UNLP, 1996).

[449] Werner Hegemann is one of the most analyzed urban theorists of the last decades. In Italy his catalogues of the 1910 and 1911 exhibitions have been republished (*Catalogo delle esposizioni internazionali di urbanistica. Berlino 1910, Düsseldorf 1911–12* [Milan: Il Saggiatore, 1975]) and *Das Steinerne Berlin* (*La Berlino di pietra. Storia della più grande città di caserme d'affitto* [Milan: Gabriele Mazzotta, 1975]), in both cases with excellent introductory studies by Donatella Calabi (in the former in collaboration with Marino Folin). See also Calabi, "Werner Hegemann, o dell'ambiguitá borghese dell 'urbanistica,'" *Casabella* (Milan) no. 428, September 1977; and Werner Oechslin, "Between America and Germany: Werner Hegemann's Approach to Urban Planning," in J. P. Kleihues and Chr. P. Kleihues and Chr. Rathberg, eds., *Berlin–New York, Like and Unlike: Essays on Architecture and Art from 1870 to the Present* (New York: 1993). On Hegemann and Civic Art, see Christiane Crasemann Collins, "Hegemann and Peets: Cartographers of an Imaginary Atlas," introductory essay in the reissue of *The American Vitruvius: An Architects' Handbook of Civic Art* (New York: Princeton Architectural Press, 1988).

of technical reforms, and plotting a dense network of institutional relations in close connection with the city's existent expansion processes.[450] Socialists closely followed Hegemann's impressions of Buenos Aires: the main figures of the Socialist Party (among others, Repetto, candidate for the national vice-presidency in the middle of the election campaign) toured the city with him and visited the housing groups of El Hogar Obrero; La Vanguardia closely followed his lectures and praised their contents. In the culture of the time, his credentials in the face of progressive sectors is exceptional. Not only did he come to represent the most solid theoretical support for the realistic reform of the capitalist city in a modernizing and progressive sense; he also had a progressive political position (which had earned him a trial in 1912, along with Käthe Kollwitz, for his denunciations of the housing conditions in Berlin and would later lead to his deportation in 1933) and in regard to urbanism which was in tune with the most committed transformations of the interwar period. Hegemann is one of those key figures of German urbanism that makes the passage from classical positions, via British-American theories, toward the determined support for modernist urban reform, like that which was being put into practice by Martin Wagner in social democratic Berlin. At the same time, his trajectory and his realistic vision allow him to tune in for different reasons with the most pragmatic local sectors, such as architect Jorge Kalnay or engineer della Paolera, who will apply a good part of his proposals in the Regulatory Plan of Rosario that he undertakes with Ángel Guido and, starting in 1932, in the Office of the Urbanization Plan of Buenos Aires. Yet his sympathy for socialist ideas and practices will be transparent in all his interventions.

However, it is Hegemann who offers Socialists what is possibly the most global and merciless criticism of their urban policy. In principle, because one of the main themes of Hegemann's interventions in Buenos Aires is the analysis of the 1928 Building Code that the Socialists voted for without arguments: a regulation that allows an abusive occupation of the land, which would allow for a population of 160 million people in the capital (if the possibilities of the code, which favored overcrowded buildings without ventilation, were exploited

---

[450] The best account of Hegemann's activities in Buenos Aires appears in a pamphlet published by Los Amigos de la Ciudad and reproduced by Hegemann in "Als Städtebauer in Südamerika," Wasmuths Monatshefte für Baukunst und Städtebau XVI (Berlin, 1932) (the article appears in three parts in consecutive issues). On his work in Rosario, see Problemas urbanos de Rosario. Conferencias del urbanista Dr. W. Hegemann (Rosario: Municipality of Rosario, 1931). See also Jorge Liernur, "Juncal y Esmeralda, Perú House, Maison Garay: fragmentos de un debate tipológico y urbanístico en la obra de Jorge Kalnay," Anales del Instituto de Arte Americano e Investigaciones Estéticas "Mario J. Buschiazzo" 25 (1988); Alicia Novick and Raúl Piccioni, "Árbitros, pares, socios. Técnicos locales y extranjeros en la génesis del urbanismo porteño" (Buenos Aires: Instituto de Arte Americano, FADU-UBA, 1990); and Jorge Tartarini, "La visita de Werner Hegemann a la Argentina en 1931," DANA 37–38 (1995).

to their limit). By oversizing that occupation, the only thing that the Code achieves, Hegemann shows, is to favor the interest of speculators by irrationally raising the potential value of urban land: anyone can erect a building that takes advantage of the maximum allowed occupation in blocks that are still populated by low-rise houses, distorting the whole game of supply and demand, to the detriment of a rationally planned occupation in which everyone is guaranteed the present and future value of their property and, therefore, the type of urban context that it produces. In this framework, the dilemma Socialists had been posing between large groups of workers' housing and the model of the tree-lined suburb with its individual houses loses all meaning, because in both cases its proposals only reproduce the serious problems implicit in the building regulations and in the deformities of land rent without public control:

> It is exciting to see with what eagerness the socialists of Buenos Aires have tried to build better houses and how the noble social passion of these men failed because of the unfavorable urban situation of Buenos Aires. These collective houses [...] have many of the inevitable defects of other collective houses in Buenos Aires built in accordance with the building regulations of this city. This collective house is built on such high-priced land that it had to take advantage of the regulations to obtain the necessary rent on the land. This collective house harms the neighbor who still owns a ground-floor house, and this collective house will be deprived of light and air as soon as the neighbor builds his house according to the regulations in force.[451]

We will see that, in this dilemma, Hegemann is ultimately on the side of the "little house with a garden." But in Buenos Aires this is also a product of the absence of urban policy and poor regulation, as he takes care to point out, this time with irony, to the de facto Mayor José Guerrico, who is proud of the individual *porteño* house as a counter-model to the danger of European "collectivizing attempts":

> I have always understood the opinion of the mayor [in favor of individual houses], although that does not prevent me from also seeing the disadvantages of low-rise houses if they are cramped, in old or poorly developed towns, without drains, without running water, and above all without sufficient gardens or large parks. Such poorly urbanized neighborhoods exist in unlimited dimensions in the city and in the immediate suburbs. It could almost be said that most of the neighborhoods of Buenos Aires have preserved the highest urban virtue, which is the private house with a garden, but

---

[451] "La vivienda barata en Buenos Aires y en otras ciudades del mundo," *Anales del Instituto Popular de Conferencias* XVII (1932): 288 (this is the second lecture he gave in Buenos Aires, October 2, 1931).

that this virtue, like some virtuous ladies, has been so abandoned that the vice of the clean tenement house is preferable to the dubious virtue of the low-rise house.[452]

It is not so much the model of the house that is important, but the irrational and indiscriminate growth. Hegemann again stresses the need for regulation and public control, but through that route, he once more necessarily links reformist ideas with the planning of expansion.

It could be said that Hegemann's thought is the exact opposite of Socialism; not only for "methodological" reasons (in the sense that his discourse shows the blindness of passing the "urban question" through the "housing question," as we saw in Palacín), but, above all, in its urban economic conception. As opposed to Socialism's exclusive Georgist reliance on a progressive tax policy that homogenizes an urban tenants' market, the theory of expansion starts from a decisive public intervention on extra-urban land (the expropriation of the land surrounding the city to prevent the "waiting" or "potential" rent produced by speculators, who acquire this land in the expectation of its valuation), from which a "natural" (in the sense that it channels market forces without stifling them) ordering of growth can be encouraged: releasing specific zones to a publicly regulated market with the instruments of *zoning*, building regulations, and the definition of regional extension plans. In other words, this theory starts from a global image of the city and its future, emphasizing certain expansion zones over others, reserving green areas for regional forests, and defining the direction of urban development through road axes and public transport.

How, then, does Hegemann see Buenos Aires from this perspective, and what can Socialists take from this view? As the opening quote reveals, the first thing that stands out in Hegemann is the link between planning, the "search for the center," and expansion: the great task for Buenos Aires is to plan the occupation of its "still almost virgin" center. This places him at the antipodes of Le Corbusier (he will make scathing references to his proposal) and of all the conservative criticisms of the Organic Project.[453] In addition, his experience in the United States makes him highlight the advantages of the open grid as a rational and equitable organization of the urban market, limiting the picturesque layout model typical of the Garden City only to restricted residential suburb projects. Faced with the existing suburbs of Buenos Aires, he does not propose an *in toto* rejection of the grid (typical of both picturesque and avant-garde perspectives), but rather of the conditions of overcrowding that nestle in the lack of regulatory control: his analyses show not only that city reform, suburban expansion, and grid layout could be made compatible, but that, in the "American city," they are inseparable.

---

[452] Ibid., 289.
[453] The ironic references to Le Corbusier in "Als Städtebauer in Südamerika II," *Wasmuths Monatshefte.*

"Authoritarian" attempts to control expansion, such as the "alignment plan" 5
of 1898–1904, generate what he calls "a desert of houses" scattered in all directions; against this, the theory of expansion proposes an overcoming of the grid aimed at extending its benefits by favoring its controlled expansion. But for that to be possible it is inevitable to take to the limit the most advanced elements of the Organic Project, such as the institution of a metropolitan area. Ironically dismissing the opposition to the establishment of "Greater Buenos Aires," Hegemann argues that the big problem is that *porteños* are "conservative" and "exaggeratedly modest," which prevents them from taking pride in the fact that their city is already much larger than its boundaries indicate, with a 60 percent larger population:

> [*Porteños*] only fixate their fascinated attention on the relatively small problems of the old city center [and] forget that today, outside the haphazard political boundaries of the so-called Federal Capital, the possibilities for healthy housing, more spacious park systems, forest reserves, and usable traffic routes are being irrationally obstructed and destroyed.[454]

With these arguments, Hegemann is going to produce one of the most significant reflections on the relationship between expansion, squared grid, and "ant speculation." Compared to the housing parameters of Berlin, where tenants are crammed into large central "barracks" (*Mietkaserne*) with the only incentive of the very small—and also overcrowded—"colonies" for vegetable gardens, "the living conditions of the small houses of Buenos Aires, from many other objectionable perspectives, become worthy of attention [...] and, in many points of view, really valid as a model."[455] For proof, upon his return, he describes to his German audience, the operations "of the Argentinean landowner of Italian origin named Fiorito," whose trail he followed in Buenos Aires, giving rise to one of the most fascinating and precise documents on the actual process of suburban expansion. On the one hand, with his usual irony, Hegemann describes the characteristics of the ferocious real estate exploitation:

> Fiorito is not only one of the most successful "urban planners" in South America, but also a benefactor of humanity. He sells his lots in installments. If the buyers get sick, not only does he not let them get worse—since if they did, they could no longer afford to pay—but he also sends them a doctor and nurse free of charge or has them admitted to the large hospital he built

[454] "Als Städtebauer in Südamerika," 148 (I thank Luis Rossi for the translation from German into Spanish).
[455] "Als Städtebauer in Südamerika III," 248–49 (trans. Luis Rossi); the system of garden colonies (allotment gardens) is widespread in German cities: they are urban plots divided into very small, privately allotted gardens.

80

for that purpose. Fiorito does not evict anyone who cannot afford his house and garden. All the buyers speak highly of him and almost without exception pay every penny or find a successor to meet their obligations. [...] [The lots are] 8.5 meters wide and 45 meters deep. Fiorito sells these lots without paved streets, sidewalks, gas, water, sewage, or electricity. The buyer must pay 120 monthly installments of 30.30 pesos each [...]. The lots shown in the illustrations and many others like them were not buildable at the time of sale but had to be filled in to prevent them from being almost completely flooded after the winter rains. The buyer must pay for at least ten truckloads of earth at a price of ten pesos each. Other people explained to me that they had obtained the backfill by digging up the neighboring lots and showed me the holes that remained. On the lot, the buyer builds his house with his own hands; in case of need he builds it with old crates or cans of gasoline or canned food.

The portrait of Fiorito coincides with that of the "auctioneer of the marsh-lands," as described in the local reformist criticism: false benefactor, he becomes a millionaire by selling unhealthy lands without the basic infrastructure, which will then be claimed from the state that will continue to add value to his new lands or those of others like him. A few years earlier, councilman Penelón denounced that "thanks" to the "filthy lots" of Fiorito, workers surround the "Big City" with "an enormous belt [of] misery, infection, and filth."[456] However, Hegemann's commentary shifts, almost seamlessly, to a dazzling description of the lifestyle that this expansion makes possible:

80

Because of the narrowness of the lot, the rooms are strung next to each other. The door of each room, which often serves as the only window, opens onto a covered veranda. For the most part each owner enjoys, despite the smallness of the lot, a great deal of privacy. [...] These long verandas to which all the windows open are often charming. [...] In the house shown in the illustration, I counted two families making a total of eleven persons. In the back barn—still within the 382 square-meter lot—there were three pigs, a goat, thirty chickens, a dog, and only four ducks, because just the week before ten had been sold. In addition to the beloved animals, a large number of vegetables were planted. Alongside the long right angle of the house and the edges of the lot, there was still room for a small but fruitful garden. The space behind the house was divided into three parts: dovecote, pigsty, and vegetable garden. The owner's family was of Spanish origin, but the adult

---

[456] See Municipalidad de la Ciudad de Buenos Aires, *Actas del Honorable Concejo Deliberante* (Buenos Aires), June 10, 1927. Hegemann's quotations are from "Als Städtebauer in Südamerika III," 249–50 (trans. Luis Rossi).

Figure 80. Werner Hegemann, *Barrio Fiorito*, 1931, photographs illustrating "Als Städtebauer in Südamerika III. Der Sieg der Randsiedlung über die Mietkaserne," *Wasmuths Monatshefte für Baukunst und Städtebau* (Berlin) 16, no. 3 (1932).

son was born in Argentina. At the moment they seemed to be all unemployed and living exclusively on their small farm of rammed earth.

In the context of the crisis of the early 1930s, the garden and the vegetable garden, a product of the spasmodic expansion of the grid that, as we have
already seen, made it possible to maintain traditional rural habits in the midst
of metropolitan production, is far from having merely hygienic or recreational
connotations; but it does not rule them out, and they are what, in the end,
make tolerable (and preferable) constructive and social situations unthinkable
in Berlin. Hegemann ends his description with the example of a Yugoslavian-
German couple:

> The couple had very few vegetables in the garden; instead, there were many
> flowers, which they both spoke of with a truly charming enthusiasm. When
> I asked if the house wasn't a bit damp, the owner lifted a neat floorboard
> and showed me with the flashlight that the whole house was over a pond. It
> had rained the week before. There was no basement, but because of the high
> price of filler material, the ground under the house had not been prepared.
> A neighboring lot, which had not yet been built on or filled in, was thickly
> covered with green, swampy mud. The owner assured me that until now he
> had never had to worry in the least about the pond below his house or the
> neighboring swamp. In this house I found as pets a large dog, three canaries,
> and nine rabbits. Since it was the school holidays at the time, the two children
> of a family friend from the center of Buenos Aires were spending the holidays
> with them on an enticing summer vacation in the countryside. When I said
> goodbye, I was presented with flowers and was told to report in Berlin that it
> is much better to live in Buenos Aires than in Berlin's rented buildings.

Fiorito is clearly not the virtuous capitalist that technical reformism (in discourses such as Selva's or Cibils') thought to have finally found, but the urban
and social effects of the economic process he leads cannot be ignored.

So, is the expansion progressive? The interesting thing about this moment
is that the different positions maintain a high degree of heterogeneity and
ambiguity, with blind spots, but with an important tension toward city models
that may lead the ambition of reform. Hegemann notices the same thing that
other travelers sensitive to the problems of reform, such as Adolfo Posada, had
warned about: there is no possibility of interpreting in a reformist key the articulation between grid expansion and "ant speculation" in Buenos Aires, without
understanding their mutual connection with processes of social ascent. From
the perspective of the idea of the "city of tenants," it was impossible for Socialists to consider it and to tune in with the actual trajectory of the new popular
sectors in the city, which brings us back to the specific theoretical limits posed
by the urban problem. For, if it cannot be denied that in politics and economics
the Socialists were extremely sensitive to the question of social ascent, at the

same time they emphasized large, centrally located workers' housing, and promoted an ideological defense of an open and politically democratic city with streets and squares traversed by mobilized masses, all of which raises a question that could easily be forgotten in the more "technical" proposals on the urban theory of expansion: What kind of society and city does restricting political responses to the self-satisfied verification of social ascent produce? We will see that in Socialism this question ends up affecting its relations with the institutions that expansion produces in society. What is certain is, for now, that the Civic Art background and the corresponding praise of the grid that underlies its theory of expansion is what saves Hegemann from the extreme nostalgia for the suburban "community" of the Garden City in his vision of Buenos Aires; what prevents a last step that will later be inevitable: the "naturalizing" transformation of the park, from the political articulator of civic and economic life that the grid favors to "green space." In fact, the political conjunction between grid and park that we saw in the Organic Project and that we still see in these vacillations between the *search for the center* and expansion, commanding the civic restructuring of the new city, will take on a completely different dimension in the theory of expansion of the thirties.

But between the late 1920s and the mid-1930s, it could be said that in the passage from the City Beautiful to the theory of expansion, and from support for specific interventions in the barrios to global and institutional management, local reformism gathered the instruments to criticize the 1898–1904 grid, proposing realistic transformations that did not cut back the publicity it had achieved for the suburbs, but that tried to enhance it qualitatively and broaden its scope to the regional sphere, seeking to make its promise of integration effective. To summarize: the Organic Project had shown that the public domain—vindicated by Socialists—and the grid—denounced by it—were mutually interdependent, and that their articulation was possible through the Plan: through a systematic public intervention capable of articulating zonal civic centers that would strengthen the relationship between the grid and the park in the process of expansion. In this framework, Hegemann ratifies the need to reunite *the search for the center* with regional expansion, showing that urban growth does not have as its only modality wild speculation, but that, precisely because it is a capitalist city, a fairer way of living was possible through public instruments of control: tax reform, plans, and building regulations that capitalize the expansion in urban and social terms.

If the reformism of the Organic Project had revealed the contradictions of socialist reformism, the cycle can be completed with a position like that of Hegemann. As he himself notes, the fact that in the three arms of metropolitan growth, to the south, west, and north, urbanization in blocks had already been consolidated, preventing the "classic" articulation between the theory of expansion and the model of the garden suburb. Neither concentrated city nor Garden City residential expansion: instead, it resulted in an expansion *by means of* representative public space. From here emerges a unitary reading of the metropolitan conglomerate that Socialism will increasingly be able to capitalize on in its interventions: thus, if technical reformism continues to have the most unitary vision of the urban process, progressively, political reformism is placed in a position to add new items to its agenda, to steer it toward different orientations and toward problems that are not contemplated by the state, even if it does not yet possess the instruments to offer answers or propose alternatives, but in the possibility of opening a horizon of potentialities that are difficult to ponder.

CHAPTER 8

"In the Shadow of the Beloved Barrios"

It could be said, then, that "socialist" Buenos Aires is the one that, hand in hand with the politicization of public space and the urban theory of expansion, goes from the barrio to the city and from the city to the metropolitan region. That is, the Buenos Aires evoked by della Paolera's phrase with which we began, which warns against the "fiction" of the current limits because the real city overflows them and demands an extended public policy. But the publicity of the barrio produces other representations of Buenos Aires, more in tune with Martínez Estrada's contrasting phrase: that of the border legions that advance upon Florida. We saw that from a political and urbanistic point of view the contradiction was apparent: both visions of Buenos Aires point to complementary impulses of the expansive reformist tension that seeks to tear down the borders of the city and society, outward into the territory and inward into society. But from the point of view of urban imaginaries, both representations of the expansive tension generate completely different cities, in which not only the place of barrios is modified, but also their role in the conformation of an expanded public space. The folkloric barrio of literature and tango, which appears simultaneously with the "cordial" and "progressive" neighborhood, will take the inverse path of its public-political conformation: an unmediated leap "from silence to nostalgia."[457] From the silence of the "spontaneous" production of the barrio cultural artifact, to the nostalgia for local color that confines it to an intimate territory of the city and society's infancy: *A la sombra de los barrios amados* (In the Shadow of the Beloved Barrios), as evoked by the title of a book by Raúl González Tuñón, one of the promoters of literary Buenos Aires, with a Proustian evocation that only ratifies the function of the barrio as a topic for intimist nostalgia.

The new "centrality" of the suburb produces, in principle, two Buenos Aires: the one that in the "cordial barrio" identifies the demand for progress and translates it into vindication and political demands of neighborhood advocacy and municipal reformism; and the "folkloric" Buenos Aires, which in the search for tradition and local color organizes new cultural products and new

---

[457] I owe to a work by Graciela Silvestri the expressive formula: "La mirada sobre el barrio: del silencio a la nostalgia," in *Cuadernos de Historia* 3 (September 1987).

modes for their consumption: tango, soccer, the literature of the margins. This is the Buenos Aires "of the barrio" that reacts against the effects that neighborhood publicity generates in the city, because in the 1920s we also witness the paradoxical results of the materialization of "the thousand subtle threads" of the grid: the universal communication that will give birth with all its cultural and urban power to the barrio as a public subject is the same that, strictly speaking, extends its death certificate, by homogenizing into the whole; the barrio can be born as a cultural subject when it ceases to be a geographic and social reality. Hence the consciously mystifying character of the cultural operation that produces it, as an explicit resistance to its disappearance.

As could not be otherwise, many of the actors in this conflict of representations were well aware of what was at stake: the following quote from socialist councilor Ángel Giménez, trying to establish a demarcation to refer to Nueva Pompeya as a modern barrio, is just one example of how, for many, the demands of "progress" and "tradition" did not exactly coincide:

> It is no longer the legendary barrio that has given rise to a certain literature of vagrants, delinquents, and *milonguitas* (loose women of tango), but a neighborhood of working-class, honest, and hard-working people who rightly demand the right to live in more humane conditions than those in which they currently find themselves, completely orphaned of any official protection.[458]

The explosive success of tango lyrics—to give the most substantial example—which since the early twenties produce their "modest mythology" cultivating that legend of bums, delinquents, and *milonguitas*, should make us think, however, that the real inhabitants of those cordial and progressive neighborhoods managed to recognize themselves in such flagrantly conflicting demands.[459]

As we anticipated, only the press will be able to make them coincide, giving them, moreover, equal stimulus. As a generic continuity with the tension present in the illustrated magazines between the celebration of modernization and the rescue of the picturesque, the new journalism of *Crítica* and *El Mundo* will be one of the few areas where the neighborhood as *project* and as *tradition* is produced simultaneously, making the dissonances between different representations coincide in the same textual space, the constitutive conflict

---

[458] In Municipalidad de la Ciudad de Buenos Aires, *Actas del Honorable Concejo Deliberante* (Buenos Aires), June 8, 1928.

[459] I take the characterization "modest mythology" from an article on tango by Blas Matamoro in the newspaper *La Opinión* (Buenos Aires), October 21, 1975, partially reproduced in José González y Cátulo Castillo, *Cancionero* (Buenos Aires: Torres Agüero Editor, 1977), 119.

of neighborhood *publicity* between its cordial progressivism and its necessary folkloric character for an effective literary processing. The differences with those magazines lie, in any case, in the character of this new folklorism: it is no longer a matter of showing, in the manner of *costumbrismo*, the past or urban marginality in its radical otherness; the new journalism and the new literature is made by writers and intellectuals who now also come "from the suburbs."[460]

But here again it is worth noting how diversified this production is in the very seat of literature:

> I am a man who ventured to write and even to publish some verses that commemorated two neighborhoods of this city that were very intertwined with his life [...].Two or three critics immediately pounced on me [...]. One treated me as a retrograde; another, with a deceitful pity, pointed out more picturesque neighborhoods than the ones luck afforded me and recommended the 56 streetcar that goes to Los Patricios instead of the 96 that goes to Urquiza; some attacked me in the name of the skyscrapers; others, in the name of the tin-can shantytowns.

Borges writes this in the mid-twenties, showing that discussions of the character of the barrios was far from being a phenomenon circumscribed to popular culture or to the "marginal" expressions of literary renovation.[461] The new neighborhoods were also the territory of dispute for the construction of a cultural tradition in the terms in which this task was undertaken by the literary and artistic avant-gardes. Borges's phrase further diversifies the map of the city, showing that there were not only confrontational representations between a generically progressive or generically folkloric suburb: the irruption of the barrio into the culture of the 1920s produced a plural map in which certain areas of the suburb had to correspond to certain cultural contents from which precise aesthetic programs could be derived. Thus, Borges's way of recalling the famous opposition between the Florida and Boedo "groups" suggests that it was not just a *boutade*:

> I would have preferred to be in the Boedo group, since I was writing about the Barrio Norte, the suburbs and the sadness and the sunsets. But I was

---

[460] Referring to this transformation in the literary field, Beatriz Sarlo has written: "The scene of the shores is no longer the literary place of the Others, considered as pure alienness, as a threat to social order, established morality, purity of blood, traditional customs; neither is it only about the Others to be understood and redeemed. They are Others who can form an "us" with the literary "I" of poets and intellectuals; they are close Others, if not *one's own*." See *Una modernidad periférica: Buenos Aires 1920 y 1930*, 180.

[461] "Profesión de fe literaria," in *El tamaño de mi esperanza* (1926) (Buenos Aires: Seix Barral, 1994), 127.

informed by one of the conspirators that I was already assigned to Florida's hosts and that it was too late to change sides.[462]

It indicates that the Florida/Boedo conflict should also be understood in the more existential terms of the east/west conflict, as Martínez Estrada put it, and not in the mere terms of the center/periphery conflict of literary cenacles or political-ideological sympathies: the cultural geography of the city is not only made up of different neighborhoods, but also of different views of "the neighborhood."[463]

This is the main novelty in the public production of the neighborhood: in the twenties and thirties the suburb appeared as a reservoir of competing cultural models that artists set out to recognize in order to identify with them and, at the same time, through that same recognition they constructed. Literary criticism has taken due note: there were few moments in Buenos Aires when culture referred so directly to urban figurations to define its programs and to put its conflicts into action, to the point that Leopoldo Marechal was able, several years later, to use the urban wandering of which he himself was the protagonist as the main resource for an ironic reading of the cultural polemics of the 1920s.[464] But if the city has been intelligently incorporated by literary criticism as a scenario that affected cultural production, here I am interested in giving that approach a twist: to try to see to what extent these representations of the city come into conflict with others that were simultaneously produced outside the literary sphere and how they operate as a whole in the very production of the neighborhood as a public space; above all, in the configuration of its roles in the process of metropolitanization. This is, perhaps, what we still need to begin

---

[462] Quoted by Horacio Salas, "El salto a la modernidad," preliminary study to *Revista Martín Fierro 1924–1927, Revista Martín Fierro 1924-1927, Edición facsimilar* (Buenos Aires: Fondo Nacional de las Artes, 1995), xii.

[463] In his work "Boedo y Florida" Adolfo Prieto quotes another significant phrase by Borges from 1927 that ratifies this role of the city in the literature of the twenties: "Demasiado se conversó de Boedo y Florida, escuelas inexistentes. Creo, sin embargo, en la correlación de la parroquia, de la sección electoral, del barrio, con la literatura." (Too much was said about Boedo and Florida, non-existent schools. I believe, however, in the correlation between the parish, the electoral section, the barrio, and literature). Cited in *Estudios de literatura argentina* (Buenos Aires: Editorial Galerna, 1969), 43.

[464] See the hilarious excursion to Saavedra in *Adan Buenosayres* (1948). Adolfo Prieto, in *Estudios de literatura argentina*, analyzed the role that "collective excursions to the suburbs" played in the avant-garde groups, recalling the way Raúl Scalabrini Ortiz had presented himself in the introduction to *El hombre que está solo y espera*; but it is Beatriz Sarlo who has taken this approach further, analyzing in several of her books the importance of the city in the literary and cultural production of the avant-garde. See especially Sarlo, *Una modernidad periférica* and *La imaginación técnica. Sueños modernos de la cultura argentina* (Buenos Aires: Nueva Visión, 1992).

to see: in a city like Buenos Aires, without traditions or prestigious or pictur-esque geographies, the barrio could exist as a product of cultural violence, in a process that articulates its emergence and apogee as a political reality and as a cultural myth, as a product of a new mass culture and as an avant-garde project.

1. The "Crooked Barrio" versus the "Cordial Barrio"

Villa Crespo!... crooked Barrio,
the one of narrow streets
and poorly made little houses
cute because you were ugly,
[...]
You were taken in by the architecture
of the municipal plan.[465]

–Alberto Vacarezza, *El conventillo de la paloma*, 1929

In his prognoses on the future of the myth of the barrio in Parque Patricios, recently converted "to decency," we noted that Enrique González Tuñón was one of those who early and most lucidly recognized the need for an operation of mystification to culturally produce the barrio: Tuñón anticipates that the neighborhood can be built as a tradition only once the obstacles to its mod-ernization have been overcome. What he does not say, but what soon becomes clear, is that this cultural production will have to try to undermine all the con-stitutive characteristics of the "progressive" neighborhood.

Tuñón's awareness of the mystifying operation can be seen in his irony—in his journalistic articles, though not in many of his stories, where he cultivates pathos. Take for example, his ironic take of the famous Café Japonés, where a good part of his stories take place (and where a good part of the gatherings of the writers "from the margins" were organized), to which he applies with-out euphemism the category of "mystifying café" (for Tuñón there are also the "bourgeois café" and "absurd café"). In the mystifying café, "everything is adulterated," starting with its own geography, since according to the needs of Tuñón's prose it is placed alternatively in Boedo, Parque Patricios, or Nueva Pompeya.[466] But, above all, Tuñón's awareness of the operation can be seen in

---

[465] "¡Villa Crespo!... Barrio reo, / el de las calles estrechas / y las casitas mal hechas / que eras lindo por lo feo, / [...] / Te engrupió la arquitectura / del plano municipal." Alberto Vacarezza, "El conventillo de la Paloma," a comedy in one act and three scenes that premiered at the Teatro Nacional on April 5, 1929, in *Teatro I* (Buenos Aires: Corregidor, 1993), 273–75.

[466] *Crítica* (Buenos Aires), July 17, 1925; series of notes continued on July 19 and 20. I have to thank Sylvia Saítta for introducing me to these articles. The Café Japonés, later

the way he seeks to modulate, in his journalistic and literary texts, different forms for the barrio, as in an exercise of trial and error: the "Parque Patricios" that in *Caras y Caretas* is cordial, naive, humble, and regenerated through work; in the series of notes he writes for *Crítica* it is the mysterious territory of an anarchizing bohemia; in the glosses of tangos, it is the bitter suburb in which failed *malevos* coexist with failed immigrants against the ghostly background of the Corrales Viejos; and in some stories of *El alma de las cosas inanimadas* (The Soul of Inanimate Things), it is the picture of misery of social denunciation.[467]

A few years later we will find even more radical oscillations in the etchings of Roberto Arlt, in which the barrio may embody anything from the space of social desolation present in the notes of "Buenos Aires se queja" (Buenos Aires Complains), to the sordid ring in which the fight for a social ascent without horizons is played out; from the magical realm of "*mafioso* charm" and "*mistonga* sweetness" (pitiable/poor sweetness), with its "*atorranta* little houses" (lazy little houses), and its "souls that only know the rhythm of tango and 'I love you,'" to the petty universe of mediocrity and tedium marking the daily life of the popular sectors, with their shoddy morals and their small worlds of deceit and hypocrisy.[468] In addition to the oscillations, it is interesting to identify in this late Arltian record a first prototypical form of condemnation of the "cordial" and "progressive barrio" as the social and cultural expression of the new middle class. With more or fewer contradictions, with a greater degree of elitism or radical criticism, many writers cultivated it along the lines initiated by Roberto Gache in 1916 in his *Glosario de la farsa urbana* (Glossary of Urban Farce) when this type of neighborhood was just emerging as a social reality: it is the "*matero* (*mate*-drinking) and progressive" Palermo that Borges sees hurrying "toward inanity" in Carriego's *La canción del barrio* ("Palermo conducted itself in a God-fearing manner, and it was a place of genteel poverty, like any other mixed community of immigrants and native Argentines"); and it is also, at times, to return to González Tuñón's Parque Patricios, "the monotonous regularity [of its] environment."[469]

Another operation that we notice early on in Tuñón is to ratify, in all cases, the local peculiarity that picturesque representations demand. The barrio can occupy a *place* in the city as long as it assumes a picturesqueness that will become

---

called Canadian (now Homero Manzi), is on Boedo and San Juan, in the heart of the Boedo neighborhood.

[467] See "Parque Patricios," *Caras y Caretas* (Buenos Aires), December 12, 1925; *Crítica* 17, July 19 and 20, 1925; *El alma de las cosas inanimadas* (Buenos Aires: Gleizer, 1927). A selection of his texts for *Crítica* in 1926 is published in *Tangos* (1926) (Buenos Aires: Editorial Borocaba, 1953).

[468] Oscar Terán has explored these oscillations in Arlt's vision of the city in "Modernos intensos en los veintes," *Prismas* 1 (1997): 91–103. I take from him the quote from *Aguafuertes*.

[469] Borges's phrase is from *Evaristo Carriego: A Book About Old-time Buenos Aires*, 82; that of Tuñón from "El hombre de los velorios," in *El alma de las cosas inanimadas*, 62.

the second line of condemnation of the "cordial barrio," since it needs to distance itself from its integrative ambition: the invention of a tradition implies the need to cut out a geographic-cultural space for the neighborhood, against the backdrop of growing urban homogenization. Picturesqueness claims a local autonomy that the inclusive structure of Buenos Aires, with its grid and developed transportation system, hinders. This is precisely what will lead those who celebrate the neighborhood's peculiarity and its "past" to settle on the few "irregularities" that progressivism was trying to erase: from the heading of the first series of notes he writes about "Parque Patricios," Tuñón needs to stress that "In the barrio there are those who don't know Avenida de Mayo!" The exclamation mark shows the awareness of artifice: in 1925 Buenos Aires will only admit such a characterization as a picturesque feature. But in pointing out its artificial necessity, Tuñón again marches ahead, showing that the activation of the myth is practically simultaneous to the public appearance of the barrios as "progressive" neighborhoods: when in the thirties the unequal commercial competition of the center, favored by the ease of communications, forces intense advertising campaigns to preserve parochial clients, localist appeals will necessarily go through the updating of foundational myths, seeking to reinforce identity barriers that are increasingly necessary, but increasingly difficult to recognize. That process will stretch the neighborhood advocacy movement's discourse in such paradoxical ways as to make the Villa Crespo newspaper, appropriately called *El Progreso*, state in 1934: "Today the streets are a hell of traffic, the sidewalks a Babel; friendship has disappeared, drowned by the selfishness of Mercantilism and the Machine."[470] From the urban point of view, the need for more stable identity barriers (*differentiation*) translates into a condemnation of the "cordial barrio" that logically reverts into a new and unexpected reason for repudiating the regular grid of the "municipal plan": contradicting the very meaning of the neighborhood's formation, González Tuñón describes a "Parque Patricios" crossed by "arbitrary streets that rejected the established symmetrical layout, refusing to grid themselves."[471] The social and urban irregularity, the peculiarities, now appear as an essential advantage to give body to identity.

César Tiempo once characterized González Tuñón's contribution to journalism by saying that his entrance into *Crítica*:

> revolutionized the national journalistic style. The news conquered the fourth dimension; the suburb took possession of the center; the municipal and thick prose of the gazetteers became luminous and variegated;

[470] It is an article by Ricardo Dulac in the extra edition of *El Progreso* (Villa Crespo), 1934. Luciano de Privitellio has shown that localist appeals in the thirties are linked with commercial competition with the center: "Inventar el barrio: Boedo 1936–1942," in *Cuadernos del Ciesal* 2–3, (1994).
[471] In *Crítica*, July 17, 1925.

metaphor took citizenship in the world of information. People began to write like Enrique, to make reports in Enrique's way, to give hierarchy to tango, whose first cultured exegete was Enrique.[472]

Beyond the accuracy of the praise—in the twenties the newspapers are populated by chroniclers coming from literature, and the cultured exegesis of tango is generalized enough to make it difficult to establish precedence—what is interesting is the linkages that Tuñón embodies for his contemporaries between new journalism, avant-garde literature, the neighborhood, and tango, entirely modern products associated in the search for a local tradition. And at this point it can be said that Tuñón presents us with one of the first literary artifacts in which the relationship appears complete: the commentaries on tangos that he published in 1926 in *Crítica*. They are short stories, each associated with a tango lyric, but in which Tuñón produces a factory of archetypes and a space of experimentation to create an urban and social framework that returns to tango, as it will increasingly hegemonize his lyrics as a representation of the "barrio." In the multiplying space of the newspaper page, through narratives that could also be celebrated by some of his fellow members of the *martinfierrista* avant-garde, Tuñón amplifies the meaning of those tangos that in the 1920s begin to design a mythic neighborhood, granting the dozens of tangos that do not directly deal with it the same setting and the same protagonists for their stories of love and loneliness.[473]

The suburb leaves behind the moment of *costumbrista* alienation, and the picturesqueness that the press had been unsuccessfully seeking in Buenos Aires to feed the urban chronicle with its main fuel, local color, which now seems to be embodied in the mixture of bohemia, social misery, and tango mythology that some artists and intellectuals offer as a "typical" product of the new suburban neighborhood. The collaboration between them and the press in the emergence of this cultural quarry far exceeds the space of the barrio chronicle or the tango commentaries found in the pages of the newspapers: Cátulo Castillo recalled, for example, how through the initiatives of the newspaper *Crítica* in the 1920s the República de La Boca and the República de Boedo were born, with painter Quinquela Martín and José González Castillo as respective presidents, and how Botana's newspaper fostered an artificial antagonism between the two to feed the picturesque chronicle.[474]

Castillo's memory, in turn, brings together two very different types of picturesque neighborhood construction: La Boca and Boedo, both fundamental to tango mythology. As Graciela Silvestri has well demonstrated, La Boca is the

---

[472] In "Cómo conocí a Enrique González Tuñón," prologue to E. González Tuñón, *Camas desde un peso* (1932) (Buenos Aires: Editorial Deucalion, 1956), 9.
[473] See *Tangos* (the excerpts selected in the book are a small part of those published in *Crítica*).
[474] See José González and Cátulo Castillo, *Cancionero*, 124.

only sector of Buenos Aires that offers from very early on a surplus of pictur-esque urban landscape: the river and the port, the isolation from the city, the first immigrant concentration with its corresponding proliferation of cultural and political initiatives of socialist and anarchist circles had already generated by the mid-nineteenth century an urban, social, and cultural space that is quite peculiar, which allows us to understand that at the beginning of this century an artistic bohemia found its own *rive gauche* on the banks of the Riachuelo and that the cultural and institutional work of Quinquela Martín later produced the only note of color (and in this case it is more than a metaphor) in Buenos Aires. If in Buenos Aires the *barrio* is an imaginary construction, La Boca is the only place where it has been able to draw on actual facts that go beyond romantic voluntarism.[475]

Boedo, on the other hand, is one of the clearest examples of neighborhoods produced on a territory completely stripped of attributes. Boedo is one of the many neighborhoods baptized after the occupation of the grid, as a result of an arbitrary and imprecise cut on the regularity of the urban plan and on the reg-ularity of the social composition of a larger area, Almagro (being on the city's central plateau, in this area there are not even "*bajos*" or differentiated spaces). It is one of those neighborhoods that is not produced around the pre-exis-tences of the "traditional" city, like Flores or Belgrano; nor by an outstanding urban event, like the park that rearticulates San Cristóbal Sur and gives origin to Parque Patricios; nor even by a speculative project that conceives it from the beginning as a unit, like Villa Devoto; but from a specific center or a commer-cial street, in this case Boedo Street, in which the neighborhood "identity" is exhausted, since a few blocks away from that place it is practically impossible, even for its own inhabitants, to differentiate it from other neighborhoods or to recognize its limits. It is a completely nondescript neighborhood, in the sense that its urban landscape is identical to that of the entire west-southwest fringe of the city; a random portion of the most homogeneous grid sprawl: an "inven-tion," strictly speaking.[476] If we saw that the cultural artifact barrio as public space can be formed from a double process of *differentiation* and *generalization*, in Boedo the differentiation is a truly uncertain operation; and yet, at the same time, it results in a *neighborhood*, one of the most defined in *porteño* culture.

---

[475] Graciela Silvestri, *El color del río. Historia cultural del paisaje del Riachuelo* (Buenos Aires: Editorial de la Universidad de Quilmes, 2003).

[476] As we saw in a previous note, this is how Privitellio titles his work on Boedo: "Inventar el barrio," focused on the thirties. Up to this point I have been careful to use the notion of "invention": in Argentine urban culture it is rather difficult to find something that has not been invented and, above all—as I am trying to show—with full awareness of the operation (we saw it from the beginning with Sarmiento); anyway, it is relevant in this case, as a way of distinguishing less differentiated neighborhoods such as Boedo, from a neighborhood with the tradition of La Boca.

The role that tango and football have played since the thirties in the ratifi-cation of this cultural invention is well-known: the lyrics of Homero Manzi and the late identification of San Lorenzo *de Almagro* with Boedo, with the ensuing celebration of one of the main barrio "classics" with Huracán, from the neigh-boring Parque Patricios. But already in the 1920s there are a number of cultural initiatives that will concentrate and gather in Boedo the representations of what Sarlo has defined as the novel margins of an expanding intellectual field: "writ-ers of immigrant origin, neighborhood residence, and culture in transition, if compared to the more homogeneous literary culture that characterized Argen-tina until the nineteenth century."[477] That margin is formed by a pleiad of jour-nalists, playwrights, poets, painters, and sculptors who were going to give the neighborhood the cultural base on which the "popular universities," the "pop-ular theaters," the "popular libraries," the *cineclubs*, the *peñas*, and the dozens of neighborhood newspapers would multiply in the 1920s. And we are already discussing a much wider "margin" than that which fits in the history of art or literature, because for every Enrique González Tuñón who finds in the barrio a subject for literary projection, there will be dozens of minor authors who, in contrast, in literature or art find a social projection in the barrio. They are the ones who will sustain the flourishing of neighborhood culture in that formida-ble expansion of culture as a popular value, a touching culture, of as good inten-tions as poor results, which will be expected above all to produce a naturalistic evocation of its own mythicized condition: that will be one of the guarantees of the success of a tango lyric or a theatrical performance in the neighborhood.

Perhaps because it brought together some artists and some initiatives of greater notoriety, Boedo was the epitome of that marginal production, a syn-thetic incarnation of all the new neighborhood culture beyond its geographical location or thematic definition. In this sense, José González Castillo, as well as its "president," is one of its most significant figures, because he is one of those who early on carried out the double function of building the neighborhood as a topic and of building in the neighborhood the cultural institutions capable of nurturing it. He was a playwright at the height of theatrical production, a tango lyricist at the beginning of tango song, and a pioneer explorer of the combina-tions between the two genres. Tango histories underline the fact that the first sung tango, "Mi noche triste" by Pascual Contursi, was included in 1918 in the *sainete* (comic sketch) "Los dientes del perro" (The Dog's Teeth) by González Castillo and Weisbach. A scriptwriter in the beginnings of cinematography, the journalist and poet González Castillo settled in Boedo after walking as a bohe-mian around the country and after having been expelled to Chile as an anarchist in the years of the centenary. Once in Boedo, he promoted a great part of the institutions that in the twenties and thirties gave it its cultural aura: the Universi-dad Popular, the Pacha Camac club, the gatherings at the Biarritz tearoom. And

---

[477] Sarlo, *Una modernidad periférica*, 179.

it is interesting to note the weight that the association bohemian-anarchist had in representations of the neighborhood, at a time when anarchism had practically disappeared as a political force. The barrio cultural artifact produced by this bohemian neighborhood is the last refuge of a romantic anarchism that, once again, proposes an image completely displaced from the "cordial barrio": it is a neighborhood of vagabonds, poets, inventors, and café philosophers. A representative capacity whose imaginary force is the only explanation for the adoption of the name Boedo by the writers who sought to oppose in the 1920s a literature of social commitment to the experiments of the Florida avant-garde, a literature of the margins to the literature of the center. As de Privitellio rightly states, it is a recurrent error in the history of literature to suppose, instead, that the Boedo neighborhood was in itself the engine of such social concerns, as a working-class factory or marginal neighborhood: Boedo is *from its birth* a typical middle-class, "progressive" neighborhood, and Boedo Avenue—"the Florida of the suburb," according to Dante Linyera, a member of the journalistic bohemia and one of the main builders of the neighborhood myth—a thriving commercial street.[478]

José González Castillo's lyrics stylize from very early for tango the description of an archetypal neighborhood from a synthetic enumeration of essential motifs: they seem like scenographic notes to represent in a *sainete* or a film the verses of Evaristo Carriego—elevated by this bohemia, but also by Borges, as "the first poet of the suburb." So, it is in *Sobre el pucho* (On the fag, or On the spot) from 1922, with music by his then very young son Cátulo:

> An alley in Pompeya
> and a lantern silvering the mud,
> And there's an ruffian who smokes
> and a little organ grinding a tango.

Motifs that would continue to be elaborated by Pascual Contursi with *Ventanita de arrabal* in 1927, by Cátulo himself in almost all his work written with Aníbal Troilo, and, finally, by Homero Manzi—even with direct quotations, in which the mixture of González Castillo with Carriego appears as a tribute to the founding fathers—closing with these constants the cycle that goes from the "narrative" tango of the twenties to the "poetic" variant of the forties. But, in the same way that irony works in González Tuñón, it could be said that in the procedures of a tango like *Silbando*, from 1923, the consciousness with which González Castillo worked the different planes of the myth he was producing becomes explicit. *Silbando* clearly differentiates two neighborhoods: the one of the "descriptive" stanzas in the "scenographic" line we mentioned:

> With its flickering light, a lantern

---

[478] De Privitellio, "Inventar el barrio: Boedo 1936–1942."

in the shadow flickers,
and in a hallway
Is a lover
talking to his love

and that of the "narrative" stanzas, in which stages the also archetypal story of fatal love and of the deception that leads to the mortal duel of two men over a woman:

A whimper and a mortal scream
and, shining in the shadows,
the glitter
with which a knife
gives its fatal slash[479]

Both "barrios" are brought together only by the artifice of tango, made evident in the continuous background of the "languid lament [...] of a monotonous accordion." Also, the music, by Cátulo Castillo and Sebastián Piana—later creators of *Tinta roja*, another fundamental tango in the production of the neighborhood myth—subtly emphasizes this contrast between two universes, creating completely different climates for each scene, between the air of a whistled *milonga*, gentle and sweet, and the dramatic counterpoint of the energetic tango.

And the fact that the action of this tango takes place in Barracas al Sur, finally, with all three authors fervent followers of the Boedo myth, points out another peculiarity of the tango production of the barrio that already appeared insinuated in Cátulo Castillo's quote on *Crítica*: the city of literature and tango, evil or romantic, bohemian or libertarian, assembles a circuit that brings together La Boca, Dock Sud, and Barracas with Patricios, Boedo, and Pompeya, that is, the "old south" and the "new south" that the municipal model of the "cordial barrio," as a humble, decent, and progressive neighborhood tried to separate in its moral map. José González Castillo, the Tuñóns, Olivari, Arlt himself, are going to literally work on that circuit, as the circuit of artistic and tango bohemia, but they are also going to traverse it daily, building a universe of images in which intellectual and social relations are confused with literature itself. Guillermo Facio Hebequer, one of the main "social engravers" of the Artistas del Pueblo group, linked to the writers of Boedo, shows how a marginal circuit of

---

[479] The original Spanish stanzas: "Un callejón en Pompeya / y un farolito plateando el fango, / y allí un malevo que fuma / y un organito moliendo un tango"; "Con su luz mortecina, un farol / en la sombra parpadea, / y en un zaguán / está un galán / hablando con su amor"; "Un quejido y un grito mortal /y, brillando entre las sombras, / el relumbrón / con que un facón / da su tajo fatal..." The lyrics of *Sobre el pucho* and *Silbando*, according to the copyright of Editorial DO RE MI FA, as they appear in José González y Cátulo Castillo, *Cancionero*, 32–35.

artists had developed—a very novel one in a city in which, until very recently, everything took place in a few central blocks—that connected the entire southern and southwestern cordon of the city through precise relationships: houses, clubs, and "stimulus" societies.[480] A radical novelty that was to show its political face dramatically in the Tragic Week: for the first time an event of such magnitude took place completely outside the traditional circuits of political protest that we had seen consolidate toward the centenary; the workers organized their shocking protest procession from the Riachuelo to the Chacarita (where they buried the comrades killed in the repression), establishing a "marginal" route ritually punctuated in union or suburban resistance homes.[481]

These are then some of the cultural, social, and political reasons why in the Buenos Aires of the 1920s the margins became visible to the center. But, in reality, there is another very direct reason, that is recurrently pointed out: for, if in a number of expressions it had been possible to set up an autonomous marginal circuit—and that was the way to appropriate a "central" place behind the center's back—the urban imaginary of the artistic and tango bohemia is going to place the center of all its marginal universe in Corrientes Street, very close to the very heart of the traditional city. Corrientes Street, that magical territory of urban nightlife in the twenties and thirties, territory of the cultural crossroads celebrated by authors like Tuñón, Arlt, or Scalabrini Ortiz as an area of metropolitan intensity and bohemian adventure, becomes the displaced heart of this new "marginal" city.[482] While reformism seeks to capitalize on the new political "centrality" of the suburbs by claiming a displacement of the traditional center toward the new neighborhoods, "marginal" literature carries out the inverse movement, ratifying a "central" heart for neighborhood culture: it is also the vindication of a plebeian outpost (that of Martínez Estrada's "frontier neighborhoods") over the constituted values of the city. Although, from many points of view, for that same imaginary it is a paradoxical center, not only because of all the oppositions that could be set up between the barrio and Corrientes Street, starting with its geographical location, but because tango will formalize in that opposition, at the same time, its first

81, 82

---

[480] See Miguel Ángel Molina and Diana Wechsler, "La ciudad moderna en la serie 'Buenos Aires' de Guillermo Facio Hebequer," *Demócrito* I, no. 2 (October 1990). It should be noted that the two articles written by Enrique González Tuñón about neighborhoods in *Caras y Caretas* are the one about Parque Patricios, already mentioned, and another about La Boca: "Una mañana de sol. *Caras y Caretas* en la Boca del Riachuelo," *Caras y Caretas* (Buenos Aires), December 5, 1925.

[481] John R. Hébert, "The Tragic Week of January, 1919, in Buenos Aires: Background, Events, Aftermaths" (PhD diss., Georgetown University, 1972).

[482] See Oscar Terán, "Modernos intensos en los veintes," and Sylvia Saítta, "Introducción" to Roberto Arlt, *Aguafuertes porteñas. Buenos Aires, vida cotidiana* (Buenos Aires: Alianza, 1993). See also José Luis Romero, "Buenos Aires: una historia," in *Historia Integral Argentina*, vol. 7 (Buenos Aires: CEAL, 1972).

The barrio and downtown:

Figure 81. Unknown photographer, *Chubut and Triunvirato Streets*, 1935. Dirección de Paseos, Museo de la Ciudad, Buenos Aires.

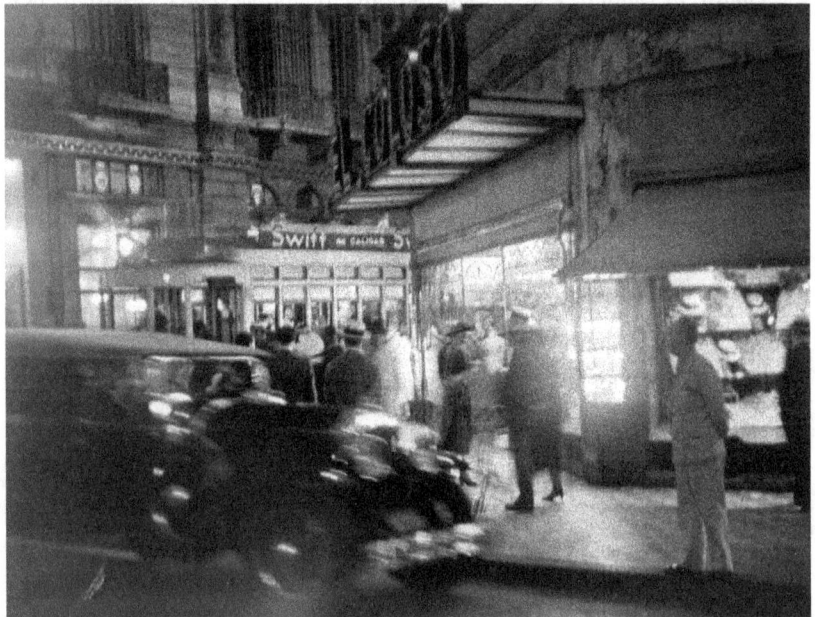

Figure 82. Horacio Coppola, *Corrientes at 900*, 1936. Horacio Coppola Archive. The street was the center of *porteño* cultural life.

urban-moral split between the lost paradise of the "suburb" and the perversion of the "center," of which the *milonguitas* would be its favorite victims.

From that first split that appears very early on in its lyrics, tango will deepen, as Noemí Ulla has pointed out, on the topic of the neighborhood as a refuge, in the correlation barrio-home-mother-childhood-shelter, that "suburban goodness" that, it could be claimed, is the only point where tango is reconciled with certain motifs of the "cordial barrio."[483] However, here appears the last front of contestation, perhaps the most radical, to the neighborhood that we already saw erected as local public space; because the cordiality of this "barrio refuge" of tango will lie forever in an intimate, familiar quality, built of childhood memories (personal and of the city), the idealization of a community space that will seek to recreate everything that the modern neighborhood had to displace to become the public, civic, and urban artifact of the twenties. Both barrios are so incompatible that tango will quickly describe the complete itinerary that leads it from the description of *its* neighborhood as a pre-modern myth, to nostalgia for the loss of what it never had, and from nostalgia to the repudiation of modernization that, within the very narrative logic of the barrio myth, would have ended up destroying it. Unlike literature, which will be able to maintain a certain ironic distance from its own mythological production, tango must complete the rejection of modernization of which it is the most genuine product.

It is the itinerary that goes from the stripped-down description of *Silbando* to the desolate evocation of *Tinta roja* ("¿Dónde estará mi arrabal? / ¿quién se robó mi niñez?"; Where is my *arrabal*? / Who stole my childhood?"), and from there to Manzi's lament for "pesadumbre de barrios que han cambiado" (the dejection of barrios that have changed); but it is not a diachronic itinerary: as happened with the literary production on the barrio, some tango lyrics show that the conflict was posed almost from the very emergence of the progressive neighborhood and tango song. For example, already in 1926, a lyric laments the modernization of Nueva Pompeya:

> Alsina Bridge, yesterday my bosom,
> the avenue caught up with you in one swipe...
> Old Bridge, solitary and confident,
> you are the mark that
> on the forehead of progress
> has left the rebellious suburb,
> that succumbed in its wake.[484]

---

[483] Noemí Ulla, *Tango, rebelión y nostalgia* (1967) (Buenos Aires: CEAL, 1982).
[484] "Puente Alsina, que ayer fuera mi regazo, / de un zarpazo la avenida te alcanzó... / Viejo Puente, solitario y confidente, / sos la marca que, en la frente, / al progreso le ha dejado / el suburbio rebelado / que a su paso sucumbió." *Puente Alsina*, lyrics and

Still with greater anti-modernizing clarity, identifying the enemies of the barrio in the "municipal plane" and the immigrant in social ascent that had precisely formed it, Alberto Vacarezza, as we anticipated, makes his character recite about Villa Crespo in the *sainete* titled *El conventillo de la Paloma* of 1929:

> Villa Crespo!... crooked *Barrio*,
> the one of narrow streets
> and poorly made little houses
> you who was nice 'cause you were ugly.
> [...]
> You're not what you used to be
> Villa Crespo of my dreams,
> other laws and other owners
> widened your sidewalks,
> and with uncouth hands
> the ragged Italian builder
> nailed in the blooming holes of
> scaffolding the networks
> and with rising walls
> your tone began changing.
> What do you want with the pose
> of your tents and your streets,
> your cinemas and your coffees,
> if you got caught in the paint?
> You were taken in by the architecture
> of the municipal plan...[485]

Despite the rejection of the modern universe of the middle-class barrio that so many lyrics like these make explicit, it is possible to see a structural connection between the emergence of the tango song and that of the "progressive" neighborhood. The appearance of lyrics in tango has been analyzed as a direct product of the emergence of the new popular barrio public rising to middle-class status, since they would have produced a "tidying up" of tango that would have made it suitable for massification, a process of which the industrialization of

---

music by Benjamín Tagle Lara, in Eduardo Romano, ed., *Las letras del Tango. Antología cronológica 1900–1980*, fifth edition (Rosario: Editorial Fundación Ross, 1995), 100.

[485] "¡Villa Crespo!... Barrio reo, / el de las calles estrechas / y las casitas mal hechas / que eras lindo por lo feo. / [...] / Ya no sos lo que eras antes / Villa Crespo de mis sueños, / otras leyes y otros dueños / te ensancharon las veredas, / y con manos chapuceras / el grébano constructor / clavó en los güecos en flor / del andamiaje las redes / y levantando paredes / te fue cambiando el color. / ¿Qué querés con la postura / de tus tiendas y tus llecas, / tus cinemas y tus fecas, / si te agarró la pintura? / Te engrupió la arquitectura / del plano municipal..." Vacarezza, "El conventillo de la Paloma," 273–75.

records and the emergence of the celebrity singer are a part.[486] The very thematization of the barrio in the lyrics would be another sign of that transformation. But I think it is necessary to emphasize the paradoxical way in which
the thematization undermined the foundations on which the middle classes
built their social and urban progress: tango, as a key product of modern urban
culture in Buenos Aires, closes the circle of the contestation of the modern
neighborhood as a product of urban integration and social ascent. The tango
barrio, then, that of "marginal" literature and anarchizing bohemia, concludes
in a full-scale negation of the "cordial barrio" by contesting its class-ridden
pettiness, its ambitions for social climbing, the monotonous regularity of its
integrative grid with the dissolution of local peculiarities that its universality,
and especially its modernity and progressive aspirations, entail. That is why it
can form a circuit completely antagonistic to the one proposed with the "model
working-class barrio" and why it can offer it a "past" that denies its entire history and is ambiguously related to its "project." As Borges pointed out, surely
that was the mission of tango: to give the Argentines, to give the barrio one
might say here, an apocryphal past.[487]

2. Barrio and Pampa: A New Reading of the Grid

It was really a city block in my district—Palermo.
A whole square block, but set down in open country.[488]
        –Jorge Luis Borges, "The Mythical Founding of Buenos Aires," 1929

But there is no critical intent in Borges's definition of tango; that was not the
issue of his polemic with tango song: no one was as aware as he was of the
importance of an apocryphal past for the constitution of a modern culture in
Buenos Aires. His quarrel—with tango song as well as, symmetrically, with *criollismo*—was about the most appropriate or effective motifs to achieve it, and
he may have been the figure who most programmatically insisted on that objective: all his poetic and essayistic production of the twenties—from *Fervor de*

---

[486] For example, see José Gobello and Eduardo Stilman, *Las letras de tango de Villoldo a
Borges* (Buenos Aires: Editorial Brújula, 1966), who claim that the lyrics allow the diffusion
"entre amplios sectores de clase media, para los cuales la lubricidad de la danza era motivo
de inquietud" (12); or Eduardo Romano, "Prologue" to *Las letras del Tango*, who speaks
of the "adecentamiento" (8), perhaps recalling Borges's famous text, "A History of the
Tango," included in *Selected Non-Fictions* (New York: Viking, 1999), in which he refers to
"the deplorable gentrification of rough and rundown neighborhoods," 399.
[487] "A History of the Tango," 397.
[488] "Fue una manzana entera y en mi barrio: en Palermo. / Una manzana entera pero en
mitá del campo." From *Cuaderno San Martín* (1929), in *Selected poems*, 53.

Buenos Aires to *Evaristo Carriego*—was destined to produce an "epic of Buenos Aires," that "literary feast that can be believed: are not the national theater and the tangos and our feelings in the face of the heartbreaking vision of the suburbs foreshadowing it?"[489] Continuing the master line of Argentine literature that had addressed the need for an epic to condense the essential values of nationality, Borges obsessively poses in those years the questions that derive from that task, proposes his own motifs and traditions, his landscapes, producing as a result of that search what has been defined as "avant-garde urban criollismo."[490] As this definition rightly points out, the novelty introduced by Borges is a radical change in the scenario of those searches, and here again the neighborhood occupies a central place, although it will be, by programmatic necessity, another neighborhood, and another circuit of neighborhoods completely different from that of the artistic tango bohemia.

The myth that Borges proposes to produce dispenses with all picturesqueness; he finds in the barrio a characteristic of Buenos Aires that allows him to locate, to give form to the double search for synthesis typical of a sector of the *porteño* avant-garde: the synthesis between modernity and tradition, and between the city and the pampas. His circuit can therefore reach from Palermo and Saavedra to Boedo, passing through Villa Urquiza and Bajo Flores, but he would never accept La Boca as part of his suburb—with its garish colors and its "rezongona quejumbre itálica" (groaning Italian grumbling)—and, even less, center it on Corrientes Street—with "the insolence" of its "false lights." Faced with the bohemian picturesque, Borges opposes a stripped suburb, that of "Buenos Aires' unintentional beauty spots" that he finds in the houses with straight, blind walls, in the legends of the carriages, in the light of the sunsets, in the straight rows of trees on the straight streets, in the ghostly memory of the primordial confrontation of two men on a corner—a confrontation that, unlike that of *Silbando* and the tango song, will always dispense with the sentimental motive: it is a matter of courage.[491]

Now, from the point of view of the literary production of the barrio, his perspective is also opposed to the pro-advocacy progressivism of the "cordial barrio"—that "decent, innocent thing"—and also, although for different reasons, affects its main quality as a public space: the barrio is, for Borges, the space of a "wide intimacy," a sphere that actualizes origins and the feeling of eternity, the

---

[489] "Invectiva contra el arrabalero," in *El tamaño de mi esperanza*, 125.

[490] Sarlo has developed this illuminating definition in several texts during the eighties; her most global vision appears in *Borges: A Writer on the Edge* (London; New York: Verso, 1993).

[491] The quotations are respectively from "Fechas," *El idioma de los argentinos* (1928) (Buenos Aires: Seix Barral, 1994), 116; from the poem "Ciudad," in *Fervor de Buenos Aires* (Buenos Aires, 1923); and from *Evaristo Carriego: A Book about Old-time Buenos Aires*, 89.

Figure 83. Horacio Coppola, *Corner of Jean Jaurés and Paraguay*, 1936. Horacio Coppola Archive. In 1929 Coppola photographed the same corner for one of the images illustrating the 1930 edition of Jorge Luis Borges's *Evaristo Carriego*.

Figure 84. Horacio Coppola, *Barrio Saavedra*, 1936. Horacio Coppola Archive.

existential place of production of social and cultural identity ("This reference to the neighborhood is just as personal, helpful, and unifying in the parish of La Piedad as it is in Saavedra"). That is why he highlights, in *Carriego*, lines in which the poet converses with a street showing his "secret, innocent possession."[492] However, there are other elements of Borges's neighborhood that generate a relation of greater ambiguity with different aspects of the suburb that, in those same years, are involved in the emergence of a metropolitan public space.

In the first place, there is the material quality of his representations. Horacio Coppola has narrated a very significant anecdote of the suburban walks he took with Borges in the 1920s: "It was interesting, (his) taste for the skin, so to speak, of Buenos Aires. For example, walking by a place where there was a wall, a plastered and peeling wall, there was a moment when Borges put his hands like this, and felt it, like this, as if it were something alive."[493] From this point of view, Coppola's own presence on the walk is even more significant than the anecdote: a modernist photographer, Coppola portrayed the images that inspired Borges, and Borges not only thought it important to incorporate two of them in the first edition of *Evaristo Carriego*, but also planned a complete book about the city—*Descubrimiento de Buenos Aires*—organized as a photographic tour.[494] Unlike the mythologizing production of the literary and tango bohemia, which constructs a neighborhood of archetypes necessarily distanced from the urban and social reality that has been shaping the neighborhood, Borges produces a mythological neighborhood from the gathering and poetic empowerment of a series of objects existing in the real neighborhood: that is why he would have wished, in the end, to be in the Boedo group, because in that area of the city, and not in Florida, he can find the same poetic-urban *objects* as in Palermo or Villa Urquiza, the same remnants of the city mixed with the pampas, the same houses, the same streets, the same sky. In any case, his provocation against the classic way of presenting the Boedo/Florida polemic consists in turning an aesthetic-ideological polemic into a topological choice. It is a provocation that aims to highlight the mythologized character of bohemian and humanitarian Boedo in order to present his own mythologization of a Creole and avant-garde Boedo and, above all, to show that, paradoxically, *his* neighborhood myth is truer; not because his cultural operation rests on the logic of realist description, but because Borges claims that for him the neighborhood is in itself the literary object that must produce the mythology and not, as in humanitarian realism or bohemian tango, an archetypal scenario in which stories take place.

At the same time, this material referentiality, this production on existing elements, allows us to think that Borges's neighborhood is not merely an

---

[492] The quotations from *Evaristo Carriego*, 83 and 93, respectively.

[493] See "Horacio Coppola: testimonios," edited from a long interview I had with the photographer in 1995, in *Punto de Vista* 53 (November 1995).

[494] Cristina Grau mentions it in *Borges y la arquitectura* (Madrid: Cátedra, 1989), 24.

Figure 85. Horacio Coppola, *Avenida del Trabajo y Lacarra*, 1936. Horacio Coppola Archives.

Figure 86. Horacio Coppola, *Dividing Walls*, 1931. Horacio Coppola Archive.

attempt at the "restitution" of an earlier Buenos Aires, as some approaches to the relationship between his literature and the city have interpreted: in his own suburban present, Borges finds the space in which to combine tradition and the new in a typically avant-garde way.[495] The *arrabal* can thus be, simultaneously, a sphere of resistance to modernization and its most bastard product, but not the mere repetition of an "essence" of the traditional city that, because of the transformations taking place in the center, must be sought more and more outside. Borges's poetry and Coppola's photographs do not collect frozen images of a city on the move: in their own flow, the ever-changing shores of Buenos Aires show the city's most specific character. "Yesterday it was countryside, today it is uncertainty": there is nothing prior to Villa Urquiza, and it is on this ambiguous edge that urban *criollismo* seeks the production of a new language that at the same time invents its tradition.[496]

Coppola's photographs of the 1920s and 1930s ratify, then, a typically avant-garde operation, not so much because they offer documentary "information" about that suburb, but because they share the same gaze that produces it: Coppola photographs the traditional "austere little houses" as if they were objects of avant-garde design, with their pure volumes and white surfaces. It is an essentialist and abstracting reduction that turns the most traditional and spontaneous elements of the city into proclamations of modernist purity: the last step of the classicism that in the centenary appeared only as a reaction, as a defense, as a call to order in the face of "eclectic chaos," and that now seems capable of proposing a new figuration; the step that leads from the "party of sobriety" to avant-garde figuration. An avant-garde, then, to multiply the oxymoron, that is not only *criollista* and urban, but also classicist.

85, 86

Thus, Borges's and Coppola's images of the barrio shape from another angle the legitimization of the version that will be most influential in local modernist architecture. The suburban houses, recomposed by a look loaded with the most radical avant-garde motifs, can only now make the "poor colonial" tradition of the Río de la Plata recoverable, in an equation that ends up closing the way to the neocolonial explorations of the centenary. A few years after the beginning of Borges and Coppola's suburban tours, the "popular house" as a modernist motif finds a much more direct external legitimation for architectural renovation: the only point of agreement in Le Corbusier and Hegemann's opposing visions of Buenos Aires, which are worth reproducing because of their similarity to the terms proposed by urban *criollismo* and because they would later be taken up again. In one of his 1929 lectures accompanied by drawings, Le Corbusier called on the architects of Buenos Aires to "open their eyes":

89

87

---

[495] The clearest interpretation of Borges's work as an attempt to "fix in durable images the past of the city," to "restore" the "Buenos Aires of the beginning of the century," is the book by Grau, *Borges y la arquitectura*, 20.

[496] "Villa Urquiza," in *Fervor de Buenos Aires*.

Here you all say: "We have nothing here, our city is all new." [...] Look, I draw a property wall; a door opens in it, the wall continues with the gable end of a lean-to, with a little window in the middle; to the left I draw a loggia, quite square, very neat. On the roof terrace, I draw this nice cylinder: a water reservoir. You think, "Well, here he is designing a modern house!" Not at all, I am drawing the houses of Buenos Aires.[497]

Two years later, Hegemann agreed with this modern rescue of the traditional house from the revaluation of the "spirit of Schinkel" in South America: 88

still today building companies erect thousands of small houses that are completely within the classical forms [which] have been simplified and purified of baroque additions and have given themselves over completely, immediately and innocently, to a very modern materialism (*Sachlichkeit*). [...] It was not necessary in South America to import post-war cubism by European architects, because it was formed on its own, as a natural and logical consequence of its healthy tradition. [...] Between these constructions and those of the young generation of architects there is only a small but decisive step.[498]

The popular suburban house, then, is an element that brings together the most traditional with the newest from an avant-garde reconsideration of its simplicity and purity: a spontaneous cubism. We saw that the suburban house,   85, 86 as a model of urban expansion through individual property, had "solved" the social and political problem of the popular sectors of the traditional city, as decompression in the first moment, as integration in the second; now we see that it also offers a decompressive solution to the aporias of architectural culture in its search for linguistic renovation. This avant-garde reading of the suburban houses solves the dilemmas of the technical nationalism of the centenary, bringing together history, climate, materials, and *place* in a concrete reference of language. Later we will analyze the role of the classicist avant-gardes in architecture and urbanism in the modernist reorganization of the city as a whole; here it is interesting to analyze their incidence in the process of construction of the suburb and the reasons why they find in that suburb a key territory to be produced.

The search for an epic for the city leads vanguard urban *criollismo* to classicist figuration because the search for an epic is at the same time the search for an essence: where does the character of this city, stubbornly changing day by day, the fulminating product of a modernization without quality, lie? We

[497] Le Corbusier, "The World City and Some Perhaps Untimely Considerations" (1930), in *Precisions on the Present State of Architecture and City Planning* (Zurich: Park Books, 2015), 227.
[498] "El espíritu de Schinkel en Sud América," *Revista de Arquitectura* 142 (October 1932).

Buenos Aires' little houses:

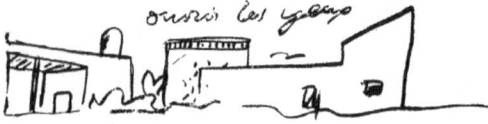

Figure 87. Le Corbusier, *Ouvrir les yeux*, from *Précisions, sur un état présent d l'architecture et de l'urbanisme*, Paris, 1931. Drawing presented by Le Corbusier in one of his conferences in Buenos Aires in 1929, explaining to the local public the "modernity" of the city's traditional houses.

Figure 88. Werner Hegemann, photograph taken in Buenos Aires in 1931 illustrating his "Schinkels Geist in Südamerika," *Wasmuths Monatshefte für Baukunst und Städtebau* (Berlin) 16, no. 7 (1932). Hegemann locates Schinkel's "spirit" in the spontaneous classicism and cubism of Buenos Aires' popular houses.

Figure 89. Horacio Coppola, *A Street in Almagro*, 1936. Horacio Coppola Archive.

have already seen how exceptional Gerchunoff's "progressive" answer is in the culture of Buenos Aires: to affirm itself in that precariousness in a futuristic and productivist way, designating the very passing of time as its essence. On the other hand, the classicist response, more prevalent among the local avant-garde, must discard time as essence: the "light" time is what passes the fastest in young countries without history, as Borges repeatedly states, so that nothing that wishes to anchor itself to that movement can do so. An essential order, something to hold on to after time passes.

It is, evidently, a counter-progressive aspiration, which will rescue in the modern city the chinks of an archaic temporality: the square of pampa in the courtyard behind a wall, the distanced cart in the bustle of the avenue. Borges writes:

> The late cart is perpetually distanced there, but that very postponement is a victory for him, as if the other's celerity were a slave's terrified urgency, and delay itself a complete possession of time, almost of eternity. (Temporal possession is the infinite Creole capital, the only one. We can elevate delay to immobility: possession of space).[499]

However, the choice of the suburb as a solution to that aspiration makes it ambiguous: what is it that leads him to the suburb? What is it that allows him to suppose that such an aspiration could be rooted in that suburb where the urban landscape did not cease to change under his eyes, to the rhythm of "the red flag of auctions," as he himself describes ironically, "sign of our civil epic about brick kilns, monthly payments, and bribes"?[500] To what can a classicist ambition in the whirlwind of modernization lead back to? The suburb, the most progressive region of the city of the twenties, which traditionalist sectors resisted including in the image of *the city* or which marginal cultural sectors incorporated as a picturesque corner, offers this modernist counter-progressivism, an essential structure for its paradoxical resolution of the modernity/tradition and city/pampa dilemmas: the grid.

Nothing more essential than this abstract structure, as abstract as the pampa, which since the beginning of the century had been appearing as the most essential part of this culture. Borges sees what the travelers of the centenary had just begun to glimpse, although he inverts its negative connotations:

---

[499] "El tardío carro es allí distanciado perpetuamente, pero esa misma postergación se le hace victoria, como si la ajena celeridad fuera despavorida urgencia de esclavo, y la propia demora, posesión entera del tiempo, casi de eternidad. (La posesión temporal es el infinito capital criollo, el único. A la demora la podemos exaltar a inmovilidad: posesión del espacio)." "Séneca en las orillas," *Sur* 1 (Summer 1931).

[500] Jorge Luis Borges, "The Language of the Argentines" (1928), in *On Argentina* (New York: Penguin Books, 2010), 80.

the grid weaves and gives meaning to every new piece of city as an invisible and powerful warp, conferring a unity of form, the block, which overcomes all social or cultural heterogeneity:

> and I was among the
> fearful and humiliated houses
> judicious as sheep in a flock,
> imprisoned in blocks
> different and the same
> as if they were all
> shuffled, overlapping memories,
> of a single block.[501]

In this way, Borges allows us to close the rounds of the different cultural attitudes through which the Buenos Aires grid was perceived. His vindication could not be Gerchunoff's utilitarian celebration of the grid as a tabula rasa; this "avant-garde urban *criollismo*" is seeking to take over the entire tradition, and therefore must offer an answer that simultaneously involves both the grid and the pampa.

In the line of culturalist analysis that began with Sarmiento, this was the conjunction demonized as traditional: the double barbarism of the colony and of nature that mutually reinforced each other in Buenos Aires and prevented modernization. But the usual regenerationist criticisms of the centenary, which repudiate the grid no longer as traditional but as modern and capitalist, break up that pair: they confront the grid with a pampa where a reserve of values is then located, an uncontaminated place, an emblem of nationality, in any case threatened by the advance of gridded rationality. At the beginning of the 1920s it could be said that the rejection of the grid has become completely independent, has superimposed different layers, even contradictory ones, identifying itself as the universal key to the evils of Buenos Aires: of ugliness and anonymity, of modernity and tradition. From the urban to the literary picturesque, a common sense has been formed that is emblematized by Alfonsina Storni's well-known verses against the city's row houses, squares, and right angles, which are translated into ideas in rows and square souls: Storni gathers in the grid Sarmiento's rejection of its Hispanic and clerical matrix ("multiplying gray moles / [....] / always making the sign / of the cross," she would say in "Selvas de ciudad") and the regenerationist rejection, in the manner of a Rusiñol, against its monotonous sadness ("Sad straight streets, grayed and even / [...] / when I wandered through them, I was buried," she wrote in "Versos a la tristeza de

---

[501] "y estuve entre las casas / miedosas y humilladas / juiciosas cual ovejas en manada, / encarceladas en manzanas / diferentes e iguales / como si fueran todas ellas / recuerdos superpuestos, barajados / de una sola manzana." See "Arrabal," in *Fervor de Buenos Aires*.

Buenos Aires").[502] But the spread of this common sense is shown even more fully in the casual way with which the following statement is inserted as shared evidence in the opening paragraph of a commentary on art in the magazine *Martín Fierro*: "Every city has its fate, like every man his way of smoking. The fate of Buenos Aires is ugliness. When it was founded, the gods said: let's give it the checkerboard layout, the monument to Columbus, the works of Peynot, the monument to the Two Congresses, etc., etc."[503]

Borges reacts in a vanguard way against that common sense by recovering the initial pair grid/pampa, as Martínez Estrada would do a few years later. But Martínez Estrada does so by also recovering Sarmiento's ominous correlation so as to derive from it his lapidary conclusions about society, with the same culturalist reflex of the nineteenth-century writer:

> The street outlines and the house plans, Gothic and Vandalic through Spain's influence, are ways of evading the problems of perspective and of the broken, undulating line rich in family motifs—natural to a race of horsemen. The shape of the drawing board is correlative to the plain and to the spiritually uncomplicated man. Only an inexpert eye, unable to perceive the shades and the tones of panoramic symphonies, could tolerate without displeasure the coarse sincerity of the perpendicular street and the edification of entire blocks of one-story houses through which the plain invades. The Gothic outline of the streets and the slablike appearance of the city blocks give the impression of a tedious geometric-administrative figure. [...] It is a symmetrical monotony typical of cities with horses and carts [...] The streets are designed to spy dangers, to see far away into the horizon and not to display architecture, fronts, and the aspect of affairs; such is the case with Rivadavia Street, long like a telescope. The countryside flows into the cities through these infinitely straight avenues, through these troughs [...] It is impossible to escape through these straight streets.[504]

Precisely because *the countryside flows into the cities through these infinitely straight avenues*, Borges, in his material recognition of the formal matrix of Buenos Aires, is going to celebrate them as part of what recovers the presence of the pampa: "to my city that opens up clear as a pampa."[505] And therefore he will

---

[502] The poem "Cuadrados y ángulos" is from her book *El dulce daño*, 1918; "Selvas de ciudad" is from *Mundo de siete pozos*, 1934; and "Versos a la tristeza de Buenos Aires," from *Ocre*, 1925; I have taken the three from Alfonsina Storni, *Obras completas, Tomo 1. Poesías* (Buenos Aires: SELA, 1968), 119, 340, and 255, respectively.

[503] L. H. "La suerte del último centauro" *Martín Fierro* 8–9, (August–September 1924), in *Revista Martín Fierro 1924-1927. Edición facsimilar*, 56.

[504] *X-ray of the Pampa*, 231.

[505] "Versos de catorce," in *Luna de enfrente* (Buenos Aires: Proa, 1925).

completely invert the valorization of the pair, beginning with the vindication of the plain and its incarnation in the straight lines of the grid:

> Buenos Aires is not a raised-up, ascendant city [...]. Rather, it is a replica of the flatness that surrounds it, and the submissive straightness of that plane continues in the straightness of streets and houses. Horizontal lines overwhelm vertical ones. Perspectives—on one or two-story dwellings lined up and facing one other all along the miles of asphalt and stone—are so easy that they don't seem improbable. Four infinities meet at every crossroad.[506]

Like Lugones, who for the first time celebrated the horizontality of the Buenos Aires landscape as a quality and consequently demanded a "reserved and philosophical art," this classicist avant-garde will postulate the value of the sequence of low-rise houses with flat roofs, a typical product of the expansion over a large empty territory, in which the "disquieting" sky of the pampas always stands out, "the enormity of the absolute and undermined plain."[507] Coppola took several photographs that he titled *A Sky of Buenos Aires*, in which we can see an indiscernible line of "city" cornered at the lower edge and an infinite sky that refers directly to certain landscapes of Figari, the old Uruguayan painter extolled by the avant-garde.[508]

But in a much more specific way than in Lugones, who only referred to the horizontality of the urban landscape, Borges is going to find the fullest synthesis of the city in the block. I believe that only in the framework of the tradition of double rejection of the grid and the pampa is the degree of provocation sought by Borges in his poem "The Mythical Founding of Buenos Aires" understandable, when he proposes the foundation of the city in a square block in the middle of the pampa: "a whole square block, but set down in open country."[509] Even more than the little white houses, the block, already resolved into a pure and perfect form, offers this avant-garde the most complete expression of the formal and ontological qualities it desires for the suburb. As in Borges's poems, the block will appear in Coppola's photographs, always present in the endless perspectives of the streets that are always the same, in the importance given to the corners—key to the constructive intelligibility of the grid—in the

83

---

[506] Borges, "Buenos Aires," from *Inquisitions* (1925) in *On Argentina*, 14.

[507] Ibid.

[508] "¡Qué no sabe y qué no puede Figari en sus cielos!," Ricardo Güiraldes wondered in "Don Pedro Figari," in *Martín Fierro* nos. 8–9 (September 6, 1924), in *Revista Martín Fierro 1924-1927. Edición facsimilar*, 61. The following phrase by Roger Caillois has been used to evoke Figari: "I thank this land that has so exaggerated the part of the sky"; in Carlos A. Herrera Mac Lean, *Pedro Figari* (Buenos Aires: Poseidón, 1943), 52. This is typical of the pampean vindications of travelers in the thirties in which the local avant-gardists so liked to recognize themselves.

[509] From *Cuaderno San Martín* (1929), in *Selected poems*, 53.

smoothness of the homogeneous facades where the "soft colors like the sky itself" are shown, in the abstract games produced by the flat superposition   86
of dividing walls—another characteristic of the peculiar layout of the Buenos Aires block, repudiated by architectural and urbanistic culture.

In addition to its geometric perfection and its indefinite extension—it is this combination that allows the city to open up "clear as a pampa"—the block is the most appropriate matrix for bringing together the most archaic, the foundational trace itself, with the newest, the metropolitan expansion that at that very moment was producing the most complete social integration of the new popular sectors in the city. Thus, seeking to capture in the block the frontier space characteristic of the mythical *criollo* city, Borges also identifies, in fact, the place which materializes the most specific quality of a purely modern city such as Buenos Aires. The suburban neighborhood then becomes the place that brings together history and the future. And the pampa thus recovers the other side of the ambiguous oscillation between horror and fascination that characterized the attitude of nineteenth-century Romantics: it is not only the place of lack, it is also the place where the modernist "new" can emerge pure, "(u)nder the impassive stars, on the earth infinitely deserted and mysterious [...] undefiled by the shadow of Any God," as the poet Dino Campana envisioned in his hallucinated pilgrimage through the pampa at the beginning of the century.[510]

This is the operation that the classicist avant-garde carried out on the neighborhood, an operation that was then more reserved and secret than that of the picturesque, although it is possible to find undifferentiated manifestations of one or the other in the avant-garde magazines or in the mass media of the period. It is not possible to identify, in the 1920s, any kind of direct urban or cultural influence of this way of thinking the suburb through the celebratory recovery of the grid and the pampa; as in the case of Gerchunoff, these are anomalous readings at the time, but they allow us to see the open possibilities of interpretation against which the most widespread imaginaries are cut back. In any case, both this avant-garde inversion of culturalism and its reaffirmation in Martínez Estrada show us the survival of a cliché, the imaginary quality with which the abstraction of the grid replicates that of the pampa. The park, the device with which Sarmiento's culturalism imagined exorcising the double barbarism of the grid and the pampa, has disappeared from these reflections; and it has disappeared at the moment of its greatest urban articulation as a public space, because the great absentee in this whole operation of refoundation in the suburb is the very notion of the city as a public space.

In contrast to the "red" Buenos Aires of socialist reformism and the "black" Buenos Aires of marginal bohemianism, classicist avant-gardism builds a neighborhood that aims to recover from the suburbs the "white" Buenos Aires

---

[510] Dino Campana, "Pampas" (c. 1908), in *Orphic Songs and Other Poems* (New York: P. Lang, 1991), 155.

that the cultural elite yearns for, with its poverty and its aesthetic dignity in the face of the eclectic chaos of the modernizing *cocoliche*. Compared to those first two Buenos Aires, the "white" Buenos Aires is undoubtedly more ambiguous: a familiar and intimate Buenos Aires that ignores the margins of political publicity won by the "cordial barrio," but that at the same time is set in that suburb despised by the dominant "central" versions that we saw in a Larreta or a Le Corbusier. Above all, it reinvokes as foundational, and therefore legitimizes, the expansion of the grid that was producing, at that very moment, the most complete integration of new popular sectors into the city, an integration rejected, in turn, by the picturesque versions of the tango neighborhood that those same sectors were paradoxically beginning to celebrate. Such was the explosive reality, open, diversified, and in full course of construction, of the representations of the barrio in a Buenos Aires that witnesses its massive publicity. In the late twenties and early thirties, the resolution of this productive cultural tension had not yet been decided.

CHAPTER 9

End of Cycle: Second Birthday

Expansion or withdrawal, integration or differentiation, universality or particularism, project or tradition, new dimension of a metropolitan public space or restoration of the traditional public space with suburban satellite communities: the debates activated by suburban publicity throughout the twenties do not recognize the year 1930 as a radical watershed; nor does publicity itself, which will continue without pause in its social, political, and cultural manifestations. The economic crisis of 1929 and the institutional rupture produced by the 1930 coup, in so many ways decisive for the future of Argentine economy and political culture, do not allow us, however, in our more limited topics of public space and urban culture in Buenos Aires, to establish a definite periodization.

In principle, this is due to the recognition, several times raised throughout this book, of different temporalities in the city, culture, society, and politics: it is well-established that an important part of the processes that we have tried to reconstruct so far is only linked through many mediations with events and political conjunctures. As the historical analyses of Gutiérrez and Romero have shown, in certain social and cultural dimensions (new popular neighborhood sociability, processes of social ascent and integration, consolidation of cultural identities) the twenties and thirties configure in Buenos Aires "a definite stage of its social evolution." Far from the well-known image of the thirties (coup, fraud, crisis, famine), the authors show a homogeneous period, which links the two decades through a series of "underground" processes that work "quietly and calmly" on a new *porteño* society. Both in the dimensions of popular mass culture (romantic imaginaries, technical imaginaries) and in those of high culture (the development of a "peripheral modernity"), it is possible to find such a periodization in Beatriz Sarlo's studies on Buenos Aires culture in those decades. It could be said that these studies permitted approaches that have finally made it possible to conceive as a unit in Argentina what in Western culture was always individualized as a defined historical unit: the interwar period.[511]

---

[511] See Gutiérrez and Romero, *Sectores populares, cultura y política. Buenos Aires en la entreguerra;* and Sarlo's trilogy: *El imperio de los sentimientos* (Buenos Aires: Catálogos, 1985); *Una modernidad periférica* and *La imaginación técnica.*

But there is a second, much more specific reason for the continuity to be found within the political situation itself: it is evident that in the municipal dimension the changes introduced by the thirties were quickly cushioned by an institutional dynamic that made it possible to believe in a radicalization of the political conditions conquered with the reform of 1918. Indeed, in the capital, the coup immediately meant the closure of the Council and the appointment as mayor of José Guerrico, a former conservative councilor—together with Adolfo Mujica, solitary survivors throughout the twenties of the once single bloc in municipal politics. A year later, in the first national elections called in November 1931 by the revolutionary government, the presidential ticket of the Civil Democratic-Socialist Alliance (Lisandro de la Torre-Nicolás Repetto) won the city against the official ticket of the Concordancia (Agustín Justo-Julio Roca), and the Socialist Party (which for the other elective posts ran alone) won comfortably the offices of deputies and senators.[512] Unlike what happened in many provinces, in the city of Buenos Aires the fraudulent practices that would characterize the Concordancia regime during the entire decade were not to be generalized. Thus, in the first election to reinstate the City Council, in January 1932, Socialism also won comfortably over independent socialism, the National Democratic Party and the anti-personalist Radicals, which led to a hyper-politicized inauguration of the new Council, with votes for the freedom of political prisoners of the regime and the near installation of a Socialist mayor.[513]

---

[512] Faced with the radical abstention produced by the contestation of the Alvear-Güemes formula, the main competition in the capital was between the Socialist Party and the Independent Socialist Party: the socialist list won twenty-two deputies against ten of the independents, and in the senatorial race they won the two positions in dispute.

[513] Socialist Andrés Justo (son of the party's founder) had been appointed president of the City Council and was almost installed as mayor to govern during the short interregnum between Guerrico's resignation and the appointment of the new mayor; it was, in fact, a way of questioning the legitimacy of the national elections, contested as a fraud by socialists, especially in the provinces of Buenos Aires and Mendoza. For this discussion see *Actas del Honorable Concejo Deliberante* (Buenos Aires: Municipalidad de la Ciudad de Buenos Aires, February 19, 1932; March 1, 1932). The same debate saw the approval of the vote for the liberty of political prisoners. Electoral results, with 60 percent participation (lower than the usual 70 percent of 1928 but higher than that of the 1922, 1924, and 1926 elections), gave the Socialist party (Partido Socialista) twelve councilmen, the Independent Socialist (Socialista Independiente) party four, the same number for the National Democratic Party (Demócrata Nacional), two for the antipersonalist radicals (Radicalismo Antipersonalista), one for the Progressist Democracy (Democracia Progresista), one for the Worker's Concentration (Concentración Obrera) (communist), one for the Popular Party (Partido Popular), and three for the Public Health Party (Partido Salud Pública) (of which more will be said here). See Walter, *Politics and Urban Growth in Buenos Aires: 1910–1942*, chap. 8 ("Conservative Resurgence").

As will be proven in 1936, with the full re-entry of Radicals to the electoral game, Socialists enjoyed the ephemeral mirage generated by its abstention; at the same time, it is evident that the Radicals' abstention completely tinged the attitude of the Socialists which, though emphatically oppositional, seemed to legitimize the new political chessboard designed by the regime. But reconstructing the coordinates of the moment, the scenario could turn out to be different: if one considers the terms of the even dispute for the electorate between Socialists and Radicals throughout the decade and until the 1928 "plebiscite," (as the election Yrigoyen won with over 60% of the vote was called) which could well be considered exceptional; if one thinks of the generalized fall of the Radical government's public image in the years prior to the coup, especially in the capital; if one thinks of the firm Socialist opposition to the coup, which maintained its democratic aura even among broad sectors of Radicalism; and if one remembers, above all, the notoriously low rates of Radical abstention in the capital in the elections of the 1930s; then it is possible to understand that Socialists could interpret their electoral triumphs as a sign of the recovery of its not so long ago undisputed representativeness. In terms of institutional functioning, the full control it exercised in the Council reinforced its preponderance in the city, and its massive presence in the discussion of public affairs and in the elaboration of its agenda gave it an image of sustained political and electoral growth, in clear recovery since its division (1927) and, above all, since the death of Juan B. Justo, its founder (1928).

In addition, the accidental episode of the resignation of the first mayor appointed by President Justo, Rómulo Naón, of Radical anti-personalist origins but better known in the period for his links with Standard Oil amid the discussions on the concessions for the sale of gasoline, will feed disproportionately the image of continuity of the "socialist Buenos Aires" in the midst of conservative restoration at the national level. Shortly after his appointment, Naón had already broken the delicate balance of support in the City Council, becoming the first mayor without his own bloc, which led to an unprecedented situation of conflict: a representative City Council, which emerged from clean elections governed by the most advanced electoral law, with a large socialist majority and absolute hegemony of the opposition, against a mayor appointed by a national government defeated in the city and a product, in turn, of a fraudulent operation in the rest of the country. The illegitimate origin of the national government produces an exasperation of the institutional conflict latent in the Municipal Organic Law (elective deliberative and executive appointed by the national government) and, as if that were not enough, in a totally anomalous situation in the framework of an important mobilization of public opinion, the conflict is resolved in favor of the Council.[514]

---

[514] Faced with repeated votes of censure and requests for his resignation with a comfortable majority, which implied a lack of recognition of the mayor's authority and

Thus, the institutional conflict and the conflict of legitimacy at this junc-ture radicalizes the image of a popular democracy institutionalized in a solid and independent political body, capable of exercising representativeness and superimposing it on the interests and negotiations of a spurious executive (and political system). In barely two years, the breakdown of the democratic system of 1930 in the capital seems to have been so well saved that the democratic institution can now return the move on a local scale, bringing down the person who represented the political meaning of that interruption in the city. The years after the coup bring about a city and a citizenry in continuous political effer-vescence, a revalidation of the institutions of representation, and a full confi-dence in the continuity of the experience of municipal reformism.[515] It could be said that all the debates that marked that experience describe an open curve that brings together the twenties and thirties: from urban debates—a cycle that starts with the Organic Project of 1925 is formalized in the First Argentine Congress of Urbanism of 1935 and in the administration of Carlos María della Paolera at the head of the Office of the Urbanization Plan—to municipal polit-ical debates, in which Socialism had the larger part as well as the capacity to mobilize diverse publics during the twenties and the first half of the thirties.

However, and this is the necessary counterpart—in my opinion—of the hypotheses that emphasize a "quiet and calm" continuity, it will quickly become clear to what extent a different logic has begun to prevail underneath that con-tinuity, like a continuous bass that will deafly end up changing the direction of the main melody, reorganizing and giving new meanings to most of the dimen-sions at play in the production of public space and urban culture. It is evident that, at this point, the metaphor of geological strata to think out different his-torical temporalities does not contribute precision: although it is possible to recognize different rhythms and different dimensions in this story we are tell-ing, the changes that take place in the thirties affect—in a differential way—all of them; in some cases, changing only a certain emphasis; in others, capitalizing on traditional components in favor of new objectives. In all cases, I believe the task is to try to understand the vertical fissures that tangentially and in a dislo-cated way connect one dimension with the others, one stratum with the others, because it is in their contacts and relations that the warp that we call history is woven. From this point of view, it is possible to affirm that, in the mid-thirties, within the framework of processes that, examined in isolation—or, better yet, in

---

growing obstacles to his daily work, Naón turned to the president of the nation, the "direct boss" of the city, who refused to support him, precipitating his resignation. See Walter, *Politics and Urban Growth in Buenos Aires: 1910–1942*.

[515] In 1933 the socialist councilman Zabala Vicondo could assume the presidency of the Council declaring himself a "soldier of the workers and socialist democracy." The anecdote captures the climate of those years. See *Actas del Honorable Concejo Deliberante* (Buenos Aires: Municipalidad de la Ciudad de Buenos Aires, April 7, 1933).

another code of intelligibility—do not seem to have changed much—the sense of the urban, social, political, and cultural transformations that Buenos Aires had been experiencing in the previous decades—was decisively disrupted.

I have already anticipated that the *quality* of the change appears in the unnoticed generalization of a new coloration, which superimposes on the reformist climate a new, exclusively modernizing climate; the *narrative form* it assumes, in turn, is that of an "end of cycle." Toward the mid-thirties Buenos Aires seems to close a cycle, to the point that the main reasons for which we still recognize it today as a *modern city*, are then completed. On the ongoing processes and the debates that open up—of the expansion, of metropolitan public space—a series of transformations are operated that have the capacity to crystallize a new universe of representations, whose main effectiveness consists of determining a point of arrival for the city. And it is the "second birthday," the celebration of the fourth centenary of the first foundation of the city in 1936, where the symbolic coalition of that point of arrival will be produced as a multiple point of arrival: of the colonizing spirit, of the Creole spirit, of the modernizing spirit. Unlike the "first birthday" on the centenary of Independence, the city seems to have saved the conflict between modernization and history through the course of a transformation that promises to lead it back to its finally discovered essences. That is the key to what I call the *de Vedia operation*: Mariano de Vedia y Mitre is the mayor who played a leading role in that period with enormous capacity; although, beyond that undoubted capacity, with the term "operation" I try to objectify him in some way, to see him as a great mediator, as a catalyst of situations and trends that emerged during his administration and that, in any case, he knew how to capitalize, but that existed outside of him and that he did not in any way control at will.

In the first part of this last chapter, I will try to analyze the two main aspects through which *de Vedia's operation* produced the scenario for the "end of cycle." On the one hand, *modernization*, through which he reorganizes the problematic of expansion, producing a new positioning with regard to the subject of the grid and the debate between center and suburb, through which he places himself as the point of arrival of the "Alvear project." On the other side, the *symbolic refoundation of the center*, through which the main explorations of traditionalism and the avant-garde are articulated to define the "essence" of the city, its *identity*. A representation is produced that turns Buenos Aires into the ideological materialization of four hundred years of utopian predestination; a utopia of origin and future: the vision of a city that recovers its *true* past—Spanish and Creole—because it has come to glimpse its future. In the second part of the chapter, we will try to question the effect of this "end of cycle" on the processes and actors that had been the protagonists of the publicity of the suburb in the previous decade, on the way it affected the very emergence of a metropolitan public space.

1. De Vedia's Operation

> The city, constrained within its limits, continues to grow with unsustainable strength. [...] This development, overwhelming and inharmonious though magnificent in its exuberance, that is manifested throughout the perimeter of the city, is one of its most outstanding characteristics.[516]
>
> –Mariano de Vedia y Mitre, 1935

Mariano de Vedia y Mitre, appointed by Justo after Naón's departure in November 1932, was the figure capable of leading that series of changes and acting as a catalyst to bring together and give new meaning to the different sets of problems and dimensions at stake. Lawyer and judge, literary man, and journalist in the family newspaper—he was the grandnephew of General Mitre—historian, university professor, and member of elite cultural circles, close friend of Justo, whom he accompanied in his electoral campaign, the new mayor seems an epitome of the social characteristics that distinguished his main predecessors. With the not inconsiderable addition, in tune with the "Alvear model," of having an external relationship with politics, in terms of party politics. He appears as a late member of the "generation of the eighties" also in his liberal-conservative-modernizing orientation and, in fact, the specialized literature will recognize him, even from the time of his administration, not only as the most faithful heir of Alvear, but as the last of his lineage.[517]

His style of government was part of that characterization: with all the effectiveness of enlightened authoritarianism, in the sense that he exacerbated, for obvious reasons of electoral reality, the typical tendencies to govern without the "obstacle" of the City Council, and that he legitimized himself at the same time in notable figures of *porteño* culture of the widest ideological spectrum. His team shows the clarity with which de Vedia managed the different aspects of his "operation," the modernizing and technical, and the refoundational and spiritual, emblematized respectively in his two secretaries: that of Public Works, Amílcar Razori, a lawyer specializing in municipal law, who would demonstrate enormous efficiency in the management of the material problems of the city; and that of Finance and Administration, Atilio dell'Oro Maini, refined intellectual, prominent in modernizing Catholic groups, founder and director of the magazine *Criterio* and of the *convivia* within the Courses of Catholic

[516] Intendencia Municipal, *Memoria 1935* (Buenos Aires, 1935), 361–62.
[517] What little has been written about de Vedia sustains this interpretation. See Ulyses Petit de Murat, "Mariano de Vedia y Mitre," in *Tres intendentes de Buenos Aires* (Buenos Aires: IHCBA/Municipalidad de la Ciudad de Buenos Aires, 1985); or Alberto Elguera and Carlos Boaglio, "Vedia y Mitre, el intendente del obelisco," *Todo es Historia* 342 (January 1996).

Culture at the end of the 1920s, where he gathered a great part of the artistic and cultural avant-garde.[518]

Let us dwell on the affiliation of the new mayor with Torcuato de Alvear. De Vedia y Mitre himself places his city as the culmination of the "Alvear project," and there lies, undoubtedly, part of the success of the "operation." In his favor was the fact that he was one of the few mayors who repeated his term of office, extending it in this case for six years: again, as we saw in the case of Alvear himself, and then of Mayors Bullrich and Anchorena (and the same should have been pointed out with Noel), time plays in favor of memorable tenures. But what makes de Vedia even more memorable within this post-Alvear saga is having "closed" the cycle inaugurated by Alvear, investing him ex post facto with the attributes of the "project." More than for its own initiatives, de Vedia's administration is marked by the inauguration of an enormous number of previous works: if at the origin of the cycle there is a mayor whose celebrity—already mythical in the thirties—consists of having begun all the works (even those he did not start), the closing of the cycle can be produced by a "great inaugurator." De Vedia's achievement was to gather the legal and administrative instruments—the political force—to conclude public works of diverse and almost forgotten origin, all of them located in the course of a process of modernization marked by the name of Alvear: the widening of the transversal avenues from Callao to the river—Alvear had begun to weave the legal plot to carry out the widening of those avenues from Callao to the west, which had, in turn, served his association with Rivadavia, drafter of the first law in that sense; finishing the north and south diagonals; beginning of the 9 de Julio Ave (the long-desired North–South Avenue); conclusion of the Costanera; completion of the subway network; rectification of the Riachuelo with the replacement of all its bridges with modern structures; the canalization of the Maldonado stream; consolidation and completion of the street structure of the 1898–1904 plan, with the corresponding infrastructure of services. The city, always undecided, always incomplete, always precarious as a frontier encampment, in a

91

---

[518] Dell'Oro Maini had also been *interventor* (comptroller) of the province of Corrientes during Uriburu's government, and he would be Minister of Education of the Revolución Libertadora. He directed the magazine *Criterio* in its first stage, from 1928 to 1930: according to Zuleta Álvarez, the "golden years" of the magazine that ended due to the pressure of the less pluralist sectors that wanted a closer link with Catholic Action. See *El nacionalismo argentino* (Buenos Aires: Ediciones La Bastilla, 1975), 1: 189. Dell'Oro founded the Cursos de Cultura Católica together with Tomás Casares and César Pico in 1922, and in 1927 he was part of the commission that convened the first *Convivio*; see *Convivio de los Cursos de Cultura Católica (Artes y Letras)*, catalogue of the exhibition at the Museo de Arte Español Enrique Larreta, April–May 1996. Razori will publish an important work: *Historia de la ciudad argentina*, 3 vols. (Buenos Aires: Imprenta López, 1945).

Mariano de Vedia y Mitre's public works:

Figure 90. Unknown photographer, *Enlargement of Corrientes Street* (with the obelisk under construction in the background), April 1936. Dirección de Paseos, Museo de la Ciudad, Buenos Aires.

Figure 91. Unknown photographer, *Construction of 9 de Julio Avenue*, 1937. Dirección de Paseos, Museo de la Ciudad, Buenos Aires.

very short time seems to assume a definite and solid form, it seems to be able to finally materialize a "project."

In a very short time: de Vedia y Mitre manages to recover the sense of urban spectacle that had characterized Alvear and that reappears only fleetingly in the following fifty years. Faced with the feeling of impotence and temporariness left by long-lasting urban works (imagine the landscape of an avenue whose widening is decreed but for which demolition cannot be finished because expropriations have not been completed and, therefore, for years it presents an irregular aspect, with abandoned houses, with the fronts of buildings responding to the different alignments); faced with that impotent city, then, de Vedia restores, once again, the dynamic imaginary of modern cities. In less than a year, Corrientes Avenue was demolished and opened from Callao to Pellegrini, and the   90
following year from there to Alem; but every two months partial inaugurations were carried out to great ritual effect—all of them were attended by President Justo, one of them was accompanied by the president of Brazil, Getúlio Vargas. In a similar timeframe, the five complete blocks that formed the beginning of 9 de Julio Avenue, between Tucumán and Mitre, were demolished (do not forget: "the widest avenue in the world"); in sixty days the obelisk, the crowning piece from a symbolic point of view of the whole "operation," was erected at the intersection of three avenues just opened, then the Diagonal, Corrientes, and 9 de Julio, and over the tunnel of two subway lines that were then also under construction. Again, Buenos Aires seemed like a place where nothing was impossible.

The photographs of the time show a city in disarray, working day and night   90, 91
in a feverish march of progress. Roberto Arlt, whose fiction had already depicted a fundamentally modernist Buenos Aires, is its enthusiastic chronicler:

> Sand clouds as in the African desert, in downtown Buenos Aires. Demolitions in Cangallo Street. In Carlos Pellegrini. On Sarmiento. Wrecked buildings. Card castles of brick and paper. [...] Card castles and the pentatonic range of five qualities of hammering. Opaque hammering of picks on brick. Dull on the cement. Metallic in the beams. Muffled in the partitions. Aquatic in the shovels. [...] The passerby can pick up modernist notes.

His exasperated reading reveals the fascination that the city's decision to accelerate the future awakens in its inhabitants:

> To see destruction is a spectacle that man most likes to witness because his instinct tells him that after what has been destroyed something new must rise up. Man desires the new, seeks it, and is excited by its possibility. Hence the repugnance that most normal beings experience toward the past because the past is always, emphatically, the negation of the present. Of course, in most people this feeling, though it exists, has not been designed with lines vigorous enough to be specified. And its effect is translated into the gesture

of open mouths, while the eyes are filled with a certain light of unexplained joy. [...] And the fact is that the demolitions have opened an extemporaneous clearing in the heart of the city, as no one could dream of, neither by closing their eyes nor by straining their imagination. [...] People are ecstatic in front of such a spectacle. Three blocks of buildings have been cut off from the surface of the city. In their place, there remains the disemboweled subsoil, the basements of white walls, with the remains of truncated columns like those of the classical ruins where tourists have their photographs taken with a Kodak in hand. [...] On the plain surrounded by skyscrapers, the zinc huts of the cranes turn rapidly on themselves, amid a clatter of engines. Their old locomotive chimneys, latticed, spew out whirlwinds of gray, thick, billowing smoke.[519]

The whole of Western history falls surrendered at the feet of the modern city, which, by evoking it, surpasses it. That is modernity: it is at the point of greatest development at which everything acquires intelligibility and meaning. Similar terms to those used by a writer as different from Arlt as Leopoldo Marechal in justifying the writing of his *Historia de la calle Corrientes* (History of Corrientes Street), not centered, precisely, on the past of that street, of such significance for the cultural bohemia, but on its vertiginous present, "when a formidable transformation shakes it to its foundations, renews it and presents it to the observer as a living index of the city in motion, as an exponent of the new rhythm that Buenos Aires assumes."[520] If the city is the sphere par excellence of continuity and slow maceration, of petrified history, the works of de Vedia y Mitre recover the Faustian magic that, by opposition, can only be offered by fulminating urban transformations, bold modifications, in the manner of Alvear and with an identical awareness of the symbolic value of each of his gestures: "The Mayor [...] seems gleefully ready to tear down the city," writes Arlt in his column—not used to praising the political class—and reminds us of the fascination that a Sansón Carrasco, a Cané, demonstrated half a century earlier for the energy of their modernizing mayor.[521]

From the urban point of view, *de Vedia's operation* shows great efficacy and far-reaching consequences; but the most interesting thing is the way in which he manages to place himself in a different place in relation to the debates we are analyzing. It is no longer a matter of pitting the interests of the old city against those of the new neighborhoods, or of opposing traditional public space to

---

[519] Aguafuertes, "Demoliciones en el centro" and "Nuevos aspectos de las demoliciones," *El Mundo* (Buenos Aires), April 19 and June 28, 1937, respectively, in Roberto Arlt, *Aguafuertes porteñas. Buenos Aires, vida cotidiana*, 106ff.

[520] Leopoldo Marechal, *Historia de la calle Corrientes* (1937) (Buenos Aires: Paidós, 1967), 11–12.

[521] Roberto Arlt, "Buenos Aires, paraíso de la tierra," *El Mundo* (Buenos Aires), September 24, 1937, in *Aguafuertes porteñas. Buenos Aires, vida cotidiana*, 114.

metropolitan public space, concentration to expansion. It can fulfill the modernizing yearnings of the center and the neighborhoods because it is capable of annulling reformist tension: that is, because it manages to redirect all specific transformations for the center and the suburbs toward the consolidation of what the very becoming of the city had established, interrupting the public pursuits—typical, even in their contradictions—that seek to transform the reality of the market. In truth, by annulling the reformist pole, de Vedia's modernization eliminates a triple tension: that which existed between the emblematic qualifying intervention in the park and the homogenization of the grid (the tension of the organic pursuit with which the imaginary of public reformism sought social and urban integration); that which began to be proposed in the 1920s between the city and the region (the expansive tension, outward into the territory); and that of the projective tension which characterized the long cycle of reformism since the mid-nineteenth century.

This appears clearly in one of the main actions to transform the city in those years: the conclusion without remainders of the 1898–1904 grid, at a time when the "border" of the city drawn in 1887, General Paz Avenue, finally materializes. In that completion, the ambiguity of the Alvear-de Vedia relationship appears fully in the mystifying way in which the latter retrospectively names the former's "project." For de Vedia, the 1898–1904 plan is no longer an abstract   5 scheme subject to reform, nor a contractual agreement between the state and the market, but a conclusive city form whose completion should be celebrated— without the reticence that had been customary in public administration—as the definitive "modernization" of the neglected neighborhoods and the vision of a Buenos Aires that "feels great, strong, thriving."[522] In the municipal reports of 1932 and 1933, from the beginning of his term of office, de Vedia unequivocally presented the version that equated the city's modernization with the completion of the layout: "the convenience of extending (to the whole municipal area) the urbanized surface of the city is evident." From the 1935 report comes a sentence from our opening quote: "The city, constrained in its limits, continues to grow with unsustainable strength."[523] *Constrained within its limits*: that is the necessary flip side of the operation to modernize the city: the materialization of what until then had been a formal border. The rectification of the Riachuelo and the completion of General Paz Avenue, although they are carried out by the national government (Ministry of Public Works and National Roads), were not only encouraged by the mayor's office but, above all, were seen by the latter—especially General Paz—as the de facto resolution of the intense debate on the new urban and institutional mechanisms for managing expansion, as the ratification of a conclusive and definitive form for the city: they are the *borders*

---

[522] Inaugural speech at the obelisk, *El Mundo* (Buenos Aires), May 24 1936, 7.
[523] Intendencia, *Memorias 1932–1933* (Buenos Aires, 1934), 311 (section "Apertura de calles"); and *Memorias 1935*, respectively.

that circumscribe the area of municipal action and densify the capital's entire territory, materializing the until then imaginary grid, excluding any possible reform that included the regional dimension.

We saw that since the mid-twenties the regional expansion of the city's jurisdiction was being proposed by the public authority itself, not only as a way of contemplating urban, social, and political processes of territorial expansion but, above all, as an indispensable resource for management. The observation that no problem affecting the urban conglomerate recognizes jurisdictional limits and, therefore, the need to define institutionally the "Greater Buenos Aires," already appears in the 1925 Organic Project. In fact, the example of the web of Obras Sanitarias de la Nación (National Sanitation Works), which in those same years had incorporated the entire metropolis into a single system without considering jurisdictional boundaries, began to be cited repeatedly as a practical response to the new management challenges. In spite of the initial resistance of the professional field of architects and engineers, already in the thirties, while de Vedia carried out his "operation," that need had become an indisputable truth among renovating sectors of those professions and in the professions that arrived with novel approaches to urban problems. If in the 1920s the existence of the suburb turned the polemic between expansion and concentration into a dispute between reformism and conservatism, from the 1930s onwards, the regional perspective on the urban issue gradually imposes itself as the core of a technical instrumentation unaffected by ideological alignments.

For example, in the middle of the decade, geographer Romualdo Ardissone points out the lack of coincidence between *city* (as a real city, in its regional dimension) and *municipality* (as a formal jurisdiction, the federal capital). Proposing that the municipal census of 1936 (again, as in the centenary, what better way than a census to celebrate the city's anniversaries) cover the entire metropolis to account for the "gigantic tentacular advance," Ardissone explains the differences between the two entities: one, the city, "constitutes a living, pulsating thing, which, in the case of Buenos Aires, manifests a formidable tendency to expand"; the other, the municipality, "is a rigid thing, it presents a crystallized limit with a strong tendency not to transform itself even though reality has long since surpassed it." In tune with the theories of expansion, he proposes to revise the dimension of the metropolitan conglomerate simultaneously outward and inward from the formal border of the municipality: "If the dress that was given in 1887 to Buenos Aires for administrative purposes was too loose [...]; now it only adheres to the body in some parts, while in several others it has been ridiculously short and narrow for many years." [524] As Hegemann had suggested,

92

60
2

---

[524] Romualdo Ardissone, "La ciudad de Buenos Aires excede los límites de la Capital Federal. Necesidad de levantar un censo que abarque la totalidad de la aglomeración urbana bonaerense" (1935), GAEA *(Anales de la Sociedad Argentina de Estudios Geográficos)* V (1937): 470.

it was a matter of capitalizing on the reality of a still partial urbanization of the municipal surface, drawing parks within the municipality but at the same time organizing and projecting urban and environmental sanitation onto the three arms already launched by the region, with regulations and unified legislation favoring a new socialization. For this reason, Ardissone continues, "one may ask if the time has not come to make [Buenos Aires] a more modern, more anatomical dress, that is, if it is not the right time to proceed to a new modification of the limits."[525]

The truth is that to do so—and this is the significant point of Ardissone's demand—was nothing more than to place oneself in line with the long cycle of urban expansion: the article points out that those who oppose the institutional creation of "Greater Buenos Aires" should not accept the "recent" limits of General Paz and the Riachuelo, created in the course of the expansionary process and in response to it, but should go back "to a much smaller expression: to the limits established by Garay in 1580, and suppress all successive expansions." The conservative utopia offered to the city by Le Corbusier or Larreta's proposals was no different. But if such positions were then still part of a debate *against* the main lines of public reformism embodied in the state, what a text like Ardissone's shows us is the deliberate rupture of the cycle produced by de Vedia y Mitre with the jurisdictional crystallization of the capital and its symbolic enhancement. Instead of adapting the municipality to the city, de Vedia y Mitre restricts "his" city to the municipality, which not only prevents reform in the interior of the capital: above all, he breaks with the tradition of successive layouts of wider and wider "beltway boulevards" to always give place to the real   1 city within its formal jurisdiction. We have seen how from the Callao boulevard, already in Rivadavia's time, through Alvear's proposal for a regularizing boulevard and up to the one projected in 1887, the boulevard had been in Buenos Aires a way of controlling the urban phenomenon that, even when caught in evocations of the "small and concentrated" city model, produced institutional gestures of inclusion of everything that the expansion produced, seeking to anticipate it with ample foresight. Time and again, formal jurisdiction had been defined far outside the real city. For the first time, however, in the 1930s in Buenos Aires the political decision was made to ratify a *cut*: an operation analogous to that of Vicuña Mackenna in Santiago de Chile at the end of the 1870s with his "camino de cintura" (beltway), differentiating between the legal and the real city, between the "proper" and the "alien" city.

De Vedia y Mitre decided that the administrative "dress" of 1887 was so well suited to the "strong and thriving" Buenos Aires of the thirties that not only should its limits be maintained outwardly, but also be punctiliously completed inwardly. It must be stressed that this is the first time that a public authority celebrates the grid without reticence; at this point of the story, it can be better

---

[525] Ibid., 471.

understood that it had not been either in its celebration or in mere resistance to it that reformist novelty had taken place in the city over the first two decades of the century. The strategy of public interventions, punctual and qualitative, from which the "reform park" was born, emerged as a product of the conflict between the public value of the grid and the resistance generated in public authorities that identified it with market forces; it was largely from this collision, between the organicism of the punctual "reparative" intervention and the universality of the grid, that the cultural artifact of the barrio emerged, as an expression of a new type of public space marked by the ambition of state intervention in the new society. The very misunderstanding of the effects of the grid device had led to the search for its qualification and its simultaneous fulfillment: it is the unstable balance that produced that conflict in public power that is articulated as a "project" in the twenties, as a resolution of progressive and communitarian tendencies, as an urbanistic expression of the necessary conjunction between expansion and integration. That is what *de Vedia's operation* will disassemble in the thirties.

But how does this celebration of the opening to the market of the entire municipal territory and the symmetrical withdrawal to the borders of the city with the region connect with the continuity and deepening of technical debates, with that new professional, regionalizing, and planning common sense, if there is no doubt that the urban planning discipline also celebrated de Vedia as a modernizing mayor who sought great advances for its institutional consolidation? In principle, because the same technical neutrality that favors the extension of this new professional common sense outside ideological alignments is, more than the generalization of a political conviction translated into ideas on the city, the product of a specialization that radicalizes the autonomy that we already saw outlined in the engineering tradition since the late nineteenth century. From the 1930s onward, the ideological affiliation of the new figures who would hegemonize the disciplinary field being consolidated under the still ambiguous heading of "urbanism" would matter little, because the link between technical aspects and politics had been severed in these matters. The will to build a professional field and effective management instruments leads the urban debate to become a growing ecumenical search for compatibility and coexistence between very different proposals; as if to say: this city is as big as its urban deficiencies, therefore there is room for all kinds of interventions, and the important thing is that they are carried out. Or, better, as if the vindication of technical specialization and professional recognition in the face of political power necessarily entailed the dissolution of the political value of urban ideas.

The effervescence of the relations between political and technical reformism in the twenties will remain only as a passing conjuncture, which put in contact the high voltage of municipal politics, the novelties produced by the publicity of the suburbs, and a moment of transition in disciplinary formation. Thus, for a long time to come, the professional field will only appear as the uncritical sum of an infinity of technical solutions that aspire at most to share a patchwork. The landscape that emerges from the First Argentine Congress of Urbanism, a foundational episode for the discipline that had been encouraged by the City Council, is similar. The Congress brought together members of older generations of architects and engineers with new generations that already define themselves as professionals of urbanism, along with officials of municipal departments from all over the country, who gathered under intentions so general so as not to be discussed, and therefore constrained to a punctilious presentation of their handful of extremely specific "technical" proposals. The following, very illustrative exchange, took place in one of the plenary sessions—where the conclusions and general recommendations were voted according to what was presented and discussed in commissions:

> Mr. Dagnino Pastore: [...] I note that in these en bloc votes we are accepting propositions that clash with each other [...] so I draw attention to the contradictions we are incurring.
> Mr. Guido: We do not vote on the proposals, but simply on the publication of the work or its submission to the respective authorities.
> Mr. Chedufau: We do not make doctrine.
> Mr. Dagnino Pastore: Very good! [526]

Even for the protagonists themselves it was evident that, by not discussing general criteria, the "technical" proposals could turn out to be contradictory: not making doctrine means, in this framework, that the professionals gathered in the Congress send "to the respective authorities" a series of dissimilar proposals, disregarding the decision-making process by which one is considered more convenient than another. It means that they have accepted that this decision is an exclusive attribution of those who politically manage the city.

Outside the necessarily homogenizing objective that characterizes the Congress, one can distinguish the same dislocation between technical debate and real management of the city, and between technical debate and politics, in the positions that are evolving in the architectural discipline and in the institutional management of urbanism itself. In 1933, an article appeared in the *Revista de Arquitectura* signed by architects Ernesto Vautier and Fermín Bereterbide that brought together all the elements with which architecture would think through the problems of the city for many years to come. [527] The article brings to the

---

[526] *Primer Congreso Argentino de Urbanismo* (Buenos Aires, 1936), 1: 270. The Congress, which had significant state support, was organized by Los Amigos de la Ciudad and the Museo Social Argentino in conjunction with a large number of public and private institutions. It was held in Buenos Aires, October 11–19, 1935, and its results were published in three volumes in 1936, 1937, and 1938, respectively.

[527] "Urbanismo," *Revista de Arquitectura* XIX, no. 146 (February 1933). Ernesto Vautier was a modernist architect responsible for the Sugar City project for Tucumán in the twenties, developed in conjunction with Alberto Prebisch, with whom he also signed

architectural discipline, a decade late, the urban reformism that we had seen in the making since the twenties in the City Council and in public management: need for regionalization, need for reconfiguration of urban form through the functional and symbolic weight of new civic centers. Its themes are technically articulated—criticism of speculation, emphasis on tax policies, demands for strong public intervention in the definition of the city—and linked to the more specific objectives of the new proposals for urban intervention—planning, building regulations in connection with zoning, green reserves, restructuring of transportation on a metropolitan scale. But this architectural progressivism weakens its conception of a plan in a sum of proposals that it takes from the most advanced examples of international urban planning while it simultaneously does not build differentiated forms of public management, focusing all its artillery on the propaganda of the need for a plan that never arrives and of the figure of the architect as a liberal professional, formal organizer of the reform's contents.

It is in institutional management, in any case, where the clearest case of this position appears: Carlos María della Paolera, ecumenically recognized even since these years as the "founding father" of urbanism as a profession. If his urban positions show to what extent in this cycle of debates the most important problems posed by the new city emerging from suburbanization were open for technical and political administration, at the same time, from his position as director of the Office of the Urbanization Plan in the administration of Mariano de Vedia y Mitre, he did nothing more than accompany, with specific "neutral" undertakings, the celebration of the completion of the grid and the qualities of the traditional city. Already in 1929, as we saw in the quotation with which we began the third part, he had already stated the impossibility of reforming the problems of the city of Buenos Aires if the metropolitan area outside the administrative limits of the federal capital was not considered. Unlike Hegemann, della Paolera's orthodoxy prevented him from including in his expansive scheme the reality of the grid, insisting on the need for a more classical link between expansion and the picturesque model of the Garden City; but, in any case, he maintained, citing the example of Paris, Berlin, or New York, that the old administrative limits "should be overwhelmed by regional organization."[528] In 1931, during the short de facto administration

92

---

articles in *Martín Fierro*, the magazine where the pair polemically and stridently introduced European proposals for artistic and architectural renovation. A year before the publication of "Urbanismo," Vautier had taken over the direction of the *Revista de Arquitectura*, highlighting the changes that were taking place among the discipline's elite; and from there he strongly projected the magazine's strong participation with innovative positions on urban issues.

[528] See "Urbanismo y problemas urbanos de Buenos Aires" (pamphlet), cited in Alicia Novick, "Della Paolera, Carlos María," in Aliata and Liernur, eds., *Diccionario de arquitectura en la Argentina*.

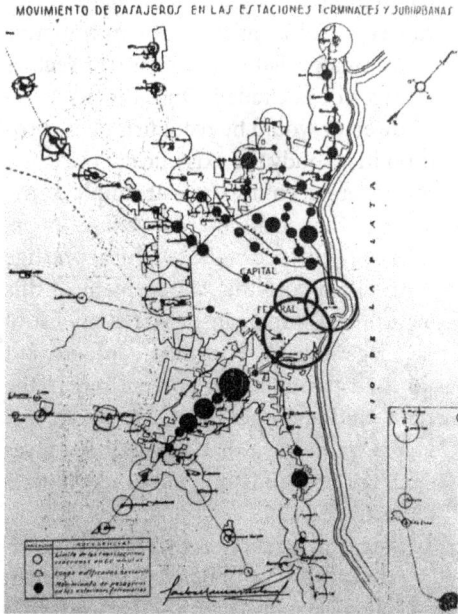

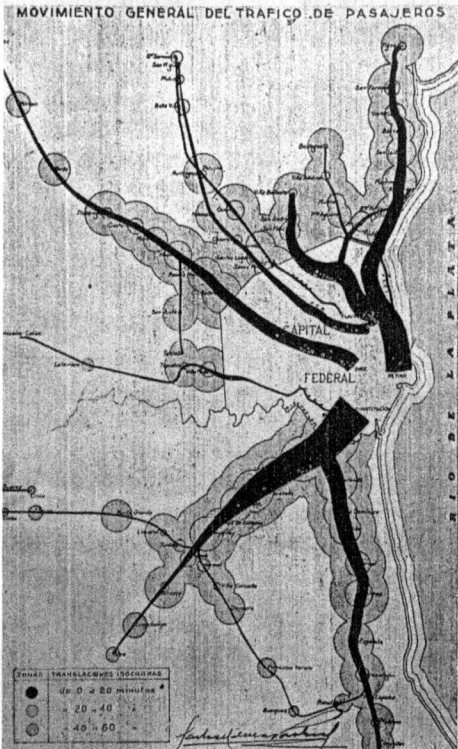

Figure 92. Carlos María della Paolera, *General Movement of Passenger Traffic*. Analysis of the unitary functioning of the metropolitan region through two graphs of the traffic and movement of passengers. Della Paolera, *Urbanismo y problemas urbanos de Buenos Aires* (Buenos Aires: Honorable Concejo Deliberante, 1929).

of Mayor Guerrico, the Office of the Urbanization Plan (Oficina del Plan de Urbanización) had been formed with della Paolera as its head, an initiative that was considered a triumph of the campaign led by professional sectors gathered in associations such as Los Amigos de la Ciudad. Once the new government was formed, the office and its director would be reconfirmed by proposal of the City Council, since in the political body the existence of the office and della Paolera's own technical figure were seen also as a triumph of the reformist demands of the previous decade. That such different groups, interests, and ideologies could coincide is already evidence of the technical prestige and political neutrality of the idea of the Plan; and the management of this office will demonstrate, in effect, how technical pragmatism works: its list of specific proposals once again rounds off generically reformist contents, but by leaving the selection of priorities or their partial realization entirely in the hands of political power, by relinquishing judgment on them, and by accepting that they can be realized without the framework that theoretically gives them meaning—expansion—the technician suspends not only the political character of his proposal, but also its effectiveness.[529]

One of the most precise examples of the mismatch between technical knowledge and city management is verified by the office's position facing the problem of the grid's incomplete spaces. Della Paolera's expansive orthodoxy leads him to culminate the cultural transformation that we already saw outlined in the previous decade, by which he unifies under the denomination "green space" the opposite poles of the civilizing paradigm of nineteenth-century reformism, the park and the pampas. These two elements no longer symbolize the confrontation between culture and nature, but the only "natural" potentiality against the unstoppable advance of the artificiality of the grid that occupies everything. Thus, we see already defined the contemporary version of an urban reformism that has "naturalized" its objective: it is no longer the enlargement of public space but the enlargement of "green"; all the ambiguity of the twenties between the "naturalizing" regional vision of the theory of expansion and the political vision of *Civic Art* has disappeared. This disaggregation undoubtedly converges with that made by de Vedia between the civic and economic value of the conjunction of grid and park; but the truth is that in the specific case of the completion of the grid, della Paolera generates an insoluble contradiction with *de Vedia's operation*, because it confronts nature and grid even more radically as the opposite poles of urban reformism and the market. Thus, della Paolera analyzes in detail and denounces the "loss of green spaces," heading the list of the office's proposals with the reconsideration of the opening of streets that the mayor's office of which he depends on has, however, fervently promoted,

---

[529] On the vicissitudes in the formation of the office, see the radio conference by Jerónimo Rocca, member of Los Amigos de la Ciudad, on September 9, 1935; in *Primer Congreso Argentino de Urbanismo*, vol. I, 46.

without this opposition modifying in any way the policy of the latter or the "reformist operability" of the former.[530]

It is in this sense that I spoke of dislocation between the topics and debates that preside over the formation of the professional field and public administration: "We want—and I express it in advance to avoid misunderstandings—to save democracy through urbanism, which is a social policy placed above parties and trade unions," said José Rouco Oliva, former councilman of the Independent Socialist Party and active member of Los Amigos de la Ciudad, at the opening of the First Argentine Congress of Urbanism.[531] During the 1930s, urban discourse, as counterpart to greater specialization, continues to strike reformist gestures through its particularized proposals, defining itself as a "social policy" so "above" parties and society that it only makes sense by linking itself unidirectionally with political power, without noticing—or without caring—that the latter, with a global intervention, gives a completely different sense to urban modernization. This only highlights one of the major paradoxes of the professionalization of the disciplines that operate in the city: the greater the technical autonomy, the greater the dependence on political power, and the greater the dependence, the greater the need for absolute political power. As we pointed out in the first chapters, urban "reformism," left to its own logic, returns again and again to the original precept of Enlightenment despotism: absolute power for reform.

The political character and the effects of urban artifacts is something in permanent mutation: in the absence of instruments to overcome it, the grid had acquired at the end of the century a reformist content, enhanced, paradoxically, by (impotent) attempts to contain or qualify it. When in the thirties the metropolitan dimension of the problem is understood, the uncritical completion of the grid implies defining it as a closed form, and its effects revert to conservatism as they restrict its regional public projection. Even in its rusticity, the 1898–1904 "alignment plan" had implied a public foresight on a collective future that was in line with the definition of the very wide boulevard. Reformist

5

---

[530] He makes comparisons in areas of the capital between 1916, 1925, and 1932 to show the "reduction of green spaces" to the compass of the completion of the grid; in *Urbanización de Buenos Aires* (Buenos Aires, 1935).

[531] *Primer Congreso Argentino de Urbanismo*, 3:31. This hypothesis of "saving democracy through urban planning" is clarified when Rouco Oliva offers examples: "The great transformations of Italian, German and Russian cities in recent times [this is written in 1935] have been possible thanks to the restrictions on [free speculation] imposed by public authorities. And the influence of these changes on the health of the population has been felt immediately. And not only in health: in all demographic experiences and in the spirit of the people. [...] there has been a renewal of man's most precious moral and intellectual values: an extraordinary strength moves his creative aptitudes, a more vital spirit characterizes the multitudes, a vital rejuvenation pushes them along the new paths of history."

critique, having revealed its technical and political limitations and by giving regional scale to the relationship between the grid and the park, exposed the completion operation as the closure of the search for answers to the new city and the new society that had emerged in the meantime. De Vedia's administration appears to complete a cycle in the sense that it materializes the grid that was still merely figured in vast areas and that it completes and finalizes an important group of projects of the modern city initiated with federalization and Alvear's administration. But that which is "completed" is not "Alvear's project," because here appears the third aspect of the reformist tension that de Vedia disassembles: the idea of the project itself.

The *de Vedia operation* looks backward, invents a "project" of a modern city that traces an affiliation with Alvear and arbitrarily places itself at its final point, for which it needs to cut out every element of urban reality that does not respond to its guidelines. In the case of accepting that Alvear had a project thus defined and that the city should complete it, what de Vedia's does is simply carry out that "mandate": for "the municipality"—following Ardissone's characterization—*de Vedia's operation* implies a complete and, in a certain way, "progressive" end, since it fulfills the postponed aspirations of the neighborhoods, ratifying the universality of communications and infrastructures; that is, modernization. On the other hand, when Alvear is placed as part of an expansive cycle in progress, which in the thirties was just entering a new stage, that "operation" becomes a brake: for "the city" (that is, the expanded territory of the regional metropolis), *de Vedia's operation* implies an attempt at closure; that is the interrupted reform.

We have pointed out that the whole reformist cycle is marked by the tension—returning to the figure of Real de Azúa that we quoted in the introduction—between *the impulse and its brake*; we know, moreover, that the city continued the expansion process in the following years, so the idea of a *brake* should be relativized: de Vedia does not stop the expansion, he disregards it, slowing down the process of integration. The ratification of the division between "city" and "municipality" at the very moment when this division was beginning to show its urban, social, and institutional consequences and at the very moment when there were technical and political instruments to give a better answer marked the whole future of the metropolis with fire, its impossibility until today to begin to process the relations between the capital and the suburbs. To reevaluate the meaning of "end of cycle" produced by *de Vedia's operation* it is sufficient to remember that immediately before, in the 1910s and 1920s, the same conflict with the suburbs had been solved through the fullest integration: what is stopped is the triple reformist tension that linked, "naturally," expansion, integration, and project.

Impulse and brake, continuity, or rupture: now we can better understand the point I raised at the beginning of the chapter about the way to consider the shift of the thirties. In contrast to traditional hypotheses, historiographical perspectives that have emphasized the "quiet and calm" continuities of the

1920s and 1930s have managed to identify with acuity a number of elements in society and culture of those decades that also pave the way to Peronism and explain many of its features as a phenomenon that does not emerge from a vacuum. I believe, however, that this perspective must be made more complex with the evidence of the profound and traumatic transformations of the city and urban culture in the 1930s: it is possible to hypothesize that many of the city's later conflicts would have been considerably different if this withdrawal of the capital into itself had not previously crystallized, not only in institutional and territorial terms, but also in symbolic ones.

A Reactive Utopia: The Avant-garde Reclaims the Center

The indispensable flip side of this withdrawal of the capital into its borders was the symbolic refoundation of its center, surely the most culturally dense aspect of *de Vedia's operation*, the point which thoroughly tested its catalytic capacity. The "search for the Center" that we saw unfolding in the previous decade from the destabilization produced by the publicity of the suburb, is resolved in the thirties by defining the character of a new public space for the metropolis. And that resolution, at the moment of greatest intensity in the confrontation of projects to requalify the Plaza de Mayo or to move the heart of the city to the "real center" of the municipality, becomes one of the keys to understanding the way in which the "end of cycle" is culturally imposed. *de Vedia's operation* can solve the problem of the center without even intervening in that "urbanistic" debate, because it is able to affect the debate on cultural identity, articulating a successful answer to questions about the character of Buenos Aires that reconciles the two conflicting poles of the centenary: modernization and history. We already saw in the 1920s the response of a sector of the avant-garde, which managed to connect a whole tradition of obsessive debates about the role of history in a fully modern city like Buenos Aires; in the 1930s, those searches are reused to produce a new public space, whose achievement is the promise of harmony of a modernization that arrives to restore an essential meaning: the main inauguration of the "great inaugurator" that was de Vedia is that of a past for the city.[532]

What should this refoundation be like? In his proposals for the recovery of the Plaza de Mayo, Larreta had already indicated, as we have seen, its main guidelines:

> Perhaps one day [...] almost everything that today is called progress will be seen as a morbid proliferation, a neoplasm. There will be a return to

---

[532] In this section I follow the hypotheses that we developed jointly with Graciela Silvestri in "El pasado como futuro. Una utopía reactiva en Buenos Aires," *Punto de Vista* 42 (April 1992).

simplicity. Slowness itself will regain its value. There will be trains for the rich who will be obliged to travel very slowly. Those who cannot afford this luxury will live protesting. The poor will be made to travel at dreadful speeds.[533]

It is a counter-progressive, anti-technological, and reactive position, which seeks to conjure up the progressive temporality of modernity to transcend the evils of civilization. *There will be a return to simplicity. Slowness itself will regain its value.* The way in which Borges posed the problem of time in the modern city, his vision of the urban ideal as the recovery of an archaic temporality, resonates immediately: the opposition between the unbridled traffic of the avenue and the essential quality of the "late cart," whose "very postponement is a victory for him, as if the other's celerity were a slave's terrified urgency."[534] But if this ideological background is common to two figures as distant as Larreta and Borges, the main novelty in the 1930s is that the conflict over the linguistic procedures for restitution in the city seems to have been resolved: the center appropriates the images of the "white city" that *criollo* avant-gardism had been rehearsing in the 1920s in the suburbs.

I tried to show that the interpretations of Borges's early work that exclusively emphasize its reactive character in the face of the city's modernization, leave aside the specificity of his literary suburb as a modern suburb. But here we must incorporate another, much more paradoxical ingredient: the *projectual quality* of the "white city" that Borges constructs reactively in the 1920s and that will contribute to providing the most effective way out of the search for cultural identity in architecture and the city in the 1930s, when not only the architectural avant-garde, but above all the state, take charge of the same representations and put them into practice. The figure that gives that last formative step to *de Vedia's operation*, closing the cycle of debates on national architecture that opened with the century, is Alberto Prebisch's obelisk, constructed as a culminating moment of the celebration of the fourth centenary, the best monument to this synthesis that all now agreed in prescribing.

It must be recognized that Borges in the thirties will express reservations about the crystallization of the "white city" of which he had been a precursor, taking a prudent distance from its official apotheosis.[535]

98

---

[533] Larreta, *Las dos fundaciones de Buenos Aires*, 66.

[534] "Séneca en las orillas."

[535] In this sense, Borges's radio conference in honor of the fourth centenary is a very valuable document to show the changes in his positions, foreshadowing the imminent

On the other hand, in Coppola's photographs for the fourth centennial tribute album, one can see one of the singular moments of the passage from that imaginary suburb to the center: the same option for classicism that allowed him to portray the traditional houses as if they were modern objects, allows him to portray the most modern sectors of the city as if time had not passed through them.[536] Faced with the dilemma of *cultural* synthesis between accelerated modernization and local tradition, again avant-garde classicism offers the way out for its paradoxical resolution: to find modernity in the traditional and the traditional in the most modern forms through an annulment of the passage of time,

93
95

---

fissures of the counter-progressive bloc. In 1936, faced with the literalness of the founding myth which, as we will see later, is resolved by decree, Borges takes an ironic distance. To begin with, he himself states: "It is enough for me, for now [he begins to say in his lecture], to promise that I will not rehearse on paper—or on the invisible paths of air—an umpteenth "foundation" of our city. For the rest, the subject is already in itself a literary genre." Thus, precisely at the moment when it seems to be resolved, Borges rejects the enterprise he began: "First [...] it is convenient to reject a pseudo-problem, capable of infinite perplexity. I am talking about the intrinsic meaning of Buenos Aires: *What* is Buenos Aires, *who* is and who has been Buenos Aires? Thus posed, the debate runs the risk of provoking a thousand and one answers, all unverifiable, all diverse, and all equally mythological. [...] Someone will discover the substance of Buenos Aires in the deep patios of the south and in the meticulous iron of its gates; another, in the street greetings of Florida; others, in the broken suburbs that inaugurate the pampas or that crumble toward the Riachuelo or the Maldonado; others, in the gloomy cafés of lonely men who feel Creole and resentful while the orchestra dispatches tangos; others, in a memory, a tree, a bronze. Which is tolerable, if we understand by it that no man can feel linked to *all* the neighborhoods and false, irreparably false, if we mistake those preferences or those customs with an explanation or an idea." Just five years after the publication of *Evaristo Carriego*, in a turn that skeptically discards one after another of the solutions proposed to resolve the vision of a harmonious past, Borges ends by disengaging himself from the counter-progressive temporality to propose a leap forward in an integrative vision. See "Tareas y destino de Buenos Aires," *Homenaje a Buenos Aires en el cuarto centenario de su fundación* (Buenos Aires: Municipalidad de la Ciudad de Buenos Aires, 1936), 520, 530–31.

[536] See *Buenos Aires 1936* (Buenos Aires: Municipalidad de la Ciudad de Buenos Aires, 1936); that timeless quality of modernism is notorious in the photographs of the Diagonal Norte, the great alternative of building order raised in front of the chaotic Avenida de Mayo; in those of the widened Corrientes, with the new skyscrapers that are never presented to us in expressionist angles, but as massive and timeless white masses; in those of the port silos, those typical artifacts of modernization, but which Coppola chooses to show by flattening the image and composing it in classical proportions, making explicit the influence of the painter Alfredo Guttero, who also portrays the "modern" city through the filter of the *call to order* of the European aesthetic avant-gardes of the twenties.

93
94

95

96

Figure 93. Horacio Coppola, *Diagonal Norte*, 1936. Horacio Coppola Archive. Classicist shape to order the modernist city.

Figure 94. Horacio Coppola, *Avenida de Mayo*, 1936. Horacio Coppola Archives. The avenue's "eclectic masks" as counterexample. In the foreground, the Barolo Palace; in the background, the National Congress.

Classicist images of the modernist city:

Figure 95. Horacio Coppola, *Port*, 1936. Horacio Coppola Archive.

Figure 96. Alfredo Guttero, *Silo*, c. 1928. Oil on cardboard. Museo Nacional de Bellas Artes collection, Buenos Aires, Argentina, Fondo Nacional de las Artes Donation, 1970.

Figure 97. Rodolfo Franco, *Murals in the Buenos Aires Subway Line D*, c. 1936. Harmonious association of modern technology, the city, and labor in the Art Deco project by artists associated with the "national renaissance."

through a deceleration of progressive temporality. In the 1920s, while that way out was in fact hypothesized in the white popular houses, in the connection of colonial tradition with the avant-garde through the "spirit of Schinkel," Alberto Prebisch sought to theoretically defend the need for that classicism in his polemical, "avant-garde" interventions in the magazine *Martín Fierro*:

> Every man, every epoch, tends to obey this pressing need for order. Order that results from a harmonious balance between inner life and outer life, spirit and nature, idea and form, to use the Hegelian expression. Each epoch seeks its equilibrium. [...] Our epoch seeks to achieve this agreement, this balance, it seeks a classicism, *its* classicism.[537]

When one sees the work of the main modernist architects of Buenos Aires, such as Antonio Vilar or Jorge Kalnay, it becomes clear that this was the most locally successful version of modernism—Vilar would say in 1931 that "the healthy tendencies of contemporary architecture" should not be called "modern style" but "classical school of the twentieth century"—a version against which a work such as that of Wladimiro Acosta is as marginal as the visions of Gerchunoff or Arlt in relation to dominant culture. And when one sees the drawings that Prebisch, the undoubted theoretician of that renovation, made for the obelisk project, one perceives the most ambitious attempt to translate that classicist version of modernist architecture into urban public space.[538]

98

Prebisch's "white city" breaks with the ambiguity that suburban precariousness gave to Borges's city: it proposes an imposing and homogeneous urban framework, which continues in the whole area surrounding the monument the

93 sober lines of the building regulations of the Diagonal Norte—building police measures that, Prebisch laments, are *now* essential as the only way to recover the harmony of the urban landscape that *was once* the "spontaneous" product of "a community of tastes and needs": continuous facades, smooth and white, with regular openings, in which only a base with delicate arches and a sober cornice stands out. In the center, the obelisk, establishing a golden ratio in the circle of the Plaza de la República and in the height of the building complex, white thanks to the covering of Cordovan flagstone (as both technical nationalism and Lugones had proposed in their own way: a monument that would be both a permanent exhibition of local traditional materials and industries),

[537] Alberto Prebisch, "Sugestiones de una visita al Salón de acuarelistas, pastelistas y aguafortistas," in *Martín Fierro*, 5–6 (May 15–June 15, 1924), in *Revista Martín Fierro 1924–1927. Edición facsimilar*, 35. On the peculiar architectural modernism of Buenos Aires, I am indebted to the luminous hypotheses of Jorge Liernur in texts like "El discreto encanto de nuestra arquitectura," *summa* (April 1986).
[538] Antonio U. Vilar, "Arquitectura contemporánea," *Nuestra Arquitectura* (August 1931).

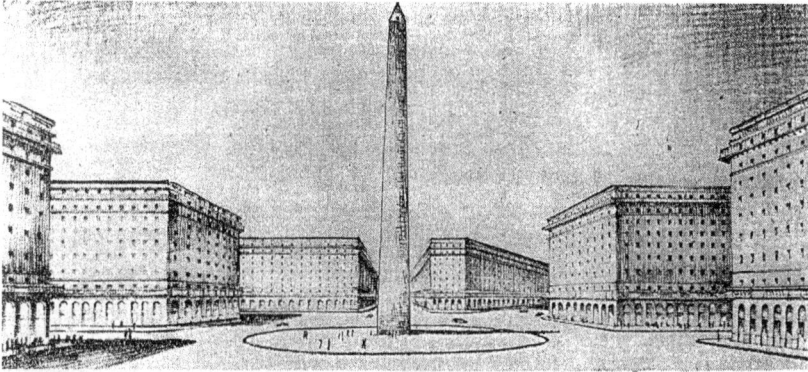

Figure 98. Alberto Prebisch, *General Perspective of Plaza de la República with the Obelisk at the Center*, 1936, as published in *La Prensa*, March 10, 1936. The image shows Prebisch's project for the entire area. Note the similarity with Diagonal Norte Avenue in Horacio Coppola's photograph.

Figure 99. Dirección General de Arquitectura, Ministry of Public Works, *Proposal for the Remodeling of the Plaza de Mayo*, 1934, published in *Revista de Arquitectura*, Buenos Aires, XX, no. 167 (November 1934). Proposal after Enrique Larreta's notes, which shares the same classicist ambitions as Prebisch's drawing.

connecting from its pure forms the modern city with universal culture and, above all, with national history.[539] In the midst of the confusion of vulgar languages of the modern metropolis, this special version of modernism is the one that manages to produce, finally, the act of *recognition* so sought after by the cultural elite.

The problem continues to be defined on the same essentialist plane of the centenary: to appear or to be; to recover history superficially or in the deepest sense. One of the best demonstrations of a resolution in the first didactic modality is given by the murals in the subways executed by figures already highlighted by Rojas in *Eurindia* as representatives of the "national renaissance" in the plastic arts, Rodolfo Franco and Alfredo Guido. The main emblem of technical modernization and urban speed, the subway, whose network was completed in the thirties, is masked in its interior by an iconography that, in an *art deco* tone—the type of figurative modernization toward which the first neocolonial artists generally drifted—proposes the same conciliated narrative of the "white city": between tradition and progress, the countryside and the city, the Spanish foundation, the Creole patriots, and the industrious contemporary inhabitants; each station of the Catedral-Palermo subway offers a series of confronting murals that didactically reconstruct a conflict-free journey from the origins to the present, seeking to demonstrate that the abrupt transformation of urban habits that the subway exemplarily put into action did not do violence to that which was inscribed in a transcendent origin. But beyond sharing with classicist avant-gardism that blind confidence in the possibility of synthesis, the great difference is once again procedural: the covering operation of the neocolonial does not affect the production of the past it seeks to recover, because it considers that past a given fact, which must only be didactically transferred to the surface of the images in order to make it present.

Modernism carries out a more complex operation with that past. The image it sets up as a goal toward which to direct its search for moral and aesthetic recovery is the paradigmatic image of the "white city": that of Vidal and Pellegrini's prints of the Creole city of the mid-nineteenth century. The reasons for this choice also coincide widely: Prebisch found in those prints a "simple and harmonious city, without great monumental pretensions, but possessing that beauty that is the expression of naturally cultured races"; Larreta, "the charm [of] a set of rough architectures, but so expressive [with its] ingenuous lines, in those simple walls—starched whiteness."[540] In fact, in his proposal for the Plaza de Mayo, Larreta moved himself to dispense with his private neocolonial

[539] Prebisch's quote on the diagonal is from "La ciudad en que vivimos," introduction to Horacio Coppola's album of photographs, *Buenos Aires 1936*, 11. His drawings of the obelisk appeared in newspapers and have been republished in *Alberto Prebisch, Monografías de artistas argentinos*, 9 (Buenos Aires: Academia Nacional de Bellas Artes, 1972).
[540] Prebisch, "La ciudad en que vivimos"; Larreta, *Las dos fundaciones de Buenos Aires*, 69.

tastes—which led him to commission Martín Noel with the design of his own house in that style—to propose a framework of classicist homogeneity also highlighted by the presence of monumental columns:

> On Victoria Street, on the blocks that on that side face north, from Bolívar to Balcarce, equal buildings, quiet, as if they had been made to last indefinitely. [...] There would not be, in fact, anywhere, a square that would have that majesty, that dominion. As contemplation, which would never tire, the distant ships, the colors of the water, and cutting with its slender shadow the immense horizon, as in Venice, as in Rhodes, two great columns, the May column and the July column.[541]

99

It would not be an exaggeration to see Prebisch's obelisk and the Plaza de la República almost as an echo of Larreta's proposal for the Plaza de Mayo. For both, it is not a matter of emulating that past, reproducing its images, but of producing an analogous gesture, in the certainty that it is possible to recreate with gestures a circuit of dormant patriotic signs. Columns, pyramids, obelisks: hieratic monuments, pure and mute, in the face of academic or neocolonial rhetoric. It is striking that two figures as different as Roberto Giusti and Arturo Cancela coincide in 1936, summoned by the intendancy, in imagining a reconciled dialogue between the May Pyramid and the obelisk. For Giusti, the dialogue is offered as a metaphor of the reciprocal need of tradition and the present in the course of an unstoppable progress; it is the reading from the modernizing and progressive side of the Concordancia.[542] For Cancela, on the other hand, gathering all the threads that stretch from Lugones to classicist avant-gardism, the dialogue shows the ratification of the elemental series of the criollo cultural milieu: Buenos Aires-pampa-grid-geometry:

98

100

> How much we have protested the regularity of our urban layout, devoid of surprises and amenity, as if it were possible to build a city on a plain without accidents and, in fact, without limits! No matter how obstinate we may be, we will never escape from geometry because it is imposed on us, as it was on the Egyptians, by the very nature of the soil. In this respect, is it not very significant that in order to perpetuate the initial splendor of our history as a Nation, the men of May raised in the center of the glorious square, the simplest and most gallant of geometric constructions; the pyramid? [...] the modest construction seems to indicate a direction for Argentine art: the cult of pure lines and the search for beauty in the Pythagorean number. If twenty-six years ago it had not been moved from where it was, it would be facing across the first diagonal of the city, with the white obelisk of the Plaza

100

---

[541] *Las dos fundaciones de Buenos Aires*, 74.
[542] "Sinfonía de Buenos Aires," in *Homenaje a Buenos Aires en el cuarto centenario*, 493ff.

Figure 100. Horacio Coppola, *Plaza de Mayo*, 1936. Horacio Coppola Archive.
Note how the photograph visually associates the May Pyramid with the Obelisk through the
Diagonal Norte Avenue, in clear affinity with Arturo Cancela's text.

de la República, a monument that boldly affirms the same aesthetic canon and that is already an indestructible feature of the city. This coincidence after more than a century, and in similarly illustrious circumstances, is not a simple effect of chance. It is the expression, instinctive in one case, more conscious in the other, of the city's own genius, which is only accommodated to the simplicity of the noble styles in which the line reigns supreme. And to confirm this approximation in time and space, there is the great diagonal that serves as a connecting link: grandiose but white and, essentially, uniform like the colonial streets.

To return to simplicity is ratified again and again as the unquestionable slogan of belonging, as the basic *trait d'union* between the past and the future; Cancela ends: "Because since '74 until yesterday, we who have tried all the styles, are returning, although within the appropriate dimensions, to primitive simplicity."[543]

The capacity of anniversaries to condense long-lasting cultural problems is remarkable in urban history: by giving them form in public works and monuments, they manage to operate, in turn, on their future definition. With the fourth centenary, the city entered into a jubilee that lasted throughout 1936, with inaugurations of public works and cultural initiatives in which history played a decisive role, again as in the centenary of the May Revolution: as a construction of the city's memory and as a contribution to the consistent definition of its "essence." The big difference with the centenary, in any case, is that the questions of cultural identity have lost their drama: now, the general tone is the celebration of a reunion. The loss of cultural direction, the confusion of languages in which the city had seemed bent over the last fifty years, had finally proved to be short-lived: the fourth centenary confirms that the "essential character" of Buenos Aires has remained on the prowl. As it is easy to see, this celebratory climate identifies a sector of the cultural elite of Buenos Aires, but here *de Vedia's operation* intervenes, broadening it and making it representative, marking by fire with its optics the definition of public space in the contemporary city and the definition of the most enduring narrative about its modernization. There are other contemporary visions of enormous future productivity, such as the ironic distance that we saw Borges take, or that of Martínez Estrada, basing himself precisely on the omissions of this festive climate of ideas—main among them the omission of the conflict implicit in the insertion in the country of that city that contentedly withdraws into itself; but in 1936 those visions do

---

[543] "Buenos Aires a vuelo de pájaro," in *Homenaje a Buenos Aires en el cuarto centenario*, 540–41. Also José Gabriel (founder of the *Cuadernos novecentistas*) in his radio lecture makes the positive articulation between city and pampa, showing the generalization of the motif initiated by Lugones and developed by Borges; see "El país y la ciudad de Buenos Aires," in ibid., 28ff.

not set the tone of that cultural atmosphere. In any case, what seems to be the norm is the negative evaluation of the city that has resulted from fifty years of immigration and modernization—which is reinforced by "pessimistic" balance of the national character essay typical of the thirties—although this evaluation of the cycle is made by most from the celebration of its end: Buenos Aires has finally found the mold in which to macerate all the contributions that have constituted it; even giving secondary participation to the most exotic, it has proven to be *criolla*.

The role de Vedia's figure in this *operation* is highly telling of the cultural changes of elites that we already outlined in the context of our discussion of the centenary. Seeming himself to be a late man of the eighties, who recalls in every inauguration his affiliation with Alvear, de Vedia steers his adminis- tration to the most diverse manifestations of the counter-progressive alliance that had been harshly censuring the process opened in the eighties: while the Concordancia sought to restore in the country the order that had forged the "outward looking economy," cultural elites complete their criticism and for- mulate, at least at the urban level, their most articulate response. In this way, de Vedia culminates the separation already insinuated in previous decades in urban culture between a mythical Alvear, the prototypical figure of the mod- ernizing "Lord Mayor," and the effective project of modernization of which he was one of its manifestations. Alberto Prebisch, for example, can characterize Avenida de Mayo in the most catastrophic way, as the kneecap that marks in Buenos Aires the passage from the previous *culture* to the present *civilization*— Prebisch appeals to the classic antinomy of central European thought, and it seems unnecessary to clarify that he endorses that assessment of each of the terms—but that does not prevent him from stating emphatically at the same time that the avenue is the work of "the great mayor that was Don Torcuato de Alvear." Radicalizing the positions of the cultural elite of the centenary, the Avenida de Mayo has become a stigma for the counter-progressive alliance, the most finished example of "progressive superstition," of "the mania of *guaranga* (vulgar) competition that translated into the eagerness to crush the neighbor with *parapetos sobradores* (arrogant parapets) and licentious ornamentations"; in short, in the sample of the babel of languages of eclecticism, generated by "the rumbustious whim" of the "parvenu" immigrant, which altered "the hier- archical ordering of society [and] the moral physiognomy of its people." [544]

But where *de Vedia's operation* is shown to be more fully of the Concordan- cia—and here is where the avant-garde seems so functional, since that will be for decades its ideology, at least in architecture—is in its capacity to redirect that repudiation toward the wager on a modernization that ratifies its more archaic sense; in its attempt to restore the social and political fabric of a traditional Argentina through a drastic leap forward. Thus, he also managed to give his

94

---

[544] Prebisch, "La ciudad en que vivimos," 11.

name to a work that could be emphatically saluted by the futuristic imagination of an Arlt, and it should be noted that without that facet substantial elements of the *operation* could not be understood. De Vedia, again like Alvear, can access the pantheon of the great mayors because of his modernizing identity: the very location of the obelisk, emblem of the "white city," on a sector of the city center affected by works of great transformative impact, but also at the very center of the site that the artistic bohemia had chosen as the vortex of the new suburban culture, Corrientes Street must be read in that sense; de Vedia completes the "thousand subtle threads" of the grid in the neighborhoods and gives it a center. How not to understand the socialist's fury against the obelisk—beyond the procedural questions in which it justified the request for its demolition—if it ratifies the two Buenos Aires—the "white" one of avant-garde counter-progressivism and the "black" one of the tango myth—that dispute the progressivism of their "red" Buenos Aires? But, at the same time, how can we not understand their impotence in the face of de Vedia's move: Could the modernizing party of Argentina turn against modernization without putting its identity in crisis?[545]

90, 91
82

Tradition and avant-garde; elitist restoration and plebeian modernization: the urban and cultural initiatives of the intendancy achieved in the 1930s a very broad "cultural front," which took advantage of the peculiar figure of de Vedia but which also took advantage, as we shall see, of a very peculiar moment. First of all, we must emphasize the ecumenical way in which de Vedia organizes his cultural administration: he appoints Victoria Ocampo and Alberto Prebisch, colleagues in *Sur*, to the board of directors of the Teatro Colón, and Enrique Larreta as president of the Commission of Celebrations of the fourth centenary; commissions Coppola, recently returned from his experiences with the German radical avant-garde—with some of whose more radical members, such as Brecht and Eisler, he ended up sharing a passing exile in London—to take the photographs of Buenos Aires for the album of homage that he commissions Prebisch and Ignacio Anzoátegui (then member of the board of the Cursos de Cultura Católica) to preface; donates a municipal building in the recently widened Corrientes to Leónidas Barletta to create the Teatro del Pueblo—mythical for the Communist left—and entrusts the historiographic projects for the centenary to the founders of the New Historical School, Ricardo Levene and Emilio Ravignani, a history of Buenos Aires to Rómulo Zabala and Enrique De Gandía, and the *History of Corrientes Street* to Marechal; finally, he organizes a series of radio talks to commemorate the foundation, inviting figures from the most

---

[545] The requests for the demolition of the obelisk were made by the socialist bench of the Council on the initiative of Councilman Alejandro Comolli, arguing that it had been decided by decree during the summer recess; see *La Razón* (Buenos Aires), April 30, 1936. That was the highest point of an intense aesthetic, technical, and political controversy—which was exploited to the point of exhaustion by all the newspapers in those months—between the defenders and detractors of the obelisk.

diverse backgrounds, such as Roberto Giusti, Francisco Luis Bernárdez, Manuel Ugarte, Barletta, Anzoátegui, Alfonsina Storni, Borges, Levene, Cancela, Samuel Medrano, Manuel Mujica Láinez, Marechal, Baldomero Fernández Moreno, or José Gabriel. A good part of the aesthetic-ideological coalitions that have been shaping the intellectual map of the twenties are harmoniously gathered here, coinciding in a significant way with the type of *refoundation* proposed.

I have insisted up to this point on the "Creole" character of this refoundation; however, as befits the event it commemorates, the most ambitious aspect of the *operation* is to establish its link with the Hispanic past: what better than the celebration of the foundation to repair the spiritual alliance of the American metropolis that had been a pioneer in becoming independent from it. This connection also continues in many ways the problems of the centenary; but beyond the ideological attempts, and beyond how advanced historiographical revision was then, it was a task of improbable resolution when what it was precisely about was the celebration of the rupture. Now, by contrast, it is possible to sustain and celebrate a vision of Spain that turns the page of the "black legend" and gives spiritual roots to the Buenos Aires of the present. The whole celebration of 1936 is marked by fire, by this need for spiritual roots, starting with the story of the origin that the commission of historians of the New School carried out at the request of the mayor's office (the mayor is also part of this commission, as a historian and surely also to ensure its results). It is well-known that there are no documents proving the date or the precise place of the city's first foundation; it is therefore significant that the leaders of the school that had led historiography to a documentary apotheosis should have relied so heavily on interpretation as to define date and place by decree. For, as Silvestri has shown, it was not a question of dispelling the haze of origin but of constituting it as a glorious certification of the Spanish spirit: between the previous hypotheses of Groussac or Madero, who maintained that the foundation had been on the Bajo (and therefore did not give the expeditioners an image of special wisdom), and the decision of Levene and company that it *must have* occurred on the plateau (in the present-day Parque Lezama), what was at stake was an opinion about Spain and about the character of the foundation.[546]

In any case, Hispanicism is only the prelude to what will serve as a more general and encompassing organizing principle in the symbolic refoundation: that which can restore the essential Buenos Aires, that which can give a transcendent meaning to the cosmopolitan Buenos Aires—"the populous city and its diabolical *balumba* (mass)" says Levene, scarcely conciliatory— is religion, the fundamental content of the Spanish heritage with which the city would have been fertilized in that original act.[547] The spiritual, modern, and traditional Bue-

---

[546] Silvestri, *El color del río*.

[547] See Ricardo Levene, "La conquista de América y la expedición de Don Pedro de Mendoza," in *Homenaje a Buenos Aires en el cuarto centenario*, 30.

nos Aires is, above all, Catholic. When the documents of the fourth centenary are reviewed, the invocations of the Spanish lineage as a way of rediscovering the Christian filiation of the city stand out overwhelmingly. Dell'Oro Maini's imprint cannot but be recognized: behind the ecumenism on which the success of *de Vedia's operation* depends so much, there is a firm thread that connects the great majority of the participants in the conferences and in the commissions: the membership of the *convivia* and the Courses of Catholic Culture. For example, Samuel Medrano, editorial secretary of *Criterio* during the years when Dell'Oro was its director, asked himself during the radio conferences:

> What can it be that will bind us to the ideal of the founders? In addition to the language that is preserved and the few family traditions that are fading away and the cult of the past that does not encourage everyone with due fervor, there is something, however, that links us to the vocational ideal of the old Buenos Aires [: the] Christian bond that transcends the common good of the city because this is not an ultimate end but is subordinated to the supreme end of man, which is God. To maintain this order [...] is the highest ministry of the city, it constitutes the true vocation of Buenos Aires, the reason for its existence as a city. The founder gave it that vocation, which must be fulfilled in time and in history as long as Buenos Aires exists, as long as it does not deserve to disappear like Babylon.[548]

A good number of other lecturers point in the same direction: Ignacio Anzoátegui, Francisco Luis Bernárdez, or Leopoldo Marechal, who writes for the occasion his "Spiritual Foundation of Buenos Aires," in which he discovers that the city was consecrated "from its origin to the loving labors of the spirit," as image and simulacrum, "in order and virtue," of the Celestial City.[549] But the insertion here of Marechal's name places the religious plea on another plane, returning us circularly to the beginning of the *operation*, because, as we know, Marechal was also an active member of vanguard aesthetic renewal, which allows us to complete a characterization.

Although it has not been studied much, the rise of Catholicism in Buenos Aires society in those years is well-known, as evidenced by the multitudinous acts of the Eucharistic Congress of 1934. Tulio Halperin described dominant sectors' adherence to the church in the period as an "abdication of conservative liberalism"; although he points out antecedents that explain its spread—for

---

[548] Samuel Medrano, "Four Centuries," 329–30.
[549] *Homenaje a Buenos Aires en el cuarto centenario*, 491. Bernárdez writes his "Oración a Nuestra Señora de los Buenos Aires" so that "Dios funde a Buenos Aires / Por vez tercera, pero en Jesucristo / [...] / Y para que la bienaventurada / Ciudad de Buenos Aires sobreviva, / Convertida en la parte más poblada / De la Jerusalén definitiva," in *Homenaje a Buenos Aires en el cuarto centenario*, 265.

example, the growth of Catholic Action in the middle sectors—he recognizes that the magnitude of the Congress did not fail to appear as a surprise with striking details of sudden transvestism: Borges and Bioy Casares will exploit it ironically in a later story—"me, such a good Catholic since the Eucharistic Congress," says Mariana Ruiz Villalba de Anglada to Don Isidro Parodi.[550] But the fact that in the period it was noticed by many with surprise or with irony, does nothing but point to a significant fact of the relations of Buenos Aires society with the church: the church appears in Buenos Aires when and where it is least expected. It is a society that has a self-image of plurality and secularism; so when religion appears, it does so surprisingly and explosively and its generalization is not accepted, remaining in representation exclusively linked to a small group and to an archaic imaginary of narrow obscurantism. Perhaps this is one of the reasons why the relationship between Catholicism and the aesthetic avant-garde, which was more than solid and productive in those years, has not been analyzed in depth.[551] Borges himself, who would later rejoice in the surprise, had been participating with some assiduity in the Courses of Catholic Culture and publishing in several Catholic magazines of the period. The truth is that, although they are also known, these links have not come to form a structured part of our representations of the cultural modernism of the 1920s and 1930s.

It is at this point that Prebisch and the obelisk complete their condensing capacity. In principle, because Prebisch is in himself, like Marechal, an unbeatable example of the relationship between Catholicism and the avant-garde, since he had an intense doctrinaire participation in the main institutions of both sectors: the magazines *Criterio* (in Dell'Oro's time), *Baluarte* and *Número*, the *convivia* and the Cursos, on the one hand; the magazines *Martín Fierro* and *Sur*, on the other. The character of the articulation achieved by de Vedia between the different spheres of Buenos Aires culture has in this conjunction of *Criterio* and *Sur* a more than synthetic manifestation, since they are the magazines that very soon—just months—after the celebration of the fourth centenary, in the new framework created by the Spanish Civil War, will emblematize the two irreconcilable sides that will organize cultural and ideological representations for much longer: Catholic Hispanism and sympathies for Franco,

---

[550] See Tulio Halperin Donghi, "1930–1960. Crónica de treinta años" (1961), in *Argentina en el callejón* (Buenos Aires: Ariel, 1995), 128; Jorge Luis Borges and Adolfo Bioy Casares, "Las previsiones de Sangiácomo" (1942), in *Six Problems for Don Isidro Parodi* (New York: Dutton, 1981), 77. After the research for this book was completed, Loris Zanatta's work documented this Catholic boom very convincingly in *Del estado liberal a la nación católica. Iglesia y Ejército en los orígenes del peronismo. 1930–1943* (Buenos Aires: Editorial de la Universidad Nacional de Quilmes, 1996).
[551] Zuleta Álvarez records these relations in the first period of *Criterio*: "The union of tradition in fundamental ideas with the aesthetic avant-garde was achieved in a way that has never been possible again in Argentine culture"; in *El nacionalismo argentino*, 190.

against modernist, cosmopolitan and democratic liberalism.[552] That is why I mentioned that it is not only the peculiar figure of de Vedia, but also the peculiar conjuncture that favors this communion—if the play on words is allowed—of cultural stances unthinkable shortly after.

But if Prebisch is already a factor in the synthesis, when we realize that Dell'Oro Maini took the initiative to build an obelisk as a monument to the fourth centenary, the meaning of the monument changes subtly and gains a new intelligibility. Dell'Oro, this refined intellectual, the main driving force behind the meeting of Catholicism and the avant-garde in the *convivia* and a modernist reestablishment of the religious imaginary, first convinced de Vedia that an obelisk was the right monument to commemorate the celebration and that Prebisch, his fellow militant, was the most suitable person to build it; and then he proposed it, with express mention of its formal characteristics and with all the institutional provisions so as to be able to execute it by decree in record time.[553] The call to order of avant-garde classicism thus finds its ulterior explanation in the call to celestial order to be carried out in the City of Men: that ends up being the "white city" in its passage from the suburbs to the center, by definitively reorganizing—until today—the public space of the expanded metropolis. The essential geometry of the monuments and of this stripped architecture no longer questions only the national history and the nature of the Pampa—the two aspects of the reconquered milieu—but above all the essential origin of a community, its spiritual foundation, what can really give it a transcendent meaning: precisely, outside the passage of time, with which the counter-progressive alliance finds its ultimate horizon.

There are no documents that show a theoretical or doctrinaire argumentation in the meeting of this type of Catholicism—its modernizing sectors—and the avant-garde—the classicist one. But I believe that this encounter has a high explanatory capacity of the series of agreements that subtended, at that precise juncture, an important part of the Buenos Aires elite, and that later external

---

[552] On these polemics, focused from the perspective of *Criterio*, see the article by Marcelo Montserrat and Carlos Floria, "El pensamiento de Gustavo Franceschi y la revista *Criterio* en la cultura política de la Argentina contemporánea," in M. Montserrat, *Usos de la memoria* (Buenos Aires: Sudamericana and Universidad de San Andrés, 1996).

[553] In a note dated February 4, 1936, Dell'Oro Maini wrote to Prebisch: "My dear friend Prebisch: On the occasion of the forthcoming completion of the Plaza de la República, I have proposed to the mayor an idea which he has taken up with great enthusiasm. It would be to erect an obelisk in the center of that square. Undoubtedly it will not be possible to build a true monolith in the oriental style, that is to say, in one piece; but as I do not wish for that reason to abandon my project, which seems to me to be really good, I would like to talk to you and ask your intelligent opinion on how best to carry it out [...]". I thank Mónica Rojas, who gave me access to a collection of documents belonging to the Prebisch family, for finding this letter, which is decisive in understanding the nature of the commission.

conflicts prevented from being clearly identified. At the same time, the social explanation of the phenomenon could be found there: that the modernism of the "white city" has had such a rapid and widespread acceptance among leading sectors of society as to produce with it the imaginary of the new public space of Buenos Aires; that it has also had so much diffusion, and that it has been liable to such a proliferation of essentialist interpretations (and it must be remembered here that also Antonio Vilar, the other founder of Argentine architectural modernism, was a fervent believer, and that a good part of his "social" interventions in the architecture of the thirties were motivated by religious philanthropic purposes).

With these components, in the 1930s a long-lasting narrative was formalized in the urban culture and historiography of the city, which canonized the vision of an idyllic colonial city, authentic in its rusticity during the nineteenth century, and sick with a suicidal disorientation from the 1880s onwards.[554] All the elements that compose it—elitist nostalgia for an origin, repudiation of modernization, anti-positivism, rejection of the dissolving effects of immigration—had long existed in different spheres of the cultural and political elites; the interesting thing about de Vedia's operation is that by responding to it by means of a finished model of a city affiliated with the aesthetic avant-garde, he articulates it as a narrative while at the same time giving it a "modern" character: in short, it was also against the eclectic masks that the avant-garde reacted in Europe and also, in many of its aspects, to turn with nostalgia toward more harmonious pasts. The peculiarity, perhaps, of Argentine hegemonic modernism—its reactive utopia—was to have been able to find in certain models of northern European modernism a mirror through which to retrospectively invent the "white" images of its colonial Buenos Aires.

---

[554] One of the first formalizations that I found of that narration is the historical introduction in the Estudio del Plan de Buenos Aires of 1948, written by Rodolfo Puiggrós and Eduardo Astesano (see "Evolución del Gran Buenos Aires en el tiempo y el espacio," Revista de Arquitectura 376–77 [1956]) and reproduced on the basis of the developmentalist Regulating Plan of 1958–64. Its power and validity are proved by the undoubted influences in the version of such a different historian as Scobie. We have analyzed it with Silvestri in "Imágenes al sur. Sobre algunas hipótesis de James Scobie para el desarrollo de Buenos Aires.""

2. The Conflicting Dimensions of Public Space

[The councilors of the Socialist Party] knew how to break with the petty politics of the neighborhood, of zones, of guilds, to protect, instead, the general
interests of the city.[555]

–Revista Socialista, 1932

Neighborhoods abandoned to their own fate by the building authorities,
have placed in you the only possibility of progress claimed in multiple and
well-founded requests, which unfortunately have been lost among the fol-
ders of the Municipal Palace, condemning us to a situation of such abandon-
ment that already exceeded, as Mr. Mayor could appreciate, the limit of what
was tolerable. No mayor to date had echoed our distressing situation; they
succeeded each other underestimating the true value of this suburban area,
and we lived resigned to suffer patiently the unjust indifference with which
we are treated by those who should have solved it with a little good will. And
that is why, Mr. Mayor, your attitude cannot go unnoticed by us, it sets a
very honorable precedent and vindicates for the commune of Buenos Aires a
beautiful gesture of equity and justice, so common in the personality of Mr.
Mayor Doctor De Vedia y Mitre, whom we sincerely consecrate as the only
benefactor of the areas of Nueva Pompeya and Soldati.[556]

–Sociedades de Fomento Edilicio y Cultural "El Despertar" and "El Pilar" of
    Nueva Pompeya. Letter to the mayor thanking him for a tour of the area, 1935

The end of an urban and cultural cycle, but also, and above all, a political one:
the end of "socialist Buenos Aires." It is one of these singular coincidences of
history that the year 1936 was also called to symbolize the end of the urban
cycle, with the consecration of a form of administration that would shape for
decades the relationship between institutions, politics, and society, marking the
definition of a new type of public space. The triumph of modernization over
reform, expressed in the withdrawal of the city into itself and the symbolic
refoundation of its center, would also have an impact on the political institution
that had emerged as a direct product of the new reformist moment opened in
1918: the City Council. Despite the growing socialist influence during the first
half of the decade, the year 1936 will show the resounding defeat of that party
not only in the electoral field, against the return of Radicalism, but in the definition of the main conflicts over public services that it had driven in the twenties and thirties sustained by much of public opinion, and around which it had

---

[555] "Vida Municipal," *Revista Socialista* II, no. 20 (January 1932): 68.

[556] Municipalidad de la Ciudad de Buenos Aires, *La obra de la Intendencia municipal en
los barrios suburbanos de la ciudad de Buenos Aires durante los años 1932–1935 (discurso
del secretario de Obras Públicas Dr. Amílcar Razori en el HCD)* (Buenos Aires: Peuser,
1935), 61.

built its reformist identity in the city, betting its political future on its outcome. For a series of intertwined factors—the skill with which the municipal executive handled the resolution of conflicts; the complete identification between the Socialist Party and the Council in the previous decade; the corruption with which the institution was globally associated, beyond specific circumstances and actors (Radicalism, especially)—1936 will mark the beginning of the debacle not only of municipal Socialism, but of the Council itself, whose discredit led to its closure shortly after, in 1941, in the face of the most complete public indifference, closing definitively the reformist cycle.

In any case, the failure of political reformism along with the exhaustion of the experience of the party and the institution that had, in truth, most clearly embodied it—and this latter point will be the main focus of this last section— does no more than mirror the particular characteristics of social reformism in the institutions that, for their part, had also exemplified it: the neighborhood advocacy associations. In other words, it does no more than show the roots of official modernization of the 1930s in urban society itself, the way in which that modernization knew how to connect with profound social tendencies that crystalized and showed all their consequences at this decisive juncture. The contrast between the opening quotes heading this section shows the growing distance between the objectives of political reformism and social reformism: while Socialism claims its rupture with "the small politics of the neighborhood," two advocacy associations, which had been linked in the reformist period with Socialism and Communism, show their full satisfaction with de Vedia's work because it solves their neighborhood's problems, introducing the main issue that the new public space "barrio" personifies in the quandary of modernization and reform: the confrontation of a local and a metropolitan dimension.

To better understand this confrontation in which the reformist experience finds its limits, in this last chapter we must take up again the threads of certain aspects of urban policy in which Socialism played a leading role: the conflicts over public services. These erupted in 1936, but to understand them as a symptom of the relations between Socialism and society it is useful to follow their outcome from the 1920s, at the height of the reformist boom. Faced with the ideological or practical difficulties it encountered in other urban issues—especially those linked to a unified vision of the city's expansion—Socialists had relied on its proposals and campaigns for public services to build their municipal political identity. In these they could harmoniously articulate the main roles with which they identified: political oversight of the state and vigilance of consumer rights, legislation, and the construction of alternatives. It could, above all, coincide punctually with demands that they found already generalized in society: especially lower tariffs, but also—in the politicized twenties and thirties—rejection of foreign monopolies with the correlate of alternatives of cooperativization or municipalization; and, additionally, they could structure a line of action that descended without contradictions from national leadership to municipal militancy. Thus, if in the face of urban reform issues we can see Socialists vacillating, supporting diverse initiatives, often coming from municipal executives and not always coherent with their own thinking—the Building Regulations of 1928, the Office of the Urbanization Plan of 1932—on the issue of public services it led with very definite proposals the main actions of an enormously mobilized public opinion and, in general, forced the whole political field to align themselves behind their project.

A paradigmatic case is that of transportation, throughout two decades in which the complexification and diversification of urban public transport was the norm in the main cities of the world. In Buenos Aires, this was a fundamental issue due to the close dependence that had arisen between the business model for operating the service and suburban expansion. In fact, the monopoly that Compañía Anglo Argentina de Tranvías (Anglo-Argentine Tram Company) had formed after the electrification of the system (1897–1904), through the purchase and annexation of most of the competing companies during the first decade, had been functional to the massive suburban expansion of the city. The technical innovation of electrification in transportation implicitly led to a tendency to merge companies and create monopolies to the extent that it allowed lower costs in proportion to the unification and rationalization of the system. Therein lies one of the keys to the 10-cent fare that the tram company imposed in 1905 as a single fare, and which decisively pushed the displacement of the popular sectors toward the suburbs by making it possible for them to locate their residence separately from their work.[557] In 1909, at the height of the company's monopolizing strategy and the expansion of suburbanization, the Anglo-Argentinian Tram Company obtained the municipal concession to build and operate three subway lines through a mixed system combined with its own tramway network that gave it complete control of urban transportation; however, as a preview of the political climate that would dominate a decade later, in the conservative City Council prior to the reform there was already strong resistance against the unification of the entire system under the command of a foreign company.[558]

---

[557] The classic study on this subject is Scobie, *Buenos Aires: Plaza to Suburb*, esp. ch. 5 See also Sargent, *The Spatial Evolution of Greater Buenos Aires*, and Torres, "Evolución de los procesos de estructuración espacial urbana"; more specifically on Anglo, see Raúl García Heras, *Transportes, negocios y política. La compañía Anglo Argentina de Tranvías, 1876–1981* (Buenos Aires: Sudamericana, 1994).

[558] See Honorable Concejo Deliberante, *Versiones Taquigráficas*, December 21, 1909. In those same years the English company was being co-opted by SOFINA, the transnational consortium based in Belgium: Raúl García Heras points out that between 1907 and 1913 it came to be controlled by the European consortium Compagnie Générale des Tramways de Buenos Aires based in Belgium, with majority participation of SOFINA (Société Financière de Transports et d'Enterprises Industrielles) and in which British

When the new Council took office in 1919, with a Socialist and Radical majority, the social and political irritation produced by the monopoly would intensify because the company, favored by its fluid relations with conservative mayors, had not fulfilled most of the commitments of the concession (it had only built the first subway line in 1913–14) and, arguing that the economic inconveniences derived from the European war had changed their situation, requested a fare increase as a necessary condition to continue the works. From then on, and over the following fifteen years, an intense public campaign led by Socialists but followed to a greater or lesser extent by the entire political spectrum due to its enormous popularity, placed the company in a pincer, attacking at the same time the two central aspects of its business policy: proposing to break the monopoly and keep fares at 10 cents (this in particular will become the rallying cry of the campaign as a symbol of its popular character). The company continued to rely on its fluid contacts with the traditional political class, including the Radical mayors, so that a sort of stalemate was reached during the 1920s: for short periods the company obtained fare increases, but against very demanding conditions that it was unable to meet (the Radical mayors could look favorably on the company's claims, but they were not willing to pay the cost of appearing subjected to it); the City Council repeatedly withdrew the 1909 monopoly concession and opened the game to new bids for subways, with great public expectation and campaigns organized by the neighborhood advocacy associations to obtain signatures in favor of different proposals, but the company also managed to stop them time and time again.[559]

The curious thing is that the equation that a decade earlier seemed irrefutable (the greater the business concentration, the greater the technical progress and the lower the fares) and the very suburban expansion with which this equation collaborated, had now turned against the company. In the first place, because the growth of the city began to make partial exploitations of zones or subsystems profitable (for example, the subway without the trams); in second place, and much more important, because the development of combustion-engine transportation—promoted by the North American automotive industry as part of the intense worldwide competition against the railroads and the British trams—allowed a high decentralization at lower cost and greater flexibility (managerial and technical, in contrast to the rigidity of the tramway

---

businessmen occupied a secondary place (this will in fact be mentioned throughout the debates in the City Council during the 1920s); See *Transportes, negocios y política.*

[559] On the ambiguous attitude of the radicals, see Walter, *Politics and Urban Growth in Buenos Aires: 1910–1942.* On the support of the Sociedades de Fomento, see for example the letters of the Sociedad de Fomento de Villa Mazzini, in Municipalidad de la Ciudad de Buenos Aires, *Actas del Honorable Concejo Deliberante* (Buenos Aires), February 12, 1927.

system). So, favored also by that situation of political stalemate that translated in a stagnation of the tramway system, automotive public transportation would grow in an explosive way in the twenties: in 1923 with the formation of the first *omnibus* lines and in 1928 with the creation of the *taxis-colectivos*; and if in the beginning these emerge to complement the tram lines, with routes that connect the track layouts with interstitial zones, they quickly begin to enter into competition. Between 1920 and 1930, while the tramway system remains stable at almost 900 kilometers of track, automobile transport reaches 4,000 kilometers of routes; thus, the tram company drops from 78 percent of the total passengers transported to 48 percent, entering a complicated vicious circle (the inverted equation: the lower the monopoly capacity the lower the economic performance and the impossibility to modernize the system, which in turn decreases the monopoly capacity). This leads the tram company to face the 1929 crisis in an extremely compromised economic situation while, at the same time, the small, self-managed bus and collective lines do not cease to multiply.[560]

Political and public sympathies had already buckled in net terms. The conservatives were clearly in favor of the Anglo-Argentine Tram Company's monopoly. During the de facto administration of Mayor Guerrico buses and collective taxis were prohibited in the center to prevent the company from what he considered "unfair competition," and during Naón's administration, in a scandalous visit to Buenos Aires, the Duke of Atholl, president of the board of directors, obtained official support to maintain the subway concessions and submit the whole system to his control. By contrast, the Socialists, accompanied by the majority of public opinion, favored business diversification in subway transport and, above all, the multiplication of automobile transport. The collective taxi, especially, represented for the socialists—and for public opinion generally—an emblem of progressive opposition to the tram company: it added the prestige of technical novelty, superior speed, the flexibility that allowed it to reach at low-cost interstitial areas of the suburbs, precisely the areas that progressive opinion considered "abandoned." And it offered an irresistible combination as a formula for its entrepreneurial identity: a *modern, national,* and *socializing* spirit of enterprise—since in the beginning the organization of the *colectivos* was cooperative—and, above all, emblematic of "*viveza criolla*" (Creole sharpness)—which brings together socialist reformism with neighborhood populism. The businessmen would conduct their campaign talking about "the capacity and spirit of progress that the nation's men have to exploit public services, without the usual foreign contribution." All the conditions were there for their cause to be taken up by the nationalist populism of a newspaper like

[560] The data in Martha Susana Páramo, *Un fracaso hecho historia. La Corporación de Transportes de la Ciudad de Buenos Aires* (Mendoza: Universidad Nacional de Cuyo, 1991), 40; and Raúl García Heras, *Transportes, negocios y política,* 73.

Crítica, which will launch a campaign in favor of the collective taxi and against "the dictatorship of the tramway." [561]

It could thus be said that the *colectivo* emerged as the most effective response to the double process of urban dispersion and homogeneity that characterized the formation of the neighborhoods: the Buenos Aires of the barrio, of "ant speculation" and "ant industrialization," already had its "ant public transport." It was a very special moment in the history of the city, when technical transformations of a particular service could be linked almost without mediation with the urban structure and with ideological-political sympathies. In effect, the two fronts on which the Socialists fought the battle for transportation—new subway concessions and defense of the emerging organization of buses and *colectivos*—coincide, beyond the issue of monopoly and fares, with the commitment to a more uniform use of urban land based on the ratification of the new expanded city: the *colectivos*, because they favor the development of interstitial areas; and the non-monopolistic subways, because they propose lines different from those serviced by the Anglo-Argentine Tram Company. In the second half of the 1920s, when competition for new concessions arose, Socialism gave its support to those proposals that sought to replace the radiocentric system of the lines concessioned to the tram company with systems that covered the territory more homogeneously; while the Anglo-Argentine Tram Company's scheme tended to converge radially on the Plaza de Mayo, alternative proposals tended to integrate the "geometric center" in a beltway scheme for the municipality. [562]

Thus, the dispute over transportation in the 1920s can also be understood within the framework of "the search for the Center" that we saw developing, which would show the certainty of Socialism on this issue, since it consequently supported the tendency to decentralize the traditional core of urban prestige. Especially if we compare this certainty with the ambiguities regarding the issue of expansion: the homogenizing vision of the new urban figure is so clear for reformism that it does not notice that the interstitial coverage that the *colectivo* favors actually contributes to the processes of urbanization it is fighting against in the still incomplete zones of the grid that it attempts to preserve from subdivision. But in the twenties the ambiguities are not limited to Socialism but affect the very reformism of the municipal apparatus: the reformist technicians, also with absolute coherence, incorporate into the 1925 Organic Project one of

---

[561] The campaigns are very forceful since the end of the twenties and reach their peak in the debates of the thirties; the quote is from April 1934. The businessmen's quote in Páramo, *Un fracaso hecho historia*, 47.

[562] These are the Dodero-Benigni and Celestino and Horacio Marcó proposals: see Benigno Benigni, "Vías de comunicación. Los subterráneos de Buenos Aires," *Revista de Ingeniería* (Buenos Aires), 1925; Municipalidad de la Ciudad de Buenos Aires, *Actas del Concejo Deliberante* (Buenos Aires), December 27, 1927.

the decentralizing subway proposals, while Mayor Noel—promoter of the Project—negotiates with the Anglo-Argentine Tram Company the maintenance in exclusivity of its radiocentric concession.

But that is another ingredient of the "tie" of the decade. The truth is that, unable to impose new global proposals, Socialism manages in 1930, before the coup, to have the City Council grant a Spanish company (CHADOPYF) the two lines that Anglo had not yet built.[563] When the Council was reopened in 1932 with a renewed socialist majority, the social situation on the issue was very tense, in the context of even greater stagnation of Anglo, the multiplication of the automotive system, and a political climate rarefied by allegations of interference of British imperialism in national sovereignty. Faced with this situation, the City Council proposed the formation of a municipal technical commission to study the coordination and municipalization of the different systems, encouraging the formation of a public monopoly.[564] This proposal should be seen in conjunction with Socialism's growing acceptance of planning toward the end of the 1920s: planning and municipalization appear as the clearest political evidence of its greater concern for active public policies and for its own insertion within the machinery of a state already openly dedicated to intervening in society and the economy, at a growing distance from previous positions that wanted a minimal state so as not to affect the development of initiatives within society itself (cooperatives, mutual societies, etc.). What took hold in Buenos Aires Socialism in the 1930s was the certainty that only a public monopoly could favor a rational coordination of the whole system, controlling fares, avoiding the exclusive exploitation of remunerative lines or the low quality of service in those that were not, preventing technological backwardness and the stagnation of peripheral urban areas. And this change is fundamental because we will see that it will also manifest itself in a search for a repoliticization of Socialism's relations with social organizations.

While the municipal technical commission was being set up, de Vedia y Mitre had already taken over, and would soon show his great political capacity (empowered by Justo's unrestricted support) to liquidate the opposition. In the first place, he vetoed the Council commission, taking advantage, as in the case of the obelisk and so many others, of the summer recess, to avoid the public reaction of Socialism and its impact on opinion, because, from the point of view of votes, as soon as the sessions reopened it would be clear that the mayor had recovered his own bloc with the support of independent Socialism, so that Socialism could hardly gather the two-thirds necessary to review a veto.

---

[563] They are lines C (Constitución-Retiro) and D (Palermo-Catedral), which started in 1933 and 1936; line B (Alem-Lacroze) had been granted by the Congress to the Lacroze company (a national capital company) in 1912 and was built in the 1930s.

[564] See *Actas*, December 29, 1932, when the Municipal Mass Transportation Study Commission is formed.

Second, he appointed a new commission but at the level of the national government, making the overlapping of jurisdictions, which the reformist mayors had traditionally perceived as a curtailment of their power, play to his advantage; he thus placed the conflict in a completely different orbit, dominated by the Concordancia. The fact that this commission was chaired by Roberto Ortiz—then minister and future president—shows the importance that the government gave to the issue (the company had begun direct talks with Justo at the beginning of his administration), already in the framework of bilateral negotiations with England from which the so-called Roca-Runciman pact would emerge to guarantee Argentina the continuity of the meat trade despite the restrictions of the crisis, with the famous trade-off promising a "benevolent treatment" to British capital in the country.[565]

The conclusions of this new national commission agreed with the municipal commission on the need to coordinate the system as a whole but, arguing strongly against the "politicization" of the issue by the City Council, they proposed that the National Congress should be responsible for the establishment by law of a Transport Corporation hegemonized by the tramway company to control competition in the automobile system; that is, they translated coordination into private monopoly. The jurisdictional dispute over the city has, as we saw in previous chapters, a long, problematic tradition: in the case of transportation there was already a partial precedent in the concession that the Congress had granted to the Lacroze company in 1912 for the realization of a subway line (line B, which was built in the early thirties); but now a much more serious cutback of attributions is proposed, because it takes away from the municipality all control over the whole of public transport and because, for the first time, the municipal government itself takes the initiative in this "dispossession."

From March 1934, when the mayor presented the conclusions of his commission to Congress with a bill, to September 1936 (in the middle of the celebration of the fourth centenary), when the law creating the Corporation was passed by the Senate, a very harsh battle took place in parliament and in public opinion in which the limitations of the socialist opposition to translate their ideological positions into effective policies became evident. Socialist deputies made long opposition speeches, the councilors formed a control commission to

---

[565] Seeking to contradict traditional hypotheses, García Heras argues that the company had a very relative place within the British interests at stake in the Roca-Runciman pact, since for the British government it would have been a transnational company (SOFINA); at the same time—and here we agree—he has shown the contradictions of the Argentine government which, along with the concessions to the company, favored large-scale automobile transport as never before with Allende Posse's road plan; but what all that does not manage to explain, anyway—beyond showing the typical incongruities of politics—is the consistent support of the Argentine government to the more global pretensions of Anglo in the city, which will be crowned with the formation of the Corporación de Transportes (Corporation of Transports).

denounce irregularities and mobilized support from social organizations and the press. But the executive of the mayor's office generated a new scenario, from which it emerged that, after more than fifteen years of confrontation, the formal transport system had stagnated, technical innovations appeared through the "spontaneous" initiative of society despite a posteriori political support, and that, in any case, it was necessary to coordinate a system whose competition threatened chaos. In a presentation to the Council, the municipality's Secretary of Public Works, Amílcar Razori, made a technically unquestionable defense of the need for coordination and regional control of transportation, recovering elements of the conclusions of the municipal commission, but proposing that, given the jurisdictional difference between the capital and the Province of Buenos Aires, only the national government could carry it out. Municipal government thus alienated the control of public transportation from the city using as argument the absence of a regional entity that, in its policy of withdrawal and in its vision contrary to the institutionalization of Greater Buenos Aires, it had itself prevented from forming. Razori's technical discourse doubled Socialism's bet on the need for control, hiding behind the simulacrum of regional coordination the elimination of municipal interference in the elaboration of public policies.[566]

Although the Corporation finally began to function three years later, 1936 was the date in which the city relinquished by law one of the main levers for metropolitan politics, which it would never recover. This shows that de Vedia had taken office determined to solve the political conflicts of his district at any cost: without fear of institutionalizing them and with an absolute lack of concern about their future consequences. But it also shows the dilemma of the City Council at the moment of greatest reformist incidence: placed in front of an executive municipality, willing to take to the limit the institutional conflict that had already appeared in the twenties, the Council is shown as an impotent institution, whose only destiny seems to be to realize the caricature that "anti-political" sectors have created of it: "obstructing" effective actions—paralyzing "progress"—and politicizing the issues that would require "technical" solutions. After the euphoria of the first years of the "Socialist Council," when it even seemed possible to impose on the national government the fall of its mayor, institutional limits show their insurmountable character: the public force of a Council headed by the opposition turns against it, because the greater its mobilizing capacity, the greater by contrast its inability to resolve the conflicts it generates, its inability to turn them into concrete urban policies, in such a way that it leads society into a spiral of confrontation for whose resolution it lacks, *by definition*, the tools. Not only because it is the legislative sphere, but also because it does not even retain the power of legislation, which can be

---

[566] See intervention of Amílcar Razori in the Council, HCD, *Actas* (Buenos Aires), June 5, 1934.

recovered at any time, opportunistically, by the National Congress. De Vedia puts the prevailing municipal power system in black and white, in such a way that the equation is the same as it was before the reform: without the executive, there is no urban administration; without the Council, there is. And from here some questions arise that society, having lost the expectations placed in the reformist process, inevitably had to ask itself: Is there anything more important in a city than management? What is the Council for? What should its relationship with society be?

In the definitive answers that were to mark reformism's "end of cycle," another conflict over public services, of greater political gravity although of lesser urban incidence than that of transportation, would exert influence: the conflict over electricity rates, which has gone down in posterity as the "CHADE scandal," one of the emblems of the "infamous decade." This is a much better known case and its links with the municipal political sphere, in terms very similar to those I pursue here, have been recently dealt with in a comprehensive way, so it will be convenient to present it succinctly.[567] Once again, it is a foreign and practically monopolistic company, which has great political leeway in negotiations with the national government and the municipal executive to impose its own strategies of service expansion and tariff modification (according to the custom of these large companies, the local board included important figures of the local establishment with quick access to government offices, such as former Mayor Joaquín de Anchorena or Carlos Meyer Pellegrini).[568] In fact, since the 1920s, within the framework of the general sociopolitical mobilization of the reformed Council, there had been a succession of criticisms against arbitrary tariff policies, in response to which Socialism demanded the construction of instruments of public control and used the municipal electric cooperatives that abounded in the rest of the country as a differential example of business management.

So, the scenario in the first half of the 1930s practically replicates that of the conflict over transportation, mutually reinforcing each other: enormous social mobilization led by Socialism and reflected in the appearance of federations of neighborhood advocacy societies that propose not to pay the fares; a

[567] See Luciano de Privitellio, *Vecinos y ciudadanos*, especially chapter 4, "¿Quién habla por la ciudad?" For a detailed analysis of the conflict in relation to municipal politics, see Walter, *Politics and Urban Growth in Buenos Aires: 1910–1942*. For the traditional analysis of the "CHADE affair" in terms of political scandal and corruption, in the report of the investigative commission formed by the revolutionary government in 1943, see *El informe Rodríguez Conde. Informe de la Comisión Investigadora de los Servicios Públicos de Electricidad* (Buenos Aires: EUDEBA, 1974).
[568] CHADE (Compañía Hispano Americano de Electricidad), successor of CATE (Compañía Alemana Transatlántica de Electricidad), a subsidiary of the German AEG that, since 1907, controlled the electric monopoly in the capital with a fifty-year concession.

majority public opinion that coincides with the opposition; public acts, parliamentary debate. But the interesting thing about this case is that the Mayor's office, instead of taking the conflict out of the municipal sphere (there were no arguments to do so), took it to the very terrain that Socialism considered intangible: the City Council and the neighborhood advocacy associations. In the first sphere, the conciliatory policy of the Mayor's office counted with the collaboration of Radicalism, which had triumphantly reappeared in 1936. Upon its return to the electoral game, Radicals confronted Socialists with the double argument of their ineffectiveness and their politicization of the conflict, but above all denounced the illegitimacy of their origins, since their previous majority would have depended—as the comfortable election of 1936 proved—on the abstention of the Radicals. The Radical councilors proposed a new contract that lowered rates but maintained the status quo for the company: the transparency with which spurious interests acted in the arrangement produced a true scandal, but while the municipality received no impact whatsoever, the Council would not recover. One of the questions we raised seems to be answered in this Radical-Socialist complement in spite of itself: the Council, which does not serve to modify the policies of the executive, serves to corrupt itself. In any case, it is the second sphere, that of the neighborhood advocacy associations, which interests us most, because it is where the peculiarities of the political relationship between reformism and society will become clearer.

As de Privitellio has proved, the CHADE conflict set in motion a real battle of legitimacy between the advocacy associations organized by the opposition and those organized by the municipality, using all the resources with which the government had traditionally sensitized the advocacy community: above all, the direct management of the neighborhood's problems, its modernization.[569] As part of this cooptation policy, in 1933 the city government set up a special office to deal directly—without "political" mediation—with all the problems of the advocacy associations, and began to carry out heavily advertised periodic tours—such as that for which the societies of Villa Soldati and Nueva Pompeya expressed their gratitude—relying in this case on the technical efficiency of Secretary Razori. Seeking to build its own base of legitimacy, it sponsored a geometric growth in the number of associations: as the reports of the municipality proudly state, in 1933 there were 95 societies and, thanks to the state

---

[569] It should be made clear, however, that de Privitellio has used the example of the CHADE precisely to dispute my hypotheses: to prove that the localist and apolitical tradition was not as preeminent, as I am trying to show, but that institutions were split by conflicts and logics that also implied a global view of the city. On the contrary, I believe that the very example of the conflicts over public services shows that the preeminence of that tradition is still the best explanation for the resounding triumph of de Vedia's strategy. See de Privitellio, *Vecinos y ciudadanos*, especially chapter 4, "¿Quién habla por la ciudad?"

initiative, by the end of 1934 there were 125 (two years later, when the conflict was resolved, there would be 140), all "purged," the official text emphasizes, of any activity "alien" to their "specific function."[570] The truth is that also in this case a real tie had been reached, with a similar number of societies on both sides. But the great triumph for the mayor's office is that, while the socialist advocacy associations are identified with "political" aims, those of the ruling party retain the legitimacy given to them by their permanent preaching of the absence of political motivations, their search for the most effective solution for the benefit of the neighbors, and their practical demonstration that they are in a position—because of their relations with the mayor's office—to achieve tangible improvements in the "real" problems of the neighborhood, those which, in short, had given meaning the neighborhood development movement.

And it is this legitimacy that will prove to be the most effective in tuning in to very basic aspects of a style of sociability built in neighborhood institutions, in direct relation to the localist and administrativist vision of urban management. Because, if in the two battles over services that we have discussed an important sector of neighborhood advocacy groups appear mobilized to accompany reformist proposals, I believe that their defeat should not be read as the mere imposition of a logic external to those institutions, but as the product of the preeminence of a series of traditions that ate away at their own reformist logic from within: faced with the resounding success of the delegitimizing tactic of the "politicized" associations, what we must analyze is what has happened in that sector of society with the image of politics.

There are numerous coincidences between the localist tradition, the negative vision of politics in which the neighborhood associations—and the barrio itself as an institution—were formed, and de Vedia's type of modernization without reform, because reform always requires a global, that is, political, vision of the city. Here it is convenient to specify the sense in which I propose to use the terms "reformism" and "politics" in relation to the barrio; to note that the "reformism" of the neighborhood is emptied of political content and remains, simply, as a social practice for consensus, as a style of peaceful and negotiated resolution of conflicts, and as a moderate imaginary about social transformation, centrally activated by the idea of "ascent." As we have seen in different passages, the importance of the emergence of the barrio also in political terms is undoubtable, in the sense that, in these decades, the effects of social and civic integration produced within it (which produces *it* as a local public space) are political, and that the consequences of the irruption of the suburban phenomenon in the institutional reorganization of the city are political, in the very way in which the city must modify its self-image in

---

[570] Municipalidad de la Ciudad de Buenos Aires, *La obra de la intendencia municipal en los barrios suburbanos*, especially the appendix that reproduces *Boletín Municipal* 3918, "Sociedades de fomento. Labor realizada por la intendencia," 87ff.

an inclusive perspective. But what I am interested in sustaining in these last pages is that these political effects do not imply that the barrio as an institution produces a political vision of the city, as an abstract space of construction of citizenship; that this internal mechanics of social reformism, in the very political evolution of the *barrio* institution did not establish relations with the logic of a political reformism capable of influencing the democratizing transformation of the city as a metropolitan public space. This perspective must prevent us, in turn, from the temptation to create excluding polarities in an extremely complex process, because the first thing to be recognized is the contribution of socialist reformism itself in the consolidation of these localist traditions; in such a way that it could be interpreted that it is not only a triumph of the modernizing administration, but, in truth, a pyrrhic triumph of political reformism, which when it decides to politicize society must confront the "apoliticism" with which it built its relations with society from the beginning: it is also the aporias of Socialism that de Vedia sets in black and white at this "end of cycle." That is why, to conclude, I propose returning to the tracing of connections between the problems of the global management of the city with those of the local dimension of public space, the *barrio*, because there we will be able to see what happens in this "second modernization" and what role the institutions that produced the public transformation of the barrio had in the face of the cancellation of its metropolitan projection.

The "Republic of Inhabitants"

The ambivalent role of the neighborhood advocacy movement could be explained, then, by noting the existence of a double face of local associations. From an internal, local perspective, we should note the role they played as shapers of neighborhood popular culture and of the public space that made it possible, a perspective we insisted on when we analyzed the emergence of the barrio as public artifact. From a global perspective, however, it is essential to understand the role they played in the construction of the city: there appears a complicated relationship with Socialism, for example, as well as the organic relationships they maintained with the municipal governments in systematic attempts to avoid political mediation. If "inside" the neighborhood they tended to function as vessels of social integration and production of a democratic local public space, amplifying the rights to the city, "outside" they tended to complement the main characteristics of traditional Creole politics. A double role that, of course, is not without mutual relations and effects, and that makes the very dynamics of the increasing decadence of these institutions more understandable: by hindering the qualitative passage from local to metropolitan public space, those tendencies reverted on the local function of neighborhood advocacy itself, affecting the democratizing qualities of the already consolidated public space. What is certain is that in the development of the city, it could be argued that what on a local scale had shaped an innovative community, rati-fying many of Gutiérrez and Romero's hypotheses on the social, cultural, and civic role of these associations, on a global scale consolidated the tendencies of the *republic of inhabitants*, that matrix of Buenos Aires society that Natalio Botana has glimpsed in the "laboratory of the eighties" as a paradox of the materialization of Alberdian legitimacy: a logic of civil integration that split the political system from society; that at the same time as it stripped the latter of a political principle capable of guiding it, condemned it to reproduce the evils of the former.[571]

It could be said that the cycle of neighborhood institutions is the same as that of "socialist" Buenos Aires: their public appearance and multiplication

---

[571] Gutiérrez and Romero in fact make many references to problems such as the ones I underline here, especially in their work "La construcción de la ciudadanía, 1912-1955," as when they show the growing elitization of neighborhood societies, or when they argue that in the late 1930s citizenship had "thick foliage and weak roots," a situation they attribute to the strong state verticality of the citizenship process. However, I try to show that this double role of neighborhood advocacy is structural, while they—in their perspective "from the inside"—tend to periodize it in terms of a before and after the satisfaction of material needs—the "function" of neighborhood advocacy—in the barrios, emphasizing, in most of their writings, the role of the neighborhood as a "nest of democracy." The mention of Botana refers to *La tradición republicana*, 482. In the last pages of his book, I have found an illuminating conceptual approach to the type of sociability that I see in the neighborhoods of Buenos Aires in the period I am studying, which has been extremely useful for the writing of this final chapter. By using Botana's figure for the title, I seek to acknowledge the debt. His thesis is that this sociability is germinating in the nineteenth century, in "the formula of a restrictive republic, generous with civil liberties and stingy with political freedom" to which society reacted by ratifying its disinterest in politics. I am more concerned with emphasizing the role of the state and of a special type of urbanization in this process, but the landscape that Botana presents is functional enough for me to quote it in extenso: "The positive effects of the freedom of resistance that the inhabitants asserted in the use of their civil rights soon became evident. Well equipped, with the guarantees opposed to the arbitrariness of rulers, they and their people created their own destiny. Thanks to that freedom, the Argentines—Creoles and foreigners—made their daily history in peace. With all that it entailed, including successes and mistakes, hopes and failures, in a short time they wove these in the fabric of the private sphere. More than the beauty of monuments and public palaces, of the precincts where eloquence shines, or of the open place where political combat breaks out, the Alberdian legitimacy illuminated an urban landscape impregnated by the discipline of work: houses and neighborhoods, means of transport, electricity, and factories. In each owner, whatever his fortune, in each civil association, whatever its size, this legitimacy set in motion the machinery of negative pluralism. It thus unwittingly deposited the seed that would later grow into innumerable individual and collective forms. It was private conduct that, in its sphere, carried out as many actions as there were possibilities open to human inventiveness and that turned toward the political, manifesting itself through an ethics of negation."

coincide with—and are part of—the public transformation of the suburb from the end of the 1910s, and their decline (in the sense of their role in activating public space) accelerates in the mid-1930s. Associationism is the main product and driving force of the reform process that gives publicity to the suburb; at the same time, it can only maintain tense links with that process. We have already mentioned Socialism's distrust of the process of urban expansion; here it is worthwhile to dwell on its diagnosis of the social consequences of such growth: the very demands of popular suburban sectors that gave advocacy meaning in the new municipal policy reproduced the logic that generated them. For example, in the middle of the debate on the use of the municipal loan of 1923 for sanitation of suburban neighborhoods (from which the Organic Project is derived), the socialist councilman Zaccagnini observed:

> We appreciate the works of the advocacy commissions for all they are worth, but it is necessary that the citizens who work so enthusiastically within them realize that we have the duty and obligation to be councilors for the whole capital and not exclusively for each of the barrios, because with local criteria it is easy to remember our own needs and forget [...] the overall vision of the whole city. [...] The works of beautification should not be solely and exclusively for certain districts but should be linked to the aesthetics of the entire city. [...] We will try to bring these improvements to all the districts that have requested them, looking at and studying the overall plan of the city, not listening to the voice of local interests, and totally disregarding the interests of unscrupulous owners who think only of selling their land to the municipality at the highest price.[572]

The criticism of localist criteria, by which Socialism is presented as the party that, as we saw, has been able to break "with the petty politics of the neighborhood" in order to "protect the general interests of the city" is made clear in this passage. But the interesting thing about Zaccagnini's intervention is that it goes beyond that: it is not only a question of local versus general interest; he is posing a structural link between those localist criteria—by which neighborhood advocacy associations appear as agents uninterested in the fate of the city—and spurious interests. As we saw, for example, the challenge of regularizing low-lying areas that have already been allotted is a problem for the Socialists: they propose it only as a last resort to which they are forced, attempting to distinguish always between the "deceived" humble inhabitants and the unscrupulous owners; to return to the example that Hegemann would give, between whoever buys a lot and Fiorito. That is already difficult: everyone perceives that in the vertigo of expansion the limits between both actors are modified at every instant, which, more often than not, makes the objectives of one and the other

---

[572] *Actas del Honorable Concejo Deliberante* (Buenos Aires), September 20, 1924.

equal. However, the great paradox of expansion, which shows the difficulty reformism has of facing it with progressive values, is that while advocacy associations of the poorest areas reclaim "ant speculation" favoring the "auctioneers of swamp areas," some better placed associations will coincide with the socialist position against the division of property, but only to defend their privileges against "families without resources" that can access the lots because they are small and then build "in sheet metal and wood," disfiguring the neighborhood. Faced with the city that results from "ant speculation," it can be stimulating to imagine the great workers' complexes of red Vienna, but in the concrete social circumstances of the expansion, it is a matter of understanding which interests are favored in each case; and the advocacy associations, with their crude localist vision, do not help establish that definition.[573]

In the very long controversy that takes place in the Council to avoid the subdivision of Bajo Flores (the main *leading case* against the completion of the grid), the attitude of the neighborhood advocacy associations necessarily coincides with that of the owners who hope to continue to plot and sell. This is demonstrated by a letter from the Sociedad de Fomento de Villa Soldati asking that the paving of Coronel Roca Avenue be accelerated:

> Some councilors who have no deep knowledge of the situation in this area
> [plan] mass expropriations, [speak] of low-lying land and unhealthy land,
> etc., etc., etc. There is none of all this, Mr. President; the people of this part
> of the city do not absolutely regret the situation of the land where they live;
> they only regret the lack of building action, they regret the negligence of
> the municipal authorities toward them, they mainly regret the lack of storm
> drains and of the first paved arteries, which would be more than enough
> to completely solve the whole problem that some people want to uselessly
> make very complex.[574]

And the same thing will happen when the advocacy associations of the southern zone support the Mayor Guerrico's efforts to lower the minimum building height allowed in the vicinity of the Riachuelo, a limit that had been achieved as a great success by reformist councilors to prevent the subdivision and "urbanization" of the lower areas and that real estate interests sought to repeal (the repeal will be one of the first measures of the de facto mayor's

---

[573] This was the case of the Sociedad de Fomento 25 de Mayo (in the western zone: Concordia and Álvarez Jonte), which, using the aforementioned argument, asked that large landowners no longer be allowed to divide plots of land; see Municipalidad de la Ciudad de Buenos Aires, *Actas del Honorable Concejo Deliberante* (Buenos Aires), April 5, 1927. I have expanded on the socialist positions against subdivision in chapter 7.

[574] Reproduced in *Actas del Honorable Concejo Deliberante* (Buenos Aires), November 6, 1928.

office).[575] Localism is, then, the real limit of the kind of reformism advocated by the neighborhood advocacy reformism, because what interests one sector of the city—its "building progress," its "modernization"—is not necessarily the best for the whole city: for reformism, the city as a public and collective artifact is not built by the simple sum of particular interests. But, at the same time, the limit of reformism resides, as we have seen, in its inability to avoid the social power of the neighborhood movement as the embodiment of an effective combination of direct popular representation and a local vision; in short, as the embodiment of the city's *reality*. Through its local role as a structuring agent of suburban society—in which a large number of Socialists also took part—advocacy associations built up a legitimacy that inevitably extended to the consideration of representativeness, even though in municipal politics it could play out in different ways. But here it is time to talk about the other distrust of reformism vis-à-vis neighborhood advocacy: political distrust.

The notorious proliferation of advocacy associations in the twenties has to do not only with the definition of the suburban neighborhoods and the growth of their material problems, not only with the new publicity that they have acquired in the light of the new City Council and the modern press that seek to represent them, but above all with the strong state impulse, through the policy of recognition of the Mayor's office. In fact, it is during the administration of Radical José Luis Cantilo in 1920 when the registry of these societies is created, and it does not escape many contemporary observers of the phenomenon that there lay one of the decisive factors of its multiplication.[576] This is the first issue that generates political distrust: the ease with which Radicalism in municipal power has been able to recreate through neighborhood associations the classic clienteles of "Creole politics." We have already mentioned this with regard to Noel and the 1923 loan: there are constant accusations that the mayor's office is using public works as a bargaining chip; the same public works demanded by reformist councilors are transformed once they are in the hands of the Mayor's office into a key for influence peddling.

And for this reason, in the 1920s, the reformist movement made the definition of a regulatory framework for associations a priority: more than the increase in the number of neighborhood institutions, what concerns Socialists is the political weight they began to have and their ambitions for electoral participation—which is a great novelty that seemed to take the Council back to the

---

[575] See, for example, the defense of the Guerrico paving plan by the Asociación de Fomento de Luis María Saavedra, because "beyond its legality," as they clarify in 1932, it was thought out in collaboration with all the advocacy associations; *Actas del Honorable Concejo Deliberante* (Buenos Aires), April 5, 1932.

[576] This will appear in the debates when the regulations of the neighborhood advocacy associations are discussed: see *Actas del Honorable Concejo Deliberante* (Buenos Aires), December 17, 1926; April 5, 1927; March 13, 1927; May 31, 1927; November 30, 1927.

times of sectoral representation. In fact, in the 1926 elections, a "federation" of neighborhood advocacy associations, the Unión de Fomento Edilicio (Union of Building Promotion), encouraged by Noel's administration to compete with the parties represented in the City Council, participated: the opposition denounced that the Union had been created directly in the public offices, where the participating associations were promised work crews and pavements; and their predictions are proven to be founded by the appearance of slogans against the very "political" functioning of the Council and in favor of a "direct" representation of the needs of the neighborhoods: "we don't want politicians," is the battle cry.[577] So, the discussion on regulation will be crossed by reformism's fear of the political use of the apolitical nature of neighborhoodism.

Socialists believe they can stop this resurgence of "Creole politics" with strict regulations that, paradoxically, aim to preserve the apolitical nature that

---

[577] Complaints about influence peddling follow one after the other in the Council: Faggioli (Radical Personalist) says that "before the last communal campaign, in some public offices some neighbors have been told: 'if you are federated you will have crews and pavements, otherwise everything is useless'"; the socialist councilman Castiñeiras shows a newspaper with a photo showing a group working in a neighborhood, under the title: "Gentileza del señor intendente, cuadrilla puesta a disposición del señor presidente de la Sociedad de Fomento" (Courtesy of the mayor, crew at the disposal of the president of the Sociedad de Fomento); in *Actas del Honorable Concejo Deliberante*, December 17, 1926. I owe to Luciano de Privitellio (*Vecinos y ciudadanos*, 114-115), the declaration of the Unión de Fomento. It is useful to reproduce it at length to see the direct relation they had drawn with Noel's politics and, above all, to see the crudeness of his vision of municipal politics: "We do not want politicians. [...] The Unión de Fomento Edilicio [...] is a group made up of sixty or seventy neighborhood associations in the different *barrios* of this capital. These associations, little known in the center, have done and are doing meritorious and effective work for the improvement and advancement of districts and parishes where neither the beauty of the diagonals nor the breezes of the riverside resort reach. They have not had until now anybody to care about them, even in the Council, and the little that these neighborhoods have achieved is the exclusive work of these societies that, aided by the goodwill of Mayor Noel, have gotten from him a little attention by the authorities of the commune. But, these steps, private and friendly in most cases, necessarily had their limit in relation to the importance of the matter. It is worth saying that when we wanted to obtain something of certain transcendence the goodwill of the impotent mayor was no longer enough in certain cases without the collaboration of the City Council. *And in this case, all efforts failed.* That is why we decided to take part in the electoral struggle for the renewal of the Council with our own candidates. We have put together our list with honest men of goodwill, totally alien to any political party discipline, *convinced that political interference in communal affairs is detrimental to the interests of the municipality.* [...] Honest men must accompany us in this campaign, in which [...] we have no purpose other than to cooperate in an honest and well-oriented administration, *without politics and without politicians*, the only way to achieve it" (emphasis added).

has favored neighborhood advocacy. To this end, they propose a system of official recognition of the institutions which, in addition to the prohibition to participate in politics, regulates the number of members, the characteristics of the neighborhoods where they can be formed (no more than 40 percent paved streets, no more than 80 percent lighting), the area of influence, etc.: it is a question of imposing a double restriction on associationism which cannot but be seen as contradictory to the ideology of socialist reformism.[578]

The first restriction is to define the neighborhood advocacy associations exclusively in terms of the material improvement of those barrios that still demonstrate they need it: the political sector that most collaborated with the cultural and civic construction of these neighborhood societies, now tries to limit its meaning to the material improvement of the area. The second one is derived from this reduction to materiality: territorial restriction. But, para-doxically, what in one sense is proposed as a restriction, in another implies a universalizing extension of the quality of its representation: within a given territory, the "area of influence," the neighborhood advocacy associations rec-ognized by the regulations will "naturally" represent all the residents of that area. An apparently inexplicable shift has occurred within the conception of Socialism: parallel to the logic of citizenship and political representation that it has defended for the electoral reform of the capital, it reintroduces a logic for associations that relies on a traditional type of representation, according to the identity of interests that in this case the common territory affords, and that, in addition, governs the state.

And this shows that the very regulatory ambition is completely opposed to the theoretical and ideological tradition in which socialism had conceived urban society. Socialism constructed its image of the city as the cradle and laboratory of democracy with Tocquevillian criteria, which assume not only that access to the public sphere should not be regulated but, above all, that the guarantee of the entire political system resides in free civil association on a local scale.[579] From this conception, the double political logic that socialism

---

[578] The Socialists' position is shared by the Personalist Radicals; here I am interested in developing the Socialist position, which undoubtedly has the advantage. Also important in the case of Radicalism is the rivalry with Mayor Noel, who took advantage of the weight of neighborhood advocacy in the internal disputes of the party.

[579] Contrasting American associationism with the European situation, Tocqueville writes: "In all European peoples there are certain associations which can only be formed after examination of their statutes and with the authorization of the State. In many, attempts are being made to extend this rule to all associations. It is not difficult to see where the success of such a proposal would lead. If the day came when the sovereign had the general right to authorize all kinds of associations under certain conditions, it would not be long before he would claim the right to supervise and direct them, so that they could not deviate from the rule that had been imposed on them." In Tocqueville, *Democracy in America*, 2:262. On the relationship between Tocqueville's statements

is arriving at (electoral citizen representation/traditional representation in the associations) is unthinkable, because it would break the chain that leads from civil associations to political participation. In fact, it will be in the opposition to this regulation of conservative groups in the Council where the liberal prevention against state corporatism that could have been expected from socialism will appear. Conservative councilors understand the good intentions that explain the will to regulate—they don't like the fact that the mayor uses the promotion societies for electoral purposes—but they warn that the regulation would give the state the power to decide which society is legitimate and which is not, which would affect the essential right of every citizen to petition without special recognition by the state; the regulation is authoritarian because it promotes a unique and compulsory representation of all the inhabitants of a territory and submits it to the will of the state which, due to the political limits of the municipal system, resides almost exclusively in the Mayor's office.

Now, can it be thought that such state despotism is driven by socialism only to prevent neighborhood advocacy from intervening in the elections? The cost in corporate structuring of sociopolitical identities in the city that reformism pays with this regulation seems too high to reduce it to reasons of electoral competition. I believe, instead, that these contradictions should be seen in the broader framework of socialism's own conception and the way in which it constructs its relationship with that popular society it sought to represent.

On the one hand, we find here again the oscillation, typical in the Argentine liberal reformist tradition, between political and administrative conceptions of "municipal democracy": the material-territorial restriction of the associations is undoubtedly reproducing a notion of the local (in this case the most local, the neighborhood) as the universe of "natural" interests, which must be managed by the interested parties themselves without the interference of "politics": that is the definition of the "neighbor" as opposed to that of the "citizen." The party that upheld the most political vision of the city as the construction of citizenship, however, reproduced at the local level this administrative subjection, limiting the political projection of the public sphere that it contributed so much to create; for socialism, it would seem that the "citizen" builder of democracy should first be constituted as a "neighbor," without it being easy to understand how and when it passes from one dimension to the other and how completely it can do so. Ultimately, the oscillation is analogous to the one we saw between a conception that imagines the city as a political public space—the possession of corners and squares by the people as evidence of the democratic spirit that

---

and the socialists, who frequently turned to him for inspiration in these years, see, for example, Juan Nigro, "El partido socialista y la política municipal," *Revista Socialista* 21 (1932), and the later works on the municipality by Carlos Mouchet, for example, in Concejo Deliberante, *Evolución institucional del municipio de la ciudad de Buenos Aires.*

Ghioldi proposed—and one that limits it to basic consumption infrastructure and popular habitation.

On the other hand, perhaps we should recognize in it a structural feature in the conformation of Socialism, which derived in something like a double identity: a political identity, which throughout the period we are dealing with was channeled through its parliamentary participation; and another sociocultural one, that had been formed prior to its entry into representative politics through a firm and widespread insertion in society across a number of initiatives that contributed greatly to shape it. A double identity from which a diagnosis on reform can be derived: unlike "conservative" political reformism that produced the transformation of the electoral system, and unlike the technical reformism that produced a series of state devices of social and urban transformation, Socialism proposes to reform politics and society at the same time. That is why it never presents itself as a "natural" emergence of existing social needs and demands, but as the representative of a set of rights, which it must both dispute with the state and build as a necessity within society. It is this double identity that, in short, takes us back to Sarmiento: that of legislator and creator of habits and customs: if state and society in the modernization of Buenos Aires had been formed autonomously—and here I follow Botana's presentation of the issue—with self-sufficient legitimacies that reciprocally deny each other but that, therefore, end up feeding back on each other, the task of reform must necessarily be double and simultaneous. But in that double logic, socialism could not avoid reproducing—perhaps because it was itself part of it—the basis of its mutual autonomy: the necessary "depoliticization" of civil society. The task of transforming customs was so strategic for socialism that it was not to be done under the petty advocation of party politics; as all those who have studied it have verified, that was the characteristic of its original insertion—an "ant"-type insertion, precisely—in all levels of civil society: unions, popular libraries, clubs, cooperatives, neighborhood advocacy associations. Socialism managed to *blend* so successfully into society that it ended up feeding the circle of apoliticism and its repudiation of party politics.

Thus, the regulation of the neighborhood advocacy associations is ratifying a modality of insertion with which socialism returns to them the image they themselves have of their role, without noticing that in that image is not where democracy resides, but the corporative integration in a policy of state perks. In the thirties, Dr. Giacobini, a representative of this way of seeing municipal action, arrived at the Council. He was a resident of Parque Patricios, founder of the Salud Pública party, whose political work would be presented as exclusively oriented to defend the interests of "his" sector, almost as an incarnation of the program of the federation of neighborhood associations of the previous decade. In addition, at a time when the material obstacles of the area he "defends" are centrally overcome, the role of Giacobini, trying to assume himself as a proponent at all costs of the most trivial issues, invariably imposing them as a matter of privilege over discussions of the general problems of the city, is both a caricature of the relationship between progressive politics and neighborhood interests and the extreme example of the impotence of reformism to implement an alternative policy, to put limits on the "legitimacy" of localist claims.

It could be thought that this strong consensus, that neighborhood advocacy is at odds with politics, is what ends up turning against Socialists in the thirties, at the time when it proposes to repoliticize its relations with society. This is what explains the success of de Vedia y Mitre in delegitimizing the social mobilization led by Socialism and bolstering his own legitimization based on the support he found in the "apolitical" neighborhood associations: there de Vedia's management will mount an indestructible liaison for its modernization, because in the *vecinalismo* movement it always finds the best defense against criticism, showing the conformity of those who, in the criteria shared also by the opposition, would be the directly affected, "the voice of the city," as Razori points out when he lists the neighborhood advocacy associations that support official administration. This also explains the success of the threat to leave out of the system *regulated by Socialism* those advocacy associations that do not comply because they are now "politicized" following socialist orientations. In terms of that consensus, "politicization" is a stain that—more and more as a shameful habit of neighborhood politics—everyone charges others with: it has the maximum effectiveness in delegitimizing social action. This is why I believe that it is not possible to speak, in the "socialist" years of the first half of the 1930s, of a politicization of the neighborhood advocacy movement. On the contrary, it was then that the tautological definition that has lasted until the present was ratified: neighborhood advocacy associations do not do politics, because when they become politicized, they cease to be advocacy associations.

Disaggregations

The ideal of direct government, of a relation without political mediations between executive authorities and the suburban population, cuts across the entire institutional development of neighborhood associations as a structural aspect to its own constitution. This brings us to the paradox that the basic agents of public space, which at the neighborhood level fulfill an effectively integrating task, at the metropolitan level will be inhabited by a logic that goes against the very definition of public space, in the sense of a public sphere. It is a conflict that confronts the quality of local public space with that of metropolitan public space, which is like confronting a social citizenship with another political one. But was it to be expected that one could "naturally" pass from one dimension to the other by means of the material contact and access to symbolic centrality that suburban neighborhoods achieved in the 1920s? It is not only a question of scale: a long theoretical tradition of reflection on public space would directly rule out the possibility of its emergence—in terms of an active public sphere—in a mass society; and, indeed, it is unquestionable that this moment of citizen formation must be placed in a more encompassing and complex framework, in which the processes of metropolitanization tended to transform the community, still perceptible in the neighborhood, into an undifferentiated mass society: as in sport or popular culture that become mass spectacles in those years, it could be thought that citizens are no longer actors but spectators. However, I think this is too partial and external to the very urban logic that we are trying to reconstruct. I think it is necessary to try to understand this phenomenon also from a perspective more focused on the local combination between the formation of political sociability and urbanization.

The 1898–1904 grid functioned in the first decades as an abstract plane, as a state *gesture* of incorporation of the new inhabitants to citizenship, provoking a tension with the specific interventions of public qualification born from the rejection of the urban effects of that same compulsive homogenization. Local public space arose from the tension between modernization and reform: from a state that applied a technical logic and at the same time reacted in horror at its results; and from a society that sought to progress in its own spheres but that, to do so, had to widen the margins of participation it had been granted to produce new urban and social spaces. Thus emerged the territory of expansion; on which the ideal of an organic relationship between public space and public sphere, and between both and the construction of citizenship, produced a political discourse that proposed to reform the city by placing at the center an urban model of precise connotations: civic centers, boulevards, perspectives with continuous classicist facades, republican monuments, parks, masses of citizens walking along the scenography of their own protagonism.

The local public space of the neighborhood was proposed as a device to fulfill the role that, in Sarmiento's tradition of reformism, was attributed to the park: to build a citizenship that stitched together the distant spheres of civil society and the political system. Was it heading in that direction before the 1930s? Could it have fulfilled that role had it not been for the dissolving action of reactive modernization? The most that can be affirmed is that the reformist ambiguity of the 1920s did not have this outcome written all over it. Local public space, the *barrio*, had demonstrated that an "ant" society could build instances of citizenship that exceeded the *private* framework of the neighborhood. While reform seemed to accompany the progress of modernization, in the ambiguity of the public tension that was debated between one and the other, the local public space of integration and the realization of the neighborhood society seemed to be the prelude to a surpassing instance, a metropolitan public space that would enhance the experience of citizenship construction to the new dimension of the city. Political reformism participates and shares the productivity and the limits of that tension. When reform and modernization showed their contradictions, however, their respective emphasis on the political and the social, the society of ascent made its anti-political reflex prevail, paradoxically nourished also by a long tradition of local reformism that had bet on the transformation of customs, confusing itself with them.

At the moment of universalizing the experience of the neighborhood, resistance to establishing a political community outside its limits appeared, opting for the passive role that is reinforced by state tutelage. This is the local retreat, a manifestation in scale of the withdrawal of the city into itself produced by de Vedia; in the neighborhood it is the exclusive triumph of the nostalgic, familiar, and anti-reformist representation of tango. Public space, having failed in its metropolitan expansion, can no longer be local either: such is the explanation for the dramatic expiration of "*vecinalismo*" (the neighborhood movement) in the late thirties, as soon as modernization improved the material conditions of the neighborhood. Once the problem of expansion is abandoned, "constrained in its limits," urban society finds no contradiction between homogeneity and the neighborhood myth: with the functionality of tango's lament for the loss of identity, or of its conversion into a refuge of traditions, the neighborhood becomes the cell of a modernization of the city that not only ratifies its traditional radial structure, in the terms inscribed in the market; but above all, it ratifies the secondary role of neighborhood sociability in the now definitively crystallized public space, which also reproduces the radial hierarchical structure: from the center to the neighborhoods. Hence the ever-growing capacity of the obelisk to emblematize *de Vedia's operation*, confirming in its own way the most bitter visions—that of an Arlt—of the duplicity of the new society that emerges from integration: Catholic and *tanguera*, conservative and anarchist, moralist, and scoundrel.

If the twenties are a contradictory but highly productive compound, in the thirties its parts are disassembled one by one. The professionalization of urban planning disaggregates technique from politics, urban management from ideological presuppositions, and separates a naturalized "green space" from the civility of the park and the integration of the grid; neighborhoodism undoes the tense balance between differentiation and equalization of local public space, breaking it apart from metropolitan public space. Urban culture separates the "white city" from suburban ambiguity and ratifies a representation of the center that can simultaneously fulfill counter-progressive expectations and the barrio myth. That is the framework in which modernist conservatism is effectively installed: functionalizing those processes in the disassembly of the triple reformist tension. De Vedia is the *realist* instance that turns reformist ambiguities into aporias: dislocating modernization and reform, he tends to strip the grid of everything that is not the modernization of the market, and neighborhoodism of everything that is not exclusively functional to the expectations of social ascent of the "republic of inhabitants." In its fulfillment lies the political aspect of the reactive utopia. Then the city completes its *project*, finally finds its center, bringing to an end the long cycle in which technical ideas, political visions, cultural representations, and social uses of the city seemed to enter into consonance with institutional forms and with a precise experience of materialization of spaces for the public.

About the Author

Adrián Gorelik (b. Mercedes, Buenos Aires, 1957) is an architect trained at the University of Buenos Aires, where he also obtained his doctoral degree in history. He is a researcher of the Argentine research council (CONICET) and full professor at the Universidad Nacional de Quilmes, where he has directed the Centro de Historia Intelectual. He has held the Guggenheim Foundation fellowship and has been a fellow of the Wissenschaftskolleg in Berlin. In 2012 he held the Simón Bolívar professorship at the University of Cambridge. He was member of the board of directors of the journal Punto de Vista and is currently part of the editorial committee of *Prismas. Revista de Historia Intelectual*. He has published widely on urban and intellectual cultural history, architecture, and urban thought in Argentina and Latin America. His books include *La sombra de la vanguardia. Hannes Meyer en México*, with Jorge F. Liernur (Buenos Aires, 1993; Santiago de Chile, 2019); *La grilla y el parque. Espacio público y cultura urbana en Buenos Aires* (Buenos Aires, 1998), *Miradas sobre Buenos Aires* (Buenos Aires, 2004); *Das vanguardas a Brasília. Cultura urbana e arquitetura na América Latina* (Belo Horizonte, 2005); and *Correspondencias. Arquitectura, ciudad, cultura* (Buenos Aires, 2011). He is an influential voice in public debates regarding urban policies and culture in Buenos Aires.

Bibliography

Dates in brackets indicate either original dates of publication or reflect when a text was first written.

Official Documents Quoted

Censo General de Población, Edificación, Comercio e Industrias de la Ciudad de Buenos Aires. Buenos Aires: 1889, 1904, and 1910.

Comisión Nacional del Centenario, *Concurso para el Monumento de la Independencia Argentina.* Buenos Aires: Kraft, 1908.

Comisión Nacional del Centenario, *1810–1910. La República Argentina en el primer Centenario de su Independencia.* Buenos Aires: Talleres Gráficos Rosso, 1911.

Comisión Nacional del Centenario, *Expedientes relativos a monumentos del Centenario con intervención del Ministerio de Obras Públicas.* Archivo General de la Nación, 1911–1920.

Congreso Nacional, Cámara de Senadores. *Diario de sesiones,* 1874.

El informe Rodríguez Conde. Informe de la Comisión Investigadora de los Servicios Públicos de Electricidad. Buenos Aires: EUDEBA, 1974.

Honorable Concejo Deliberante, Comisión de monumentos para el Centenario. *Memorándum sobre las estatuas inauguradas en 1910.* Buenos Aires: Talleres Gráficos Rinaldi, 1912.

Honorable Concejo Deliberante. *Diario de Sesiones,* 1905, 1909, 1923.

Intendencia Municipal. *Memorias,* 1887, 1901, 1908, 1913, 1932, 1933, and 1935.

Intendencia Municipal y Comisión de Estética Edilicia. *Proyecto orgánico de urbanización del municipio.* Buenos Aires: Peuser, 1925.

Municipalidad de Buenos Aires. *Memoria del Presidente de la Comisión Municipal al Concejo.* 1881.

Municipalidad de la Ciudad de Buenos Aires. *Actas del Honorable Concejo Deliberante.* 1924, 1925, 1926, 1927, 1928, 1932, and 1933.

Municipalidad de la Ciudad de Buenos Aires. *Tratamiento y eliminación de las basuras. Informe teórico práctico de la Comisión especial.* June 1904.

Ministerio de Obras Públicas. *Leyes, contratos y resoluciones referentes a los ferrocarriles y tranvías*, IV, part II. Compiled by Eduardo Schlatter. Buenos Aires, 1902.

Primer Congreso Argentino de Urbanismo. 3 vols. (1936–1938).

Periodicals and Magazines (Buenos Aires)

Arquitectura
Arquitectura. Suplemento de la Revista Técnica
Atlántida
Caras y Caretas
Diarios *Crítica, El Mundo, La Nación, La Prensa, La Razón, La Vanguardia*
El Monitor de la Educación Común
Las Avenidas
La Revista del Plata
Nosotros
Revista de Ingeniería
Revista Martín Fierro
Revista Municipal
Revista Socialista

Books and Articles

Agulhon, Maurice. *Histoire vagabonde*. Paris: Gallimard, 1988.
Aliata, Fernando, and Graciela Silvestri. "Continuidades y rupturas en la ciudad del Ochocientos. El caso de los mataderos porteños (1820–1900)," 26. In *Anales del Instituto de Arte Americano e Investigaciones Estéticas "Mario J. Buschiazzo."* 1988.
Aliata, Fernando. *La ciudad regular. Arquitectura, programas e instituciones en el Buenos Aires posrevolucionario, 1821–1835*. Buenos Aires: Editorial de la Universidad Nacional de Quilmes, 2006.
Altamirano, Carlos, and Beatriz Sarlo. "La Argentina del Centenario: campo intelectual, vida literaria y temas ideológicos." In *Ensayos argentinos. De Sarmiento a la vanguardia*. Buenos Aires: Centro Editor de América Latina, 1983.
Alwood, John. *The Great Exhibitions*. London: Studio, 1977.
Ansay, Pierre, and René Schoonbrodt. *Penser la ville. Choix de textes philosophiques*. Brussels: AAM Editions, 1989.
Antonio, Eduardo, and Fernando García Molina. "Las tres clausuras del Concejo Deliberante." *Todo es Historia* 329 (December 1994).
Archetti, Eduardo. "El imaginario del fútbol: estilo y virtudes masculinas en *El Gráfico*." *Punto de Vista* 50 (November 1994).

Arcondo, Mariana, Eduardo Gentile and Juan Carlos Pignataro. "Centros cívicos para Buenos Aires: 1923–1943." Paper presented at the conference Buenos Aires moderna. Historia y perspectiva urbana, IAA, Buenos Aires, 1990.

Ardissone, Romualdo. "La ciudad de Buenos Aires excede los límites de la Capital Federal. Necesidad de levantar un censo que abarque la totalidad de la aglomeración urbana bonaerense." In GAEA (Anales de la Sociedad Argentina de Estudios Geográficos) V. 1937 [1935].

Arendt, Hannah. The Human Condition. Chicago: University of Chicago Press, 1958.

Aricó, José. "La hipótesis de Justo." La ciudad futura 30–31 (December–February, 1991–92).

Arlt, Roberto. "La gran manga." Originally published in El Mundo (Buenos Aires: March 24, 1929). In Tratado de la delincuencia. Aguafuertes inéditas de Roberto Arlt. Edited by Sylvia Saítta. Buenos Aires: Biblioteca, 1996.

Arlt, Roberto. "Buenos Aires, paraíso de la tierra." Originally published in El Mundo (September 24, 1937); "Demoliciones en el centro." Originally published in El Mundo (April 19, 1937); "Nuevos aspectos de las demoliciones." Originally published in El Mundo (June 28, 1937). In Roberto Arlt, Aguafuertes porteñas. Buenos Aires, vida cotidiana. Edited by Sylvia Saítta. Buenos Aires: Alianza, 1993.

Asociación Amigos de la Ciudad. Cinco lustros al servicio de la ciudad, 1924–1949. Buenos Aires: Ediciones de Amigos de la Ciudad, 1951.

Astesano, Eduardo, and Rodolfo Puiggrós. "Introducción histórica al estudio del plan de Buenos Aires" (1948). In "Evolución del Gran Buenos Aires en eltiempo y el espacio." Revista de Arquitectura 376–77, 1956.

Augé, Marc. Non-Places: Introduction to an Anthropology of Supermodernity. Translated by John Howe. London and New York: Verso, 2008 [1992].

Auza, J. "Buenos Aires y sus reglamentos industriales desde 1900 hasta la actualidad." In II Jornadas de Historia de Buenos Aires. Buenos Aires: IHBCA, 1988.

Bahrdt, Hans Paul. La moderna metrópoli. Reflexiones sociológicas sobre la construcción de las ciudades. Buenos Aires: Eudeba, 1970 [1961] .

Ballent, Anahi. "Manuel Gálvez: barrio y reforma social. Algunas relaciones entre literatura y ciudad." In Anahi Ballent, Adrián Gorelik, and Graciela Silvestri, "Para un estudio de la ciudad y sus barrios." Actas de las Primeras Jornadas del Instituto de Historia "Mario J. Buschiazzo." Buenos Aires: FADU-UBA, 1985.

Ballent, Anahi. Socialismo, vivienda y ciudad: la Cooperativa El Hogar Obrero. Buenos Aires, 1905–1940. https://www.eho.coop/historia_documentos.php, 1989.

Ballent, Anahi. Las huellas de la política. Vivienda, ciudad, peronismo en Buenos Aires, 1943– 1955. Buenos Aires, Editorial de la Universidad Nacional de Quilmes, 2005.

Barabino, Santiago. "La Plaza del Congreso." *Arquitectura. Suplemento de la Revista Técnica* (September 30, 1904).

Baracchini, Hugo. "Evolución urbanística de Montevideo." In *250 años de Montevideo (Ciclo conmemorativo)*. Montevideo: GERGU, 1980.

Beccar Varela, Adrián, and Enrique Udaondo. *Plazas y calles de Buenos Aires (significación histórica de sus nombres)*. Buenos Aires: Talleres gráficos de la Penitenciaría Nacional, 1910.

Beccar Varela, Adrián. *Torcuato de Alvear. Primer Intendente municipal de la ciudad de Buenos Aires*. Buenos Aires: Kraft, 1926.

Benevolo, Leonardo. *Orígenes de la urbanística moderna*. Buenos Aires: Ediciones Tekné, 1967 [1963].

Benigni, Benigno. "Vías de comunicación. Los subterráneos de Buenos Aires." *Revista de Ingeniería* (1925).

Berensztein, Sergio. *Un partido para la Argentina moderna. Organización e identidad del partido socialista (1896–1916)*. Buenos Aires: Documento CEDES, 1991.

Bergeron, Louis, ed. *Parigi*. Bari: Laterza, 1989.

Berjman, Sonia. "Los espacios verdes de Buenos Aires, 1887–1925." PhD diss., University of Buenos Aires, 1987.

Berjman, Sonia. "Proyectos de Bouvard para la Buenos Aires del centenario: barrio, plazas, hospital y exposición."*DANA* 37/38 (1995).

Berjman, Sonia. *Plazas y parques de Buenos Aires: los paisajistas franceses, 1860–1930*. Buenos Aires: Fondo de Cultura Económica, 1998.

Berjman, Sonia. "Carrasco, Benito." In *Diccionario de arquitectura en la Argentina*. Edited by Jorge Francisco Liernur and Fernando Aliata. Vol. 2. Buenos Aires: Agea, 2004.

Bernárdez, Francisco Luis. "Oración a Nuestra Señora de los Buenos Aires." In *Homenaje a Buenos Aires en el cuarto centenario de su fundación*. Buenos Aires: Municipalidad de la Ciudad de Buenos Aires, 1936.

Bernárdez, M. "La quema de las basuras." *Caras y Caretas*, January 21, 1899.

Bertoni, Lilia Ana. "La educación 'moral': visión y acción de la elite a través del sistema nacional de educación primaria, 1881–1916." Buenos Aires: Instituto Ravignani, 1991.

Bianco, José. *Transmisión inmobiliaria*. Buenos Aires: G. Mendesky e Hijo, 1912.

Bioy, Adolfo. *Antes del Novecientos (Recuerdos)*. Buenos Aires: Talleres Gráficos Compañía Impresora Argentina, S.A., 1958.

Blot, Pablo, and Alfredo Ebelot. *Proyecto de un canal de circunvalación de Buenos Aires y Puerto de Cabotage*. Buenos Aires: Imprenta de La Nación, 1884.

Bontempelli, Massimo. *Noi, gli Aria. Interpretazioni sudamericane*. Palermo: Sellerio Editore, 1994 [1933].

Borges, Jorge Luis. *Fervor de Buenos Aires*. Buenos Aires: Imprenta Serrantes, 1923.

Borges, Jorge Luis. *Luna de enfrente*. Buenos Aires: Proa, 1925.

Borges, Jorge Luis. "Buenos Aires." In *On Argentina*. New York: Penguin Books, 2010 [1925].

Borges, Jorge Luis. *El tamaño de mi esperanza*. Buenos Aires: Seix Barral, 1994 [1926].

Borges, Jorge Luis. "The Language of the Argentines." In *On Argentina*. New York: Penguin Books, 2010 [1928].

Borges, Jorge Luis. *El idioma de los argentinos*. Buenos Aires: Seix Barral, 1994 [1928].

Borges, Jorge Luis. "The Mythical Founding of Buenos Aires." In *Cuaderno San Martín*. Translated in *Selected Poems*. New York: Viking, 1999 [1929].

Borges, Jorge Luis. *Evaristo Carriego: A Book About Old-time Buenos Aires*. Translated by Norman Thomas Di Giovanni. New York: Dutton, 1984 [1930].

Borges, Jorge Luis. "Séneca en las orillas." *Sur* 1 (Summer 1931).

Borges, Jorge Luis. "Tareas y destino de Buenos Aires." In *Homenaje a Buenos Aires en el cuarto centenario de su fundación*. Buenos Aires: Municipalidad de la Ciudad de Buenos Aires, 1936.

Borges, Jorge Luis. "A History of the Tango." In *Selected Non-Fictions*. New York: Viking, 1999 [1953].

Borges, Jorge Luis, and Adolfo Bioy Casares. "Las previsiones de Sangiácomo." In *Six Problems for Don Isidro Parodi*. New York: Dutton, 1981 [1942].

Botana, Natalio. *El orden conservador. La política argentina entre 1880 y 1916*. Buenos Aires: Hyspamérica, 1986 [1977].

Botana, Natalio. "Conservadores, radicales y socialistas." In *Buenos Aires, historia de cuatro siglos*. Edited by José Luis Romero and Luis Alberto Romero. Buenos Aires: Abril, 1983.

Botana, Natalio. *La tradición republicana*. Buenos Aires: Sudamericana, 1984.

Bourdé, Guy. *Buenos Aires: urbanización e inmigración*. Buenos Aires: Huemul, 1977.

Bravo, Mario. *La ciudad libre*. Buenos Aires: Ferro y Gnoatto, 1917.

Bridges, William. "Commissioner's Remarks." In *Map of the City of New York and Island of Manhattan*. New York, 1811.

Bucich Escobar, Ismael. *Buenos Aires Ciudad, 1880–1930*. Buenos Aires: El Ateneo, 1930.

Bullrich, Adolfo. "Discurso del Intendente Bullrich." *El Diario* (Buenos Aires), September 11, 1902.

Bunge, Augusto. "El anticarrasco." *Nosotros* 21, no. 81 (January 1916).

Buschiazzo, Juan. "El parque Tres de Febrero." *La Prensa* (Buenos Aires), March 21, 1893. Quoted in Sonia Berjman, "Los espacios verdes de Buenos Aires, 1887–1925."

Calabi, Donatella. "Nota introdutiva." In Werner Hegemann, *Catalogo delle esposizioni internazionali di urbanistica. Berlino 1910–Düsseldorf 1911–12*. Milan: Il Saggiatore, 1975.

Calabi, Donatella. "Werner Hegemann, o dell'ambiguitá borghese dell'urbanística."" *Casabella* 428. Milan: September, 1977.

Calabi, Donatella. "L'arte urbana e i suoi teorici europei." In *Camilo Sitte e i suoi interpreti*. Edited by Guido Zucconi. Milan: FrancoAngeli, 1992.

Calzadilla, Santiago. *Las beldades de mi tiempo*. Buenos Aires: Editorial Sudestada, 1969 [1891].

Campana, Dino. "Pampas." In *Orphic Songs and Other Poems*. New York: P. Lang, 1991 [c. 1908].

Cancela, Arturo. "Buenos Aires a vuelo de pájaro." In *Homenaje a Buenos Aires en el cuarto centenario de su fundación*. Buenos Aires: Municipalidad de la Ciudad de Buenos Aires, 1936.

Cané, Miguel. *En viaje*. Buenos Aires: Claridad, 1995 [1884].

Cané, Miguel. "Carta al Intendente Torcuato de Alvear desde Viena (January 14, 1885)." In Adrián Beccar Varela, *Torcuato de Alvear. Primer Intendente municipal de la ciudad de Buenos Aires*. Buenos Aires: Kraft, 1926.

Cané, Miguel. "Sobremesa." Archivo General de la Nación, sala VII, 2.214, Leg. 13." Quoted in "El modelo ideal y la realidad de la traza. Buenos Aires en el pensamiento de Miguel Cané" by Elisa Radovanovic. In *Pensar Buenos Aires (X Jornadas de Historia de la ciudad de Buenos Aires)*. Buenos Aires: Instituto Histórico de la Ciudad de Buenos Aires, 1994.

Capron, Horace. "Report of the Commissioner of the United States Department of Agriculture." *Both Americas* 1, no. 4 (July 1868).

Carbia, Rómulo. "El alma nuestra." *Nosotros* 3 (Buenos Aires), November–December 1908.

Carranza, Adolfo B. *Origen del nombre de las calles de Buenos Aires*. Buenos Aires: Kraft, 1910.

Carranza, Arturo B. *La cuestión Capital de la República, 1826–1887*. Buenos Aires: Talleres Gráficos Rosso, 1927.

Carranza, Arturo B. *La Capital de la República. El ensanche de su municipio, 1881 a 1888*. Buenos Aires: Talleres Gráficos Rosso, 1938.

Carrasco Benito. *Algunas consideraciones sobre la urbanización de las ciudades*. Buenos Aires: Los Amigos de la Ciudad, 1927.

Carrasco, Benito. "La ciudad del porvenir." *Caras y Caretas*, February 22, 1908.

Carrasco, Sansón (Daniel Muñoz). "La gran Capital del Sud." *El Nacional* (Buenos Aires), June 12, 1884. Reprinted in Adrián Beccar Varela, *Torcuato de Alvear. Primer Intendente municipal de la ciudad de Buenos Aires*. Buenos Aires: Kraft, 1926.

Chadwick, G. F. *The Park and the Town: Public Landscape in the 19th and 20th Centuries*. London: The Architectural Press, 1966.

Chanourdie, Enrique. "Sarmiento y su estatua." *Revista Técnica* 104–105. (Buenos Aires), June 15, 1900.

Chanourdie, Enrique. "Conferencia sobre transformación edilicia de Buenos Aires." *Arquitectura. Suplemento de la Revista Técnica* 39 (Buenos Aires), July and August 1906.

Chaquesien, Donato. *Los partidos porteños en la vía pública*. Buenos Aires: Talleres Gráficos Araujo, 1919.

Chase, Jeanne. "New York City reinventata: utili riflessioni su un ordine in continuo evolversi." In *La città e le sue storie* Edited by Carlo Olmo and Bernard Lepetit. Turin: Einaudi, 1995.

Châtelet, Anne-Marie. "Joseph Antoine Bouvard, 1840–1920." In Programa Internacional de Investigaciones sobre el campo urbano, *Documento de Trabajo N° 1. Seminario Internacional Vaquerías*. 1996.

Choay, Françoise. *The Modern City: Planning in the 19th Century*. New York: Braziller, 1969.

Choay, Françoise. "Haussmann et le système des espaces verts parisiens."*La Revue de l'Art* 29 (1975).

Christophersen, Alejandro. "Conmemoración del gran centenario. Proyecto sometido a la Comisión Nacional." *Arquitectura: Suplemento de la Revista Técnica* 39 (Buenos Aires), July–August 1906.

Cibils, F. R. "La descentralización urbana de la ciudad de Buenos Aires."*Boletín del Departamento Nacional del Trabajo* 16 (Buenos Aires), March 31, 1911.

Clemenceau, Georges. *South America Today; A Study of Conditions, Social, Political and Commercial in Argentina, Uruguay and Brazil*. New York, London: G. P. Putnam's Sons, 1911.

Collins, George R., and Christiane Collins. *Camillo Sitte and the Birth of Modern City Planning*. New York: Random House, 1965.

Cominges, Juan de. "Informe sobre Palermo." *Revista del Jardín Zoológico de Buenos Aires* (Buenos Aires), May 1916 [1882].

Coni, Gabriela L. de. "El barrio de las ranas." *La Prensa* (Buenos Aires), February 7, 1902.

Coppola, Horacio. *Buenos Aires 1936*. Buenos Aires: Municipalidad de la Ciudad de Buenos Aires, 1936.

Costa, Eduardo. "Avenida de Mayo." In *Memoria de la Intendencia Municipal de 1887*. Buenos Aires: Imprenta La Universidad, 1888.

Crasemann Collins, Christiane. "Hegemann and Peets: Cartographers of an Imaginary Atlas." Introduction to Werner Hegemann and Elbert Peets, *The American Vitruvius: An Architects' Handbook of Civic Art*. New York: Princeton Architectural Press, 1988.

Crespo, Eduardo. "Monografías y disertaciones históricas."*Sarmiento y la ciudad de Buenos Aires*, 9. Buenos Aires: Museo Histórico Sarmiento, 1942.

Crispiani, Alejandro. "Alejandro Christophersen y el desarrollo del eclecticismo en la Argentina."*Cuadernos de Historia*, 6. Buenos Aires: Instituto de Arte Americano, FADU-UBA, April 1995.

Cutolo, Vicente. *Nuevo diccionario biográfico argentino, 1750–1930*. Vol. V. Buenos Aires: Elche, 1978.

Daguerre, Mercedes. "Eclecticismo." In *Diccionario de arquitectura en la Argentina* Edited by Jorge Francisco Liernur and Fernando Aliata. Vol. 3. Buenos Aires: Agea, 2004.

Daireaux, Émile. *Vida y costumbres en el Plata*. Vol. 1. Buenos Aires: Félix Lajouane, 1888.

Dal Co, Francesco. "From Parks to the Region: Progressive Ideology and the Reform of the American City." In Giorgio Ciucci, Francesco Dal Co, Mario Manieri-Elia, and Manfredo Tafuri. *The American City: From the Civil War to the New Deal*. Cambridge, MA: MIT Press, 1979 [1973].

De la Serna, Gerónimo. "Disquisiciones edilicias referentes al 'Proyecto de la Municipalidad para la urbanización del municipio.'" Lecture delivered at the Centro Argentino de Ingenieros and published in *La Ingeniería*, 1927.

De Paula, Alberto. "Una modificación del diseño urbano porteño proyectada en 1875." *Anales del Instituto de Arte Americano e Investigaciones Estéticas* 19 (1966).

De Paula, Alberto, and Ramón Gutiérrez. *La encrucijada de la arquitectura argentina, 1822–1875. Santiago Bevans — Carlos Pellegrini*. Resistencia: Universidad Nacional del Nordeste, 1974.

De Privitellio, Luciano. "Inventar el barrio: Boedo 1936–1942." In *Cuadernos del Ciesal* 2–3 (1994).

De Privitellio, Luciano. *Vecinos y ciudadanos. Política y sociedad en la Buenos Aires de entreguerras*. Buenos Aires: Siglo XXI, 2003.

De Ramón, Armando. *Santiago de Chile (1541–1991). Historia de una sociedad urbana*. Madrid: MAPFRE, 1992.

De Vedia y Mitre, Mariano. Inaugural speech at the obelisk, *El Mundo* (Buenos Aires), May 24, 1936.

Della Paolera, Carlos María. "Servidumbres estéticas en las construcciones edilicias." *La Ingeniería* XX, no. 5, January 9, 1916.

Della Paolera, Carlos María. *Urbanismo y problemas urbanos de Buenos Aires*. Lecture published as a pamphlet. Instituto Popular de Conferencias, September 13, 1929. Reprinted in *La Ingeniería* 660 (October 1929).

Devoto, Fernando. "Los orígenes de un barrio italiano en Buenos Aires a mediados del siglo XIX." *Boletín del Instituto de Historia Argentina y Americana Dr. E. Ravignani* 1 (1989).

Díaz, Tony, and Damián Quero. *Buenos Aires Ideal*. Buenos Aires and Madrid, 1995.

Dickens, Charles. *American Notes*. New York: Modern Library, 1996 [1842].

Elguera, Alberto, and Carlos Boaglio. "Vedia y Mitre, el intendente del obelisco." *Todo es Historia* 342 (January 1996).

Esteban, Francisco. *El Departamento Topográfico de la Provincia de Buenos Aires (actual Dirección de Geodesia). Su creación y desarrollo*. Buenos Aires: Dirección de Geodesia de la Provincia de Buenos Aires, 1962.

Estrada, José María. Letter to the City Council *Revista Nacional* XIII, November 11, 1891 [1883].

Fein, Albert. *Landscape into Cityscape: Frederick Law Olmsted's Plans for a Greater New York City*. Ithaca, New York: Cornell University Press, 1968.

Fernández Moreno, Baldomero. "Callejuela Rauch." In *Ciudad, 1915-1949*. Buenos Aires: Ediciones de la Municipalidad, 1949 [1917].

Foot Hardman, Francisco. *Trem fantasma. A modernidade na selva*. São Paulo: Companhia Das Letras, 1988.

Forestier, Jean Claude Nicolas. "Los parques de juego o jardines de barrio en las grandes ciudades." *Revista Municipal* 146, November 5, 1906

Fraser, Nancy. "Rethinking the Public Sphere: A Contribution to the Critique of Actually Existing Democracy." In *Habermas and the Public Sphere*. Edited by Craig Calhoun. Cambridge, MA: MIT Press, 1991.

Fray Mocho (José S. Álvarez). "Me mudo al norte."*Caras y Caretas*, December 10, 1898. Reprinted in Fray Mocho, Carlos M. Pacheco, and others. *Los costumbristas del 900*. Edited with prologue by Eduardo Romano. Buenos Aires: Centro Editor de América Latina, 1980.

Gabriel, José. "El país y la ciudad de Buenos Aires." In *Homenaje a Buenos Aires en el cuarto centenario de su fundación*. Buenos Aires: Municipalidad de la Ciudad de Buenos Aires, 1936.

Gache, Roberto. *Glosario de la farsa urbana*. Buenos Aires: Cooperativa Editorial, 1919.

Gache, Samuel. *Les logements ouvriers à Buenos Aires*. Paris, 1899.

Gálvez, Manuel. *El diario de Gabriel Quiroga*. Buenos Aires: Arnoldo Moen y Hno., 1910

Gálvez, Víctor (Vicente Quesada). *Memorias de un viejo. Escenas de costumbres de la República Argentina*. Buenos Aires: Solar, 1942 [1889].

García de Enterría, Eduardo. *Revolución francesa y administración contemporánea*. Madrid: Taurus, 1981.

García Heras, Raúl. *Transportes, negocios y política. La compañía Anglo Argentina de Tranvías, 1876-1981*. Buenos Aires: Sudamericana, 1994.

García Molina, Fernando, and Cecilia Devia de Ovadía. *Domingo Faustino Sarmiento. Concejal porteño*. Buenos Aires: Honorable Concejo Deliberante, 1988.

García, Martín. "Inauguración de los nuevos mataderos." *Caras y Caretas*, March 31, 1900.

Geertz, Clifford. *The Interpretation of Cultures*. London: Fontana Press, 1993.

Gentile, Eduardo. "Los centros cívicos y el ideal City Beautiful. Propuestas para Buenos Aires 1925-1943." In *Materiales para la historia de la arquitectura, el hábitat y la ciudad en la Argentina*. Edited by Fernando Aliata and Fernando Gandolfi. La Plata: FAU-UNLP, 1996.

Gerchunoff, Alberto. "Buenos Aires, metrópoli continental." *La revista de América* 23-24, January–April and May 1914. Reprinted in Alberto Gerchunoff. *Buenos Aires, la metrópoli de mañana, Cuadernos de Buenos Aires*. Buenos Aires: Municipalidad de la Ciudad de Buenos Aires. 1960.

Ghioldi, Américo. Speech upon the resignation of Mayor Noel In *Actas del Honorable Concejo Deliberante*. Buenos Aires: Municipalidad de la Ciudad de Buenos Aires, May 3, 1927.

Ghioldi, Américo. "Las reuniones en las plazas y esquinas de la ciudad." *La Vanguardia,* October 27, 1929.

Giménez, Ángel. Intervention in *Actas del Honorable Concejo Deliberante,* Municipalidad de la Ciudad de Buenos Aires, September 20, 1924.

Giunta, Rodolfo. "Buenos Aires en el Correo del Domingo." *Seminarios de Crítica 1994,* 54. Buenos Aires: Instituto de Arte Americano, FADU-UBA, November 1994.

Giusti, Roberto. *"La restauración nacionalista* por Ricardo Rojas." *Nosotros* V, no. 26 (February 1910).

Giusti, Roberto. "Sinfonía de Buenos Aires." In *Homenaje a Buenos Aires en el cuarto centenario.* Buenos Aires: Municipalidad de la Ciudad de Buenos Aires, 1936.

Gobello, José, and Eduardo Stilman. *Las letras de tango de Villoldo a Borges.* Buenos Aires: Editorial Brújula, 1966.

Gómez Carrillo, Enrique. *El encanto de Buenos Aires.* Madrid: Perlado, Páez y Comp., 1914.

González Bernaldo, Pilar. "L'Urbanisation de la mémoire. Politique urbaine de l'État de Buenos Aires pendant les dix annés de sécession (1852–1862)." In *Colloque International de l'AFSSAL* (Les enjeux de la mémoire. L'Amérique Latine à la croisée du cinquième centenaire. Commémorer ou remémorer?). Paris, December 1992.

González Tuñón, Enrique. "Una mañana de sol. Caras y Caretas en la Boca del Riachuelo." *Caras y Caretas,* December 5, 1925.

González Tuñón, Enrique. "Parque Patricios." *Caras y Caretas,* December 12, 1925.

González Tuñón, Enrique. Series of articles published in *Crítica,* July 17, 19 and 20, 1925.

González Tuñón, Enrique. *Tangos.* Buenos Aires: Editorial Borocaba, 1953 [1926].

González Tuñón, Enrique. *El alma de las cosas inanimadas.* Buenos Aires: Gleizer, 1927.

González Tuñón, Enrique. *Camas desde un peso.* Buenos Aires: Editorial Deucalion, 1956 [1932].

González, Joaquín V. *La expropiación ante el derecho público argentino.* Buenos Aires: Librería La Facultad, 1915.

González Castillo, José, and Cátulo Castillo. *Cancionero.* Buenos Aires: Torres Agüero Editor, 1977.

González, Ricardo. "Lo propio y lo ajeno. Actividades culturales y fomentismo en una asociación vecinal. Barrio Nazca (1925–1930)." In *Mundo urbano y cultura popular. Estudios de Historia social Argentina.* Edited by Diego Armus. Buenos Aires: Sudamericana, 1990.

Gorelik, Adrián. "La búsqueda del Centro. Ideas y dimensiones de espacio público en la gestión urbana y en las polémicas sobre la ciudad, 1925–1936." *Boletín del Instituto de Historia Argentina y Americana Dr. E. Ravignani* 9, third series (1994).

Gorelik, Adrián. "Horacio Coppola: testimonios." *Punto de Vista* 53 (November 1995).

Gorelik, Adrián, and Graciela Silvestri. "Imágenes al sur. Sobre algunas hipótesis de James Scobie para el desarrollo de Buenos Aires." *Anales del Instituto de Arte Americano e Investigaciones Estéticas "Mario J. Buschiazzo"* 27–28 (1991).

Gorelik, Adrián, and Graciela Silvestri. "San Cristóbal Sur entre el Matadero y el Parque: acción municipal, conformación barrial y crecimiento urbano en Buenos Aires, 1895–1915." *Boletín del Instituto de Historia Argentina y Americana Dr. E. Ravignani* 3 (1991).

Gorelik, Adrián, and Graciela Silvestri. "El pasado como futuro. Una utopía reactiva en Buenos Aires." *Punto de Vista* 42 (April 1992).

Gover de Nasatsky, M. E. *Bibliografía de Alberto Gerchunoff*. Buenos Aires: Fondo Nacional de las Artes and Sociedad Hebraica Argentina, 1976.

Gramuglio, María Teresa. "La primera épica de Lugones." *Prismas* 1 (1997).

Grau, Cristina. *Borges y la arquitectura*. Madrid: Cátedra, 1989.

Güiraldes, Ricardo. "Don Pedro Figari." *Martín Fierro* no. 8–9 (September 6, 1924). In *Revista Martín Fierro 1924–1927. Edición facsimilar*. Buenos Aires: Fondo Nacional de las Artes, 1995.

Gutiérrez, Leandro, and Luis Alberto Romero. *Sectores populares, cultura y política. Buenos Aires en la entreguerra*. Buenos Aires: Sudamericana, 1995.

Gutiérrez, Leandro, and Luis Alberto Romero. "La construcción de la ciudadanía, 1912-1955." In Leandro Gutiérrez and Luis Alberto Romero. *Sectores populares, cultura y política. Buenos Aires en la entreguerra*.

Habermas, Jürgen. "The Public Sphere: An Encyclopedia Article." *New German Critique* 3 (1974 [1964]).

Habermas, Jürgen. *The Structural Transformation of the Public Sphere: An Inquiry Into a Category of Bourgeois Society*. Cambridge, MA: MIT Press, 1991 [1962].

Halperin Donghi, Tulio. "Un nuevo clima de ideas." In *La Argentina del ochenta al Centenario*, compiled by Gustavo Ferrari and Ezequiel Gallo. Buenos Aires: Sudamericana, 1980.

Halperin Donghi, Tulio. *Una nación para el desierto argentino*. Buenos Aires: Centro Editor de América Latina, 1982.

Halperin Donghi, Tulio. *El espejo de la historia. Problemas argentinos y perspectivas latinoamericanas*. Buenos Aires: Sudamericana, 1987.

Halperin Donghi, Tulio. "1930–1960. Crónica de treinta años." *Argentina en el callejón*. Buenos Aires: Ariel, 1995 [1961].

Hardoy, Jorge B. "Consideraciones sobre urbanización de la ciudad de Buenos Aires. Contribución al estudio de su plano regulador." *Revista de Arquitectura* 83 (November 1927).

Hardoy, Jorge Enrique. "Teorías y prácticas urbanísticas en Europa entre 1850 y 1930. Su traslado a América Latina." In *Repensando la ciudad de América Latina*. Edited by Jorge Enrique Hardoy and Richard Morse. Buenos Aires: GEL, 1988.

Hardoy, Jorge Enrique, and Margarita Gutman. *Buenos Aires. Historia urbana del Área Metropolitana*. Madrid: Mapfre, 1992.

Haussmann, Georges-Eugène. *Mémoires*. Paris: Victor-Havard, 1890–93.

Hébert, John R. "The Tragic Week of January, 1919, in Buenos Aires: Background, Events, Aftermaths." PhD diss., Georgetown University, 1972.

Hegemann, Werner. *Problemas urbanos de Rosario. Conferencias del urbanista Dr. W. Hegemann*. Rosario: Municipality of Rosario, 1931.

Hegemann, Werner. "El espíritu de Schinkel en Sud América." *Revista de Arquitectura* 142 (October 1932).

Hegemann, Werner. "La vivienda barata en Buenos Aires y en otras ciudades del mundo." *Anales del Instituto Popular de Conferencias* XVII (1932).

Hegemann, Werner. "Als Städtebauer in Südamerika." *Wasmuths Monatshefte für Baukunst und Städtebau* XVI (1932).

Hegemann, Werner. *La Berlino di pietra. Storia della piú grande città di caserme d'afitto*. Milan: G. Mazzotta, 1975 [1930].

Hegemann, Werner. *Catalogo delle Esposizioni Internazionali di Urbanistica. Berlino 1910–Düsseldorf 1911–12*. Edited by Donatella Calabi and Marino Folin. Milan: Il Saggiatore, 1975.

Hegemann, Werner, and Elbert Peets. *The American Vitruvius: An Architects' Handbook of Civic Art*. New York: Architectural Book Pub. Co., 1922

Hénard, Eugène. *Études sur les transformations de Paris*, in *Alle origini dell'urbanistica: la costruzione della metropoli*. Edited by Donatella Calabi and Marino Folin. 1903. Padova: Marsilio, 1972 [1903].

Herf, Jeffrey. *Reactionary Modernism: Technology, Culture, and Politics in Weimar and the Third Reich*. Cambridge and New York: Cambridge University Press, 1984.

Hernández, Carlos y Cía. "Propuesta de Plano Triangulado del Municipio de Buenos Aires con su Ensanche y Mejoramiento." Archivo Histórico Municipal, Caja 12, Obras Públicas series, March 1881.

Herrera Mac Lean, Carlos A. *Pedro Figari*. Buenos Aires: Poseidón, 1943.

Hogg, Ricardo. *Recuerdos del siglo pasado*, quoted in Ricardo M. Llanes, *Historia de la calle Florida*. 1976.

Huret, Jules. *De Buenos Aires al Gran Chaco*. Buenos Aires: Hyspamérica, 1988 [1911].

Insolera, Italo. "Europa XIX secolo: ipotesi per una nuova definizione della città." In *Dalla città preindustriale alla città del capitalism*. Edited by Alberto Caracciolo. Bologna: Il Mulino, 1975.

Jacobs, Jane. *The Death and Life of Great American Cities.* New York: Modern Library, 1993 [1968].

Jaeschké, Víctor Julio. *A propósito de mejoras y embellecimientos urbanos en Buenos Aires. Carta abierta dirigida al nuevo Intendente Municipal de la Capital de la República Argentina, Señor D. Adolfo Bullrich.* Buenos Aires: Imprenta y Encuadernación de Juan Schurer Stolle, 1898.

Jaeschké, Víctor Julio. "Ver para creer. ¿A dónde están nuestros edificios públicos?" *El Tiempo,* April 21, 1909.

Jaeschké, Víctor Julio. "Inútil ensanche de la ciudad de Buenos Aires." in *Revista de Arquitectura* 45 (September 1924).

Jauretche, Arturo. *El medio pelo.* Buenos Aires: Peña Lillo, 1966.

Jiménez Muñoz, Jorge H. *La traza del poder. Historia de la política y los negocios urbanos en el Distrito Federal, de sus orígenes a la desaparición del Ayuntamiento (1824–1928).* Mexico City: Dédalo-Códex, 1993.

Koolhaas, Rem. *Delirious New York. A Retroactive Manifesto for Manhattan.* Rotterdam: 010 Publishers, 1994 [1978].

Korn, Francis, and Lidia de la Torre. "La vivienda en Buenos Aires, 1887–1914." *Desarrollo Económico* 98 (July–September 1985).

L. H. "La suerte del último centauro." *Martín Fierro* 8–9 (August–September 1924). In *Revista Martín Fierro 1924-1927. Edición facsimilar.* Buenos Aires: Fondo Nacional de las Artes, 1995.

Larreta, Enrique. *Las dos fundaciones de Buenos Aires.* Buenos Aires: EMECE, 1943 [c. 1929].

Le Corbusier. *Urbanisme.* Paris: Éditions Crès, 1924.

Le Corbusier. *Precisions on the Present State of Architecture and City Planning.* Zurich: Park Books, 2015 [1930].

Lefebvre, Henri. "The Right to the City." In *Writings on Cities.* Oxford and Cambridge, MA: Blackwell Publishers, 1996 [1968].

Levene, Ricardo. "La conquista de América y la expedición de Don Pedro de Mendoza." In *Homenaje a Buenos Aires en el Cuarto Centenario de su Fundación.* Buenos Aires: Municipalidad de la Ciudad de Buenos Aires, 1936.

Liernur, Jorge Francisco. "Buenos Aires del centenario: en torno a los orígenes del movimiento moderno en la Argentina." *Materiales* 4 (December 1983).

Liernur, Jorge Francisco. "La estrategia de la casa autoconstruida."In *Sectores populares y vida urbana.* Edited by Diego Armus. Buenos Aires: CLACSO, 1984.

Liernur, Jorge Francisco. "El discreto encanto de nuestra arquitectura." *summa* (April 1986).

Liernur, Jorge Francisco. "Juncal y Esmeralda, Perú House, Maison Garay: fragmentos de un debate tipológico y urbanístico en la obra de Jorge Kalnay." *Anales del Instituto de Arte Americano e Investigaciones Estéticas "Mario J. Buschiazzo"* 25 (1988).

Liernur, Jorge Francisco, ed. "Formación y desarrollo del barrio de San Cristóbal (1870–1940)." Informe Final PID-CONICET. Buenos Aires, 1991.

Liernur, Jorge Francisco. "¿Arquitectura del Imperio español o arquitectura criolla? Notas sobre las representaciones 'neocoloniales' de la arquitectura producida durante la dominación española en América." *Anales del Instituto de Arte Americano e Investigaciones Estéticas "Mario J. Buschiazzo"* 27–28 (1992).

Liernur, Jorge Francisco. "La ciudad efímera." In *El umbral de la metrópolis. Transformaciones técnicas y cultura en la modernización de Buenos Aires (1870–1930)*. Edited by Jorge Francisco Liernur and Graciela Silvestri. Buenos Aires: Sudamericana, 1993.

Liernur, Jorge Francisco, and Pablo Pschepiurca. "Precisiones sobre los proyectos de Le Corbusier en la Argentina 1929/1949." *summa* 243 (November 1989).

Liernur, Jorge Francisco, and Fernando Aliata, eds. *Diccionario de arquitectura en la Argentina*. 6 vols. Buenos Aires: Agea, 2004.

Livacich, Serafín. *Buenos Aires. Páginas históricas para el primer centenario de la Independencia*. Buenos Aires: Compañía Sudamericana de Billetes de Banco, 1907.

Llanes, Ricardo. *La avenida de Mayo*. Buenos Aires: Kraft, 1955.

Llanes, Ricardo. *El barrio de Parque de los Patricios, Cuadernos de Buenos Aires*, XLII. Buenos Aires: Municipalidad de la Ciudad de Buenos Aires, 1974.

Llanes, Ricardo. *Historia de la calle Florida*. Buenos Aires: Municipalidad de la Ciudad de Buenos Aires, 1976.

López, Lucio V. *La gran aldea. Costumbres bonaerenses*. Buenos Aires: Centro Editor de América Latina, 1980 [1884].

Loudet, Osvaldo. *Ensayos de crítica e historia*. Buenos Aires: Academia Argentina de Letras, 1975.

Ludmer, Josefina. "Latin American Cultural Coalitions and Liberal States," *Travesia. Journal of Latin American Cultural Studies* 2, no. 2 (1993).

Lugones, Leopoldo. *Didáctica*. Buenos Aires: Otero y Cía., 1910.

Lugones, Leopoldo. *Piedras liminares. Las limaduras de Hephaestos*. Buenos Aires: A. Moen y Hno., 1910.

Mallea, Eduardo. *History of an Argentine Passion*. Pittsburgh: Latin American Literary Review Press, 1983 [1937].

Mangone, Carlos. "La república radical entre *Crítica* y *El Mundo*." In *Yrigoyen, entre Borges y Arlt (1916–1930)*. Edited by Graciela Montaldo. Buenos Aires: Contrapunto, 1989.

Manieri-Elia, Mario. "Toward an Imperial City: Daniel H. Burnham and the City Beautiful Movement." In Giorgio Ciucci, Francesco Dal Co, Mario Manieri-Elia, and Manfredo Tafuri. *The American City: From the Civil War to the New Deal*. Cambridge, MA: MIT Press, 1979 [1973].

Marcuse, Peter. "The Grid as City Plan: New York City and Laissez-faire Planning in the Nineteenth Century." *Planning Perspectives* 2 (1987).

Marechal, Leopoldo. *Historia de la calle Corrientes*. Buenos Aires: Paidós 1967 [1937].

Marechal, Leopoldo. *Adán Buenosayres*. In *Obras completas*, vol. III. Edited by Jorge Lafforgue. Buenos Aires: Perfil Libros, 1998 [1948].

Martel, Julián. *La Bolsa*. Buenos Aires: Editorial Huemul, 1979 [1891].

Martínez Estrada, Ezequiel. *X-ray of the Pampa*. Austin: University of Texas Press, 1971 [1933].

Martínez, Alberto. "Estudio topográfico de Buenos Aires." *Censo General de Población, Edificación, Comercio e Industrias de la Ciudad de Buenos Aires*. Buenos Aires: Compañía Sudamericana de Billetes de Banco, 1889.

Medrano, Samuel. "Cuatro siglos." In *Homenaje a Buenos Aires en el cuarto centenario de su fundación*. Buenos Aires: Municipalidad de la Ciudad de Buenos Aires, 1936.

Merquior, José Guilherme. "El otro Occidente." In *El complejo de Próspero. Ensayos sobre cultura, modernidad y modernización en América Latina*. Edited by Felipe Arocena and Eduardo de León. Montevideo: Vintén, 1993.

Molina, Miguel Ángel, and Diana Wechsler. "La ciudad moderna en la serie 'Buenos Aires' de Guillermo Facio Hebequer." *Demócrito* I, no. 2 (October 1990).

Monteleone, Jorge. "Lugones: canto natal del héroe." In *Yrigoyen, entre Borges y Arlt (1916–1930)*. Edited by Graciela Montaldo. Buenos Aires: Contrapunto, 1989.

Montserrat, Marcelo, and Carlos Floria. "El pensamiento de Gustavo Franceschi y la revista *Criterio* en la cultura política de la Argentina contemporánea." In Marcelo Montserrat, *Usos de la memoria*. Buenos Aires: Sudamericana and Universidad de San Andrés, 1996.

Morales, Carlos María. "Algunos datos relativos al trazado general del Municipio." *Anales de la Sociedad Científica Argentina* 46 (1898).

Morales, Carlos María. "Las mejoras edilicias de Buenos Aires. Memoria presentada al Segundo Congreso Científico Latino-Americano reunido en Montevideo." *Anales de la Sociedad Científica Argentina*, no. 51 (1901).

Morales, Carlos María. "Estudio topográfico y edilicio de la ciudad de Buenos Aires." In *Censo General de Población, Comercio e Industrias de la Ciudad de Buenos Aires*. Vol. 1. Buenos Aires: Compañía Sudamericana de Billetes de Banco, 1906.

Mosser, Monique, and Georges Teyssot. "L'architettura del giardino e l'architettura nel giardino." In *L'architettura dei giardini d'Occidente. From the Renaissance to the Twentieth Century*. Edited by Monique Mosser and Georges Teyssot. Milan: Electa, 1990.

Mouchet, Carlos. "Las ideas sobre el municipio en la Argentina hasta 1853." In Honorable Concejo Deliberante, *Evolución institucional del municipio de la ciudad de Buenos Aires*. Buenos Aires: Ediciones del H. Concejo Deliberante, 1963.

Mumford, Lewis. *The Brown Decades: A Study of Arts in America, 1865–1895*. New York: Dover Publications, 1955 [1931].

Mumford, Lewis. *The City in History: Its Origins, Its Transformations, and Its Prospects*. New York: Harcourt Brace Jovanovich, 1961.

Nairn, Tom. *The Break-up of Britain: Crisis and Neo-nationalism*. London: NLB, 1977.

Nigro, Juan. "El partido socialista y la política municipal." *Revista Socialista* 21 (1932).

Nora, Pierre. *Les lieux de mémoire*. 7 vols. Paris: Gallimard, 1981.

Novick, Alicia, and Raúl Piccioni. *Árbitros, pares, socios. Técnicos locales y extranjeros en la génesis del urbanismo porteño*. Buenos Aires: Instituto de Arte Americano, FADU-UBA, 1990.

Novick, Alicia. "Técnicos locales y extranjeros en la génesis del urbanismo argentino. Buenos Aires, 1880–1940." *Area* 1 (1992).

Novick, Alicia. "Della Paolera, Carlos María." In *Diccionario de arquitectura en la Argentina*. Edited by Jorge Francisco Liernur and Fernando Aliata. Vol. 2. Buenos Aires: Agea, 2004.

Ocampo, Victoria, Horacio Butler and Amancio Williams. *Alberto Prebisch*. Monografías de artistas argentinos, volume 9. Buenos Aires: Academia Nacional de Bellas Artes, 1972.

Oechslin, Werner. "Between America and Germany: Werner Hegemann's Approach to Urban Planning." In *Berlin-New York, Like and Unlike: Essays on Architecture and Art from 1870 to the Present*. Edited by J. P. Kleihues, Chr. P. Kleihues and Chr. Rathberg. New York: Rizzoli, 1993.

Olmo, Carlo, and Bernard Lepetit, eds. *La città e le sue storie*. Turin: Einaudi, 1995.

Olmsted, Frederick Law. "Public Parks and the Enlargement of Towns." *American Social Science Association*. Cambridge: Riverside Press, 1870. Republished in *The Public Face of Architecture: Civic Culture and Public Space*. Edited by Nathan Glazer and Mark Lilla. New York and London: The Free Press, 1987.

Olmsted Jr., Frederick Law, and Theodora Kimball, eds. *Olmsted: Forty Years of Landscape Architecture*. Cambridge, MA, and London: MIT Press, 1973 [1928].

Onelli, Clemente. "El jardín zoológico en 1916." *Revista del Jardín Zoológico de Buenos Aires* XII, no. 48 (December 1916).

Ortiz, Federico, J. Mantero, Ramón Gutiérrez, and Abelardo Levaggi. *La arquitectura del liberalismo en la Argentina*. Buenos Aires: Sudamericana, 1968.

Otaola, Julio. *El Centro Cívico de la ciudad de Buenos Aires*. Buenos Aires: Los Amigos de la Ciudad, 1933.

Palacín, Manuel. "Vivienda, expansión y urbanización." *La Vanguardia*, September 1, 1929.

Páramo, Martha Susana. *Un fracaso hecho historia. La Corporación de Transportes de la Ciudad de Buenos Aires*. Mendoza: Universidad Nacional de Cuyo, 1991.

Payá, Carlos, and Eduardo Cárdenas. *El primer nacionalismo argentino en Manuel Gálvez y Ricardo Rojas.* Buenos Aires: Peña Lillo, 1978.

Payró, Roberto. "Las píldoras del centenario." In Roberto Payró, *Crónicas.* Buenos Aires: M. Rodríguez Giles 1909 [1906].

Pellegrini, Carlos (Enrique). "Plano de la ciudad." *La Revista del Plata* 4 (December 1853).

Pellegrini, Carlos (Enrique). "Traza y abertura de calles y plano de la ciudad." *La Revista del Plata* 6 (February 1854).

Pellegrini, Carlos (Enrique). "Departamento de Ingenieros." *La Revista del Plata* 7 (March 1854).

Pellegrini, Carlos (Enrique José). Letter to Torcuato de Alvear, London, July 18, 1883. In Adrián Beccar Varela, *Torcuato de Alvear. Primer Intendente municipal de la ciudad de Buenos Aires.* Buenos Aires: Kraft, 1926.

Peña, Enrique. *Documentos y planos relativos al período colonial en la ciudad de Buenos Aires.* 5 vols. Buenos Aires: Peuser, 1910.

Perulli, Paolo. *Atlante metropolitano. Il mutamento sociale nelle grandi città.* Bologna: Il Mulino, 1992.

Petit de Murat, Ulyses. "Mariano de Vedia y Mitre." In *Tres intendentes de Buenos Aires.* Buenos Aires: IHCBA/Municipalidad de la Ciudad de Buenos Aires, 1985.

Piccinato, Giorgio. *La costruzione dell'urbanistica. Germania 1871–1914.* Rome: Officina, 1974.

Pillado, José Antonio. *Buenos Aires colonial. Edificios y costumbres.* Buenos Aires: Compañía Sudamericana de Billetes de Banco, 1910.

Pisano, Natalio J. *La política agraria de Sarmiento. La lucha contra el latifundio.* Buenos Aires: Depalma, 1980.

Ponte, Alessandra. "Il parco pubblico in Gran Bretagna e negli Stati Uniti. Dal *genius loci* al 'genio della civilizzazione.'" In *L'architettura dei giardini d'Occidente. From the Renaissance to the Twentieth Century.* Edited by Monique Mosser and Georges Teyssot. Milan: Electa, 1990.

Ponte, Jorge Ricardo. *Mendoza, aquella ciudad de barro. Historia de una ciudad andina desde el siglo XVI hasta nuestros días.* Mendoza: Municipalidad de la Ciudad de Mendoza, 1987.

Posada, Adolfo. *La República Argentina. Impresiones y comentarios.* Buenos Aires: Hyspamérica, 1986 [1912].

Prebisch, Alberto. "Sugestiones de una visita al Salón de acuarelistas, pastelistas y aguafortistas." In *Martín Fierro*, 5–6, May 15–June 15, 1924. In *Revista Martín Fierro 1924–1927. Edición facsimilar.* Buenos Aires: Fondo Nacional de las Artes, 1995.

Prebisch, Alberto. "La ciudad en que vivimos." Introduction to Horacio Coppola, *Buenos Aires 1936.* Buenos Aires: Municipalidad de la Ciudad de Buenos Aires, 1936.

Prieto, Adolfo. *Estudios de literatura argentina.* Buenos Aires: Editorial Galerna, 1969.

Riegl, Aloïs. "The Modern Cult of Monuments: Its Character and Its Origin." Translated by Kurt W. Forster and Diane Ghirardo. *Oppositions* 25 1982 [1903].

Rocca, Jerónimo. Radio conference, Buenos Aires. September 9, 1935. In *Primer Congreso Argentino de Urbanismo.* Vol. 1. 1936.

Rocchi, Fernando. "La armonía de los opuestos: industria, importaciones y la construcción urbana de Buenos Aires en el período 1880–1920." *Entrepasados* no. 7 (1994).

Rojas, Ricardo. *Eurindia*. Buenos Aires: Librería La Facultad, 1924.

Rojas, Ricardo. *La restauración nacionalista*. Buenos Aires: Peña Lillo, 1971 [1909].

Romano, Eduardo. Prologue to *Las letras del Tango. Antología cronológica 1900-1980*. 5th ed. Rosario: Editorial Fundación Ross, 1995.

Romero, José Luis. *Las ideas políticas en Argentina*. Mexico City: Fondo de Cultura Económica, 1956.

Romero, José Luis. "Buenos Aires: una historia." In *Historia Integral Argentina*. Vol. 7, *El sistema en crisis*. Buenos Aires: Centro Editor de América Latina, 1972.

Romero, José Luis, and Luis Alberto Romero, eds. *Buenos Aires, historia de cuatro siglos*. Buenos Aires: Abril, 1983.

Romero, Luis Alberto. "Buenos Aires en la entreguerra: libros baratos y cultura de los sectores populares." In Leandro Gutiérrez and Luis Alberto Romero. *Sectores populares, cultura y política. Buenos Aires en la entreguerra*. Buenos Aires: Sudamericana, 1995.

Romero, Luis Alberto. "Nueva Pompeya, libros y catecismo." In Leandro Gutiérrez and Luis Alberto Romero. *Sectores populares, cultura y política. Buenos Aires en la entreguerra*. Buenos Aires: Sudamericana, 1995.

Roncayolo, Marcel. "L'esperienza e il modello." In *La città e le sue storie*. Edited by Carlo Olmo and Bernard Lepetit. Turin: Einaudi, 1995.

Rossi, Luis. "Los primeros años de la *Revista de Filosofía, Cultura, Ciencias y Educación*: la crisis del positivismo y la filosofía en la Argentina." Buenos Aires: CEI-UNQUI (mimeo), 1996.

Rubione, Alfredo. *En torno al criollismo. Textos y polémica*. Buenos Aires: Centro Editor de América Latina, 1983.

Rusiñol, Santiago. *Un viaje al Plata*. Translated from Catalan by G. Martínez Sierra. Madrid: V. Prieto y Compañía, 1911.

Ruskin, John. *The Seven Lamps of Architecture*. New York: John Wiley & Sons, 1889 [1849].

Sabato, Hilda. *La política en las calles. Entre el voto y la movilización. Buenos Aires, 1862-1880*. Buenos Aires: Sudamericana, 1998.

Sabugo, Mario. "Las canchas, monumentos bohemios." *Ambiente* 40 (1984).

Sabugo, Mario. "Placeres y fatigas de los barrios." *Anales del Instituto de Arte Americano e Investigaciones Estéticas "Mario J. Buschiazzo"* 27-28 (1992).

Saítta, Sylvia. Introduction to *Aguafuertes porteñas. Buenos Aires, vida cotidiana* by Roberto Arlt. Buenos Aires: Alianza, 1993.

Saítta, Sylvia, ed. *Tratado de la delincuencia. Aguafuertes inéditas de Roberto Arlt*. Buenos Aires: Biblioteca Página/12, 1996.

Saítta, Sylvia. *Regueros de tinta: el diario "Crítica" en la década de 1920*. Buenos Aires: Sudamericana, 1998.

Salas, Horacio. "El salto a la modernidad." Preliminary study to *Revista Martín Fierro 1924–1927. Edición facsimilar*. Buenos Aires: Fondo Nacional de las Artes, 1995.

Santos Gómez, Susana. *Bibliografía de viajeros a la Argentina*, 2 vols. Buenos Aires: FECIC/IAHH, 1983.

Sargent, Charles. *The Spatial Evolution of Greater Buenos Aires, Argentina, 1870–1930*. Tempe: Arizona State University, 1974.

Sarlo, Beatriz. *El imperio de los sentimientos. Narraciones de circulación periódica en la Argentina (1917–1927)*. Buenos Aires: Catálogos, 1985.

Sarlo, Beatriz. *Una modernidad periférica: Buenos Aires 1920 y 1930*. Buenos Aires: Nueva Visión, 1988.

Sarlo, Beatriz. "Arlt, ciudad real, ciudad imaginaria, ciudad reformada." *Punto de Vista* 42 (April 1992).

Sarlo, Beatriz. *La imaginación técnica. Sueños modernos de la cultura argentina*. Buenos Aires: Nueva Visión, 1992.

Sarlo, Beatriz. *Borges: A Writer on the Edge*. London; New York: Verso, 1993.

Sarlo, Beatriz. "Cabezas rapadas y cintas argentinas." *Prismas* 1 (1997).

Sarmiento, Domingo Faustino. *Obras completas (BS)*. 52 vols. Edited by A. Belín Sarmiento. Buenos Aires: Imprenta y Litografía Mariano Moreno, 1884–1903.

Sarmiento, Domingo Faustino. *Obras completas (LD)*. 53 vols. Buenos Aires: Editorial Luz del Día, 1948–1956.

Sarmiento, Domingo Faustino. "Proyecto de Ley del Poder Ejecutivo." In *Cámara de Senadores, Sesión de 1874*. Buenos Aires, 1875.

Sarmiento, Domingo Faustino. *Viajes por Europa, Africa y América, 1845–47, and Diario de Gastos* Edited by Javier Fernández. Buenos Aires: Colección Archivos, Fondo de Cultura Económica, 1993.

Sartre, Jean-Paul. "New York, Colonial City." In *The Aftermath of War (Situations III)*. London and New York: Seagull Books, 2008 [1949].

Scalabrini Ortiz, Raúl. *El hombre que está solo y espera*. Buenos Aires: Manuel Gleizer, 1931.

Scaltriti, Mabel. "Surgimiento de las sociedades barriales en Buenos Aires. El caso de Nueva Pompeya." *Jornadas del Instituto Histórico de la Ciudad de Buenos Aires* VII (September 1990).

Schiaffino, Eduardo. *Urbanización de Buenos Aires*. Buenos Aires: Manuel Gleizer, 1927.

Schild, Erich. *Dal palazzo di cristallo al Palais des Illusions*. Florence: Vallecchi, 1971.

Scobie, James. *Buenos Aires: Plaza to Suburb, 1870–1910*. New York: Oxford University Press, 1974.

Sebreli, Juan José. *Buenos Aires, vida cotidiana y alienación*. Buenos Aires: Siglo Veinte, 1965 [1964].

Secchi, Bernardo. "Le condizione sono cambiate." In *Un progetto per l'urbanistica*. Turin: Einaudi, 1989 [1984].

Seeber, Francisco. "Carta al Intendente Torcuato de Alvear." London, July 29, 1886. In Adrián Beccar Varela, *Torcuato de Alvear. Primer Intendente municipal de la ciudad de Buenos Aires*. Buenos Aires: Kraft, 1926.

Selva, Domingo. "La habitación higiénica para el obrero." Paper presented at the 2nd Latin American Medical Congress. *Revista Municipal* 46, 47, 49, December 5, 12 and 19, 1904.

Selva, Domingo. "Edificación obrera." *Arquitectura. Suplemento de la Revista Técnica* 63 (May–June 1910).

Sennett, Richard. *The Conscience of the Eye: The Design and Social Life of Cities*. New York: Alfred Knopf, 1900.

Sica, Paolo. *Historia del urbanismo. El siglo XIX*. Madrid: Instituto de Estudios de Administración Local, 1981 [1977].

Silvestri, Graciela. "1880–1910: la federalización de Buenos Aires y la construcción de los barrios." In Anahi Ballent, Adrián Gorelik and Graciela Silvestri, "Para un estudio de la ciudad y sus barrios." *Actas de las Primeras Jornadas del Instituto de Historia "Mario J. Buschiazzo."* Buenos Aires: FADU-UBA, 1985.

Silvestri, Graciela. "La mirada sobre el barrio: del silencio a la nostalgia." *Cuadernos de Historia* 3, Instituto de Arte Americano, FADU-UBA, September 1987.

Silvestri, Graciela. "La ciudad y el río." In *El umbral de la metrópolis. Transformaciones técnicas y cultura en la modernización de Buenos Aires (1870–1930)*. Edited by Jorge Francisco Liernur and Graciela Silvestri. Buenos Aires: Sudamericana, 1993.

Silvestri, Graciela. *El color del río. Historia cultural del paisaje del Riachuelo*. Buenos Aires: Editorial de la Universidad de Quilmes, 2004.

Silvestri, Graciela, and Fernando Aliata. *El paisaje en el arte y las ciencias humanas*. Buenos Aires: Centro Editor de América Latina, 1994.

Simmel, Georg. "The Metropolis and the Life of the Spirit." In *The Art of the City. Rome, Florence, Venice*. London: Pushkin Press, 2018 [1903].

Storni, Alfonsina. *Obras completas, Tomo 1. Poesías*. Buenos Aires: SELA, 1968.

Tafuri, Manfredo. *The Sphere and the Labyrinth: Avant-gardes and Architecture from Piranesi to the 1970s*. Cambridge, MA: MIT Press, 1987 [1980].

Tagle Lara, Benjamín. *Puente Alsina*. In *Las letras del Tango. Antología cronológica 1900–1980*. Edited by Eduardo Romano. 5th edition. Rosario: Editorial Fundación Ross, 1995 [1926].

Taine, Hippolyte. *Notes on England*. London: W. Isbister and Co., 1874. Quoted in Monica Charlot. "El spleen de los exiliados franceses." *Londres 1851–1901. La era victoriana o el triunfo de las desigualdades*. Edited by Monica Charlot and Roland Marx. Madrid: Alianza, 1993.

Tarán, Marina E. "Juan Kronfuss: un registro de nuestra arquitectura colonial." *summa* 215/216 (August 1985).

Tartarini, Jorge. "El Plan Bouvard para Buenos Aires (1907–1911). Algunos antecedents." *Anales del Instituto de Arte Americano e Investigaciones Estéticas Mario J. Buschiazzo"* 27–28 (1992).

Tartarini, Jorge. "La visita de Werner Hegemann a la Argentina en 1931." *DANA* 37–38 (1995).

Taullard, Alfredo. *Nuestro antiguo Buenos Aires*. Buenos Aires: Peuser, 1927.

Terán, Oscar. "El primer antiimperialismo latinoamericano." *Punto de Vista* 12 (July–October 1981).

Terán, Oscar. *En busca de la ideología argentina*. Buenos Aires: Catálogos, 1986.

Terán, Oscar. *Positivismo y nación en la Argentina*. Buenos Aires: Puntosur, 1987.

Terán, Oscar. *"El decadentismo argentino."* Buenos Aires: Instituto Ravignani, 1990.

Terán, Oscar. "Modernos intensos en los veintes." *Prismas* 1 (1997).

Ternavasio, Marcela. "Debates y alternativas acerca de un modelo de institución local en la Argentina decimonónica." *Anuario*, Escuela de Historia, Universidad Nacional de Rosario, 14 (1991).

Ternavasio, Marcela. "Municipio y representación local en el sistema político argentino de la segunda mitad del siglo XIX." *Anales del Instituto de Arte Americano e Investigaciones Estéticas "Mario J. Buschiazzo"* 27–28 (1992).

Teyssot, Georges. "Il sistema dei Batiments civils in Francia e la pianificazione di Le Mans (1795–1848)." In *Le macchine imperfette. Architettura, programma, istituzioni nel XIX secolo*. Edited by Paolo Morachiello and Georges Teyssot. Roma: Officina, 1980.

Tiempo, César. "Cómo conocí a Enrique González Tuñón." Prologue to *Camas desde un peso* by Enrique González Tuñón. Buenos Aires: Editorial Deucalion, 1956.

Tocqueville, Alexis de. *Democracy in America*. Garden City, NY: Doubleday, 1969 [1835–40].

Torres, Horacio. "Evolución de los procesos de estructuración espacial urbana. El caso de Buenos Aires." *Desarrollo Económico* 58 (July–September 1975).

Troncoso, Oscar. "Las formas del ocio." *Buenos Aires, historia de cuatro siglos*. Edited by José Luis Romero and Luis Alberto Romero. Buenos Aires: Abril, 1983.

Ulla, Noemí. *Tango, rebelión y nostalgia*. Buenos Aires: CEAL, 1982 [1967].

Vacarezza, Alberto. "El conventillo de la Paloma." In Alberto Vacarezza. *Teatro I*. Buenos Aires: Corregidor, 1993 [1929].

Vautier, Ernesto, and Fermín Bereterbide. "Urbanismo." *Revista de Arquitectura* XIX, no. 146 (February 1933).

Vezzetti, Hugo. *La locura en la Argentina*. Buenos Aires: Folios, 1983.

Vicuña Mackenna, Benjamín. *La transformación de Santiago. Notas e indicaciones respetuosamente sometidas a la Ilustre Municipalidad al Supremo Gobierno y al Congreso Nacional por el Intendente de Santiago.* Santiago: Imprenta de la Librería del Mercurio, 1872.

Vicuña Mackenna, Benjamín. *El Santa Lucía. Guía popular y breve descripción de este Paseo para el uso de las personas que lo visiten.* Santiago: Imprenta de la Librería del Mercurio, 1874.

Viguera, Aníbal. "El primero de mayo en Buenos Aires, 1890–1950: revolución y voz de una tradición." *Boletín del Instituto de Historia Argentina y Americana Dr. E. Ravignani* 3 (1991).

Vilar, Antonio U. "Arquitectura contemporánea." *Nuestra Arquitectura* (August 1931).

Viñas, David. *Literatura argentina y realidad política.* Buenos Aires: Centro Editor de América Latina, 1982 [1964].

Walter, Richard J. *Politics and Urban Growth in Buenos Aires: 1910–1942.* Cambridge: Cambridge University Press, 1993.

Weber, Max. *The City.* Glencoe, IL: Free Press, 1958 [1921].

Wilde, Eduardo. "A Palermo." In *Páginas escogidas* by Eduardo Wilde. Vol. IX. Edited by José María Monner Sans. Buenos Aires: Editorial Estrada, 1939 [1875].

Yujnovsky, Oscar. "Políticas de vivienda en la ciudad de Buenos Aires, 1880–1914." *Desarrollo Económico* 54 (July–September 1975).

Zabala, Rómulo. *Historia de la Pirámide de Mayo.* Buenos Aires: Academia Nacional de la Historia, 1962.

Zanatta, Loris. *Del estado liberal a la nación católica. Iglesia y Ejército en los orígenes del peronismo. 1930–1943.* Buenos Aires: Editorial de la Universidad Nacional de Quilmes, 1996.

Zimmermann, Eduardo. *Los liberales reformistas. La cuestión social en la Argentina, 1890–1916.* Buenos Aires: Sudamericana and Universidad de San Andrés, 1995.

Zuleta Álvarez, Enrique. *El nacionalismo argentino.* Buenos Aires: Ediciones La Bastilla, 1975.

Index

About Latin America Research Commons

Latin America Research Commons (LARC) is the first open-access publishing press dedicated to the publication of monographs in Spanish and Portuguese. It is an editorial project originated in the Latin American Studies Association (LASA), and its main goal is to ensure the widest possible dissemination of original monographs and journals in all disciplines related to Latin American studies. It is oriented to ensure that scholars from around the world are able to find and access the research they need without economic or geographic barriers.

In translation. Key Books in Latin American Studies is LARC series dedicated to publish classic Latin American books that has never been translated before and urge to reach new readers.

* 9 7 8 1 9 5 1 6 3 4 2 4 7 *